CIMA
STUDY TEXT

Intermediate level Paper 10

Systems and Project Management

IN THIS JULY 2002 EDITION

- Targeted to the **syllabus** and **learning outcomes**
- **Quizzes** and **questions** to check your understanding
- Clear layout and style designed to save you time
- Plenty of **exam-style questions**, some with **NEW** detailed guidance from BPP
- **Chapter Roundups** to help revision
- **Mind Maps** to integrate the key points

BPP's **MCQ cards** and **i-Learn** and **i-Pass** products also support this paper.

BPP Publishing
July 2002

First edition July 2000

Third edition July 2002

ISBN 0 7517 3764 X (Previous edition 0 7517 3166 8)

British Library Cataloguing-in-Publication Data
*A catalogue record for this book
is available from the British Library*

Published by

*BPP Publishing Limited
Aldine House, Aldine Place
London W12 8AW*

www.bpp.com

Printed in Great Britain by Ashford Colour Press

All our rights reserved. No part of this publication may be reproduced, stored in a retrieval system or transmitted, in any form or by any means, electronic, mechanical, photocopying, recording or otherwise, without the prior written permission of BPP Publishing Limited.

We are grateful to the Chartered Institute of Management Accountants for permission to reproduce the Pilot Paper. The suggested solutions to the questions have been prepared by BPP Publishing Limited.

©

BPP Publishing Limited
2002

Contents

	Page
THE BPP STUDY TEXT	(v)
HELP YOURSELF STUDY FOR YOUR CIMA EXAMS The right approach - developing your personal study plan - suggested study sequence	(vii)
SYLLABUS AND LEARNING OUTCOMES	(xii)
THE EXAM PAPER	(xix)
WHAT THE EXAMINER MEANS	(xxii)
TACKLING SCENARIO QUESTIONS	(xxiii)

PART A: PROJECT MANAGEMENT

1	Introducing project management	3
2	Project stages and management tools	19
3	Business meetings and presentations	62

PART B: INFORMATION TECHNOLOGY AND SYSTEMS

4	Systems and information theory	89
5	Systems development	118
6	Feasibility, investigation, analysis and design	140
7	Implementation, maintenance and review	173
8	Selecting and managing information technology	202
9	Effective communication	247

PART C: CONTROL

10	Control of activities and resources	261

PART D: AUDIT OF ACTIVITIES AND SYSTEMS

11	Internal audit	297
12	Information technology and the audit process	329

PART E: QUALITY

13	The management of quality	355

QUESTION BANK QUESTIONS	369
QUESTION BANK SUGGESTED SOLUTIONS	387
INDEX	427
REVIEW FORM & FREE PRIZE DRAW	
ORDER FORM	

MULTIPLE CHOICE QUESTION CARDS

Multiple choice questions do not feature in the Paper 10 exam. However, multiple choice questions are a useful study aid - allowing you to test your knowledge retention and identify areas requiring further study. We have produced a bank of **150 multiple choice question cards**, covering the syllabus. This bank contains MCQ questions in a format to help you **revise on the move**.

COMPUTER-BASED LEARNING PRODUCTS FROM BPP

If you want to reinforce your studies by **interactive** learning, try BPP's **i-Learn** product, covering major syllabus areas in an interactive format. For **self-testing**, try **i-Pass,** which offers a large number of **objective test questions**.

See the order form at the back of this text for details of these innovative learning tools.

VIRTUAL CAMPUS

The Virtual Campus uses BPP's wealth of teaching experience to produce a fully **interactive** e-learning resource **delivered via the Internet**. The site offers comprehensive **tutor support** and features areas such as **study, practice, email service, revision** and **useful resources**.

Visit our website www.bpp.com/virtualcampus/cima to sample aspects of the campus free of charge.

LEARNING TO LEARN ACCOUNTANCY

BPP's ground-breaking **Learning to learn accountancy** book is designed to be used both at the outset of your CIMA studies and throughout the process of learning accountancy. It challenges you to consider how you study and gives you helpful hints about how to approach the various types of paper which you will encounter. It can help you **get your studies both subject and exam focused**, enabling you to **acquire knowledge, practice and revise efficiently and effectively**.

THE BPP STUDY TEXT

Aims of this Study Text

To provide you with the knowledge and understanding, skills and application techniques that you need if you are to be successful in your exams

This Study Text has been written around the **Systems and Project Management** syllabus.

- It is **comprehensive**. It covers the syllabus content. No more, no less.
- It is written at the **right level**. Each chapter is written with CIMA's precise learning outcomes in mind.
- It is targeted to the **exam**.

To allow you to study in the way that best suits your learning style and the time you have available, by following your personal Study Plan (see page (ix))

The BPP Study Test has a variety of features, highlighted by icons. You can use these features in different ways to suit your learning style. You may be studying at home on your own, or you may be attending a full-time course. You may like to (and have time to) read every word, or you may prefer to (or only have time to) skim-read and devote the remainder of your time to question practice. Wherever you fall in the spectrum, you will find the BPP Study Text meets your needs in designing and following your personal Study Plan.

To tie in with the other components of the BPP Effective Study Package to ensure you have the best possible chance of passing the exam (see page (vi))

The BPP Study Text

Recommended period of use	Elements of the BPP Effective Study Package
From the outset and throughout	**Learning to learn accountancy** Read this invaluable book as you begin your studies and refer to it as you work through the various elements of the BPP Effective Study Package. It will help you to acquire knowledge, practice and revise, both efficiently and effectively.
Three to twelve months before the exam	**Study Text and i-Learn** Use the Study Text to acquire knowledge, understanding, skills and the ability to use application techniques. Use BPP's **i-Learn** product to reinforce your learning.
Throughout	**Virtual Campus** Study, practice, revise and take advantage of other useful resources with BPP's fully interactive e-learning site with comprehensive tutor support.
Throughout	**MCQ cards and i-Pass** Revise your knowledge and ability to apply techniques, with 150 multiple choice questions. **i-Pass**, our computer-based testing package, provides objective test questions in a variety of formats and is ideal for self-assessment.
One to six months before the exam	**Practice & Revision Kit** Try the numerous examination-format questions, for which there are realistic suggested solutions prepared by BPP's own authors. Then attempt the two mock exams.
From three months before the exam until the last minute	**Passcards** Work through these short, memorable notes which are focused on what is most likely to come up in the exam you will be sitting.
One to six months before the exam	**Success Tapes** These audio tapes cover the vital elements of your syllabus in less than 90 minutes per subject. Each tape also contains exam hints to help you fine tune your strategy.
Three to twelve months before the exam	**Breakthrough Videos** Use a Breakthrough Video to supplement your Study Text. They give you clear tuition on key exam subjects and allow you the luxury of being able to pause or repeat sections until you have fully grasped the topic.

HELP YOURSELF STUDY FOR YOUR CIMA EXAMS

Exams for professional bodies such as CIMA are different from those set at college or university. They place you under **greater time pressure before** the exam - as you may be combining your study with work - as well as in the exam room. There are many different ways of learning and so the BPP Study Text offers you a number of different tools to help you through. Some tips are included in the approach suggested below.

The right approach

1 **The right attitude**

Believe in yourself	Yes, there is a lot to learn. Yes, it is a challenge. But thousands have succeeded before and you can too.
Remember why you're doing it	Studying might seem a grind at times, but you are doing it for a reason: to advance your career.

2 **The right focus**

Read through the syllabus and learning outcomes section	These tell you what you are expected to know and are supplemented by Exam Focus Points in the text.
Study the Exam Paper section	Past papers are a reasonable guide of what you should expect in the exam. Take note of the form of assessment that will be used in the exam *you* will be facing.

3 **The right method**

The big picture	You need to grasp the detail - but keeping in mind how everything fits into the big picture will help you understand better. • The **Introduction** of each chapter puts the material in context. • The **Syllabus content**, **Learning outcomes** and **Exam focus points** show you what you need to **grasp**. • **Mind Maps** show the links and key issues in key topics.
In your own words	To absorb the information (and to practise your written communication skills), it helps **put it into your own words**. • **Take notes.** • Answer the **questions** in each chapter. As well as helping you absorb the information you will practise your written communication skills, which become increasingly important as you progress through your CIMA exams. • Draw **mind maps**. We have some examples. • Try 'teaching' to a colleague or friend.

Give yourself cues to jog your memory	The BPP Study Text uses **bold** to **highlight key points** and **icons** to identify key features, such as **Exam focus points** and **Key terms**.
	• Try **colour coding** with a highlighter pen.
	• Write **key points** on cards.

4   **The right review**

Review, review, review	It is a **fact** that regularly reviewing a topic in summary form can **fix it in your memory**. Because **review** is so important, the BPP Study Text helps you in many ways.
	• **Chapter roundups** summarise the key points in each chapter. Use them to recap each study session.
	• The **Quick quiz** is another review technique to ensure that you have grasped the essentials.
	• Go through the **Examples** in each chapter a second or third time.

Help yourself study for your CIMA exams

Developing your personal Study Plan

One thing that the BPP Learning to learn accountancy book emphasises (see page (iv)) is the need to prepare (and use) a study plan. Planning and sticking to the plan are key elements of learning success. There are **four steps** you should work through.

Step 1. How do you learn?

First you need to be aware of your style of learning. The BPP Learning to learn accountancy book commits a chapter to this **self-discovery**. What types of intelligence do you display when learning? You might be advised to brush up on certain study skills before launching into this Study Text.

> BPP's **Learning to learn accountancy** book helps you to identify what intelligences you show more strongly and then details how you can tailor your study process through your preferences. It also includes handy hints on how to develop intelligences you exhibit less strongly, but which might be needed as you study accountancy.

Are you a **theorist** or are you more **practical**? If you would rather get to grips with a theory before trying to apply it in practice, you should follow the study sequence on page X. If the reverse is true (you like to know why you are learning theory before you do so), you might be advised to flick through Study Text chapters and look at questions, case studies and examples (Steps 7, 8 and 9 in the **suggested study sequence**) before reading through the detailed theory.

Step 2. How much time do you have?

Work out the time you have available per week, given the following.

- The standard you have set yourself
- The time you need to set aside later for work on the Practice & Revision Kit and Passcards
- The other exam(s) you are sitting
- Very importantly, practical matters such as work, travel, exercise, sleep and social life

Note your time available in box A. A [ ] Hours

Step 3. Allocate your time

- Take the time you have available per week for this Study Text shown in box A, multiply it by the number of weeks available and insert the result in box B. B [ ]

- Divide the figure in Box B by the number of chapters in this text and insert the result in box C. C [ ]

Remember that this is only a rough guide. Some of the chapters in this book are longer and more complicated than others, and you will find some subjects easier to understand than others.

Step 4. Implement

Set about studying each chapter in the time shown in box C, following the key study steps in the order suggested by your particular learning style.

This is your personal **Study Plan**. You should try and combine it with the study sequence outlined below. You may want to modify the sequence a little (as has been suggested above) to adapt it to your **personal style**.

Help yourself study for your CIMA exams

Suggested study sequence

Tackle the chapters in the order you find them in the Study Text. Taking into account your individual learning style, you could follow this sequence.

Key study steps	Activity
Step 1 **Topic list**	Each numbered topic is a numbered section in the chapter.
Step 2 **Introduction**	This gives you the **big picture** in terms of the **context** of the chapter, the **content** you will cover, and the **learning outcomes** the chapter assesses - in other words, it sets your **objectives for study.**
Step 3 **Knowledge brought forward boxes**	In these we highlight information and techniques that it is assumed you have 'brought forward' with you from your earlier studies. If there are topics which have changed recently due to legislation for example, these topics are explained in more detail.
Step 4 **Explanations**	Proceed methodically through the chapter, reading each section thoroughly and making sure you understand. Where a topic has been examined, we state the month and year of examination against the appropriate heading. You should pay particular attention to these topics.
Step 5 **Key terms and Exam focus points**	• **Key terms** can often earn you *easy marks* if you state them clearly and correctly in an appropriate exam answer (and they are indexed at the back of the text). • **Exam focus points** give you a good idea of how we think the examiner intends to examine certain topics.
Step 6 **Note taking**	Take brief notes if you wish, avoiding the temptation to copy out too much.
Step 7 **Examples**	Follow each through to its solution very carefully.
Step 8 **Case examples**	Study each one, and try to add flesh to them from your own experience - they are designed to show how the topics you are studying come alive (and often come unstuck) in the real world.
Step 9 **Questions**	Make a very good attempt at each one.
Step 10 **Answers**	Check yours against ours, and make sure you understand any discrepancies.
Step 11 **Chapter roundup**	Work through it very carefully, to make sure you have grasped the major points it is highlighting.
Step 12 **Quick quiz**	When you are happy that you have covered the chapter, use the **Quick quiz** to check how much you have remembered of the topics covered.

Key study steps	Activity
Step 13 **Question(s) in the Question bank**	Either at this point, or later when you are thinking about revising, make a full attempt at the **Question(s)** suggested at the very end of the chapter. You can find these at the end of the Study Text, along with the **Answers** so you can see how you did. We highlight those that are introductory, and those which are of the standard you would expect to find in an exam.

Short of time: *Skim study technique?*

You may find you simply do not have the time available to follow all the key study steps for each chapter, however you adapt them for your particular learning style. If this is the case, follow the **skim study** technique below (the icons in the Study Text will help you to do this).

- Study the chapters in the order you find them in the Study Text.

- For each chapter, follow the key study steps 1-3, and then skim-read through step 4. Jump to step 11, and then go back to step 5. Follow through steps 7 and 8, and prepare outline answers to questions (steps 9/10). Try the Quick quiz (step 12), following up any items you can't answer, then do a plan for the Question (step 13), comparing it against our answers. You should probably still follow step 6 (note-taking), although you may decide simply to rely on the BPP Passcards for this.

Moving on...

However you study, when you are ready to embark on the practice and revision phase of the BPP Effective Study Package, you should still refer back to this Study Text, both as a source of **reference** (you should find the index particularly helpful for this) and as a **refresher** (the Chapter roundups and Quick quizzes help you here).

And remember to keep careful hold of this Study Text - you may find it useful in your work.

SYLLABUS AND LEARNING OUTCOMES

Syllabus overview

This syllabus introduces students to the concepts, tool and issues of the management of Information Technology and Systems, the process and tools of project management, and the control of organisational systems. It is assumed that students will have basic knowledge and understanding of the following areas, either from their earlier studies or from their work experience, prior to commencing study for this examination.

(a) The features and function of common IT hardware, software, peripherals and networks, and their application to management accounting and other parts of the organisation.

(b) The characteristics and components of a simple information system (data input, processing, storage, information output).

(c) The most common controls in computerised systems (security measures, verification, validation, access controls, backup).

Although Chartered Management Accountants are finance specialists they are often given early responsibility for the design, development, implementation and control of Information Systems. This work normally consists of a series of projects, of which the Chartered Management Accountant may be manager.

Another major aspect of the work of Chartered Management Accountants is control. Either through their day-to-day activities or as part of an internal audit function, Chartered Management Accountants are tasked with ensuring that the various systems within an organisation achieve their objectives.

One of the objectives of this syllabus is to introduce and develop some of the skills required for success in the case study at the Final level.

Aims

The syllabus aims to test the student's ability to:

- Contribute to the management of key projects
- Evaluate an organisation's Information Systems and recommend appropriate solutions
- Recommend improvements to the control of organisational activities and resources
- Advise management on the audit of systems and activities
- Evaluate and recommend improvements in the management of quality

Assessment

There will be a written paper of 3 hours. All questions are based upon a single substantial scenario. The pages containing the questions are detachable from the paper so that the questions can be referred to at the same time as the scenario. Answers will normally be required in the form of memorandum, letter, briefing notes, presentation slides or report.

The paper contains two sections (questions in both sections are based upon the scenario):

Section A (80 marks). Three compulsory questions (10, 30 and 40 marks).

Section B (20 marks). Answer one question from two.

Syllabus and learning outcomes

Learning outcomes and syllabus content

(i) Project management *(study weighting 30%)*

Learning outcomes

On completion of their studies students should be able to:

- Explain the skills required of a project manager
- Evaluate the project management process
- Produce a management plan for a simple project
- Apply project management tools
- Analyse the issues relating to the selection and management of an effective project team
- Evaluate the relationships between the project manager, the project team and organisational project sponsors
- Identify problems with the interpersonal relationships of project staff and recommend solutions to those problems
- Explain why meetings are commonly used in organisations
- Explain the planning and conduct of a meeting and the roles of the various participants in a typical meeting
- Identify the main problems associated with meetings and recommend how those problems might be avoided or solved
- Recommend changes to the management and conduct of a meeting in order to avoid or solve problems identified
- Produce a presentation on a management accounting topic
- Explain the process of post-completion audit and its importance in the project management process

Syllabus content

	Covered in Chapter(s)
The skills of a project manager	1
The scope of project management	1
Project objectives, performance measurement and control	2
Building and managing a project team	1
The stages of a project (eg initiation, formation, objective setting, planning, feasibility, fact finding, position analysis, options generation, options evaluation, design and development, implementation, review, completion)	2
The major tools and techniques used at each of the project stages (ie project initiation document, SWOT analysis, critical path analysis, Gantt chart, resource histogram, budget, progress report, completion report)	2
The purpose, conduct and limitations of meetings in a business context	3

Syllabus and learning outcomes

Covered in Chapter(s)

- The roles which may be adopted by participants in a business meeting (eg chair, secretary, facilitator, advisor, protagonists, antagonists) and how the chair should manage those participants to retain control of the meeting — 3

- The stakeholders of a project (eg organisation, customers, steering committee, project manager, project team, vendors, specialists, users) and the relationships between them — 1

- Managing project stakeholder conflict — 1

(ii) Information technology and systems   *(study weighting 35%)*

Learning outcomes

On completion of their studies students should be able to:

- Explain the features and operation of commonly-used Information Technology hardware and software
- Evaluate the use and relative merits of different hardware and applications architectures
- Identify opportunities for the use of Information Technology in organisations, particularly in the implementation and running of the Information System
- Apply General Systems Theory to the design of Information Systems in organisations
- Recommend how the value of information can be increased by careful design of an organisation's data and information architecture
- Explain the importance of effective communication and the consequences of failure in the communication process
- Analyse communication problems in a range of organisational situations
- Recommend changes or action to avoid or correct communication problems
- Evaluate the operation of the various parts of the Information System of an organisation and the relationships between them
- Explain the issues involved in planning and managing an Information Systems project and produce a management plan for such a project
- Apply the main tools and techniques used in the gathering, recording and analysis of information relating to an existing Information System
- Explain the processes of system design and development and analyse the main issues arising at those stages
- Identify and evaluate the main issues relating to the development of an Information Systems solution, and the risks involved in implementation
- Explain the nature and purpose of system maintenance and performance evaluation

Covered in Chapter(s)

Syllabus content

- The various types of Information Technology hardware and software in common use in organisations — 8

- The different hardware and applications architectures (ie centralised, distributed, client-server) available to organisations, and the Information Technology required to operate them (eg PCs, servers, networks, peripherals) — 8

(xiv)

Syllabus and learning outcomes

Covered in Chapter(s)

- The concepts of General Systems Theory and their application to Information Systems (ie system definition, system components, system behaviour, system classification, entropy, requisite variety, coupling and decoupling) — 4
- The qualities of information — 4
- Designing data and information architectures to assist and improve planning, decision-making and control — 4
- The use of information for decision-making at the various levels of the organisation, and the components of the Information System which can support those decisions (ie transaction processing systems, management information systems, decision support systems, executive information systems, expert systems) — 4
- The purpose and process of communication — 9
- Communication problems and solutions — 9
- The main communication tools (ie conversation, meeting, presentation, memorandum, letter, report, telephone, facsimile, electronic mail, video-conference), their features and limitations — 9
- Systems evaluation — 7
- The concept of the systems development life-cycle when applied to an Information Systems project — 2, 5, 6
- The stages in the systems development life-cycle — 5
- Assessing the feasibility of systems projects (ie cost-benefit analysis, technical feasibility, time feasibility) — 6
- Information gathering techniques (ie interviews, questionnaires, observation, simulation, document review) — 6
- Recording and documenting tools used during the analysis and design of systems (ie entity-relationship model, logical data structure, entity life history, dataflow diagram, and decision table) — 6
- Databases and database management systems (Note: Knowledge of database structures will not be required) — 5
- The nature and purpose of data normalisation and Structured English (Note: students will not be expected to apply these techniques) — 6
- Performance and technical specification (Note: Knowledge of computer programming is not required) — 7
- Prototyping, including the use of fourth generation languages to improve productivity — 5
- The features, benefits and drawbacks of structured methodologies (eg SSADM) for the development of Information Systems (Note: detailed knowledge of any specific methodology will not be required) — 5
- The problems associated with the management of in-house and vendor solutions and how they can be avoided or solved — 8
- System testing (ie off-line, on-line and user-acceptance) — 7
- System documentation (ie user and technical manuals) — 7
- Training and user support — 7
- File conversion procedures — 7
- System changeover methods (ie direct, parallel, pilot, phased) — 7
- Maintenance of systems (ie corrective, adaptive, preventive) — 7

Syllabus and learning outcomes

(iii) Control of activities and resources *(study weighting 10%)*

Learning outcomes

On completion of their studies students should be able to:

- Evaluate and recommend appropriate control systems for the management of organisations
- Evaluate the control of activities and resources within the organisation
- Recommend ways in which the problems associated with control systems could be avoided or solved
- Evaluate and recommend improvements to the control of Information Systems including those using Information Technology

Covered in Chapter(s)

Syllabus content

• The way in which systems are used to achieve control within the framework of the organisation (eg contracts of employment, policies and procedures, discipline and reward, reporting structures, performance appraisal and feedback)	10
• The views of classical and contemporary management writers relating to control	10
• The application of control systems and related theory to the design of management accounting systems and information systems in general (ie control system components, primary and secondary feedback, positive and negative feedback, open and closed-loop control)	10
• The controls which can be designed into an information system, particularly one using information technology (eg security, integrity and contingency controls)	10

(iv) Audit of activities and systems *(study weighting 15%)*

Learning outcomes

On completion of their studies students should be able to:

- Explain the process of internal audit
- Produce a plan for the audit of various organisational activities including management, accounting and information systems
- Analyse problems associated with the audit of activities and systems, and recommend action to avoid or solve those problems
- Recommend action to improve the efficiency, effectiveness and control of activities
- Evaluate specific problems associated with the audit of systems which use information technology

Covered in Chapter(s)

Syllabus content

• The process of review and audit of internal controls	11
• The major tools available to assist with such a review (eg audit planning, documenting systems, internal control questionnaires, sampling and testing)	11, 12
• The identification and prevention of fraud	11, 12
• The role of the internal auditor and the relationship between the internal auditor and the external audit	11

Syllabus and learning outcomes

	Covered in Chapter(s)
• The techniques available to assist audit in a computerised environment	12
• The use of Information Technology to assist the audit process (ie CAATs)	12
• The operation of internal audit, the assessment of audit risk and the process of analytical review	11
• The different types of benchmarking, their use and limitations	11, 13
• The analysis of business risks and approaches to risk management	11
• Value for money audit and management audit	11

(v) Management of quality *(study weighting 10%)*

Learning outcomes

On completion of their studies students should be able to:

- Analyse problems with the management of quality in an organisation
- Evaluate the features, benefits and drawbacks of contemporary approaches to the management of quality
- Produce and communicate a plan for the implementation of a quality improvement programme

	Covered in Chapter(s)
Syllabus content	
• The concept of quality and how the quality of products, services and activities can be assessed, measured and improved	13
• Quality circles	13
• The use of benchmarking in quality measurement and improvement	13
• The various approaches to the management of quality (ie quality inspection, quality control, quality assurance, total quality)	13
• External quality standards (eg the various ISO standards appropriate to products and organisations)	13
• Contemporary developments in the management of quality	13

Syllabus and learning outcomes

Syllabus Mind Map

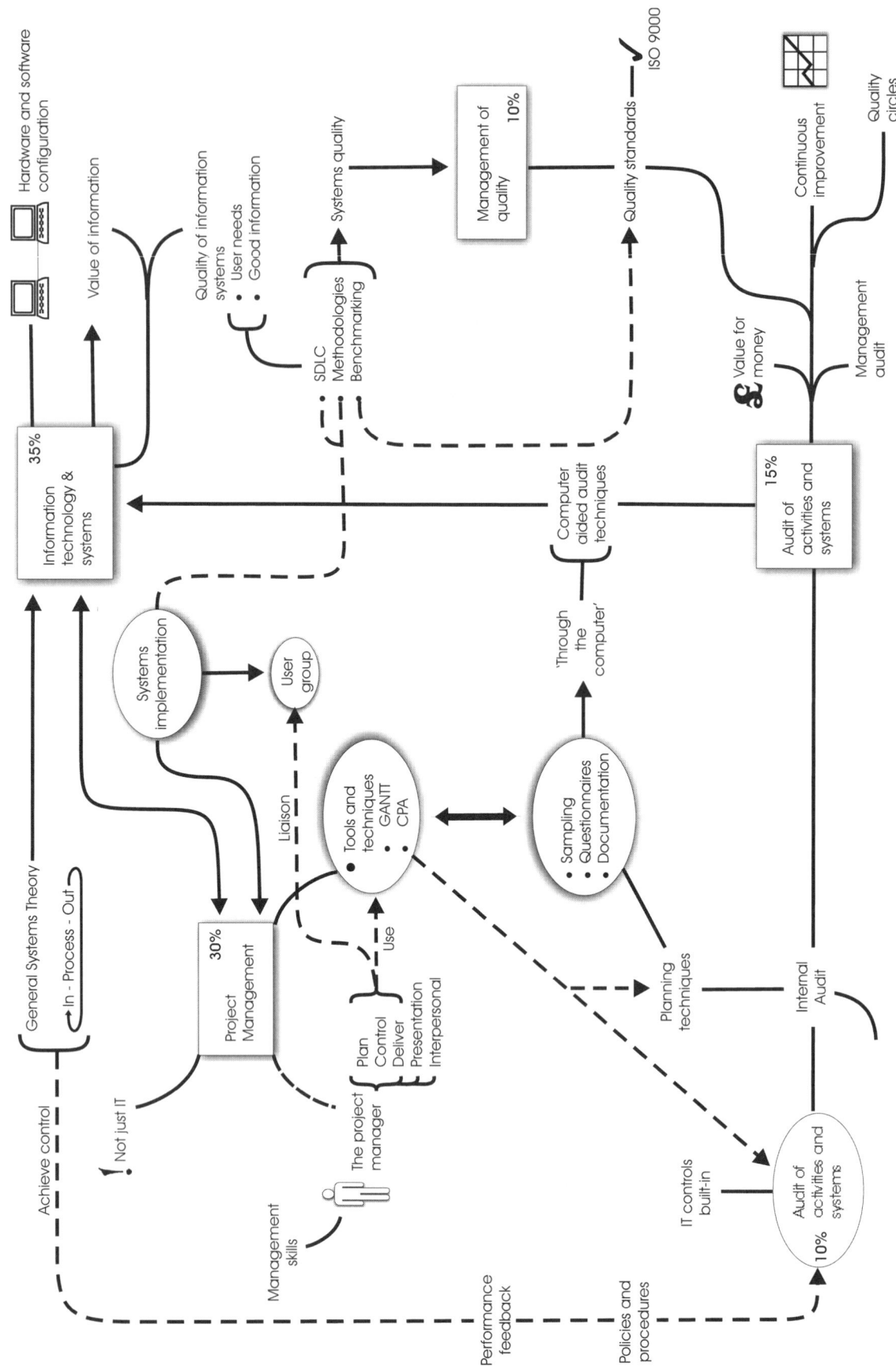

THE EXAM PAPER

Format of the paper

The paper consists of a **single substantial scenario** on which **all** questions are based. Responses will normally be in the form of memorandum, letter, briefing notes, presentation slides or report.

The format of the exam **changed** with effect from May 2002. Before then, the paper consisted of four compulsory questions. Under the new format, the exam provides candidates with a limited amount of choice. The current exam format is explained below.

All questions are based on the same scenario. The pages containing the questions are detachable from the paper so that the questions can be referred to at the same time as the scenario. There are two sections to the paper:

Section A (80 marks). **Three compulsory** questions (10, 30 and 40 marks).

Section B (20 marks). Answer **one** question **from two**.

Time allowed: 3 hours

Total marks: 100

Analysis of past papers

May 2002

A four page scenario regarding a health authority connecting to a national information network.

Section A (three compulsory questions)

Question 1

Produce briefing notes relating to benchmarking. (10 marks)

Question 2

(a) Produce a memorandum discussing the relationship of the project manager to various stakeholders and potential conflicting objectives. (20 marks)
(b) Discuss potential project management problems that may arise from allowing separate terms to be negotiated by individual hospitals/medical centres. (10 marks)

Question 3

Prepare a maximum of ten presentation slides with accompanying notes that:
(a) Explain the importance of communication and consequences of communication failure. (15 marks)
(b) Identifies opportunities for the use of IT and explains the benefits of an intranet. (15 marks)
(c) Identifies the features and advantages of an expert system. (10 marks)

Section B (answer one question from the two available)

Question 4

(a) Identify security problems and recommend items for a code of conduct. (11 marks)
(b) Discuss problems that could be encountered conducting a Value for Money Audit. (9 marks)

Question 5

(a) Explain the importance of using performance measures for project objectives. (5 marks)
(b) Produce a set of performance measures. (15 marks)

The exam paper

November 2001 (old format)

This paper followed the old examination format – four compulsory questions based on a scenario. The four page scenario (including a one page Data Flow Diagram) concerned a joint venture manufacturing project.

1 A memorandum for project team members containing a project SWOT analysis and an analysis of project selection and leadership issues, and an outline agenda for a post-completion review. (31 marks)

2 A set of briefing notes explaining the project reporting procedures shown in a Data Flow Diagram and identifying weaknesses in the procedures. (25 marks)

3 A memorandum explaining the purpose of quality standards and evaluating the benefits of quality management. A second memorandum regarding internal quality audits. (22 marks)

4 The first draft of a report regarding cost management and risk management issues. (22 marks)

May 2001 (old format)

The three page scenario concerned a medium-sized manufacturing company introducing an integrated production planning and management reporting system.

1 Prepare a report for the Board:
   - Describing a standard management process for IT projects
   - Explaining problems that occurred in the project management process
   - Evaluating project team relationships
   - Explaining how communications and team meetings should have been undertaken

   (30 marks)

2 Write an individual memorandum to the project team:
   - Analysing and recommending data controls
   - Explaining the internal audit function compared to external audit
   - Explaining audit problems with integrated real-time systems

   (25 marks)

3 Prepare briefing notes for the steering committee:
   - Explaining planning and managing an IS project using the SDLC
   - Identifying the risks associated with the tendering process
   - Produce a Gantt chart using project plan data

   (31 marks)

4 Prepare outline slides and a set of accompanying notes:
   - Evaluating the importance of quality management
   - Produce a plan to communicate this information

   (14 marks)

Pilot paper (old format)

A three page scenario about an information system implementation project at a small chain of retail outlets.

1 Prepare a report for the chief executive explaining processing options, system merits and how decision making will be improved. (25 marks)

2 Prepare a memorandum to the chief executive explaining the benefits of using a structured methodology and how the concept of quality can be applied to information systems. (20 marks)

3 Prepare a briefing report for the management team that describes the project management issues, evaluates project management tools and produces a critical path analysis. (30 marks)

4 Prepare slides and supporting notes for a presentation to be given to shop managers explaining the role of the internal auditor, internal controls and how IT could assist the audit process. (25 marks)

WHAT THE EXAMINER MEANS

The table below has been prepared by CIMA to help you interpret exam questions.

Learning objective	Verbs used	Definition
1 Knowledge What you are expected to know	• List • State • Define	• Make a list of • Express, fully or clearly, the details of/facts of • Give the exact meaning of
2 Comprehension What you are expected to understand	• Describe • Distinguish • Explain • Identify • Illustrate	• Communicate the key features of • Highlight the differences between • Make clear or intelligible/state the meaning of • Recognise, establish or select after consideration • Use an example to describe or explain something
3 Application Can you apply your knowledge?	• Apply • Calculate/ compute • Demonstrate • Prepare • Reconcile • Solve • Tabulate	• To put to practical use • To ascertain or reckon mathematically • To prove with certainty or to exhibit by practical means • To make or get ready for use • To make or prove consistent/compatible • Find an answer to • Arrange in a table
4 Analysis Can you analyse the detail of what you have learned?	• Analyse • Categorise • Compare and contrast • Construct • Discuss • Interpret • Produce	• Examine in detail the structure of • Place into a defined class or division • Show the similarities and/or differences between • To build up or compile • To examine in detail by argument • To translate into intelligible or familiar terms • To create or bring into existence
5 Evaluation Can you use your learning to evaluate, make decisions or recommendations?	• Advise • Evaluate • Recommend	• To counsel, inform or notify • To appraise or assess the value of • To advise on a course of action

TACKLING SCENARIO QUESTIONS

All questions in the examination for Paper 10 are based on a written scenario (ie a case study). Responses will normally be in the form of memorandum, letter, briefing notes, presentation slides or report.

A case study or scenario is simply a history or description of an organisation facing a particular set of circumstances. There is usually some discussion of how the organisation's current situation developed, and there is often one or more central characters charged with the task of resolving the problem, or exploiting the opportunity.

Cases may be based around activities of real people and organisations (although candidates do *not* require any specialist knowledge of any particular organisation), or they may be fictitious.

The essential function of this type of examination is to test a candidate's ability to tackle relatively complex, unstructured problems. There **may be several feasible solutions** and candidates should not necessarily expect there to be a single definitive answer. The solution will involve the use of techniques which have been learned, but usually also requires the exercise of judgement and (possibly) creative thinking. Preparation to answer case incident/scenario-based questions cannot rely on reading alone, but must be heavily supplemented **by question practice under examination conditions**.

It is important to realise that in case study questions marks are earned by the quality of the reasoning and exposition displayed. The **ability to structure a coherent report** which leads logically to its conclusion is regarded as essential. Recommendations are often required. Acceptable recommendations may vary but must be sensible and fully justified. Drawing on your own practical experience is often useful.

Candidates' chances of success will be significantly enhanced if they are **familiar with the current business environment**. An easy way to achieve this is to read selectively from the *Financial Times* and to visit relevant business oriented websites. Examination answers are enhanced by examples drawn from the real world.

Key points to remember when tackling case study questions

- Answer the question asked – tailor what you know to fit the scenario
- Plan your answer – this will help clarify your thoughts
- Structure your answer eg introduction, body of answer, conclusion
- Justify your recommendations

Part A
Project management

Chapter 1

INTRODUCING PROJECT MANAGEMENT

Topic list		Syllabus reference	Ability required
1	The scope of project management	(i)	Application
2	The project manager	(i)	Comprehension
3	The project team	(i)	Evaluation
4	Project stakeholders	(i)	Evaluation

Introduction

Welcome to **project management**, a topic that has grown in significance in both the 'real' and academic worlds over recent years.

This chapter will introduce the subject of project management, explain what project management is and outline what a **project manager** does. Later in the chapter we look at how a **project team** should be put together, and examine the **stakeholders** of a project and the relationships between them.

Project management tools and techniques will be covered in Chapter 2.

Learning outcomes covered in this chapter

- **Evaluate** the project management process
- **Explain** the skills required of a project manager
- **Analyse** the issues relating to the selection and management of an effective project team
- **Identify** problems with the interpersonal relationships of project staff and recommend solutions to these problems
- **Evaluate** the relationships between the project manager, the project team and organisational project sponsors

Syllabus content covered in this chapter

- The scope of project management
- The skills required of a project manager
- Building and managing a project team
- The stakeholders of a project and the relationships between them
- Managing project stakeholder conflict

Part A: Project management

1 THE SCOPE OF PROJECT MANAGEMENT

What is a project?

1.1 To understand project management it is necessary to first define what a project is.

KEY TERMS

A **project** is 'an undertaking that has a beginning and an end and is carried out to meet established goals within cost, schedule and quality objectives'. (Haynes, *Project Management*)

Resources are the money, facilities, supplies, services and people allocated to the project.

1.2 In general, the work which organisations undertake involves either **operations** or **projects**. Operations and projects are planned, controlled and executed. So how are projects distinguished from 'ordinary work'?

Projects	Operations
Have a defined beginning and end	On-going
Have resources allocated specifically to them, although often on a shared basis	Resources used 'full-time'
Are intended to be done only once (eg organising the 2002 London Marathon – the 2003 event is a separate project)	A mixture of many recurring tasks
Follow a plan towards a clear intended end-result	Goals and deadlines are more general
Often cut across organisational and functional lines	Usually follows the organisation or functional structure

1.3 An activity that meets the first four criteria above can be classified as a project, and therefore falls within the **scope of project management**. Whether an activity is classified as a project is important, as projects should be managed using **project management techniques**.

1.4 Common examples of projects include:

- Producing a new product, service or object
- Changing the structure of an organisation
- Developing or modifying a new information system
- Implementing a new business procedure or process

What is project management?

KEY TERM

Project management is the combination of systems, techniques, and people used to control and monitor activities undertaken within the project. Project management co-ordinates the resources necessary to complete the project successfully.

1: Introducing project management

1.5 The objective of project management is a successful project. A project will be deemed successful if it is completed at the **specified level of quality**, **on time** and **within budget**.

Objective	Comment
Quality	The end result should conform to the project specification. In other words, the result should achieve what the project was supposed to do.
Budget	The project should be completed without exceeding authorised expenditure.
Timescale	The progress of the project must follow the planned process, so that the 'result' is ready for use at the agreed date. As time is money, proper time management can help contain costs.

1.6 Projects present some management challenges.

Challenge	Comment
Teambuilding	The work is carried out by a team of people often from varied work and social backgrounds. The team must 'gel' quickly and be able to communicate effectively with each other.
Expected problems	Expected problems should be avoided by careful design and planning prior to commencement of work.
Unexpected problems	There should be mechanisms within the project to enable these problems to be resolved quickly and efficiently.
Delayed benefit	There is normally no benefit until the work is finished. The 'lead in' time to this can cause a strain on the eventual recipient who is also faced with increasing expenditure for no immediate benefit.
Specialists	Contributions made by specialists are of differing importance at each stage.
Potential for conflict	Projects often involve several parties with different interests. This may lead to conflict.

1.7 Project management ensures responsibilities are clearly defined and that resources are **focussed** on specific objectives. The **project management process** also provides a structure for communicating within and across organisational boundaries.

1.8 All projects share similar features and follow a similar process. This has led to the development of **project management tools and techniques** that can be applied to all projects, no matter how diverse. For example, with some limitations similar processes and techniques can be applied whether building a major structure (eg The Millennium Dome) or implementing a company-wide computer network.

1.9 All projects require a person who is ultimately responsible for delivering the required outcome. This person (whether officially given the title or not) is the **project manager**.

2 THE PROJECT MANAGER

2.1 Some project managers have the job title 'Project Manager'. These people usually have one major responsibility: the project. Most people in business will have 'normal work' responsibilities outside their project goals – which may lead to conflicting demands on their time. Anybody responsible for a project (large or small) is a project manager.

Part A: Project management

> **KEY TERMS**
>
> The person who takes ultimate responsibility for ensuring the desired result is achieved on time and within budget is the **project manager**.
>
> The way in which a project manager co-ordinates a project from initiation to completion, using project management and general management techniques, is known as the **project management process**.

2.2 The role a project manager performs is in many ways similar to those performed by other managers. There are however some important differences, as shown in the table below.

Project manager	Operations manager
Are often 'generalists' with wide-ranging backgrounds and experience levels	Usually specialists in the areas managed
Oversee work in many functional areas	Relate closely to technical tasks in their area
Facilitate, rather than supervise team members	Have direct technical supervision responsibilities

2.3 A person should only take on the role of project manager if they have the time available to do the job effectively. Also, if somebody is to be held responsible for the project, they must be given the resources and authority required to complete project tasks.

2.4 The duties of a project manager are summarised below.

Duty	Comment
Outline planning	Project planning (eg targets, sequencing) <ul><li>Developing project targets such as overall costs or timescale needed (eg project should take 20 weeks).</li><li>Dividing the project into activities and placing these activities into the right sequence, often a complicated task if overlapping.</li><li>Developing a framework for the procedures and structures, manage the project (eg decide, in principle, to have weekly team meetings, performance reviews etc).</li></ul>
Detailed planning	Work breakdown structure, resource requirements, network analysis for scheduling.
Teambuilding	Build cohesion and team spirit.
Communication	The project manager must let superiors know what is going on, and ensure that members of the project team are properly briefed.
Co-ordinating project activities	Between the project team and users, and other external parties (eg suppliers of hardware and software).
Monitoring and control	The project manager should estimate the causes for each departure from the standard, and take corrective measures.
Problem-resolution	Even with the best planning, unforeseen problems may arise.
Quality control	There is often a short-sighted trade-off between getting the project out on time and the project's quality.

1: Introducing project management

2.5 Project management as a discipline developed because of a need to co-ordinate resources to obtain desired results within a set timeframe. Common project management tasks include establishing goals and objectives, developing a work-plan, scheduling, budgeting, co-ordinating a team and communicating.

2.6 The project management process helps project managers maintain control of projects and meet their responsibilities.

The responsibilities of a project manager

2.7 A project manager has responsibilities to both management and to the project team.

Responsibilities to management

- Ensure resources are used efficiently – strike a balance between cost, time and results
- Keep management informed with timely and accurate communications
- Manage the project to the best of his or her ability
- Behave ethically, and adhere to the organisation's policies
- Maintain a customer orientation (whether the project is geared towards an internal or external customer) - customer satisfaction is a key indicator of project success

Responsibilities to the project and the project team

- Take action to keep the project on target for successful completion
- Ensure the project team has the resources required to perform tasks assigned
- Help new team members integrate into the team
- Provide any support required when members leave the team either during the project or on completion

The skills required of a project manager

2.8 To meet these responsibilities a project manager requires a wide range of skills. The skills required are similar to those required when managing a wider range of responsibilities. Some of the skills required are described in the following table.

Type of skill	How the project manager should display the type of skill
Leadership and team building	Be **enthusiastic** about what the project will achieve.
	Be **positive** (but realistic) about all aspects of the project.
	Understand where the project fits into the '**big picture**'.
	Delegate tasks appropriately – and not take on too much personally.
	Build team spirit through encouraging **co-operation.**
	Do not be restrained by organisational structures – a high tolerance for ambiguity (lack of clear-cut authority) will help the project manager.

Part A: Project management

Type of skill	How the project manager should display the type of skill
Organisational	Ensure all project **documentation** is clear and distributed to all who require it.
	Use project **management tools** to analyse and monitor project progress.
Communication	**Listen** to project team members.
	Use **persuasion** to coerce reluctant team members or stakeholders to support the project.
	Ensure management is kept **informed** and is never surprised.
Technical	By providing (or at least providing access to) the **technical expertise** and experience needed to manage the project.
Personal	Be **flexible**. Circumstances may develop that require a change in plan.
	Show **persistence.** Even successful projects will encounter difficulties that require repeated efforts to overcome.
	Be **creative**. If one method of completing a task proves impractical a new approach may be required.
	Patience is required even in the face of tight deadlines. The 'quick-fix' may eventually cost more time than a more thorough but initially more time-consuming solution.

Leadership styles and project management

2.9 As in other forms of management, different project managers have different styles of leadership. There is no 'best' leadership style, as individuals suit and react to different styles in different ways. The key is adopting a style that suits both the project leader and the project team.

2.10 Managers will usually adopt a style from the range shown in the following diagram.

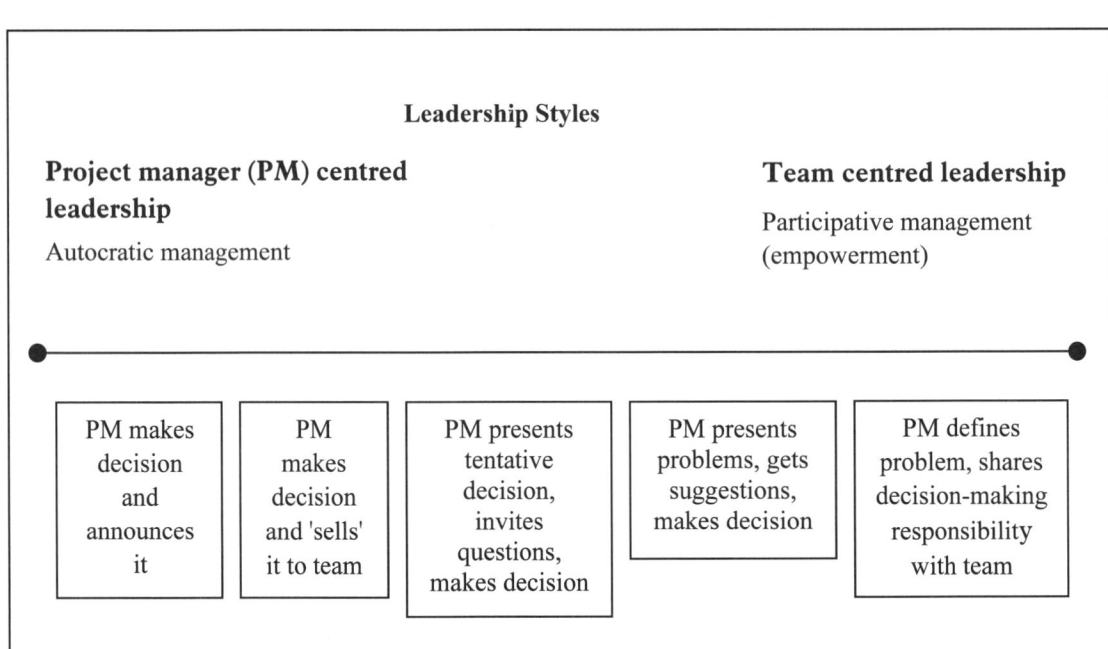

2.11 The leadership style adopted will affect the way decisions relating to the project are made. Although an autocratic style may prove successful in some situations (eg 'simple' or 'repetitive' projects), a more consultative style has the advantage of making team members feel more a part of the project. This should result in greater **commitment**.

2.12 Not all decisions will be made in the same way. For example, decisions that do not have direct consequences for other project personnel may be made with no (or limited) consultation. A **balance** needs to be found between ensuring decisions can be made efficiently, and ensuring adequate consultation.

2.13 The type of people that comprise the project team will influence the style adopted. For example, professionals generally dislike being closely supervised and dictated to. (Many non-professionals dislike this too!) Some people however, prefer to follow clear, specific instructions and not have to think for themselves.

2.14 Project management techniques encourage **management by exception** by identifying, from the outset, those activities which might threaten successful completion of a project.

3 THE PROJECT TEAM 5/01

Building a project team

> **KEY TERM**
>
> The **Project Team** comprises the people who report directly or indirectly to the project manager.

3.1 Project success depends to a large extent on the team members selected. The ideal project team achieves project completion on time, within budget and to the required specifications - with the minimum amount of direct supervision from the project manager.

3.2 The team will comprise individuals with **differing skills and personalities**. The project manager should choose a balanced team that takes advantage of each team member's skills and compensates elsewhere for their weaknesses.

3.3 The project team will normally be drawn from existing staff, but highly recommended **outsiders with special skills** may be recruited. When building a team the project manager should ask the following questions.

(a) **What skills** are required to complete each task of the project? (This list will be based on the project goals established previously – this process is explained in Chapter 2.)

(b) **Who** has the talent and skills to complete the required tasks, whether inside or outside the organisation?

(c) Are the people identified **available, affordable**, and able to join the project team?

(d) What level of **supervision** will be required?

3.4 This information should be **summarised in worksheet format**, as shown in the following example.

Part A: Project management

Project Skill Requirements		
Project Name: _____ **Date worksheet completed:** _____		
Project Manager: _____		
Task	**Skill needed**	**Responsibility**

3.5 The completed worksheet provides a document showing the skills required of the project team. Deciding who has the skills required for each task and if possible seconding those identified to the project team, should be done **as early as possible**. Team members should then be able to **participate** in the planning of schedules and budgets. This should encourage the acceptance of agreed deadlines, and a greater commitment to achieve project success.

3.6 The individuals selected to join the team should be told **why they have been selected**, referring both to their technical skills and personal qualities. This should provide members with guidance as to the role they are expected to play.

3.7 In an ideal world the project team would contain staff already capable of performing all tasks to the standard required. However, **compromises** will often need to be made. For example, the outsiders required to complete certain tasks might prove **too expensive**. An alternative would be to provide **training** for in-house staff. However, the complexity of the skills required, and/or the time it would take to teach those skills may mean this is not feasible.

3.8 Although the composition of the project team is critical, project managers often find it is not possible to assemble the ideal team, and have to do the best they can with the personnel available. If the project manager feels the best available team does not possess the skills and talent required, the project should be **abandoned or delayed.**

3.9 Once the team has been selected each member should be given a (probably verbal) project briefing, outlining the overall aims of the project, and detailing the role they are expected to play. (The role of documentation is discussed later).

1: Introducing project management

Managing the project team

3.10 **Group cohesiveness** is an important factor for project success. It is hoped that team members will **develop and learn from each other**, and solve problems by drawing on different resources and expertise.

3.11 The performance of the project team will be enhanced by the following.
- Effective communication
- All members being aware of the team's purpose and the role of each team member
- Collaboration and creativity among team members
- Trusting, supportive atmosphere in group
- A commitment to meeting the agreed schedule
- Innovative/creative behaviour
- Team members highly interdependent, interface effectively
- Capacity for conflict resolution
- Results orientation
- High energy levels and enthusiasm
- An acceptance of change

3.12 Collaboration and interaction between team members will help ensure the skills of all team members are utilised, and should result in 'synergistic' solutions. Formal (eg meetings) and informal channels (eg e-mail links, a bulletin board) of **communication** should be set up to ensure this interaction takes place.

3.13 Team members should be responsible and accountable. The project manager should provide **regular updates** on project progress and timely **feedback** on team and individual performance.

3.14 Most **effective project managers** display the ability to:
- Select the right people
- Connect them to the right cause
- Solve problems that arise
- Evaluate progress towards objectives
- Negotiate resolutions to conflicts
- Heal wounds inflicted by change

Managing conflict within the project team

3.15 It is inevitable when people from wide-ranging backgrounds combine to form a project team that **conflict** will occasionally occur. Some conflicts may actually be **positive**, resulting in fresh ideas and energy being input to the project. Other conflicts can be **negative** and have the potential to bring the project to a standstill.

3.16 Most conflicts are able to be resolved, but some would require more effort to achieve a resolution than is justified. In these instances it may be more efficient to use creativity to devise a method of working **around the problem**.

3.17 An open exchange of views between project personnel should be encouraged as this will help ensure all possible courses of action and their consequences are considered. The project manager should keep in touch with the relationships of team members and act as a conciliator if necessary.

Part A: Project management

3.18 Ideally, conflict should be harnessed for productive ends. Conflict can have **positive effects** such as those listed below.

- Results in better, well thought-out ideas
- Forces people to search for new approaches
- Causes persistent problems to surface and be dealt with
- Forces people to clarify their views
- Causes tension which stimulates interest and creativity

Negotiation and resolution techniques

3.19 When conflict occurs the project manager should avoid displaying bias and adopt a logical, ordered approach towards achieving resolution. The following principles should be followed.

- Focus on the problem, not the personalities
- Define the problem carefully
- Try to develop options that would result in mutual gain
- Look for a wide variety of possible solutions

3.20 Ideally the conflict will be resolved by the parties involved **agreeing** on a course of action. In cases where insufficient progress towards a resolution has occurred the project manager should attempt to bring about a resolution.

3.21 The project manager should employ the following **techniques** in an attempt to resolve the conflict.

(a) Work through the problem using the **negotiation techniques** listed in 3.19 above.

(b) Attempt to establish a **compromise** - try to bring some degree of satisfaction to all parties through give and take.

(c) Try to **smooth out any differences** and downplay the importance of any remaining differences.

(d) Emphasise areas of **agreement**.

(e) If all else fails, and resolution is vital, the project manager should force the issue and **make a decision**. He or she should emphasise to all parties that their commitment to the project is appreciated, and that the conflict should now be put behind them.

A computerised information system project team

3.22 In a modern organisation it may be that the IS department has a very limited number of staff. An **hierarchical structure** of manager, analysts, programmers, etc may prove to be **very inflexible** in terms of getting individual projects done. For instance, someone who officially has the 'status' of 'Project Manager' may find that he or she has no projects to manage at a particular time but may have four or five projects to manage at another time.

3.23 This situation is likely to arise frequently because much of the work of a dedicated IS department is **project-based**. One project may require a considerable amount of programming from scratch, while the next is largely 'tweaking' an existing system, requiring analyst skills, and someone who can motivate staff and control progress but very little programming.

3.24 A solution adopted increasingly in organisations is to organise the IS department according to a **flat** structure that recognises that multi-talented individuals will adopt **different roles**

1: Introducing project management

at different times rather than occupying a particular 'status' whether or not there is any work for someone of that status to do. Staff are selected from a pool of available staff and perform different roles depending upon demand.

3.25 To operate such a system the organisation needs to devise a **remuneration system** that recognises **skills** and work done rather than status.

3.26 We will cover the systems development process in depth later in this text. In the context of explaining the roles of analysts and programmers, developing a computer system can be divided into two parts.

  (a) **Designing** a program or programs that will do the data processing work that the user department wants, and to the user's specification (for example about response times, accuracy etc).

  This involves deciding what hardware there should be, what the input and files should be, how output should be produced, and what programs there should be to do this work.

  This is the task of the **systems analyst**.

  (b) **Writing the software** – this is the job of the programmer.

Systems analysts

3.27 In general terms, the tasks of the systems analyst are as follows.

3.28 **Systems analysis** - involves carrying out a methodical study of a **current system** (manual or computerised) to establish:

  (a) What the current system **does**.

  (b) Whether it does what it is **supposed to do**.

  (c) What the user department would **like it to do**, and so what the required objectives of the system are.

3.29 **Systems design** - having established what the proposed system objectives are, the next stage is to design a system that will **achieve these objectives**.

3.30 **Systems specification** - in designing a new system, it is the task of the systems analyst to **specify** the system in detail.

3.31 This involves identification of inputs, files, processing, output, hardware, costs, accuracy, response times and controls.

3.32 The system design is spelled out formally in a document or manual called the **systems specification** (which includes a program specification for each program in the system).

3.33 The analyst will be responsible for **systems testing**.

3.34 Once installed, the analyst will keep the system under **review**, and control system **maintenance** with the co-operation of **user** departments.

Programmers

3.35 Programmers write the programs. This involves:

Part A: Project management

(a) Reading the **system specification** and understanding it.

(b) Recognising what the processing requirements of the program are, in other words, **defining the processing problem in detail**.

(c) Having defined and analysed the processing problem, **writing the program** in a programming language.

(d) Arranging for the program to be **tested**.

(e) Identifying **errors** in the program and getting rid of these 'bugs' - ie **debugging** the program.

(f) Preparing full documentation for each program within the system.

Case example

BUSINESS DAY SURVEY - PROJECT MANAGEMENT - STAFF ARE THE KEY TO SUCCESS

People who have left the comfort of their traditional management environment are often the most important ingredient in successful project management.

You can have the best tools and techniques, the most advanced systems and methods and most innovative structure, but ultimately it is the committed project team of people who choose to make it happen, says Mark Wright, MD of Scott Wilson's project management division. The faster the markets change and the technology advances, the greater need there will be for successful project management implementation to satisfy goals.

As the project management profession continues to evolve, globalisation is often seen as a threat. But it need not be seen as such, says David Sparrow, managing partner of global operations for EC Harris, an international capital project and facilities consultancy company. The reality is that through globalisation, various world-class processes are exposed to the local market. Similarly, clients are globalising and changing to remain competitive, he says.

Project managers need to be focused on client needs and thus the technical consultancy skill is now just a mere tool that needs to be applied in innovative ways. Trevor Lowen, GM of business development for Axis Interim Management, says the problem most organisations have is the lack of project management experience within their ranks. He says the use of interim management is creating a growing project management resource for business.

Interim management is the provision of short-term senior managers, industry or functional specialists to companies to undertake an assignment which they lack the resources to undertake themselves. The launch of a new product is an example of project work undertaken by interim managers.

Business Day (South Africa) Nov 1999

---

4 PROJECT STAKEHOLDERS 5/02

KEY TERM

Project stakeholders are the individuals and organisations who are involved in or may be affected by project activities.

4.1 We have already looked at the role of the **Project Manager** and the **Project Team**. Other key stakeholders are defined as follows.

1: Introducing project management

> **KEY TERMS**
>
> **Project sponsor** is the generic name given to the source of the project manager's authority. The sponsor may be owner, financier, client etc., or their delegate.
>
> **Project owner** is the party responsible for financing the project.
>
> A **Project supplier** is anyone who makes goods and/or services available at a price for use on a project.
>
> **Project support team** is a term used to designate the personnel working on a project who do not report to the project manager administratively.
>
> **Users** are the group that will utilise the end product, process or service produced by the project.

4.2 Project stakeholders should all be **committed towards a common goal** – successful project completion. The Project Plan (covered in Chapter 2) should be the common point of reference that states priorities and provides cohesion.

4.3 However, the individuals and groups that comprise the stakeholders all have different roles. A **stakeholder matrix** is a useful tool for identifying and clarifying the role of stakeholders. An example follows.

Case example

STAKEHOLDER ANALYSIS – CALL CENTRE IMPLEMENTATION PROJECT

Stakeholder	Reason for Involvement	Importance[2]			Nature of Communic-ations	Current Attitude[1]				Detail of Attitude	Required Attitude[1]		Required Outcome	Knowledge	Previous Communications
		H	M	L		H	S	A	R		H	S			
Call Centre Team Managers	Will be significant user of system	✓			Awareness & Training		✓			Positive		✓	High commitment, understanding context and of need to upgrade	Awareness of the broad concept but low understanding of detail	Limited (some mention in team meetings), Internal newsletter article
User Group	Vehicle for communication of project details to other key stakeholders	✓			Awareness, consultation and work group		✓			Largely positive, not fully engaged, gap in understanding of role (lack of willingness to train own people)	✓		High knowledge of project, use of position to relay information to Users and Owners	High	Active involvement in process through user group meetings, Internal newsletter article
Group / Div Managers and Directors	Need to be aware of developments, impacts and potential for their area		✓		Awareness			✓	✓	Varying from ambivalence to positive / supportive		✓	Awareness of impact and potential	Low	Internal newsletter article
Users	Will be significant user of system	✓			Awareness & Training		✓		✓	Likely to be positive, maybe some resistance to need for greater structure	✓		Acceptance of system along with high technical knowledge and understanding of reasons for the change	Should be reasonably high (through user group reps)	Regular updates from UG reps, visits from IRT, informal discussion w/ CCC people as part of normal business, Internal newsletter article
Owners	Will be significant user of system and system output; increased accountability reliant on system use	✓			Awareness & Training, consultation through user group		✓			Likely to be positive (as they can see the benefits)	✓		Acceptance of system, high technical knowledge, impact on other areas	Should be reasonably high (through user group reps & direct dealings)	Regular updates from UG reps, visits from IRT, informal discussion w/ CCC people as part of normal business, Internal newsletter article
Wider Organisation	Support for direction / use of CCC; possible potential for use of system by others			✓	Awareness		✓	✓		Largely ambivalent, positive for those that see potential		✓	Awareness of the broad concept of integrated incident management	Very low	Internal newsletter article

Notes
1. H = High commitment, S = supportive, A = ambivalent, R = resistant
2. H = High commitment, M = medium, L = low

15

Part A: Project management

Managing stakeholder disputes

4.4 The first step is to establish a **framework** to predict the potential for disputes. This involves **risk management**, since an unforeseen event (a risk) has the potential to create conflict, and **dispute management**: the matching of dispute procedures with minimum impacts on costs, goodwill and progress. (Risk management is covered in Chapter 2.)

4.5 The potential for disputes should be considered when managing all areas of a project. A skilled project manager should be able to organise working methods in such a way that minimises the likelihood of disputes.

Dispute resolution processes

4.6 **Resolution** is the solution of a conflict. **Settlement** is an arrangement which brings an end to the conflict, but does not necessarily address the underlying causes.

4.7 Wherever there is a potential for conflict, a **process to resolve** it should be established before the conflict occurs.

4.8 We have already discussed negotiation and resolution techniques in the context of project team conflict in Section 3 of this chapter. Many of the principles discussed previously can be applied to stakeholder conflicts, although the relative positions of the stakeholders involved can complicate matters. Conflict between project stakeholders may be resolved by:

- **Negotiation** (perhaps with the assistance of others)
- **Mediation**
- **Partnering**
- A third party neutral may judge or intervene to **impose a solution**

4.9 **Negotiation** involves the parties discussing the problem. This may or may not settle or resolve the dispute, but it should certainly be the first step.

4.10 **Mediation** or 'assisted negotiation' may be necessary. This involves a third-party neutral (the mediator) intervening to reach a mutually agreeable outcome.

4.11 **Partnering** focuses on creating communication links between project participants with the intention of directing them to a common goal - the project outcome - ahead of their own self-interest.

4.12 On very large projects a **Disputes Review Board** (DRB) may be formed. This may comprise persons directly involved in the project engaged to maintain a 'watching brief' to identify and attend upon disputes as they arise. Usually there is a procedure in place which provides for the DRB to make an 'on the spot' decision before a formal dispute is notified so that the project work can proceed, and that may be followed by various rights of review at increasingly higher levels.

4.13 In practice, disputes are often resolved by the acceptance of the view of the party that has financial responsibility for the project. In such a situation mediation and negotiation may only deliver an outcome which is a reflection of the original power imbalance.

1: Introducing project management

> # Chapter roundup
>
> - A **project** is an undertaking that has a beginning and an end and is carried out to meet established goals within cost, schedule and quality objectives.
>
> - A **project** often has the following characteristics:
>   - A defined beginning and end
>   - Have resources allocated specifically to them
>   - Intended to be done only once (although similar separate projects could be undertaken)
>   - Follow a plan towards a clear intended end-result
>   - Often cut across organisational and functional lines
>
> - **Project management** is the combination of systems, techniques, and people used to control and monitor activities undertaken within the project.
>
> - A project will be deemed successful if it is completed at the specified level of **quality**, **on time** and within **budget**.
>
> - The person who takes ultimate responsibility for ensuring the desired result is achieved on time and within budget is the **project manager**.
>
> - **Duties** of the project manager include: Planning, teambuilding, communication, co-ordinating project activities, monitoring and control, problem-resolution and quality control.
>
> - Project managers require the following **skills**: Leadership and team building, organisational ability, communication skills (written, spoken, presentations, meetings), some technical knowledge of the project area and inter-personal skills.
>
> - Project **success** depends to a large extent on the **team members** selected.
>
> - **Project stakeholders** are the individuals and organisations who are involved in, or may be affected by, project activities.
>
> - Wherever there is a potential for conflict a **process to resolve** it should be established before the conflict occurs.
>
> - Most conflicts that arise during a project should be able to be resolved using **negotiation** and **resolution** techniques.
>
> - The wide range of people and skills required to successfully complete a systems development project has led to the acceptance of **flat management structures** being the most appropriate for this process.

Quick quiz

1. What is a successful project?

2. List four areas a project manager should be skilled in.

    1. ....
    2. ....
    3. ....
    4. ....

3. Who is the project sponsor?

4. 'Project management techniques encourage management by exception'.

    True ☐

    False ☐

5. List four ways a dispute between project stakeholders could be settled.

    1. ....
    2. ....

Part A: Project management

  3 ....

  4 ....

6 Do you agree with the following statement: 'To be an effective systems analyst requires skills in computer programming'?

> **Answers to quick quiz**
>
> 1 One that is completed on time, within budget and to specification.
>
> 2 [Four of] Leadership, team building, organisational, communication, technical, personal.
>
> 3 The project sponsor may be the owner, financier, client etc., or their delegate. The sponsor is accountable for the resources invested into the project and responsible for the achievement of the project's business objectives.
>
> 4 True.
>
> 5 Negotiation (perhaps with the assistance of others).
> Partnering.
> Mediation.
> A third party neutral may judge or intervene to impose a solution.
>
> 6 Disagree. Systems analysts require a logical mind and an ability to understand the workings of a system – knowledge of programming is not essential.

The material covered in this Chapter, together with the material in Chapter 2, is tested in Questions 8(b), 10, 13(a) and 17 in the Question Bank. Study Chapter 2 before attempting these Questions.

Chapter 2

PROJECT STAGES AND MANAGEMENT TOOLS

Topic list		Syllabus reference	Ability required
1	The project life cycle	(i)	Application
2	Project phases and stages	(i)	Evaluation
3	Management tools and techniques	(i)	Evaluation
4	Project management software	(i)	Application
5	Documentation and reports	(i)	Evaluation
6	Risk management	(i)	Application
7	Information systems projects – common problems	(i)	Application

Introduction

In this chapter we study the stages a project moves through from initiation to completion. Be aware that other books may refer to **project stages** with different names or may include more or fewer stages. This does not mean one description is incorrect. The principles behind the process and techniques are more important than the labels used.

Later in the chapter we study the various **management tools and techniques** used in project management.

Learning outcomes covered in this chapter

- **Produce** a management plan for a simple project
- **Apply** project management tools
- **Explain** the issues involved in planning and managing an Information Systems project and produce a plan for such a project. *(Also see Chapters 6-8.)*
- **Explain** the process of post-completion audit and its importance in the project management process

Syllabus content covered in this chapter

- The stages of a project
- The major tools and techniques used at each of the project stages
- Project objectives, performance measurement and control

1 THE PROJECT LIFE CYCLE

1.1 A successful project relies on two activities – **planning** first, and then **doing**. These two activities form the basis of every project.

Part A: Project management

1.2 Projects can be divided into several phases to provide better management control. Collectively these phases comprise the **Project Life Cycle**.

> **KEY TERM**
>
> **Project Life Cycle**. The major time periods through which any project passes. Each period may be identified as a phase and further broken down into stages.

1.3 Although the principles of the project life cycle apply to all projects, the number and name of the phases identified will vary depending on what the project aims to achieve, and the project model referred to.

1.4 When studying Project Management it is convenient to give generic names to the phases of the **Project Life Cycle**. Remember though, in '**real**' situations (or in examination questions!) the model can be modified to suit circumstances.

1.5 The diagram below shows a generic model of the **five main phases of a project**.

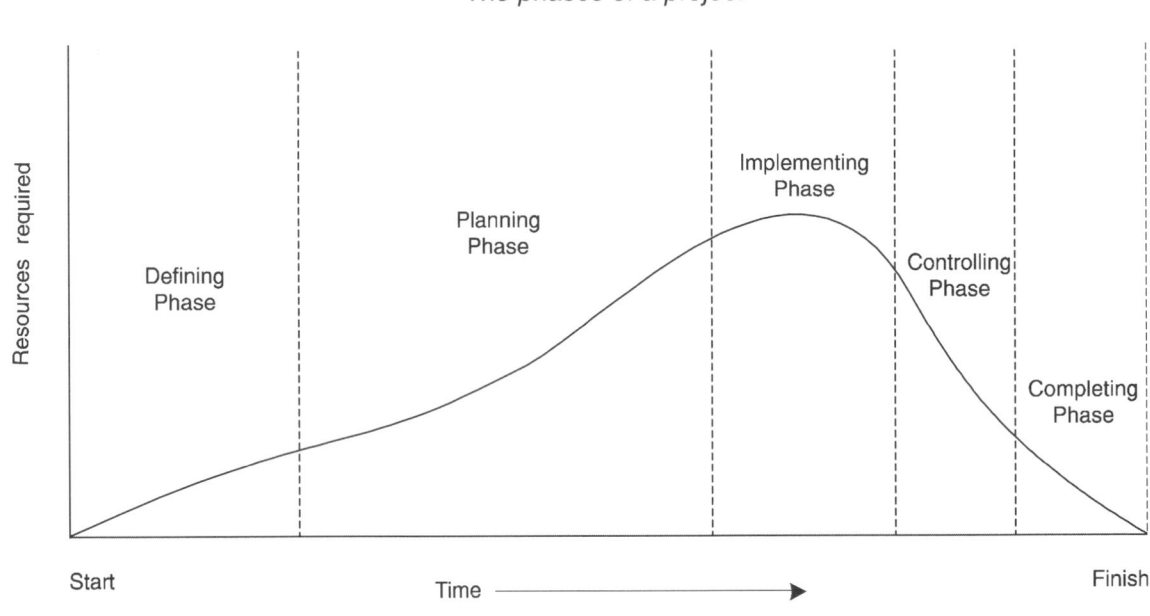

The phases of a project

[Diagram: A curve on axes showing Resources required (y-axis) against Time (x-axis from Start to Finish). The curve rises gradually, peaks, and falls rapidly. The phases labelled along the curve are: Defining Phase, Planning Phase, Implementing Phase, Controlling Phase, Completing Phase.]

1.6 As shown on the diagram, resource use (such as funds and staff hours required) is low at the start of the project, higher towards the end and then drops rapidly as the project draws to a close.

1.7 Risk and uncertainty are highest at the start of the project. This is when the probability of successfully completing the project is lowest. The likelihood of successful completion increases the longer the project continues.

1.8 The cost of making changes to the project increases the further into the life cycle the project has progressed.

2 PROJECT PHASES AND STAGES   Pilot paper

2.1 The phases of a project can be broken down into a number of **stages**. Again, the number of stages identified varies depending on type of project and the conventions of the organisation undertaking the project. In the syllabus for this paper *CIMA* identify thirteen project stages. These are shown in the following diagram.

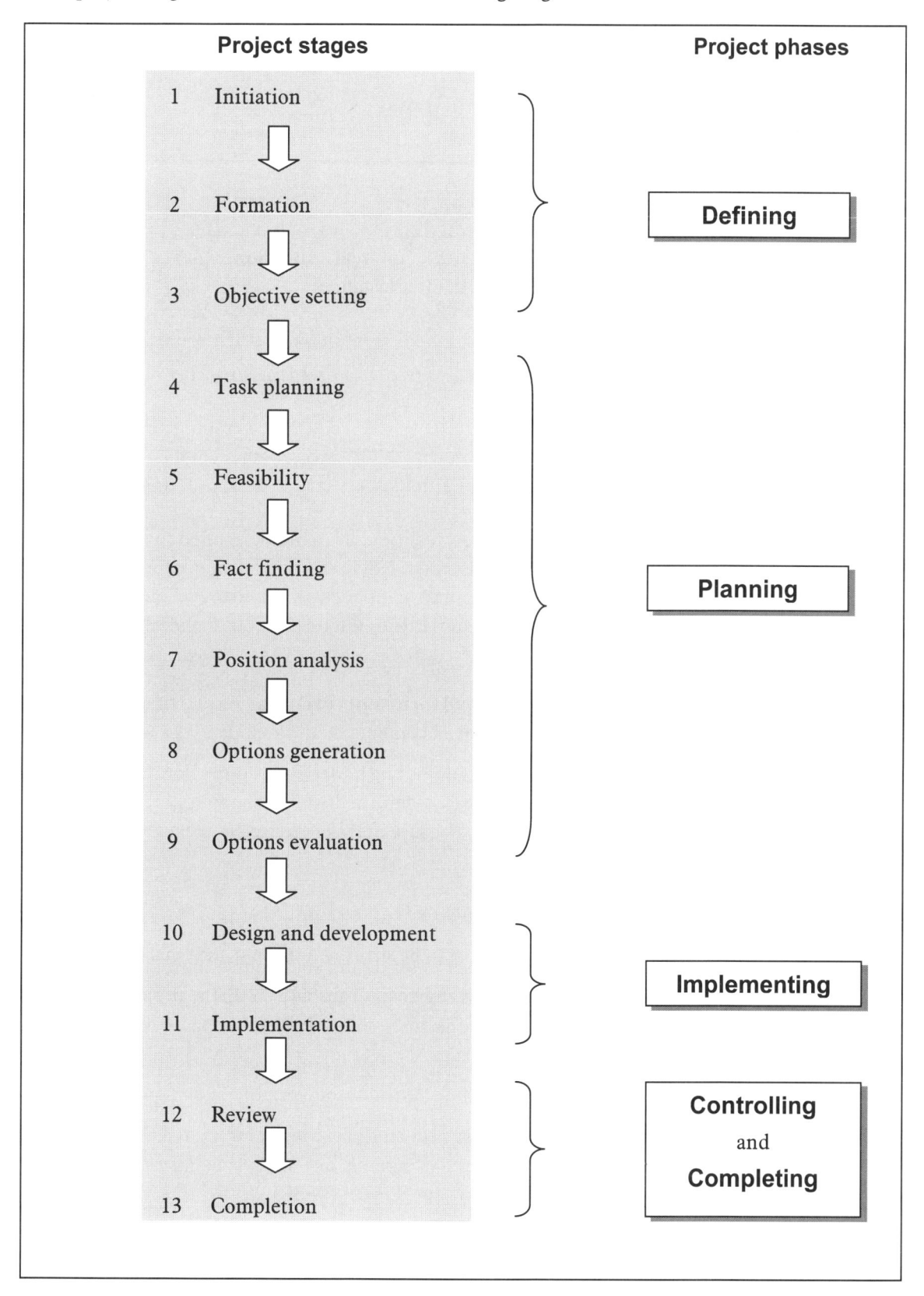

Project stages	Project phases
1 Initiation	Defining
2 Formation	
3 Objective setting	
4 Task planning	Planning
5 Feasibility	
6 Fact finding	
7 Position analysis	
8 Options generation	
9 Options evaluation	
10 Design and development	Implementing
11 Implementation	
12 Review	Controlling and Completing
13 Completion	

2.2 We now will look at each of these phases and stages.

Part A: Project management

Defining Phase

> **KEY TERM**
>
> The **defining phase** of a project is concerned with deciding whether a project should begin and committing to do so.

Initiation stage

> **KEY TERM**
>
> **Project initiation** describes the beginning of a project at which point certain management activities are required to ensure that the project is established with clear reference terms and an appropriate management structure.

2.3 Projects originate from someone attempting to resolve a **problem,** or seeing an **opportunity** to do something new.

2.4 It is often not clear precisely what the problem is. The project team should study, discuss and **analyse** the problem, from a number of different aspects (eg technical, financial).

2.5 Not all ideas will result in viable projects. A 'reality test' should be applied to all ideas. This is not a detailed feasibility study, and is intended to eliminate only concepts that are **obviously not viable**. For example, a small construction company should not waste resources investigating the possibility of submitting a tender to build the second channel tunnel.

2.6 At the start of a project, a **Project Initiation Document (PID)** may be drawn up, setting out the **terms of reference** for the project. Typical contents might include.

(a) The **business objectives**. Projects should not be undertaken simply for their own sake: the business advantages should be clearly identified and be the first point of reference when progress is being reviewed, to make sure that the original aim is not lost sight of.

(b) **Project objectives.**

(c) The **scope** of the project: what it is intended to cover and what it is not.

(d) **Constraints,** such as maximum amount to be spent and interim and final deadlines.

(e) The **ultimate customer** of the project, who will resolve conflicts as they occur (for example between two different divisions who will both be using the new system) and finally accept it.

(f) The **resources** that will be used – staff, technical resources, finance.

(g) An **analysis of risks** inherent in the project and how they are to be avoided or reduced (for example, the consequences of replacing the old sales ledger system and only discovering after the event that the new one does not work).

(h) A preliminary **project plan** (targets, activities and so on) and details of how the project is to be organised and managed.

(i) **Purchasing and procurement policy,** perhaps specifying acceptable suppliers and delivery details.

2: Project stages and management tools

> **KEY TERM**
>
> **Project scope** is a concise description of the end products or deliverables to be expected from the project.

Formation stage

2.7 The formation stage involves selecting the personnel who will be involved with the project. First to be selected are usually the **Project Manager** (whose role was discussed in Chapter 1) and the **Project Board**.

> **KEY TERM**
>
> The **Project Board** is the body to which the Project Manager is accountable for achieving the project objectives.

2.8 The project manager should **select and build the project team**. This process was explained in Chapter 1.

Objective setting stage

2.9 Before specific objectives can be set it is necessary to establish more general **project goals**. Clear goals and objectives give team members **quantifiable targets** to aim for. This should improve motivation and performance, as attempting to achieve a challenging goal is more inspiring than simply being told 'do your best.'

2.10 The **overall project goal** or project definition will be developed. On complex projects it is likely that the goal will be written in stages, with each definition being more detailed and refined than before. The project goal might be defined in a:

- Contract
- Product specification
- Customer's specification

> **KEY TERMS**
>
> A **goal** is a result or purpose that is determined for a project. Goals are broader than objectives.
>
> An **objective** is a specific project outcome required – including required resources and timing.

2.11 Objectives are developed from broad goals. In an accounting software installation project a project goal could be 'to produce timely and accurate management accounting reports.' An objective of the same project could be 'to have the nominal ledger system live and fully operational by November 1 200X.'

2.12 Project objectives should be **SMART**:

- **S**pecific - so all involved are working towards the same end
- **M**easurable - how will success be measured

Part A: Project management

- **A**greed upon - by all team members and stakeholders
- **R**ealistic - to motivate goals and objectives must be achievable
- **T**ime-bound - a date must be allocated to provide focus and aid priority setting
- Allocated - in terms of responsibility

Planning Phase

> **KEY TERM**
>
> The **planning phase** of a project aims to devise a workable scheme to accomplish the overall project goal.

Task planning stage

2.13 After the project team is in place and project goals and objectives have been set, the project should be broken down into **manageable tasks**. This process is often referred to as **Work Breakdown Structure (WBS)**. A brief overview of the process follows. We cover WBS in greater detail later in this chapter.

> **KEY TERMS**
>
> A **task** is an individual unit of work that is part of the total work needed to accomplish a project.
>
> An **activity** is a set of tasks that are carried out in order to create a deliverable.
>
> A **deliverable** is another name for a required outcome (eg product, service, document etc) from a project.

2.14 By breaking the project down into a series of manageable tasks it is easier to determine the skills needed to complete the project. A **task list** should be produced showing what tasks need to be done and the work sequences necessary.

2.15 Building a task list for a complex project can be an involved and lengthy process. It can be difficult deciding what constitutes a task, and where one task ends and another begins.

2.16 Tasks should be:

(a) **Clear**. Eg 'Design the layout of the fixed asset depreciation schedule.'

(b) **Self-contained**. No gaps in time should be apparent on work-units grouped together to form a task. All work-units within a task should be related.

Feasibility and fact finding stage

2.17 Once all the tasks have been defined a basic **network diagram** can be developed, together with a **complete list of resources** required. Network diagrams are covered later in this chapter.

2.18 A more realistic judgement as to the **overall feasibility** of the project can now be made. Some large projects may involve a **pre-project feasibility study**, which establishes whether it is feasible to undertake the project at all. Feasibility and fact finding activities undertaken after the project has been initiated are more detailed.

2.19 For complex projects, a detailed **feasibility study** may be required to establish if the project can be achieved within acceptable **cost and time constraints**.

> **KEY TERM**
>
> A **feasibility study** is a formal study to establish what type of solution could be implemented to meet the needs of the organisation. Practice will vary between different organisations.

2.20 We cover the feasibility study in detail in Chapter 6, in the context of a systems development project.

2.21 Fact finding may be performed substantially during the feasibility study.

2.22 The activities carried out will differ depending on the nature of the project. For information systems projects the fact finding exercise would take the form of a systems investigation. This is covered in detail in Chapter 6.

Position analysis, options generation and options evaluation stages   **11/01**

2.23 Once the current position has been clearly established options can be generated with the aim of utilising the internal strengths identified.

2.24 The process may involve options generation for a range of projects, only one of which can be chosen, eg should a new sales outlet be built in location C or should the limited finance available be spent on implementing a website that provides for on-line purchasing.

2.25 The general management technique of **SWOT analysis** can be applied to establish the current position, generate available options and evaluate those options.

> **KEY TERM**
>
> **SWOT analysis** is a process that aims to determine:
>
> What **Strengths** do we have? (How can we take advantage of them?)
>
> What **Weaknesses** do we have? (How can we minimise them?)
>
> What **Opportunities** are there? (How can we capitalise on them?)
>
> What **Threats** might prevent us from getting there? (eg Consider technical obstacles, competitive responses.)

2.26 The purpose of SWOT analysis (in the context of project management) is to ensure full consideration is given to possible approaches to the project and the effect the project will have on the organisation and its environment. The analysis should also ensure the project is compatible with the **overall strategy** of the organisation.

2.27 A variety of techniques are used to assess and value the options generated. Some will be assessed on financial criteria, such as **net present value**. Where this is not possible, or where the uncertainty in the environment is great, other models are used. **Scenario building** postulates a number of possible 'futures' (eg world-wide economic growth, interest rates, competitors).

2.28 A **strengths and weaknesses analysis** should identify:

(a) Strengths the organisation has that the project may be able to exploit.

(b) Organisational weaknesses that may impact on the project. Strategies will be required to improve these areas or minimise their impact.

2.29 The **strengths** and **weaknesses** analysis has an **internal** focus. The identification of shortcomings in skills or resources could lead to a decision to purchase from outsiders or to train staff.

2.30 An **external appraisal** is required to identify **opportunities** which can be exploited by the company and also to anticipate environmental **threats** (a declining economy, competitors' actions, government legislation, industrial unrest etc) against which the company must protect itself.

2.31 For **opportunities**, it is necessary to decide the following.

(a) What opportunities exist in the business environment?
(b) What is their inherent profit-making potential?
(c) Whether the organisation can exploit the worthwhile opportunities.
(d) What is the comparative capability profile of competitors?
(e) What is the company's comparative performance potential in this field of opportunity?

2.32 For **threats**, it is necessary to decide the following.

(a) **What threats** might arise, to the company or its business environment?
(b) How market players will be **affected.**

2.33 Opportunities and threats might relate to:

(a) **Political**: legislation may affect a company's (or an individual project's) prospects through the threats/ opportunities of pollution control or a ban on certain products, for example.

(b) **Economic**: a recession might imply poor sales.

(c) **Social attitudes.**

(d) **Technology**: new products or means of distribution may be developed.

(e) Competitors can threaten to increase their market-share with better and/or cheaper products or services.

(Note: (a) to (d) are often referred to as **PEST factors**.)

2.34 The internal and external appraisals of SWOT analysis will be brought together.

(a) Major **strengths** and profitable opportunities can be **exploited** especially if strengths and opportunities are matched with each other.

(b) Major **weaknesses** and threats should be **countered,** or a contingency strategy or corrective strategy developed.

2.35 It is likely that **alternative strategies** will emerge from the identification of strengths, weaknesses, opportunities and threats.

2.36 The elements of the SWOT analysis can be summarised and shown on a **cruciform chart**. The following chart relates to a project that proposes to install a new computerised accounting system.

2.37 EXAMPLE: NEW COMPUTERISED ACCOUNTING SYSTEM

STRENGTHS	WEAKNESSES
£1 million of funds allocated	Workforce has very limited experience of computerised systems
Willing and experienced workforce	Seems to be an expectation that the new system will 'do everything'
THREATS	OPPORTUNITIES
The software vendor is rumoured to be in financial trouble and may 'disappear'	Chance to introduce compatible systems in other departments at a later date
Choosing a poor system will result in increased risk of system failure	Later integration with e-commerce functions is possible

Potential strategy

Significant benefits can be obtained from the project, which should be able to achieve its aims within the £1 million budgeted.

Assurances should be sort from the software vendor as to their future plans and profitability. Contractual obligations should be sought in regard to this. If the rumours are justified, either another supplier should be approached or the possibility of employing the original vendor's staff on a contract basis could be explored. *(This is an example of an alternative strategy coming out of the SWOT analysis.)*

The end users of the system must be involved in all aspects of system design. Training of staff must be thorough and completed before the system 'goes live'. Management and users must be educated as to what the system will and will not be able to do.

A contingency plan should be in place for repairing or even replacing hardware at short notice.

2.38 Where a range of potential strategies have been identified, they each need to be **evaluated**.

2.39 Four steps are taken.

Step 1. The gap between the current position and the targeted position (project completion) is estimated.

Step 2. One or more courses of action are proposed.

Step 3. Each course is analysed in terms of how well it would meet the project aims. A weighted scoring or ranking system may be useful here.

Step 4. A course is chosen.

2.40 Examples of projects where a wide-ranging SWOT analysis would be of value include.
- New product launches
- Proposed advertising campaign

Part A: Project management

- Move into a new market
- Change in selling method eg Launch of e-commerce
- Open a new factory
- Relocation of operations
- New brand launch
- Organisation re-structuring

2.41 A course of action has been chosen, it now needs to be incorporated into the project plan. The following techniques (outlined in the following section of this chapter) could be used to incorporate the actions into the project plan.

- Work breakdown structure (WBS)
- Gantt charts
- Critical path analysis (CPA)
- Project evaluation review technique (PERT)
- Resource histogram

Implementing Phase

> **KEY TERM**
>
> The **implementing phase** is concerned with co-ordinating people and other resources to carry out the project plan.

Design and development stage

2.42 The design and development stage is where the actual product, service or process that will be the end result of the project is worked on.

2.43 The activities carried out in this stage will vary greatly depending on the type of project. For example, in a software implementation this is when the programming of the software would take place; in a construction project, the building design would be finalised.

Implementation stage

2.44 After the process, service or product has been developed it will be **implemented or installed** so it is available to be used.

2.45 If the project involves a new system or process, a period of **parallel running** alongside the existing system or process may be carried out. This enables results to be checked, and any last-minute problems to be ironed out before the organisation is fully reliant on the new system or process.

Controlling Phase

> **KEY TERM**
>
> The **controlling phase** is concerned with ensuring project objectives are met by monitoring and measuring progress and taking corrective action when necessary.

2: Project stages and management tools

Review stage

2.46 Actual performance should be reviewed against the objectives identified in the project plan. If performance is not as expected, control action will be necessary.

Completing Phase

> **KEY TERM**
>
> **Completion** involves formalising acceptance of the project and bringing it to an orderly end.

Completion stage

2.47 Following installation and review there should be a meeting of the Project Board to:

- Check that all products are complete and delivered
- Check the status of any outstanding requests for change
- Check all project issues have been cleared
- Approve the project completion report (covered in section 5 of this chapter)
- Arrange for a post completion audit (also covered in section 5 of this chapter)

Comment

2.48 We have summarised the thirteen stages identified by *CIMA*. In real life, **projects do not break down conveniently into thirteen sequential stages**. The activities we have identified with a certain stage may in fact be carried out at other stages, depending on the requirements of the project.

3 MANAGEMENT TOOLS AND TECHNIQUES   Pilot paper, 5/01, 11/01, 5/02

The Project Budget

> **KEY TERM**
>
> **Project budget.** The amount and distribution of resources allocated to a project.

3.1 Building a project budget should be an orderly process that attempts to establish a realistic estimate of the cost of the project. There are two main methods for establishing the project budget; **top-down** and **bottom-up**.

3.2 **Top-down budgeting** describes the situation where the budget is imposed 'from above'. Project Managers are allocated a budget for the project based on an estimate made by senior management. The figure may prove realistic, especially if similar projects have been undertaken recently. However the technique is often used simply because it is quick, or because only a certain level of funding is available.

3.3 In **bottom-up budgeting** the project manager consults the project team, and others, to calculate a budget based on the tasks that make up the project. Work breakdown structure (WBS) is a useful tool in this process. WBS is explained later in this section.

Part A: Project management

3.4 It is useful to collate this information on a **Budgeting Worksheet**.

Budgeting Worksheet				
Project Name: _____ **Date worksheet completed:** _____ **Project Manager:** _____					
Task (code)	Responsible staff member or external supplier	Estimated material costs	Estimated labour costs	Total cost of task

3.5 Estimates (and therefore budgets) cannot be expected to be 100% accurate. Business **conditions may change**, the project plan may be amended or estimates may simply prove to be incorrect.

3.6 Any **estimate** must be accompanied by some **indication of expected accuracy**.

3.7 Estimates can be **improved** by:

- **Learning** from past mistakes
- Ensuring sufficient design **information**
- Ensuring as **detailed a specification as possible** from the customer
- Properly **analysing the job** into its constituent units

3.8 The overall level of cost estimates will be influenced by:

(a) **Project goals**. If a high level of quality is expected costs will be higher.

(b) **External vendors**. Some costs may need to be estimated by outside vendors. To be realistic, these people must understand exactly what would be expected of them.

(c) **Staff availability**. If staff are unavailable, potentially expensive contractors may be required.

(d) **Time schedules**. The quicker a task is required to be done the higher the cost is likely to be – particularly with external suppliers.

3.9 The budget may express all resources in monetary amounts, or may show money and other resources - such as staff hours. A monetary budget is often used to establish the current cost variance of the project. To establish this we need:

(a) **The Actual Cost of Work Performed (ACWP)**. This is the amount spent to date on the project.

(b) **The Budgeted Cost of Work Scheduled (BCWS)**. The amount that was budgeted to be spent to this point on scheduled activities.

(c) **The Budgeted Cost of Work Performed (BCWP)**. This figure is calculated by pricing the work that has actually been done – using the same basis as the scheduled work.

BCWP – ACWP = The **cost variance** for the project.
BCWP – BCWS = The **schedule variance** for the project.

3.10 During the project, actual expenditure is tracked against budget on either a separate **Budget Report,** or as part of a regular **Progress Report.** We will be looking at project documentation and reports later in this chapter.

3.11 Budgets should be presented for approval and **sign-off** to the stakeholder who has responsibility for the funds being used.

3.12 Before presenting a budget for approval it may have to be revised a number of times. The 'first draft' may be overly reliant on rough estimates, as insufficient time was available to obtain more accurate figures.

3.13 On presentation, the Project Manager may be asked to find ways to cut the budget. If he or she agrees that cuts can be made, the consequences of the cuts should be pointed out - eg a reduction in quality.

3.14 It may be decided that a project costs more than it is worth. If so, scrapping the project is a perfectly valid option. In such cases the budgeting process has highlighted the situation before too much time and effort has been spent on an unprofitable venture.

Gantt charts

3.15 A Gantt chart, named after the engineer Henry Gantt who pioneered the procedure in the early 1900s, is a horizontal bar chart used to plan the **time scale** for a project and to estimate the amount of **resources** required.

3.16 The Gantt chart displays the time relationships between tasks in a project. Two lines are usually used to show the time allocated for each task, and the actual time taken.

3.17 A simple Gantt chart, illustrating some of the activities involved in a network server installation project, follows.

Part A: Project management

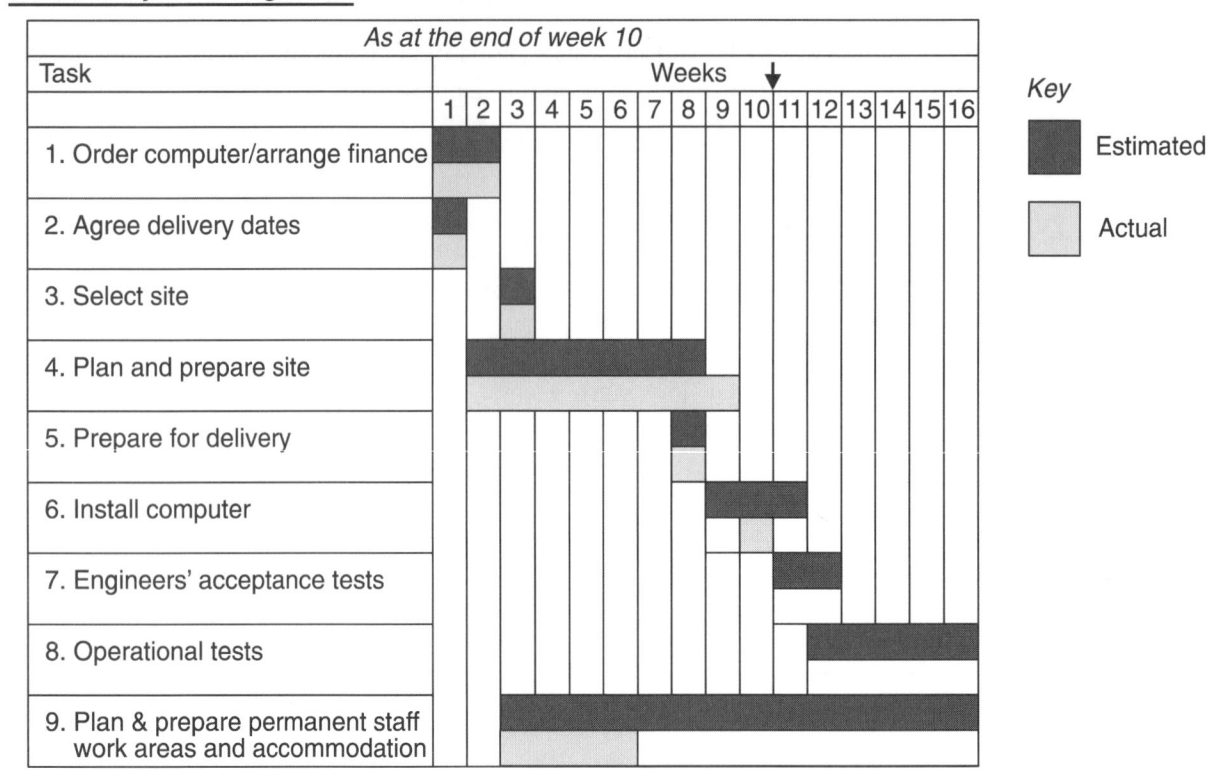

Task	As at the end of week 10
	Weeks
	1 2 3 4 5 6 7 8 9 10 11 12 13 14 15 16
1. Order computer/arrange finance	
2. Agree delivery dates	
3. Select site	
4. Plan and prepare site	
5. Prepare for delivery	
6. Install computer	
7. Engineers' acceptance tests	
8. Operational tests	
9. Plan & prepare permanent staff work areas and accommodation	

Key: Estimated / Actual

3.18 The chart shows that at the end of the tenth week Activity 9 is running behind schedule. More resources may have to be allocated to this activity if the staff accommodation is to be ready in time for the changeover to the new system.

3.19 Activity 4 had not been completed on time, and this has resulted in some disruption to the computer installation (Activity 6), which may mean further delays in the commencement of Activities 7 and 8.

3.20 A Gantt chart does not show the interrelationship between the various activities in the project as clearly as a **network diagram** (covered later in this chapter). A combination of Gantt charts and network analysis will often be used for project planning and resource allocation.

Network analysis   Pilot paper

3.21 **Network analysis,** also known as **Critical Path Analysis** (CPA), is a useful technique to help with planning and controlling large projects, such as construction projects, research and development projects and the computerisation of systems.

> **KEY TERMS**
>
> **Network analysis** requires breaking down the project into tasks, arranging them into a logical sequence and estimating the duration of each.
>
> This enables the series of tasks that determines the minimum possible duration of the project to be found. These are the **critical activities**.

3.22 CPA aims to ensure the progress of a project, so the project is completed in the **minimum amount of time**.

3.23 It pinpoints the tasks which are **on the critical path**, ie those parts which, if delayed beyond the allotted time, would **delay the completion** of the project as a whole.

3.24 The technique can also be used to assist in **allocating resources** such as labour and equipment.

3.25 Critical path analysis is quite a simple technique. The events and activities making up the whole project are represented in the form of a **diagram**.

3.26 Drawing the diagram or chart involves the following steps.

   Step 1. Estimating the time needed to complete each individual activity or task that makes up a part of the project.

   Step 2. Sorting out what activities must be done one after another, and which can be done at the same time, if required.

   Step 3. Representing these in a network diagram.

   Step 4. Estimating the critical path, which is the longest sequence of consecutive activities through the network.

3.27 The duration of the whole project will be fixed by the time taken to complete the largest path through the network. This path is called the **critical path** and activities on it are known as **critical activities**.

3.28 Activities on the critical path **must be started and completed on time**, otherwise the total project time will be extended. The method of finding the critical path is illustrated in the example below.

3.29 Network analysis shows the **sequence** of tasks and how long they are going to take. The diagrams are drawn from left to right.

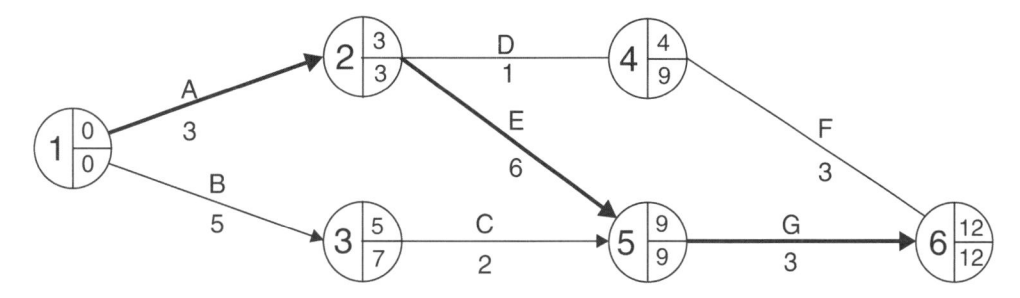

(a) **Events** (eg 1 and 2) are represented by circles. **Tasks** (eg A) connect events.

(b) The **critical path** is represented by drawing an extra line or a thicker line between the tasks on the path. It is the **minimum amount of time** that the project will take.

(c) It is the convention to note the earliest start date of any task in the *top* right hand corner of the circle.

(d) We can then work **backwards** identifying the **latest** dates when tasks have to start. These we insert in the bottom right quarter of the circle.

3.30 The **critical path** in the diagram above is AEG. Note the **float time** of five days for Activity F. Activity F can begin any time between days 4 and 9, thus giving the project manager a degree of flexibility.

Part A: Project management

Activity-on-node presentation

3.31 The method of drawing network diagrams explained here closely follows the presentation that you would see if you used the **Microsoft Project** software package. It is easier and clearer than old-fashioned method of using divided circles.

3.32 EXAMPLE: ACTIVITY ON NODE

Suppose that a project includes three activities, C, D and E. Neither activity D nor E can start until activity C is completed, but D and E could be done simultaneously if required.

This would be represented as follows.

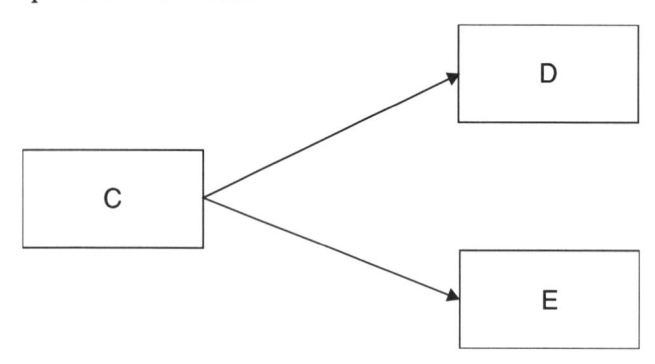

3.33 Note the following.

(a) An **activity** within a network is represented by a rectangular box. (Each box is a **node**.)
(b) The **'flow'** of activities in the diagram should be from **left to right**.
(c) The diagram clearly shows that **D and E must follow C**.

3.34 A second possibility is that an activity cannot start until two or more activities have been completed. If activity H cannot start until activities G and F are both complete, then we would represent the situation like this.

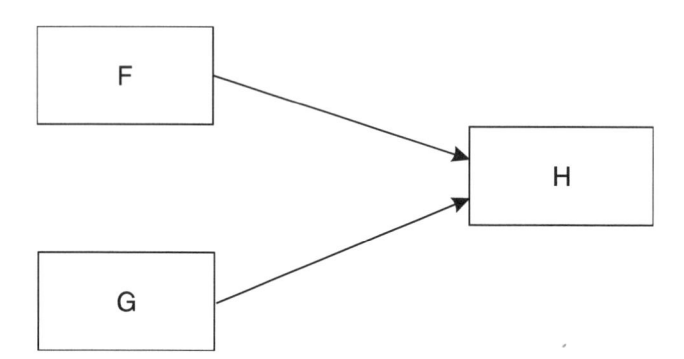

3.35 In some conventions an extra node is introduced at the start and end of a network. This serves absolutely no purpose (other than to ensure that all the nodes are joined up), so we recommend that you do not do it. Just in case you ever see a network presented in this way, both styles are shown in the next example.

2: Project stages and management tools

3.36 EXAMPLE: STARTS AND ENDS

Draw a diagram for the following project. The project is finished when both D and E are complete.

Activity	Preceding activity
A	-
B	-
C	A
D	B & C
E	B

3.37 SOLUTION

Microsoft Project style

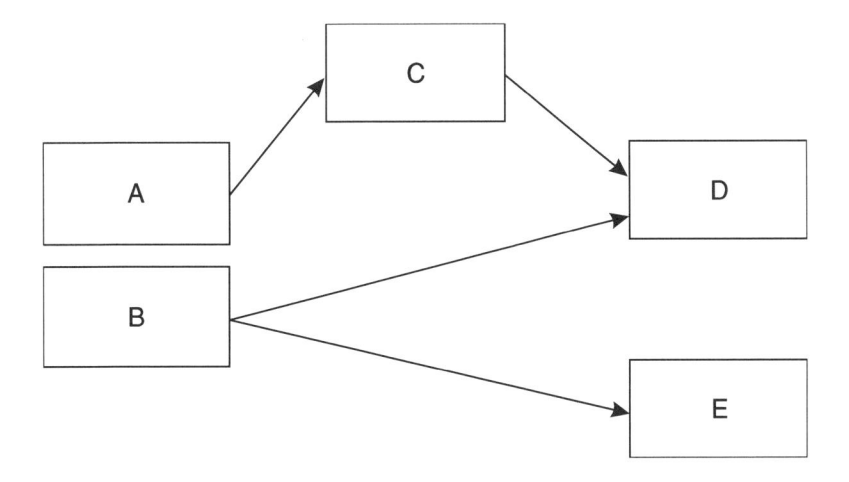

With start and end nodes

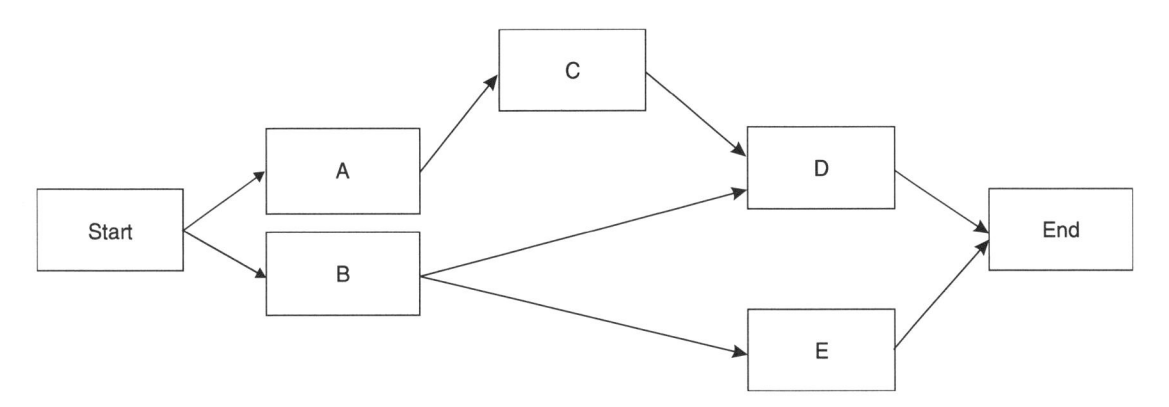

3.38 Any network can be analysed into a number of different paths or routes. A path is simply a sequence of activities which can take you from the start to the end of the network. In the example above, there are just three routes or paths.

(a) A C D.
(b) B D.
(c) B E.

Part A: Project management

3.39 The time needed to complete each individual activity in a project must be estimated. This **duration** is shown within the node as follows. The reason for and meaning of the other boxes will be explained in a moment.

Task A	
ID	6 days

3.40 EXAMPLE: THE CRITICAL PATH

Activity	Immediately preceding activity	Duration (weeks)
A	-	5
B	-	4
C	A	2
D	B	1
E	B	5
F	B	5
G	C, D	4
H	F	3
I	F	2

(a) What are the paths through the network?
(b) What is the critical path and its duration?

3.41 SOLUTION

The first step in the solution is to draw the network diagram, with the time for each activity shown.

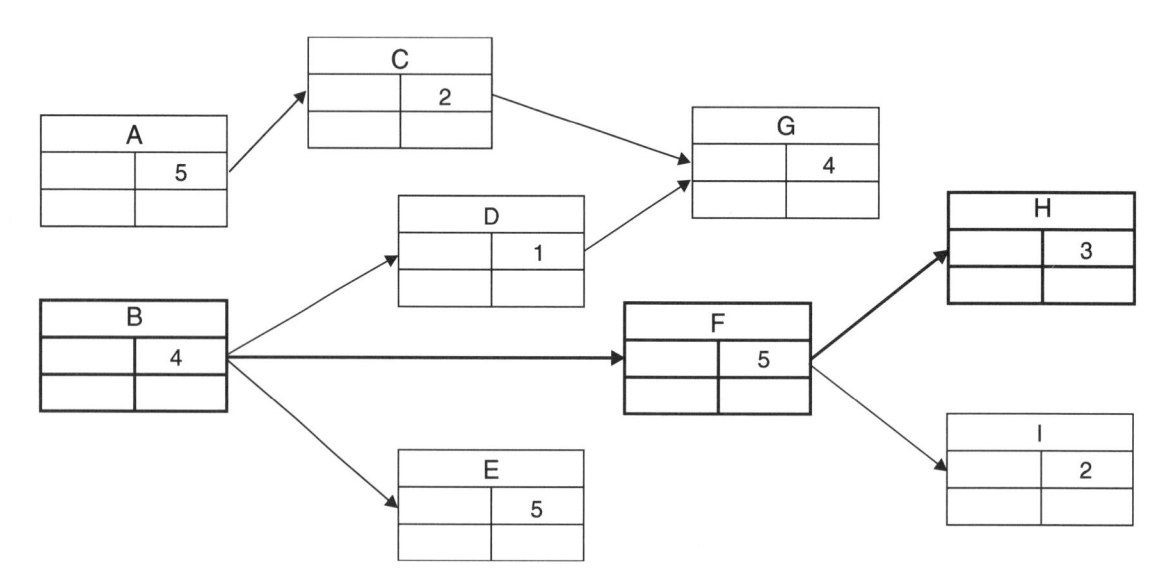

3.42 We could list the paths through the network and their overall completion times as follows.

Path	Duration (weeks)	
A C G	(5 + 2 + 4)	11
B D G	(4 + 1 + 4)	9
B E	(4 + 5)	9
B F H	(4 + 5 + 3)	12
B F I	(4 + 5 + 2 + 0)	11

3.43 The critical path is the longest, **BFH**, with a duration of 12 weeks. This is the **minimum time needed** to complete the project.

3.44 The **critical path** is indicated on the diagram by drawing **thick** (or **double-line**) arrows, as shown above. In Microsoft Project the arrows and the nodes are highlighted in **red**.

3.45 **Listing paths** through the network in this way should be easy enough for small networks, but it becomes a **long and tedious task** for bigger and more complex networks. This is why **software packages** are used in real life.

3.46 Conventionally it has been recognised as useful to calculate the **earliest and latest times for activities to start or finish**, and show them on the network diagram. This can be done for networks of any size and complexity.

3.47 Project management software packages offer a much larger variety of techniques than can easily be done by hand. Microsoft Project allows **each activity** to be assigned to any one of a variety of types: 'start as late as possible', 'start as soon as possible', 'finish no earlier than a particular date', 'finish no later than a particular date', and so on.

3.48 In real life, too, activity times can be shortened by working **weekends and overtime**, or they may be constrained by **non-availability of essential personnel**. In other words with any more than a few activities the possibilities are mind-boggling, which is why software is used.

3.49 Nevertheless, a simple technique is illustrated in the following example.

3.50 EXAMPLE: EARLIEST AND LATEST START TIMES

One way of showing earliest and latest **start** times for activities is to divide each event node into sections. This is similar to the style used in Microsoft Project except that Project uses real dates, which is far more useful, and the bottom two sections can mean a variety of things, depending what constraints have been set.

These sections record the following things.

(a) The **name** of the activity, for example Task A. This helps humans to understand the diagram.

(b) An **ID number** which is unique to that activity. This helps computer packages to understand the diagram, because it is possible that two or more activities could have the same name. For instance two bits of research are done at different project stages might both be called 'Research'.

(c) The **duration** of the activity.

(d) The **earliest start time**. Conventionally for the first node in the network, this is time 0.

(e) The **latest start time**.

(**Note**. Don't confuse start times with the '**event**' times that are calculated when using the **activity-on-arrow** method, even though the approach is the same.)

Task D	
ID number: 4	Duration: 6 days
Earliest start: Day 4	Latest start: Day 11

Part A: Project management

Earliest start times

3.51 To find the earliest start times, always start with activities that have no predecessors and give them an earliest starting time of 0. In the example we have been looking at, this is week 0.

Then work along each path from **left to right** through the diagram calculating the earliest time that the next activity can start.

For example, the earliest time for activity C is week 0 + 5 = 5. The earliest time activities D, E and F can start is week 0 + 4 = 4.

To calculate an activity's earliest time, simply look at the box for the **preceding** activity and add the bottom left figure to the top right figure.

If **two or more** activities precede an activity take the **highest** figure as the later activity's earliest start time: it cannot start before all the others are finished!

Latest start times

3.52 The latest start times are the latest times at which each activity can start **if the project as a whole is to be completed in the earliest possible time,** in other words in 12 weeks in our example.

Work backwards from **right to left** through the diagram calculating the latest time at which the activity can start, if it is to be completed at the latest finishing time. For example the latest start time for activity H is 12 - 3 = week 9 and for activity E is 12 - 5 = week 7.

3.53 Activity F might cause difficulties as two activities, H and I, lead back to it.

(a) Activity H must be completed by week 12, and so must start at week 9.
(b) Activity I must also be completed by week 12, and so must start at week 10.

Activity F takes 5 weeks so its latest start time F is the either 9 – 5 = week 4 or 10 – 5 = week 5. However, if it starts in week 5 it not be possible to start activity H on time and the whole project will be delayed. We therefore take the **lower** figure.

3.54 The final diagram is now as follows.

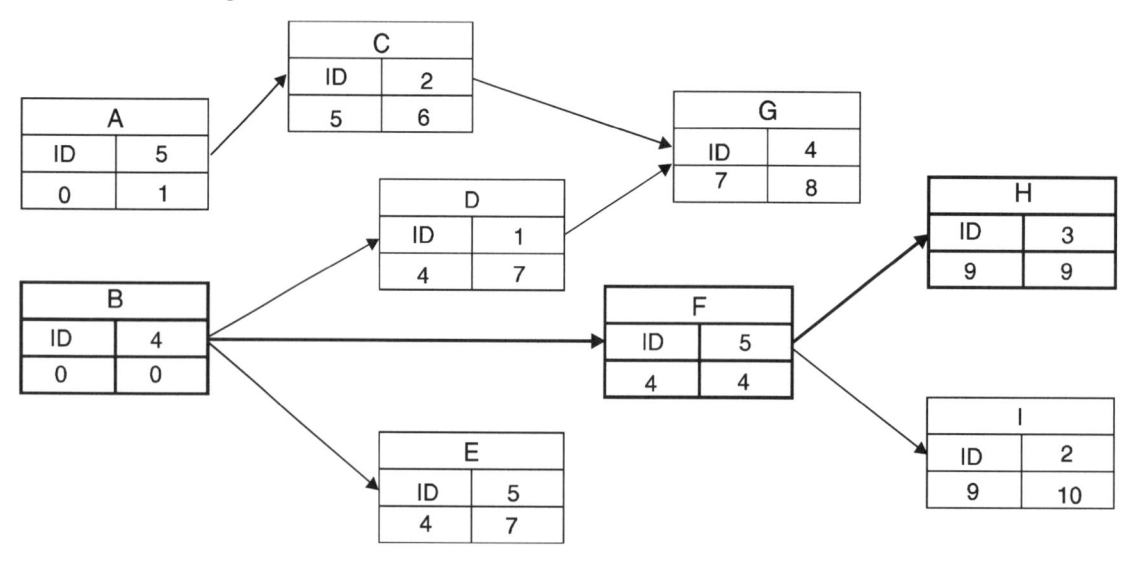

	C	
ID		2
5		6

	A	
ID		5
0		1

	G	
ID		4
7		8

	D	
ID		1
4		7

	H	
ID		3
9		9

	B	
ID		4
0		0

	F	
ID		5
4		4

	E	
ID		5
4		7

	I	
ID		2
9		10

3.55 **Critical activities** are those activities which must be started on time, otherwise the total project time will be increased. It follows that each event on the critical path must have the same earliest and latest start times. The critical path for the above network is therefore **B F H**.

2: Project stages and management tools

Criticisms of critical path/network analysis

3.56 (a) It is not always possible to devise an effective WBS for a project.

(b) **It assumes a sequential relationship** between activities. It assumes that once Activity B starts after Activity A has finished. It is not very good at coping with the possibility that an activity 'later' in the sequence may be relevant to an earlier activity.

(c) There are **problems in estimation**. Where the project is completely new, the planning process may be conducted in conditions of relative ignorance.

(d) Although network analysis plans the use of resources of labour and finance, it **does not appear to develop plans for contingencies, other than crashing time**.

(e) CPA **assumes a trade-off between time and cost.** This may not be the case where a substantial portion of the cost is **indirect overheads** or where the direct labour proportion of the total cost is limited.

3.57 EXAMPLE: GANTT CHARTS AND RESOURCES

This example is provided as an illustration of the use of Gantt charts to manage resources efficiently.

A company is about to undertake a project about which the following data is available.

Activity	Preceded by activity	Duration Days	Workers required
A	–	3	6
B	–	5	3
C	B	2	4
D	A	1	4
E	A	6	5
F	D	3	6
G	C, E	3	3

There is a multi-skilled workforce of nine workers available, each capable of working on any of the activities.

Draw the network to establish the duration of the project and the critical path. Then draw a Gantt chart, using the critical path as a basis, assuming that jobs start at the earliest possible time.

3.58 SOLUTION

Here are the diagrams.

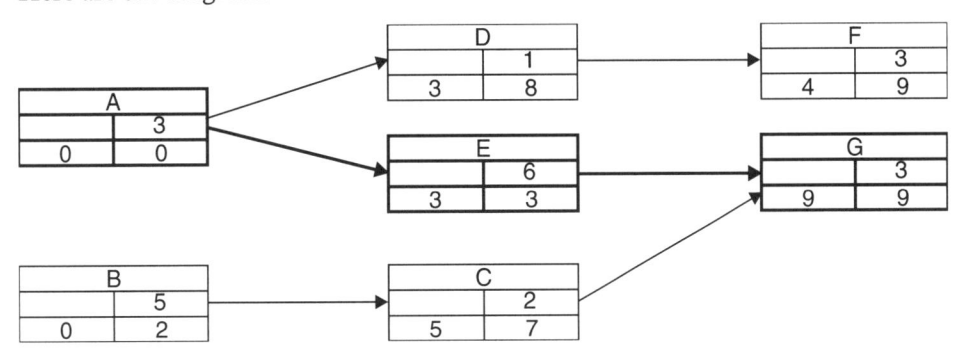

Part A: Project management

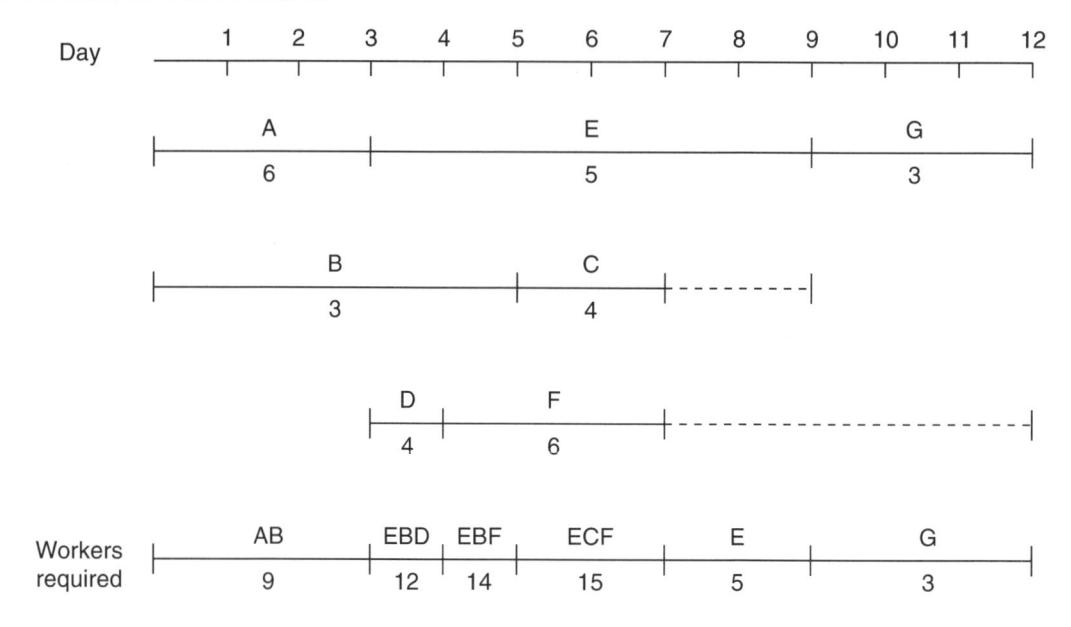

```
Day    1   2   3   4   5   6   7   8   9   10  11  12

       |------A------|---------E---------|------G------|
              6                  5                3

           |-----B-----|------C------|- - - - -|
                3              4

                |--D--|------F------|- - - - - - - - - -|
                   4        6

Workers  |----AB----|-EBD-|-EBF-|---ECF---|----E----|----G----|
required      9       12    14      15         5         3
```

3.59 It can be seen that if all activities start at their earliest times, as many as 15 workers will be required on any one day (days 6-7) whereas on other days there would be idle capacity (days 8-12).

3.60 The problem can be reduced, or removed, by using up spare time on non-critical activities. Suppose we **deferred the start** of activities D and F until the latest possible days. These would be days 8 and 9, leaving four days to complete the activities by the end of day 12.

3.61 The Gantt chart would be redrawn as follows.

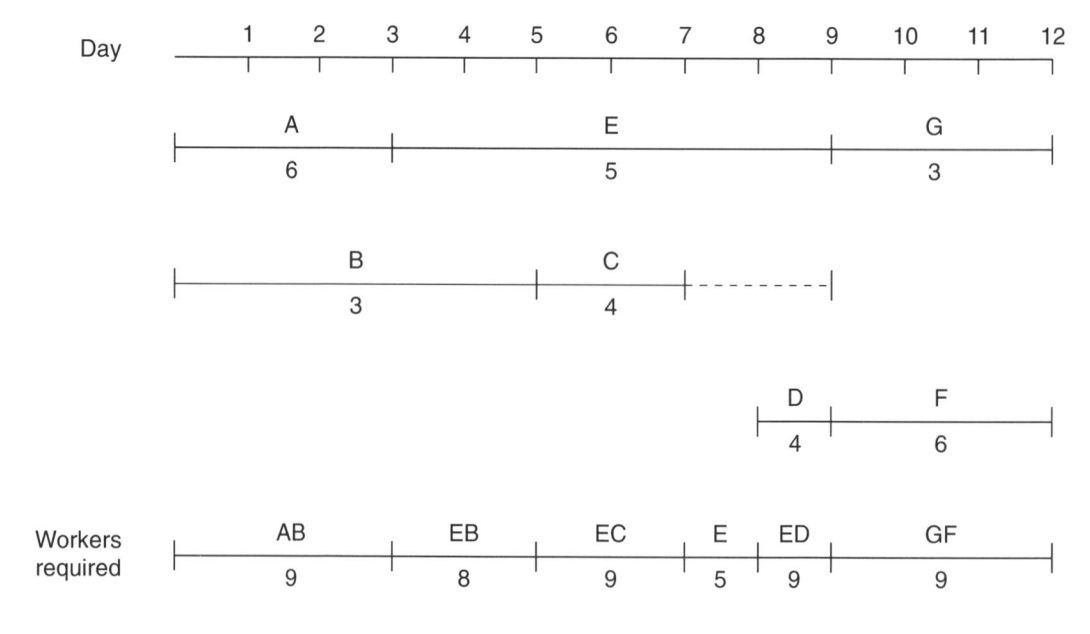

```
Day    1   2   3   4   5   6   7   8   9   10  11  12

       |------A------|---------E---------|------G------|
              6                  5                3

           |-----B-----|------C------|- - - - -|
                3              4

                                    |--D--|------F------|
                                       4        6

Workers  |----AB----|----EB----|----EC----|-E-|-ED-|----GF----|
required      9          8          9       5    9       9
```

Project evaluation review technique (PERT)

3.62 **Project evaluation and review technique (PERT)** is a technique for allowing for uncertainty in determining project duration. Each task is assigned a best, worst, and most probable completion time estimate. These estimates are used to determine the average completion time. The average times are used to establish the critical path and the standard deviation of completion times for the entire project.

3.63 PERT is a modified form of network analysis designed to account for **uncertainty**. For each activity in the project, optimistic, most likely and pessimistic estimates of times are made,

2: Project stages and management tools

on the basis of past experience, or even guess-work. These estimates are converted into a mean time and also a standard deviation.

3.64 Once the mean time and standard deviation of the time have been calculated for each activity, it should be possible to do the following.

(a) Estimate the **critical path** using expected (mean) activity times.
(b) Estimate the **standard deviation of the total project time**.

> **Exam focus point**
>
> PERT is not mentioned in the syllabus, so we have not included a worked example. Just be aware that it exists and that it is designed to build in an allowance for time uncertainty.

Resource histogram

3.65 A useful planning tool that shows the amount and timing of the requirement for a resource (or a range of resources) is the resource histogram.

> **KEY TERM**
>
> **A resource histogram** shows a view of project data in which resource requirements, usage, and availability are shown against a time scale.

3.66 A simple resource histogram showing programmer time required on a software development program is shown below.

Programmer Time Required

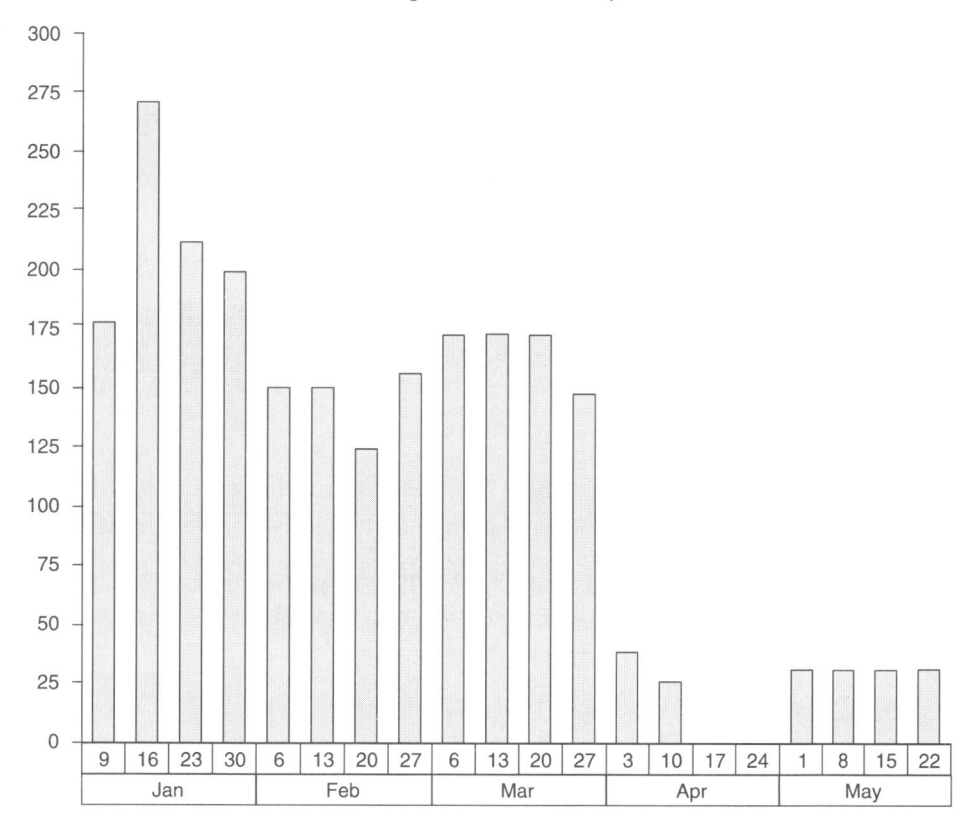

Week ending

Part A: Project management

3.67 Some organisations add another bar (or a separate line) to the chart showing resource availability. The chart then shows any instances when the required resource hours exceed the available hours. Plans should then be made to either obtain further resource for these peak times, or to re-schedule the work plan. Alternately the chart may show times when the available resource is excessive, and should be re-deployed elsewhere. An example follows.

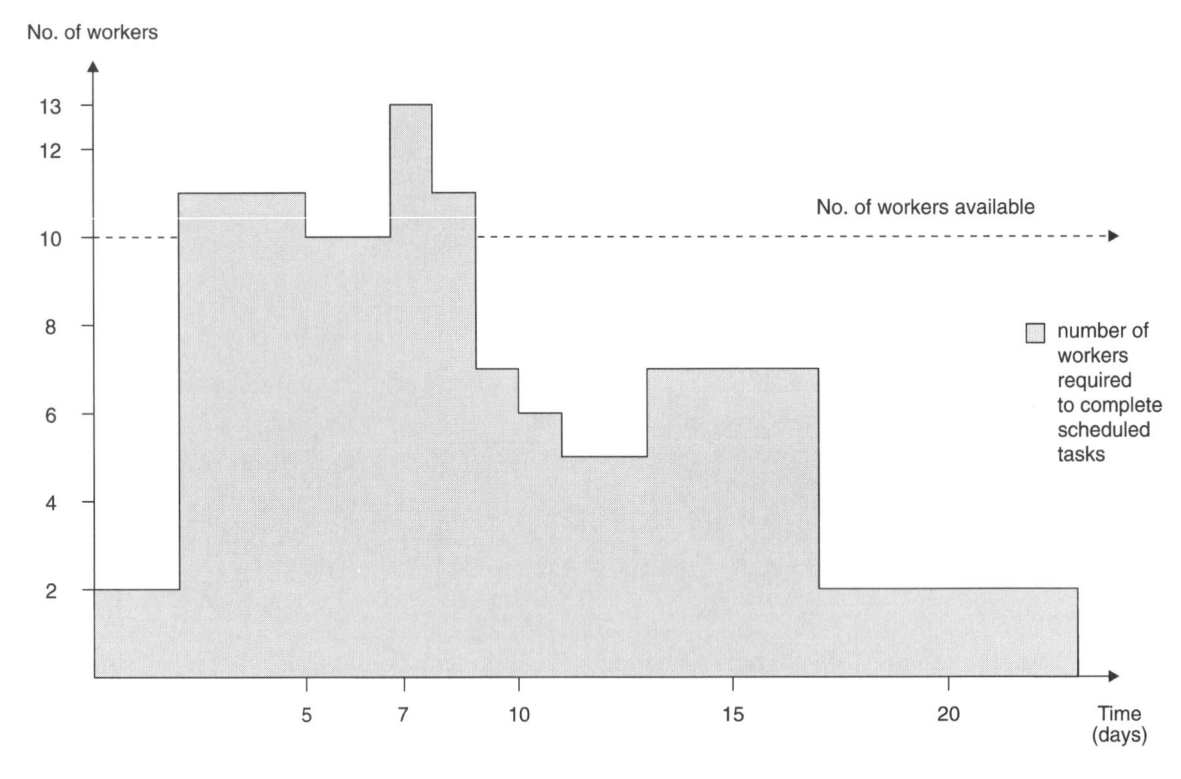

3.68 The number of workers required on the seventh day is 13. Can we re-schedule the non-critical activities to reduce the requirement to the available level of 10? We might be able to re-arrange activities so that we can make use of the workers available from day 9 onwards.

Float times and costs

3.69 **Float time** is the time built in to allow for unforeseen circumstances.

(a) **Total float** on a job is the time available (earliest start date to latest finish date) *less* time needed for the job. If, for example, job A's earliest start time was day 7 and its latest end time was day 17, and the job needed four days, total float would be:

$(17 - 7) - 4 = 6$ days

(b) **Free float** is the delay possible in an activity on the assumption that all preceding jobs start as early as possible and all subsequent jobs also start at the earliest time.

(c) **Independent float** is the delay possible if all preceding jobs have finished as late as possible, and all succeeding jobs have started as early as possible.

4 PROJECT MANAGEMENT SOFTWARE

4.1 Project management techniques are ideal candidates for computerisation. Project management software packages have been available for a number of years. Microsoft Project and Micro Planner X-Pert are two popular packages.

2: Project stages and management tools

4.2 Software might be used for a number of purposes.

(a) **Planning**

Network diagrams (showing the critical path) and Gantt charts (showing resource use) can be produced automatically once the relevant data is entered. Packages also allow a sort of 'what if?' analysis for initial planning, trying out different levels of resources, changing deadlines and so on to find the best combination.

(b) **Estimating**

As a project progresses, actual data will become known and can be entered into the package and collected for future reference. Since many projects involve basically similar tasks (interviewing users and so on), actual data from one project can be used to provide more accurate estimates for the next project. The software also facilitates and encourages the use of more sophisticated estimation techniques than managers might be prepared to use if working manually.

(c) **Monitoring**

Actual data can also be entered and used to facilitate monitoring of progress and automatically updating the plan for the critical path and the use of resources as circumstances dictate.

(d) **Reporting**

Software packages allow standard and tailored progress reports to be produced, printed out and circulated to participants and senior managers at any time, usually at the touch of a button. This helps with co-ordination of activities and project review.

4.3 Most project management packages feature a process of identifying the main steps in a project, and breaking these down further into specific tasks.

4.4 A typical project management package requires four **inputs**.

(a) The length of **time** required for each activity of the project.
(b) The **logical relationships** between each activity.
(c) The **resources** available.
(d) **When** the resources are available.

4.5 The package is able to analyse and present this information in a number of ways. The views available within Microsoft Project are shown in the following illustration – on the drop down menu.

Part A: Project management

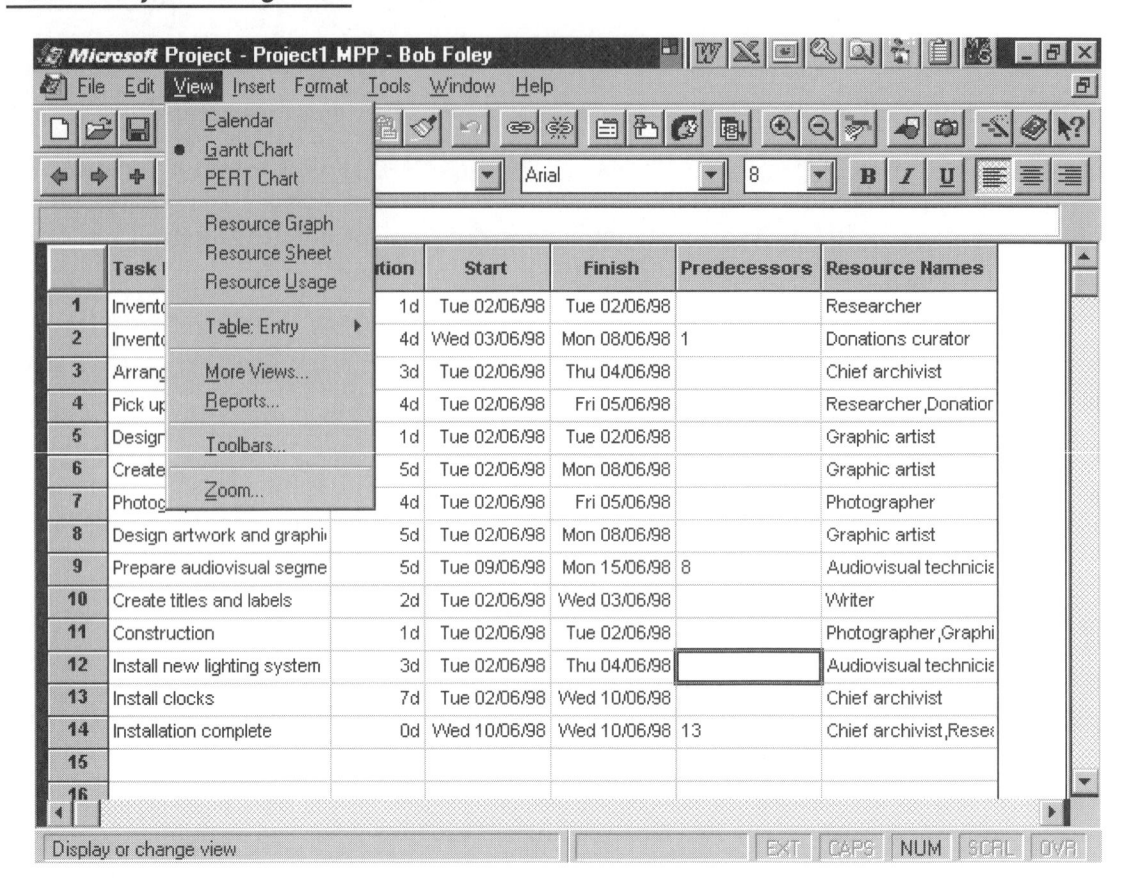

4.6 The advantages of using project management software are summarised on the following table.

Advantage	Comment
Enables quick re-planning	Estimates can be **changed many times** and a new schedule produced almost instantly. Changes to the plan can be reflected immediately.
Document quality	Well-presented plans give a **professional** impression and are easier to understand.
Encourages constant progress tracking	The project manager is able to compare **actual** progress against **planned** progress and investigate problem areas promptly.
What if? analysis	Software enables the effect of various scenarios to be calculated quickly and easily. Many project managers conduct this type of analysis using **copies** of the plan in separate computer files – leaving the actual plan untouched.

4.7 Two **disadvantages** of project management software are:

(a) Some packages are difficult to use.

(b) Some project managers become so interested in producing perfect plans that they spend too much time producing documents and not enough time managing the project.

5 DOCUMENTATION AND REPORTS

5.1 We will now look at the main **documents and reports** used in project management. The name allocated to documents will vary across different organisations. What is constant is the need for clear and relevant documentation that helps monitor and control the project.

5.2 Remember that reports are not a substitute for **face-to-face communication**. Too many (or too lengthy) reports will result in **information overload**.

5.3 When outlining possible content of documents some duplication of items occurs. This does not mean that information should be repeated, but that the information may appear in one or other of the documents depending on the format adopted by the organisation.

Project Charter

> **KEY TERM**
>
> The **Project Charter or Project Brief** is a document approved by the project board that provides the project manager with the authority to apply resources to project activities. In some cases it also defines the terms of reference for the project.

5.4 The Project Charter is presented at the **Project Initiation Meeting**. This meeting agrees the project organisation structure and the initial project plans, which may then be incorporated into the Project Charter. The aim of the meeting is to ensure:

- That everyone knows their role
- All agree on what job is to be done
- There are good business reasons for the project
- That any risks involved have been assessed

It is likely that the Charter will evolve as the project develops, until it is ultimately incorporated into the Project Management Plan.

5.5 The Project Charter defines the **terms of reference** for the project. The charter should contain the statements of project manager, team, stakeholders and sponsors about:

- The **scope** of the project - what it is intended to cover and what it is not
- The desirable attitudes and behaviours for the project
- The objectives for the team during the project, and for the completed project
- The processes the team commits to, to help it work efficiently and effectively

5.6 The charter is more 'abstract' than the project documentation that will follow it. The team must be involved in discussing the expectations that the charter raises for them about the behaviour of others. This will combat the cynicism of the 'yet another mission statement' attitude.

5.7 The charter is not likely to give many specifics about how the team and the project are to proceed. The Project Management Plan will do that.

Project Management Plan

5.8 The project manager should also develop a **Project Management Plan**. (In some organisations what is described here as the Project Management Plan would simply be

Part A: Project management

called the Project Plan. In other organisations the Project Plan refers only to the project schedule, usually in the form of a network diagram.)

> **KEY TERM**
>
> The **Project Management Plan** is used as a reference tool for **managing the project**. The plan is used to guide both project execution and project control. It outlines how the project will be planned, monitored and implemented.

5.9 The **project management plan** should include:

- Project objectives and how they will be achieved and verified
- How any **changes** to these procedures are to be **controlled**
- The **management and technical procedures**, and **standards**, to be used
- The **budget** and **time-scale**
- **Safety**, health and environmental policies
- Inherent **risks** and how they will be managed

5.10 An example of a simple **Project Plan / Project Management Plan** is shown over the page. This plan was produced by an American organisation - the Project Management Institute (PMI) - to manage a project to produce formal project management principles.

5.11 The Project Plan **evolves** over time. A high-level plan for the whole project and a detailed plan for the current and following stage is usually produced soon after project start-up. At each subsequent stage a detailed plan is produced for the following stage and, if required, the overall project plan is revised.

Case example

Project Management Plan	
Project Name	The full name of this project is 'Project Management Principles.'
Project Manager	The project manager is Joe Bloggs. The project manager is authorised to (1) initiate the project, (2) form the project team and (3) prepare and execute plans and manage the project as necessary for successful project completion.
Purpose / Business Need	This project addresses a need for high-level guidelines for the project management profession through the identification and presentation of project management principles. The project sponsor and accepting agent is the Project Management Institute (PMI) Standards Program Team (SPT). The principal and beneficial customer is the membership of PMI. Principles are needed to provide high-level context and guidance for the profession of project management. These Principles will provide benefit from the perspectives of practice, evaluation, and development.
Product Description and Deliverables	The final deliverable of this project is a document containing a statement of project management Principles. The text is to be fully developed and ready for publication. As a research and development project, it is to be approached flexibly in schedule and resource requirements, with an initially proposed publication date of June 2001.
Project Management	The project team will use project methodology consistent with PMI Standards. The project is to be managed with definitive scope and acceptance criteria fully established as the project progresses and the product is developed.
Assumptions, Constraints and Risks	The project faces some increased risk that without a clearly prescribed definition of a Principle, standards for product quality will be more difficult to establish and apply. To mitigate this risk, ongoing communication between the project team and the project sponsor on this matter will be required.

2: Project stages and management tools

Resources	The PMI Standards Program Team (SPT) is to provide the project team with the following. **Financial.** SPT will provide financial resources as available. The initial amount for the current year is $5,000. The project manager must not exceed the allocated amount, and notify the SPT when 75% of the allocation has been spent. **Explanation of Standards Program.** SPT will provide guidance at the outset of the project, updates as changes occur, and clarifications as needed. **Personnel / Volunteers.** SPT will recruit volunteer team members from within the membership of PMI through various media and liaisons. The project team is to consist of no less than ten members, including the project manager. General qualifications to be sought by SPT in recruiting will be: **Mandatory**<ul><li>Acceptance of project plan</li><li>Demonstrated capability for strategic, generalised or intuitive thinking</li><li>Capability to write clearly on technical subject matter for general audiences</li><li>Capability to work co-operatively with well-developed interpersonal skills</li><li>Be conversant in English and be able to use telephone and Internet email telecommunications</li></ul>**As possible**<ul><li>Time availability (Team members may contribute at different levels. An average of approximately five to ten hours per month is desired.)</li><li>Diversity (Team members collectively may represent diverse nationalities, types of organisations or corporate structure, business sectors, academic disciplines, and personal experience)</li><li>Travel (As determined mutually by the project sponsor and manager, some travel for face-to-face meetings may be requested)</li></ul>
Approach	The project will progress through the following phases. **Phase 1: Team formation** – Recruit and orient volunteer team members. Establish procedures and ground rules for group process and decision making. **Phase 2: Subject Matter Clarification** – Identify and clarify initial scope and definitions of project subject matter. **Phase 3a: Exploration** – Begin brainstorming (through gathering, sharing, and discussion) of data and views in unrestricted, non-judgmental process. **Phase 3b: Selection** – Conclude brainstorming (through evaluation and acceptance or rejection) of collected data and views. As the conclusion to this phase, the SPT will review as an interim deliverable the selection made by the project team. **Phase 4: Development** – Conduct further research and discussion to develop accepted subject matter. **Phase 5: Articulation** - Write a series of drafts to state the accepted and developed subject matter as appropriate for the project business need and product description. **Phase 6: Adoption** – Submit product to SPT for the official PMI standards approval and adoption process. Revise product as needed. **Phase 7: Closeout** – Perform closure for team and administrative matters. Deliver project files to SPT.
Communication and Reporting	The project manager and team will communicate with and report to the PMI Standards Program Team as follows. **Monthly Status Reports** – Written monthly status and progress reports are to include:<ul><li>Work accomplished since the last report</li><li>Work planned to be performed during the next reporting period</li><li>Deliverables submitted since the last report</li><li>Deliverables planned to be submitted during the next reporting period</li><li>Work tasks in progress and currently outside of expectations for scope, quality, schedule or cost</li><li>Risks identified and actions taken or proposed to mitigate</li><li>Lessons learned</li><li>Summary statement for posting on PMI website</li></ul>

Part A: Project management

	Monthly Resource Reports – Written monthly resource reports are to include: **Financial resources** • Total funds allocated • Total funds expended to date • Estimated expenditures for the next reporting period • Estimated expenditures for entire project to completion **Human resources** • List of all volunteer team members categorised by current involvement (i.e., active, new (pre-active), inactive, resigned) • Current number of new and active volunteer team members • Estimated number of volunteer team members needed for project completion **Milestone and Critical Status Reports** – Additional status reports are to be submitted as mutually agreed upon by SPT and the project manager and are to include at least the following items. • Milestone Status Reports are to include the same items as the Monthly Status reports, summarised to cover an entire project phase period since the last milestone report, or entire project to date. • Critical Status Reports are to focus on work tasks outside of expectations and other information as requested by SPT or stipulated by the project manager.
Acceptance	The project manager will submit the final product and any interim deliverables to the Standards Program Team (SPT) for formal acceptance. The SPT may (1) accept the product as delivered by the project team, or (2) return the product to the team with a statement of specific requirements to make the product fully acceptable. The acceptance decision of the SPT is to be provided to the project manager in writing.
Change Management	Requests for change to this plan may be initiated by either the project sponsor or the project manager. All change requests will be reviewed and approved or rejected by a formal proceeding of the Standards Program Team (SPT) with input and interaction with the project manager. Decisions of the SPT will be documented and provided to the project manager in writing. All changes will be incorporated into this document, reflected by a new version number and date.

Plan Acceptance	Signature and Date
By PMI Standards Program Team	_____ 12 July 1999 Fred Jones - PMI Technical Research & Standards Manager
By Project Manager	_____ 20 July 1999 Joe Bloggs - PMI Member

5.12 The format and contents of a Project Management Plan will **vary** depending on the organisation involved and the complexity of the project. The contents page and introduction from a detailed Project Management Plan relating to a software implementation project at a call centre follow.

Case example

Call centre software implementation - Project Management Plan

CONTENTS

Page

1. INTRODUCTION
2. PROJECT ROLES
3. COMMUNICATIONS PLAN
4. TRAINING PLAN
5. CHANGE MANAGEMENT PLAN
6. QUALITY MANAGEMENT
7. PROJECT DOCUMENTATION
8. FINANCIAL MANAGEMENT
9. PROGRAMME MANAGEMENT

SECTION 1

INTRODUCTION

1.1 **Purpose of the Project Management Plan**

The purpose of this Plan is to define the working relationship between Project Team (PT) and the Manager, Customer Centres Group (MCCG). It details the level of service to be provided by Project Team to the client and the associated cost. If the nature of the project changes, or if situations develop which indicate a need for modification, then this plan will be altered accordingly in consultation with the Client. This Plan details key milestones, the methods for delivering these milestones, and responsibilities of the project manager, project owner and the project team representatives.

1.2 **Project Objective**

To develop and fully support a call centre environment that promotes the achievement of '80% of all incoming calls resolved at the first point of contact.'

1.3 **Project Deliverable**

To deliver to the MCCG, fully commissioned and operational system upgrades as defined within this project plan, including an appropriately skilled call centre team, by 15 April 1999 at an estimated Project Team cost of £ 123,975.

Note: Only the contents page and introduction of this comprehensive plan are reproduced here.

Project quality plan

5.13 An important element of the overall Project Plan is the Project Quality Plan.

> **KEY TERM**
>
> The **Project Quality Plan** outlines the quality strategy to be followed and links this to any formal quality management approach the organisation has chosen to follow.

5.14 There is no generally accepted format for a quality plan - in fact the **distinction** between a **project management plan** and a **quality plan** is becoming **increasingly blurred**.

Part A: Project management

5.15 Key elements of a quality plan include:
- The formal stages of the project
- Standards to be used throughout the project
- Controls that aim to ensure quality
- Checks to ensure quality

Progress report 5/02

> **KEY TERM**
>
> A **progress report** shows the current status of the project, usually in relation to the planned status.

5.16 The frequency and contents of progress reports will vary depending on the length of, and the progress being made on, a project.

5.17 The report is a **control tool** intended to show the discrepancies between where the project is, and where the plan says it should be.

5.18 A common form of progress reports uses two columns – one for **planned** time and expenditure and one for **actual**.

5.19 Any additional content will depend on the format adopted. Some organisations include only the 'raw facts' in the report, and use these as a basis for discussion regarding reasons for variances and action to be taken, at a project review meeting.

5.20 Other organisations (particularly those involved in long, complex projects) produce more comprehensive progress reports, with more explanation and comment.

5.21 The report should monitor progress towards key **milestones.**

> **KEY TERM**
>
> A **milestone** is a significant event in the project, usually completion of a major deliverable.

5.22 A progress report may include a milestone slip chart which compares planned and actual progress towards project milestones. Planned progress is shown on the X-axis and actual progress on the Y-axis. Where actual progress is slower than planned progress **slippage** has occurred.

2: Project stages and management tools

Milestone slip chart

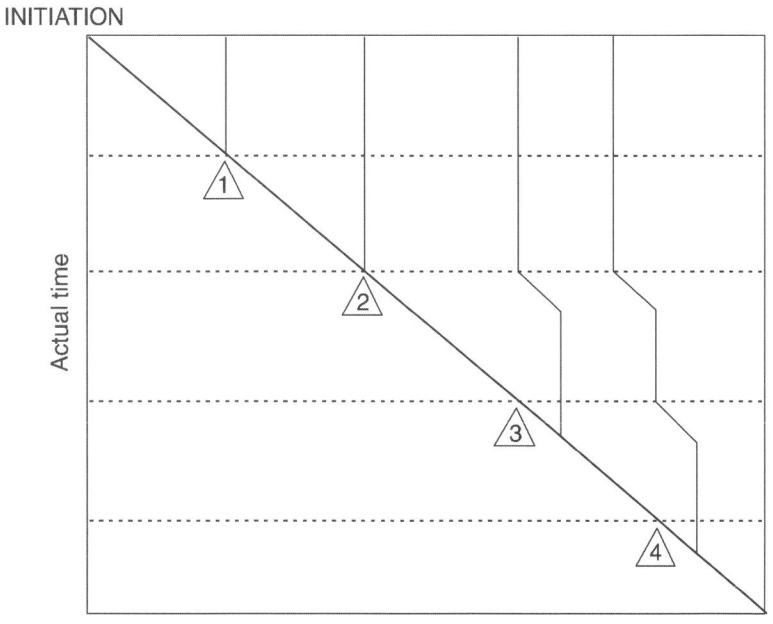

5.23 On the chart above milestones are indicated by a triangle on the diagonal planned progress line. The vertical lines that meet milestones 1 and 2 are straight – showing that these milestones were achieved on time.

5.24 At milestone 3 some slippage has occurred. The chart shows that no further slippage is expected as the progress line for milestone 4 is the same distance to the right as occurred at milestone 3.

5.25 We look at ways of dealing with slippage later in this chapter.

5.26 The progress report should also include an updated budget status – such a report could adopt the format shown in the following example.

Part A: Project management

Case Example

PROJECT STATUS REPORT

Project title: Software Implementation   To date: 11 May 2000

OVERALL STATUS	Behind XX days	On target	Ahead.........days

KEY MILESTONES

	Plan	Actual
1. Project scope and plans signed off		
2. SLA / contract signed off		
3. Acceptance criteria signed off		
4. Training plan signed off		
5. Business processes signed off		
6. User training complete (on existing 'test' system)		
7. Pilot system established		
8. Pilot system reviewed		
9. Go live date confirmed		
10. Go live		

IMPACT OF SLIPPAGES

M/s	Details / planned remedial action	Date

KEY RISKS

Ref	Description	Management actions	Date

KEY ISSUES

Ref	Description	Resolve by date

FINANCIAL STATUS

$ 000's	"a" Initial budget	"b" Curr budget (inc app'd changes)	"c" Actual spend to date	"d" R/cast - to complete	"e" Var	Reason
Capital						
Fixed						
Variable						
Ongoing						
Fixed						
Variable						
Total						

Note: Var = (c+d) - b

Other comments (notable achievements / major changes / planned absences etc.):

Project Manager:..

Project Sponsor...

Completion report

> **KEY TERM**
>
> The **completion report** summarises the results of the project, and includes client sign-off.

5.27 On project completion the project manager will produce the **Completion Report.** The main purpose of the completion report is to document (and gain client sign-off for) the end of the project.

5.28 The report should include a **summary** of the project outcome. The completion report should contain:

(a) Project objectives and the outcomes achieved.

(b) The final project budget report showing expected and actual expenditure (If an external client is involved this information may be sensitive - the report may exclude or 'amend' the budget report).

(c) A brief outline of time taken compared with the original schedule.

5.29 The completion report will also include provision for any **on-going issues** that will need to be addressed after completion. Such issues would be related to the project, but not part of the project. (If they are part of the project the project is not yet complete!) An example of an on-going issue would be a procedure for any 'bugs' that become apparent **after** a new software program has been tested and approved.

5.30 Responsibilities and procedures relating to any such issues should be laid down in the report.

5.31 The manager may find it useful to distribute a provisional report and request **feedback**. This should ensure the version presented for client sign-off at the completion meeting is acceptable to all parties.

5.32 A more detailed review of the project follows a few months after completion, the post-completion audit.

The post-completion audit   11/01

> **KEY TERM**
>
> The **post-completion audit** is a formal review of the project that examines the lessons that may be learned and used for the benefit of future projects.

5.33 The audit looks at all aspects of the project with regard to two questions.

(a) Did the end result of the project meet the **client's expectations**?
- The actual **design** and **construction** of the end product
- Was the project achieved **on time**?
- Was the project **completed within budget**?

(b) Was the **management of the project** as successful as it might have been, or were there bottlenecks or problems? This review covers:

  (i) Problems that might occur on future projects with similar characteristics.
  (ii) The performance of the team individually and as a group.

In other words, any project is an opportunity to learn how to manage future projects more effectively.

5.34 The post-completion audit should involve **input from the project team**. A simple questionnaire could be developed for all team members to complete, and a reasonably informal meeting held to obtain feedback, on what went well (and why), and what didn't (and why).

5.35 This information should be formalised in a report. The **post-completion audit report** should contain the following.

(a) A **summary** should be provided, emphasising any areas where the structures and tools used to manage the project have been found to be **unsatisfactory**.

(b) A **review** of the end result of the project should be provided, and compared against the results expected. Reasons for any significant **discrepancies** between the two should be provided, preferably with suggestions of how any future projects could **prevent these problems recurring**.

(c) A **cost-benefit review** should be included, comparing the forecast costs and benefits identified at the time of the feasibility study with actual costs and benefits.

(d) **Recommendations** should be made as to any steps which should be taken to **improve** the project management procedures used.

5.36 Lessons learnt that relate to the way the **project was managed** should contribute to the smooth running of future projects.

5.37 A starting point for any new project should be a **review** of the documentation of any **similar projects** undertaken in the past.

6 RISK MANAGEMENT 11/01

6.1 The identification of risks involves an overview of the project to establish what could go wrong, and the consequences.

- What are the sources of risk?
- What is the likelihood of the risk presenting itself?
- To what extent can the risk be controlled?
- What are the consequences of that risk presenting itself?
- To what extent can those consequences be controlled?

6.2 The likelihood and consequences of risks can be plotted on a matrix.

Risk Assessment Matrix

Potential impact			
High	M	H	VH
Med	L	M	H
Low	VL	L	M
	Low	Med	High

Threat Likelihood

6.3 Developing a **contingency plan** that contains strategies for risks that fall into the VH quadrant should have priority, followed by risks falling into the two H quadrants. Following the principle of **management by exception**, the most efficient way of dealing with risks outside these quadrants may be to do nothing unless the risk presents itself.

6.4 There are four main strategies that could be employed when managing risk:

(a) **Avoidance**: the factors which give rise to the risk are removed.

(b) **Reduction**: the potential for the risk cannot be removed but analysis has enabled the identification of ways to reduce the incidence and / or the consequences.

(c) **Transference**: the risk is passed on to someone else - or is perhaps financed by an insurer.

(d) **Absorption**: the potential risk is accepted in the hope or expectation that the incidence and consequences can be coped with if necessary.

7 INFORMATION SYSTEMS PROJECTS – COMMON PROBLEMS

7.1 It is not uncommon for information systems projects to be years late, wildly over budget, and produce a system that does not meet user requirements.

7.2 A number of factors can combine to produce these expensive disasters.

Project managers

7.3 IS project managers were often **technicians,** not managers. Technical ability for IS staff is no guarantee of management skill - an individual might be a highly proficient analyst or programmer, but not a good manager.

Part A: Project management

7.4 The project manager has a number of **conflicting requirements**.

(a) The **systems manager**, usually the project manager's boss, wants the project **delivered on time**, to specification and within budget.

(b) **User** expectations may be misunderstood, ignored or unrealistic.

(c) The project manager has to plan and supervise the work of **analysts** and **programmers** and these are rather different roles.

7.5 The project manager needs to develop an **appropriate management style**. What he or she should realise is the extent to which the project will fail if users are not consulted, or if the project team is unhappy. As the project manager needs to encourage participation from users, an excessively authoritarian style is not suitable.

Other factors

7.6 Other factors can be identified.

(a) The project manager may accept **an unrealistic deadline** - the timescale is fixed early in the planning process. User demands may be accepted as deadlines before sufficient consideration is given to the realism of this.

(b) **Poor or non-existent planning** is a recipe for disaster. Unrealistic deadlines would be identified much earlier if a proper planning process was undertaken.

(c) A lack of **monitoring** and **control**.

(d) Users **change their requirements**, resulting in costly changes to the system as it is being developed.

(e) **Poor time-tabling and resourcing**. It is no use being presented on day 1 with a team of programmers, when there is still systems analysis and design work to do. The development and implementation of a computer project may take a considerable length of time (perhaps 18 months from initial decision to operational running for a medium-sized installation); a proper plan and time schedule for the various activities must be drawn up.

7.7 A project is affected by a number of factors, often in **conflict** with each other.

(a) **Quality** of the system required, in terms of basic system requirements.

(b) **Time,** both to complete the project, and in terms of the opportunity cost of time spent on this project which could be spent on others.

(c) **Costs** and resources allocated to the project.

7.8 The balance between the constraints of time, cost and quality will be different for each project.

(a) If a system aims to provide competitive advantage then time will tend to be the dominant factor.

(b) If safety is paramount (eg an auto-pilot system) then quality will be most important.

(c) If the sole aim of a project is to meet administrative needs that are not time dependent, then cost may be the dominant factor.

7.9 The relationship can be shown as a triangle.

The Time/Cost/Quality Triangle

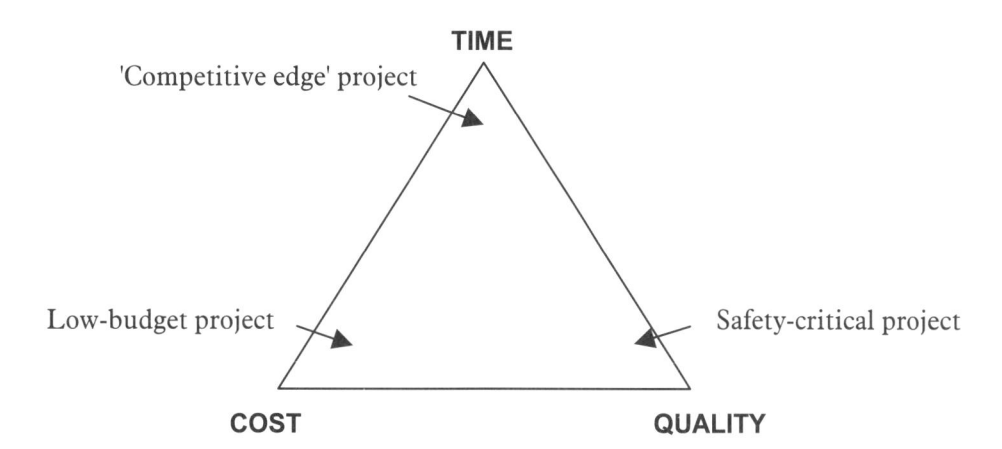

```
                    TIME
    'Competitive edge' project ↘
                     /\
                    /  \
                   /    \
                  /      \
                 /        \
    Low-budget  /          \  Safety-critical project
      project ↘/            \↙
              /_____\
            COST           QUALITY
```

7.10 The balance of time, cost and quality will influence decision making throughout the project – for example whether to spend an extra £5,000 to fix a problem completely or only spend £1,000 on a quick fix and implement a user work-around?

Dealing with slippage

7.11 When a project has slipped behind schedule there are a range of options open to the project manager. Some of these options are summarised in the following table.

Action	Comment
Do nothing	After considering all options it may be decided that things should be allowed to continue as they are.
Add resources	If capable staff are available and it is practicable to add more people to certain tasks it may be possible to recover some lost ground. Could some work be subcontracted?
Work smarter	Consider whether the methods currently being used are the most suitable – for example could prototyping be used.
Replan	If the assumptions the original plan was based on have been proved invalid a more realistic plan should be devised.
Reschedule	A complete replan may not be necessary – it may be possible to recover some time by changing the phasing of certain deliverables.
Introduce incentives	If the main problem is team performance, incentives such as bonus payments could be linked to work deadlines and quality.
Change the specification	If the original objectives of the project are unrealistic given the time and money available it may be necessary to negotiate a change in the specification.

Project change procedure

7.12 Some of the reactions to slippage discussed above would involve changes that would significantly affect the overall project. Other possible causes of changes to the original project plan include:

Part A: Project management

- The availability of new technology
- Changes in personnel
- A realisation that user requirements were misunderstood
- Changes in the business environment
- New legislation eg Data protection

7.13 The **earlier** a change is made the **less expensive** it should prove. However, changes will cost time and money and should not be undertaken lightly.

7.14 When considering a change **an investigation** should be conducted to discover:

(a) The consequences of **not** implementing the proposed change.

(b) The impact of the change on **time, cost** and quality.

(c) The expected costs and benefits of the change.

(d) The risks associated with the change, and with the status-quo.

7.15 The process of ensuring that proper consideration is given to the impact of proposed changes is known as **change control.**

7.16 Changes will need to be implemented into the project plan and communicated to all stakeholders.

Case example

WHY CAN'T WE BUILD SOFTWARE LIKE WE BUILD BUILDINGS?

Introduction

The software development industry has a reputation for poor project performance. This makes many organisations reluctant to undertake large development projects.

The Project Manager's Responsibility

The project manager plays the same role within a software development as they would in a construction project: their aim is to finish the job within time and cost to the quality required.

Get the Right Person for the Job

Just imagine that you have built a garden shed and a passer-by compliments you on your achievement. The passer-by then asks since you've made such a good job of the shed would you build a new three-bedroom house. After all, it will utilise the same materials, just more of them. It's not very likely is it?

Yet many people learned how to use a PC-based database development application such as Microsoft Access, Dbase, or Paradox, and then went on to build 'commercial' systems. In many cases these were not designed to be commercial systems, they just started as a useful place to store information, then grew until they became a vital source of information.

Appropriate Methodology

Every size of building project requires its own set of processes to most cost effectively complete. Software is no different. Applying skyscraper standards to a house will be expensive and result in over-engineering. When setting up a software development project the same rules apply. Select the right methodology and ensure that your developer is experienced with this methodology.

Reusable Components

When building, there is little point in designing non-standard sizes into a building then trying to fit standard components into the design. These components are often as simple as the garage or interior doors, but could well include items which cannot easily be built on site, such as sealed unit double glazing.

2: Project stages and management tools

In the software industry, the reuse of code or objects is a relatively recent development. As with buildings, if you are going to use existing components, the design must be created in such a way as to accommodate them. In the early years of software development these components would be simple subroutines which could be copied into the code to perform simple tasks such as date verification. More recently the advent of commercially successful component infrastructures such as CORBA, the Internet, ActiveX or Java Beans, has triggered a whole industry of off-the-shelf components for various domains, allowing you to buy and integrate components rather than developing them all in-house. Reusability shifts software development from programming software (a line at time) to composing software (by assembling components) just as a modern builder does not fabricate their own material but assembles the delivered components.

Responsibility of the Project Manager

The project manager is key to the success of any project and must be able to manage both people and other resources. The key role of the manager is not simply in monitoring progress but is in fixing things when they go wrong. This is the case in both industries.

Create the Environment

The project manager can create a little bit of 'project magic' by establishing a project environment which allows project participants to operate effectively and co-operatively. This type of project environment is significantly more effective than an aggressive environment.

Issue Resolution

In the building industry, the issues that arise are more likely to be physical in nature. If a team is gathered around a hole in the ground or a piece of building which doesn't quite fit, they can start to suggest solutions by measuring, drawing or simply explaining what they think will fix it.

In the software industry, the issues that arise are more likely to be abstract. However, the need for the sponsor to understand the problem is just as important. Any explanation that can be given in terms which mere mortals can understand is worth far more than the exact technical definition, especially if the Sponsor is required to make a decision on how to resolve the issue.

Conclusion

The use of modern methodologies and modelling techniques allows much of the risk of software development to be reduced. The rigorous use of CASE tools applies standards which are as close to regulations the software industry has at present. The development environments, frameworks and object libraries of software developers are gaining in sophistication to a point where many of the risks are already written out of a new development.

It may take a few years to come to terms with the international implications of electronic commerce over the Internet. The changes in taxable revenue of having a business process independent of location will have far-reaching effects. This is likely to be the next challenge of the technology industry.

Adapted from a paper prepared by Synergy International 1999

Summary

7.17 The following Mind Map provides a useful **overview of the project management process**. It is slightly more detailed than the syllabus requires, but should help you understand the inter-relationships between the various techniques and methodologies we have looked at.

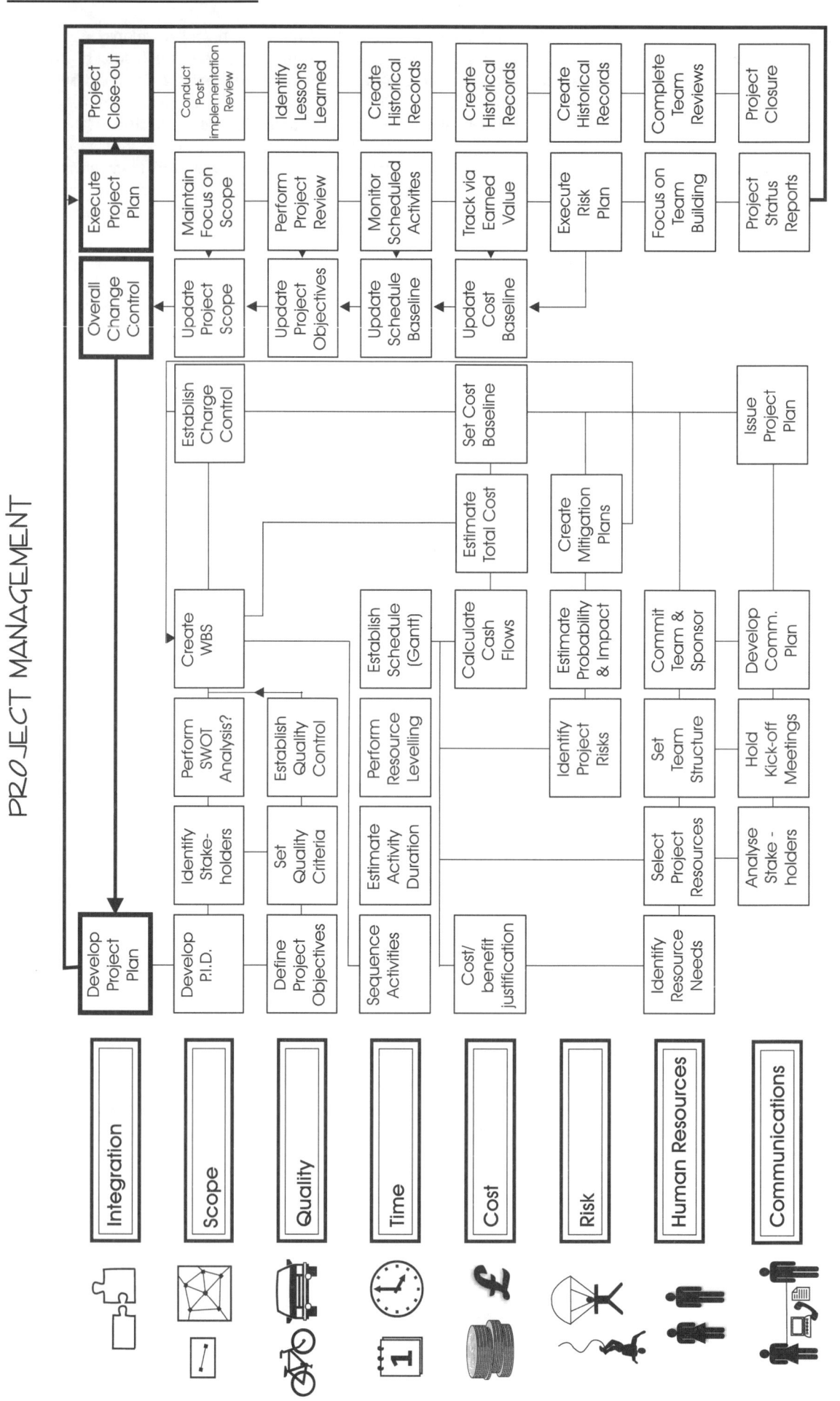

Part A: Project management

PROJECT MANAGEMENT

Integration:
- Develop Project Plan
- Overall Change Control
- Execute Project Plan
- Project Close-out
- Conduct Post-implementation Review

Scope:
- Develop P.I.D.
- Identify Stakeholders
- Perform SWOT Analysis?
- Create WBS
- Establish Charge Control
- Update Project Scope
- Maintain Focus on Scope
- Identify Lessons Learned

Quality:
- Define Project Objectives
- Set Quality Criteria
- Establish Quality Control
- Update Project Objectives
- Perform Project Review
- Create Historical Records

Time:
- Sequence Activities
- Estimate Activity Duration
- Perform Resource Levelling
- Establish Schedule (Gantt)
- Update Schedule Baseline
- Monitor Scheduled Activities
- Create Historical Records

Cost:
- Cost/benefit justification
- Calculate Cash Flows
- Estimate Total Cost
- Set Cost Baseline
- Update Cost Baseline
- Track via Earned Value
- Create Historical Records

Risk:
- Identify Project Risks
- Estimate Probability & Impact
- Create Mitigation Plans
- Execute Risk Plan

Human Resources:
- Identify Resource Needs
- Select Project Resources
- Set Team Structure
- Commit Team & Sponsor
- Focus on Team Building
- Complete Team Reviews

Communications:
- Analyse Stakeholders
- Hold Kick-off Meetings
- Develop Comm. Plan
- Issue Project Plan
- Project Status Reports
- Project Closure

2: Project stages and management tools

> **Chapter roundup**
>
> - A project typically passes through five **phases**: defining, planning, implementing, controlling and completing.
> - CIMA identify thirteen **project stages**, although in 'real' situations the number and sequence of stages will vary.
> - Various **tools and techniques** are available to plan and control projects.
> - Project **documentation** plays an important part in project control and communication.
> - The Mind Map on the previous page 'rounds-up' many of the issues discussed in this chapter.

Quick quiz

1. List five typical stages of a project.
   1. ....
   2. ....
   3. ....
   4. ....
   5. ....
2. What would you expect a Project Initiation Document to contain?
3. What is Work Breakdown Structure?
4. What is the purpose of a Gantt chart?
5. What is the Project Quality Plan used for?
6. Why do many project managers prefer to use project management software?
7. Briefly outline the relationship between quality, cost and time in the context of an information systems project.
8. What should the risk management process achieve?

> **Answers to quick quiz**
>
> 1. Defining, Planning, Implementing, Controlling, Completing.
> 2. Contents could include: Project objectives, the scope of the project, overall budget, final deadlines, the ultimate customer, resources, risks inherent in the project, a preliminary project plan (targets, activities and so on) and details of how the project is to be organised and managed.
> 3. Work Breakdown Structure (WBS) is the process of breaking down the project into manageable tasks.
> 4. A Gantt chart displays the time relationships between tasks in a project. It is a horizontal bar chart used to estimate the amount and timing of resources required.
> 5. The Project Quality Plan is used to guide both project execution and project control. It outlines how the project will be planned, monitored and implemented.
> 6. A project management software package saves time and produces high quality output. As with all software, it is dependant on the quality of the data fed into the package - the length of time required for each activity of the project, the logical relationships between each activity, the resources available and when the resources are available.
> 7. The quality of information system produced is dependant upon (among other things) the time available to develop the system and the resources (ie cost) available to the project. Insufficient time and / or resources will have an adverse effect on the quality of system produced.
> 8. The risk management process should identify and quantify the risks associated with the project, and decide on how the risks should be managed.

The material covered in this Chapter is tested in questions 2, 8(b), 10, 13, 17 and 19 in the Question Bank.

Chapter 3

BUSINESS MEETINGS AND PRESENTATIONS

Topic list		Syllabus reference	Ability required
1	The purpose of meetings	(i)	Evaluation
2	The conduct of meetings	(i)	Evaluation
3	Managing meetings	(i)	Evaluation
4	Project meetings	(i)	Evaluation
5	Producing a presentation	(i)	Analysis

Introduction

This chapter is included within the project management part of this Study Text to remain consistent with the CIMA syllabus structure.

Firstly we examine the use and conduct of **meetings** in a business setting, before looking at techniques to increase the efficiency of meetings. Although this material applies to meetings held under the banner of project management, it applies also to other meetings held in a business context.

The same applies to the information on producing a **presentation**. While this may be required in the context of project management, the syllabus allows for this material to be examined in any management accounting context.

Learning outcomes covered in this chapter

- **Explain** why meetings are commonly used in organisations
- **Evaluate** the planning and conduct of a meeting and the roles of the various participants in a typical meeting
- **Identify** the main problems associated with meetings and recommend how those problems might be avoided or solved
- **Recommend** changes to the management and conduct of a meeting in order to avoid or solve problems identified
- **Produce** a presentation on a management accounting topic

Syllabus content covered in this chapter

- The purpose, context and limitations of meetings in a business context
- The roles which may be adopted by participants in a business meeting and how the chair should manage those participants to retain control of the meeting

1 THE PURPOSE OF MEETINGS

1.1 Meetings play an important part in the life of any organisation. Meetings include:

(a) **Formal meetings** required by government legislation or the Articles of a company

(b) Regular or 'one-off' **internal management meetings**. These may involve the gathering of, communication of, or review of, information. Alternately, the meeting may have a problem-solving or decision-making purpose.

(c) Some **discussions held informally** may 'qualify' as a meeting – there are no hard and fast rules as to what constitutes an informal meeting.

> **KEY TERM**
>
> A **meeting** consists of people gathering in the same room for one or more of the following purposes.
>
> - Gather information
> - Disseminate information or instructions
> - Generate ideas
> - Make or implement decisions

Why are meetings used in organisations?

1.2 A well-organised, well-aimed and well-led meeting can be effective in many different contexts.

(a) **Decision-making**, for example, by a group of directors, managers, or employees.
(b) The **relaying of decisions** and instructions.
(c) The **provision of advice** and information.
(d) Participative **problem-solving**.
(e) **Brainstorming**: free exchanges with a view to generating new approaches and ideas.

1.3 The wider organisational purposes of meetings may include the following.

(a) **Ritual.** A manager's 'ceremonial' role is acted out in meetings. Often, meetings form the ritual ending of months of negotiation: the final 'handshake'.

(b) **Communication and personal contact**. A meeting helps people to get to know one another. Establishing good personal relationships is important in organisational life.

(c) **'Letting off steam'**. There is sometimes a good purpose in having a session in which grievances get aired. Disagreement might be seen as a useful way of generating new ideas.

(d) **Motivation and satisfaction**. The fact, or at least the illusion, of participation in decisions may improve individual motivation.

(e) **Representation**. Meetings enable the various different interests in a decision to be represented as 'equals'.

(f) **Inspiration**. Some meetings can be inspirational, if they are used to persuade, cajole or encourage a sense of values.

(g) **Unification**. Finally, bringing people together underlines the fact that they belong to the same organisation, and in theory should be working to the same purpose.

Part A: Project management

2 THE CONDUCT OF MEETINGS

2.1 To achieve their purpose, those who attend a meeting must generally conform or respond to a measure of **organisation** and **procedure**.

   (a) There is usually a **Chairperson**, or at least an organiser, who guides the proceedings of the meeting and aims to maintain order.

   (b) There should be an **agenda** outlining what is to be covered.

2.2 An **informal meeting** may take the form of a group discussion 'chaired' by a leader and informally documented. Notes may be taken during the meeting, a summary of arguments and decisions reached provided afterwards.

2.3 **Formal meetings** follow conventions and generate formal documentation for the announcement, planning, conduct and recording of the proceedings. Principal among the documents are the:

   - Notice - the announcement of, and 'invitation' to, the meeting
   - Agenda - the list of items of business to be discussed at the meeting
   - Minutes - the written record of a meeting, approved by those present

2.4 The **rules and regulations** for holding formal meetings will vary across organisations, and even within organisations depending on the subject matter. For example, a formal meeting to communicate the announcement of redundancies would follow a rigid structure designed to ensure the required level of formality and cover all legal obligations. A meeting to discuss a new advertising campaign would be structured, but not as rigidly.

Arranging a meeting

Who should take part?

2.5 The participants for a meeting may be predetermined. For example, if it is a meeting of members of a department, club, society, or committee, or parties to a negotiation or conflict.

2.6 In other instances, who should attend should be decided according to the purpose of the meeting.

   (a) Consideration should be given to the **mix of attendees** that would comprise an effective problem-solving, task-oriented group.

   (b) The personal qualities of each attendee should be considered. The group requires a **balanced combination of qualities** including creativity, enthusiasm, analysis, and 'people' skills.

   (c) Individuals with the required **technical** information or experience will be required to enable informed decisions to be made.

   (d) Individuals who have an interest or concern in the **outcome** of the meeting - 'meeting stakeholders' - should be invited to the meeting if:

      (i) Their acceptance of decisions is desirable.

      (ii) Their involvement is not detrimental to the interests of the organisation or group calling the meeting.

   (e) If a meeting aims to make a decision, a person with the authority to ratify and enforce decisions taken by the meeting must attend.

3: Business meetings and presentations

Convening the meeting

2.7 Most meetings are conducted according to informal rules. The guiding principles are civility and efficiency. Much of the material that follows applies only to formal meetings, though the principles, in a watered-down form, may well help to ensure smooth-running meetings in less formal contexts.

2.8 **Convening** a meeting means making arrangements for people to attend. A formal meeting should be convened in accordance with any regulations laid down in the Articles of Association. Otherwise the proceedings may be challenged on the basis that procedures have not been followed.

2.9 There are two main ways of convening or calling together a meeting.

(a) If a meeting is one of a series or cycle of similar gatherings it may be convened 'automatically'. For example, an informal Finance Team Briefing may be held in the boardroom at 10 am on the first Monday of each month.

(b) By issuing a notice of each meeting.

2.10 **Notice** of a meeting will be prepared and circulated in advance (according to any regulations laid down). The notice may be communicated by:

- An internal notice board
- E-mail
- A card or note, like an invitation
- A personal letter (for a small committee)
- A memorandum (for internal organisational meetings)

2.11 The **agenda** is often included with the notice, to give participants a guide to the business to be discussed and the preparations they will need to make. The minutes of the previous meeting may also be attached so that any objections or queries relating to them may be prepared.

Agenda 11/01

2.12 A meeting can only discuss one subject at a time. The agenda lists the items to be discussed in sequence. Conducting a meeting without an agenda would be like making a journey without having a map.

2.13 The agenda is usually drawn up by the Chair or secretary, and distributed to those participating in the meeting, so that:

(a) Everyone knows **what is to be covered**, and can prepare speeches, questions etc. accordingly.

(b) All are aware of the **order of business**, and can if necessary arrange to attend only the relevant session of the meeting.

(c) The Chairperson can keep the meeting to a **schedule**, and within a framework of which everyone is already aware.

Location and facilities

2.14 Attention should be given to the following.

(a) **Accessibility**. Is the location easy to find? Signs at reception may be required within a large building.

Part A: Project management

(b) **Size**. Can the room comfortably accommodate the number of people attending? Is the room so big that people may feel swamped?

(c) **Facilities**. There should be provision for:

  (i) Equipment – PC facilities, network connections, power points, screens, desks or tables etc.

  (ii) Participants' comfort – rest rooms, refreshments, cloak-rooms, access to telephones etc. You may wish to provide a note pad and pen for each participant.

(d) **Seating arrangements.**

  (i) An informal discussion meeting may be best conducted in a close circle or cluster of chairs, without the barrier of tables.

  (ii) A large formal meeting may be more appropriately seated around a table: a circular table is less confrontational and less status-conscious.

  (iii) In a formal meeting, or where authority is required, the 'head' of the table' may be used by the Chair or leader.

  (iv) In a small meeting, it may be possible to consider a detailed seating plan. Individuals could be placed achieve a good spread of skills and personalities around the table.

Constituting the meeting

2.15 A meeting may only proceed to business if it has been properly **constituted**. This means it must meet criteria laid down regarding attendance and conduct.

2.16 To qualify as constituted, a meeting must have a **quorum**. The quorum is the minimum number of people the organisation has specified must be present for certain types of meetings to be valid. If there is no quorum, or the quorum is 'lost' during the meeting by people leaving, the meeting must be suspended or adjourned.

2.17 Procedures may also be defined for the conduct of the meeting. Each item of business may be required to be put before the meeting in the form of a **proposal** which defines:

- The matter for discussion
- The point to be decided - in straightforward 'Yes or No' terms

2.18 The proposal put to a meeting is called a **motion**. It usually requires a proposer and a seconder. If it is 'carried' (or approved) the motion becomes a **resolution** (or decision).

2.19 The original motion is sometimes amended (or altered) in the course of debate and may then be carried in altered form as a 'substantive motion'. An **amendment** is a proposal to alter a motion which has been put before the meeting, but has not yet been put to the vote. An amendment which simply adds words to the original motion is called an **addendum**.

2.20 An **adjournment** is an interruption of the proceedings of a meeting before they have been completed. It may be:

(a) An adjournment of a particular debate, to be resumed later in the same meeting.

(b) An adjournment of the meeting itself, with a view to its resumption at some time later that day or on a later date.

2.21 It is not possible to cancel or postpone a formal meeting, once a notice to convene it has been issued. If there are reasons for not holding it at the appointed time, the correct

3: Business meetings and presentations

procedure is to hold the meeting but propose a motion for an adjournment before any business is done. The secretary may issue an advance notice to members that the adjournment will be proposed.

2.22 A **point of order** is an objection to the Chair about an alleged irregularity in the convening, constitution or conduct of the meeting. The Chair should make an immediate ruling.

2.23 Points of order are designed to ensure that regulations are observed, so that:

(a) The proceedings cannot be disputed later as **invalid**.

(b) Members are protected from attempts to **manipulate** procedures. eg By giving inadequate notice, or voting without the right to do so.

2.24 There may be procedural problems over who is permitted to speak at a formal meeting. For example, at some meetings **proxies,** or 'stand-ins' for absent members, have the right to be present - but not to speak.

Voting

2.25 Voting is the means by which participants in a formal meeting inform the Chair of their decision with regard to a motion.

2.26 In informal meetings the Chair may simply look round the table, saying something like: 'Well, I think we are all agreed ' and, unless there is dissent, the discussion will close.

2.27 Where it is necessary (or usual) to vote on a motion, one of the following methods will should be adopted.

(a) **A show of hands**. At the invitation of the Chair those 'In favour' raise a hand and then 'Those against'. The Chair declares the result of the count. This is a 'one person, one vote' system, requiring the presence of the individual or an appointed proxy.

(b) **A poll**. This is a feature of company voting procedures. Each person entitled to vote does so in writing on an individual voting paper or on a polling list. The number of votes a person is entitled to cast may vary (eg by shareholding).

(c) **A ballot**. Each voter completes an individual voting paper (out of the view of others) and puts it into a ballot box to be counted later. Parliamentary and local government elections follow this procedure.

(d) **A division**. Those present rise from their places and walk into separate 'lobbies' ('For' and 'Against') where their numbers are counted.

(e) **A voice vote,** or '**vote by acclamation**'. The Chair calls for those in favour to say 'Aye' and those against to say 'No'. The volume of votes determines the result. This is used for conventional votes of thanks, or matters on which there is almost certainly unanimous feeling.

2.28 Whatever the method of voting, the Chair declares the result, which is entered in the minutes. In formal meetings once an item of business is concluded, it cannot be raised again in the same meeting.

The Chair or Chairperson

2.29 Meetings should have a leader or **Chair** to guide proceedings.

2.30 The Chair has responsibility for the following.

Part A: Project management

(a) **Keeping the meeting to the agenda.** All meetings are held for a purpose. The Agenda is designed to ensure issues relevant to the purpose are discussed.

(b) **Maintaining order.** Only one person at a time should speak. If there is conflict, the Chair decides who is to speak. If opinion at the meeting is sharply divided, it may be tactful to call on speakers from each side in turn.

(c) **Ensuring correct procedure is observed** in convening and constituting the meeting, and during the meeting.

(d) Ensuring that all entitled to speak have the opportunity to do so, and that there is adequate discussion of each item.

(e) Ascertaining 'the sense of the meeting' (the consensus view or decision of the meeting) by summing up, or putting the issue to the vote and declaring the result.

(f) Depending on the level of formality of the meeting - checking and signing the minutes.

2.31 There are a number of recognised **qualities of a good Chair**.

(a) In formal meetings immediate rulings on points of order may be required, so the Chair should have:

   (i) A sound **knowledge** of the relevant regulations.
   (ii) The ability to be **decisive**.
   (iii) Skill in communicating rulings **clearly** but **tactfully**.

(b) The Chair should be, and be seen to be, **impartial**, giving all parties a reasonable opportunity to express their views.

Secretary

2.32 In addition to a chairperson, there may be administrative support from an elected **secretary** of the meeting, whose duties may include the following.

(a) **Before the meeting**

- Fixing the date and time of the meeting
- Choosing and preparing the location
- Preparing and issuing the agenda and other relevant documents

(b) **At the meeting**

- Assisting the chairman
- Making notes

(c) **After the meeting**

- Preparing minutes
- Acting on and communicating decisions

Minutes

2.33 Minutes are a written record of the proceedings of a meeting. They provide a **source of reference** particularly in regard to decisions and 'action points' agreed.

2.34 Notes should be made during the meeting by an appointed person and written up into minute format as soon as possible afterwards. The Chair (and possibly all other attendees) should be asked to check the draft minutes.

3 MANAGING MEETINGS

Effective meetings

3.1 Meetings can be an effective form of business communication. The following steps should help ensure meetings are effective and productive.

Step 1. **Purpose.** The purpose of the meeting should be clearly defined.

Step 2. **Attendees.** Establish who needs to attend - don't waste the time of those who are not required.

Step 3. **Agenda.** Determine the agenda and distribute it before the meeting.

Step 4. **Time and place.** A time and location should be selected that ensures those required to attend are able to.

Step 5. **Discussion.** The chair should facilitate discussion and if required manage conflict to ensure all attendees feel free to contribute.

Step 6. **Summarise.** At key stages throughout the discussion the chair should summarise and clarify key points and agreed future action plans.

Step 7. **Publish.** The results of the meeting and of activities decided upon at the meeting should be reported as soon as possible to maintain team focus.

3.2 Some meetings achieve very little. Hindrances to productive meetings are shown in the following table.

Hindrance	How to avoid
Participants are unclear as to what the meeting hopes to achieve.	Agree goals in advance.
Attendees have conflicting aims.	The goals agreed provide a common aim. Use negotiation skills.
The meeting lacks focus and direction.	Prepare a focussed agenda and ensure people stick to it.
'Action points' agreed on in the meeting are not performed.	Name the person responsible for completing each action point, and assign a completion date. Include all actions required and the assigned dates in the minutes.

Running a meeting

3.3 The chairperson aims to ensure the **successful completion** of business.

3.4 The chair should **maintain control** of the meeting without talking excessively. A group mentality should be encouraged where all feel willing and able to contribute.

3.5 Several **techniques that may be used by the chair** to encourage the best utilisation of the skill-set present at the meeting are shown in the following table.

Part A: Project management

Technique	Desired result
Make opening statements.	Clarify the scope and objectives of the meeting.
Ask 'opening questions'.	These should relate to the opening statements and stimulate thought of the group as a whole.
Ask a specific question to a specific participant.	Can be used to encourage 'shy' attendees to participate and/or to ensure those with specialist knowledge contribute when appropriate.
Use summaries.	Consolidate points agreed on as a basis for moving on.

Handling undesirable behaviour

3.6 The participants at a meeting may be drawn from wide-ranging backgrounds, with their own (undisclosed) 'agendas'. As with any group of people, different personalities and attitudes can be expected.

3.7 Undesirable behaviour is anything that could prevent the meeting achieving its objectives in the most efficient manner. The chair has a range of options available to deal with participants displaying undesirable behaviour.

Undesirable behaviour	'Typical' personality	Chair tactic to modify behaviour
Dismissive of others' ideas.	'Know-it-all'	Ask for their views early in the discussion and tactfully point out areas where others may be able to suggest improvements.
Contributes regularly, but rarely relevantly!	'Unfocused'	Stress the agenda and objectives.
Looks disinterested. Yawns!	'Bored'	Ask a direct question. Should encourage them to pay attention in future!
Talks too much, shouts others down.	'Aggressor'	Re-direct their comments back to them ('reverse' questioning) or to the group ('relay' questioning.) A warning may be required, with the ultimate sanction of expulsion.
Attempts to catch the chair or participants out.	'Devious'	Re-direct their comments back to them (reverse questioning). Eg 'Fair enough. Do you have a better suggestion?'
Unenthusiastic, 'seen it all before' attitude.	'Cynic'	Emphasise the authority the group has to act on decisions taken. Encourage positive contributions through questioning.
Plays no part in proceedings.	'Timid'	Ask a direct question you are reasonably sure they know the answer to. This should build confidence.

Handling difficult situations

3.8 The chair may be presented with a difficult situation such as those described outlined below.

3: Business meetings and presentations

Difficult situation	Suggested approach
Bad news (eg redundancies) needs to be communicated.	Prepare thoroughly to gain a thorough knowledge of the issues. Ignorance is likely to be interpreted as not caring.
Personal tension between participants	Select the group carefully. Use the seating plan to reduce the possibility of confrontation.
Lack of enthusiasm / interest.	Only those who need to be at the meeting should be invited.
	If a topic is particularly uninteresting stress the need to reach a decision/cover ground quickly, so the meeting can move on.
	Suggest taking a break.
Too much digression.	Allow digression to continue for a short time to allow the issues to be explored. If participants don't 'right' themselves use frequent summaries to refocus the discussion.

Cost

3.9 Meetings are time-consuming, costly events. The major cost is to some extent hidden – participants' time. As the saying goes, 'time is money'.

3.10 If a meeting is proposed ensure that:

- It is really needed
- Only those that need to be there are invited
- The aims and agenda are clear to all
- A good chair with the required skills is appointed

4 PROJECT MEETINGS 5/01

4.1 Project team members should **meet regularly** to maintain and improve team relationships and to ensure project objectives, progress and current priorities are communicated and understood.

Project status meetings

4.2 Project status meetings should be held regularly to keep project stakeholders informed of project status and plans. The attendees of such a meeting would usually include:

- Project manager
- Team members
- Customer/client representatives

4.3 A typical agenda of a project status meeting may include the following items:

- Objectives achieved since the previous meeting
- Current project status
- Expected future project progress
- Current expenditure/resource use compared to forecast
- Task assignment with due dates

Part A: Project management

Project problem-solving meetings

4.4 It may be necessary over the course of a project to call additional meetings to address specific problems. If a problem that has the potential to impact on project progress is identified, a meeting of all those affected may be the best way to establish an effective course of action.

4.5 The project manager should ensure all are aware of the level of authority the problem-solving team has to make decisions, and it is clear who is responsible for ensuring the action decided on is carried out.

Project evaluation meeting

4.6 At the end of a project the project manager should meet each team member to thank him or her for their work, assess their contribution to the project and consider how this may be improved on future projects.

4.7 The project manager should also call the whole project team together for a project evaluation meeting to see what lessons can be learnt from the project that may help with future projects.

4.8 A typical agenda of a project evaluation meeting may include the following items:

- Was the overall objective achieved?
- Resource use compared with the budget
- Time taken compared with the schedule
- The effectiveness of the project plan and management
- Problem identification and resolution
- Team relationships and working arrangements
- Customer liaison, communication and satisfaction

4.9 The results of the meeting should be incorporated into the post-completion audit report.

5 PRODUCING A PRESENTATION

5.1 In the final part of this chapter we look at the steps involved in producing a presentation on a management accounting topic.

> **KEY TERM**
>
> A **presentation** is the act of making something (eg information) available to an audience. Presentations are usually planned acts of communication.

5.2 A **management accounting presentation** could be made in a wide range of contexts, which may vary in terms of a number of aspects.

(a) The size and composition of the audience. This could range from a single manager to a small group of decision-makers or a large conference. The audience may be known to you or be complete strangers. They may have prior knowledge of the area you are speaking about or be complete 'laymen'.

All these factors will affect the audience's ability to accept your message.

(b) The purpose and approach of the presentation. You may be offering:
- Technical information
- Instruction
- A comparison
- A recommendation
- Persuasion

(c) The complexity of the subject matter

(d) The level of formality. A staff briefing may be informal while a presentation to senior management is likely to be formal.

(e) The time available. The purpose of the presentation should be a guide as to time required - but time available may be different, placing constraints on your content and style.

Purpose

5.3 As a starting point in your preparation you should devise **clear objectives for your presentation**. If your objectives are going to help you plan your presentation they need to be **specific** and **measurable**.

5.4 Your objectives should be stated in terms of what the audience will do, or how they will be changed, at the end of the presentation: eg they will believe, be persuaded, agree, be motivated, do, understand, be able – or something similar.

5.5 Start with your primary objective, then move on to secondary objectives you will need to achieve along the way. This hierarchy of objectives provides a useful aid to planning the content and structure of your presentation.

Audience

5.6 You are likely to have a fair idea of the audience composition – from senior decision-makers to trainees.

5.7 The **audience's motivations and expectations** will influence their perceptions of you and your message. Why might they be at your presentation?

(a) They are **required to be there**.
  (i) Attendance may be compulsory. Unless interest can be stimulated by the presentation, compulsory attendance may create resistance to the message.
  (ii) Attendance may be recommended by a superior. Participants may be motivated because they perceive it to be in their own interest to do so.

(b) They are **interested in the topic** of the presentation. This often means there is a fine line to tread between telling the audience what they already know, and losing them by assuming more knowledge than they possess.

(c) They **need specific information**. An audience which is deliberately seeking information, and intending to use it to further their own objectives, is highly motivated.

5.8 Taking into account audience needs and expectations, your message needs to have the following qualities.

Part A: Project management

(a) **Relevance**. It should be relevant to the audience's needs and interests, eg making a difficult decision easier, or satisfying a need.

(b) **Credibility**. It should be consistent in itself, and with known facts; apparently objective; and from a source perceived to be trustworthy.

(c) **Accessibility**. This means both:

  (i) Audible and visible. Do you need to be closer to the audience? Do you need a microphone? Enlarged visual aids?

  (ii) Understandable. What is the audience's level of knowledge of the topic? What technical terms or 'jargon' will need to be avoided or explained?

The room

5.9 You should also consider all factors which will affect the audience's ability and willingness to keep listening attentively. Some of these may not be in your control, but as far as possible, give attention to the following.

(a) **Listening conditions**, eg background noise.
(b) **Freedom from outside distractions**, eg others entering the room.
(c) **Adequate ventilation, heating and lighting**.
(d) **Seating comfort and layout**, eg formal or informal.

Developing content

5.10 Armed with your clearly-stated objectives and audience profile, you can plan the content of your presentation.

5.11 One approach, which may help to clarify your thinking, is as follows.

Step 1. **Brainstorm**. Think laterally about the subject, noting down your thoughts. Do not worry about the order or relevance of the ideas - just keep them coming, until your brain 'dries up'.

Step 2. **Prioritise**. Select the **key points**, and a **storyline** or theme that gives your argument a unified sense of 'direction'. The fewer points you make (with the most emphasis) and the clearer the direction in which your thoughts are heading, the easier it will be for the audience to grasp and retain your message. Discard - or de-emphasise - points which do not further your simple design.

Step 3. **Structure / Outline**. Make notes that show the selected main points and how they link to each other. Then flesh out your message. The outline should include an introduction; supporting evidence, examples and illustrations; notes of where (and what) visual aids will be required; signals of logical progressions and a conclusion.

Step 4. **Practise**. Learn the basic outline, or sequence of ideas, rather than a word-for-word 'script': if you repeat a speech by rote, it will sound stilted and mechanical. Practice runs will give you confidence and should identify:

- Difficult logical leaps
- Dull patches
- Jargon and other potential barriers to understanding that may require further explanation
- The length of your presentation

3: Business meetings and presentations

You should attempt **at least one full, timed 'dress' rehearsal**, preferably in front of a mock audience.

Step 5. **Develop your cue and visual aids.** Your outline may be too unwieldy to act as a cue or aide for the talk itself. Cards small enough to fit into the palm of your hand are ideal memory 'joggers'. If you are using slides, either on an overhead projector or via a PC and presentation software (eg Microsoft PowerPoint), these will also guide you and the audience. They should contain very brief, clear notes (verbal or pictorial) which provide:

- Key words for each topic and the logical links between them
- The full text of any (brief) detailed information you wish to quote

The Introduction

5.12 You only get one chance to make a good first impression!

Purpose of the Introduction	Suggested approach(es)	Example
Establish your credibility on the subject.	Very briefly (eg two sentences) outline your qualifications and / or experience, emphasising the parts most relevant to the topic. An 'old' unsuccessful anecdote may demonstrate the need for proficiency in the subject.	'My first experience of an accounting package was not an enjoyable experience - due in equal measures to the quality of the package and the quality of my skills! However, the last decade has seen rapid developments in accounting packages, and hopefully a steady development of my knowledge and skills.'
Gain the audience's attention and interest	Establish the relevance of the topic to the audience – problems or opportunities they may be able to apply the material to. Surprise them with an interesting fact.	'The techniques explained in this session have the potential to save you on average ten hours a week.' 'In 1985 60% of management accountants used a computer less than three times a week!'
Establish a rapport with the audience	Anecdote, humour or identify with them.	
Prepare the audience for the content and structure of your presentation	Define and describe the topic. Make it clear why the presentation is being made. What are the objectives? Set the scene, introduce the topic and state your 'theme'.	'The techniques explained in this session have the potential to save you on average ten hours a week.'

The 'body' of the presentation - clarifying the message

5.13 Your structured notes and outline should contain cues that clarify the shape and progression of your information or argument. This will help keep you 'on track' and enable the audience to:

(a) Maintain a sense of purpose and motivation
(b) Follow your argument, so that they arrive with you at the conclusion.

5.14 Logical cues indicate the links between one topic or statement and the next. Here are some examples.

Part A: Project management

    (a) You can simply begin each point with *linking words or phrases* like:

        This has led to...

        Therefore ...   [conclusion, result or effect, arising from previous point]
        So...
        As a result...
        However...
        But ...   [contradiction or alternative to previous point]
        On the other hand...
        Similarly ...   [confirmation or additional example of previous point]
        Again...
        Moreover ...   [building on the previous point]

    (b) You can set up a **framework** for the whole argument, giving the audience an overview and then filling in the detail. For example:

        'There are three main reasons why ... Firstly ... Secondly ... Thirdly....'

        'So what's the answer? You could take two sides, here. On the one hand.... On the other hand....'

        'Let's trace how this came about. On Monday 17th.... Then on Tuesday....'

        'Of course, this isn't a perfect solution. It has the advantages of.... But there are also disadvantages, in that....'

        'You might like to think of communication in terms of the 5 C's. That's: concise, clear, correct, complete, and courteous. Let's look at each of these in turn'.

    (c) You can use devices that **summarise or repeat the previous point** and lead the audience to the next. These have the advantage of giving you, and the listener, a 'breather' in which to gather your thoughts.

5.15 Other ways in which content can be used to clarify the message include the following.

    (a) **Examples** and illustrations - showing how an idea works in practice.

    (b) **Anecdotes** - inviting the audience to relate an idea to a real-life situation.

    (c) **Questions** - rhetorical, or requiring the audience to answer, raising particular points that may need clarification.

    (d) **Explanation** - showing how or why something has happened.

    (e) **Description** - helping the audience to visualise the setting you are describing.

    (f) **Definition** - explaining the precise meaning of terms that may not be understood.

    (g) The use of facts, **quotations** or **statistics** - to 'prove' your point.

5.16 Your **vocabulary** and style should contribute to the clarity of the message. Use short, simple sentences. Avoid jargon, unexplained acronyms, colloquialisms, double meanings and vague expressions.

Adding emphasis

5.17 Emphasis is the 'weight', importance or impact given to particular words or ideas. This can be achieved through delivery - the tone and volume of your voice, eye contact and gestures. Emphasis can also be provided through the following techniques:

Technique	Comment
Repetition	'If accuracy in **income estimation** is vital to our investment decisions, then accurate **income estimation** techniques must be developed.'
Rhetorical questions	'Do you know how many of our departmental heads are unhappy with the management information we provide? Fifty percent. Do you think that's acceptable?'
Quotation	'Information overload is the number one issue in the information we are producing. That's the conclusion of our survey.'
Statistics	'One in two of our internal customers have complained this year: that's 20% more complaints than last year. If the trend continues, we will soon have more complainers than satisfied customers!'
Exaggeration	'We have to look at our quality control system, because if the current trend continues, we are going to end up without any customers at all.'

Adding interest

5.18 Simple, clear information may only be interesting to those already motivated by the subject. You should strike a balance between the need for clarity and the need to make your message vivid, attention-grabbing and memorable.

Here are some further suggestions:

(a) **Analogy.** Comparing something to something else which is in itself more colourful or interesting.

(b) **Anecdote or narrative.** Telling a story that illustrates the point, using suspense, humour or a more human context.

(c) **Curiosity or surprise.** For example, 'If you put all the widgets we've sold this year end to end, they would stretch twice around the equator.'

(d) **Humour.** Used well, this will add entertainment value, and serve as a useful 'breather' for listeners. Be careful, humour may not travel well, the audience may not be on the speaker's wavelength. Use with caution!

(e) **Emotion.** You may wish to appeal to the audience's emotions. As with humour you have to be sure of your audience before you attempt this. Your appeal may come across as patronising, manipulative or just irrelevant. Emotion does add human interest, and can be used to stress the humanity and involvement of the speaker.

'When I first heard about this technique, I was sceptical about it: *surely* it couldn't be as effective as they were trying to claim? But when I tried it for myself - Wow! I was just ... so excited. So impressed. Perhaps I can share some of that with you today.'

Question 1

You are preparing a presentation to management on the benefits of flexitime hours. What techniques might you use?

Part A: Project management

Answer

Some options are outlined below. The **techniques** listed below are applicable to a range of presentations.

1 As part of your **introduction**, **explain** what flexitime is and the philosophy behind it.
2 Include **statistics** on staff absenteeism and turnover to support your argument.
3 Offer a **case study** of another organisation that introduced flexitime to their benefit.
4 Present **quotes and opinions** of staff who are working 9-5, and others in a flexitime scheme.
5 Present a **series of scenarios** (from the organisation's and employees' points of view) in which a problem - seasonal demand, dentist's appointment, travel delays etc - would be solved by flexitime.
6 Compare flexitime, in **an analogy**, with a school day of fixed hours, with pupils completing homework outside those hours.

Visual aids

5.19 Visual aids use a visual image to aid communication. The purpose of visual aids is not to look good for their own sake, but to support the message. Michael Stevens (*Improving Your Presentation Skills*) notes:

> 'The proper use of aids is to achieve something in your presentation that you cannot do as effectively with words alone. They are only *a means to an end*, for instance to clarify an idea, or prove a point. A good aid is one that does this efficiently.'

Slides (Used with an overhead projector or PC and projector)

5.20 Slides may include photographs, text, diagrams and other images projected onto a screen or other surface. Slides have several useful features.

(a) They allow the use of images that can be used to create a mood or impression. As they are perceived as an image of reality, they are also powerful tools if you wish to 'prove a point'.

(b) They are pre-prepared. The slides for a Management Accounting presentation would now usually be prepared using presentation software. This allows careful planning and execution, and slides can be finished to a very high degree of style, quality and 'professionalism'.

(c) The sequence and timing of slides is controlled by the presenter, allowing the synchronisation of images with relevant points in the presentation. Slides are therefore flexible in keeping pace with the presenter and audience.

(d) The swiftness with which one image follows another is particularly suited to messages of contrast or comparison: two products, say, or before and after scenarios.

3: Business meetings and presentations

5.21 Here is an example of a set of slides produced using Microsoft PowerPoint. A range of design templates can be applied at the click of a button.

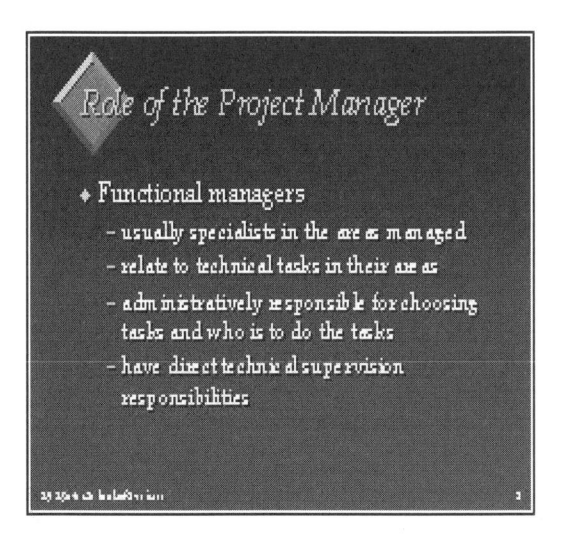

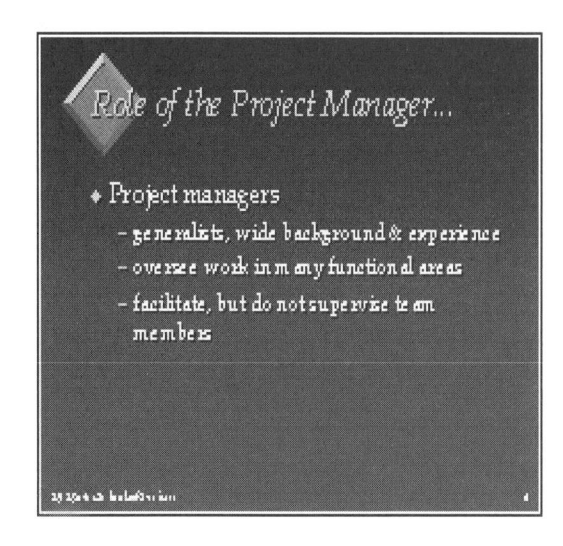

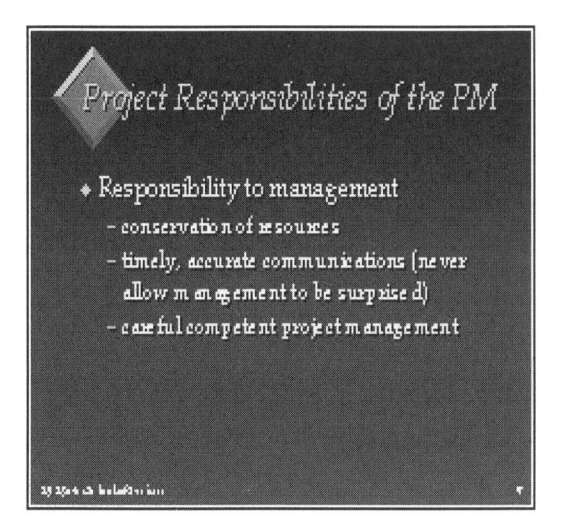

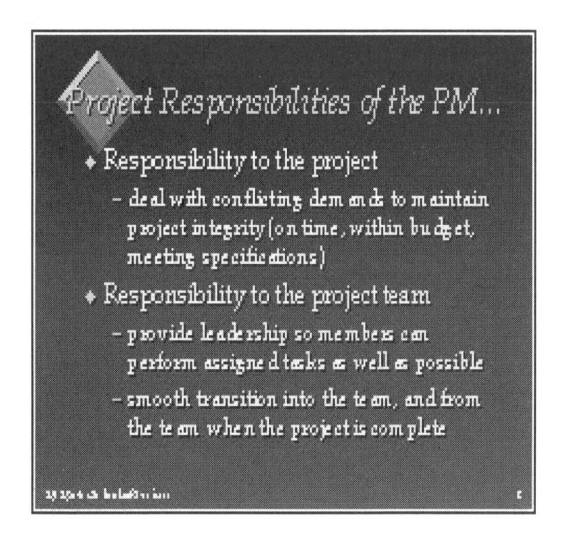

Slide 1: Role of the Project Manager
- Functional managers
  - usually specialists in the areas managed
  - relate to technical tasks in their areas
  - administratively responsible for choosing tasks and who is to do the tasks
  - have direct technical supervision responsibilities

Slide 2: Role of the Project Manager...
- Project managers
  - generalists, wide background & experience
  - oversee work in many functional areas
  - facilitate, but do not supervise team members

Slide 3: Project Responsibilities of the PM
- Responsibility to management
  - conservation of resources
  - timely, accurate communications (never allow management to be surprised)
  - careful competent project management

Slide 4: Project Responsibilities of the PM...
- Responsibility to the project
  - deal with conflicting demands to maintain project integrity (on time, within budget, meeting specifications)
- Responsibility to the project team
  - provide leadership so members can perform assigned tasks as well as possible
  - smooth transition into the team, and from the team when the project is complete

5.22 The **drawbacks to slides** are as follows.

(a) They require a room that is **not too bright** for effective projection, which may hinder the taking of notes by the audience.

(b) Malfunctions or incompetent use of the OHP or PC and projector are frustrating and distracting.

(c) There is a temptation to base a presentation around a sequence of slides. The images should clarify and support the message, not drive it.

Question 2

Produce a presentation slide and supporting notes that could be used to start a presentation entitled 'What is the Internet?'

Part A: Project management

Answer

> **What is the Internet?**
>
> Technology
>
> www
>
> Web browsers
>
> Websites
>
> Internet Service Providers

Technology. The Internet is the name given to the technology that allows any computer with a telecommunications link to exchange information with any other suitably equipped computer.

The Internet is also called the *World Wide Web* (**www**), information superhighway or cyberspace, although technically it is the 'Web' that makes the Internet easy to use.

Web browsers are the software loaded on Internet-enabled computers to allow them to view information from the Internet.

Internet information is contained on *Websites*, which range from a few pages about one individual to large sites offering a range of services such as Amazon.co.uk and Lastminute.com.

Access to the Internet is provided by *Internet Service Providers*. An Internet connection may be made via a telephone line (or an ISDN or ASDL line) to the ISP and then onto the www.

Flipcharts

5.23 If the presenter intends to write notes or draw diagrams in the course of the presentation, a flipchart can be used.

5.24 A drawback is that the flipchart presents a **smaller image** which may be difficult to see clearly in a larger room. It also relies on the immediate drawing and writing skills of the presenter – mistakes will be seen by all.

5.25 An advantage is that the 'picture' can evolve during the presentation. Words or drawings can be added to the existing ones as you go along. Earlier 'pages' of the flipchart can be easily referred to again if required - for a conclusion or to answer questions.

Handouts

5.26 Handouts may include notes or diagrams referred to during the presentation, or additional **supporting information**. They fulfil much the same function as other pre-prepared aids, with the following added advantages.

(a) The audience can **take them away** as a reminder.

(b) The audience is relieved of the requirement to take notes, which may **eliminate some distractions** (although note-taking is a part of active listening and need not generally be discouraged).

(c) If presentation software such as Microsoft PowerPoint is used, **printed versions of the slides** can easily be printed and distributed.

Props and demonstrations

5.27 Objects and processes can be displayed or demonstrated to the audience. This gives credibility to the message. Demonstrations are particularly effective to illustrate how efficient a process is, or how easy a device is to operate. For example, a **demonstration** is common before a new software package is purchased.

The effective use of visual aids

5.28 (a) Ensure that the aid is:

(i) **Appropriate** to your message, in content and 'style' or mood.
(ii) Easy to see and **understand**.
(iii) Only used when there is support to be gained from it.

(b) Ensure that all equipment and materials are available and **working** and that you can **operate them** efficiently and confidently.

(c) Ensure that the aid does **not become a distraction**.

(i) Show each image long enough to be absorbed and noted, but not so long as to merge with following idea.

(ii) Maintain voice and eye contact with your audience, so they know that it is you who are the communicator, not the machine.

(iii) Introduce your aids and what they are for, placing the focus on the verbal presentation.

(iv) Hand out supporting material either well before the presentation (to allow reading beforehand) or at the relevant point. If you hand out material just before starting it will distract the audience from your presentation.

(v) If you need to write or draw during the presentation, do so as quickly and efficiently as possible (given the need for legibility and neatness).

The conclusion

5.29 The conclusion should be used to:

(a) Clarify and **draw together the points you have made.** Use an example, anecdote, review, summary or conclusion - but do not introduce any new ideas at this stage.

(b) State, reinforce or imply what you expect your audience to do, know, believe, feel, or agree to. You should leave the audience with the seed of response or action in their minds.

Part A: Project management

(c) **Reinforce the content** and the audience response expected. You may use repetition, a joke or anecdote, quotation or surprising statistic to make your main message memorable.

Choosing a title

5.30 This may be devised after you have planned your talk, to **reflect its content and style**, or may be given to you. The title is part of the message, and - as a first impression - an important part. It should be:

- Brief
- Meaningful - a clear indication of what your presentation is about
- Interesting - curiosity-arousing, motivating
- Accurate and honest, so that the audience do not feel cheated

For example:

- 'Accountants - ten myths exposed'
- 'A career in accountancy - have you got what it takes?'

Delivering the presentation

Nerves

5.31 'Stage-fright' is common before standing up to talk in front of a group of people. Fears include making a fool of yourself, forgetting the material, being unable to answer questions, or being faced by blank incomprehension.

5.32 Fear can make vocal delivery hesitant or stilted and body language stiff and unconvincing. Memory lapse and physical fumbling can be caused by fear in a 'self-fulfilling prophecy'.

5.33 A **controlled amount of fear**, or stress, is actually good for you: it stimulates the production of adrenaline, which can contribute to alertness and dynamic action. If you can manage your stress it will help you to be alert to feedback from your audience, to think 'on your feet' in response to questions, and to project vitality and enthusiasm.

5.34 **Nervousness can be controlled** by the following means.

(a) Reduce uncertainty and risk.

(i) **Preparing thoroughly**, including rehearsal and anticipating questions.

(ii) **Checking** equipment and seating conditions are as required.

(iii) Preparing whatever is necessary for **your own confidence and comfort** (glass of water, tissues, note cards etc).

(iv) Keeping your **notes** to hand.

(b) **Ensure that you look and feel your best:** Professional appearance, good night's sleep, no hangover!

(c) **Focus on the desired outcome.** Believe in what you are saying, it will make it easier to project enthusiasm and energy.

(d) **Control physical symptoms**.

(i) Breathe deeply and evenly.
(ii) Control your gestures and body movements.
(iii) Maintain an upright (but not stiff) posture.

3: Business meetings and presentations

    (iv)   Put down the piece of paper that is shaking in your hand!
    (v)   Pause to collect your thoughts if necessary.
    (vi)   Smile, and maintain eye contact with members of the audience.
    (vii)   Act calm, the calm will follow!

Inviting questions

5.35   Inviting or accepting questions can be a helpful - if slightly nerve-wracking - part of a presentation. Questions provide an opportunity to:

(a)   **Clarify** any misunderstandings the audience may have perceived.

(b)   **Address specific doubts** or resistance the audience may have.

5.36   Ignorance or excessive hesitation in the face of a (relevant) question may cast doubt on your credibility. As this is usually the last stage of the presentation, your response to questions will leave a **lasting impression**.

5.37   The way to tackle questions effectively is to **anticipate** them. Put yourself in your audience's shoes, **what questions might they ask** and why? When questions arise, listen to them carefully, assess the questioner's manner, and draw the questioner out if necessary, in order to ascertain exactly **what** is being asked, and **why**. People might ask questions:

(a)   To seek **additional information** of particular interest to them.

(b)   To seek **clarification** of a point that is not clear.

(c)   To **add information** of their own, which may be relevant, helpful and accurate - or not!

(d)   To **undermine** the speaker's authority.

Incorporate the answers to expected questions into your outline notes.

5.38   The important points about answering questions are as follows.

(a)   You may seek limited feedback throughout your presentation - it is common to invite the audience to let you know if anything is unclear - but you should encourage **more involved questions to be held until the end** of your presentation. Questions should not be allowed to disrupt your message to the audience as a whole.

(b)   You should **add or clarify information if required** to achieve your purpose. An honest query deserves a co-operative answer.

(c)   To **maintain your credibility** and authority strong tactics may be required, without in any way ridiculing or 'putting down' the questioner.

    (i)   If a question is based on a false premise or incorrect information, correct it. An answer may, or may not, then be required.

    (ii)   If a question is rambling, clarify what the question is and answer it. If it is completely irrelevant, say politely that it is **outside the scope** of the presentation.

    (iii)   If a question is hostile or argumentative, you may wish to **show understanding** of how the questioner has reached his or her conclusion, or why the feeling is apparent. However, you then need to reinforce, repeat or explain your own view.

    (iv)   If a questioner tries to pin you down or 'corner' you on an area in which you do not wish to be specific or to make promises, be **straightforward** about it.

    (v)   If a question exposes an area in which you do not know the answer, admit your limitations with **honesty and dignity**.

Part A: Project management

(vi) Try and answer all questions with points already made in your speech, or related to them. This reinforces the impression that your speech was in fact complete and correct.

(d) Repeat any question that you think might not have been heard by all in the room.

(e) **Clarify** any question that you think is ambiguous or uses jargon not shared by the audience as a whole.

(f) Answer **briefly**, keeping to the point.

(g) Keep an eye on the overall **time-limit**.

'I'll take one more question ... ' or 'I'm afraid that's all we have time for' is standard practice which should not offend. Leaving an audience wishing there was time for more is a sign of their interest and your success.

Chapter roundup

- **Meetings** are used in organisations to gather information, disseminate information, generate ideas and make decisions.
- Meetings should have an agenda. The formality of proceedings will depend on the type and purpose of the meeting.
- Meetings need to be **managed** to ensure they are productive.
- A **presentation** makes something (eg information) available to an audience.
- **Planning** and **preparation** are essential in formulating an effective presentation.

Quick quiz

1 List five common purposes of a business meeting.

    1 ....
    2 ....
    3 ....
    4 ....
    5 ....

2 What factors should be considered in deciding who should attend a meeting?

3 What is the purpose of an agenda?

4 List five responsibilities of the chair.

    1 ....
    2 ....
    3 ....
    4 ....
    5 ....

5 Why do some meetings achieve very little?

6 List seven steps that help ensure meetings are effective.

    1 ....
    2 ....
    3 ....

    4 ....

    5 ....

    6 ....

    7 ....

7   What three key qualities should the message conveyed in a presentation have?

    1 ....

    2 ....

    3 ....

8   What should the conclusion to a presentation be used for?

Answers to quick quiz

1   Decision-making, relaying decisions, provision of advice, problem-solving and brainstorming.

2   Relevant factors include; the purpose of the meeting, the mix of attendees, technical expertise, implications of expected decisions and the authority required to take decisions.

3   To inform attendees of the meeting purpose, what is to be discussed and the order of business.

4   Keeping the meeting to the agenda.
    Maintaining order.
    Managing conflict.
    Ensuring all have an equal opportunity to speak.
    Summarising the key points decided upon.
    (You may have come up with other responsibilities.)

5   The purpose of the meeting is unclear.
    Attendees have different aims.
    The meeting lacks focus.
    Action points agreed on are not followed up.
    (You may have come up with other reasons.)

6   *Step 1.* Establish the purpose of the meeting.

    Step 2. Establish who needs to attend.

    Step 3. Determine the agenda and distribute it before the meeting.

    Step 4. Select a suitable time and place.

    Step 5. Facilitate discussion.

    Step 6. Summarise and clarify key points and agreed future action plans.

    Step 7. Publish the results of the meeting and of agreed action plans.

7   Relevance.
    Credibility.
    Accessibility.

8   To clarify and draw together points made.
    Reinforce the content.
    Reinforce what you expect the audience to feel or agree to.

The material covered in this Chapter is tested by the *format and style* of answers to Questions 5, 7, 8, 9, 10, 12, 13, 14, 15, 16 and 18 in the Question Bank.

Part B
Information Technology and Systems

Chapter 4

SYSTEMS AND INFORMATION THEORY

Topic list	Syllabus reference	Ability required
1 Systems theory	(ii)	Application
2 Information theory	(ii)	Application
3 The systems view of organisations	(ii)	Evaluation
4 Types of system	(ii)	Evaluation
5 Systems concepts	(ii)	Application
6 Information systems and decision making	(ii)	Evaluation

Introduction

In this chapter we look at **systems and information theory**, and how these concepts can be applied to information systems.

There are lots of **terms** and **concepts** to learn, but remember that in the exam you are likely to be asked to give practical business **examples** or apply the theory to a practical scenario, so it is important to take note of the examples within the chapter too.

Learning outcomes covered in this chapter

- **Apply** General Systems Theory to the design of Information Systems in organisations
- **Recommend** how the value of information can be increased through the design of the data and information architecture
- **Evaluate** the operation of the various parts of the Information System of an organisation and the relationships between them.
- **Identify** opportunities for the use of Information Technology in organisations, particularly in the implementation and running of the Information System

Syllabus content covered in this chapter

- The concepts of General Systems Theory and their application to Information Systems
- Designing data and information architectures to assist and improve planning, decision making and control
- The qualities of information
- The use of information for decision making at various levels of an organisation, and the components of the Information System which can support these decisions (transaction processing systems, MIS, DSS, EIS, expert systems)

Part B: Information technology and systems

1 SYSTEMS THEORY

1.1 The term **system** is widely used - the 'respiratory system', the 'political system', the 'long ball system', and so on.

1.2 A system is a set of parts co-ordinated to accomplish a goal or a set of goals.

Question 1

Apply the idea of connections to any 'systems' you can think of - the London Underground system, a computer system, the idea of working 'systematically', or anything else that comes to mind.

KEY TERMS

A **system** is set of interacting components that operate together to accomplish a purpose.

A **business system** is a collection of people, machines and methods organised to accomplish a set of specific functions.

Why study systems theory?

1.3 An understanding of the concepts of systems theory is relevant to the design of **financial and management accounting systems** and it presents a particularly useful way of describing and analysing **computer systems**. The application of systems theory may:

(a) Create an awareness of **subsystems** (the different parts of an organisation), each with potentially conflicting goals which must be brought into line with each other.

(b) Help in the design and development of **information systems** to help **decision makers** ensure that decisions are made for the benefit of the organisation as a whole.

(c) Help identify the effect of the **environment** on systems. The external factors that affect an organisation may be wide-ranging. For example, the government (in all its forms), competitors, trade unions, creditors and shareholders all have an interactive link with an organisation.

(d) Highlight the **dynamic aspects** of the business organisation, and the factors which influence the growth and development of all its subsystems.

The component parts of a system

1.4 A system has three component parts: inputs, processes and outputs. Other key characteristics of a system are the environment and the system boundary - as shown in the following diagram.

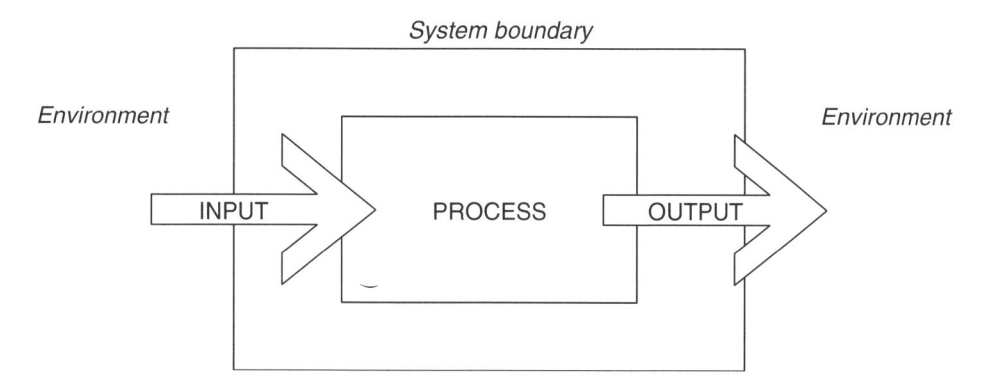

4: Systems and information theory

```
                    System boundary
Environment                                    Environment
         ┌──────────────────────────────┐
         │   ┌──────────────────────┐   │
    INPUT├──▶│       PROCESS        ├──▶│ OUTPUT
         │   └──────────────────────┘   │
         └──────────────────────────────┘
```

Inputs

1.5 Inputs **provide the system with what it needs** to be able to operate. Input may vary from matter, energy or human actions, to information.

- Matter might include, in a manufacturing operation, adhesives or rivets.
- Human input might consist of typing an instruction booklet or starting up a piece of machinery.

1.6 Inputs may be **outputs from other systems**, for example, the output from a transactions processing system forms the input for a management information system.

Processes

1.7 A process **transforms an input into an output**. Processes may involve tasks performed by humans, plant, computers, chemicals and a wide range of other actions.

1.8 Processes may consist of **assembly**, for example where electronic consumer goods are being manufactured, or **disassembly**, for example where oil is refined.

1.9 There is **not necessarily a clear relationship** between the number of inputs to a process and the number of outputs.

Outputs

1.10 Outputs are the **results of the processing**. They could be said to represent the **purpose** for which the system exists.

1.11 Many outputs are used as **inputs to other systems**.

1.12 Alternatively outputs may be discarded as **waste** (an input to the ecological system) or **re-input** to the system which has produced them, for example, in certain circumstances, defective products.

The system boundary

1.13 Every system has a boundary that **separates it from its environment**. For example, a cost accounting department's boundary can be expressed in terms of who works in it and what work it does. This boundary will separate it from other departments, such as the financial accounts department.

1.14 System boundaries may be natural or artificially created (an organisation's departmental structures are artificially created).

Part B: Information technology and systems

1.15 There may be **interfaces** between various systems, both internal and external to an organisation, to allow the exchange of resources. In a commercial context, this is most likely to be a reciprocal exchange, for example money for raw materials.

The environment

1.16 Anything which is outside the system boundary belongs to the system's environment and not to the system itself. A system **accepts inputs** from the environment and **provides outputs** into the environment. The parts of the environment from which the system receives inputs may not be the same as those to which it delivers outputs.

1.17 The environment exerts a considerable influence on the behaviour of a system; at the same time the system can do little to **control** the behaviour of the environment.

Question 2

The environment affects the performance of a system. Using a business organisation as an example of a system, give examples of environmental factors which might affect it.

Answer

(a) Policies adopted by the government or ruling political body.
(b) The strength of the domestic currency of the organisation's country of operation.
(c) Social attitudes: concern for the natural environment.
(d) The regulatory and legislative framework within which the company operates.
(e) The number of competitors in the marketplace and the strategies they adopt.
(f) The products of competitors; their price and quality.

Subsystems

1.18 A system itself may contain a number of systems, called **subsystems**. Each subsystem consists of a process whereby component parts interact to achieve an objective. Separate subsystems **interact** with each other, and **respond** to each other by means of **communication** or observation. The goals of subsystems must be consistent with the goal of the overall system.

1.19 Subsystems may be **differentiated** from each other by:
- Function
- Space
- Time
- People
- Formality
- Automation

Question 3

Using each of the above six factors by which subsystems may be differentiated, give examples of how an organisation may be structured. (For example, an organisation structured by function might have a production department, a sales department, an accounts department and a personnel department.)

Answer

(a) Functional departments might include production, sales, accounts and personnel.

(b) Differentiation by space might include the geographical division of a sales function (subsystem) into sales regions (sub-subsystems).

4: Systems and information theory

(c) A production system might be subdivided into three eight-hour shifts.

(d) The hierarchy may consist of senior management, middle management, junior (operational) management and the workforce.

(e) There may be a formal management information system and a 'grapevine'.

(f) Some systems might be automated (sales order processing, production planning), while others may be 'manual' (public relations, staff appraisal).

1.20 Often, whether something is a system or a subsystem is a matter of definition, and depends on the context of the **observer**. For example, an organisation is a social system, and its 'environment' may be seen as society as a whole. Another way of looking at an organisation would be to regard it as a *subsystem* of the entire social system.

1.21 **Information** links up the different subsystems in an organisation.

2 INFORMATION THEORY 5/02

Why do organisations need information?

2.1 Organisations require information for a range of purposes.

- Planning
- Controlling
- Recording transactions
- Performance measurement
- Decision making

Planning

2.2 Once any decision has been made, it is necessary to plan **how to implement** the steps necessary to make it effective. Planning requires a knowledge of, among other things, available **resources**, possible **time-scales** for implementation and the likely **outcome under alternative scenarios**.

Controlling

2.3 Once a plan is implemented, its actual performance must be controlled. Information is required to assess **whether it is proceeding as planned** or whether there is some unexpected deviation from plan. It may consequently be necessary to take some form of corrective action.

Recording transactions

2.4 Information about **each transaction or event** is required for a number of reasons. Documentation of transactions can be used as **evidence** in a case of dispute. There may be a **legal requirement** to record transactions, for example for accounting and audit purposes. Detailed information on production costs can be built up, allowing a better **assessment of profitability**. Similarly, labour utilised in providing a particular service can be measured. Structured systems can be installed to capture transactions data.

Performance measurement

2.5 Just as individual operations need to be controlled, so overall performance must be measured in order to enable **comparisons against budget or plan** to be carried out. This may involve the collection of information on, for example, costs, revenues, volumes, time-scale and profitability.

Decision making

2.6 Information is also required to make informed decisions. This completes the full circle of organisational activity.

The qualities of good information

2.7 The **qualities of good information** are outlined below - in mnemonic form. If you think you have seen this before, note that the second A here stands for '**Authoritative**', an increasingly important concern given the huge **proliferation of information sources** in the new millennium.

Quality		Example
A	ccurate	Figures should **add up**, the degree of **rounding** should be appropriate, there should be **no typos**, items should be allocated to the **correct category**, **assumptions should be stated** for uncertain information (no spurious accuracy).
C	omplete	Information should includes everything that it **needs** to include, for example external data if relevant, or comparative information.
C	ost-beneficial	It should not **cost more** to obtain the information than the **benefit** derived from having it. Providers of information should be given efficient means of collecting and analysing it. Presentation should be such that users do not waste time working out what it means.
U	ser-targeted	The **needs of the user** should be borne in mind, for instance senior managers may require summaries, junior ones may require detail.
R	elevant	Information that is **not needed** for a decision should be omitted, no matter how 'interesting' it may be.
A	uthoritative	The **source** of the information should be a reliable one (**not**, for instance, 'Joe Bloggs Predictions Page' on the Internet unless Joe Bloggs is known to be a reliable source for that type of information.
T	imely	The information should be available **when it is needed**.
E	asy to use	Information should be **clearly presented, not excessively long**, and sent using the **right medium** and **communication channel** (e-mail, telephone, hard-copy report etc).

2.8 The table on the following page shows some **examples** of problems, weaknesses and deficiencies in information. Please note that the allocation of a problem to one heading or another is fairly arbitrary. For instance information that is not **easy to use** is also not **cost-beneficial** because it wastes time. Information that is not **user-targeted** is not as **relevant** as it should be.

2.9 Please note that in an exam you would be expected to give specific examples, drawn from the case study information.

4: Systems and information theory

Feature	Example of problems/weaknesses/deficiencies
Accurate	Information is collated in **too much of a hurry** and so **mistakes** are common.
	Assumptions used in forecasts are not stated, making it look as if future information is known for certain and stated accurately.
Complete	Information does **not take into account past data** and therefore it does not take account of past **trends**.
	On the other hand information may look **only** at past data, which is not necessarily a good guide to what will happen in the **future**.
	Information omits **potential** developments such as **new** products.
	Information **does not look far enough ahead.**
	Senior managers have to obtain additional information
	No budget information is given, such as standard costs and variances
	No comparative information is given, such as previous month's figures.
	There is **no indication of how many weeks** the project has taken to date.
Cost-beneficial	**Time is wasted** producing material that is filed without being read!
User-targeted	Information currently provided is of an **operational** level and **not suitable** for **senior** managers.
	Information is too detailed for the intended users. They would not be able to spot trends or even identify quickly the areas that needed special attention.
	The **summary is not at a high enough level** for senior managers.
Relevant	A report may have little relevance to the **purpose for which it is used**. Some of the information given may **not be necessary** at all.
Authoritative	Information is prepared by inexperienced staff who do not **have a full understanding** of the company or the industry.
	Information is derived from the Internet which is not necessarily a **reliable** source.
Timely	**Information is nearly three weeks out of date** and may bear no resemblance to current operating conditions.
Easy-to-use	Information is presented in such a way that it is **difficult to view** on screen and therefore the **impact of the information is lost**.
	It is **not possible to see how the figures link up:** how one figure is related to or derives from another.
	A **mass of figures over several pages** will be extremely **difficult to read** and **impossible to take in at a glance**.
	No overall summary.
	Some figures are stated to two decimal places and others are rounded. This is **inconsistent and confusing.**
	Figures are **not consistently aligned.**
	It is not clear what **units are being used.**
	The **layout makes at-a-glance comparison impossible**.

Part B: Information technology and systems

Problems with systems

2.10 In many cases the information problem arises because of some problem with the underlying **system** or systems that generate the information. Here are some examples.

(a) **Compatibility problems**

Hardware and software are **not compatible** from one system (eg a department) to another. This makes it difficult to share data and raises the possibility of **re-inputting of the same data**, inevitably leading to **inconsistencies** due to inputting **errors** and discrepancies between overlapping information in each system.

Different departments base their decisions on different information and **come to different conclusions**.

If some systems are **computerised** and others are **manual** this will lead to problems such as **time-delays**. Manual processes probably take longer than computerised ones, and this will cause problems if computer input depends upon manual processes being completed first. The system will never be fully **up-to-date**.

(b) **Functional problems**

Systems simply **do not process** data and files **as they should do,** perhaps because they have been modified by inexperienced users. This will lead to inconsistent and inaccurate information.

(c) **Inadequate systems**

Systems are **working beyond the capacity** that they were designed for.

(i) For **computerised** systems this could result in the systems being **overloaded and crashing** frequently. Unless the operating system and the various applications offer strong protection in the case of a crash this will result in some **corruption and/or loss of data**.

(ii) For **manual systems** it means that work will be rushed, shortcuts will be taken, and matters perceived as non-essential by tired human information processors will be neglected. Mistakes will be made, procedures will be ignored and information will be incomplete.

Older computer systems may be unable to provide **real-time information.**

A system may **fail to collect** data that is needed completely because the **need** for such data was **not foreseen** when the system was devised.

Improvements to information

2.11 The following table contains suggestions as to how bad information can be **improved**. Obviously, to some extent this is the other side of the coin to the information problems identified in the previous table.

Feature	Example of possible improvements
Accurate	Use **computerised** systems with automatic input checks rather than manual systems.
	Allow **sufficient time** for collation and analysis of data if pinpoint accuracy is crucial.
	Incorporate elements of **probability** within projections so that the required response to **different future scenarios** can be assessed.
Complete	Include **past data** as a reference point for future projections.
	Include any **planned developments,** such as new products.
	Information about **future demand** would usually be more useful than information about past demand.
	Include **external** data.
Cost-beneficial	Always bear in mind whether the benefit of having the information is greater than the cost of obtaining it.
User-targeted	Information should be **summarised** and presented together with relevant **ratios or percentages**.
Relevant	The **purpose** of the report should be defined. It may be trying to fulfil too many purposes at once. Perhaps **several shorter reports** would be more effective.
	Information should include **exception reporting**, where only those items that are worthy of note - and the **control actions taken** by more junior managers to deal with them - are reported.
Authoritative	Use **reliable sources** and **experienced personnel**.
	If some figures are derived from other figures the **method of derivation** should be explained.
Timely	Information **collection and analysis** by production managers needs to be **speeded up** considerably, probably by the introduction of better information systems.
Easy-to-use	**Graphical** presentation, allowing **trends** to be quickly assimilated and relevant action decided upon.
	Alternative methods of presentation should be considered, such as **graphs or charts**, to make it easier to review the information **at a glance**. **Numerical** information is sometimes best summarised in **narrative** form, or vice versa.
	A '**house style**' for reports should be devised and adhered to by all. This would cover such matters as number of decimal places to use, table headings and labels, paragraph numbering and so on.

Internal information

2.12 Data and information come from sources both inside and outside an organisation, and an information system should be designed so as to obtain - or **capture** - all the relevant data and information from whatever source. Capturing data/information from **inside** the organisation involves the following.

(a) A **system** for collecting or measuring **transactions** data - for example sales, purchases, stock turnover etc – which sets out procedures for **what** data is **collected,** how frequently, by whom, and by what methods, and how it is **processed**, and **filed** or **communicated**.

(b) **Informal communication** of information between **managers and staff** (for example, by word-of-mouth or at meetings).

(c) **Communication between managers**.

Internal data sources

The accounting records

2.13 You should be very familiar with the idea of a system of **sales ledgers** and **purchase ledgers, general ledgers, cash books** and so on. Some of this information is of great value outside the accounts department, for example, sales information for the **marketing** function.

2.14 You will also be aware that to maintain the integrity of its accounting records, an organisation of any size will have systems for and **controls** over transactions. These also give rise to valuable information. A stock control system is the classic example: besides actually recording the monetary value of purchases and stock in hand for external financial reporting purposes, the system will include **purchase orders, goods received notes, goods returned notes** and so on, and these can be analysed to **provide management information** about **speed of delivery**, say, or the **quality** of supplies.

Other internal sources

2.15 Much information that is not strictly part of the accounting records nevertheless is closely tied in to the accounting system.

(a) Information about **personnel** will be linked to the **payroll** system. Additional information may be obtained from this source if, say, a project is being costed and it is necessary to ascertain the availability and rate of pay of different levels of staff, or the need for and cost of recruiting staff from outside the organisation.

(b) Much information will be produced by a **production** department about machine capacity, fuel consumption, movement of people, materials, and work in progress, set up times, maintenance requirements and so on. A large part of the traditional work of cost accounting involves ascribing costs to the **physical information** produced by this source.

(c) Many **service** businesses, notably accountants and solicitors, need to keep detailed records of the **time spent** on various activities, both to justify fees to clients and to assess the efficiency and profitability of operations.

2.16 **Staff** themselves are one of the primary sources of internal information. Information may be obtained either informally in the course of day-to-day business or through meetings, interviews or questionnaires.

External information

2.17 Capturing information from **outside** the organisation might be entrusted to particular individuals, or might be 'informal'.

4: Systems and information theory

2.18 **Formal** collection of data from outside sources includes the following.

(a) A company's **tax specialists** will be expected to gather information about changes in tax law and how this will affect the company.

(b) Obtaining information about any new legislation on health and safety at work, or employment regulations, must be the responsibility of a particular person - for example the company's **legal expert** or **company secretary** - who must then pass on the information to other managers affected by it.

(c) Research and development (R & D) work often relies on information about other R & D work being done by another company or by government institutions. An **R & D official** might be made responsible for finding out about R & D work in the company.

(d) **Marketing managers** need to know about the opinions and buying attitudes of potential customers. To obtain this information, they might carry out market research exercises.

2.19 **Informal** gathering of information from the environment **goes on all the time, consciously or unconsciously**, because the employees of an organisation learn **what is going on in the world around** them - perhaps from newspapers, television reports, meetings with business associates or the trade press.

External data sources

2.20 Obviously an organisation's files are full of external information such as invoices, letters, advertisements and so on **received from customers and suppliers**. But there are many occasions when an active search outside the organisation is necessary.

> **KEY TERM**
>
> The phrase **environmental scanning** is often used to describe the process of gathering external information, which is available from a wide range of sources.

(a) The government.

(b) Advice or information bureaux.

(c) Consultancies of all sorts.

(d) Newspaper and magazine publishers.

(e) There may be specific reference works which are used in a particular line of work.

(f) Libraries and information services.

(g) Increasingly businesses can use each other's systems as sources of information, for instance via electronic data interchange (EDI).

(h) Electronic sources of information are becoming ever more important.

(i) Companies like **Reuters** operate primarily in the field of provision of information, offering access to a range of predominantly business related information. The trend is towards information provision services being provided over the Internet.

(ii) The **Internet** is a vast network linking millions of computers across the world via telecommunications links. Information can be found on virtually any topic using a network browser, and the net can also be used to exchange information.

Question 4

(a) Think about the relative importance of internally-produced and external information. What sort of problems might, say, Marks and Spencer face if it decided **not** to collect external information?

(b) Also think about how information needs vary for different types of organisation, such as commercial, public sector and charities.

---

3 THE SYSTEMS VIEW OF ORGANISATIONS

3.1 Organisations can be viewed as a system. **Inputs** are received and **processed** to produce **outputs** of goods and services. The **objectives** of the organisation are thereby fulfilled.

The systems approach

3.2 The systems approach uses three steps.

- Identify what the **whole system** is
- Identify the overall **objectives** of the system as a whole
- Make **plans** with these objectives in mind

3.3 For example, in a business, the total system is the **business as a whole**. Its objective might be to **maximise profits**. The plans for the business should then be made with this objective in view.

3.4 To achieve systems objectives, it is usually necessary to set objectives and targets for **individual parts** of the system. The systems approach involves development of plans and controls for subsystems within the framework of the overall objectives of the total system.

3.5 However, the organisation must also remain sensitive to its **external environment**. It must respond to threats and opportunities, restrictions and challenges posed by markets, consumer trends, competitors, the government and so on.

Hierarchy of systems

3.6 The organisation as system can be viewed as being composed of subsystems arranged in a **system hierarchy**.

Corporate level

3.7 Corporate systems support the organisation as a whole. They are concerned with its **strategic** outlook and its relationship with the external elements and systems in the environment. Systems at this level might include business and economic **forecasting** systems and corporate **financial planning** systems.

Divisional level

3.8 Many organisations are divided into a number of distinct units which may operate in different industrial sectors, provide different services or sell different products. Legally,

4: Systems and information theory

these units may be divisions of a single company or separate subsidiary companies or a combination of the two. Systems at this level might include **market analysis** systems and **industry performance** forecasting systems.

Departmental level

3.9 At departmental level, the emphasis is on the implementation of the organisation's strategy. This involves managing available resources within the constraints imposed. Systems at this **tactical** level include **credit control** and **quality control** systems.

Operational level

3.10 At **operational** level, the emphasis is on the control of day-to-day operations. The systems usually found at this level are **transaction processing systems**, such as sales order processing or production control systems.

Socio-technical systems

3.11 Another point of view suggests that an organisation is a 'structured **socio-technical** system', that is, it consists of at least three subsystems.

(a) A structure.

(b) A technological system (concerning the work to be done, and the machines, tools and other facilities available to do it).

(c) A social system (concerning the people within the organisation, the ways they think and the ways they interact with each other).

4 TYPES OF SYSTEM

Open systems and closed systems

4.1 In systems theory a distinction is made between open systems and closed systems.

> **KEY TERM**
>
> A **closed system** is a system which is isolated from its environment and independent of it. No environmental influences affect the behaviour of the system, nor does the system exert any influence on its environment.

4.2 Some scientific systems might be described as closed systems. An example of a closed system is a chemical reaction in a sealed, insulated container. Another is the operation of a thermostat. However, all **social** systems, including business organisations, have some interaction with their environment, and so cannot be closed systems.

> **KEY TERM**
>
> An **open system** is a system connected to and interacting with its environment. It takes in influences (or 'energy') from its environment and also influences this environment by its behaviour (it exports energy).

4.3 Open and closed systems can be described by diagram as follows.

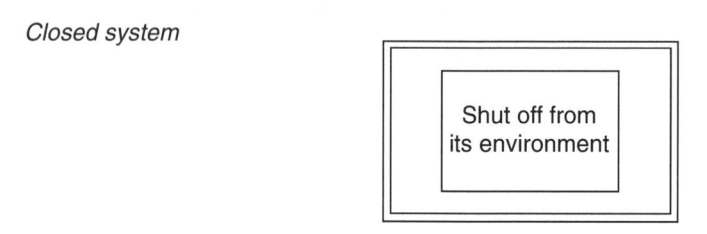

Closed system

[Diagram: A box labelled "Shut off from its environment" enclosed within an outer boundary.]

Open system

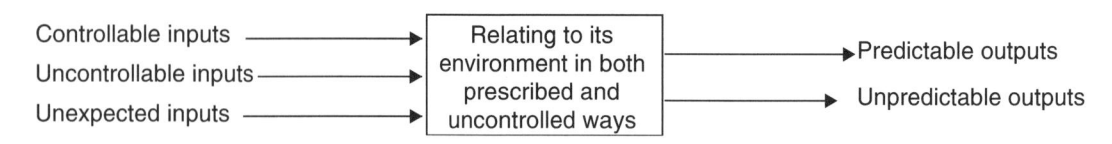

[Diagram: Controllable inputs, Uncontrollable inputs, and Unexpected inputs feed into a box labelled "Relating to its environment in both prescribed and uncontrolled ways", which produces Predictable outputs and Unpredictable outputs.]

4.4 For example, a **business** is an open system where management decisions are influenced by or have an influence on suppliers, customers, competitors, society as a whole and the government.

4.5 Employees are obviously influenced by what they do in their job, but as members of society at large, they are also a part of the **environment**, just as their views and opinions expressed within the business are often a reflection of their opinions as members of society at large.

4.6 Every system has a boundary. An open system will have considerable cross-influences with its environment **across its boundary**, whereas a closed system's boundary would shut it off from its environment.

Deterministic systems

4.7 A deterministic system is one in which various states or activities follow on from each other in a completely **predictable** way, ie A will happen, then B, then C. A fully-automated production process is a typical example. A computer program is another.

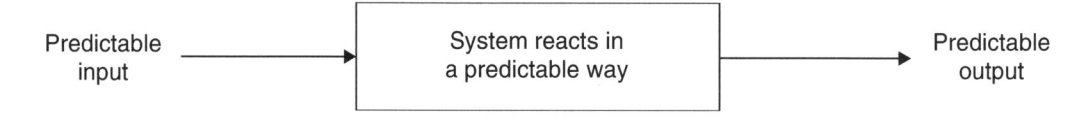

[Diagram: Predictable input → System reacts in a predictable way → Predictable output]

Probabilistic systems

4.8 A probabilistic system is one in which, although some states or activities can be predicted with certainty, others will occur with **varying degrees of probability**. In business, many systems can be regarded as probabilistic systems.

(a) A company's **credit control department** can analyse customers' payment schedules as 10% cash with order, 50% within 1 month of invoice and 40% within 2 months of invoice.

(b) A **purchasing department** might assess a supplier's delivery times as 75% on schedule, 20% one week late and 5% two weeks late.

4: Systems and information theory

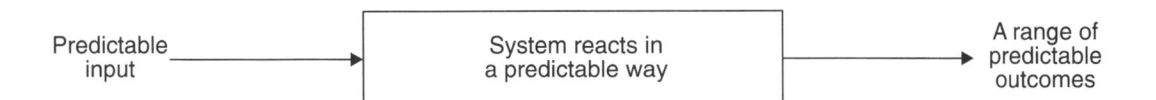

```
Predictable  ──▶  System reacts in   ──▶  A range of
input              a predictable way        predictable
                                            outcomes
```

Self-organising systems

4.9 A self-organising system is one which **adapts and reacts** to a stimulus. The way in which it adapts is uncertain and the same input (stimulus) to the system will not always produce the same output (response). Social and psychological systems come within this category. Examples might be as follows.

(a) A bank which pays a rate of interest to depositors depending on the amount of money in the deposit account. Interest calculations (the output of the system is the calculated interest) will **vary** as the money in each depositor's account goes up or down.

(b) A stock re-ordering system where the quantity of a stock item that is ordered from a supplier **varies** according to changes in the usage of the item. For example, if consumption of stock item 12345 goes up by 20% per week, the reorder quantity of the item will be increased.

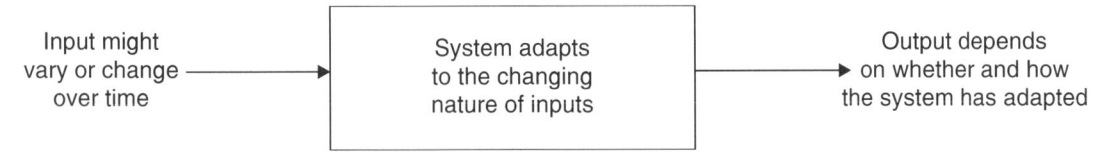

```
Input might          System adapts           Output depends
vary or change  ──▶  to the changing   ──▶   on whether and how
over time            nature of inputs        the system has adapted
```

4.10 The three classifications are **not mutually exclusive**, and a system may contain elements of all three types.

5 SYSTEMS CONCEPTS

Filtering

> **KEY TERM**
>
> **Filtering** means removing 'impurities' such as excessive detail from data as it is passed up the organisation hierarchy.

5.1 We met this concept in the context of good information. Operational staff may need all the detail to do their jobs, but when they report to higher and higher subsystems the data can be progressively **summarised**. Extraneous detail is filtered out leaving only the important points.

5.2 The **problem** with this is that sometimes the 'filter' may let through unimportant information and/or remove important information, with the result that the message is **distorted** at the next level.

Coupling and decoupling

5.3 If systems or subsystems are very closely linked or **coupled** this may cause difficulties.

5.4 For example, in order to sell goods, a manufacturing company must first of all make them. If the sales and production subsystems are closely coupled, the company may be able to produce almost exactly the amount required for a given period's sales. However the system would be prone to inefficiency through a 'mishap', such as a late delivery of raw materials, a machine breakdown, or a strike, as then goods would not be available to meet sales demand.

5.5 From a traditional point of view, greater efficiency is achieved between the production and sales systems by **decoupling** them. In the example above, this would mean reducing the interaction between sales and production by creating a finished goods stock.

5.6 From a modern point of view, holding finished goods stock is expensive, and greater efficiency is achieved by adopting **quality management** philosophies to try to ensure that mishaps do not occur. If this is successful this means that a **Just-In-Time (JIT)** approach to production and purchasing can be adopted. JIT closely couples the sales and production subsystems and closely couples one organisation's purchasing function with another's supplying function.

Requisite variety

5.7 The so-called 'law' of requisite variety is a principle of general system theory, developed by Ross Ashby.

> **KEY TERM**
>
> The **law of requisite variety** states that the variety *within a system* must be at least as great as the *environmental variety* against which it is attempting to regulate itself.

5.8 In other words, if there is **variety** in the environmental influences in the system, then the system itself must be suitably varied and variable to adapt itself successfully to its environment.

5.9 If a system does not have the requisite amount of variety, it will be **unable to adapt to change** and will eventually die or be replaced. History is full of examples of political systems that could not adapt to social, economic or political changes, and so were overthrown.

5.10 The law of requisite variety applies to self-regulating systems in general, but one application of the law relates to control systems. A control system (which is a sub-system of a larger system) must be sufficiently flexible to be able to deal with the variety that occurs naturally in the system that it is attempting to control.

Case example

A company making heavy equipment suddenly found its raw materials and in-process inventory climbing, but, at the same time, it was experiencing reduced sales and reduced production. The system was out of control.

The cause was traced to the materials analysts who made the detailed inventory decisions. They had been furnished with decision rules for ordering, cancelling, etc, under normal conditions, but they had no rules governing how to handle the inventory when production was decreasing and production lots were being cancelled.

4: Systems and information theory

In other words, the system did not provide the requisite variety of control responses. In this case, the urgency of remedy did not allow new rules to be formulated and validated. Instead, each materials analyst was treated as a self-organising system, given a target inventory, and told to achieve it. With the analysts given the freedom to generate control responses, the inventory was reduced in a few months.

5.11 Ways of introducing the requisite variety into a control system include the following.

(a) **Allowing a controller some discretion,** to judge what control action is needed.

In a business system, managers should not be instructed that a problem must be handled in a particular way, especially when the problem involves labour relations, disciplinary procedures, motivating the workforce or any other such 'behavioural' matters. The response of individuals to control action by managers will be variable because people are different, and even one person's moods change from day to day. The control system must be flexible enough to use different methods to achieve the same ends.

(b) **Introducing tolerance limits**.

When actual results differ from planned results, control action should not be instigated automatically in every instance. Control action should only be applied when the variance becomes excessive and exceeds allowable tolerance limits. Tolerance limits recognise that plans are based on an 'average' or 'norm' of what is expected to happen, and some variation around this average will be due to 'natural' causes which there should be no reason to get alarmed about.

Entropy

5.12 A final important term in information and systems theory is entropy.

> **KEY TERM**
>
> **Entropy** is the amount of disorder or randomness present in any system.

5.13 Entropy arises because of the natural tendency of objects, and systems, to fall into a state of disorder. All inanimate systems display this tendency to move towards a state of disorder. If they remain unattended they will gradually lose all motion and degenerate into an inert state. When this state is reached and no observable systems activity can be discerned, the system has reached maximum entropy.

5.14 The term **entropy is therefore used as a measure of disorganisation**. A system will increase its entropy unless it receives **negative entropy** in the form of information or inputs from the environment.

5.15 For instance if a business does not listen to its customers' complaints about its products it will eventually fail because it will not be able to sell what it produces. The system will fall into a state of disorder, in the sense that it is ignoring its purpose, which is to sell things and not just to produce them. Negative entropy is needed in the form of new or improved products or perhaps new, more open-minded management.

5.16 The system concepts of **control** and **feedback** are discussed in Chapter 10.

6 INFORMATION SYSTEMS AND DECISION MAKING   Pilot paper

Structured and unstructured decisions

6.1 A distinction can be drawn between structured and unstructured problems and decisions.

> **KEY TERMS**
>
> A **structured problem** is one in which there is a defined number of elements, and it is possible to go about solving the problem in a systematic way.
>
> An **unstructured problem**, on the other hand, is less easy to analyse as it appears to lack any obvious logic, underlying procedures or rules for solving it.

6.2 A **structured** decision can also be described as a **programmable** decision, in that unambiguous decision rules can be specified in advance. Structured decisions can often be characterised as **routine** and **frequently repeated**.

6.3 Little or **no human judgement** is required. An organisation can prepare a **decision procedure** for a structured decision. This consists of a series of steps to be followed, and may be expressed in the form of, for example, a flowchart or a decision table.

6.4 An **unstructured** decision is said to be **non-programmable**. It will usually occur less frequently and will be non-routine. There is **no** prepared decision **procedure** for an unstructured decision. Data requirements cannot be fully known in advance. Unstructured decisions usually involve a high degree of **human judgement.**

6.5 A **semi-structured** decision falls somewhere between the two categories described. It is likely to involve an element of **human judgement** and to have characteristics of **standard procedures** with some programmed elements.

Levels of decision making

6.6 There are three **areas of decision making**:
- Strategic
- Tactical
- Operational

(This is sometimes referred to as the **Anthony hierarchy,** after the writer Robert Anthony.)

> **KEY TERM**
>
> **Strategic decisions** relate to the overall objectives of the organisation.

6.7 Strategic decision making:
- Is medium- to **long-term**
- Involves high levels of **uncertainty** and risk (the future is unpredictable)
- Involves situations that **may not recur**
- Deals with **complex** issues

4: Systems and information theory

> **KEY TERM**
>
> **Tactical decisions** are concerned with ensuring that resources are obtained and used effectively and efficiently.

6.8 Tactical control decisions are taken within the framework of strategic plans and objectives which have previously been made, or set.

> **KEY TERM**
>
> **Operational decisions** relate to the efficiency and effectiveness of tasks carried out within the guidelines issued by strategic planning and tactical control decisions.

6.9 Many operational control decisions can be **automated** or programmed.

Decision level	Structured	Semi-structured	Unstructured
Operational	Stock control procedures	Selection of new supplier	Hiring supervisor
Tactical	Selection of products to discount	Allocation of budget	Expanding into a new design
Strategic	Major investment decisions	Entry to new market; new product line	Reorganisation of whole company

Operational information

6.10 Operational information is used to ensure that specific tasks are planned and carried out properly within a factory or office.

6.11 In a payroll office for example, operational information would include the hours worked by each employee and the rate of pay per hour.

6.12 Operational information is:

- Derived almost **entirely** from **internal** sources
- Highly **detailed**, being the processing of raw data
- Relates to the **immediate** term
- **Task-specific**
- Prepared constantly, or very **frequently**
- Largely **quantitative**

Tactical information

6.13 Tactical information is used to decide how the resources of the business should be employed, and to monitor how they are being, and have been, employed.

6.14 Examples include **productivity measurements** (output per staff hour or per machine hour) **budgetary control** or variance analysis reports.

6.15 Tactical information is:

- Primarily generated from **internal** sources
- **Summarised**
- Relevant to the **short** and **medium-term**
- Describes or analyses **activities** or **departments**
- Prepared **routinely** and **regularly**
- Based on **quantitative** measures

6.16 A variety of systems can be used at this level, and there may be a greater reliance than at operational level on **exception** reporting, **informal** systems and some **external** sources.

6.17 Tactical information may be generated in the same processing operation as operational level information. For example, tactical level information **comparing** actual costs incurred to budget can be produced by a system in which those costs are **recorded**.

Strategic information

6.18 Strategic information is used to plan the **objectives** of the organisation, and to assess whether the objectives are **being met** in practice.

6.19 Such information includes **overall profitability**, the profitability of different segments of the business, future **market prospects**, the availability and cost of raising **new funds**, total cash needs, total manning levels and **capital equipment** needs.

6.20 Strategic information is:

- Derived from both **internal** and **external** sources
- **Summarised** at a high level
- Relevant to the **long-term**
- Deals with the **whole organisation**
- Often prepared on an '**ad hoc**' basis
- Both **quantitative and qualitative**
- **Uncertain,** given that the future cannot be predicted

6.21 At strategic level it is not always possible to quantify or program strategic information, and much of the information might come from environmental sources.

6.22 The following table shows the typical inputs, processes and outputs of information systems dealing with information at different levels of an organisation.

	Inputs	*Processes*	*Outputs*
Strategic	Plans Competitor information Market information	Summarise Investigate Compare Forecast	Key ratios Ad hoc market analysis Strategic plans
Tactical	Historical data Budget data	Compare Classify Summarise	Variance analyses Exception reports
Operational	Customer orders Programmed stock control levels	Update files Output reports	Updated files Listings Invoices

Types of information system 5/02

Executive Support Systems (ESS)

> **KEY TERM**
>
> An **Executive Support System (ESS)** pools data from internal and external sources and makes information available to senior managers in an easy-to-use form. ESS help senior managers make strategic, unstructured decisions.

6.23 An ESS should provide senior managers with easy access to key **internal** and **external** information. The system summarises and tracks strategically critical information, possibly drawn from internal MIS and DSS, but also including data from external sources eg competitors, legislation, external databases such as Reuters.

6.24 Executive Support Systems are sometimes referred to as **Executive Information Systems** (EIS). An ESS/EIS is likely to have the following **features**.

- Flexibility
- Quick response time
- Sophisticated data analysis and modelling tools

6.25 A model of a typical ESS follows.

Part B: Information technology and systems

An Executive Support System (ESS)

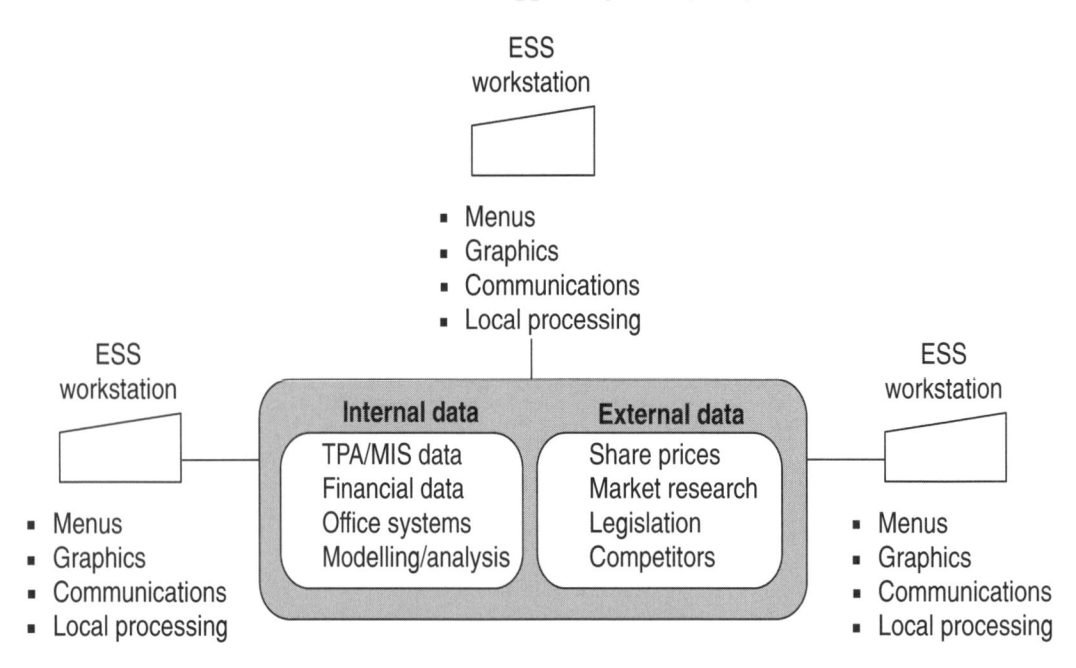

```
                        ESS
                     workstation

                      • Menus
                      • Graphics
                      • Communications
                      • Local processing

ESS                                                          ESS
workstation      ┌─ Internal data ──── External data ─┐   workstation
                 │  TPA/MIS data      Share prices     │
                 │  Financial data    Market research  │
• Menus          │  Office systems    Legislation      │  • Menus
• Graphics       │  Modelling/analysis Competitors     │  • Graphics
• Communications └─────────────────────────────────────┘  • Communications
• Local processing                                        • Local processing
```

Management Information Systems (MIS)

> **KEY TERM**
>
> **Management Information Systems (MIS)** convert data from mainly internal sources into information (eg summary reports, exception reports). This information enables managers to make timely and effective decisions for planning, directing and controlling the activities for which they are responsible.

6.26 An MIS provides regular reports and (usually) on-line access to the organisation's current and historical performance.

6.27 MIS usually transform data from underlying transaction processing systems into summarised files that are used as the basis for management reports.

6.28 MIS have the following characteristics:

- Support **structured** decisions at operational and management control levels
- Designed to report on **existing** operations
- Have little analytical capability
- Relatively **inflexible**
- Have an **internal** focus

Decision Support Systems (DSS)

> **KEY TERM**
>
> **Decision Support Systems (DSS)** combine data and analytical models or data analysis tools to support semi-structured and unstructured decision making.

6.29 DSS are used by management to assist in making decisions on issues which are subject to high levels of uncertainty about the problem, the various **responses** which management could undertake or the likely **impact** of those actions.

6.30 Decision support systems are intended to provide a wide range of alternative information gathering and analytical tools with a major emphasis upon **flexibility** and **user-friendliness**.

6.31 DSS have more analytical power than other systems enabling them to analyse and condense large volumes of data into a form that aids managers make decisions. The objective is to allow the manager to consider a number of **alternatives** and evaluate them under a variety of potential conditions.

Knowledge Work Systems (KWS)

> **KEY TERMS**
>
> **Knowledge Work Systems (KWS)** are information systems that facilitate the creation and integration of new knowledge into an organisation.
>
> **Knowledge Workers** are people whose jobs consist of primarily creating new information and knowledge. They are often members of a profession such as doctors, engineers, lawyers and scientists.

6.32 KWS help knowledge workers create new knowledge and expertise. Examples include:
- Computer Aided Design (CAD)
- Computer Aided Manufacturing (CAM)
- Specialised financial software that analyses trading situations

Office Automation Systems (OAS)

> **KEY TERM**
>
> **Office Automation Systems (OAS)** are computer systems designed to increase the productivity of data and information workers.

6.33 OAS support the major activities performed in a typical office such as document management, facilitating communication and managing data. Examples include:
- Word processing, desktop publishing, and digital filing systems
- E-mail, voice mail, videoconferencing, groupware, intranets, schedulers
- Spreadsheets, desktop databases

Transaction Processing Systems (TPS)

> **KEY TERM**
>
> A **Transaction Processing System (TPS)** performs and records routine transactions.

6.34 TPS are used for **routine tasks** in which data items or transactions must be processed so that operations can continue. TPS support most business functions in most types of organisations. The following table shows a range of TPS applications.

	Transaction processing systems				
	Sales/ marketing systems	Manufacturing /production systems	Finance/ accounting systems	Human resources systems	Other types (eg university)
Major functions of system	• Sales management • Market research • Promotion Pricing • New products	• Scheduling • Purchasing • Shipping/ receiving • Engineering • Operations	• Budgeting • General ledger • Billing • Management accounting	• Personnel records • Benefits • Salaries • Labour relations • Training	• Admissions • Student academic records • Course records • Graduates
Major application systems	• Sales order information system • Market research system • Pricing system	• Materials resource planning • Purchase order control • Engineering • Quality control	• General ledger • Accounts receivable /payable • Budgeting • Funds management	• Payroll • Employee records • Employee benefits • Career path systems	• Registration • Student record • Curriculum/ class control systems • Benefactor information system

Expert systems 5/02

6.35 Expert systems are a form of DSS that allow users to benefit from expert knowledge and information. The system will consist of a **database** holding specialised data and **rules** about what to do in, or how to interpret, a given set of circumstances.

6.36 For example, many financial institutions now use expert systems to process straightforward **loan applications**. The user enters certain key facts into the system such as the loan applicant's name and most recent addresses, their income and monthly outgoings, and details of other loans. The system will then:

(a) **Check the facts** given against its database to see whether the applicant has a good credit record.

(b) **Perform calculations** to see whether the applicant can afford to repay the loan.

(c) **Match up other criteria**, such as whether the security offered for the loan or the purpose for which the loan is wanted is acceptable, and to what extent the loan applicant fits the lender's profile of a good risk (based on the lender's previous experience).

6.37 A decision is then suggested, based on the results of this processing. This is why it is now often possible to get a loan or arrange insurance **over the telephone**, whereas in the past it would have been necessary to go and speak to a bank manager or send details to an actuary and then wait for him or her to come to a decision.

6.38 There are many other **business applications** of expert systems.

(a) **Legal** advice.

(b) **Tax** advice.

4: Systems and information theory

(c) **Forecasting** of economic or financial developments, or of market and customer behaviour.

(d) **Surveillance**, for example of the number of customers entering a supermarket, to decide what shelves need restocking and when more checkouts need to be opened, or of machines in a factory, to determine when they need maintenance.

(e) **Diagnostic systems**, to identify causes of problems, for example in production control in a factory, or in healthcare.

(f) **Project management**.

(g) **Education** and **training**, diagnosing a student's or worker's weaknesses and providing or recommending extra instruction as appropriate.

6.39 An organisation can use an expert system when a number of conditions are met.

(a) The problem is **reasonably well-defined**.

(b) The expert can define some **rules** by which the problem can be solved.

(c) The problem cannot be solved by **conventional** transaction processing or data handling.

(d) The **expert could be released** to more difficult problems. Experts are often highly paid, meaning the value of even small time savings is likely to be significant.

(e) The **investment** in an expert system is **cost-justified**.

6.40 This is a diagram of an expert system.

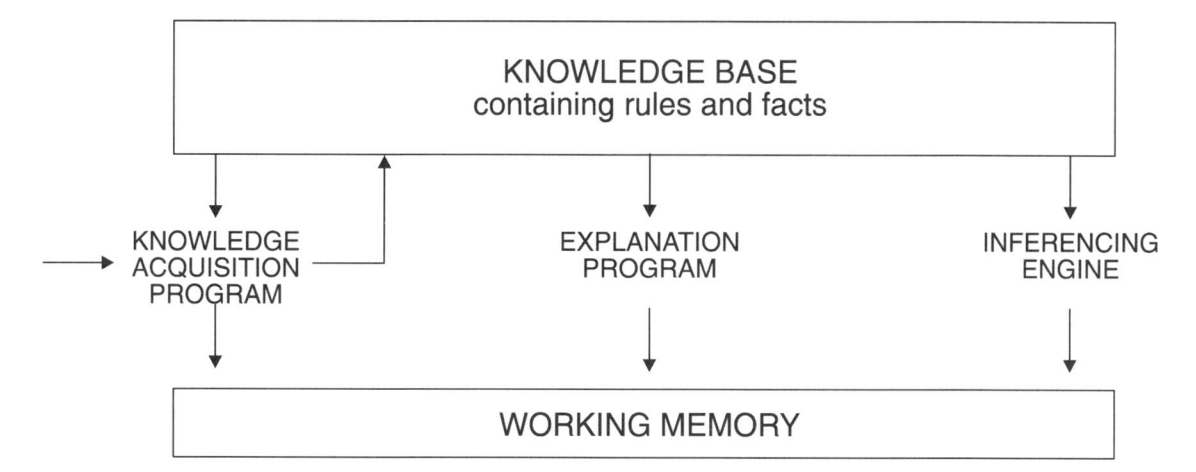

```
                    ┌─────────────────────────────────┐
                    │         KNOWLEDGE BASE          │
                    │     containing rules and facts  │
                    └─────────────────────────────────┘
                        ↓↑            ↓             ↓
          ┌──────────────┐   ┌──────────────┐   ┌──────────────┐
       →  │  KNOWLEDGE   │   │  EXPLANATION │   │  INFERENCING │
          │  ACQUISITION │   │   PROGRAM    │   │    ENGINE    │
          │   PROGRAM    │   │              │   │              │
          └──────────────┘   └──────────────┘   └──────────────┘
                  ↓                  ↓                  ↓
                    ┌─────────────────────────────────┐
                    │         WORKING MEMORY          │
                    └─────────────────────────────────┘
```

(a) The **knowledge base** contains facts (for example 'Postcode AX9 9ZZ had 104 reported burglaries in 2002') and rules ('next year the burglary rate is likely to be 5% higher than last year'). These facts and rules enable the system to make a 'judgement' such as; 'In 2003 homes in postcode AX9 9ZZ have a 6% chance of being burgled'.

(b) The **knowledge acquisition program** is a program which enables the expert system to acquire new knowledge and rules.

(c) The **working memory** is where the expert system stores the various facts and rules used during the current enquiry, and the current information given to it by the user.

(d) The **inferencing engine** is the software that executes the reasoning. It needs to discern which rules apply, and allocate priorities.

Part B: Information technology and systems

Question 5
Why do you think organisations need to automate reasoning or decision-making tasks which humans are naturally better able to perform than computers?

Answer

(a) The primary reason has to do with the relative cost of information. An expert can spend a great deal of time acquiring a specialised body of knowledge, but the commercial value of this expertise ceases with the expert's retirement or departure from the labour force.

(b) Secondly, enshrining an expert's accumulated wisdom in a computer system means that this wisdom can be accessed by more people. Thus, the delivery of complicated services to customers, decisions whether or not to extend credit and so forth, can be made by less experienced members of staff if the expert's knowledge is available to them. If a manufacturing company has a complicated mixture of plant and machinery, then the repair engineer may accumulate a lot of knowledge over a period of time about the way it behaves: if a problem occurs, the engineer will be able to make a reasoned guess as to where the likely cause is to be found. If this accumulated expert information is made available to less experienced staff, it means that some of their learning curve is avoided.

An expert system is advantageous because it saves time, like all computer systems (in theory at least) but it is particularly useful as it possesses both knowledge and a reasoning ability.

6.41 **Advantages** of expert systems include the following.

(a) The recorded information and knowledge is **permanent,** whereas human experts may leave the business.

(b) It is **easily copied,** so that one bank branch say, can have access to the same expertise as any other branch.

(c) It is **consistent,** whereas human experts and decision makers may not be.

(d) It can be **documented**. The reasoning behind a recommendation produced by a computer will be recorded.

(e) Depending on the task the computer may be **faster** than the human being.

6.42 The limitations of expert systems include:

(a) Specialised systems are likely to be expensive.

(b) The technology is still relatively new. Systems are likely to require extensive testing and amendment.

(c) People are naturally more creative.

(d) Systems have a very **narrow focus**.

Intranets and Extranets 5/02

6.43 Organisations are increasingly using **intranets** and **extranets** to **disseminate information**.

(a) An **intranet** is like a mini version of the Internet. Organisation members use networked computers to access information held on a server. The user interface is a browser – similar to those used on the Internet. The intranet offers access to information on a wide variety of topics, and often includes access to the Internet.

(b) An **extranet** is an intranet that is accessible to **authorised outsiders,** using a valid username and password. The user name will have access rights attached - determining which parts of the extranet can be viewed. Extranets are becoming a very popular means for business partners to exchange information.

4: Systems and information theory

> **Chapter roundup**
>
> - A system receives **inputs** which it **processes** and generates into **outputs**. Any system can be thought of in terms of inputs, processing and outputs.
>
> - A system exists in an environment. An environment surrounds the system but is not part of it. A **system boundary** separates the system from its environment.
>
> - An **open** system has a relationship with its environment which has both prescribed and uncontrolled elements. A **closed** system is shut off from its environment and has no relationship with it.
>
> - The terms **coupling** and **decoupling** relate to how closely one system depends on another.
>
> - Information is used for planning, controlling, recording transactions, performance measurement and decision making. Users may be internal or external.
>
> - Good information has a number of specific qualities: the mnemonic ACCURATE is a useful way of remembering them.
>
> - Data can be collected from within and beyond an organisation. Information systems are used to convert this data into information and to communicate it to management at all levels.
>
> - **Filtering** means ensuring information is relevant and required before disseminating.
>
> - The law of **requisite variety** states that the variety within a system must be at least as great as the environmental variety against which it is attempting to regulate itself.
>
> - **Entropy** is the amount of disorder or randomness there is in a system. Systems tend to fall into disorder unless they receive negative entropy in the form of information or inputs from the environment.
>
> - **Structured decisions** are routine, and are able to be solved in a systematic way.
>
> - **Unstructured decisions** require human judgement.
>
> - There are three areas of decision making - **strategic**, **tactical** and **operational**.
>
> - Different **types of information systems** exist with different characteristics - reflecting the different roles they perform.

Quick quiz

1 What are the three component parts of a system?

   1 ....
   2 ....
   3 ....

2 What does the mnemonic ACCURATE stand for?

   A ....
   C ....
   C ....
   U ....
   R ....
   A ....
   T ....
   E ....

3 Identify the three steps to 'the systems approach'.

   1 ....

Part B: Information technology and systems

    2   ....

    3   ....

4   List the three subsystems of a socio-technical system.

    1   ....

    2   ....

    3   ....

5   Define the terms open system and closed system.

6   Define the terms deterministic system and probabilistic system.

7   Why do coupled systems have increased potential for problems?

8   How can requisite variety be introduced into a control system?

9   'The more entropy present in a system the more efficient the system is likely to be'.

    True ☐

    False ☐

Answers to quick quiz

1   Inputs, processes and outputs.

2   A ccurate
     C omplete
     C ost-beneficial
     U ser-targeted
     R elevant
     A uthoritative
     T imely
     E asy to use

3   *Step 1.* Identify what the whole system is.

    Step 2. Identify the overall objectives of the system.

    Step 3. Make plans with these objectives in mind.

4   A structure.
    A technological system.
    A social system.

5   An open system is a system connected to and interacting with its environment. A closed system is a system which is isolated from its environment and independent of it.

6   A deterministic system is one in which various states or activities follow on from each other in a completely predictable way. A probabilistic system is one in which, although some states or activities can be predicted with certainty, others will occur with varying degrees of probability.

7   Linking systems together may improve efficiency when things go to plan, but also means that the impact of any 'mishap' is likely to spread to coupled systems.

8   Two examples are: by allowing a controller discretion over what control action is needed, or by introducing tolerance limits.

9   False.

The material covered in this Chapter is tested in Questions 1, 5 and 14(b) in the Question Bank.

4: Systems and information theory

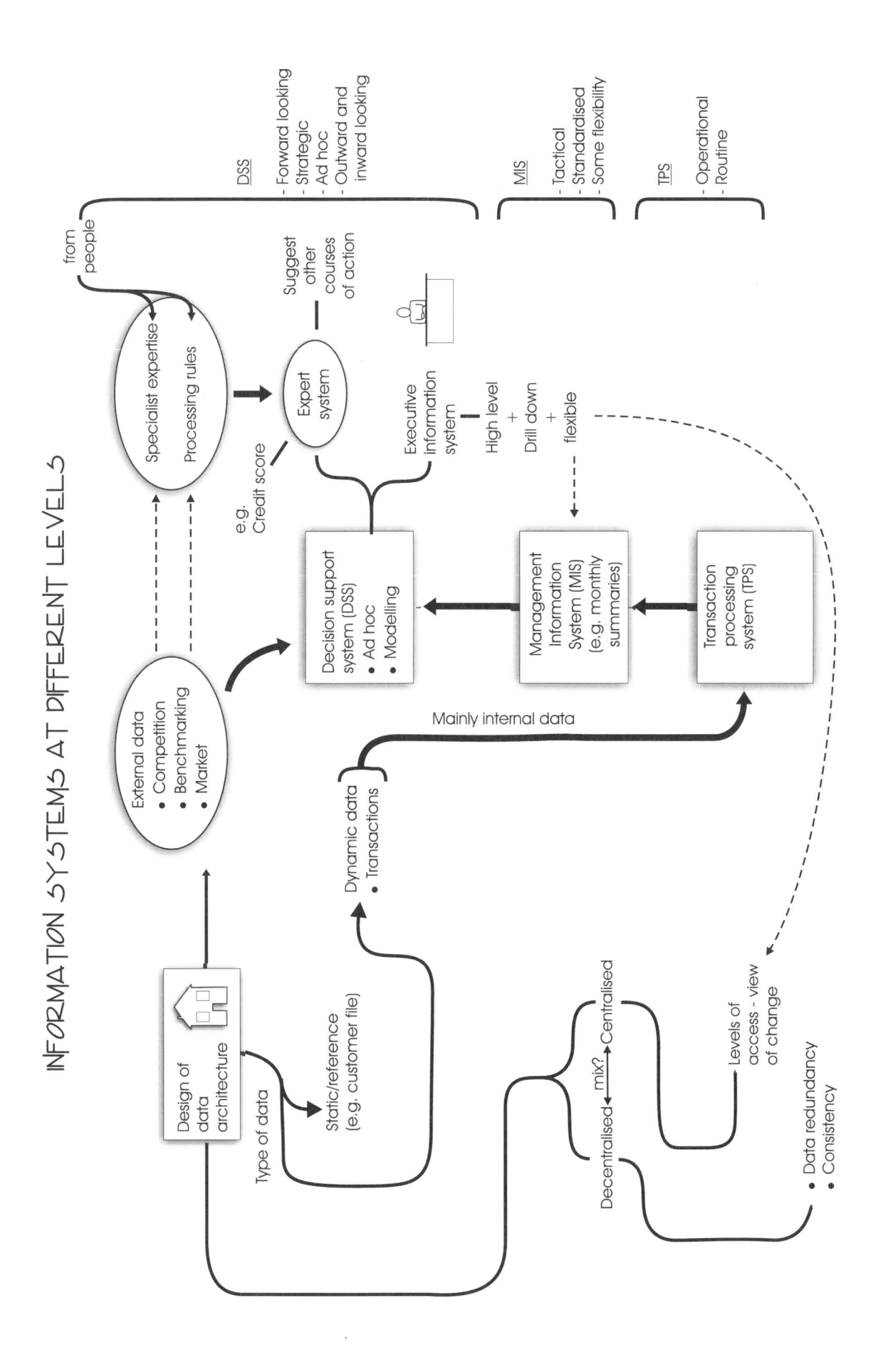

INFORMATION SYSTEMS AT DIFFERENT LEVELS

DSS
- Forward looking
- Strategic
- Ad hoc
- Outward and inward looking

MIS
- Tactical
- Standardised
- Some flexibility

TPS
- Operational
- Routine

Specialist expertise / Processing rules (from people) → Expert system → Suggest other courses of action

e.g. Credit score

Executive information system — High level + Drill down + flexible

External data
- Competition
- Benchmarking
- Market

→ Decision support system (DSS)
- Ad hoc
- Modelling

← Management Information System (MIS) (e.g. monthly summaries)

← Transaction processing system (TPS)

Mainly internal data

Design of data architecture

Type of data:
- Static/reference (e.g. customer file)
- Dynamic data
  - Transactions

Decentralised ↔ Centralised mix?

Levels of access - view of change

- Data redundancy
- Consistency

Chapter 5

SYSTEMS DEVELOPMENT

Topic list		Syllabus reference	Ability required
1	The systems development life-cycle	(ii)	Comprehension
2	Drawbacks of the SDLC	(ii)	Comprehension
3	Systems development methodologies	(ii)	Comprehension
4	CASE tools, Fourth generation languages and Prototyping	(ii)	Comprehension
5	Database systems	(ii)	Comprehension
6	User involvement	(ii)	Comprehension

Introduction

In this chapter we introduce the **systems development life-cycle (SDLC)**, a framework for the development of information systems.

We look at **methodologies** that have been developed to add discipline to the systems development process, and at other **tools** that can be utilised in systems development and implementation.

Towards the end of the chapter, **database systems** are discussed, and we finish off by considering how the **needs of the user** can best be satisfied in systems development.

Subsequent chapters will explain aspects of systems development in more detail.

Learning outcomes covered in this chapter

- **Explain** the processes of system design and development and analyse the issues arising at those stages *(Also see Chapter 6)*
- **Explain** the nature and purpose of systems maintenance and performance evaluation *(Also see Chapter 7)*

Syllabus content covered in this chapter

- The stages in the systems development life-cycle
- The concept of the systems development life-cycle when applied to an Information Systems project *(Also see Chapters 2 and 6)*
- The features, benefits and drawbacks of structured methodologies
- Prototyping including the use of fourth generation languages
- Databases and database management systems

1 THE SYSTEMS DEVELOPMENT LIFE-CYCLE

1.1 **In the early days of computing**, systems were developed in a fairly haphazard fashion. Systems development was piecemeal, involving automation of existing procedures rather than forming part of a planned strategy. **The development of systems was not properly planned**. The consequences were often poorly designed systems, which cost too much to make and which were not suited to users' needs.

1.2 In the 1960s the National Computing Centre developed a more disciplined approach to systems development, which could be applied almost anywhere. This was called the **systems development life-cycle**. It is important to note that this is only a **model** of the development life-cycle. It contains seven stages.

Stage	Comment
Identification of a problem or opportunity	This involves an analysis of the organisation's information requirements.
Feasibility study	This involves a review of the existing system and the identification of a range of possible alternative solutions. A feasible (technical, operational, economic, social) solution will be selected – or a decision not to proceed made. We look at the feasibility study in greater detail in Chapter 6.
System investigation	A fact finding exercise which investigates the existing system to assess its problems and requirements and to obtain details of data volumes, response times and other key indicators.
System analysis	Once the workings of the existing system have been documented, they can be analysed. This process examines why current methods are used, what alternatives might achieve the same, or better, results, and what performance criteria are required from a system.
System design	System design will examine existing computerised and manual procedures, addressing, in particular, inputs, outputs, program design, file design and security. New processes will also be considered allowing a detailed specification of the new system to be produced.
System implementation	This stage carries development through from design to operations. It involves acquisition (or writing) of software, program testing, file conversion or set-up, acquisition and installation of hardware and 'going live'.
Review and maintenance	This is an ongoing process which ensures that the system meets the objectives set during the feasibility study, that it is accepted by users and that its performance is satisfactory.

Part B: Information technology and systems

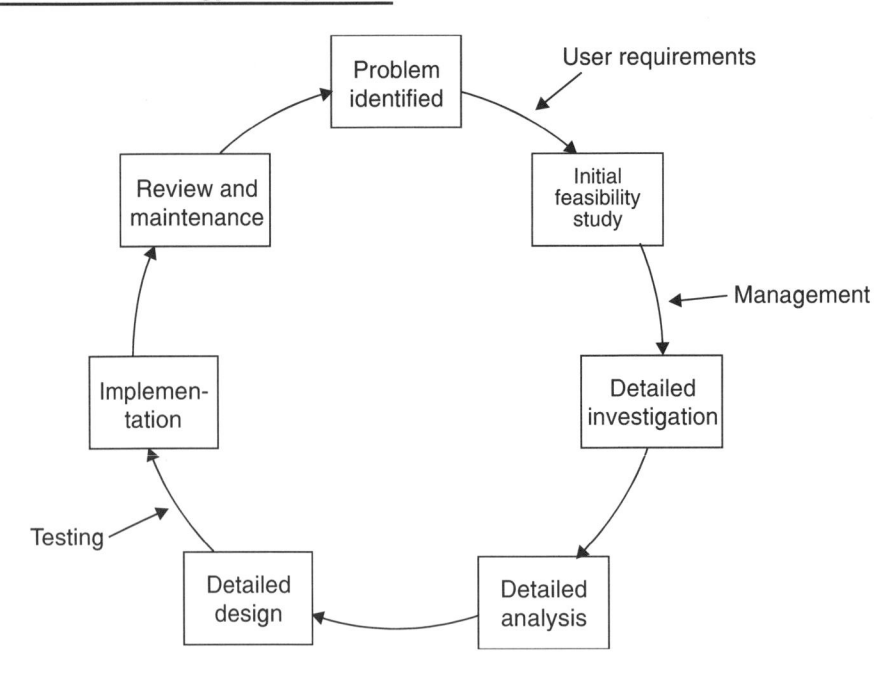

[Diagram: Systems Development Lifecycle cycle showing the following stages connected in a circle: Problem identified → Initial feasibility study → Detailed investigation → Detailed analysis → Detailed design → Implementation → Review and maintenance → (back to Problem identified). Annotations: "User requirements" points to Problem identified; "Management" points to Initial feasibility study; "Testing" points to Implementation.]

1.3 The systems development lifecycle approach to systems development was adopted by many organisations. It provided a model of how systems should be developed. It imposed a **disciplined** approach to the development process, it encouraged **communication** between systems professionals and 'ordinary' users and it recognised the importance of **analysis** and **design**.

2 DRAWBACKS OF THE SDLC

2.1 While the basic SDLC approach has some advantages, it has a number of drawbacks **if not properly implemented**.

> **Exam focus point**
> Expect the emphasis to be upon applied knowledge, rather than reproducing the theory.

Ignored information needs

2.2 While it was efficient at **automating** operational areas within easily defined processing requirements, such as payroll, the **information needs** of middle and senior management were ignored. Computerisation was a means of speeding up high-volume routine transaction processing, not providing information for decision making. Computerisation was seen as a means to save money which would otherwise be spent on an army of clerks.

No radical rethink of current operations

2.3 When computer systems were first introduced, they were modelled after the manual systems they were replacing. All that happened was that clerical procedures carried out by people were computerised. Had the computerisation been more ambitious, it might have led to a potentially beneficial rethink of the way the organisation carried out its activities.

5: Systems development

User requirements poorly defined

2.4 Much systems design is based around what the user, at an early stage in the development of a system, has specified as to what output is required. This ultimately determines what is input to the system, the file structures introduced and so forth. However, **output requirements can be altered, even during systems development**, and this can result in substantial design modifications. It has been estimated that a simple change in user requirements costs over 20 times as much to rectify after acceptance testing than after the design phase. Software maintenance consumes about 70% of the cost of developing a system. (Maintenance occurs after the system has gone live, and involves the correction of any errors that have been revealed during operations, and adding system enhancements.)

Dissatisfied users

2.5 A result of the problems mentioned above was that **new systems rarely lived up to users' expectations**. Even with packaged software, users may be disappointed. It becomes increasingly difficult to change system requirements the further a system is developed, and users were required to 'sign off' at an early stage.

Documentation

2.6 Much system documentation was **written for programmers and specialists**. It was highly technical, more of a technical manual than a guide for the user. Problems could also occur, if inadequately documented modifications led to 'bugs' elsewhere in the system.

Systems not complete

2.7 Many routine transaction processing systems **could not cope with unusual situations**, and so some complicated processing was still performed manually.

Applications backlog

2.8 Time overruns mean that systems take a long time to develop. The **applications backlog** is the systems in the pipeline whose development has been delayed. One of the causes is the time spent maintaining old systems.

3 SYSTEMS DEVELOPMENT METHODOLOGIES   Pilot paper

Overcoming the problems of the SDLC

3.1 All of these problems can be overcome if systems developers are aware of them. The modern approach is to use some kind of **methodology** such as **Structured Systems Analysis and Design**. A methodology will modify the basic elements of the SDLC to avoid problems such as those described above.

> **KEY TERM**
>
> A systems development '**methodology**' is a collection of procedures, techniques, tools and documentation aids which will help systems developers in their efforts to implement a new information system.

Part B: Information technology and systems

Characteristics of methodologies

Characteristic	Comment
Separation of logical and physical	The initial focus is on business benefits – on what the system will achieve (the logical design).
	Physical design and implementation issues are looked at later.
User involvement	User's information requirements determine the type of data collected or captured by the system.
	Users are involved throughout the development process.
Diagrammatic documentation	Diagrams rather than text-based documentation are used as much as possible to ensure the focus is on what the system is trying to achieve – and to aid user understanding of the process.
Data driven	Most structured methods focus on data items regardless of the processes they are related to.
	The type of data within an organisation is less likely to change than either the processes which operate on it or the output information required of it.
Defined structure	Most methodologies prescribe a consistent structure to ensure a consistent and complete approach to the work. For example, the Structured Systems Analysis and Design Method (**SSADM**) suggests five modules: Feasibility, Requirements Analysis, Requirements Specification, Logical Systems Specification and Physical Design.

3.2 *Jayaratna* (*Understanding and Evaluating Methodologies*, 1994) estimates that there are **over 1,000 brand named methodologies** in use in the world. The Structured Systems Analysis and Design Method (**SSADM**) was originally designed for use by the UK Government in 1980 – but is now widely used in many areas of business.

3.3 All methodologies seek to facilitate the **'best'** solution. But 'best' may be interpreted in a number of ways, such as **most rapid** or **least cost** systems. Some methodologies are highly **prescriptive** and require rigid adherence to stages whilst others are highly **adaptive** allowing for creative use of their components.

3.4 In choosing the **most appropriate methodology**, an organisation must consider the following questions.

- How **open** is the system?
- To what extent does the methodology facilitate **participation**?
- Does it generate **alternative solutions**?
- Is it **well-documented, tried, tested and proven** to work?
- Can **component 'tools'** be selected and used as required?
- Will it benefit from **computer aided tools** and **prototyping**?

3.5 Ultimately it is important to remember that whilst methodologies may be valuable in the development their use is a matter of great skill and experience. They **do not, by themselves, produce good systems solutions.**

> **Question 1**
>
> Why does it matter how 'open' a system is?
>
> **Answer**
>
> An open system is much affected by unpredictable and rapidly changing environmental factors (a hospital admissions system, for instance) and it needs an approach that takes account of 'soft' problems. A highly stable system, such as a payroll system, simply needs to follow predefined rules (payroll rules change, but even the changes are relatively predictable) and may have less need for 'soft' thinking.

Advantages and disadvantages

3.6 The **advantages** of using a methodology are as follows.

(a) Detailed **documentation** is produced.

(b) **Standard methods** allow less-qualified staff to carry out some of the analysis work, thus **cutting the cost** of the exercise.

(c) Using a standard development process leads to **improved system specifications**.

(d) Systems developed in this way are **easier to maintain and improve**.

(e) **Users are involved** with development work from an early stage and are required to sign off each stage.

(f) The emphasis on **diagramming** makes it easier for relevant parties, including users, to **understand** the system than if purely narrative descriptions were used.

(g) The structured framework of a methodology **helps with planning**. It defines the tasks to be performed, sets out when they should be done and identifies an end product. This allows control by reference to actual achievements rather than to estimates of progress.

(h) A logical design is produced that is **independent of hardware and software**.

(i) Techniques such as data flow diagrams, logical data structures and entity life histories **allow information to be cross-checked** between diagrams and ensure that the system delivered does what is required. These techniques are explained in Chapter 6.

3.7 The use of a methodology in systems development also has **disadvantages**.

(a) It has been argued that methodologies are ideal for analysing and documenting processes and data items at an operational level, but are perhaps **inappropriate for information of a strategic nature** that is collected on an ad hoc basis.

(b) Some are a little **too limited in scope**, being too concerned with systems design, and not with their impact on actual work processes or social context of the system.

(c) Arguably, methodologies encourage excessive documentation and **bureaucracy** and are just as suitable for documenting bad design as good.

4 SOFTWARE SUPPORT FOR THE SYSTEMS DEVELOPMENT PROCESS

4.1 There are a number of software tools that can be used to facilitate systems development process. We will examine three of the most widely used software tools – CASE tools, fourth generation languages and prototypes.

Computer aided software engineering (CASE)

4.2 Computer Aided Software Engineering tools are used in systems development to automate some development tasks, such as the production of documentation, and to provide an efficient tool to control developmental activities.

> **KEY TERM**
>
> **CASE tools** are software tools used to automate some tasks in the development of information systems eg generating documentation and diagrams. The more sophisticated tools facilitate software prototyping and code generation.

4.3 There are a range of CASE tools available. Some focus on certain phases of development such as analysis and design, others may be used throughout the complete development lifecycle.

4.4 The range of facilities offered by CASE tools are shown in the following table.

Stage of system development project	Possible use of CASE tools
Project initiation	• Generate project schedules in various formats
Analysis and design	• Produce diagrams eg flowcharts, DFDs, ERMs, ELHs • Generate data dictionary
Design (logical and physical)	• Produce system model diagrams • Data structures • Automate screen and report design
Implementation	• Installation schedule • Program code generator
Maintenance	• Version control • Change specification and tracking

4.5 CASE tools can be grouped into Upper CASE tools (sometimes referred to as analysts' workbenches) and Lower CASE tools (sometimes referred to as programmers' workbenches).

Upper CASE tools (analysts' workbenches)

4.6 Upper CASE tools are geared towards automating tasks associated with systems analysis. They include:

(a) **Diagramming tools** that automate the production of diagrams using a range of modelling techniques.

(b) **Analysis tools** that check the logic, consistency and completeness of system diagrams, forms and reports.

(c) A **CASE repository** that holds all data and information relating to the system. The **Data dictionary** records all data items held in the system and controls access to the repository. The dictionary will list all data entities, data flows, data stores, processes, external entities and individual data items.

Lower CASE tools (programmers workbenches)

4.7 Lower CASE tools are geared towards automating tasks later in the development process (after analysis and design). They include:

(a) **Document generators** that automate the production of diagrams using a range of modelling techniques.

(b) **Screen and report layout generators** that allow prototyping of the user-interface to be produced and amended quickly.

(c) **Code generators** that automate the production of code based on the processing logic input to the generator.

Advantages of using CASE tools

4.8 Advantages of CASE include the following.

(a) **Document/diagram preparation** and amendment is quicker and more efficient.

(b) **Accuracy of diagrams** is improved. Diagram drawers can ensure consistency of terminology and maintain certain standards of documentation.

(c) **Prototyping** (see later in this section) is made easier, as re-design can be effected very quickly.

(d) **Blocks of code can be re-used**. Many applications incorporate similar functions and processes; blocks of software can be retained in a library and used (or modified) as appropriate.

Examples of CASE tools

4.9 Examples of CASE tools include Select's SSADM Professional, Rational's ClearCase and AxiomSys from STG.

Example 1: Automated diagram production

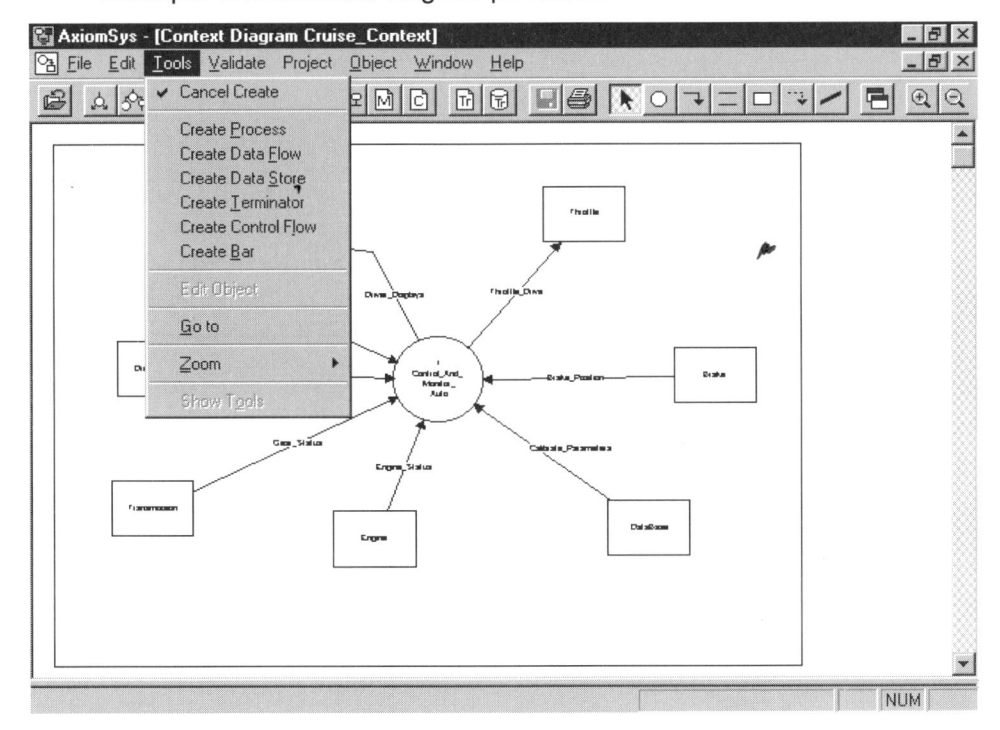

Part B: Information technology and systems

Example 2: Code generating and checking

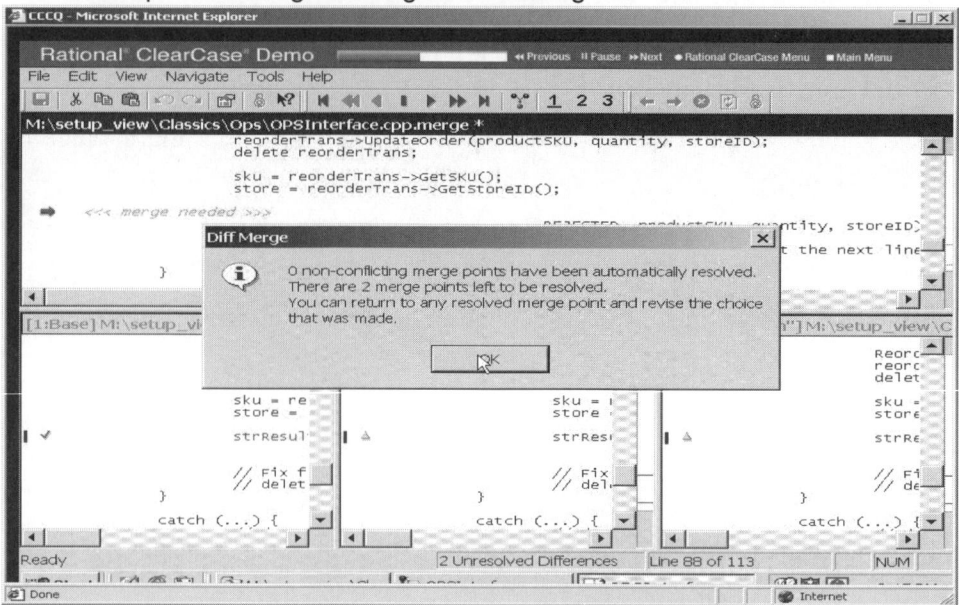

Example 3: Version/change control

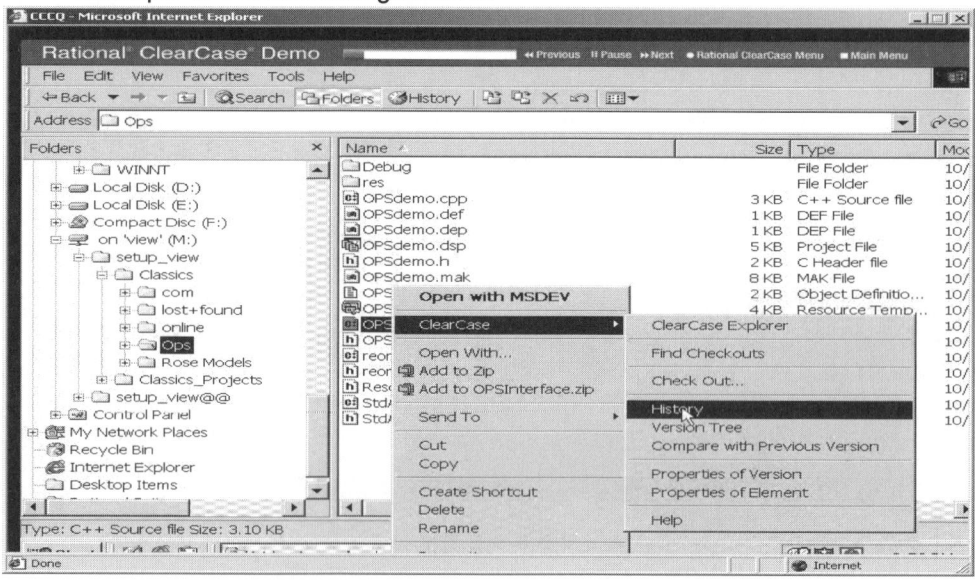

Fourth generation languages (4GLs)

4.10 As computer languages have developed over time, certain types of computer languages have become identified with a generation of languages. The four generations are explained in the following table.

Generation	Comment
First	Machine code. Program instructions were written for individual machines in binary form (a series of 1s and 0s).
Second	Assembly languages. Still machine specific, programs were written using symbolic code which made them easier to understand and maintain.
Third	High-level languages such as COBOL, BASIC and FORTRAN. These languages have a wider vocabulary of words, enabling commands to be closer to everyday language. Programs produced are able to be moved between similar computers.

5: Systems development

Generation	Comment
Fourth	There is no formal definition of a Fourth Generation Language (4GL). Fourth-generation languages are programming languages closer to human languages than typical high-level or third generation languages. Most 4GLs use simple query language such as 'FIND ALL RECORDS WHERE NAME IS 'JONES'

4.11 A fourth generation language is a programming language that is easier to use than languages like COBOL, PASCAL and C++. Well known examples include **Informix** and **Powerhouse**.

> **KEY TERM**
>
> A **Fourth Generation Language (4GL)** is a high-level computer language that uses commands that are closer to everyday speech than previous languages. 4GLs usually also include a range of features intended to automate software production.

4.12 Most fourth generation languages use a graphical user interface. Icons, objects, help facilities, pull down menus and templates present programmers with the options for building the software. Sections of code are often treated as components, which may be used (maybe with slight modifications) in a variety of applications. A 4GL will often include the following features (many of these features could also be provided by a CASE tool).

- Relatively easy to learn and use
- Often centred around a database
- Includes a data dictionary
- Uses a relatively simple query language
- Includes facilities for screen design and dialogue box design
- Includes a report generator
- Code generation is often automated
- Documenting and diagramming tools

4.13 4GLs are often used to facilitate **object-oriented programming**. With object-oriented programming, programmers define the types of operations (functions) that can be applied to data structures (in programming, a data structure refers to a scheme for organising related pieces of information). In this way, the data structure becomes an object that includes both data and functions. In addition, programmers can create relationships between one object and another. For example, objects can inherit characteristics from other objects.

4.14 One of the principal advantages of object-oriented programming techniques over procedural programming techniques is that they enable programmers to create modules that do not need to be changed when a new type of object is added. A programmer can simply create a new object that inherits many of its features from existing objects. This makes object-oriented programs easier to modify (a group of objects with some common properties may be referred to as a **class**).

4.15 4GLs enable a more flexible approach to be taken to software production than under the traditional Systems Development Lifecycle. Using a 4GL, changes to the program design and to the code itself can be made relatively easily and quickly. This allows development to follow a pattern like the Spiral model, with users able to make amendments based on prototypes.

Part B: Information technology and systems

Examples taken from 4GLs

4.16 The following screenshots are taken from the Metamill 4GL.

Example 1: Automated diagram production

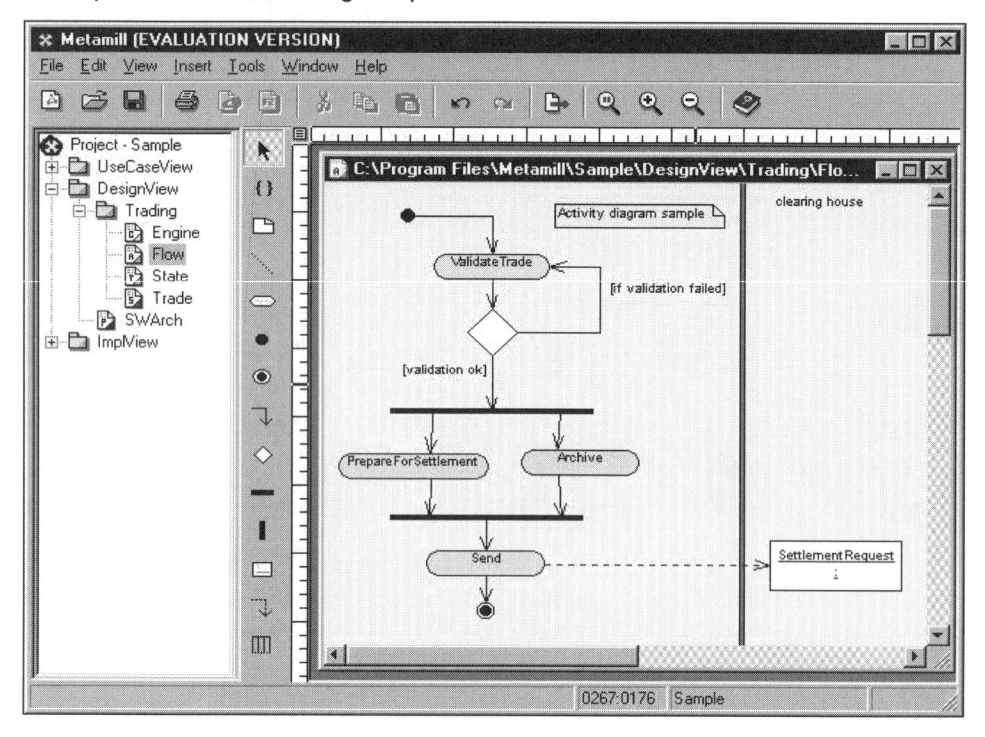

Example 2: Class properties window

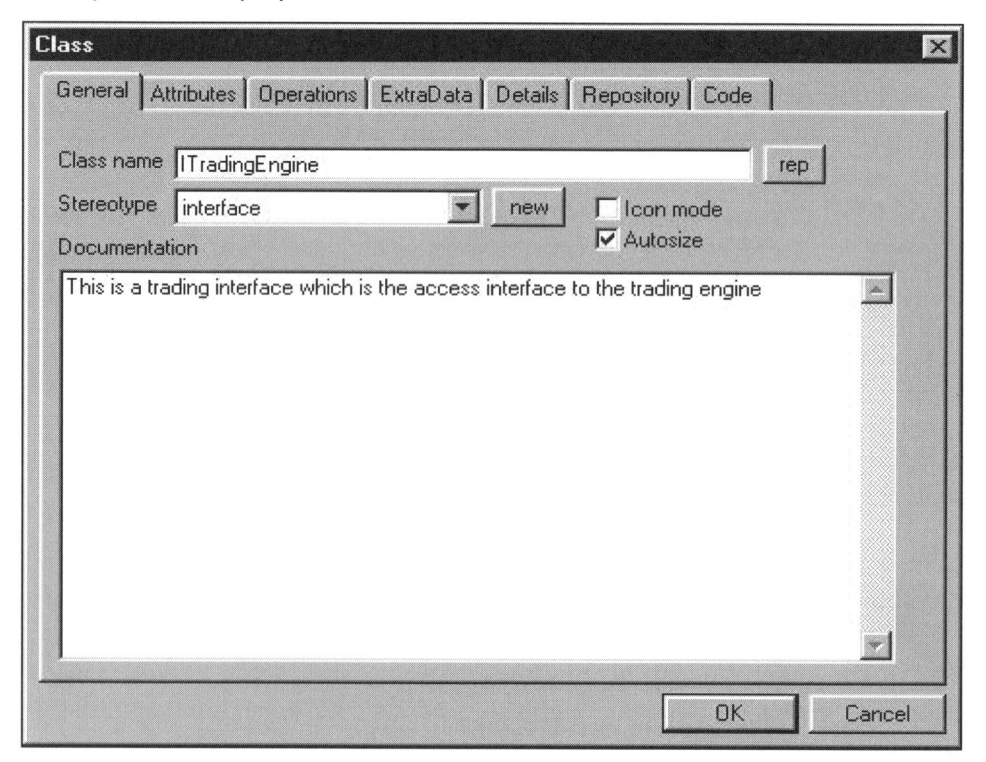

Case example: Informix

The following is an extract from marketing material on the Informix website.

The INFORMIX-4GL Product Family, comprised of INFORMIX-4GL Rapid Development System, INFORMIX-4GL Interactive Debugger, and INFORMIX-4GL Compiler, is a comprehensive fourth-generation application development and production environment that provides power and flexibility without the need for third-generation languages like C or COBOL. INFORMIX-4GL version 4.1 provides more enhancements to the product line than any other release since 4GL was introduced in 1986 giving you more functionality than ever before!

Wouldn't you like to find a self-contained application development environment that:

- Provides rapid development and interactive debugging capabilities
- Offers high performance in the production environment
- Integrates all the functionality you could possibly need for building even the most complex applications
- Doesn't require the use of a third-generation language
- Allows you to easily maintain your applications for years to come
- Is based on industry-standard SQL
- Is easily portable?

Look no further. You've just described INFORMIX-4GL.

Whether you're building menus, forms, screens, or reports, INFORMIX-4GL performs all development functions, and allows for easy integration between them, eliminating the need for external development packages. Because our INFORMIX-4GL products are source-code compatible, portability is ensured.

Prototyping

4.17 The use of 4GLs, together with the realisation that users need to see how a system will look and feel to assess its suitability, have contributed to the increased use of **prototyping**.

> **KEY TERM**
>
> A **prototype** is a model of all or part of a system, built to show users early in the design process how it is envisaged the completed system will appear.

4.18 As a simple example, a prototype of a formatted screen output from a system could be prepared using a graphics package, or even a spreadsheet model. This would describe how the screen output would appear to the user. The user could make suggested amendments, which would be incorporated into the next model.

4.19 Using prototyping software, the programmer can develop **a working model of application program quickly**. He or she can then **check with the data user** whether the prototype program that has been designed appears to **meet the user's needs**, and if it doesn't it can be amended.

Part B: Information technology and systems

The prototyping process

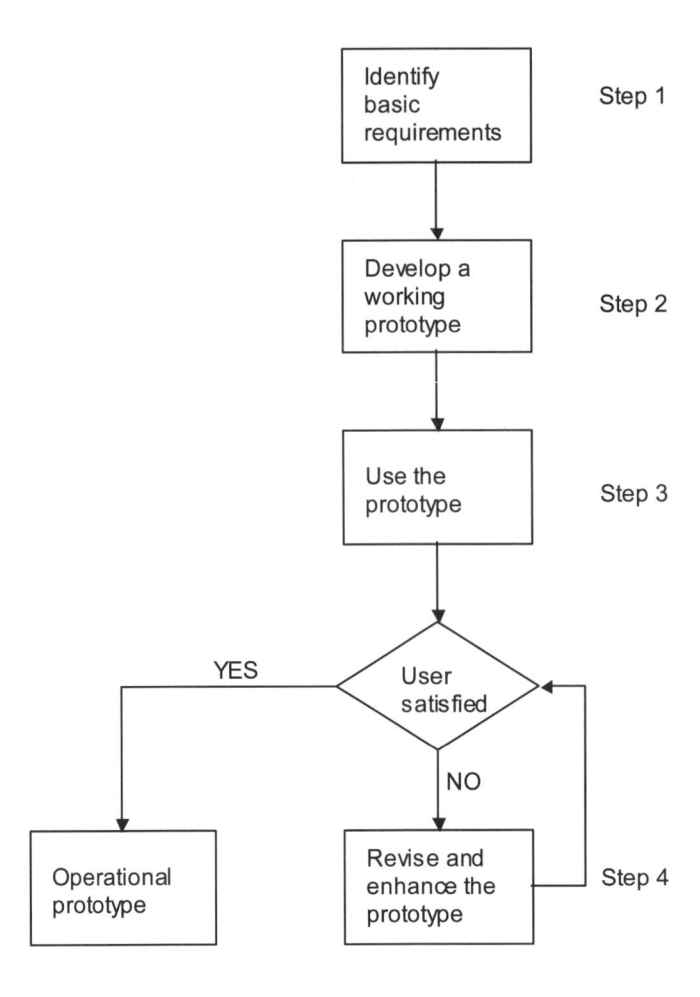

```
Step 1: Identify basic requirements
   ↓
Step 2: Develop a working prototype
   ↓
Step 3: Use the prototype
   ↓
User satisfied?
   YES → Operational prototype
   NO  → Step 4: Revise and enhance the prototype → (back to User satisfied)
```

Advantages and disadvantages of prototyping

4.20 The **advantages** of prototyping.

(a) It makes it possible for programmers to present a 'mock-up' version of an envisaged system to users **before a substantial amount of time and money** have been committed. The user can judge the prototype before things have gone too far to be changed.

(b) The process facilitates the production of **'custom built' application software** rather than off-the-shelf packages which may or may not suit user needs.

(c) It makes **efficient use of programmer time** by helping programmers to develop programs more quickly. Prototyping may speed up the 'design' stage of the systems development lifecycle.

(d) A prototype does not necessarily have to be written in the language of what it is prototyping, so prototyping is not only a tool, but a **design technique**.

4.21 **Disadvantages** of prototyping.

(a) Some prototyping tools are **tied** to a particular make of **hardware**, or a particular **database system**.

(b) It is sometimes argued that prototyping tools are **inefficient** in the program codes they produce, so that programs are bigger and require more memory than a more efficiently coded program.

(c) Prototyping may help users to steer the development of a new system towards an **existing system**.

(d) As prototyping encourages the attitude that changes and amendments are likely, some believe prototyping tools encourage programmers to produce programs quickly, but to neglect program quality.

5 DATABASE SYSTEMS

5.1 The term 'database system' is used to describe a wide range of systems that utilise a central pool of data. As shown in the following illustration, a 'database system' can, (and for our purposes usually does), involve much more than a single database package such as Microsoft Access.

> **KEY TERMS**
>
> A **database** is a collection of structured data which may be manipulated to select or sort some or all of the data held. The database provides convenient access to data for a wide variety of users and user needs.
>
> A **database management system (DBMS)** is the software that builds, manages and provides access to a database. It allows a systematic approach to the storage and retrieval of data.
>
> The independence of logical data from physical storage, and the independence of data items from the programs which access them, is referred to as **data independence**.
>
> Duplication of data items is referred to as **data redundancy**.

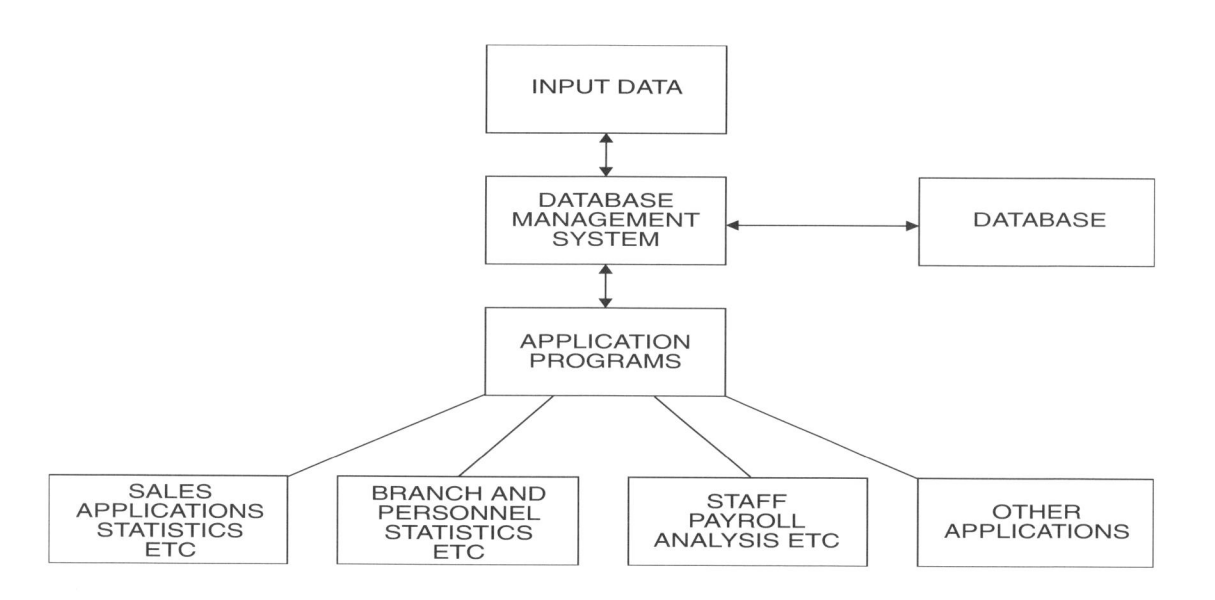

```
                    ┌─────────────┐
                    │ INPUT DATA  │
                    └──────┬──────┘
                           ↕
    ┌─────────────┐  ┌──────────────┐  ┌──────────┐
    │             │  │   DATABASE   │  │          │
    │             │←→│  MANAGEMENT  │←→│ DATABASE │
    │             │  │    SYSTEM    │  │          │
    └─────────────┘  └──────┬───────┘  └──────────┘
                            ↕
                    ┌──────────────┐
                    │ APPLICATION  │
                    │  PROGRAMS    │
                    └──────┬───────┘
        ┌──────────┬───────┴───────┬──────────┐
   ┌────────┐ ┌─────────┐    ┌─────────┐ ┌────────┐
   │ SALES  │ │BRANCH AND│   │  STAFF  │ │ OTHER  │
   │APPLIC. │ │PERSONNEL │   │ PAYROLL │ │APPLIC. │
   │STATS   │ │STATISTICS│   │ANALYSIS │ │        │
   │ ETC    │ │   ETC    │   │   ETC   │ │        │
   └────────┘ └──────────┘   └─────────┘ └────────┘
```

5.2 A database has three major **characteristics**.

(a) It should be **shared**.

(b) It should provide for the **needs of different users** who each have their own processing requirements and data access methods.

Part B: Information technology and systems

(c) The database should be **capable of evolving.** It must be able to meet the **future** data processing needs of users.

5.3 The **advantages** of a database system are as follows.

(a) Avoidance of **unnecessary duplication** of data.

(b) Data is looked upon as serving the **organisation as a whole**, not just for individual departments. The database concept encourages management to regard data as a resource that must be **properly managed.**

(c) The installation of a database system encourages management to **analyse data**, relationships between data items, and how data is used in different applications.

(d) **Consistency** - because data is only held once, the possibility of departments holding conflicting data on the same subject is reduced.

(e) Data on file is independent of the user programs that access the data. This allows **greater flexibility** in the ways that data can be used. New programs can be easily introduced to make use of existing data in a different way.

(f) Developing **new application programs** with a database system is easier because the programmer is not responsible for the file organisation.

5.4 The **disadvantages** of database systems relate mainly to security and control.

(a) There are problems of **data security** and **data privacy**. There is potential for unauthorised access to data. Administrative procedures for data security must supplement software controls.

(b) Since there is only one set of data, it is essential that the data should be **accurate** and free from corruption.

(c) Since data is held once, but its use is widespread, the impact of **system failure** would be greater.

(d) If an organisation develops its own database system from scratch, **initial development costs** will be high.

Database administrator (DBA)

5.5 Control over data and systems development can be facilitated by the appointment of a **database administrator,** who controls and sets standard for:

- The input of data
- Its definition, for instance the development of logical data models
- Physical storage structures
- System performance
- Security and integrity of data, eg maintenance of the data dictionary (see later)
- Back-up and recovery strategies

5.6 The principal role of a DBA can be described as ensuring that the database **functions correctly and efficiently** at all times. To achieve these aims the DBA will carry out a variety of tasks, including some or all of those discussed below. The DBA must be a person who is **technically competent** and possesses a **good understanding** of the **business and operational needs** of the organisation.

5: Systems development

> **KEY TERM**
>
> A **data dictionary** is an index of data held in a database, used to assist in maintenance and any other access to the data.

5.7 A data dictionary is a feature of many database systems and CASE tools. As the term might suggest, it provides a method for **looking up the items of data** held in the database, to establish the following.

(a) **Field names, types, lengths and default values**. For instance a 'year' field would be numeric with four digits and may have a default value of the current year.

(b) A list of the **entity, attribute and relationship types**.

(c) A list of the **aliases** (see below).

(d) A list of all the **processes** which use data about each entity type.

(e) **How to access** the data in whatever manner is required (a data dictionary is sometimes called a data directory).

(f) What the **data codes and symbols mean**.

(g) The **origin** of the data.

(h) Possible **range of values**.

(i) **Ownership** of the data.

(j) Other comments.

5.8 A data dictionary is a record of each **data store** in the system and each **data flow** in the system.

5.9 The data dictionary is a form of technical documentation. It is also a **control tool** and ensures that all in the organisation define data **consistently**. This is extremely important for large projects which involve several programmers.

5.10 A data dictionary helps with systems analysis, systems design and systems maintenance.

(a) During systems analysis a data dictionary helps the analyst **organise information** about the data elements in the system, where they come from, where they go to, what fields are used (name, type, length).

(b) During systems design a data dictionary helps the analyst and programmers to ensure that **no data elements are missed** out.

(c) Defining data items (ie building the dictionary) is a major part of the process of **producing the physical system**, and some data dictionaries can even generate program code automatically.

(d) Once the system is operational, and an **amendment** is required to a program, a data dictionary will help the programmer to understand what each data element is used for, so the impact of any amendments can be established. This is sometimes called **impact analysis**.

(e) Future **maintenance** work on the system is unlikely to be carried out by the people who originally wrote it. A data dictionary records the original work and helps to ensure continuity.

Using a database

5.11 There are four main operations in using a database.

(a) Creating the database **structure**, ie the structure of files and records.
(b) **Entering data** on to the database files, and **amending/updating** it.
(c) **Retrieving and manipulating** the data.
(d) Producing **reports**.

Creating the database structure

5.12 The creation of the database structure involves carrying out an **analysis** of the data to be included. It is necessary to specify what **files** will be held in the database, what **records** (entities) and the **fields** (attributes) they will contain, and how many **characters** will be in each field. The files and fields must be named, and the characteristics of particular fields (for example **all-numeric** or **all-alphabetic** fields) should be specified.

5.13 When the database structure has been established, the data user can **input data** and create a file (or files) or **derive data** from existing records.

Entering and maintaining data

5.14 When entering data into a new database the following issues may have to be addressed.

(a) The **compatibility** between systems is not just a matter of whether one system's files are computer-sensible to another system. It may extend to matters such as **different systems of coding**, different formats for personal data (with/without a contact name? with/without phone or fax number, and so on), different field sizes.

(b) There is potential for **loss or corruption of data** during the conversion process. This could mean a small amount of re-keying or it could be a disastrous, permanent loss of valuable information.

Full **back-ups** should be taken at the start of the process, and back-ups of information on the old system should continue during any period of parallel running.

(c) Existing application-specific systems are unlikely to have sufficient **storage** space to accommodate the combined data. This can easily be resolved, but it must be resolved with an eye to the **future growth** of the business and future use of the database.

(d) **Access to data must not suffer.** Operational users will be attempting to extract information from a much larger pool, and the system must be designed in such a way that they do not have to wade through large amounts of data that is irrelevant.

Those developing the system must consult those users who do the processing to ensure their information needs are met by the new data architecture.

(e) As well as offering the potential for new kinds of report the system must continue to **support existing reporting**.

Once more, **extensive consultation** with users is essential.

(f) Once the data has been amalgamated the business faces the task of ensuring that it is **secure**. A systems failure will now mean that no part of the business can operate, rather than at most just one part.

Retrieval and manipulation of data

5.15 Data can be retrieved and manipulated in a variety of ways.

5: Systems development

(a) By **specifying the required parameters** - for example from a database of employee records, records of all employees in the sales department who have been employed for over 10 years and are paid less than £12,000 pa could be extracted. Search and retrieve parameters that are used regularly, can be stored on a search parameters file for future use.

(b) Retrieved data can be **sorted** on any specified field (for example for employees, sorting might be according to grade, department, age, experience, salary level etc).

(c) Some **calculations** on retrieved data can be carried out - such as calculating **totals** and **average** values.

Query languages

5.16 A database can be interrogated by a **query language**. A query language is a formalised method of constructing queries in a database system. A query language provides the ways in which you ask a database for data. Some query languages can be used to change the contents of a database.

5.17 The illustration below shows the screen from within the query building area of Microsoft Access.

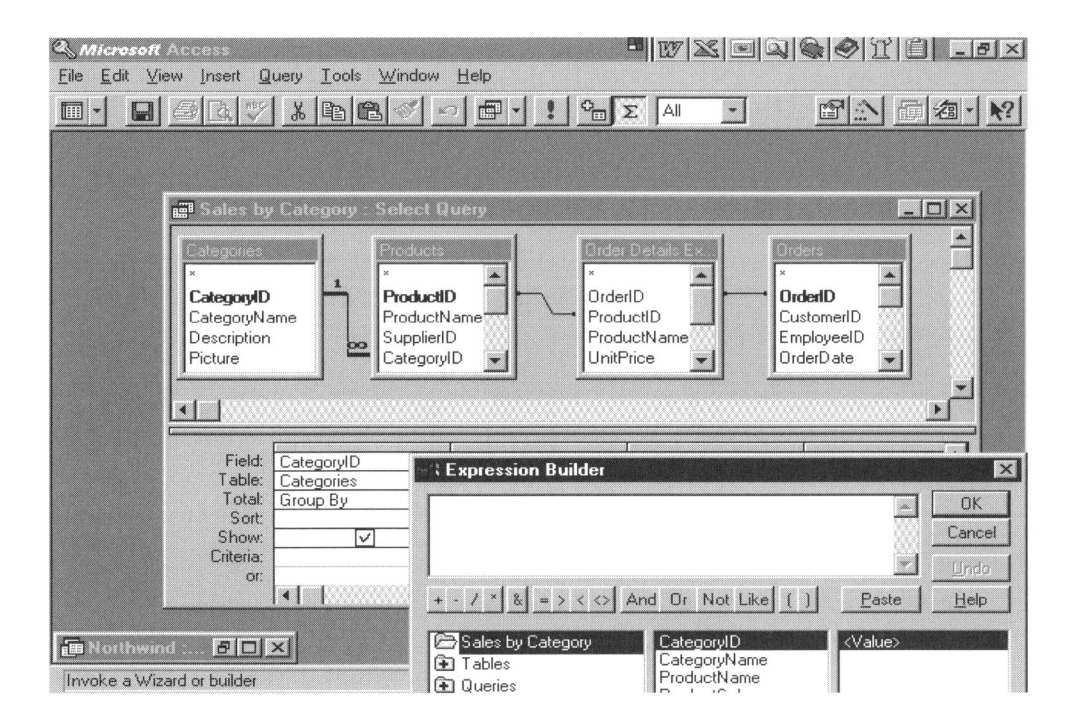

Report production

5.18 Most database packages include a **report generator facility** which allows the user to design report structures in a format which suits the user's requirements and preferences. Report formats can be stored on disk, if similar reports are produced periodically, and called up when required.

6 USER INVOLVEMENT

6.1 The importance of user involvement in the development process cannot be over-estimated. This section looks at a number of approaches intended to ensure that the required level of involvement is achieved.

Part B: Information technology and systems

Structured walkthroughs

6.2 Structured walkthroughs are a technique used (often in conjunction with SSADM) by those responsible for the design of some aspect of a system (particularly analysts and programmers) to present their design to interested **user groups** – in other words to 'walk' them through the design. Structured walkthroughs are **formal meetings**, in which the **documentation produced during development is reviewed and checked** for errors or omissions.

6.3 These presentations are used both to **introduce and explain** the new systems to users and also to offer the users the opportunity of **making constructive criticism** of the proposed systems, and suggestions for further amendments/improvements, before the final systems specification is agreed.

6.4 Users are involved in structured walkthroughs because their knowledge of the desired system is more extensive than that of the systems development personnel. Walkthroughs are sometimes referred to as **user validation**.

The importance of signing off work

6.5 At the end of each stage of development, the resulting output is presented to users for their approval. There must be a **formal sign-off** of each completed stage before work on the next stage begins.

6.6 This **minimises reworking**, as if work does not meet user requirements, only the immediately preceding stage must be revisited. More importantly, it clarifies responsibilities and leaves little room for later disputes.

(a) If the systems developers fail to deliver something that both parties formally agreed to, it is the **developers' responsibility** to put it right, at their own expense, and compensate the user for the delay.

(b) If users ask for something extra or different, that was not formally agreed to, the developers cannot be blamed and **the user must pay** for further amendments and be prepared to accept some delay.

Question 2

What, besides identification of mistakes (errors, omissions, inconsistencies etc), would you expect the benefits of a walkthrough to be?

Answer

(a) Users become involved in the systems analysis process. Since this process is a critical appraisal of their work, they should have the opportunity to provide feedback on the appraisal itself.

(b) The output from the development is shown to people who are not systems development personnel. This encourages its originators to prepare it to a higher quality and in user-friendly form.

(c) Because the onus is on users to approve design, they are more likely to become committed to the new system and less likely to 'rubbish' it.

(d) The process focuses on quality of and good practice in operations generally.

(e) It avoids disputes about who is responsible for what.

5: Systems development

Joint applications development

6.7 Joint Applications Development (JAD) describes the partnership between users and system developers.

6.8 JAD was originally developed by *IBM* to promote a more participative approach to systems development. The potential value to an organisation may be as follows.

   (a) It creates a **pool of expertise** consisting of interested parties from all relevant functions.

   (b) Reduced risk of systems being **imposed** by systems personnel.

   (c) This **increases user ownership** and responsibility for systems solutions.

   (d) Emphasises the **information needs of users** and their relationship to business needs and decision making.

6.9 There are a number of possible **risks** affecting the potential value of JAD.

   (a) The relative **inexperience of many users** may lead to misunderstandings and possibly unreasonable expectations/demands on the system performance.

   (b) The danger of **lack of co-ordination** leading to fragmented, individual, possibly esoteric information systems.

6.10 The shift of emphasis to applications development by end-users must be well-managed and controlled. An organisation may wish to set up an **information centre** to provide the necessary support and co-ordination.

Rapid applications development

6.11 **Rapid Applications Development (RAD)** can be described as a quick way of building software. It combines a managed approach to systems development with the use of modern software tools such as **prototyping**. RAD also involves the **end-user** heavily in the development process.

6.12 RAD has become increasingly popular as the pace of change in business has increased. To develop systems that provide **competitive advantage** it is often necessary to build and implement the system quickly.

6.13 RAD can create **difficulties for the project manager** as RAD relies to a certain extent on a **lack of structure** and control.

User groups

6.14 User groups enable users to share ideas and experience relating to a particular product; usually a software package.

6.15 User groups are usually set up either by the **software manufacturers** themselves (who use them to maintain contact with customers and as a source of new product ideas) or by groups of users who were not satisfied with the level of support they were getting from suppliers of proprietary software.

6.16 Users of a particular package can meet, or more usually exchange views over the Internet, to discuss ideas to improve productivity. An (electronic) newsletter service might be appropriate, based on views exchanged by members, but also incorporating ideas culled from the wider IT environment.

6.17 Sometimes user groups are set up **within individual organisations**. Where an organisation has written its own application software, or is using tailor-made software, there will be a very small knowledge base initially, and there will obviously not be a national user group, because the application is unique.

> ## Chapter roundup
>
> - The **systems development life-cycle** was developed by the National Computing Centre in the 1960s to add discipline to many organisations' approach to system development. It is a model of how systems should be developed. However, in its original form it had a number of **drawbacks**, most notably that it **ignored users'** needs.
>
> - A **methodology** is a collection of procedures, techniques, tools and documentation aids which are designed to help systems developers in their efforts to implement a new system. Methodologies are usually broken down into phases.
>
> - Methodologies may be **process-driven or data-driven**. Process-driven methodologies are based on the processes which are performed, rather than the data which is the subject of the processing. Data-driven methodologies focus on data, the rationale being that the type of data in a system is less likely to change than the processes through which it passes.
>
> - A **CASE tool** may be used to support the construction and maintenance of a system model - often allowing the construction of a prototype.
>
> - A **4GL** enables programs to be constructed more quickly, as English-like commands can be taken to produce high-level code.
>
> - **Database systems** are now common. The term 'database system' describes any system that utilises a central pool of information for a range of purposes.
>
> - **Structured walkthroughs** are a technique used by those responsible for systems design to present their design to **users**. A structured walkthrough is a meeting in which the output from a phase or stage of development is presented to users for discussion and for formal approval.
>
> - **Joint applications development** is an approach to development based on a partnership between users and IT specialists.
>
> - One way of ensuring full user involvement in and commitment to design is the technique of **prototyping**. Prototyping assists programmers by helping them to write application programs much more quickly and easily, and they involve little coding effort on the part of the programmer.

5: Systems development

Quick quiz

1 List the stages identified in the National Computing Centre systems development lifecycle model.

   1 ....
   2 ....
   3 ....
   4 ....
   5 ....
   6 ....
   7 ....

2 List four drawbacks of the SDLC.

   1 ....
   2 ....
   3 ....
   4 ....

3 Define 'systems development methodology'.

4 What would a CASE tool be used for?

5 Explain an advantage of prototyping.

6 Define the terms 'database' and 'database management system'.

7 Distinguish between JAD and RAD.

Answers to quick quiz

1 Identification of a problem or opportunity, Feasibility study, Systems investigation, Systems analysis, Systems design, Systems implementation, Review and maintenance.

2 Four drawbacks are given below. You may have thought of others.

   Ignored information needs.

   No radical rethink of operations.

   User requirements were often poorly defined.

   Led to time overruns.

3 A systems development 'methodology' is a collection of procedures, techniques, tools and documentation aids which will help systems developers in their efforts to implement a new information system.

4 A CASE tool is used to aid with system design and program coding.

5 Prototyping makes it possible for developers to present a 'mock-up' version of the envisaged system without committing too much time and effort. Users can then suggest improvements which can be incorporated in the actual system.

6 A database is a collection of structured data that is able to be accessed by a variety of users to meet a wide range of user needs. A database management system is the software that builds, manages and provides access to the data held in a database.

7 Joint Applications Development (JAD) describes the partnership between users and system developers. **Rapid Applications Development (RAD) is** a quick way of building software. It combines a managed approach to systems development with the use of modern software tools such as **prototyping** and **object oriented design methods**. As RAD involves the **end-user** heavily in the development process it is one example of JAD.

The material covered in this Chapter is tested in Questions 8(a), 9 and 16(a) in the Question Bank.

Chapter 6

FEASIBILITY, INVESTIGATION, ANALYSIS AND DESIGN

	Topic list	Syllabus reference	Ability required
1	The feasibility study	(ii)	Evaluation
2	Systems investigation	(ii)	Evaluation
3	Analysis and design methods	(ii)	Evaluation
4	The process of analysis and design	(ii)	Evaluation

Introduction

Before moving onto a closer examination of the SDLC, we will look at how the general **project management** principles and techniques covered in Chapters 1 and 2 may be applied to Information Systems projects.

In the majority of the chapter we look at the SDLC in more detail. We start with the **feasibility study**, the first stage, and systems **investigation**, the second stage, examining the common techniques of systems investigation, including the use of interviews and questionnaires.

The examiner does not expect you to be an expert systems analyst or computer programmer, but he does expect you to understand the process of analysis and design in broad terms. In section 5 of this chapter we look at a number of **techniques** that are used in systems analysis and design.

Learning outcomes covered in this chapter

- **Explain** the processes of system design and development and analyse the issues arising at those stages (*Also see chapter 5*)

- **Apply** the main tools and techniques used in the gathering, recording and analysis of information relating to an existing Information System

Syllabus content covered in this chapter

- Assessing the feasibility of systems projects (ie cost-benefit analysis, technical feasibility, time feasibility)

- Information gathering techniques (ie interviews, questionnaires, observation, simulation, document review)

- Recording and documenting tools used during the analysis and design of systems

- The nature and purpose of data normalisation and Structured English

1 THE FEASIBILITY STUDY

> **KEY TERM**
>
> A **feasibility study** is a formal study to decide what type of system can be developed which best meets the needs of the organisation.

The feasibility study team

1.1 A feasibility study team should be appointed to carry out the study (although individuals might be given the task in the case of smaller projects).

   (a) Members of the team should be drawn from the **departments affected by the project**.

   (b) At least one person must have a **detailed knowledge of computers and systems design** (in a small concern it may be necessary to bring in a systems analyst from outside).

   (c) At least one person should have a **detailed knowledge of the organisation** and in particular of the workings and staff of the departments affected. Managers with direct knowledge of how the current system operates will know what the **information needs** of the system are, and whether any proposed new system (for example an off-the-shelf software package) will do everything that is wanted. They are also most likely to be in a position to recognise **improvements that can be made in the current system.**

   (d) It is possible to hire **consultants** to carry out the feasibility study, but their **lack of knowledge about the organisation** may adversely affect the usefulness of their proposals.

   (e) Before selecting the members of the study group, the steering committee must ensure that they possess **suitable personal qualities**, eg the ability to be **objectively critical**.

   (f) All members of the study group should ideally have some knowledge of information technology and systems design. They should also be encouraged to read as widely as possible and take an **active interest in current innovations.**

1.2 With larger projects it may well be worthwhile for a small firm to employ a **professional systems analyst** and then appoint a management team to work with the analyst.

Conducting the feasibility study

1.3 Some of the work performed at the feasibility study stage may be similar to work performed later on in the development of the project. This is because some of the information necessary to decide whether to go ahead with a project or trying to define a problem is common to both phases.

1.4 **Reasons for having a feasibility study** include that new systems can:

   (a) Be complicated and **cost** a great deal to develop.

   (b) Be **disruptive** during development and implementation (eg staff and management time).

   (c) Have **far-reaching consequences** in the way an organisation conducts its business or is structured.

Part B: Information technology and systems

Terms of reference

1.5 The terms of reference for a feasibility study group may be set out by a steering committee, the information director or the board of directors, and might consist of:

(a) To **investigate** and report on an **existing system**, its procedures and costs.
(b) To define the **systems requirements**.
(c) To establish whether these requirements are being met by the **existing** system.
(d) To establish whether they could be met by an **alternative** system.
(e) To specify **performance criteria** for the system.
(f) To recommend the **most suitable system** to meet the system's objectives.
(g) To prepare a detailed **cost budget**, within a specified budget limit.
(h) To prepare a draft **plan for implementation** within a specified timescale.
(i) To establish whether the hoped-for **benefits** could be realised.
(j) To establish a detailed design, implementation and operating **budget**.
(k) To **compare** the detailed budget with the costs of the current system.
(l) To set the **date** by which the study group must **report back**.
(m) To decide which **operational managers** should be approached by the study group.

1.6 The remit of a feasibility study may be narrow or wide. The feasibility study team must engage in a substantial effort of fact finding. These facts may include matters relevant to the project which are not necessarily of a data processing nature.

Problem definition

1.7 In some circumstances the '**problem**' (for example the necessity for a real-time as opposed to a batch-processed application) may be quite **exact**; in others it may be characterised as '**soft**' (related to people and the way they behave).

1.8 The problem definition stage should result in the production of a set of documents which define the problem.

(a) A set of **diagrams** representing, in overview:

(i) The current physical flows of data in the organisation (**documents**).
(ii) The activities underlying them (**data flows**).

(b) A description of all the people, jobs, activities and so on (**entities**) that make up the system, and their relationship to one another.

(c) The **problems/requirements** list established from the terms of reference and after consultation with users.

The problems/requirements list

1.9 The problems/requirements list may cover, amongst other things, the following areas.

(a) Details of data **input** to the current system.
(b) The nature of current system **output** (contents, timing etc).
(c) Methods of **processing**.
(d) The expected **growth** of the organisation and so **future volumes** of processing.
(e) The systems **control** in operation.
(f) **Staffing** arrangements and organisational **structure**.
(g) The **operational costs** of the system.
(h) **Response times**.
(i) Details of any relevant system related **problems**.

6: Feasibility, investigation, analysis and design

Option evaluation

1.10 This stage involves suggesting a number of **options** for a new system, evaluating them and recommending one for adoption. It concludes with a final **feasibility study report**.

Step 1. Create the **base constraints** in terms of expenditure, implementation and design time, and system requirements, which any system should satisfy.

(a) **Operations** (for example faster processing, larger volumes, greater security, greater accuracy, better quality, real-time as opposed to other forms of processing).

(b) Information **output** (quality, frequency, presentation, eg GUIs, database for managers, EIS facilities).

(c) **Volume of processing**.

(d) **General system requirements** (eg accuracy, security and controls, audit trail, flexibility, adaptability).

(e) **Compatibility/integration** with existing systems.

Step 2. Create outlines of **project options**, describing, in brief, each option. The number will vary depending on the complexity of the problem, or the size of the application, but is typically between three and six.

Step 3. Assess the **impact** each proposal has on the work of the relevant user department and/or the organisation as a whole.

Step 4. **Review** these proposals with users, who should indicate those options they favour for further analysis.

System justification

1.11 A new system should not be recommended unless it can be justified. The justification for a new system would have to come from:

(a) An evaluation of the **costs and benefits** of the proposed system, and/or
(b) Other **performance criteria**.

Areas of feasibility

1.12 There are five key areas in which a project must be feasible if it is to be selected.

- Technical feasibility
- Operational feasibility
- Social feasibility
- Ecological feasibility
- Financial feasibility

Technical feasibility

1.13 The requirements, as defined in the feasibility study, must be technically achievable. This means that any proposed solution must be capable of being implemented using available **hardware, software and other equipment**. The type of requirement which might depend for success on technical feasibility might be one of the following.

(a) **Volume** of transactions which can be processed within a given time.
(b) **Capacity** to hold files or records of a certain size.
(c) **Response times** (how quickly the computer does what you ask it to).
(d) **Number of users** which can be supported without deterioration in the other criteria.

Operational feasibility

1.14 Operational feasibility is a key concern. If a solution makes technical sense but **conflicts with the way the organisation does business,** the solution is not feasible. Thus an organisation might reject a solution because it forces a change in management responsibilities, status and chains of command, or does not suit regional reporting structures, or because the costs of redundancies, retraining and reorganisation are considered too high.

Social feasibility

1.15 An assessment of social feasibility will address a number of areas, including the following.

- **Personnel** policies
- Redrawing of **job specifications**
- Threats to **industrial relations**
- Expected **skills requirements**
- **Motivation**

Ecological feasibility

1.16 Ecological feasibility relates to environmental considerations. A particular course of action may be rejected on the basis that it would cause too much damage to the environment. In some markets customers may prefer to purchase ecologically sound products. Ecological feasibility issues could include the following.

- What **waste** products are produced?
- How is waste **disposed**?
- Is use of the product likely to damage the **environment**?
- Could the production process be '**cleaner**'?
- How much **energy** does the process consume?

Financial feasibility

1.17 Any project will have financial costs and benefits. Financial feasibility has three strands.

(a) The **benefits must justify the costs**.

(b) The project must be the **'best' option** from those under consideration for its particular purpose.

(c) The project must **compete with projects in other areas of the business** for funds. Even if it is projected to produce a positive return and satisfies all relevant criteria, it may not be chosen because other business needs are perceived as more important.

1.18 **Cost-benefit analysis** before or during the development of information systems is complicated by the fact that many of the system cost elements are **poorly defined** (particularly for development projects) and that benefits can often be highly qualitative and subjective in nature.

The costs of a proposed system

1.19 In general the best cost estimates will be obtained for systems bought from an **outside vendor** who provides a cost quotation against a specification. Less concrete cost estimates are generally found with development projects where the work is performed by the organisation's own employees.

1.20 The costs of a new system will include costs in a number of different categories – see the following table.

Cost	Example
Equipment costs	- Computer and peripherals - Ancillary equipment - The initial system supplies (disks, tapes, paper etc)
Installation costs	- New buildings (if necessary) - The computer room (wiring, air-conditioning if necessary)
Development costs	These include costs of measuring and analysing the existing system and costs of looking at the new system. They include software/consultancy work and systems analysis and programming. Changeover costs, particularly file conversion, may be very considerable.
Personnel costs	- Staff training - Staff recruitment/relocation - Staff salaries and pensions - Redundancy payments - Overheads
Operating costs	- Consumable materials (tapes, disks, stationery etc) - Maintenance - Accommodation costs - Heating/power/insurance/telephone - Standby arrangements, in case the system breaks down

Question 1

Draw up a table with three headings: capital cost items, one-off revenue cost items and regular annual costs. Identify at least three items to be included under each heading. You may wish to refer back to the preceding paragraphs for examples of costs.

Answer

Capital cost items	'One-off' revenue cost items	Regular annual costs
Hardware purchase costs	Consultancy fees	Operating staff salaries/wages
Software purchase costs	Systems analysts' and programmers' salaries	Data transmission costs
Purchase of accommodation (if needed)	Costs of testing the system (staff costs, consumables)	Consumable materials
Installation costs (new desks, cables, physical storage etc)	Costs of converting the files for the new system	Power
	Staff recruitment fees	Maintenance costs
		Cost of standby arrangements
		Ongoing staff training

Part B: Information technology and systems

The benefits of a proposed system

1.21 The benefits from a proposed new system must also be evaluated. These ought to consist of benefits of several types.

(a) **Savings** because the **old system** will no longer be operated. The savings should include:

(i) Savings in **staff costs**.
(ii) Savings in **other operating costs**, such as consumable materials.

(b) Extra **savings** or revenue benefits because of the improvements or enhancements that the **new system** should bring:

(i) Possibly **more sales revenue** and so additional contribution.
(ii) **Better stock control** (with a new stock control system) and so fewer stock losses from obsolescence and deterioration.
(iii) Further savings in **staff time**, resulting perhaps in reduced future staff growth.

(c) Possibly, some one-off revenue benefits from the **sale of equipment** which the existing system uses, but which will no longer be required. Second-hand computer equipment does not have a high value, however! It is also possible that the new system will use **less office space**, and so there may be benefits from selling or renting the spare accommodation.

1.22 Some benefits might be **intangible**, or impossible to give a money value to.

(a) Greater **customer satisfaction**, arising from a more prompt service (eg because of a computerised sales and delivery service).
(b) Improved **staff morale** from working with a 'better' system.
(c) **Better decision making** is hard to quantify, but may result from better MIS, DSS or EIS.

1.23 The main **financial selection** techniques are listed below. The syllabus does not include a detailed analysis of these techniques – although you may draw on your knowledge of these techniques when discussing project feasibility.

- The payback method
- Discounted cashflow
- Accounting rate of return
- Return on investment

SWOT analysis

1.24 SWOT analysis may also be used to assess project or system feasibility. We covered this technique in detail in Chapter 2.

The feasibility study report

1.25 Once each area of feasibility has been investigated, a number of possible projects may be put forward. The results are included in a **feasibility report**. This should contain the following items.

- **Terms of reference**
- Description of **existing system**
- **System requirements**

- Details of the **proposed system(s)**
- **Cost/benefit analysis**
- **Development** and **implementation** plans
- **Recommendations** as to the preferred option

2 SYSTEMS INVESTIGATION

2.1 The systems investigation is a detailed fact-finding exercise about the areas under consideration. It may be performed substantially **during the feasibility study**.

2.2 The project team has to determine the **inputs, outputs, processing methods and volumes of the current system**. It also examines **controls, staffing and costs** and reviews the **organisational structure**. It should also consider the **expected growth** of the organisation and its **future requirements**.

2.3 The stages involved in this phase of the study are as follows.

(a) **Fact finding** by means of questionnaires, interviews, observation, reading handbooks, manuals, organisation charts, or from the knowledge and experience of members of the study team.

(b) **Fact recording** using flowcharts, decision tables, narrative descriptions, organisation and responsibility charts.

(c) **Evaluation**, assessing the strengths and weaknesses of the existing system.

2.4 At this phase, when the team is trying to discover the details of a system with which they are generally quite unfamiliar, they will be interested in all sorts of facts about the organisation. After all, the **organisational context of the system will affect its operation**. Consequently, fact finding in a user department can cover a broad area, as demonstrated by a few examples, below. The emphasis in each area will be on the potential for **improvement**.

(a) **Plans and objectives.** Does the department have clear plans and objectives and are these consistent with the objectives of the organisation as a whole?

(b) **Organisation structure**. Is the structure geared towards achieving the department's objectives? Are responsibilities clearly delegated and defined?

(c) **Policies, systems and procedures**. How has the department established its current policies? Are they written down and formally reviewed? How does management ensure that policies are adhered to?

(d) **Personnel**. Are there adequate systems/procedures for job specifications and appraisals? Are there adequate systems for staff development and training?

(e) **Equipment and the office.** What is the general condition of office equipment? Is it used to full advantage?

(f) **Operations and control.** What exceptional cases are dealt with, and how are they dealt with? Are there bottlenecks in operations; if so, what can be done to ease them?

2.5 There are many items about which facts ought to be obtained, and so the systems investigators should begin by drafting a **checklist of points** before they start asking questions.

2.6 This 'top-down' approach **focuses first on management needs**, ignoring operational requirements until later on.

Interviews

2.7 **Interviews** with members of staff can be an effective method of fact finding. although they can be **time consuming** for the analyst, who may have several to conduct, and therefore expensive.

(a) In an interview **attitudes** not apparent from other sources may be obtained.

(b) **Immediate clarification** can be sought to unsatisfactory/ambiguous responses.

(c) Interviews require a response – some staff may ignore a questionnaire.

(d) A well-conducted interview should provide staff with reassurance regarding the upcoming change.

2.8 Some guidelines to consider when conducting fact-finding interviews are explained below.

(a) The interviewer must appreciate that he or she is dealing with many different individuals with different attitudes and personalities. The approach should be adopted to suit the individual interviewee.

(b) The interviewer should be **fully prepared**, having details of the interviewee's name and job position, and a plan of questions to ask.

(c) **Employees ought to be informed** before the interview that a systems investigation is taking place, and its **purpose explained**.

(d) The interviewer must ask questions at the **level appropriate** to the employee's position within the organisation (for example top management will be concerned with policy, supervisors with functional problems).

(e) The interview should **not be too formal** a question-and-answer session, but should be allowed to develop into a **conversation** whereby the interviewee offers his or her opinions and suggestions.

(f) The interviewer must not **jump to conclusions** or confuse opinions with facts, accepting what the interviewee has to say (for the moment) and refraining from interrupting.

(g) The interviewer should gain the **interviewee's confidence** by explaining what is going on. This confidence may be more easily obtained by allowing the interview to take place on the interviewee's 'home ground' (desk or office). The purpose of note taking should also be explained.

(h) If possible, the interviewer may find it helps understanding to move **progressively** through the system, for example interviewing input personnel first, then supervisor then manager.

(i) The interviewer should refrain from making **off the record** comments during the course of the interview, for example about what is going to be recommended.

(j) The interview should be **long** enough for the interviewer to obtain the information required and to ensure an understanding of the system, but **short** enough to ensure that concentration does not wander.

(k) The interview should be **concluded** by a resumé of its main points and the interviewer should **thank** the interviewee for their time.

Question 2

Draw up a checklist of do's and don'ts for conducting fact-finding interviews.

Answer

A useful checklist for **guidance in conducting interviews** is suggested by Daniels and Yeates in *Basic training in systems analysis* as follows:

Do	Don't
Plan	Be late
Make appointments	Be too formal or too casual
Ask questions at the right level	Interrupt
Listen	Use technical jargon
Use the local terminology	Confuse opinion with fact
Accept ideas and hints	Jump to conclusions
Hear both sides	Argue
Collect documents and forms	Criticise
Check the facts back	Suggest
Part pleasantly	

Questionnaires

2.9 The use of questionnaires may be useful whenever a **limited** amount of **information** is required from a large number of individuals.

2.10 Questionnaires may be used as the **groundwork for interviews** with some respondents being interviewed subsequently. Alternatively, interviews may be carried out in one site/department, and questionnaires designed on the basis of experience and used elsewhere.

2.11 Many respondents find questionnaires **less imposing than interviews** and may therefore be more prepared to express their opinion.

(a) Employees ought to be informed of the questionnaire's **purpose**. This should remove any staff suspicion and hopefully ensure a good proportion of sensible responses.

(b) Question design is a very important issue. Questions should obtain the specific information necessary for the study, but should not be worded in such a way to influence the response given.

(c) Questionnaires must not be too long – a questionnaire of many pages is likely to end up in a 'pending' tray indefinitely, or worse, the bin.

(d) Staff may prefer **anonymity**. This should result in grater honesty, but has the disadvantage of preventing follow-up of uncompleted questionnaires, and of 'interesting' responses.

2.12 Questionnaires, by themselves, are useful for gathering specific information. In a systems development context, it is likely that further methods of gathering information, such as interview or observation, would also be required.

2.13 When designing a questionnaire, the following guidelines should be considered.

(a) Questionnaires should **not contain too many questions** (people tend to lose interest quickly and become less accurate in their answers).

(b) They should be **organised in a logical sequence**.

(c) Ideally, they should be designed so that each question can be answered with a limited range of answers, such as **'yes' or 'no'** or a 'tick' in a numbered box eg 1 = Strongly agree, 4 = Strongly disagree.

(d) They should be **tested independently** before being issued. This should enable the systems analyst to establish the effectiveness of the questions.

(e) Questionnaires should take into account the **sensitivity** of individuals in respect of any threat to their job security, change of job definition etc.

Observation

2.14 An analyst, after establishing the methods and procedures used in the organisation, may wish to undertake further investigation through **observing operations**.

2.15 Observation may be used to check facts obtained by interview or questionnaire. It may well be that staff work differently to the answers provided in interviews, and differently to written policies and procedures.

2.16 The observer must remember that staff may act differently simply because they know they are being observed – this is a difficult problem to overcome as observing staff without their knowledge may not be **ethical**.

User workshops

2.17 A workshop is a meeting with the emphasis on **practical exercises.** User workshops are often used in systems analysis to help establish and record user requirements.

2.18 At a user workshop, user input is obtained by the analyst to analyse business functions and define the data associated with the current and future systems. An outline of the proposed new system is produced, which is used to design more detailed system procedures.

2.19 Depending on the complexity of the system, the workshop may devise a **plan for implementation**. More complex systems may conduct a workshop early in the design stage and hold a later workshop with the aim of producing a **detailed system model. Prototyping** may be used at such a workshop to prepare preliminary screen layouts.

2.20 User workshops should be facilitated by a **facilitator.** The facilitator co-ordinates the workshop activities with the aim of ensuring the objectives of the session are achieved.

2.21 The facilitator would most likely be a systems analyst with excellent **communication** and leadership skills. The skills of the person in this role are critical to the success of the workshop.

2.22 Many user workshops also utilise a **scribe**. The scribe is an active participant who is responsible for producing the outputs of the workshop. The scribe may use a **CASE tool** (as explained in Chapter 5).

Document review

2.23 The systems analyst must investigate the **documents** that are used in the system for input and output. One way of recording facts about document usage is the **document description form**, which is simply a standard form which the analyst can use to describe a document.

2.24 This may be a wide ranging investigation, using for example organisation charts, procedures manuals and standard operational forms.

2.25 One risk, however, is that **staff do not follow** documented policies and procedures or that these documents have **not been properly updated**. Document review should therefore be used in tandem with one or more other investigative techniques.

2.26 An analysis of documents, together with historical operational data, should help the analyst estimate future processing requirements and volumes.

Existing computerised systems

2.27 User requirements for a new computerised system can also be collected from existing computerised systems.

2.28 It is important to take into account changes in the way work is being carried out – it is unlikely that the new system will be performing an identical role to the old system.

2.29 With this in mind, areas where the existing system can provide useful information include:

- File structures
- Transaction volumes
- Screen design
- User satisfaction
- User complaints
- Help-desk/Information centre records
- Causes of system crashes
- Processor speed

2.30 It is important to remember however that a duplicate of the existing system is not required. The aim is to produce a better system – which is likely to involve changes to existing working methods.

Question 3

How would you investigate an existing operational system in a company which operates through a network of regional branches controlled from a centrally located head office?

Answer

Because the company operates through a network of regional branches controlled from a centrally located head office, it may be appropriate for the systems analysis team to visit head office and a single representative branch. Interviews will be used with key head office staff and on the branch visit, where document analysis and observation can be used for corroborative purposes. Questionnaires can then be designed for use at other branches and, if necessary, followed up if the results do not appear compatible with those obtained by direct contact/observation at the branch visited.

3 ANALYSIS AND DESIGN METHODS

3.1 The **systems analysis** process examines why **current methods** are used and what **alternatives** might achieve the same or better results.

3.2 A variety of fact-finding techniques are available to determine how a system operates, what document flows occur, what work processes are involved and what personnel are involved.

Data flow diagrams (DFD)   11/01

3.3 Data flow diagrams show the ways in which data is processed. The production of a data flow diagram is often the first step in a structured systems analysis, because it provides a **basic understanding of how the system works**.

3.4 Four symbols are used in data flow diagrams.

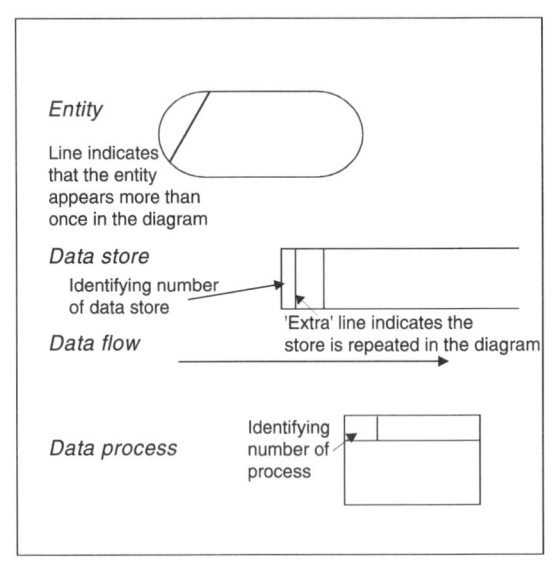

Entity — Line indicates that the entity appears more than once in the diagram

Data store — Identifying number of data store; 'Extra' line indicates the store is repeated in the diagram

Data flow

Data process — Identifying number of process

KEY TERMS

An **external entity** is a **source** or **destination** of data which is considered **external to the system** (not necessarily external to the organisation). It may be people or groups who provide data or input information or who receive data or output information.

A **data store** is a point which receives a data flow and holds data. Most data stores would be either digital (ie computer files) or paper.

A **data flow** represents the movement or transfer of data from one point in the system to another.

Data processes involve data being used or altered. The processes could be manual, mechanised or computerised.

3.5 A data flow could 'physically' be anything - for example a letter, a telephone call, a fax, an e-mail, a link between computers, or a verbal statement. When a data flow occurs, a copy of the data transferred may also be retained at the transmitting point.

3.6 A process could involve changing the data in some way, or simply using the data. For example, a mathematical computation or a process such as sorting would alter data, whereas

6: Feasibility, investigation, analysis and design

a printing data out does not change data – the process makes the same data available in a different form.

3.7 DFDs may be drawn to represent different levels of detail. The top level (least detailed) diagram would show one process only. The source of the data for this process, and its destination(s) are also shown. This type of diagram is known as a **Level 0 DFD**, or a Context diagram.

3.8 The Level 0 DFD may be 'exploded' into a more detailed data flow diagram, known as a **Level-1 DFD**. Further detail can be represented on a **Level-2 DFD**, and so on until all individual entities, stores, flows and processes are shown.

3.9 The diagram below illustrates how **levels of DFDs** are built up.

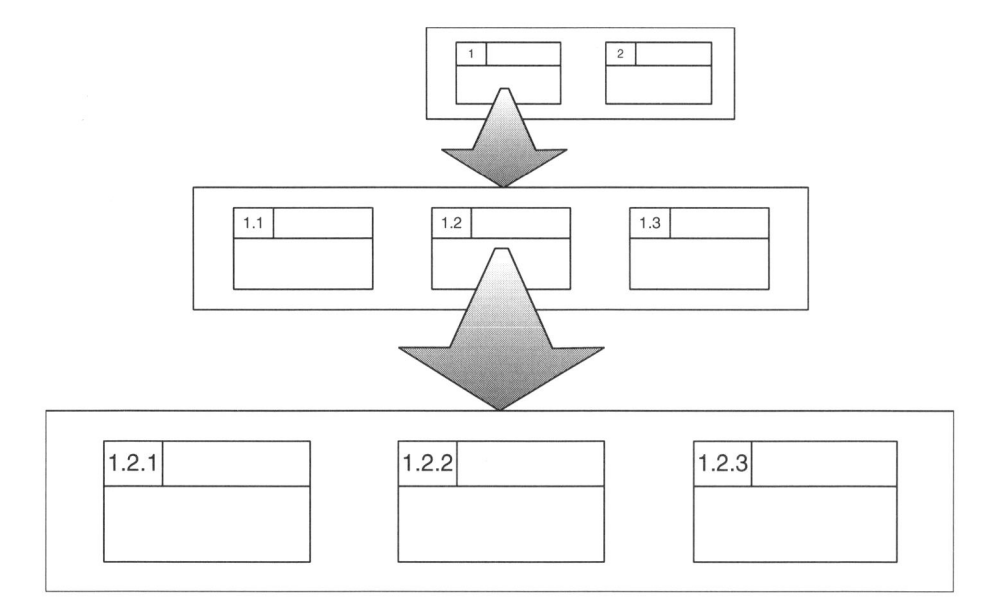

3.10 EXAMPLE: DATA FLOW DIAGRAM

The following example is based upon a system used for purchasing in a manufacturing company. Three data flow diagrams are shown; each is prepared to record a certain level of detail.

Level-0 DFD (context diagram)

3.11 The Level-0 DFD or context diagram would show the source of the purchasing process, its destination and the inputs and outputs. (Data stores are not shown on Context diagrams).

3.12 The central box represents the purchasing system as a whole. In this case only one external entity is shown. In some cases more than one entity will be required, but a context diagram will only ever show one process.

3.13 Note that we are only showing flows of data. The physical resources (the goods supplied) can be shown (by means of broad arrows ⇨), but this tends to overcomplicate the diagram.

Part B: Information technology and systems

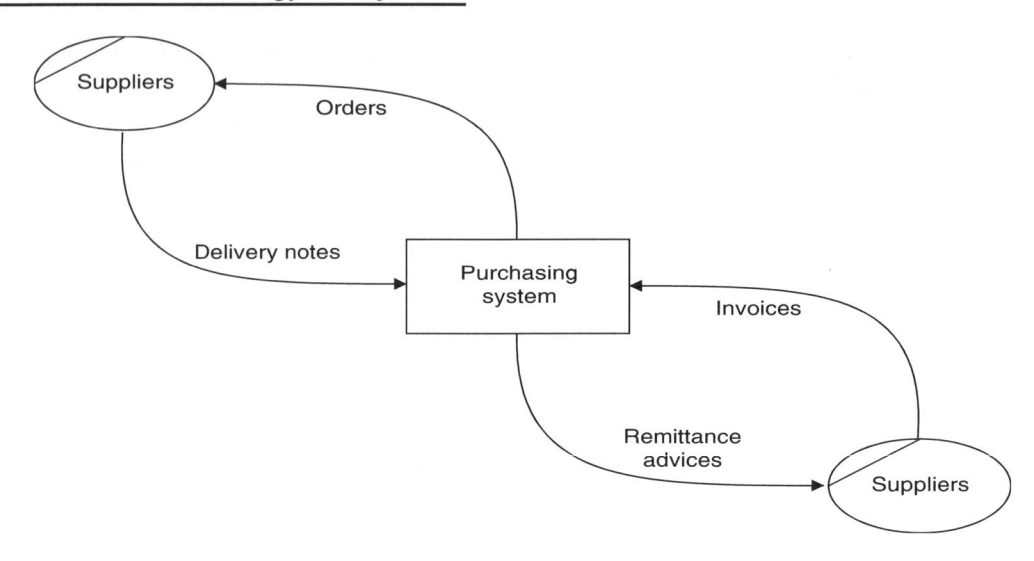

Level 1 DFDs

3.14 Within the purchasing system as a whole in this organisation there are two **subsystems**: the **Stores department** places requests for purchases and accepts delivery of the goods themselves; the **Purchasing department** places orders, and receives and pays invoices.

3.15 A **Level-1 DFD** for the purchasing department is shown below.

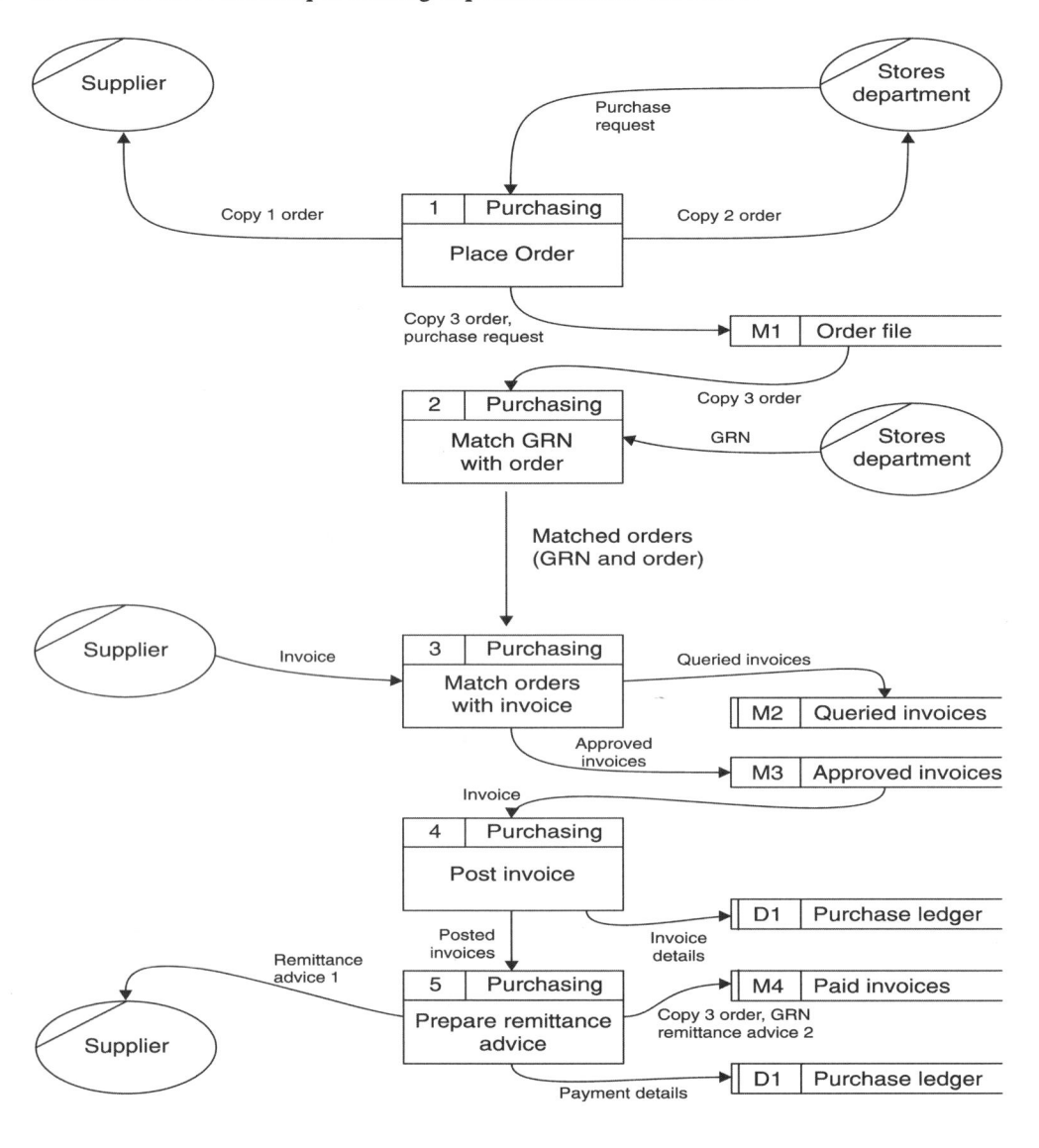

6: Feasibility, investigation, analysis and design

3.16 The following points relate to the Level 1 DFD.

(a) Each process is numbered, but this is only for ease of identification: the numbers are not meant to show the strict sequence of events.

(b) Each process box has a heading, showing where the process is carried out or who does it. The description of the process should be a clear verb like 'prepare', 'calculate', 'check' (not 'process', which is too vague).

(c) The same entity or store may appear more than once on the same diagram (to prevent diagrams becoming overly complicated with arrows crossing each other). When this is done an additional line is put within the symbol. The supplier entity and several of the data stores have extra lines for this reason.

(d) Data stores are given a reference number (again sequence is not important). Some analysts like to use 'M' with this number if it is a **manual** store, and a 'D' if it is a digital or **computerised** store.

Level-2 DFDs

3.17 A separate DFD (Level-2) could be prepared for **each of the numbered processes** shown in the Level 1 DFD. This is known as decomposing a process.

3.18 For example, the diagram below shows the data flows for process 1, Place Order.

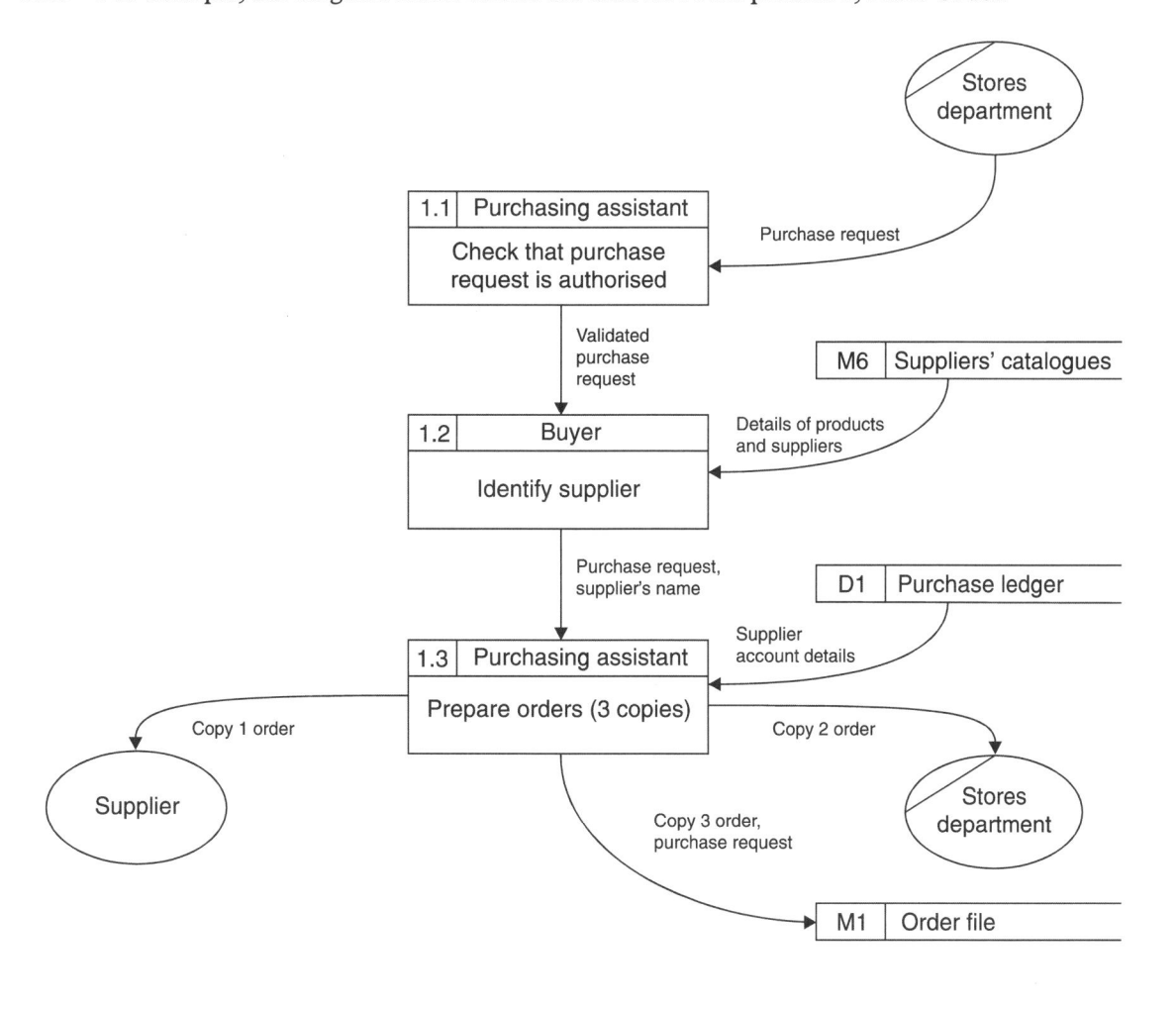

Part B: Information technology and systems

Question 4

Compare this diagram with the Level-1 DFD and note how it is possible to trace the same data flows from one level to the next.

3.19 In turn, box 1.1 could be **further decomposed** in a Level-3 DFD, with processes 1.1.1, 1.1.2 and so on, and box 1.2 could be decomposed into processes 1.2.1, 1.2.2 etc. In theory there is no limit to the number of lower levels, but **three levels is usually enough**.

Question 5

Construct a DFD that models, from the point-of-view of an on-line retailer such as Amazon.com, the process of receiving and filling an on-line order from a customer paying with a credit card.

Answer

Examination questions will not normally specify what level of DFD would be best. You should provide enough detail to show the entities, stores and flows required to answer the question.

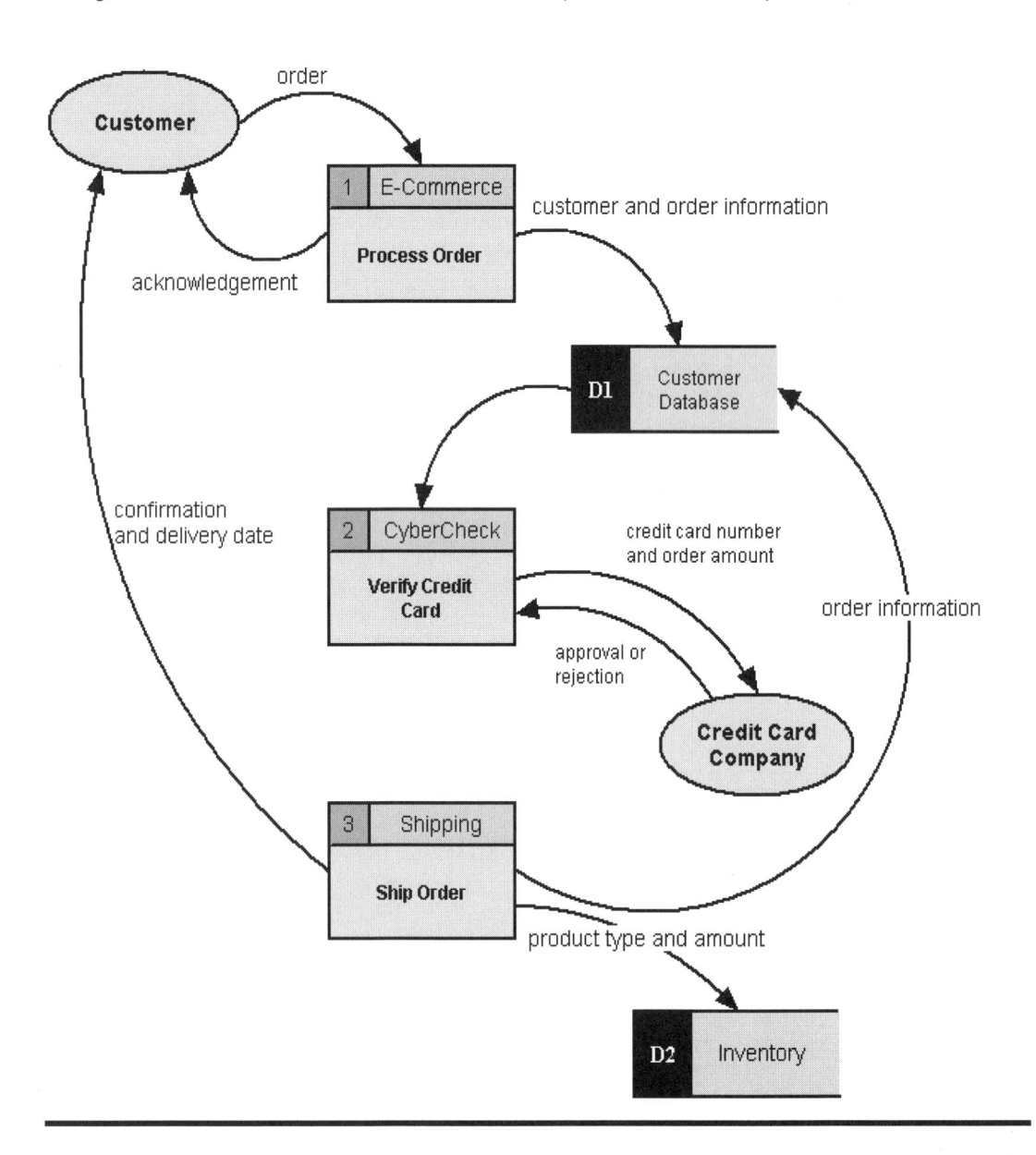

6: Feasibility, investigation, analysis and design

Entity modelling

3.20 An **entity**, as we have seen, is an item (a person, a job, a business, an activity, a product or stores item etc) about which information is stored.

> **KEY TERM**
>
> An **Entity** is any item, role, object, organisation, activity or person that is relevant to the data held in a system.

3.21 An **attribute** is a characteristic or property of an entity. For a customer, attributes include customer name and address, amounts owing, date of invoices sent and payments received, credit limit etc.

> **KEY TERM**
>
> An **Entity Relationship Model (ERM)** (also known as an **entity model** or a **logical data structure**) provides an understanding of the logical data requirements of a system independently of the system's organisation and processes.

3.22 The following relationships may be identified between attributes and entities.

One-to-one relationship (1:1)

3.23 With a one-to-one relationship, an entity is related to only one of the other entity shown. For example, a one-to-one relationship exists between *company* and *finance director*. The model below shows one company which employs one finance director. (These diagrams are sometimes called Bachmann diagrams.)

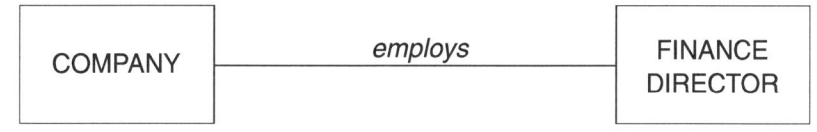

```
[COMPANY] ———employs——— [FINANCE DIRECTOR]
```

One-to-many relationship (1:M)

3.24 For example, the relationship **employs** also exists between *company* and *director*. The company employs more than one director.

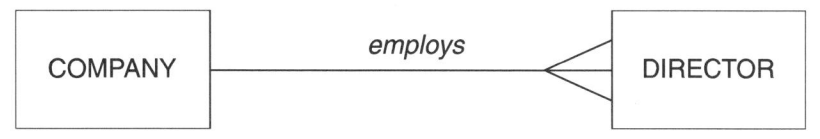

```
[COMPANY] ———employs———< [DIRECTOR]
```

Many-to-one relationship (M:1)

3.25 This is really the same as the previous example, but **viewed from the opposite direction**. For example, many *sales managers* report to one *sales director*.

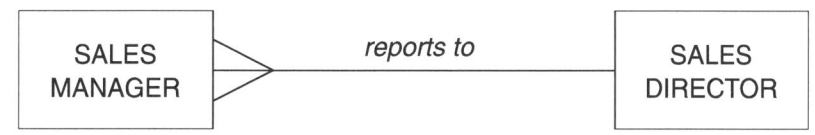

```
[SALES MANAGER] >———reports to——— [SALES DIRECTOR]
```

Part B: Information technology and systems

Many-to-many relationship (M:M)

3.26 The relationship between *product* and *part* is **many-to-many**. A product is composed of many parts, and a part might be used in many products.

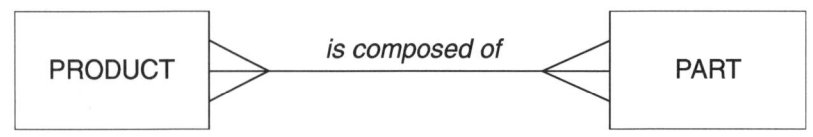

```
PRODUCT >----- is composed of -----< PART
```

3.27 When analysing relationships the correct classification is important. If the one-to-many relationship customer order contains part numbers is incorrectly described as one-to-one, a system designed on the basis of this ERM might allow an order to be entered with one item and one item only.

3.28 EXAMPLE: BUILDING AN ERM

A diagram modelling part of a warehousing and despatch system is shown below. This indicates that:

(a) A customer may make many orders.

(b) That an order form can contain several order lines.

(c) That each line on the order form can only detail one product, but that one product can appear on several lines of the order.

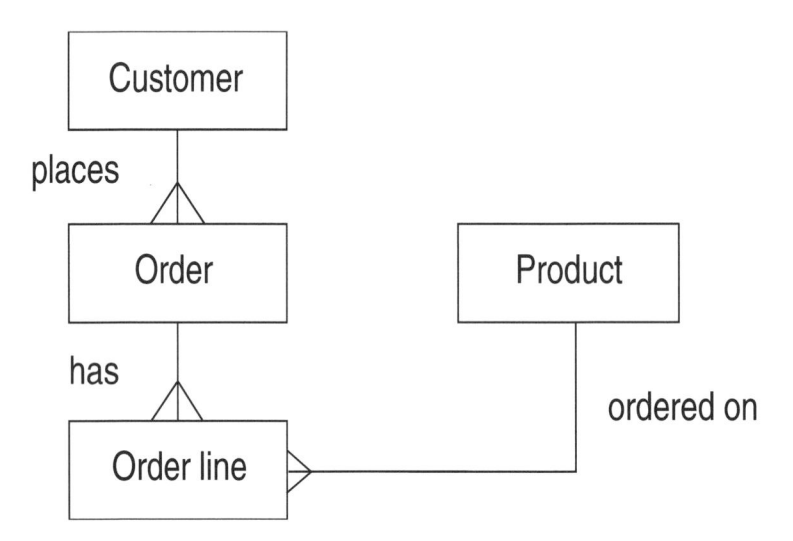

```
         Customer
            |
   places  /\
            |
          Order            Product
            |                 |
     has  /\                  |
            |                 |
        Order line >---ordered on
```

3.29 Another example of an entity model follows. Note the structure of the accompanying narrative (follows the diagram).

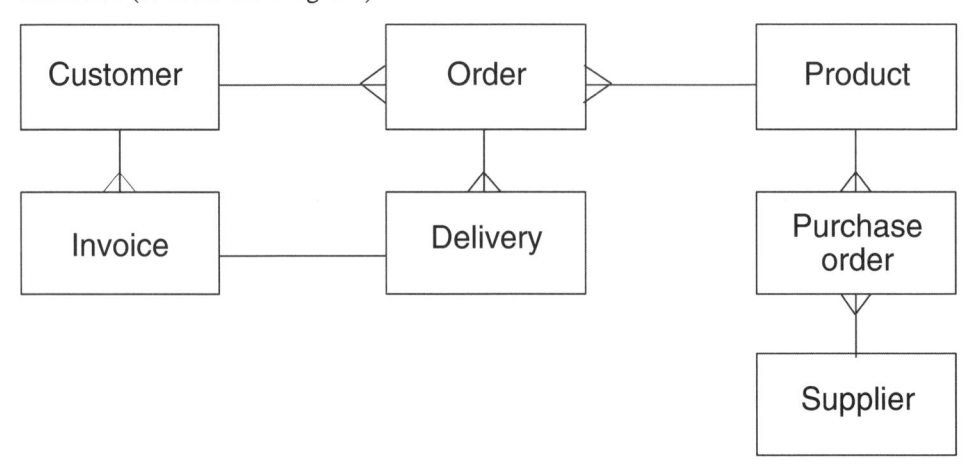

```
Customer >----- Order -----< Product
    |             |             |
    |             |             |
 Invoice ----- Delivery      Purchase
                                order
                                  |
                               Supplier
```

Entity	*Relationship*	*Entity*
Customer	Places many	Orders
Order	Has many	Deliveries
Product	Is ordered on many	Orders
Product	Is ordered on many	Purchase orders
Supplier	Receives many	Purchase orders
Invoice	Is for one	Delivery
Customer	Receives many	Invoices

Entity life histories (ELH)

3.30 As we have seen, **Entity Relationship Models** take a **static** view of data. We will now look at a modelling tool that focuses on data processes.

> **KEY TERM**
>
> An **Entity Life History (ELH)** is a diagram of the *processes* that happen to an *entity*. An entity life history gives a **dynamic** view of the data.

3.31 Data items do not always remain unchanged - they may come into existence by a specific operation and be destroyed by another. For example, a customer order forms part of a number of processes, and is affected by a number of different events. At its simplest, an entity life history displays the following structure.

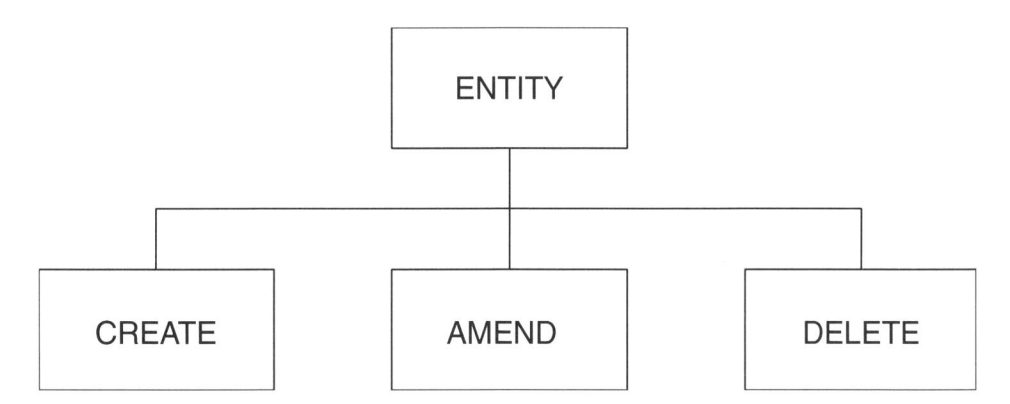

```
           ┌─────────┐
           │ ENTITY  │
           └────┬────┘
       ┌────────┼────────┐
  ┌────┴───┐ ┌──┴───┐ ┌──┴────┐
  │ CREATE │ │AMEND │ │DELETE │
  └────────┘ └──────┘ └───────┘
```

3.32 Entity life histories identify the various states that an entity can legitimately be in. It is really the functions and events which cause the state of the entity to change that are being analysed, rather than the entity itself.

3.33 The following notation rules are used for Entity life histories.

(a) Three symbols are used. The main one is a rectangular box. Within this may be placed an asterisk or a small circle, as explained below.

(b) At the top level the first box (the 'root node') shows the entity itself.

(c) At lower levels the boxes represent events that affect the life of the entity.

(d) The second level is most commonly some form of 'create, amend, delete', as explained earlier (or birth, life, death if you prefer). The boxes are read in **sequence** from top to bottom and left to right.

Part B: Information technology and systems

(e) If an event may affect an entity many times (**iteration**) this is shown by an **asterisk** in the top right hand corner of the box. A customer account, for example, will be updated many times.

(f) If events are alternatives (**selection**) - for example accept large order or reject large order - a **small circle** is placed in the top right hand corner.

3.34 Note the three types of process logic referred to:

- Sequence
- Iteration (or repetition)
- Selection

3.35 Here is a very simple example.

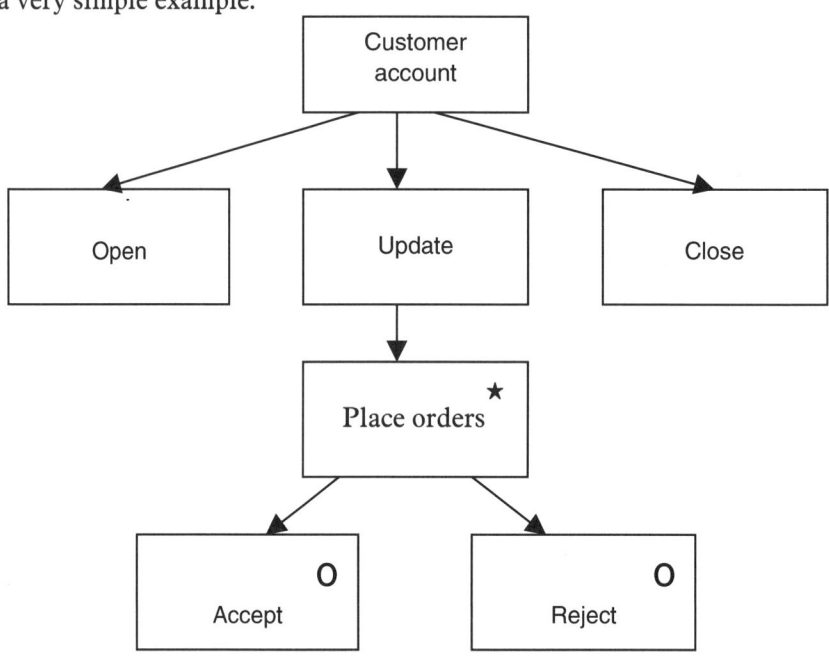

```
                    Customer
                    account
         ┌─────────────┼─────────────┐
         ▼             ▼             ▼
       Open          Update         Close
                       │
                       ▼
                  Place orders *
                   ┌────┴────┐
                   ▼         ▼
                  O         O
                Accept    Reject
```

Decision tables

3.36 Decision tables are used as a method of defining the logic of a process (ie the processing operations required) in a compact manner. They are particularly useful in situations where a **large number of logical alternatives exist**.

3.37 The basic format consists of four quadrants divided by intersecting double lines.

Condition stub	Condition entry
Action stub	Action entry

3.38 SIMPLE EXAMPLE: A DECISION TABLE

We start by considering a very simple decision that most of us face every day: whether to get up or stay in bed.

Suppose you have to get up at around 8 am during the week to enable you to get to work on time. You go to work on Monday to Friday only. If you woke up one Tuesday morning at 8.02 you would be faced with the following appalling dilemma. An X marks the action you should take.

Conditions	Entry
Is it 8 o' clock yet?	Yes
Is it the weekend?	No
Actions	Entry
Get up	X
Stay in bed	

3.39 We can expand this table so that it takes account of **all the possible combinations** of conditions and shows the action that would be taken in each case.

(a) Because a condition can only apply or not apply (Yes or No), **the number of combinations (or 'rules') is 2^n, where n is the number of conditions.**

Here there are 2 conditions (n = 2) so the number of combinations is $2^2 = 4$. There are four columns.

	1	2	3	4
Is it 8 o' clock yet? Is it the weekend?				
Get up Stay in bed				

(b) The conditions can either have a Yes or No answer (Y or N).

(i) As there are **two** possible outcomes, fill **half** of each row with Ys and the other half with Ns. So, write in Y for the first half of the columns in row 1 (columns 1 and 2) and N for the other half (columns 3 and 4).

(ii) For row 2, write in Ys and Ns for **half** the number of columns of each group in the previous row. In this example row 1 has Ys in groups of twos, so row 2 will have Ys in groups of 1.

(iii) If there are more conditions continue **halving** for each row until you reach the final condition, which will always be consecutive Ys and Ns.

	1	2	3	4
Is it 8 o' clock yet?	Y	Y	N	N
Is it the weekend?	Y	N	Y	N
Get up Stay in bed				

Part B: Information technology and systems

(c) Now **consider what action** you would take if the condition(s) specified in each column applied. For column 1 it is 8 o'clock but it is the weekend so you can stay in bed. For column 2 it is 8 o' clock but it is not the weekend so you must get up. Explain the logic of columns 3 and 4 yourself.

	1	2	3	4
Is it 8 o' clock yet?	Y	Y	N	N
Is it the weekend?	Y	N	Y	N
Get up		X		
Stay in bed	X		X	X

(d) In more complicated problems you may find that there are some columns that do not have any Xs in the Action entry quadrant because **this combination of conditions is impossible**. We will show you how to deal with these columns later.

Question 6

Mr L Bones decided to draw up a decision table demonstrating the decision-making process he executed when he woke up each day.

He identified 3 conditions, mirroring his early-morning thought processes, and 2 possible actions.

Conditions   Is it 8 o' clock yet? Is it a weekday? Is it the weekend?

Actions   Get up. Stay in bed.

Draw up and complete the decision table.

Answer

There are 3 conditions so there will be 2^3 = 8 columns.

	1	2	3	4	5	6	7	8
Is it 8 o' clock yet?	Y	Y	Y	Y	N	N	N	N
Is it a weekday?	Y	Y	N	N	Y	Y	N	N
Is it the weekend?	Y	N	Y	N	Y	N	Y	N
Get up		X						
Stay in bed			X			X	X	

Columns 1, 4, 5 and 8 do not have any Xs because it cannot be both a weekday *and* a weekend. In more complex decision situations it may only become clear that certain combinations are impossible once the table has been drawn up.

In this example we could simplify the table by deleting columns 1, 4, 5 and 8. We then end up with the same decision table as the one we saw earlier (although with the columns in a different order.)

A more formal explanation

3.40 We can now explain this more formally and look at a business example.

- The purpose of the **condition stub** is to specify the values of the data that we wish to test for.

- The **condition entry** specifies what those values might be.

3.41 Between them, the condition stub and condition entry show what values an item of data might have that a computer program should test for. Establishing conditions will be done within a computer program by means of **comparison checks**.

6: Feasibility, investigation, analysis and design

3.42 The **action entry** quadrant shows the action or actions that will be performed for each rule. The columns are marked with an 'X' opposite the actions(s) to be taken. In the computer program, instructions specify the action to take, given the conditions established by comparison checks.

3.43 EXAMPLE: A DECISION TABLE

There are **three conditions** which might be encountered by a sales order processing clerk taking a telephone order.

- The caller may have an existing overdue balance on their account
- The caller's account balance may already be in excess of their credit limit
- The caller may not have an account at all

3.44 The number of columns in the decision table is the number of options to the power of the number of conditions. In this example there are two options - 'Y' or 'N' and three conditions. The number of rules is therefore (2^3) - **eight rules**.

Rule	1	2	3	4	5	6	7	8
Account overdue?	Y	Y	Y	Y	N	N	N	N
Credit limit exceeded?	Y	Y	N	N	Y	Y	N	N
New customer (no account)?	Y	N	Y	N	Y	N	Y	N

3.45 The three conditions in this example are **not** totally **independent**. Therefore some rules can be eliminated as **impossible**. For example, a customer that does not currently have an account cannot have an overdue balance and therefore will not have a credit limit. In cases such as this you should **start with a complete table** like that shown above - and deal with the impossible combinations later.

3.46 Continuing the above example, suppose that the **actions** are as follows.

Orders from existing customers who do not have an overdue balance and have not exceeded their credit limit should **be processed**.

This organisation decides that customers requiring an account must **provide credit references** for checking before the account can be opened. If these customers attempt to place an order before an account is set up, the order is **placed on hold**.

The policy for orders from existing customers with a balance in **excess of their credit limit** is that these orders are **placed on hold** and **referred to the section head**.

The policy for existing customers who have overdue balances, but are within their credit limit, is to **process the order** but to **also generate a reminder** letter for overdue balances.

3.47 From this description we can isolate five actions.

- Process order
- Obtain reference
- Place order on hold
- Refer to head
- Send reminder

Part B: Information technology and systems

3.48 Consider the fourth rule in the following table. There is an overdue balance on the account, but the customer would remain within their credit limit. The action entry will therefore show an X against 'Process order' and 'Send reminder'.

Rule	1	2	3	4	5	6	7	8
Account overdue?	Y	Y	Y	Y	N	N	N	N
Credit limit exceeded?	Y	Y	N	N	Y	Y	N	N
New customer (no account)?	Y	N	Y	N	Y	N	Y	N
Process order				X				
Obtain reference								
Place order on hold								
Refer to head								
Send reminder				X				

3.49 By considering each rule in turn the table can be completed. The rules that are **logically not possible** are shaded in the lower half of the table – and crossed out in the top half of the table.

Rule	1	2	3	4	5	6	7	8
Account overdue?	~~Y~~	Y	~~Y~~	Y	~~N~~	N	N	N
Credit limit exceeded?	~~Y~~	Y	~~N~~	N	~~Y~~	Y	N	N
New customer (no account)?	~~Y~~	N	~~Y~~	N	~~Y~~	N	Y	N
Process order	▓		▓	X	▓			X
Obtain reference	▓		▓		▓		X	
Place order on hold	▓	X	▓		▓	X	X	
Refer to head	▓	X	▓		▓	X		
Send reminder	▓		▓	X	▓			

Question 7

Sales orders are processed and approved by a computer. Management has laid down the following conditions. Construct a decision table to reflect these procedures.

(a) If an order is between £10 and £100 a 3% discount is given, if the credit rating is good. If the customer has been buying from the company for over 5 years, the discount is increased to 4%.

(b) If an order is more than £100 a 5% discount is given, if the credit rating is good. If the customer has been buying from the company for over 5 years, the discount is increased to 6%.

(c) If the credit rating is not good in either case the order is referred to the supervisor.

(d) For all orders under £10, no discount is given.

Answer

There are five *conditions.*

(1) Is the order < £10?
(2) Is the order £10 - £100?
(3) Is the order > £100?
(4) Is the credit rating good?
(5) Has the customer been buying > 5 years?

Note that the 'cut-off' values must be precisely stated.

There are seven *actions:* approve, refer on, give one of 5 levels of discount.

32 rules are required (2^5). This results in the following table.

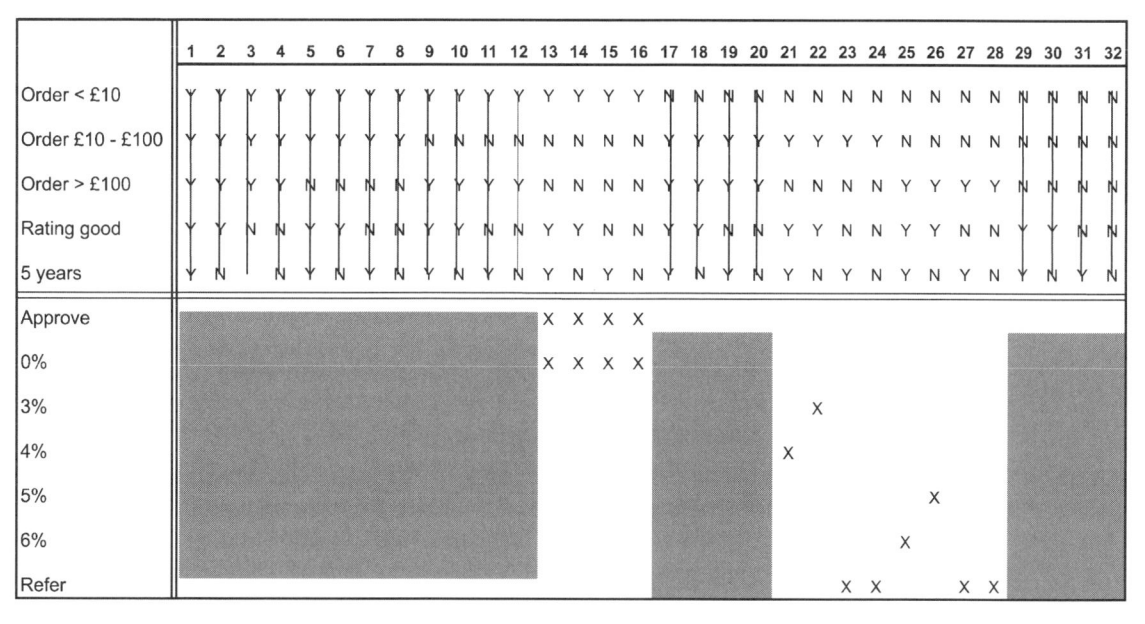

	1	2	3	4	5	6	7	8	9	10	11	12	13	14	15	16	17	18	19	20	21	22	23	24	25	26	27	28	29	30	31	32
Order < £10	Y	Y	Y	Y	Y	Y	Y	Y	Y	Y	Y	Y	Y	Y	Y	Y	N	N	N	N	N	N	N	N	N	N	N	N	N	N	N	N
Order £10 - £100	Y	Y	Y	Y	Y	Y	Y	Y	N	N	N	N	N	N	N	N	Y	Y	Y	Y	Y	Y	Y	Y	N	N	N	N	N	N	N	N
Order > £100	Y	Y	Y	Y	N	N	N	N	Y	Y	Y	Y	N	N	N	N	Y	Y	Y	Y	N	N	N	N	Y	Y	Y	Y	N	N	N	N
Rating good	Y	Y	N	N	Y	Y	N	N	Y	Y	N	N	Y	Y	N	N	Y	Y	N	N	Y	Y	N	N	Y	Y	N	N	Y	Y	N	N
5 years	Y	N	Y	N	Y	N	Y	N	Y	N	Y	N	Y	N	Y	N	Y	N	Y	N	Y	N	Y	N	Y	N	Y	N	Y	N	Y	N
Approve													X	X	X	X																
0%													X	X	X	X																
3%																					X											
4%																					X											
5%																									X							
6%																					X											
Refer																					X	X			X	X						

This means unwieldy construction (particularly in an examination). Condition 3 can be removed from the decision table. For example, if the answers to conditions 1 and 2 are NO then the answer to condition 3 must be YES, (unless there is an error) and so it need not be tested. In this way the decision table will be reduced to 16 rules.

	1	2	3	8	13	14	15	16	21	22	23	24	25	26	27	28
Order < £10	Y	Y	Y	Y	Y	Y	Y	Y	N	N	N	N	N	N	N	N
Order £10 - £100	Y	Y	Y	Y	N	N	N	N	Y	Y	Y	Y	N	N	N	N
Rating good	Y	Y	N	N	Y	Y	N	N	Y	Y	N	N	Y	Y	N	N
5 years	Y	N	Y	N	Y	N	Y	N	Y	N	Y	N	Y	N	Y	N
Approve					X	X	X	X								
0%					X	X	X	X								
3%											X					
4%									X							
5%														X		
6%											X					
Refer											X	X			X	X

Part B: Information technology and systems

In addition, the over 5 year condition is only relevant to orders for £10 or more, and so we need not test this condition when the order is below £10. This cuts the number of rules to 8.

Original rule no	21	22	23	24	25	26	27	28
Order < £10	N	N	N	N	N	N	N	N
Order £10-£100	Y	Y	Y	Y	N	N	N	N
Rating good	Y	Y	N	N	Y	Y	N	N
5 years	Y	N	Y	N	Y	N	Y	N
Approve								
0%								
3%		X						
4%	X							
5%						X		
6%					X			
Refer			X	X			X	X

Three points arise from the exercise.

(a) Orders under £10 are processed whether the credit rating is good or not. Although this results in lack of control over small orders, management may feel that the risk is justified by the savings made in processing time.

(b) After the first construction (the draft) the decision table should be redrawn to take into account:

  (i) The impossible combinations - these rules can be removed.

  (ii) Take rules which result in identical actions. These indicate which conditions need not be tested by the computer program, and highlight the order in which the conditions should be examined (to save processing time). In the example, rules 13/15 can be combined and it then becomes apparent that credit rating is immaterial if the order is less than £10; but if the credit rating is bad, it is immaterial whether the order is between £10 and £100, or over £100.

(c) For the customer > 5 years check, customers are given an extra 1% discount if they have been with the company over 5 years. Instead of 2 action entries, discount 4% and discount 6%, we can have a single action entry - add 1% to discount. The decision table could be refined still further.

Exam focus point
Decision tables are not referred to by name in the syllabus. However, the syllabus refers to 'the recording and documenting tools used during the analysis and design of systems'.

Data normalisation

KEY TERM
Normalisation is a step-by-step process in which a set of related data fields are refined into new sets having progressively simpler and more regular structure.

3.50 When thinking about how data should be organised in a computer system two features are particularly desirable.

(a) **Links** between items of data that are related, such as **customer name** and **customer address**, should be preserved.

(b) **Duplication** of data items should be avoided, for efficiency of design and processing, and to eliminate the possibility **inconsistencies** between examples of the same data stored in different places.

6: Feasibility, investigation, analysis and design

3.51 **Normalisation** describes the process undertaken to achieve a regular and efficient data structure.

Structured English

3.52 A 'structured narrative' is a systems design tool which describes the logic of a process in narrative form.

3.53 This method uses **English** as the language but **severely limits the available vocabulary** and tries to follow the layout and logical operation of a computer program.

3.54 This tool is best suited for describing **specific activities** or functions, while the broader and more general concerns of system design are typically analysed by using data flow diagrams and decision tables.

3.55 Structured English is more **like standard English** than normal programming languages and so is more user-friendly. It is concise and precise.

3.56 Structured English uses **keywords** (eg IF, ADD) which, by some conventions, are written in capitals and have a **precise logical meaning** in the context of the narrative.

3.57 **Disadvantages** of structured English are that it must be learned to be used effectively and that complex processes can be difficult to represent.

> **Exam focus point**
> The syllabus states you should be aware of the nature and purpose of normalisation and structured English – you will not be required to apply these techniques yourself. However, you should be able to explain how these techniques are used in systems analysis and design.

4 THE PROCESS OF ANALYSIS AND DESIGN

Investigation of the current environment

4.1 In this stage the current system is **investigated**, described and analysed using the techniques of observation, questionnaires, document description forms and so forth. Some of the work may have been done already during the **feasibility study**.

4.2 A major requirement of this phase is that the current system is properly documented in dataflow diagrams (DFDs) and the **logical data structure** is described to show the relationships between **entities** in the system and their **attributes** (eg an ERM).

4.3 One of the most important products of this stage is a detailed **problems/requirements** list.

   (a) **Problems** might relate, say, to the age of an existing system, and its compatibility with a proposed new system or with another business's systems.

   (b) **Requirements** may simply be the **solutions** to the problems identified in the current system, but could also imply a completely **new way** of doing things. For instance it may be decided that the existing system should be dispensed with entirely.

Business system options

4.4 The next stage is to discover **in detail** what data will have to be dealt with and what information is required as output.

4.5 There will normally be a number of possible solutions and those considered the best will be put forward to users as **Business System Options**. For each option on the shortlist there is drawn up a level-1 dataflow diagram, descriptions of the basic processes that transform data, a logical data structure, a cost/benefit analysis (in brief) and an assessment of the impact of the proposed system. Users are then asked to make a choice.

Requirements specification

4.6 This stage has several steps.

(a) Detailed dataflow diagrams etc are drawn up, and the **required** system matched with the **current** system to ensure that all necessary processing will be performed. The DFDs are modified by the solutions to the problems/requirements identified earlier.

(b) Specifications for **input** and **output** from the chosen system are prepared. These detail what appears on screen, or on documents. An input/output description of a **booking confirmation**, for instance, will list what should appear on the confirmation (customer number, name, address, date of confirmation, dates of stay, type of accommodation required and so on).

(c) Relational data analysis (**normalisation**) is performed on the input and output descriptions. This is to identify any entities that might not have been noticed, or drawn in enough detail, in the existing **logical data structure.** (Normalisation is a way of **analysing and simplifying the relationships** between items of data.)

(d) **Entity life histories** are drawn up, indicating what happens to each entity, ie what functions (processes) it is subjected to, and so forth.

Technical system options

4.7 The organisation will have to make choices concerning the means by which the system should be **implemented.**

4.8 There might be a number of ways of implementing a system physically. These can include:

(a) **Hardware configuration** (for example mainframe, mini, PC; centralised or distributed processing).

(b) **Software** (use of a database or a conventional file structure).

4.9 The technical system may need to be capable of **communicating** over quite a wide area and managing **Internet connections**.

4.10 **Performance objectives** for the system are then specified in detail so that these can be followed in the actual design of the system.

Logical design

4.11 Logical design refers to the design of data and file structures for the new system.

4.12 This stage includes the development of **output formats**, and specifying the type of **dialogue** that users will have with the system, to ensure that it is consistent with what has been prepared so far.

4.13 **Prototyping** may be used so that users can actually see what the system will look like and get a feel for how it will work.

Physical design

4.14 Physical design involves the following tasks.

(a) **Initial physical design** (obtaining the design rules from the chosen database, and applying them to the logical data design drawn up in the previous stages).

(b) Further define the **processing** required. For instance requirements for **audit, security and control** are considered, such as **controls over access** to the system; controls **incorporated within programs** (eg data validation, error handling); and **recovery procedures**, in case processing is interrupted.

(c) **Program specifications** are created. These provide in detail exactly what a particular program is supposed to achieve.

(d) Program specifications are assessed for their **performance** when implemented. For example, it should be possible to make some estimate of the times that some programs will take to run.

(e) **File and database specifications** are designed in detail

(f) **Operating instructions** are drawn up (user documentation). These will include such items as error correction and detailed instructions for operators and users (eg the sort of screen format that will appear).

Chapter roundup

- As with other major projects, systems implementation projects require skilled **project management** to achieve a successful implementation.

- The **feasibility study** is the first stage of a systems development project. The feasibility study is a formal study to decide what type of system can be developed which meets the needs of the organisation. There are three key areas in which a project must be feasible if it is to be selected. It must be justifiable on **technical, operational, social, ecological and financial** grounds.

- One of the most important elements of the feasibility study is the **cost-benefit analysis**. Costs may be analysed in different ways, but include equipment costs, installation costs, development costs, personnel costs and running costs. Benefits are usually more intangible, but include cost savings, revenue benefits and qualitative benefits.

- The **systems investigation** is a detailed **fact finding exercise** which involves investigating and recording the current system. Methods employed include the use of **interviews** and **questionnaires**. Care should be taken in planning how to carry out an investigation of this type, to ensure the most useful response.

- **Systems analysis** examines why **current methods** are used, what **alternatives** might achieve the same, or better, results, what **restricts the effectiveness** of the system and what **performance criteria** are required from a system.

- **Systems design** is a technical phase which addresses in particular **inputs, outputs, program design, dialogue design, file design and storage matters, and security**. The conclusion of this phase is a detailed specification of the new system.

- **Dataflow diagrams** are used to record the ways in which data is processed.

- An **entity relationship model** provides an understanding of a system's logical data requirements independently of the system's processes.

- An **entity life history** shows the processes that happen to an entity.

- A **decision table** may be used to define the logic of a process. Alternatively, the logic could be described using **structured English**.

- **Normalisation** describes the process by which data is standardised - allowing data to be used more efficiently.

Quick quiz

1 List three reasons why an organisation considering the implementation of a new information system should undertake a feasibility study.

  1 ....
  2 ....
  3 ....

2 What five areas should a feasibility study ensure a project is feasible in?

  1 ....
  2 ....
  3 ....
  4 ....
  5 ....

6: Feasibility, investigation, analysis and design

3   List four methods used in systems investigations.

   1   ....
   2   ....
   3   ....
   4   ....

4   What four symbols are used in data flow diagrams?

   1   ....
   2   ....
   3   ....
   4   ....

5   List the three types of relationship an Entity Relationship Model (ERM) may portray.

   1   ....
   2   ....
   3   ....

6   What three types of process logic may an Entity Life History (ELH) show?

   1   ....
   2   ....
   3   ....

7   Decision tables consist of four quadrants. Label the four quadrants below.

8   Distinguish between logical design and physical design.

Part B: Information technology and systems

Answers to quick quiz

1. A feasibility study should be undertaken when considering a new information system because new systems can:

    Be complicated and cost a great deal to develop.

    Be disruptive during development and implementation.

    Have far-reaching consequences in the way an organisation conducts its business or is structured.

2. Technical, Operational, Social, Ecological and Financial.

3. Questionnaires, interviews, observation and document review.

4. The following four symbols are used in data flow diagrams.

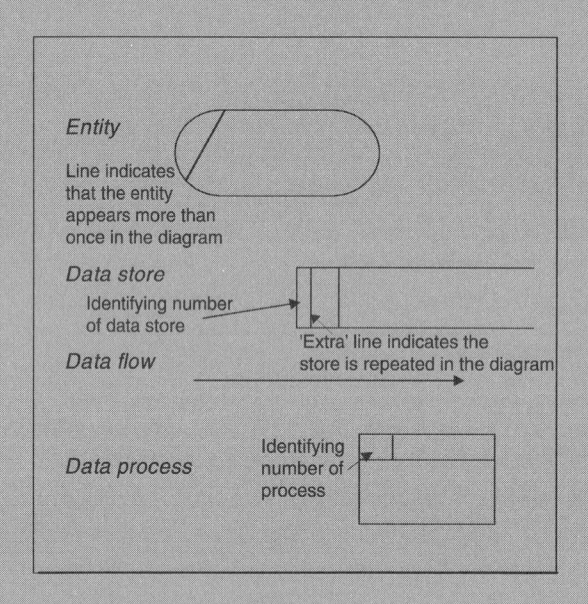

    Entity — Line indicates that the entity appears more than once in the diagram

    Data store — Identifying number of data store; 'Extra' line indicates the store is repeated in the diagram

    Data flow — →

    Data process — Identifying number of process

5. One-to-one, one-to-many and many-to-many.

6. Sequence, iteration, selection.

7.

Condition stub	Condition entry
Action stub	Action entry

8. Logical design is concerned with the nature of data or information viewed independently from the physical details of storage or output.

    Physical design involves the physical aspects of data storage and presentation.

    In general, the logical design is more relevant to the systems analyst while programmers will require details of physical design.

The material covered in this Chapter is tested in Question 11(a) in the Question Bank.

Chapter 7

IMPLEMENTATION, MAINTENANCE AND REVIEW

Topic list	Syllabus Reference	Ability Required
1 Installation	(ii)	Evaluation
2 Testing	(ii)	Evaluation
3 Training	(ii)	Evaluation
4 Documentation	(ii)	Evaluation
5 File conversion and changeover	(ii)	Evaluation
6 System maintenance	(ii)	Evaluation
7 Systems evaluation	(ii)	Evaluation
8 Systems performance	(ii)	Evaluation
9 Post-implementation review	(ii)	Evaluation

Introduction

Even if you have designed the best system in the world things can still go wrong when you actually try to put it in place. Implementation covers a **wide range of issues**, ranging from simple things like remembering that computers need desks to sit on and cables to link them up, to strategic issues like whether to change systems overnight or take a softly, softly approach.

Throughout its life, a system should operate effectively and efficiently. To do this, the system needs to be **maintained.** The last three sections look at **evaluation and review of systems.** This should be an ongoing process to ensure the system continues to meet requirements.

Learning outcomes covered in this chapter

- **Explain** the nature and purpose of systems maintenance and performance evaluation (*Also see Chapter 5*)
- **Identify** and **evaluate** the main issues relating to the development of an Information Systems solution, and the risks involved in implementation

Syllabus content covered in this chapter

- System testing (ie off-line, on-line and user-acceptance)
- Systems evaluation
- System documentation (ie user and technical manuals)
- Training and user support
- File conversion procedures
- System changeover methods (ie direct, parallel, pilot, phased)
- Maintenance of systems (ie corrective, adaptive, preventative)
- Performance and technical specification

Part B: Information technology and systems

1 INSTALLATION

1.1 The main stages in the implementation of a computer system once it has been designed are as follows.

(a) Installation of the **hardware and software.**
(b) **Testing.**
(c) **Staff training** and production of documentation.
(d) **Conversion** of files and database creation.
(e) **Changeover.**

1.2 The items in this list **do not** necessarily happen in a set **chronological order**, and some can be done at the same time - for example staff training and system testing can be part of the same operation.

1.3 The requirements for implementation **vary** from system to system.

Installation of equipment

1.4 Installing a **mainframe** computer or a large network is a major operation that is carried out by the manufacturer/supplier.

1.5 If just a few PCs are being installed in a small network, the customer may have to install the hardware.

1.6 Installing software used to be tedious and lengthy, taking perhaps half an hour for a package, but most new software is provided on CD-ROM and can be installed in minutes.

1.7 Software should be **registered** with the manufacturer, either by filling in a registration form and posting it or often by completing a form on screen and sending it in via the web.

Installation of a mainframe

1.8 If a mainframe installation is to be successful it must be carefully planned. The particular problems of planning a large installation include the following.

Site selection

1.9 The site selected for the main computer might be in an existing or a new building. Factors in the choice of site are the need for the following.

(a) Adequate **space** for computer and peripherals, including servicing room.
(b) **Room for expansion**.
(c) **Easy access** for computer equipment and supplies (it should be unnecessary to knock holes in outside walls, as has happened, in order to gain access for equipment).
(d) **Nearness** to principal **user** departments.
(e) Space available for a **library, stationery** store, and **systems maintenance** staff.
(f) **Security.** How easily can access to the site be controlled?

Site preparation

1.10 The site preparation may involve consideration of certain potential problems.

(a) **Air conditioning** (temperature, humidity and dust).
(b) Special **electricity supplies**.
(c) **Raised floor** (or **false ceiling**) so that **cables** may pass easily from one piece of equipment to another.
(d) **Fire protection devices.**
(e) **Furnishings.**

7: Implementation, maintenance and review

Standby equipment

1.11 Standby equipment should be arranged, to ensure **continuity of processing** in the event of power or computer failure. Such equipment may include standby **generators** and standby **computers**.

2 TESTING

2.1 A system must be thoroughly tested before implementation, otherwise there is a danger that the new system will **go live with faults** that might prove costly. The scope of tests and trials will again **vary with the size** of the system.

The 'V' model

2.2 The 'V' model shows the relationship between system development, testing and quality throughout a systems development project. An illustration of the V model follows. The 'V' refers to the two legs of the diagram - system design runs down the left leg of the V and testing runs up the right leg.

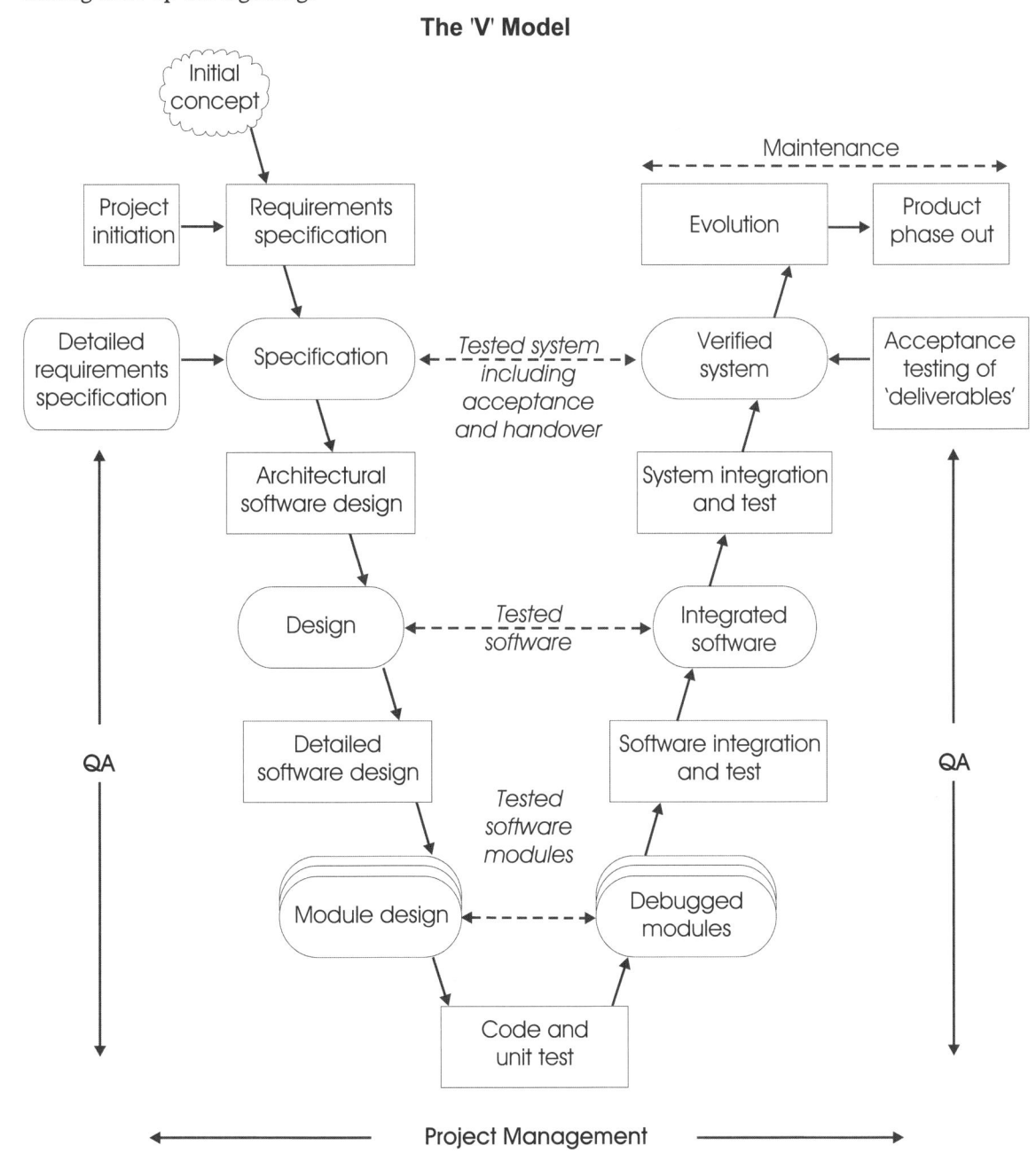

The 'V' Model

2.3 The left leg of the V shows the system development stages of analysis and design - including programming. The upward leg covers the assembly and testing phases and product delivery.

2.4 Four basic stages of testing can be identified: system logic, program testing, system testing and user acceptance testing.

Testing system logic

2.5 Before any programs are written, the logic devised by the systems analyst should be checked. This process would involve the use of flow charts or structure diagrams such as data flow diagrams.

2.6 The path of different types of data and transactions are manually plotted through the system, to ensure all possibilities have been catered for and that the processing logic is correct. When all results are as expected, programs can be written.

Program testing

2.7 Program testing involves processing test data through all programs. Test data should be of the type that the program will be required to process and should include invalid/exceptional items to test whether the program reacts as it should. Program testing should cover the following areas:

- Input validity checks
- Program logic and functioning
- Interfaces with related modules \ systems
- Output format and validity

2.8 The testing process should be fully documented - recording data used, expected results, actual results and action taken. This documentation may be referred to at a later date, for example if program modifications are required.

2.9 Two types of program testing are unit testing and unit integration testing.

Unit testing and unit integration testing

> **KEY TERM**
>
> **Unit testing** means testing one function or part of a program to ensure it operates as intended.
>
> **Unit integration testing** involves testing two or more software units to ensure they work together as intended. The output from unit integration testing is a debugged module.

2.10 Unit testing involves detailed testing of part of a program - refer back to the V model and you will see unit testing referred to at the lowest point of the V. If it is established during unit testing that a program is not operating as intended, the cause of the error must be established and corrected. Automated diagnostic routines, that step through the program line by line may be used to help this process.

2.11 Test cases should be developed that include test data (inputs), test procedures, expected results and evaluation criteria. Sets of data should be developed for both unit testing and

7: Implementation, maintenance and review

integration testing. Cases should be developed for all aspects of the software.

System testing

2.12 When it has been established that individual programs and interfaces are operating as intended, overall system testing should begin. System testing has a wider focus than program testing. System testing should extend beyond areas already tested, to cover:

- Input documentation and the practicalities of input eg time taken
- Flexibility of system to allow amendments to the 'normal' processing cycle
- Ability to produce information on time
- Ability to cope with peak system resource requirements eg transaction volumes, staffing levels
- Viability of operating procedures
- Ability to produce information on time

2.13 System testing will involve testing both before installation (known as off-line testing) and after implementation (on-line testing). As many problems as possible should be identified before implementation, but it is likely that some problems will only become apparent when the system goes live.

User acceptance testing

> **KEY TERM**
>
> **User acceptance testing** is carried out by those who will use the system to determine whether the system meets their needs. These needs should have previously been stated as acceptance criteria. The aim is for the customer to determine whether or not to accept the system.

2.14 It is vital that users are involved in system testing to ensure the system operates as intended when used in its operating environment. Any problems identified should be corrected - this will improve system efficiency and should also encourage users to accept the new system as an important tool to help them in their work.

2.15 Users process test data, system performance is closely monitored and users report how they felt the system meets their needs. Test data may include some historical data, because it is then possible to check results against the 'actual' output from the old system.

Methods of testing

2.16 In the previous section we looked at system testing in four chronological stages. In this section we explain in greater detail how testing is performed. The terms used to describe testing procedures in this section are not prescriptive or mutually exclusive - a variety of techniques may be used to test different aspects of the same system.

Static testing and dynamic testing

2.17 Software testing may be carried out in a static environment or a dynamic environment.

Part B: Information technology and systems

> **KEY TERMS**
>
> **Static testing** describes the process of evaluating a system or component based on its form, structure and content. The program or process is not executed or performed during static testing.
>
> **Dynamic testing** is testing that is performed by executing a program. It involves running the program and checking the results are as expected.

2.18 Both static and dynamic testing play an important role in software development. Static testing allows the program or part of program to be looked at in isolation - which means that other programs or parts of the system do not influence the test, and are not affected by the test. Many logical and coding errors are able to be found by simply checking and reviewing code.

2.19 However, it is only when actually running a program that some errors will be discovered. Dynamic testing will reveal any potential conflicts between the program and other elements of the system (hardware and software).

Test scripts and decision tables

2.20 A **test script** is a document that lists all tests that a new piece of software will be subjected to. It is likely that some tests from the script would be carried out by the programmer, and some by users. The script should include procedures for noting the results of the test, and for details of any suspected errors.

2.21 **Decision tables** (previously covered in Chapter 6) may be applied in the context of system testing.

2.22 EXAMPLE: DECISION TABLE AND SYSTEM TESTING

An accounts payable module includes a facility for entering invoices. A test script has been devised to ensure the checks built-in to the 'Value' field within the Invoice entry field are operating as intended. Possible actions to be taken depending on the results of testing have been laid out in a decision table, as shown below.

Invoice entry screen: value field testing	Rules															
	1	2	3	4	5	6	7	8	9	10	11	12	13	14	15	16
Numeric values only	Y	Y	Y	Y	Y	Y	Y	Y	N	N	N	N	N	N	N	N
Positive values only	Y	Y	Y	Y	N	N	N	N	Y	Y	Y	Y	N	N	N	N
Maximum value 999,999.99	Y	Y	N	N	Y	Y	N	N	Y	Y	N	N	Y	Y	N	N
Field must not be empty	Y	N	Y	N	Y	N	Y	N	Y	N	Y	N	Y	N	Y	N
Test passed	X															
Amend exit condition for Invoice entry screen		X		X		X		X		X		X		X		X
Amend field properties - maximum value			X	X			X	X			X	X			X	X
Amend field properties - minimum value					X	X	X	X					X	X	X	X
Amend field properties - numeric only									X	X	X	X	X	X	X	X

7: Implementation, maintenance and review

Performance testing

2.23 Tests can also be classified according to **what** they are testing – specifically performance and usability.

> **KEY TERM**
>
> **Performance testing** is conducted to evaluate the compliance of a system or component with specified performance requirements.

2.24 The specific performance requirements which performance testing uses will vary depending on the nature of the system. The initial specification for the software should provide suitable performance testing criteria.

2.25 As it is possible that the demands placed on the system and software may increase over time, it is useful to know what volume of transactions the system can cope with. Performance testing is therefore taken a 'step-further', to establish the volume of transactions or data the system can process before the software ceases to operate. This process is known as 'stress testing'.

Usability testing

> **KEY TERM**
>
> **Usability testing** is conducted to establish the relative ease with which users are able to learn and use a system.

2.26 Usability testing is vital as a system may look great on paper and perform well when tested by analysts and programmers, but prove inefficient when used by users in the required operating environment.

2.27 Usability testing has a slightly different emphasis than user acceptance testing. Usability testing is concerned with lessons that could be learned regarding system design, in order to produce a system that is easier to learn and use. It is possible to improve usability without actually changing system capabilities - by making something more user-friendly. User acceptance testing is more specific – its purpose is to establish whether users are satisfied that the system meets the system specification when used in the actual operating environment.

Automated testing tools

2.28 Software testing can be very time consuming – often accounting for 30 percent of software development effort and budget. The need for thorough testing to achieve a quality product often conflicts with the requirement to produce the system on time and within budget.

2.29 The need for more efficient testing has led to the development of automated software testing. Automated testing involves using computer programs that automatically run the software to be tested, and record the results.

Part B: Information technology and systems

2.30 Automated testing tools are sometimes referred to as **Computer Aided Software Testing** (**CAST**) tools. There are products available that can automate a variety of tasks, including:

- Executing various command combinations and recording the results
- Testing software in a variety of operating environments and comparing results
- The debugging of some 'obvious' programming errors
- Facilities to track and document all testing and quality assurance information

2.31 Automated testing routines may be written by the same organisation that is writing the software, or, a specialised software testing product could be used. The following illustration shows how a software error is recorded in the testing package produced by a prominent testing software provider - Rational.

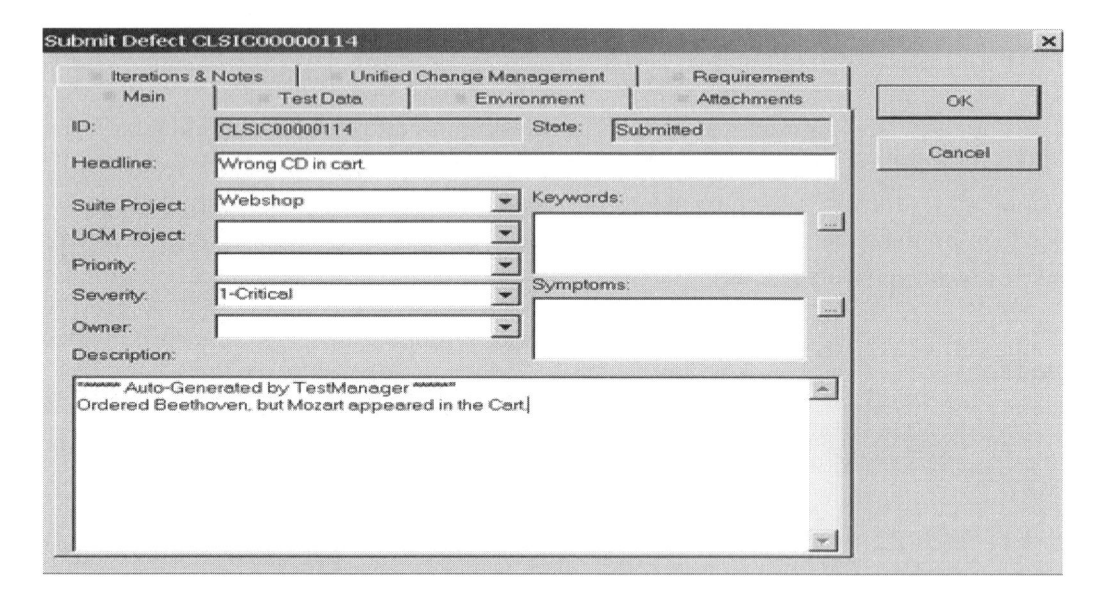

2.32 The facility provided by Rational to track software errors and testing is shown below.

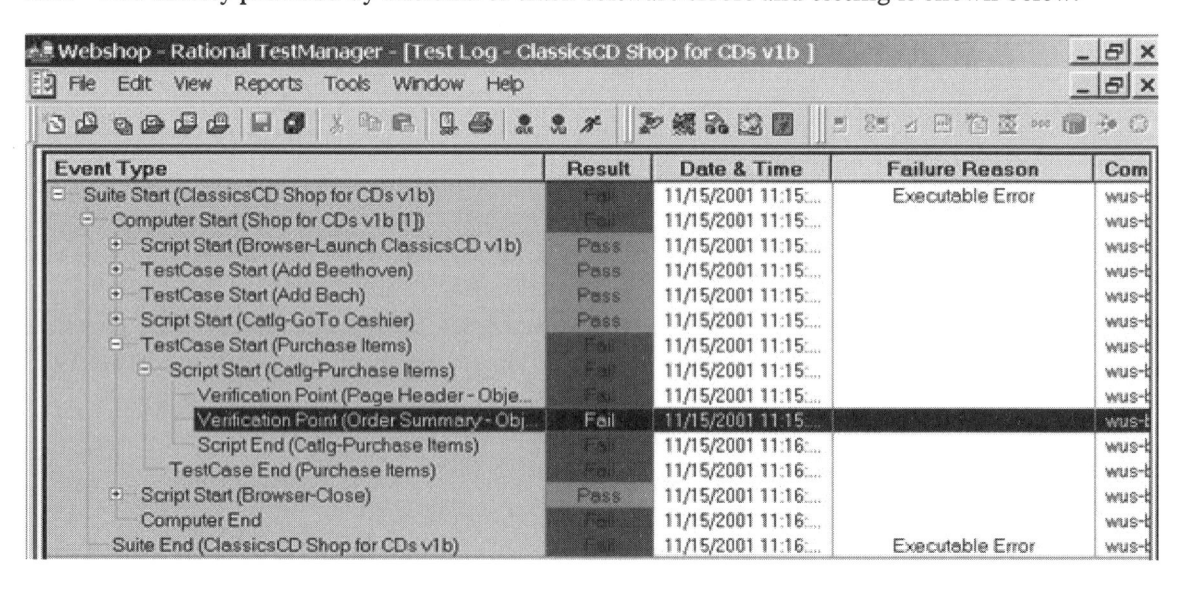

Beta versions

2.33 Commercial software producers often carry out user acceptance testing through the use of beta versions of software. A beta version is an almost finalised package, that has been tested in controlled conditions, but has not been used 'in the field'. Some users are prepared to use beta versions - and report any remaining bugs.

7: Implementation, maintenance and review

Developing a testing strategy

2.34 To ensure a coherent, effective approach to testing, a testing plan should be developed. This plan would normally form part of the overall software development quality plan.

2.35 A testing strategy should cover the following areas.

Testing strategy area	Comment
Strategy approach	A testing strategy should be formulated that details the approach that will be taken to testing, including the tests to be conducted and the testing tools/techniques that will be used.
Test plan	A test plan should be developed that states: • What will be tested • When it will be tested (sequence) • The test environment
Test design	The logic and reasoning behind the design of the tests should be explained.
Performing tests	Detailed procedures should be provided for all tests. This explanation should ensure tests are carried out consistently, even if different people carry out the tests.
Documentation	It must be clear how the results of tests are to be documented. This provides a record of errors, and a starting point for error correction procedures.
Re-testing	The re-test procedure should be explained. In many cases, after correction, all aspects of the software should be re-tested to ensure the corrections have not affected other aspects of the software.

2.36 The presence of 'bugs' or errors in the vast majority of software/systems demonstrates that even the most rigorous testing plan is unlikely to identify all errors. The limitations of software testing are outlined below.

Limitation	Comment
Poor testing process	The test plan may not cover all areas of system functionality. Testers may not be adequately trained. The testing process may not be adequately documented.
Inadequate time	Software and systems are inevitably produced under significant time pressures. Testing time is often 'squeezed' to compensate for project over-runs in other areas.
Future requirements not anticipated	The test data used may have been fine at the time of testing, but future demands may be outside the range of values tested. Testing should allow for future expansion of the system.
Inadequate test data	Test data should test 'positively' - checking that the software does what it should do, and test 'negatively' - that it doesn't do what it shouldn't. It is difficult to include the complete range of possible input errors in test data.
Software changes inadequately tested	System/software changes made as a result of testing findings or for other reasons may not be adequately tested as they were not in the original test plan.

Part B: Information technology and systems

3 TRAINING

3.1 Staff training in the use of information systems and information technology is essential if the return on investment in IS/IT is to be maximised.

3.2 Training is not simply an issue that affects operational staff. Training in information technology **affects all levels** in an organisation, from senior managers learning how to use an executive information system for example, to accounts clerks learning how to use an accounting package.

3.3 Training will be needed when:

- A new system is implemented
- An existing system is significantly changed
- Job specifications change
- New staff are recruited
- Skills have been forgotten

3.4 A **systematic approach** to training can be illustrated in a flowchart as follows.

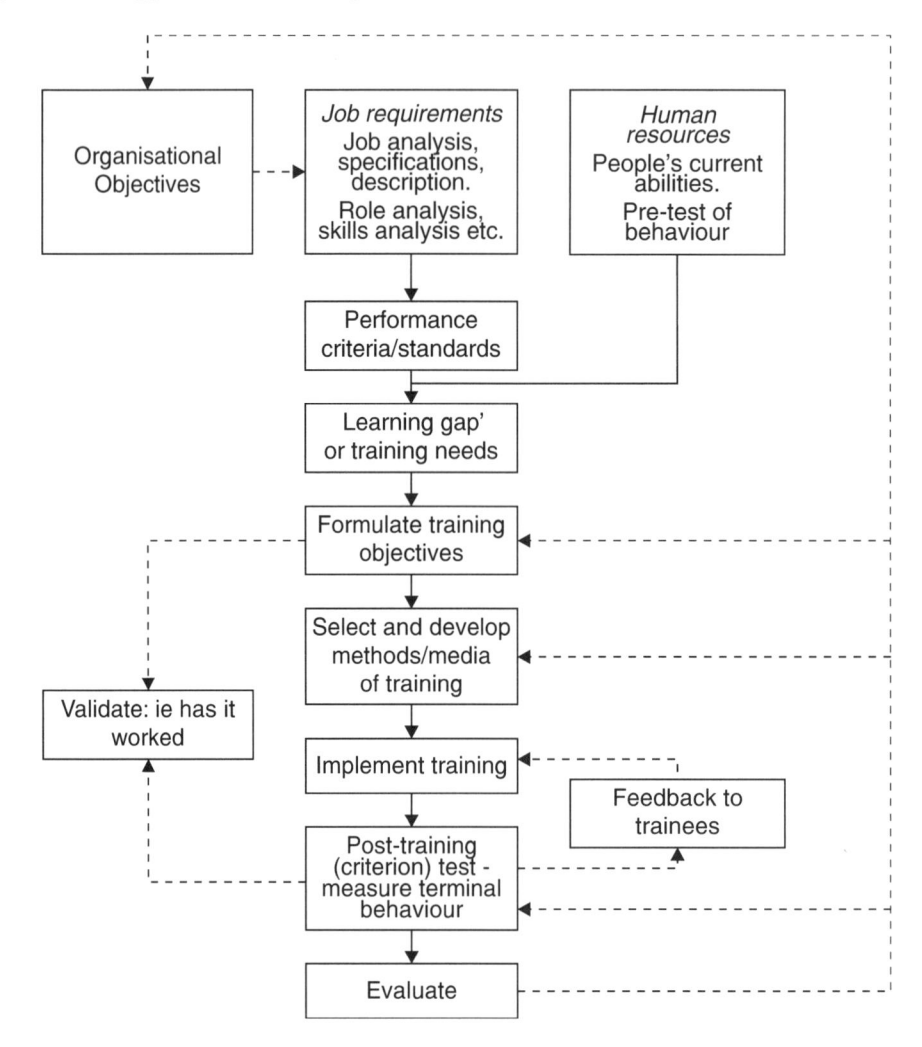

```
                    Organisational      Job requirements            Human
                    Objectives   -->    Job analysis,               resources
                                        specifications,             People's current
                                        description.                abilities.
                                        Role analysis,              Pre-test of
                                        skills analysis etc.        behaviour
                                              |                         |
                                              v                         |
                                        Performance      <--------------'
                                        criteria/standards
                                              |
                                              v
                                        Learning gap'
                                        or training needs
                                              |
                                              v
                                        Formulate training
                                        objectives
                                              |
                                              v
                                        Select and develop
                                        methods/media
                                        of training
                                              |
                    Validate: ie has it       v
                    worked                Implement training
                                              |              Feedback to
                                              v              trainees
                                        Post-training
                                        (criterion) test -
                                        measure terminal
                                        behaviour
                                              |
                                              v
                                        Evaluate
```

3.5 Note the following points in particular.

(a) Training is provided primarily to help the **organisation** achieve its **objectives**.
(b) An individual's **training need** is generally defined as follows.

7: Implementation, maintenance and review

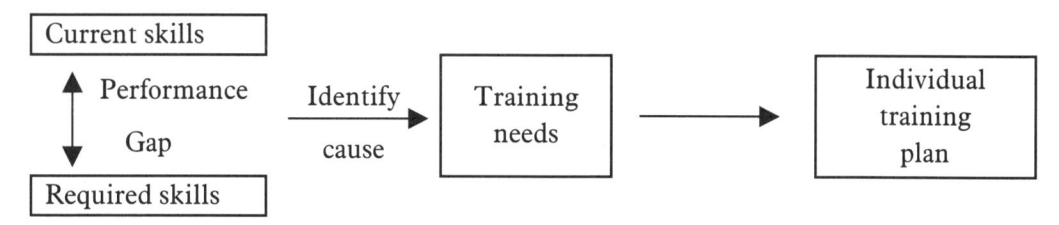

```
Current skills
    ↕ Performance      Identify      Training              Individual
      Gap              cause    →    needs      →          training
Required skills                                             plan
```

(c) Training should be **evaluated** to make sure that it has worked. If not the method may have been wrong. Whatever the cause, the training need still exists.

Senior management training

3.6 Senior manager are most likely to require training in the use of Executive Support Systems and Decision Support Systems (including spreadsheets).

3.7 Senior managers may also require an awareness of information technology in general, and project management skills to enable them to manage the acquisition and use of IS/IT within the organisation.

3.8 Training relevant to the management of information systems should therefore form part of a managers development plan.

Middle managers/supervisors training requirements

3.9 Staff operating at this level are likely to require a range of computing skills. They should be able to extract the information they require from various elements of the Management Information System.

3.10 Staff at this level should also be competent using 'office' type software (eg word-processing, spreadsheets, databases).

Operational staff

3.11 Operational staff are most likely to be involved in processing transactions. This could involve the use of bar-code readers (eg supermarket checkout operators), or keying into a transaction processing system.

3.12 Training should focus on the specific tasks the user is required to perform eg entering an invoice or answering a query.

3.13 There are a range of options available to deliver training.

Training method	Comment
Individual tuition 'at desk'	A trainer could work with an employee observing how they use a system and suggesting possible alternatives
Classroom course	The software could be used in a classroom environment, using 'dummy' data.
Computer-based training (CBT)	Training can be provided using CDs, or via an interactive website.
Case studies and exercises	Regardless of how training is delivered, it is likely that material will be based around a realistic case study relevant to the user.
Software reference material	Users may find on-line help, built-in tutorials and reference manuals useful.

Part B: Information technology and systems

3.14 The training method applicable in a given situation will depend on the following factors:

- Time available
- Software complexity
- User skill levels
- Facilities available
- Budget

4 DOCUMENTATION

> **KEY TERM**
>
> **Documentation** includes a wide range of technical and non-technical books, manuals, descriptions and diagrams relating to the design, use and operation of a computer system. Examples include user manuals, hardware and operating software manuals, system specifications and program documentation.

Technical manual

4.1 The technical manual is produced as a reference tool for those involved in producing and installing the system. The technical manual should include the following.

- Contact details for the original developers
- System overview
- System specifications including performance details
- Hardware technical specification
- System objectives
- Flowcharts or Data Flow Diagrams
- Entity models and life histories
- Individual program specifications
- Data dictionary

4.2 The technical manual should be referred to when future modifications are made to the system. The technical manual should be updated whenever system changes are made.

User manual

4.3 The system should be documented from the point-of-view of **users**. User documentation is used to **explain** the system to users and in training. It provides a **point of reference** should the user have problems with the system. Much of this information **may be available on-line** using context-sensitive help eg 'Push F1 for help'.

4.4 The manual provides full documentation of the **operational procedures** necessary for the 'hands-on' running of the system. Amongst the matters to be covered by this documentation would be the following.

(a) **Systems set-up procedures.** Full details should be given for each application of the necessary file handling and stationery requirements etc.

(b) **Security procedures.** Particular stress should be placed on the need for checking that proper authorisation has been given for processing operations and the need to restrict use of machine(s) to authorised operators.

7: Implementation, maintenance and review

(c) **Reconstruction control procedures**. Precise instructions should be given in relation to matters such as back-up and recovery procedures to be adopted in the event of a systems failure.

(d) **System messages**. A listing of all messages likely to appear on the operator's screen should be given together with an indication of the responses which they should evoke.

(e) Samples, including input screens and reports.

4.5 When a system is developed in-house, the user documentation might be written by a systems analyst. However, it might be considered preferable for the user documentation to have some input from **users.** As user-documentation is intended to help users, it must be written in a way that users are able to understand. The aim is to **ensure the smooth operation of the system,** not to turn users into analysts.

4.6 As with the technical manual, the content of the user manual must be updated to reflect any system changes.

5 FILE CONVERSION AND CHANGEOVER

> **KEY TERM**
>
> **File conversion**, means converting **existing files** into a format suitable for the new system.

5.1 Most computer systems are based around files containing data. When a new system is introduced, files must be created that conform to the requirements of that system.

5.2 The various scenarios that file conversion could involve are outlined in the following table.

Existing data	Comment
Held in manual (ie paper) files	Data must be entered manually into the new system – probably via the use of input forms, so that data entry operators have all the data they require in one document. This is likely to be a time-consuming process.
Held in existing computer files	How complex the process is in converting the files to a format compatible with the new system will depend on various technical issues such as whether coding systems are changing. It may be possible to automate much of the conversion process.
Held in both manual and computer files	Two separate conversion procedures are required
Existing data is incomplete	If the missing data is crucial, it must be researched and made available in a format suitable for the new-system – or suitable for the file conversion process.

5.3 The file conversion process is shown in the following diagram, which assumes the original data is held in manual files.

Part B: Information technology and systems

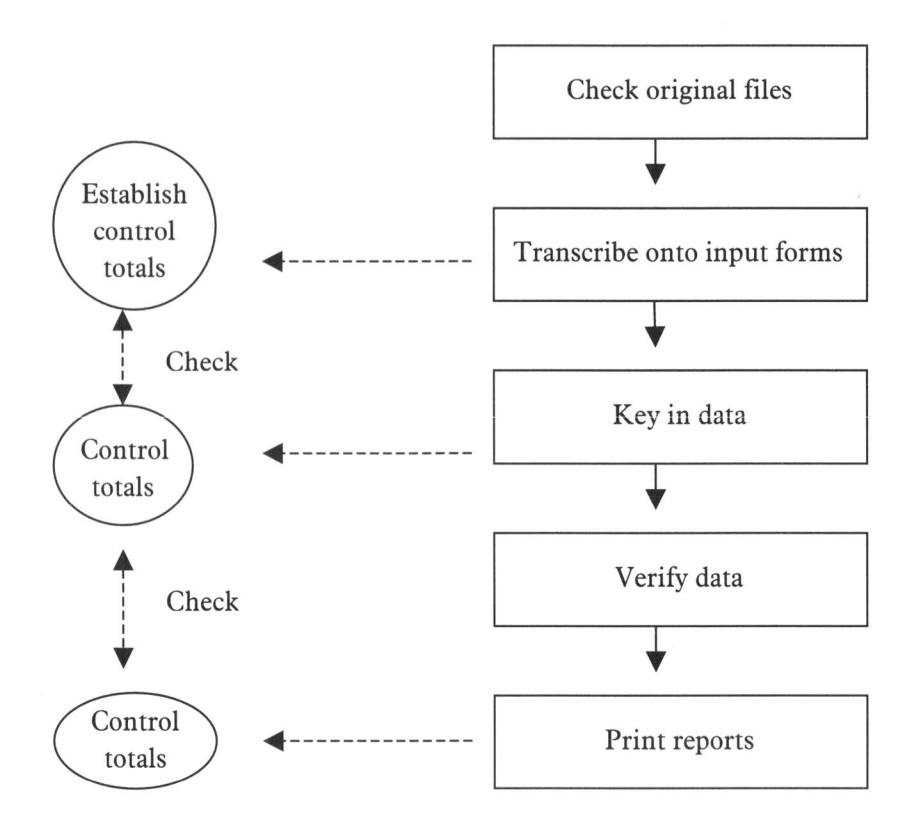

```
Check original files
        ↓
Transcribe onto input forms  ←------  Establish control totals
        ↓                                      ↕ Check
Key in data                  ←------  Control totals
        ↓                                      ↕ Check
Verify data
        ↓
Print reports                ←------  Control totals
```

- Ensure data is complete
- Remove redundant records
- Input forms should be in the same format as data entry screens
- Validation and verification checks should be built-in to the system
- These provide a standing record of the 'starting point' for the new system

5.4 It is essential that the 'new' converted files are accurate. Various controls can be utilised during the conversion process.

(a) **One-to-one checking** between records on the old and new systems.

(b) **Sample checking**. Selecting and checking a sample of records, as there are too many to check individually.

(c) **Built-in data validation** routines in automated conversion processes.

(d) **Control totals** and **reconciliations**. These checks could include checking the total number of records, and the value of transactions.

Question 1

You have been asked to transfer 400 Sales Ledger manual record cards to a PC-based system. The program menu has a 'record create' option. Explain how you would set about this process, and the steps you would take to ensure that the task was completed successfully.

Answer

The steps that should be taken are as follows.

(a) Check the manual records, and remove any dead accounts.

(b) Assign account codes to each record, ideally with codes that incorporate a check digit.

(c) If necessary transcribe the data from the card records to documents which can be used for data input.

(d) Add up the number of accounts and the total value of account balances as control totals (perhaps using a spreadsheet).

7: Implementation, maintenance and review

(e) Select the 'record create' option from the program menu and key the standing data and current data onto the new computer file. This should ideally be done at a quiet time, perhaps over a weekend.

(f) Input that is rejected by a data validation check should be re-keyed correctly.

(g) A listing of the records input should be printed out. This listing should be checked for errors, ideally by someone who did not do the keying in. Errors should be reported, and corrected data keyed in to amend the data on file.

(h) The program should produce control totals of the number of records put on to the file, and the total value of account balances. These control totals should be checked against the pre-prepared control totals. Discrepancies should be investigated, and any errors or omissions put right.

(i) A back-up copy of the new file should be made.

(j) The file and the new system should then be ready for use.

5.5 Once the new system has been fully and satisfactorily tested the changeover can be made. This may be according to one of four approaches.

- Direct changeover
- Parallel running
- Pilot operation
- Phased or 'staged' changeover

Direct changeover

5.6 The old system is **completely replaced** by the new system **in one move**.

5.7 This may be unavoidable where the two systems are substantially different, or where the costs of parallel running are too great.

5.8 While this method is comparatively **cheap** it is **risky** (system or program corrections are difficult while the system has to remain operational).

5.9 The new system should be introduced during **a quiet period**, for example over a bank holiday weekend or during an office closure.

Parallel running

5.10 The **old and new** systems are **run in parallel** for a period of time, both processing current data and enabling cross checking to be made.

5.11 This method provides a **degree of safety** should there be problems with the new system. However, if there are differences between the two systems cross-checking may be difficult or impossible.

5.12 There is a **delay** in the actual implementation of the new system, a possible indication of **lack of confidence,** and a need for **more staff** to cope with both systems running in parallel.

5.13 This cautious approach, if adopted, should be properly planned, and the plan should include:

(a) A firm **time limit** on parallel running.

(b) Details of **which data** should be **cross-checked**.

(c) Instructions on how **errors** are to be dealt with eg previously undiscovered errors in the old system.

Part B: Information technology and systems

(d) Instructions on how to report and act on any **major problems** in the new system.

Pilot operation

5.14 Pilot operation involves selecting part or parts of an organisation (eg a department or branch) to operate running the new system in parallel with the existing system. When the branch or department piloting the system is satisfied with the new system, they cease to use the old system. The new system is then piloted in another area of the organisation.

5.15 Pilot operation is **cheaper** and **easier to control** than running the whole system in parallel, and provides a **greater degree of safety** than does a direct changeover.

Phased changeover

5.16 Phased changeover involves selecting a complete section of the system for a direct changeover, eg in an accounting system the purchase ledger. When this part is running satisfactorily, another part is switched – until eventually the whole system has been changed.

5.17 A phased series of direct changeovers is less risky than a single direct changeover, as any problems and disruption experienced should be isolated in an area of operations.

5.18 The relative advantages and disadvantages of the various changeover methods are outlined in the following table.

Method	Advantages	Disadvantages
Direct changeover	Quick Minimal cost Minimises workload	Risky Could disrupt operations If fails, will be costly
Parallel running	Safe, built-in safety Provides way of verifying results of new system	Costly-two systems need to be operated Time-consuming Additional workload
Pilot operation	Less risky than direct changeover Less costly than complete parallel running	Can take a long time to achieve total changeover Not as safe as complete parallel running
Phased changeover	Less risky than a single direct changeover Any problems should be in one area – other operations unaffected	Can take a long time to achieve total changeover Interfaces between parts of the system may make this impractical

6 SYSTEM MAINTENANCE

Types of maintenance

6.1 There are three types of maintenance activity.

- Corrective
- Perfective
- Adaptive

> **KEY TERMS**
>
> **Corrective maintenance** is carried out when there is a systems failure of some kind, for example in processing or in an implementation procedure. Its objective is to ensure that systems remain operational.
>
> **Perfective maintenance** is carried out in order to perfect the software, or to improve software so that the processing inefficiencies are eliminated and performance is enhanced.
>
> **Adaptive maintenance** is carried out to take account of anticipated changes in the processing environment. For example new taxation legislation might require change to be made to payroll software.

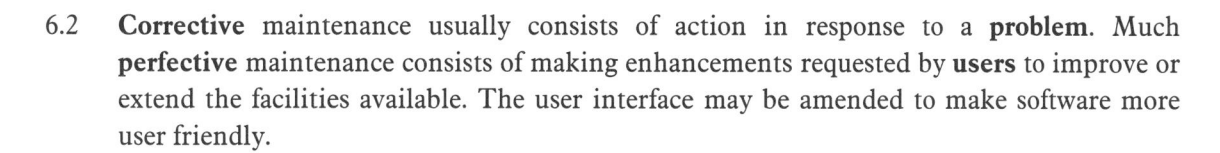

6.2 **Corrective** maintenance usually consists of action in response to a **problem**. Much **perfective** maintenance consists of making enhancements requested by **users** to improve or extend the facilities available. The user interface may be amended to make software more user friendly.

6.3 The key features of system maintenance ought to be **flexibility** and **adaptability**.

(a) The system, perhaps with minor modifications, should cope with changes in the computer user's procedures or volume of business.

(b) The computer user should benefit from advances in computer hardware technology without having to switch to another system altogether.

The causes of system maintenance

6.4 Besides environmental changes, three factors contribute to the need for maintenance.

Factor	Comment
Errors	However carefully and diligently the systems development staff carry out systems testing and program testing, it is likely that **bugs** will exist in a newly implemented system. Most should be identified during the first few runs of a system. The effect of errors can obviously vary enormously.
Changes in requirements	Although users should be consulted at all stages of systems development, problems may arise after a system is implemented because users may have found it difficult to express their requirements, or may have been concerned about the future of their jobs and not participated fully in development.

Part B: Information technology and systems

Factor	Comment
	Cost constraints may have meant that certain requested features were not incorporated. Time constraints may have meant that requirements suggested during development were ignored in the interest of prompt completion.
Poor documentation	If old systems are accompanied by poor documentation, or even a complete lack of documentation, it may be very difficult to understand their programs. It will be hard to update or maintain such programs. Programmers may opt instead to patch up the system with new applications using newer technology.

The systems maintenance lifecycle

6.5 Corrective and adaptive maintenance should be carried out **as and when** problems occur, but perfective maintenance may be carried out on a more scheduled system-by-system basis.

6.6 If maintenance requires major changes to software, this should involve all the tasks, processes and consultation involved in new system development.

6.7 Systems should have a certain amount of flexibility built-in, so that the system can be adapted to meet future demands. Changing a system carries the risks associated with systems development. Any proposed change should pass through a formal change procedure.

Components of a formal system change procedure	
Purpose of the component	Comment
Raise the change request	This is a definition of the required change in business functionality. It is usually specified in business terms. For example, 'the ability to support three regions rather than one'. The reason for the required change should be specified, with business benefits defined and quantified.
Evaluate the impact of the requested change	The change is investigated and the time and cost taken to develop, test and implement the change is estimated. This time and cost must take into account the total impact of the change on the system. The cost of the change is compared with the benefits that it will bring (defined in the previous stage) and if the decision is taken to proceed, then a priority is allocated to the change.
Specify the change request	A detailed specification for the change is prepared by the systems developer. This detailed specification must be developed in consultation with, and subsequently signed off by, user representatives.
Program and unit testing the change	Programmers write the program code, and then unit testing is carried out.
Regression, system and acceptance testing	Following unit testing, the amended program is tested in a realistic environment. (Regression testing is explained later in this section.)

7: Implementation, maintenance and review

Purpose of the component	Comment
Implement the change	Following user acceptance testing, the changes are implemented on the live system.

In-house maintenance

6.8 With **large computer systems**, developed by the organisation itself, **in-house** systems analysts and programmers might be given the responsibility for **software** maintenance.

6.9 To ensure that maintenance is carried out efficiently, the principles of **good programming practice** should be applied.

(a) Any change must be **properly authorised** by a manager in the user department (or someone even more senior, if necessary).

(b) The new program requirements must be **specified in full and in writing**. These specifications will be prepared by a systems analyst. A programmer should use these specifications to produce an amended version of the program.

(c) In developing a new program version, a programmer should keep **working papers**. He or she can refer back to these papers later to check in the event that there is an error in the new program or the user of the program asks for a further change in the program.

(d) The new program version should be **tested** when it has been written. A programmer should prepare test data and establish whether the program will process the data according to the specifications given by the systems analyst.

(e) **Provisions** should be made for **further program amendments** in the future. One way of doing this is to leave space in the program instruction numbering sequence for new instructions to be inserted later. For example, instructions might be numbered 10,20,30,40 etc instead of 1,2,3,4.

(f) A **record** should be kept of **all program errors** that are found during 'live' processing and of the corrections that are made to the program.

(g) Each **version** of a program (versions that are produced with processing modifications or corrections to errors) should be **separately identified**, to avoid a mix-up about what version of a program should be used for 'live' operating.

6.10 A problem with systems development and maintenance is that it is **hard to predict all the effects of a change** to the system.

6.11 A 'simple' software change in one area of the system may have unpredicted effects elsewhere. It is important therefore to carry out **regression testing**.

KEY TERM

Regression testing involves the retesting of software that has been modified to fix 'bugs'. It aims to ensure that the bugs have been fixed **and** that no other previously working functions have failed as a result of the changes.

6.12 Regression testing involves **repeating system tests** that had been executed correctly before the recent changes were made.

Part B: Information technology and systems

6.13 Only the changes expected as a result of the system maintenance should occur under the regression test – other changes could be due to errors caused by the recent change.

6.14 Problems with regression testing include:
- Deciding on the extent of testing required
- Envisaging all areas possibly affected
- Convincing users and programmers that the tests are necessary

Purchased software maintenance

6.15 With **purchased software** (whether off-the-shelf or bespoke), the **software house** or **supplier** is likely to provide details of any new versions of the software as they are produced, simply for marketing purposes.

Maintenance contracts

6.16 There is also likely to be an agreement between the supplier of software and the customer for the provision of a software support service. A maintenance contract typically includes the following services.

(a) **Help**

When a customer runs into difficulties operating the system, help is usually offered via a telephone help line. If a telephone call does not resolve the problem, arrangements may be made for a software analyst to visit the customer's premises (within a period of time agreed in the contract), although this would be rare for standard packages.

(b) **Information**

Extra information about using the package may be provided through factsheets or a magazine sent free to subscribers. This may include case studies showing how other users have benefited from using the package in a particular way and technical tips for common user problems

(c) **Updates**

Fixes for significant 'bugs' should be provided at no additional cost. Licensed users may also receive free upgrades if changes in the environment require a change to the software. For example, payroll software must be changed to reflect changes in taxation rates.

(d) **Upgrades**

If a significantly revised package is released, licensed users of the existing package are often able to upgrade at a discounted price. Upgrades usually include new features not found in the previous versions or updates.

(e) **Legal conditions**

Common terms include the duration of the contract, the circumstances in which the contract terminates, obligations relating to how the software is used and provisions relating to unauthorised copying of the software. A term attempting to limit the liability of the software supplier (exclusion clause) is common.

Hardware maintenance

6.17 Provision must also be made to ensure computer hardware is maintained. A hardware maintenance contract should specify service response times in the event of a breakdown,

7: Implementation, maintenance and review

and include provision for temporary replacement equipment if necessary. Maintenance services may be provided by the computer manufacturers or suppliers, or by a third-party maintenance company.

7 SYSTEMS EVALUATION

7.1 A system should be **reviewed** after implementation, and periodically, so that any unforeseen problems may be solved and to confirm that it is achieving the desired results.

7.2 The system should have been designed with clear, specified **objectives**, and justification in terms of **cost-benefit analysis** or other **performance criteria**.

7.3 Just as the feasibility of a project is assessed by reference to **technical, operational, social and economic factors**, so the same criteria can be used for evaluation. We need not repeat material that you have covered earlier, but here are a few pointers.

Cost-benefit review

7.4 A cost-benefit review is similar to a cost-benefit analysis, except that **actual** data can be used.

7.5 For instance when a large project is completed, techniques such as **DCF appraisal** can be performed **again**, with actual figures being available for much of the expenditure.

Question 2

A cost-benefit review might categorise items under the five headings of direct benefits, indirect benefits, development costs, implementation costs and running costs.

Give two examples of items which could fall to be evaluated under each heading.

Answer

Direct benefits might include reduced operating costs, for example lower overtime payments.

Indirect benefits might include better decision-making and the freeing of human 'brainpower' from routine tasks so that it can be used for more creative work.

Development costs include systems analysts' costs and the cost of time spent by users in assisting with fact-finding.

Implementation costs would include costs of site preparation and costs of training.

Running costs include maintenance costs, software leasing costs and on-going user support.

Efficiency and effectiveness

7.6 In any evaluation of a system, two terms recur. Two key reasons for the introduction of information systems into an organisation are to improve the **efficiency** or the **effectiveness** of the organisation.

Part B: Information technology and systems

> **KEY TERM**
>
> **Efficiency** can be measured by considering the resource **inputs** into, and the **outputs** from, a process or an activity.

7.7 An activity uses **resources** such as staff, money and materials. If the same activity can be performed using **fewer resources**, for example fewer staff or less money, or if it can be completed **more quickly**, the efficiency of the activity is improved. An improvement in efficiency represents an improvement in **productivity**.

7.8 Automation of an organisation's activities is usually expected to lead to greater efficiency in a number of areas.

   (a) The **cost** of a computer system is lower than that of the manual system it replaces, principally because jobs previously performed by human operators are now carried out by computer.

   (b) The **accuracy** of data information and processing is improved, because a computer does not make mistakes.

   (c) The **speed** of processing is improved. Response times, for example in satisfying customer orders, are improved.

> **KEY TERM**
>
> **Effectiveness** is a measurement of how well the organisation is achieving its **objectives**.

7.9 Effectiveness is a **more subjective** concept than efficiency, as it is concerned with factors which are less easy to measure. It focuses primarily on the relationship of the organisation with its environment. For example, automation might be pursued because it is expected that the company will be more effective at **increasing market share** or at satisfying **customer needs**.

7.10 Computing was originally concerned with the automation of **'back office'** functions, usually aspects of data processing. Development was concerned with improving **efficiency**.

7.11 Recent trends are more towards the development of **'front office'** systems, for example to improve an organisation's decision-making capability or to seek competitive advantage. This approach seeks to improve the **effectiveness** of the organisation.

Metrics

> **KEY TERM**
>
> **Metrics** are quantified measurements used to measure system performance.

7.12 The use of metrics enables some aspects of **system quality** to be **measured**. Metrics may also allow the early identification of problems - for example, by highlighting instances of system failure, the causes of which may then be investigated.

7.13 **Examples** of metrics include system response time, the number of transactions that can be processed per minute, the number of bugs per hundred lines of code and the number of system crashes per week.

7.14 Metrics should be devised that suit the system in question – those given above are simply typical examples.

7.15 Many facets of system quality are not easy to measure statistically (eg user-friendliness). Indirect measurements such as the number of calls to the help-desk per month can be used as an indication of overall quality/performance.

7.16 Metrics should be carefully thought out, objective and **stated clearly**. They must measure significant aspects of the system, be used consistently and agreed with users.

Computer based monitoring

7.17 Computers themselves can be used in systems evaluation. Three methods used are hardware monitors, software monitors and systems logs.

Hardware monitors

7.18 Hardware monitors are devices which measure the presence or absence of electrical signals in selected circuits in the computer hardware. Monitors measure factors such as idle time and CPU levels of activity. These findings are then analysed by specialised software.

7.19 Findings could include, for example, inefficient co-ordination of processors and peripherals or uneven workloads between different processors.

Software monitors

7.20 Software monitors are computer programs which monitor and record data related to the software application currently in use. They might identify, for example, excessive waiting time during program execution. Unlike hardware monitors, they may slow down the operation of the program being monitored.

Systems logs

7.21 Many computer systems provide automatic log details, for example job start and finish times or which employee has used which program and for how long. The systems log can therefore provide useful data for analysis.

(a) Unexplained variations in job running times might be recorded.
(b) Excessive machine down-time is sometimes a problem.
(c) Mixed workloads of large and small jobs might be scheduled inefficiently.

8 SYSTEMS PERFORMANCE

Performance measurement

8.1 It is not possible to identify and isolate every consequence of using a specific information system. To achieve some approximation to a complete evaluation, therefore, certain **indirect measures** must be used.

(a) Some measure of impact can be obtained by observing the **significant tasks** that a system is used for.

For example, procedures manuals held on an intranet should be more easily accessible than their paper equivalents. Increased reference to these documents should, logically, result in greater adherence to organisation policies and procedures.

(b) The **willingness** of users **to pay** might give an indication of value.

Charge-out mechanisms may provide an indication of how much users would be prepared to pay in order to gain the benefit of a certain upgrade, for example the availability of a particular report.

(c) **Systems logs** may give an indication of the value of the system if it is a 'voluntary use' system, such as an external database.

(d) **User information satisfaction** is a concept which attempts to find out, by asking users, how they rate their satisfaction with a system. They may be asked for their views on timeliness, quality of output, response times, processing and their overall confidence in the system.

(e) The adequacy of system **documentation** may be measurable in terms of how often manuals are actually used and the number of errors found or amendments made. However, low usage of a user manual, for instance, may mean either that the manual is unclear or that the system is easy to operate.

Question 3

Operational evaluation should consider, among other issues, whether input data is properly provided and output is useful. Output documents are often produced simply because 'we always print it'.

How might you identify whether a report is being used?

Answer

You could simply ask recipients if they would object to the report being withdrawn.

A questionnaire could be circulated asking what each recipient of the report does with it and assess its importance.

A charge-out system could be implemented - this would be a strong incentive to cancel requests for unnecessary output.

8.2 **Performance reviews** will vary in content from organisation to organisation, but the matters which will probably be looked at are as follows.

(a) The **growth** rates in file sizes and the number of transactions processed by the system. Trends should be analysed and projected to assess whether there are likely to be problems with lengthy processing time or an inefficient file structure due to the volume of processing.

(b) The **staffing** requirements of the system, and whether they are more or less than anticipated.

7: Implementation, maintenance and review

(c) The identification of any **delays** in processing and an assessment of the consequences of any such delays.

(d) An assessment of the efficiency of **security** procedures, in terms of number of breaches, number of viruses encountered.

(e) A check of the **error rates** for input data. High error rates may indicate inefficient preparation of input documents, an inappropriate method of data capture or poor design of input media.

(f) An examination of whether **output** from the computer is being used to good purpose. (Is it used? Is it timely? Does it go to the right people?)

(g) Operational **running costs**, examined to discover any inefficient programs or processes. This examination may reveal excessive costs for certain items although in total, costs may be acceptable.

Improving performance

8.3 **Computer systems efficiency audits** are concerned with improving **outputs** from the system and their use and/or reducing the costs of system **inputs**. With falling costs of computer hardware and software, and continual technological advances, there should often be **scope for improvements** in computer systems.

Outputs from a computer system

8.4 With regard to outputs, the efficiency of a computer system would be enhanced in any of the following ways.

(a) **More outputs** of some value could be produced by the **same input** resources.

For example:

(i) If the system could process **more transactions** per minute.

(ii) If the system could produce **better quality management information** (eg sensitivity analysis).

(iii) If the system could make information **available to more people**.

(b) **Outputs of little value** could be **eliminated** from the system, thus making savings in the cost of inputs, processing and handling.

For example:

(i) If reports are produced **too frequently**, should they be produced less often?
(ii) If reports are **distributed too widely**, should the distribution list be shortened?
(iii) If reports are **too bulky**, can they be reduced in size?

(c) The **timing** of outputs could be better.

Information should be available in good time for the information-user to be able to make good use of it. Reports that are issued late might lose their value. Computer systems could give managers **immediate** access to the information they require, by means of file enquiry or special software (such as databases or spreadsheet modelling packages).

(d) It might be found that outputs are not as satisfactory as they should be, perhaps because:

(i) **Access** to information from the system is limited, and could be improved by the use of a **database** and a **network** system.

Part B: Information technology and systems

(ii) Available outputs are **restricted** because of the **method of data processing** used (eg batch processing instead of real-time processing) or the **type of equipment** used (eg stand-alone PCs compared with client/server systems).

Question 4
What elements of hardware and software might restrict the capabilities of a system?

Answer
A system's capabilities might be limited by the following restrictions.
(a) The size of the computer's memory.
(b) The power of the processor.
(c) The capacity of the computer's backing storage.
(d) The number of printers available.
(e) The number of terminals.
(f) The software's capabilities.

Inputs to a computer system

8.5 The efficiency of a computer system could be improved if the same volume (and frequency) of output could be achieved with **fewer input** resources, and at **less cost**. Here's how.

(a) **Multi-user or network systems might be more efficient than stand-alone systems.** Multi-user systems allow several input operators to work on the same files at the same time, so that if one person has a heavy workload and another is currently short of work, the person who has some free time can help his or her busy colleague - thus improving operator efficiency.

(b) **Real-time** systems might be more efficient than batch processing.

(c) Using computers and external storage media with **bigger storage** capacity. A frequent complaint is that '**waiting time**' for the operator can be very long and tedious. Computer systems with better backing storage facilities can reduce this operator waiting time, and so be more efficient.

(d) Using more **up-to-date software**.

8.6 Management might also wish to consider whether time spent **checking and correcting** input data can be eliminated. An **alternative method of input** might be chosen. For example bar codes and scanners should eliminate the need to check for input errors.

9 POST-IMPLEMENTATION REVIEW 11/01

9.1 A **post-implementation review** should establish whether the objectives and targeted performance criteria have been met, and if not, why not, and what should be done about it.

9.2 In appraising the operation of the new system immediately after the changeover, comparison should be made between **actual and predicted performance**. This will include:

(a) Consideration of **throughput speed** (time between input and output).
(b) Use of computer **storage** (both internal and external).
(c) The number and type of **errors/queries**.
(d) The **cost** of processing (data capture, preparation, storage and output media, etc).

7: Implementation, maintenance and review

9.3 A special **steering committee** may be set up to ensure that post-implementation reviews are carried out, although the **internal audit** department may be required to do the work of carrying out the reviews.

9.4 The post-implementation measurements should **not be made too soon** after the system goes live, or else results will be abnormally affected by 'teething' problems, lack of user familiarity and resistance to change.

The post-implementation review report

9.5 The findings of a post-implementation review team should be formalised in a **report**.

(a) A **summary** of their findings should be provided, emphasising any areas where the system has been found to be **unsatisfactory**.

(b) A review of **system performance** should be provided. This will address the matters outlined above, such as run times and error rates.

(c) A **cost-benefit review** should be included, comparing the forecast costs and benefits identified at the time of the feasibility study with actual costs and benefits.

(d) **Recommendations** should be made as to any **further action** or steps which should be taken to improve performance.

Chapter roundup

- The implementation of a new computer system is a **complex task** that requires careful **planning**. Staff should be involved and kept **fully informed** at all stages of system development and implementation.

- A system must be thoroughly **tested** to ensure it operates as intended. The nature and scope of testing will vary depending on the size and type of the system and user acceptance testing. The **'V' model** shows the relationship between system development, testing and quality throughout a systems development project.

- Four basic **stages of testing** can be identified: system logic, program testing, system testing and user acceptance testing. Software testing may be carried out in a **static environment** or a **dynamic environment**. A **test script** is a document that lists all tests that a new piece of software will be subjected to.

- **Performance testing** is conducted to evaluate the compliance of a system or component with specified performance requirements. **Usability testing** is conducted to establish the relative ease with which users are able to learn and use a system. **Performance testing** is conducted to evaluate the compliance of a system or component with specified performance requirements.

- The need for more efficient testing has led to the development of **automated software testing** using computer programs that automatically run the software to be tested, and record the results.

- **Staff training** is essential to ensure that information systems are utilised to **their full potential**. Training is needed when
    - A new system is implemented
    - An existing system is significantly changed
    - Job specifications change
    - New staff are recruited
    - Skills have been forgotten

(Chapter roundup continues on the next page)

Part B: Information technology and systems

- **Training** should be targeted to ensure those involved receive training relevant to the tasks they perform. There are a range of options available to **deliver training**
    - Individual tuition 'at desk'
    - Classroom course
    - Computer based training (CBT)
    - Software reference material
    - Case studies and exercises

- The **technical manual** is produced as a reference tool for those involved in producing and installing the system. The **user manual** is used to explain the system to users.

- File creation involves creating new files or **converting** existing files for use with the new system. There are four approaches to system **changeover**: direct changeover, parallel running, pilot operation and phased implementation. These vary in terms of time required, cost and risk.

- There are three types of systems maintenance. **Corrective** maintenance is carried out to correct an error, **perfective** maintenance aims to make enhancements to systems and **adaptive** maintenance takes account of anticipated changes in the processing environment.

- The criteria for **systems evaluation** mirror those used in the feasibility study. A system can be evaluated by reference to technical, operational, social and economic factors.

- Metrics may be used to measure system **performance**. Systems **evaluation** may also use **computer-based monitoring**. Methods include the use of hardware monitors, software monitors and systems logs.

- **Performance reviews** can be carried out to look at a wide range of systems functions and characteristics. Technological change often gives scope to improve the quality of **outputs** or reduce the extent or cost of **inputs**.

- During the **post-implementation review**, an evaluation of the system is carried out to see whether the targeted performance criteria have been met and to carry out a review of costs and benefits. The review should culminate in the production of a report and recommendations.

Quick quiz

1. List the main steps involved in a major computer installation.
2. List five situations where training is required.
3. What factors are relevant when considering how training should be delivered?
4. Which method of system changeover is usually safest?
5. Which method of system changeover is probably most expensive?
6. List four different stages of testing applicable through a systems development project.
7. Define 'unit testing'.
8. Distinguish between 'static testing' and 'dynamic testing'.
9. What is the purpose of user-acceptance testing?
10. What is the purpose of regression testing?
11. How does a cost-benefit review differ from a cost-benefit analysis?
12. What are metrics?

Answers to quick quiz

1   The main steps involved in a major computer installation are:

   Step 1   Select location/site
   Step 2   Choose and order hardware
   Step 3   Design and write software (or purchase off-the shelf)
   Step 4   Program testing
   Step 5   Staff training
   Step 6   Produce user documentation
   Step 7   Produce systems documentation
   Step 8   File conversion
   Step 9   Testing (including user acceptance testing)
   Step 10 System changeover (and further testing and training if issues arise)

2
   - A new system is implemented
   - An existing system is significantly changed
   - Job specifications change
   - New staff are recruited
   - Skills have been forgotten

3   The time available, how the complex the software is, the existing user-skill level, the training facilities available and the cost.

4   Parallel running.

5   Parallel running.

6   Four basic stages of testing can be identified: system logic, program testing, system testing and user acceptance testing.

7   Unit testing means testing one function or part of a program to ensure it operates as intended.

8   Static testing describes the process of evaluating a system or component based on its form, structure and content. The program or process is not executed or performed during static testing. Dynamic testing is testing that is performed by executing a program. It involves running the program and checking the results are as expected.

9   User acceptance testing is carried out by those who will use the system to determine whether the system meets their needs. These needs should have previously been stated as acceptance criteria. The aim is for the customer to determine whether or not to accept the system.

10 To ensure a change to a program has not resulted in unforeseen changes elsewhere in the system.

11 The review uses actual data. The analysis relies on estimates.

12 Metrics are quantified measurements used to measure system performance.

The material covered in this Chapter is tested in Questions 3, 4, 7, 14(a), 16(b) and 21 in the Question Bank.

Chapter 8

SELECTING AND MANAGING INFORMATION TECHNOLOGY

Topic list	Syllabus reference	Ability required
1 Manual systems	(ii)	Evaluation
2 The computer	(ii)	Evaluation
3 Input devices	(ii)	Evaluation
4 Output devices	(ii)	Evaluation
5 Storage devices	(ii)	Evaluation
6 Software	(ii)	Evaluation
7 Data processing in a computerised environment	(ii)	Evaluation
8 Architectures	(ii)	Evaluation
9 Purchasing hardware and software	(ii)	Evaluation
10 Information systems development and outsourcing	(ii)	Evaluation
11 The Internet	(ii)	Evaluation

Introduction

Management accountants now require a **working knowledge of Information Technology** to perform their role effectively. This does not mean that the management accountant needs to be an IT expert - just as an IT specialist cannot be expected to possess accounting expertise. What is required is sufficient knowledge to understand how IT can impact on the accounting function, and upon other business functions.

The Internet is not mentioned specifically in the syllabus. However, we have included this material as the syllabus refers to commonly-used Information Technology hardware and software. The Internet is undoubtedly one of the most useful and widely-used technologies in the modern business environment.

Learning outcomes in this chapter

- **Explain** the features and operation of commonly-used Information Technology hardware and software
- **Evaluate** the use and merits of different hardware and applications architectures

Syllabus content covered in this chapter

- The various types of Information Technology hardware and software in common use in organisations
- The different hardware and applications architectures available to organisations (centralised, distributed, client-server)
- The problems associated with the management of in-house and vendor solutions, and how they can be avoided or solved

8: Selecting and managing information technology

1 MANUAL SYSTEMS

1.1 Many tasks (and people) are still better suited to manual methods of working, for example a single quick calculation may best be done mentally or by using a pocket calculator.

1.2 Many people also prefer **communicating face to face** with their colleagues, rather than using tools such as e-mail. People may prefer to interact both to fulfil social needs and because they find this form of communication more effective eg use of body language, tone of voice etc.

1.3 The use of poorly designed computer systems, or using 'good systems' with inadequately trained users, will result in inefficiencies that negate the benefits computerised processing should bring.

Manual systems v computerised systems

1.4 However, in many situations manual systems are inferior to computerised systems. Some **disadvantages of manual systems** are outlined in the following table.

Disadvantage	Comment
Productivity	**Productivity** is usually lower, particularly in routine or operational situations such as transaction processing.
Slower	Processing is **slower** where large volumes of data need to be dealt with. Slower processing means that some information that could be provided if computerised systems were used, will **not be provided** at all, because there is not time.
Risk of errors	The **risk of errors** is greater, especially in repetitive work like payroll calculations.
Less accessible	Information is generally **less accessible**. Access to information is often restricted to one user at a time. Paper files can easily be mislaid or buried in in-trays, in which case the information they contain is not available at all.
Alterations	It is difficult to make **corrections**. If a manual document contains errors or needs updating it is often necessary to recreate the **whole** document from scratch, rather than just a new version with the relevant details changed.
Quality of output	**Quality of output** is less consistent and often not well-designed. At worst, hand-written records may be illegible and so completely useless. Poorly presented information may fail to communicate key points.
Bulk	Paper based systems are generally very **bulky** both to handle and to store, and office space is expensive.

2 THE COMPUTER

2.1 A computer is a device which accepts input data, processes it according to programmed rules, calculates results and then stores and/or outputs these results.

Part B: Information technology and systems

Types of computer

2.2 Computers can be classified as follows.

- Supercomputers
- Mainframe computers
- Minicomputers
- Microcomputers, now commonly called PCs

2.3 A **supercomputer** is used to process **very large amounts of data very quickly**. They are particularly useful for occasions where high volumes of calculations need to be performed, for example in meteorological or astronomical applications.

2.4 A **mainframe** computer system uses a powerful central computer, linked by cable or telecommunications to terminals. A mainframe has many times more **processing power** than a PC and offers **extensive data storage** facilities.

2.5 Mainframes are used by organisations such as banks that have very large volumes of processing to perform and have special security needs. Many organisations have now replaced their old mainframes with networked 'client-server' systems of mid-range computers and PCs because this approach is thought to be cheaper and offer more flexibility.

2.6 A **minicomputer** is a computer whose size, speed and capabilities lie somewhere between those of a mainframe and a PC. The term was originally used before PCs were developed, to describe computers which were cheaper but less well-equipped than mainframe computers.

2.7 With the advent of PCs and of mainframes that are much smaller than in the past, the definition of a minicomputer has become rather vague. There is really no definition which distinguishes adequately between a PC and a minicomputer.

2.8 PCs are now the norm for small to medium-sized business computing and for home computing, and most larger businesses now use them for day-to-day needs such as word-processing. Often they are linked together in a **network** to enable sharing of information between users.

Portables

2.9 The original portable computers were heavy, weighing around five kilograms, and could only be run from the mains electricity supply. Subsequent developments allow true portability.

(a) The **laptop** or **notebook** is powered either from the electricity supply or using a rechargeable battery and can include all the features and functionality of desktop PCs.

(b) The **palmtop** or handheld is increasingly compatible with true PCs. Devices range from basic models which are little more than electronic organisers to relatively powerful processors running 'cut-down' versions of Windows and Microsoft Office, and including communications features.

2.10 It is estimated that portable computers now represent over 50% in volume of all types of personal computer sold.

A typical PC specification

2.11 Here is the specification for a powerful PC, from an advertisement that appeared in mid 2002. This PC cost around £1000.

PC SPECIFICATION	
Intel 1.8 GHz Pentium 4 Processor	3.5" Floppy Disk Drive
25 GB hard disk drive	15" SVGA Monitor
56 kbps internal modem	Optical mouse
128MB RAM	2 serial ports, 1 parallel port
8 Speed CD-ROM/DVD Combo Drive	4 USB ports
Windows XP pre-loaded	

The processor

2.12 The processor is the '**brain**' of the computer. The processor may be defined as follows. The processor (sometimes referred to as the central processing unit or CPU) is divided into three areas:

- Arithmetic and logic unit
- Control unit
- Main store or memory

2.13 The processing unit may have all its elements - arithmetic and logic unit, control unit, and the input/output interface on a single '**chip**'. A chip is a small piece of silicon upon which is etched an integrated circuit, on an extremely small scale.

2.14 The chip is mounted on a carrier unit which in turn is 'plugged' on to a circuit board - called the motherboard - with other chips, each with their own functions.

2.15 The most common chips are those made by the Intel company. Each generation of Intel CPU chip has been able to perform operations in fewer clock cycles than the previous generation, and therefore works more quickly.

MHz and clock speed

2.16 The processor receives program instructions and sends signals to peripheral devices. The signals are co-ordinated by a **clock** which sends out a 'pulse' - a sort of tick-tock sequence called a **cycle** - at regular intervals.

2.17 The number of cycles produced per second is usually measured in **MegaHertz** (MHz) or **GigaHertz** (GHz).

- 1 MHz = one **million** cycles per second
- 1 GHz = one **billion** cycles per second

A typical modern business PC might run at 750 MHz, but models with higher clock speeds (eg 1 GHz) are now common.

Memory

2.18 Each individual storage element in the computer's memory consists of a simple circuit which can be switched **on** or **off**. These two states can be conveniently expressed by the numbers 1 and 0 respectively.

Part B: Information technology and systems

2.19 Each 1 or 0 is a **bit**. Bits are grouped together in groups of eight to form **bytes**. A byte may be used to represent a **character**, for example a letter, a number or another symbol.

2.20 Business PCs now make use of **32 bit** processors. Put simply, this means that data travels around from one place to another in groups of 16 or 32 bits, and so modern PCs operate considerably faster than the original 8 bit models.

2.21 The processing capacity of a computer is in part dictated by the capacity of its memory. Capacity is calculated in kilobytes (1 kilobyte = 2^{10} (1,024) bytes) and megabytes (1 megabyte = 2^{20} bytes) and gigabytes (2^{30}). These are abbreviated to Kb, Mb and Gb.

RAM

2.22 RAM (Random Access Memory) is memory that is directly available to the processing unit. It holds the data and programs in current use. RAM in microcomputers is 'volatile' which means that the contents of the memory are erased when the computer's power is switched off.

2.23 The RAM on a typical business PC is likely to have a capacity of 32 to 128 megabytes. The amount of RAM available is extremely important. A computer with a 750 MHz clock speed and 64 Mb of RAM will not be as efficient as a 500 MHz PC with 128 Mb of RAM.

ROM

2.24 ROM (Read-Only Memory) is a memory chip into which fixed data is written permanently at the time of its manufacture. When you turn on a PC you may see a reference to BIOS (basic input/output system). This is part of the ROM chip containing all the programs needed to control the keyboard, screen, disk drives and so on.

Cache

2.25 The cache is a small but extremely fast part of memory which holds a second copy of data most recently read from or written to main memory – to enable quick retrieval. When the cache is full, older entries are 'flushed out' to make room for new ones.

2.26 RAM, ROM and cache are different to **hard disk storage**. Hard disks are storage devices that may hold vast amounts of data (eg 20 Gigabytes). Files are stored on storage media such as a hard disk. When files are opened to be referred to or amended, they are stored in RAM. We cover storage devices later in this chapter.

3 INPUT DEVICES

Data collection and input

3.1 A computerised information system receives data and instructions via input devices, stores data and programs on storage devices and outputs processed data (information) using output devices. The system may also interact with other systems via communications devices.

8: Selecting and managing information technology

3.2 Data must be input into a computer system in a form the computer is able to interpret. There are a number of various methods of data input. When choosing a method of data input for a given situation, key considerations are:

- Speed
- Accuracy
- Cost
- Volume of data\transactions
- System reliability
- Flexibility required

3.3 Some common methods of input are explained in the following paragraphs.

The keyboard

3.4 Almost all computer terminals and personal computers include a keyboard based on the basic QWERTY typewriter keyboard. The user inputs data by hitting the relevant combination of keys.

3.5 Keyboard input is a labour-intensive process, but is the only suitable option in many circumstances eg producing a unique letter in which accuracy is vital.

The VDU or monitor

3.6 A VDU (visual display unit) or 'monitor' displays text and graphics. The screen's resolution is the number of pixels that are lit up. More and smaller pixels enable detailed high-resolution display. Super VGA, or SVGA, is the standard for newer monitors and offers resolutions up to $1,280 \times 1,024$.

Mouse

3.7 A wheeled mouse is a handheld device with a rubber ball protruding from a small hole in its base. The mouse is moved over a flat surface, and as it moves, internal sensors pick up the motion and convert it into electronic signals which instruct the cursor on screen to move in the same direction.

3.8 The wheeled mouse is slowly being replaced by the optical mouse. The optical mouse has a small light-emitting diode (LED) that bounces light off the surface the mouse is moved across. The mouse contains sensors that convert this movement into co-ordinates the computer can understand.

3.9 A typical mouse has two or three buttons which can be pressed (clicked) to send specific signals. For example, a 'click' on the left hand button can be used to send the cursor to a new cell in a spreadsheet and a 'double click' can select a particular application from a Windows menu. The latest variety also have a wheel to facilitate scrolling up and down a screen display.

3.10 Similar to the mouse is the trackball, which is often found on laptop computers. Trackballs comprise a casing fixed to the computer, and a ball which protrudes upwards. The user moves the ball by hand. Other mobile computers use a touch sensitive pad for mouse functions; others have a tiny joystick in the centre of the keyboard.

Magnetic ink character recognition (MICR)

3.11 Magnetic ink character recognition (MICR) involves the recognition by a machine of special formatted characters printed in magnetic ink. The characters are read using a specialised reading device. The main advantage of MICR is its speed and accuracy, but MICR documents are expensive to produce. The main commercial application of MICR is in the banking industry – on cheques and deposit slips.

Optical mark reading (OMR)

3.12 Optical mark reading involves the marking of a pre-printed form with a ballpoint pen or typed line or cross in an appropriate box. The card is then read by an OMR device which senses the mark in each box using an electric current and translates it into machine code. Applications in which OMR is used include National Lottery entry forms (in the UK), and answer sheets for multiple choice questions.

Scanners and Optical Character Recognition (OCR)

3.13 A scanner is device that can read text or illustrations printed on paper and translate the information into a form the computer can use. A scanner works by digitising an image, the resulting matrix of bits is called a bit map.

3.14 To edit text read by an optical scanner, you need Optical Character Recognition (OCR) software to translate the picture into text format. Most scanners sold today come with OCR software.

Bar coding and EPOS

3.15 **Bar codes** are groups of marks which, by their spacing and thickness, indicate specific codes or values. Look at the back cover of this book for an example of a bar code.

3.16 Large retail stores have Electronic Point of Sale (EPOS) devices, which include bar code readers. This enables the provision of immediate sales and stock level information.

EFTPOS

3.17 Many retailers have now introduced EFTPOS systems (Electronic Funds Transfer at the Point of Sale). An EFTPOS terminal is used with a customers credit card or debit card to pay for goods or services. The customer's credit card account or bank account will be debited automatically. EFTPOS systems combine point of sale systems with electronic funds transfer.

Magnetic stripe cards

3.18 The standard magnetic stripe card contains machine-sensible data on a thin strip of magnetic recording tape stuck to the back of the card. The magnetic card reader converts this information into directly computer-sensible form. The widest application of magnetic stripe cards is as bank credit or service cards.

Smart cards

3.19 A smart card is a plastic card in which is embedded a microprocessor chip. A smart card would typically contain a memory and a processing capability. The information held on smart cards can therefore be updated (eg using a PC and a special device).

Touch screens

3.20 A touch screen is a display screen that enables users to make selections by touching areas of the screen. Sensors, built into the screen surround, detect which area has been touched. These devices are widely used in vending situations, such as the selling of train tickets.

Voice recognition

3.21 Computer software has been developed that can convert speech into computer-sensible form via a microphone. Users are required to speak clearly and reasonably slowly.

Question 1

The next time you are at the supermarket check-out, think of the consequences of the operator simply scanning one bar code. What effect does this quick and simple action have?

Answer

(a) The price of the item is added to your bill.

(b) The supermarket stock 'number on shelf' is reduced by one, and if the predetermined minimum has been reached the 'shelf restock required' indicator will be activated.

(c) The overall stock on hand figure will be reduced, and if the minimum stock holding has been reached the 'reorder from supplier' indicator will be activated.

(d) The relevant accounting entries will be made, or be sent to a pending file awaiting the running of the month-end routine.

(e) Marketing information will be obtained – what time the purchase was made, what else was purchased and if your loyalty card was swiped – who purchased it.

You may have thought of others. The key point to grasp from this exercise is that **efficient information collection** can be achieved using appropriate technology.

4 OUTPUT DEVICES

4.1 The two most common methods of computer output are output to a printer and output to the screen. Other methods include output to a computer file or onto microfilm (known as Computer Output on Microfilm or COM).

The choice of output medium

4.2 Choosing a suitable output medium depends on a number of factors.

Factor	Comment
Hard copy	Is a printed version of the output needed?
Quantity	For example, a VDU screen can hold a certain amount of data, but it becomes more difficult to read when information goes 'off-screen' and can only be read a 'page' at a time.

Factor	Comment
Speed	For example if a single enquiry is required it may be quicker to make notes from a VDU display.
Suitability for further use	Output to a file would be appropriate if the data will be processed further, maybe in a different system. Large volumes of reference data might be held on microfilm or microfiche.
Cost	The 'best' output device may not be justifiable on the grounds of cost - another output medium should be chosen.

Printers

4.3 Character printers, such as dot matrix printers, print a single character at a time. Dot matrix printers may still be found in some accounting departments. Their main drawback is their low-resolution. They are also relatively slow and noisy, but cheap to run.

4.4 Inkjet printers are small and reasonably cheap (under £100), making them popular where a 'private' output device is required. They work by sending a jet of ink on to the paper to produce the required characters – a line at a time. They produce print of a higher quality than dot matrix printers, and most models can print in colour. Running costs can be high.

4.5 Laser printers print a whole page at a time, rather than line by line. The quality of output with laser printers is very high. Compared with inkjet printers, running costs are relatively low.

The VDU

4.6 Screens were described earlier, as they are used together with computer keyboards for input. They can be used as an output medium, primarily where the volume of output is low, for example a single enquiry.

5 STORAGE DEVICES

Hard disks

5.1 Disks offer **direct access** to data. A modern business PC invariably has an **internal hard disk**. At the time of writing the average new **PC** has a hard disk size of around 5 **Gigabytes**, but 15 Gb disks are not uncommon. In larger computer systems **removable disk packs** are commonly used.

Floppy disks

5.2 The floppy disk provides a **cost-effective** means of on-line storage for **small** amounts of information. A $3^1/_2$" disk can hold up to **1.44 Mb** of data.

5.3 A **Zip disk** is a different type of **removable** disk, with much larger capacity (100 Mb) that requires a special Zip drive. A Zip disk is suitable for back-up, storage or for moving files between computers.

Tape storage

5.4 Tape cartridges have a **much larger capacity** than floppy disks and they are still widely used as a **backing storage** medium. Fast tapes which can be used to create a back-up file very quickly are known as **tape streamers**.

5.5 Like an audio or video cassette, data has to be recorded **along the length** of a computer tape and so it is **more difficult to access** than data on disk (ie direct access is not possible with tape). Reading and writing are separate operations.

CD-ROM (Compact Disc – Read Only Memory)

5.6 A CD-ROM can store 650 megabytes of data.

5.7 The **speed** of a CD-ROM drive is relevant to how fast data can be retrieved: an **eight speed** drive is quicker than a **four speed** drive.

5.8 CD recorders are now available for general business use with blank CDs (CD-R) and **rewritable disks** (CD-RW) are now available.

DVD (Digital Versatile Disc)

5.9 The CD format has started to be superseded by DVD. DVD development was encouraged by the advent of multimedia files with video graphics and sound - requiring greater disk capacity.

5.10 **Digital Versatile Disk (DVD)** technology can store almost 5 gigabytes of data on one disk. Access speeds are improved as is sound and video quality. Many commentators believe DVD will not only replace CD-ROMs, but also VHS cassettes, audio CDs and laser discs.

Question 2

Briefly outline two features and one common use of magnetic disks, magnetic tapes and optical disks (CD-ROMs).

Answer

(a) *Magnetic disks* offer fast access times, direct access to data and offer suitability for multi-user environments. Magnetic disk storage is therefore the predominant storage medium in most commercial applications currently. Direct access is essential for many commercial applications (eg databases) and in addition speed is necessary for real-time applications.

(b) *Magnetic tapes* offer cheap data storage, portability and serial or sequential access only. Magnetic tape is most valuable as a backup medium.

(c) *Optical disks* (eg CD-ROMs) offer capacity to store vast amounts of data but offer slower access speeds than magnetic disks. They are most suitable for backup and archiving, or keeping old copies of files which might need to be retrieved. However, the technology behind optical drives is still in development, and it may not be too long before they are a viable alternative to magnetic disk drives for most applications.

---

6 SOFTWARE

6.1 The different types of computer software can be classified into five types, as shown in the following table.

Part B: Information technology and systems

Type	Comment
Operating systems	The operating system provides the interface between the computer hardware and both the user and the other software. An operating system will typically perform the following tasks. • Initial set-up of the computer, when it is switched on • Communication between the user and hardware • Calling up of files from storage into memory • File management The most widely-used operating system is Microsoft Windows. Other operating systems include UNIX, the Apple Macintosh O/S system and Linux.
Utilities	Software utilities are relatively small software packages, usually designed to perform a task related to the general operation of a computer system. An example of a utility is software designed to perform back-ups.
Programming tools	Some software is designed specifically to help programmers produce computer programs. Examples include program compilers and assemblers, and Computer Assisted Software Engineering (CASE) tools.
Off-the-shelf applications	This term is used to describe software produced by a software manufacturer and released in a form that is ready to use. 'Office' type software (spreadsheet, word-processing, database etc) and integrated accounting systems such as Sage Line 50 are examples.
Bespoke applications	Bespoke software is tailor-made to meet the needs of an organisation. Bespoke software is relatively expensive, but may be the only feasible solution in unusual situations. We cover the factors to consider when deciding upon off-the-shelf or bespoke software in Chapter 8.

7 DATA PROCESSING IN A COMPUTERISED ENVIRONMENT

7.1 In data processing a data **file** is a collection of **records** with similar characteristics. Examples of data files include the sales ledger, the purchase ledger and the nominal ledger.

7.2 A **record** in a file consists of data relating to one logically definable unit of business information. A collection of similar records makes up a file. For example, the records for a sales ledger file consist of customer records (or 'customer accounts').

7.3 Records in files consist of **fields** of information. For example, a customer record on the sales ledger file will include name, address, customer reference number, balance owing, and credit limit.

7.4 Records on a file should contain one **key field**. This is an item of data within the record by which it can be uniquely identified.

7.5 Files are conventionally classified into **transaction** files, and **master** files. These distinctions are particularly relevant in batch processing applications.

7.6 A transaction file is a file containing records that relate to individual transactions. The sales day book entries are examples of transaction records in a transaction file.

7.7 A **master file** contains reference data and also cumulative transaction data. For example, in a purchase ledger system, the master file would consist of:

(a) **Reference data** for each supplier (supplier name and address, reference number, amount currently owed etc) and

(b) **Cumulative transaction data** for each supplier – periodic totals for purchases, purchase returns and payments.

7.8 Both manual and computer data processing can be divided into two broad types: batch processing and real-time processing. Batch processing systems are becoming less common, particularly if the process concerned impacts on customer service.

Batch processing

7.9 **Batch processing** involves transactions being **grouped** and **stored** before being processed at regular intervals, such as daily, weekly or monthly. Because data is not input as soon as it is received the system will not always be up-to-date.

7.10 Transactions will be collected up over a period of time, and will then be dealt with together in a batch. Some **delay** in processing the transactions must therefore be acceptable.

7.11 The lack of up-to-date information means batch processing is usually not suitable for systems involving customer contact. Batch processing is suitable for internal, regular tasks such as payroll.

7.12 EXAMPLE: BATCH PROCESSING OF SALES LEDGER APPLICATION

A company operates a computerised sales ledger using batch processing based on paper records. The main stages of processing are as follows.

Step 1.	Sales invoices are hand-written in a numbered invoice book (in triplicate ie three copies per invoice). At the end of the day all invoices are clipped together and a batch control slip is attached. The sales clerk allocates the next unused batch number from the batch control book. He or she enters the batch number on the control slip, together with the total number of documents and the total value of the invoices. These details are also entered in the control book.
Step 2.	The batch of invoices is then passed to the accounts department for processing. An accounts clerk records the batch as having been received.
Step 3.	The relevant account codes are written on the invoices and control slip. Codes are checked, and the batch is keyed into the computerised sales ledger system.
Step 4.	The clerk reconciles the totals on the batch control slip with the totals for valid and rejected data.
Step 5.	The ledger update program is run to post data to the relevant accounts.
Step 6.	A report is printed showing the total of invoices posted to the ledger and the clerk reconciles this to the batch totals.

Part B: Information technology and systems

Step 7. All rejected transaction records are carefully investigated and followed up, usually to be amended and then re-input with the next processing run.

On-line processing

7.13 On-line processing involves transactions being input and processed immediately, in 'real time'. On-line refers to a machine which is under the **direct control** of the main **processor** for that system. (The term 'on-line' is also used to describe an active Internet connection.)

7.14 On-line, real time processing is appropriate when immediate processing is required, and the delay implicit in batch processing would not be acceptable.

7.15 On-line systems are practically the **norm** in modern business. **Examples** include the following.

(a) As a sale is made in a department store or a supermarket, the item barcode is scanned on the **point of sale terminal** and the stock records are updated immediately.

(b) In **banking and credit card** systems whereby customer details are often maintained in a real-time environment. There can be immediate access to customer balances, credit position etc and authorisation for withdrawals (or use of a credit card).

(c) **Travel agents, airlines** and **theatre ticket** agencies all use real-time systems. Once a hotel room, plane seat or theatre seat is booked up everybody on the system must know about it immediately so that they do not sell the same holiday or seat to two (or more) different customers.

7.16 The workings of both batch and on-line processing methods are shown in the following diagram.

Batch processing and on-line processing

Batch Processing

[Diagram: Transactions grouped in batches → Keyboard input → Sorted transaction file; Old master file; both feed into Validate and update, which produces Error reports, Reports, and New master file]

On-line processing

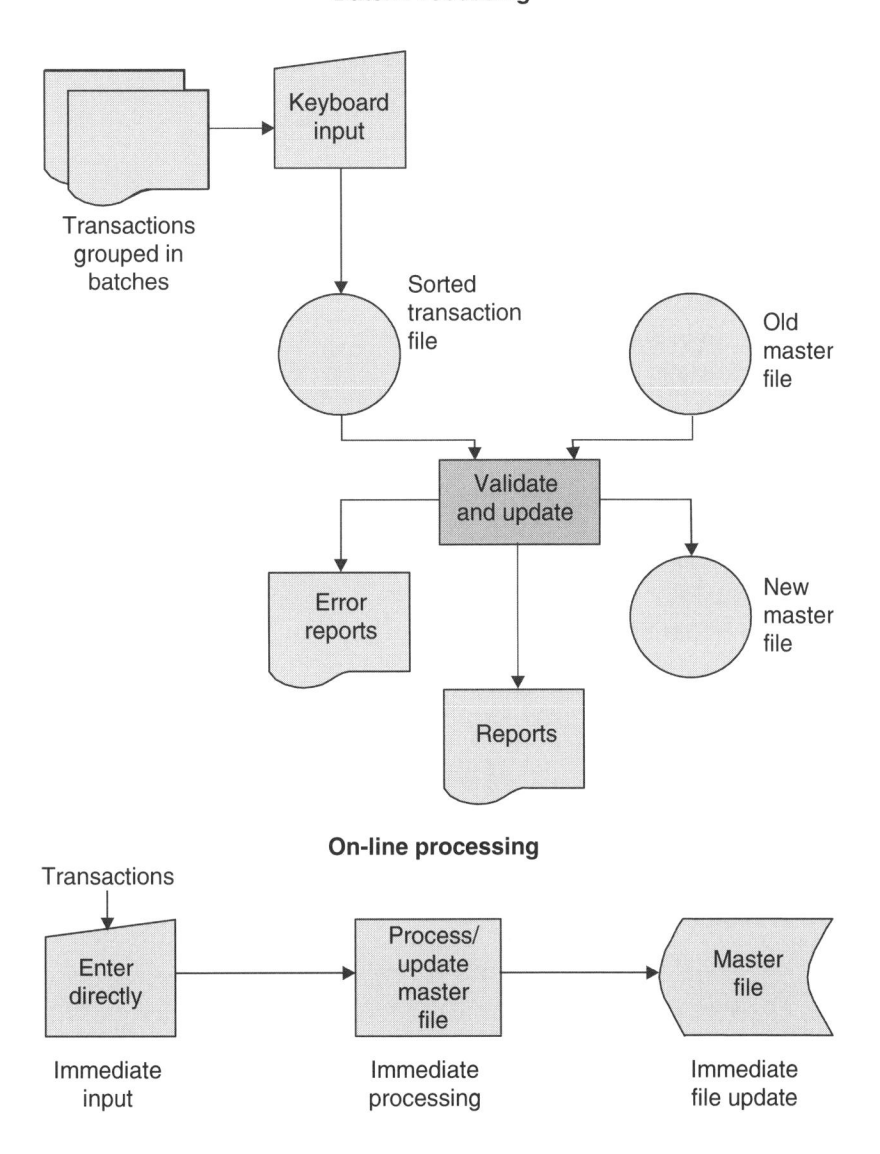

[Diagram: Transactions → Enter directly (Immediate input) → Process/update master file (Immediate processing) → Master file (Immediate file update)]

8 ARCHITECTURES   Pilot paper

8.1 The term **system architecture** refers to the way in which the various components of an information system are linked together, and the way they relate to each other. In the following paragraphs we discuss the theory behind centralised and distributed systems. However, in reality many systems include elements of both.

Centralised architecture

> **KEY TERM**
>
> A **centralised architecture** involves all computer processing being carried out on a single central processor. The central computer is usually a mainframe or minicomputer designed to be accessed by more than one user.

Part B: Information technology and systems

8.2 A centralised system using a central mainframe linked to 'dumb terminals' (which do not include a CPU and therefore rely on the central computer for processing power) is shown below.

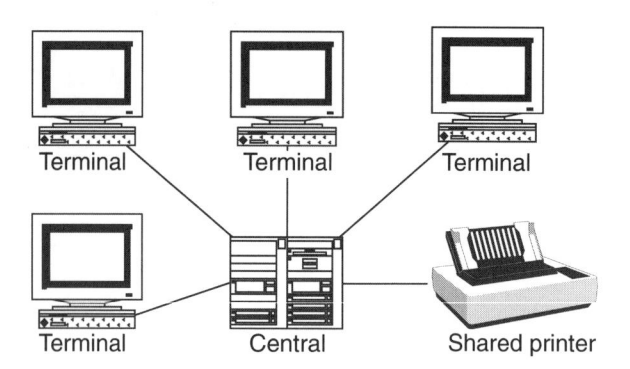

8.3 Many centralised systems also have shared peripherals, such as printers, linked to the central computer.

8.4 Centralised architectures could be based in a single location or spread over multiple locations. For example, both a local area network (LAN) and a wide area network (WAN) could utilise a centralised architecture.

8.5 A LAN is a network that spans a relatively small area. Most LANs are confined to a single building or group of buildings. A wide area network (WAN) is a computer network that spans a relatively large geographical area. A centralised WAN would have only one computer with processing power. (LANs may be linked to form a WAN – although such a configuration would not be considered a centralised architecture.)

8.6 **Advantages** of centralised architectures.
  (a) There is one set of files. Everyone uses the same data and information.
  (b) It gives better security/control over data and files. It is easier to enforce standards.
  (c) Head office (where the computer is usually based) is able to control computing processes and developments.
  (d) An organisation might be able to afford a very large central computer, with extensive processing capabilities that smaller 'local' computers could not carry out.
  (e) There may be economies of scale available in purchasing computer equipment and supplies.

8.7 **Disadvantages** of centralised architectures.
  (a) Local offices might experience processing delays or interruptions.
  (b) Reliance on head office. Local offices rely on head office to provide information they need.
  (c) If the central computer breaks down, or the software develops a fault, the entire system goes out of operation.

8: Selecting and managing information technology

Decentralised or distributed architectures

> **KEY TERM**
>
> **Distributed architectures** spread the processing power throughout the organisation at several different locations. With modern distributed systems, the majority of processing power is held on numerous personal computers (PCs) spread throughout the organisation.

8.8 An example of a distributed architecture, with a combination of stand-alone PCs and networks spread throughout an organisation, is shown in the following diagram.

Distributed architecture

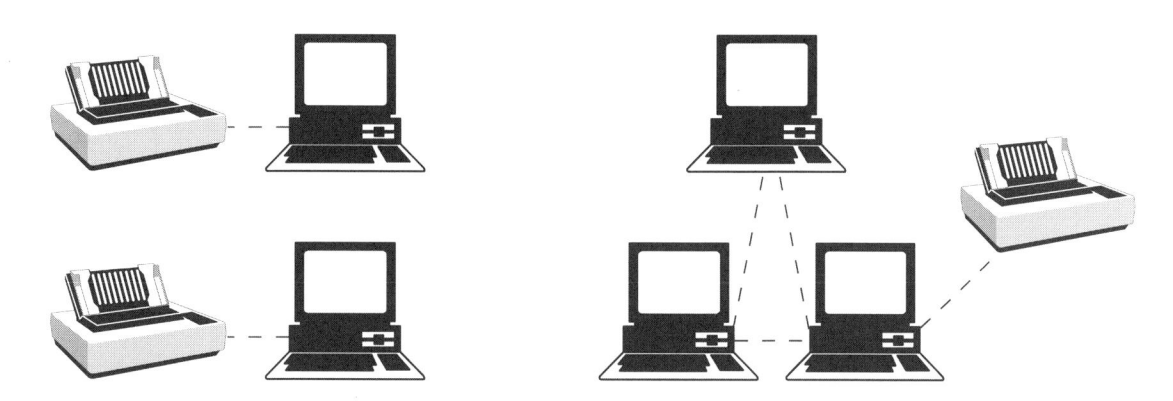

8.9 Key **features** of distributed architectures.

(a) Many computers have their own processing capability (CPU).

(b) Some sharing of information is possible via communication links.

(c) The systems are usually more user-friendly than mainframe based systems.

(d) End-users are given responsibility for, and control over, programs and data.

Advantages and disadvantages of distributed architectures

8.10 **Advantages**.

(a) There is greater flexibility in system design. The system can cater for both the specific needs of each local user of an individual computer and also for the needs of the organisation as a whole, by providing communications between different local computers in the system.

(b) Since data files can be held locally, data transmission is restricted because each computer maintains its own data files which provide most of the data it will need. This reduces the costs and security risks in data transmission.

(c) Speed of processing.

(d) There is a possibility of a distributed database. Data is held in a number of locations, but any user can access all of it for a global view.

(e) The effect of breakdowns is minimised, because a fault in one computer will not affect other computers in the system.

(f) Allows for better localised control over the physical and procedural aspects of the system.

(g) May facilitate greater user involvement and increase familiarity with the use of computer technology.

8.11 **Disadvantages** of distributed architectures.

(a) There may be some duplication of data on different computers, increasing the risk of data inaccuracies.

(b) A distributed network can be more difficult to administer and to maintain, as several sites require access to staff with IT skills.

Client-server architecture

8.12 With a client-server architecture each computer or process on the network is either a 'client' or a 'server'. Servers are powerful computers or processes dedicated to managing disk drives (file servers), printers (print servers), or network traffic (network servers). Clients are PCs or workstations on which users run applications. Clients rely on servers for resources, such as files, devices, and sometimes processing power.

> **KEY TERMS**
>
> A **client** is a machine which requests a service, for example a PC running a spreadsheet application which the user wishes to print out.
>
> A **server** is a machine which is dedicated to providing a particular function or service requested by a client. Servers include file servers (see below), print servers, e-mail servers and fax servers.

8.13 A typical client-server system includes three **hardware** elements.

- A central server (sometimes called the corporate server)
- Local servers (sometimes called departmental servers)
- Client workstations

8.14 A server computer (such as a file server) may be a powerful PC or a minicomputer. As its name implies, it **serves** the rest of the network offering a generally-accessible hard disk and sometimes offering other resources, such as a **shared printer**.

8.15 A typical client-server architecture is shown in the following illustration.

8: Selecting and managing information technology

Client-server architecture

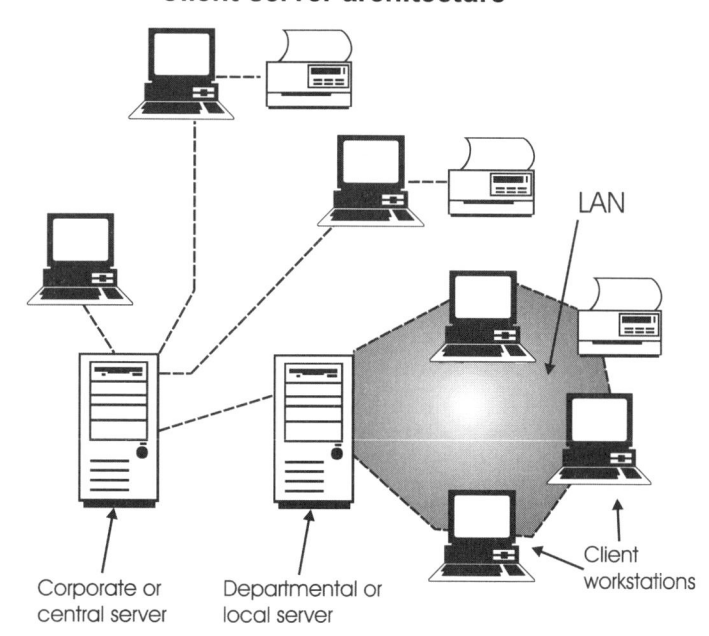

[Diagram: Client-server architecture showing Corporate or central server, Departmental or local server, LAN, and Client workstations]

8.16 Client-server systems aim to locate software where it is most efficient - based on the number and location of users requiring access and the processing power required. There are three main types of software applications.

(a) **Corporate applications** are run on the central (or corporate) server. These applications are accessed by people spread throughout the organisation, and often require significant processor power (eg a centralised Management Information System).

(b) **Local applications** are used by users within a particular section or department, and therefore are run on the relevant local or departmental server (eg a credit-scoring expert system may be held on the server servicing the loans department of a bank).

(c) **Client applications** may be unique to an individual user, eg a specialised Executive Support System (ESS). Other software that may be run on client hardware could include 'office' type software, such as spreadsheet and word processing programs. Even though many people may use these applications, individual copies of programs are often held on client hardware - to utilise the processor power held on client machines.

The advantages of a client-server architecture

8.17

Advantage	Comment
Greater resilience	Processing is spread over several computers. If one server breaks down, other locations can carry on processing.
Scalability	They are highly scalable. Instead of having to buy computing power in large quantities you can buy just the amount of power you need to do the job.
Shared programs and data	Program and data files held on a file server can be shared by all the PCs in the network. With stand-alone PCs, each computer would have its own data files, and there might be unnecessary duplication of data. A system where everyone uses the same data will help to improve data processing and decision making.

Advantage	Comment
Shared work-loads	The processing capability of each computer in a network can be utilised. For example, if there were separate stand-alone PCs, A might do job 1, B might do job 2 and C might do job 3. In a network, any PC, (A, B or C) could do any job (1, 2 or 3). This is more efficient.
Shared peripherals	Peripheral equipment can be shared. For example, five PCs might share a single printer.
Communication	LANs can be linked up to the office communications network, thus adding to the processing capabilities in an office. Electronic mail, calendar and diary facilities can also be used.
Compatibility	Client/server systems are likely to include interfaces between different types of software used on the system, making it easier to move information between applications.
Flexibility	For example, if a detailed analysis of existing data is required, a copy of this data could be placed on a separate server, allowing data to be manipulated without disrupting the main system.

The disadvantages of a client-server architecture

8.18 The client/server approach has some drawbacks.

(a) A single **mainframe** may be more efficient performing some tasks, in certain circumstances. For example, where the process involves routine processing of a very large number (eg millions) of transactions.

(b) It is easier to **control** and **maintain** a centralised system. In particular it is easier to keep data **secure**.

(c) It may be **cheaper** to 'tweak' an existing mainframe system rather than throwing it away and starting from scratch: for example it may be possible to give it a graphical user interface and to make data exchangeable between Windows and non-Windows based applications.

(d) Each location may need its own **network administrator** to keep things running smoothly - there may be unnecessary duplication of **skills** and staff.

(e) Duplication of information may be a problem if individual users do not follow a disciplined approach.

Peer-to-peer architecture

8.19 'Peer-to-peer' refers to a type of network in which each workstation has equivalent capabilities and responsibilities. This differs from client-server architectures, in which some computers are dedicated to serving the others. Peer-to-peer networks are generally simpler, but they usually do not offer the same performance under heavy workloads.

Question 3

When would you expect a **stand-alone** computer to be used?

Answer

Stand-alone computers are used in the following situations.

(a) When the data processing requirements can be handled by one user with one computer, for example for developing a personal spreadsheet model.

(b) When security could be compromised by the use of a multi-user system.

9 PURCHASING HARDWARE AND SOFTWARE 5/01

9.1 A computer user might buy hardware and software direct from a manufacturer, or through an intermediate supplier. Given that the expense is often considerable, the purchasing procedure must be carefully controlled.

Software sources

9.2 An organisation has a range of options when sourcing software for information systems. The four main options are described in the following table.

Source	Comment
Standard off-the-shelf package	This is the simplest option. The organisation purchases and installs a ready-made solution.
Amended standard package	A standard package is purchased, but some customisation is undertaken so that the software meets the organisations requirements. This may require access to the source code.
Standard package plus additions	The purchased standard package is not amended itself, but additional software that integrates with the standard package is developed. This also may require access to the source code.
Bespoke package	Programmers write an application to meet the specific needs of the organisation. This can be a time-consuming and expensive process.

9.3 In this section we discuss the process and relative advantages of the two main options - purchasing an application off-the-shelf and developing a bespoke solution. The other two options include elements of both of these two main options.

KEY TERMS

Bespoke software is designed and written either 'in-house' by the IS department or externally by a software house.

An **off-the-shelf package** is one that is sold to a wide range of users. The package is written to handle requirements that are common to a wide range of organisations.

Choosing an application package off-the shelf

9.4 Off-the-shelf packages are generally available for functions that are likely to be performed similarly across a range of organisations eg accounting. The following table describes some of the factors to consider when choosing an off-the-shelf application package.

Factor	Comment
User requirements	Does the package fit the user's particular requirements? Matters to consider include data volumes, data validation routines, number of users and the reports available.
Processing times	Are the processing times fast enough? If response times to enquiries is slow, the user might consider the package unacceptable.
Documentation	Is there full and clear documentation for the user? A comprehensive user manual, a quick reference guide and on-line help should be considered.
Compatibility	Is the package compatible with existing hardware and software? Can data be exchanged with other related systems?
Controls	Access and security controls (eg passwords) should be included, as should processing controls that enable the accuracy of processing operations to be confirmed.
User-interface	Users are most affected by the user-interface design. The interface should be clear, logical, and consistent, and should follow standard interface conventions such as those used on most packages produced for use with the Microsoft Windows operating system.
Modification	Can the package be modified by the user - allowing the user to tailor it to meet their needs?
Support, maintenance and updates	The availability and cost of support, such as a telephone help-line, should be considered, as should the arrangements for updates and upgrades. This is particularly important if software is likely to be affected by changes in legislation eg a payroll package.
Cost	An organisation should aim to purchase a package that will meet their requirements. However, a package should not be purchased if the cost outweighs the value of the benefits it should bring.

Developing a bespoke application

9.5 Producing a bespoke software system involves all the tasks included in the software development and testing cycle.

9.6 The process is summarised in the diagram below, and explained in the table that follows.

The software development cycle

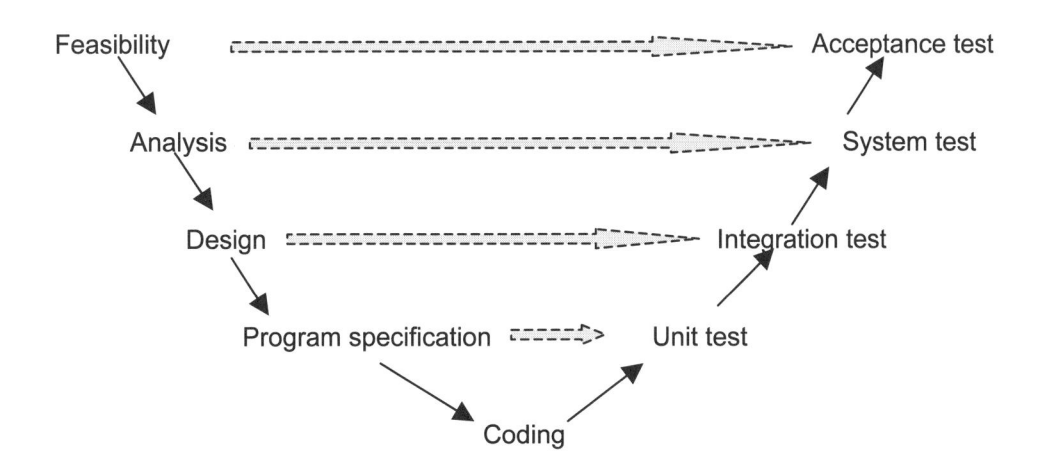

Feasibility ----------------------------------→ Acceptance test

Analysis ----------------------------------→ System test

Design ----------------------------→ Integration test

Program specification ----→ Unit test

Coding

9.7	Stages of software development	Comment
	Feasibility and analysis	The feasibility of software solutions would have usually been covered during the overall system feasibility study. An analysis of the software requirements should therefore be available.
	Design and program specification	The software requirements are used to develop a systems design specification, which in turn is used to produce a detailed program specification. The specification would be used by in-house software developers, or would be distributed to software producers (as part of the invitation to tender - covered below).
	Coding	Software producers will decide how to build the package, for example identifying parts of existing programs that may be used, and establishing what will need to be coded (ie written) from scratch. Prototyping may be used to help ensure user requirements are met.
	Testing Unit; Integration; System; Acceptance	We covered testing, in Chapter 7. To briefly re-cap, unit testing tests individual programs (or units) operating alone. Integration testing tests how two or more units of the software interact with each other. System testing tests the complete package and how it interacts with other software programs. User acceptance testing aims to ensure all user requirements included in the software specification have been met.

Part B: Information technology and systems

Invitations to tender (ITT)

9.8 A number of suppliers may be invited to tender (bid) to supply specific software (the tendering procedure could also be used for hardware, or for a complete system).

> **KEY TERM**
>
> An **Invitation To Tender** is a document that invites suppliers to bid for the supply of specified software, or hardware, or both.

9.9 There are a number of possible options available to identify possible suppliers who may be in a position to submit a realistic tender:

- **Trade magazines and websites** may include software advertisements and reviews
- **Computer consultants** may have experience and/or knowledge of suitable suppliers
- **Establish who supplies other similar organisations** - it is likely these suppliers could also meet the requirements of a similar organisation

9.10 The contents of a typical invitation to tender (ITT) are outlined in the following table. This format could be used when inviting tenders for bespoke or off-the-shelf software - although sections such as the development methodology would be shorter for off-the-shelf tenders, as this would refer only to any proposed amendments to the package.

ITT section	Comment
Covering letter	An ITT will include a letter inviting the supplier to tender. The letter should specify: • Contact names for queries relating to the tendering process and for technical queries • The closing date for submitting tenders
Instructions	Instructions to tenderers should specify the information required in a tender. Instructions are likely to require tenderers to specify: • Areas of their tender that do not comply with the software specification provided, and the reasons why • The period of validity for the tender • The basis for calculating prices, whether prices are estimates or a quote • An indication of timescale - when work could start and an approximate completion date • Alternative ways of approaching parts of the software design than indicated in the requirements specification

ITT section	Comment
Detailed software requirements	The ITT must include a detailed requirements specification so tenderers know exactly what they are tendering for. This should include: • The purpose of the system • The volume of data to be processed. • Processing requirements (including details of inputs and outputs, and interfaces with other systems). • The number of locations and users requiring access. • The speed of processing required, eg response times. • Expected life of the system. • Possible upgrades or expansion anticipated. When submitting their bids, some potential suppliers may come up with alternative specifications - these must be fully explained.
Details of development model/methodology	This section of the ITT requires tenderers to provide a description of the methodology or systems development model used to develop their software. The aim is to ensure that the supplier produces software using accepted development techniques - reducing the possibility of poor quality software.
Request for details of the proposed software contract	The ITT document should request information from potential suppliers relating to the key terms of any future software contract. We cover software contracts later in this chapter.

Evaluating supplier proposals

9.11 Once vendor proposals have been obtained, they should be evaluated against what was requested within the ITT. There are many factors that should be considered when evaluating proposals. The factors to consider fit into three general categories:

- **Technical,** how well does the proposal meet the specified technical requirements?
- **Support,** what after-sales support is included?
- **Cost,** what do we get for our money?

9.12 Some of the main factors to consider when evaluating supplier proposals are described in the following table. Some of the relevant points are the same as those considered when choosing off-the-shelf software.

Factor	Comment
Organisation needs	How well does the software meet the requirements of the organisation? If some requirements aren't met, how important are they - can they be satisfied through other means?
Speed	Can the system cope with data volumes; is response time affected by high data volumes?
Documentation	Is there full and clear documentation for the user, and a technical manual that would allow further development?

Part B: Information technology and systems

Factor	Comment
Compatibility	Is the package compatible with existing hardware and software? Can data be exchanged with other related systems?
Controls	Access and security controls (eg passwords) should be included, as should processing controls that enable the accuracy of processing operations to be confirmed.
User-friendly	Software should be relatively easy to use and tolerant to user errors. Menu structures should be logical, the software should follow standard user-interface conventions.
Modification	Can the package be modified by the user - allowing the organisation to tailor it to meet their specific needs?
Demonstration	A demonstration version of the software may be available - this should provide a good idea of how the finished product would look, feel and operate.
Training provided	Training is essential for the organisation to utilise the software effectively.
Support, maintenance and updates	The availability and cost of support, such as a telephone help-line, should be considered, as should the arrangements for updates and upgrades. This is particularly important if software is likely to be affected by changes in legislation eg a payroll package.
Conditions included in the software contract	The software contract includes terms relating to the actual supply and use of the software.
Supplier size, reputation and customer base	Software suppliers that have been in business for a reasonable amount of time, and who have an established client base, are more likely to remain in business - and therefore be in a position to provide support. References may be available from existing customers, attesting to the quality of software and support.
Cost	An organisation should aim to purchase a package that will meet their requirements. However, a package should not be purchased if the cost outweighs the value of the benefits it should bring.

Comparing supplier proposals

9.13 An organisation may receive a number of apparently viable tenders. Tenders are likely to have different strengths and weaknesses - a process to establish the 'best' tender needs to be established. Two common ways of comparing software or systems are benchmark tests and weighted ranking scores.

Benchmark tests

9.14 There are several factors involved in measuring the capability of a system. Benchmark tests are particularly useful to compare system speed and capacity.

8: Selecting and managing information technology

> **KEY TERM**
>
> **Benchmark tests** test how long it takes a machine and program to run through a particular routine or set of routines.

9.15 Benchmark tests are carried out to compare the performance of a piece of hardware or software against pre-set criteria. Typical criteria which may be used as benchmarks include speed of performance of a particular operation, acceptable volumes before a degradation in response times is apparent and the general user-friendliness of equipment. Benchmarks can cover subjective tests such as user-friendliness, although it may be harder to reach definitive conclusions.

9.16 For example, an organisation comparing accounting software packages may test a number of different packages on its own existing hardware to see which performed the best according to various predefined criteria (eg speed of response, ability to process different volumes of transactions, reporting capabilities and so on).

9.17 Once the performance of the software package under consideration has been evaluated, the acquiring organisation should consider other features of the proposal, possibly using a weighted ranking system.

Weighted ranking

> **KEY TERM**
>
> A **weighted ranking** system involves establishing a number of factors important to a system, giving each factor a numerical weighting to reflect its importance, and using these weightings to calculate a score for each supplier (or software, or system).

9.18 The factors chosen to be used in the weighted ranking, and the relative importance of each factor will vary according to the purpose of the software/system under consideration. Judgements need to be made in the selection of criteria, the weightings applied to the criteria and the scores allocated. These judgements must be made by people who have a good understanding of the software/system requirements.

9.19 The following example shows how weighted ranking scores could be calculated.

Case example

An organisation must chose between three software suppliers.

The decision-makers within the organisation have decided on the relevant criteria and weightings that will be used to judge the suppliers. This information is shown in the following model, together with the scores that have been allocated to each supplier.

Part B: Information technology and systems

Ranking scale: 3 = best supplier, 1 = worst		Supplier A software		Supplier B software		Supplier C software	
Weighted ranking							
Criteria	Weight	Rank	Weighted rank score	Rank	Weighted rank score	Rank	Weighted rank score
User friendliness	9	2	18	3	27	1	9
Cost	4	1	4	2	8	3	12
Controls/Security	8	1	8	3	24	2	16
Processing speed	7	3	21	2	14	1	7
Support	10	2	20	1	10	3	30
		Total score	**71**	**Total score**	**83**	**Total score**	**74**

The weighted ranking calculation shows that the software supplied by Supplier B appears to best meet the organisation's needs.

The advantages and disadvantages of bespoke and off-the-shelf software

Bespoke software

9.20 **Advantages** of having software specially written include the following.

(a) If it is well-written, the software should meet the organisation's specific needs.

(b) Data and file structures may be chosen by the organisation rather than having to meet the structures required by standard software packages.

(c) The company may be able to do things with its software that competitors cannot do with theirs. In other words it is a source of competitive advantage.

(d) Similar organisations may wish to purchase the software.

(e) The software should be able to be modified to meet future needs.

9.21 Key **disadvantages** are.

(a) As the software is being developed from scratch, there is a risk that the package may not perform as intended.

(b) There is a greater chance of 'bugs'. Widely used off-the-shelf software is more likely to have had bugs identified and removed.

(c) Development will take longer than purchasing ready-made software.

(d) The cost is considerable when compared with a ready-made package.

(e) Support costs are also likely to be higher than with off-the-shelf software.

Overcoming the risks of bespoke development

9.22 Building a bespoke software application involves much time, effort and money. The risks associated with such an undertaking are that the resulting software:

- Does not meet user needs
- Does not interact as intended with other systems

8: Selecting and managing information technology

- Is produced late
- Is produced over-budget

9.23 These risks can be minimised or overcome by:

(a) Good project management.

(b) Involving users at all stages of development.

(c) Ensuring in-house IT staff are able to maintain and support bespoke systems supplied from outside parties.

(d) Ensuring the ITT document includes details of all file structures required, and details of interfaces with other systems.

Off-the-shelf packages

9.24 **Advantages** of an off-the-shelf package

(a) The software is likely to be available immediately.

(b) A ready-made package will almost certainly cheaper because it is 'mass-produced".

(c) The software is likely to have been written by software specialists and so should be of a high quality.

(d) A successful package will be continually updated by the software manufacturer.

(e) Other users will have used the package already, and a well-established package should be relatively free of bugs.

(f) Good packages are well-documented, with easy-to-follow user manuals or on-line help.

(g) Some standard packages can be customised to the user's specific needs (see below).

9.25 The **disadvantages** of ready-made packages are as follows.

(a) The organisation is purchasing a standard solution. A standard solution may not be well suited to the organisation's particular needs.

(b) The organisation is dependent on the supplier for maintenance of the package - ie updating the package or providing assistance in the event of problems. It is unlikely that the supplier would give access to the code that would allow organisations with the relevant expertise to amend the software themselves.

(c) Competitors may well use the same package, removing any chance of using IS/IT for competitive advantage.

Customised versions of standard packages

9.26 Standard packages can be customised so that they fit an organisation's specific requirements. This can be done by purchasing the source code of the package and making modifications in-house, or by paying the producer of the package to customise it.

9.27 **Advantages** of customisation are similar to those of producing a bespoke system, with the additional advantages that:

(a) Development time should be much quicker, given that most of the system will be written already.

(b) If the work is done in-house the organisation gains considerable knowledge of how the software works and may be able to 'tune' it so that it works more efficiently with the company's hardware.

9.28 **Disadvantages** of customising a standard package include the following.

(a) It may prove more costly than expected, because new versions of the standard package will also have to be customised.

(b) Customisation may delay delivery of the software.

(c) Customisation may introduce bugs that do not exist in the standard version.

(d) If done in-house, the in-house team may have to learn new skills.

(e) If done by the original manufacturer disadvantages such as those for off-the-shelf packages may arise.

Add-ons and programming tools

9.29 Two other ways of trying to give a computer user more flexibility with packages are:

(a) The sale of 'add-ons' to a basic package, which an organisation may purchase if the add-ons suit their particular needs.

(b) The provision of programming tools (such as fourth generation languages) with a package, which allows users to write amendments to the software (without having to be a programming expert).

Software contracts and licences

Software contracts

9.30 The agreement to supply bespoke software should be formally laid out in a contract. The contract to supply the software is likely to include terms relating to:

(a) The cost, and what this figure does and does not include.

(b) Delivery date.

(c) Ownership of the source code, sometimes referred to as ownership rights.

(d) Right to make copies.

(e) Number of licensed users.

(f) Performance criteria, such as what the software will and will not do, processing speed.

(e) Warranty period.

(f) Support available.

(g) Arrangements for upgrades.

(h) Maintenance arrangements.

Software licences

9.31 Packaged software generally has a licence, the terms of which users are deemed to have agreed to the moment the package is unwrapped or a seal is broken.

9.32 A licence typically covers matters such as:

(a) How many users can use the software.

(b) Whether it can be modified without the manufacturer's consent.

(c) In what circumstances the licence is terminated.

(d) A limitation of liability should the software contain bugs or be mis-used (in an 'exclusion clause'). This is a complex area that is still developing. The representations that the software supplier makes regarding the package's capabilities would also be taken into account in any legal dispute.

9.33 When a user purchases software they are merely buying the rights to use the software in line with the terms and conditions within the licence agreement. The licence will be issued with the software, on paper or in electronic form. It contains the terms and conditions of use, as set out by the software publisher or owner of the copyright. A breach of the licence conditions usually means the owners' copyright has been infringed. In the UK, computer software is defined as a Literary Work in the Copyright, Designs and Patents Act (1988).

9.34 The unauthorised copying of software is referred to as software piracy. If an organisation is using illegal copies of software, the organisation may face a civil suit, and corporate officers and individual employees may have criminal liability. In the UK, remedies for civil copyright infringement may include damages to compensate the copyright owners for damage caused to their business, including reputation, and for loss of sales. Criminal penalties can include unlimited fines and two years' imprisonment or both.

9.35 The most common type of software piracy in a business setting is referred to as Corporate Over-Use. This is the installation of software packages on more machines than there are licences for. For example if a company purchases five single-user licences of a software program but installs the software on ten machines, then they will be using five infringing copies. Similarly, if a company is running a large network and more users have access to a software program than the company has licences for, this too is Corporate Over-Use.

9.36 A grey area is the installation of programs on portable or laptop computers for use off-site. Generally speaking, if a person has a program installed on their desktop in the office and the same person has the same program on their laptop for off-site use, then this usually counts as one user under the licence rather than two. However, the terms in different licences may differ.

9.37 To ensure they do not infringe copyright organisations should:
- Make sure they receive and keep licences - these are valuable documents
- Track the number of users with access to licensed programs
- Periodically check all computers for unlicensed software
- Buy from reputable dealers
- Get a written quote listing hardware/software specification and version
- Require an itemised invoice giving details of all hardware and software supplied

9.38 In the UK, the Copyright, Designs and Patents Act 1998 specifically allows the making of back-up copies of software, but only providing it is for lawful use.

Part B: Information technology and systems

Choosing hardware

9.39 In general terms, the choice of computer hardware will depend on the following factors.

Factor	Comment
User requirements	The ease with which the computer configuration fits in with the user's requirements (eg direct access facilities, hard-copy output in given quantities).
Power	The power of the computer must be sufficient for current and foreseeable requirements. This is measured by: • Processor type • RAM in Mb • Clock speed in MHz • Hard disk size in Mb or Gb
Reliability	There should be a low expected 'break-down' rate. There should be back-up hardware available to limit any down-time in case of hardware failure.
Simplicity	Systems should be as simple as possible, whilst still capable of performing the tasks required.
Ease of communication	The system (hardware and software) should be able to communicate well with the user. Software is referred to as 'user-friendly' or 'user-unfriendly' but similar considerations apply to hardware (eg not all terminals are of standard screen size; the number and accessibility of terminals might also have a bearing on how well the user is able to put data into the computer or extract information).
Flexibility	The hardware should be able to meet new requirements as they emerge. More powerful CPUs tend to be more flexible.
Security	Keeping out 'hackers' and other unauthorised users is easier with more powerful systems, although security can be a major problem for any computer system.
Cost	The cost must be justified in terms of the benefits the hardware will provide.
Changeover	Whether the choice of hardware will help with a smooth changeover from the old to the new system.
Networking	Networking capacity, if a PC has been purchased.
Software	The hardware must be capable of running whatever software has been chosen.

10 INFORMATION SYSTEMS DEPARTMENT AND OUTSOURCING

Information systems department

10.1 Most organisations choose have an information systems department, or team responsible for the tasks and responsibilities associated with information systems. Information systems increasingly utilise information technology.

10.2 At the head of the information systems/information technology function will be either the IS/IT manager, or the IS/IT director.

8: Selecting and managing information technology

10.3 The IS/IT director would have responsibility for the following areas.

IS/IT director responsibility	Comment
IS/IT strategy development	The IS/IT strategy must compliment the overall strategy of the organisation. The strategy must also be achievable given budgetary constraints. Returns on investments in IS/IT should be monitored.
IS/IT risk management	This is a wide ranging area including legal risks, such as ensuring compliance with relevant data protection legislation, ensuring adequate IS/IT security measures and disaster recovery arrangements.
Steering committee	The IS/IT director should play a key role in a steering committee set up to oversee the role of IS/IT within the organisation. There is more on steering committees later in this chapter.
IS/IT infrastructure	Standards should be set for the purchase and use of hardware and software within the organisation.
Ensuring employees have the IS/IT support and tools the require	Efficient links are required between IS/IT staff and the rest of the organisation. Technical assistance should be easily obtainable.

10.4 An IS/IT director therefore requires a wide range of skills. The ideal person would possess technical know-how, excellent general management ability, a keen sense of business awareness and a good understanding of the organisations' operations.

IS/IT steering committee

10.5 The general purpose of an IS/IT steering committee would be to make decisions relating to the future use and development of IS/IT by the organisation. The steering committee should contain representatives from all departments of the organisation.

10.6 Common tasks of such a committee could include:

- Ensuring IS/IT activities comply with IS/IT strategy
- Ensuring IS/IT activities compliment the overall organisation strategy
- Ensuring resources committed to IS/IT are used effectively
- Monitoring IS/IT projects
- Providing leadership and guidance on IS/IT

10.7 Committee members should be chosen with the aim of ensuring the committee contains the wide range of technical and business knowledge required. The committee should liase closely with those affected by the decisions it will make.

Database administrator

10.8 A key information systems role is that of database administrator. A database administrator is responsible for all data and information held within an organisation. Key tasks include:

- Preparing and maintaining a record of all data held within the organisation (the data dictionary)

- Co-ordinating data and information use to avoid duplication and maximise efficiency
- Analysing the data requirements of new applications
- Implementing and controlling procedures to protect data integrity
- Recording data ownership

Operations control

10.9 Operations control is concerned with ensuring IS/IT systems are working and available to users. Key tasks include:

- Maintaining the IS/IT infrastructure
- Monitoring network usage and managing network resources
- Keeping employees informed, eg advance warning of service interruptions
- Virus protection measures eg ensuring anti-virus software updates are loaded
- Fault fixing

Systems development staff

10.10 In medium to large organisations in is likely that the IS department will include staff with programming and systems analysis skills. Key tasks for staff involved in systems development include:

- Systems analysis
- Systems design and specification
- Systems testing
- Systems evaluation and review

Data processing staff

10.11 Over the past two decades the traditional centralised data processing department has become less common. Most departments now process their own data using on-line systems, rather than batching up transactions and forwarding paper copies of them to a centralised department for processing.

10.12 Staff involved in data processing today are spread throughout the organisation, for example a call centre employee may input an order, an accounts clerk may process journal entries etc. Accurate data entry skills and an understanding of the task they are performing are key skills.

Information centre staff

> **KEY TERM**
>
> An **Information Centre (IC)** is a small unit of staff with a good technical awareness of computer systems, whose task is to provide a support function to computer users within the organisation.

10.13 Information centres, sometimes referred to as **support centres**, are particularly useful in organisations which use distributed systems and so are likely to have hardware, data and software scattered throughout the organisation.

8: Selecting and managing information technology

Help

10.14 An IC usually offers a **Help Desk** to solve IT problems. Help may be via the telephone, e-mail, through a searchable knowledge base or in person.

10.15 **Remote diagnostic software** may be used which enables staff in the IC to take control of a computer and sort out the problem without leaving their desk.

10.16 The help desk needs sufficient staff and technical expertise to respond quickly and effectively to requests for help. IC staff should also maintain good relationships with hardware and software suppliers to ensure their maintenance staff are quickly on site when needed.

Problem solving

10.17 The IC will maintain a record of problems and identify those that occur most often. If the problem is that users do not know how to use the system, training is provided.

10.18 Training applications often contain analysis software, drawing attention to trainee progress and common problems. This information enables the IC to identify and address specific training needs more closely.

10.19 If the problem is with the system itself, a solution is found, either by modifying the system or by investment in new hardware or software.

Improvements

10.20 The IC may also be required to consider the viability of suggestions for improving the system, and to bring these improvements into effect.

Standards

10.21 The IC is also likely to be responsible for setting, and encouraging users to conform to, common **standards**.

(a) Hardware standards ensure that all of the equipment used in the organisation is compatible and can be put into use in different departments as needed.

(b) Software standards ensure that information generated by one department can easily be shared with and worked upon by other departments.

(c) Programming standards ensure that applications developed by individual end-users (for example complex spreadsheet macros) follow best practice and are easy to modify.

(d) Data processing standards ensure that certain conventions such as the format of file names are followed throughout the organisation. This facilitates sharing, storage and retrieval of information.

Security

10.22 The IC may help to preserve the security of data in various ways.

(a) It may develop utility programs and procedures to ensure that back-ups are made at regular intervals.

(b) The IC may help to preserve the company's systems from attack by computer viruses, for instance by ensuring that the latest versions of anti-virus software are available to

Part B: Information technology and systems

all users, by reminding users regularly about the dangers of viruses, and by setting up and maintaining 'firewalls', which deny access to sensitive parts of the company's systems.

End-user applications development

10.23 An IC can help applications development by providing technical guidance to end-user developers and to encourage comprehensible and well-documented programs. Understandable programs can be maintained or modified more easily. Documentation provides a means of teaching others how the programs work. These efforts can greatly extend the usefulness and life of the programs that are developed.

Centralisation and decentralisation

10.24 We now look at how the IS/IT department could be structured. There are two main options – centralised or decentralised. (Note that we are now discussing IS/IT department structure, rather than system architecture which was covered earlier in this chapter.)

> **KEY TERMS**
>
> A **centralised** IS/IT department involves all IS/IT staff and functions being based out at a single central location, such as head office.
>
> A **decentralised** IS/IT department involves IS/IT staff and functions being spread out throughout the organisation.

10.25 There is no single 'best' structure for an IS/IT department – an organisation should consider its IS/IT requirements and the merits of each structure.

10.26 **Advantages** of a centralised IS/IT department.

   (a) Assuming centralised processing is used, there is only one set of files. Everyone uses the same data and information.

   (b) It gives better security/control over data and files. It is easier to enforce standards.

   (c) Head office is in a better position to know what is going on.

   (d) There may be economies of scale available in purchasing computer equipment and supplies.

   (e) Computer staff are in a single location, and more expert staff are likely to be employed. Career paths may be more clearly defined.

10.27 **Disadvantages** of a centralised IS/IT department.

   (a) Local offices might have to wait for IS/IT services and assistance.
   (b) Reliance on head office. Local offices are less elf-sufficient.
   (c) A system fault at head office will impact across the organisation.

10.28 **Advantages** of a decentralised IS/IT department.

   (a) Each office can introduce an information system specially **tailored** for its individual needs. Local changes in business requirements can be taken into account.

   (b) Each office is more self-sufficient.

8: Selecting and managing information technology

(c) Offices are likely to have quicker access to IS/IT support/advice.

(d) A decentralised structure is more likely to facilitate accurate IS/IT cost/overhead allocations.

10.29 **Disadvantages** of a decentralised IS/IT department.

(a) Control may be more difficult - different and uncoordinated information systems may be introduced.

(b) Self-sufficiency may encourage a lack of co-ordination between departments.

(c) Increased risk of data duplication, with different offices holding the same data on their own separate files.

Outsourcing IT/IS services

> **KEY TERM**
>
> **Outsourcing** is the contracting out of specified operations or services to an external vendor.

10.30 There are four **broad classifications** of outsourcing.

Classification	Comment
Ad-hoc	The organisation has a short-term requirement for increased IS/IT skills. An example would be employing programmers on a short-term contract to help with the programming of bespoke software.
Project management	The development and installation of a particular IS/IT project is outsourced. For example, a new accounting system. (This approach is sometimes referred to as **systems integration.**)
Partial	Some IT/IS services are outsourced. Examples include hardware maintenance, network management or ongoing website management.
Total	An external supplier provides the vast majority of an organisation's IT/IS services. Eg a third party owns or is responsible for IT equipment, software and possibly staff.

Levels of service provision

10.31 The degree to which the provision and management of IS/IT services are transferred to the third party varies according to the situation and the skills of both organisations.

(a) **Time-share**. The vendor charges for access to an external processing system on a time-used basis. Software ownership may be with either the vendor or the client organisation.

(b) **Service bureaux** usually focus on a specific function. Traditionally bureaux would provide the same type of service to many organisations, eg payroll processing. As organisations have developed their own IT infrastructure, the use of bureaux has decreased.

(c) **Facilities management (FM)**. The terms 'outsourcing' and 'facilities management' are sometimes confused. Facilities management traditionally involved contracts for premises-related services such as cleaning or site security.

In the context of IS/IT, facilities management involves an outside agency managing the organisation's IS/IT facilities. All equipment usually remains with the client, but the responsibility for providing and managing the specified services rests with the FM company. FM companies operating in the UK include Accenture, Cap Gemini, EDS and CFM.

10.32 The following table shows the main features of each of the outsourcing arrangements described above.

Feature	Outsourcing arrangement		
	Timeshare	Service bureaux	Facilities Management (FM)
Management responsibility	Mostly retained	Some retained	Very little retained
Focus	Operational	A function	Strategic
Timescale	Short-term	Medium-term	Long-term
Justification	Cost savings	More efficient	Access to expertise; higher quality service provision. Enables management to concentrate on the areas where they do possess expertise.

Organisations involved in outsourcing

Facilities management companies

10.33 FM arrangements have been covered in paragraph 10.31(c).

Software houses

10.34 Software houses concentrate on the provision of 'software services'. These services include feasibility studies, systems analysis and design, development of operating systems software, provision of application program packages, 'tailor-made' application programming, specialist systems advice, and so on. For example, a software house might be employed to write a computerised system for the London Stock Exchange.

Consultancy firms

10.35 Some consultancy firms work at a fairly high level, giving advice to management on the general approach to solving problems and on the types of system to use. Others specialise in giving more particular systems advice, carrying out feasibility studies and recommending computer manufacturers/software houses that will supply the right system. When a consultancy firm is used, the terms of the contract should be agreed at the outset.

10.36 The use of consultancy services enables management to learn directly or indirectly from the experience of others. Many larger consultancies are owned by big international accountancy firms; smaller consultancies may consist of one-or-two person operations with a high level of specialist experience in one area.

10.37 The following categories of **consulting activity** have been identified by *Beaumont and Sutherland*.

8: Selecting and managing information technology

(a) **Strategic studies**, involving the development of a business strategy or an IS strategy for an organisation.

(b) **Specialist studies**, where the consultant provides a high level of expertise in one area, for example Enterprise Resource Management software.

(c) **Project management**, involving supervision of internal and external parties in the completion of a particular project.

(d) **Body-shopping**, where the necessary staff, including consultants, project managers, systems analysts and programmers, for a project are identified.

(e) **Recruitment**, involving the supply of permanent or temporary staff.

Hardware manufacturers and suppliers

10.38 Computer manufacturers or their designated suppliers will provide the **equipment** necessary for a system. They will also provide, under a **maintenance contract**, engineers who will deal with any routine servicing and with any breakdown of the equipment.

Case example

The retailer Sears outsourced the management of its vast information technology and accounting functions to Accenture. First year *savings* were estimated to be £5 million per annum, growing to £14 million in the following year, and thereafter. This is clearly considerable, although re-organisation costs relating to redundancies, relocation and asset write-offs are thought to be in the region of £35 million. About 900 staff were involved: under the transfer of undertakings regulations (which protect employees when part or all of a company changes hands), Accenture was obliged to take on the existing Sears staff. This provided new opportunities for the staff who moved, while those who remained at Sears are free to concentrate on strategy development and management direction.

Developments in outsourcing

10.39 Outsourcing arrangements are becoming increasingly flexible to cope with the ever-changing nature of the modern business environment. Three trends are:

(a) **Multiple sourcing**. This involves outsourcing different functions or areas of the IS/IT function to a range of suppliers. Some suppliers may form alliances to present a stronger case for selection.

(b) **Incremental approach**. Organisations progressively outsource selected areas of their IT/IS function. Possible problems with outsourced services are solved before progressing to the next stage.

(c) **Joint venture sourcing**. This term is used to describe an organisation entering into a joint venture with a supplier. The costs (risks) and possible rewards are split on an agreed basis. Such an arrangement may be suitable when developing software that could be sold to other organisations.

(d) **Application Service Providers (ASP)**. ASPs are third parties that manage and distribute software services and solutions to customers across a Wide Area Network. ASP's could be considered the modern equivalent of the traditional computer bureaux.

Managing outsourcing arrangements

10.40 Managing outsourcing arrangements involves deciding **what** will be outsourced, **choosing and negotiating** with suppliers and managing the supplier **relationship**.

Part B: Information technology and systems

10.41 When considering whether to outsource a particular service the following questions are relevant.

(a) Is the system of **strategic importance**? Strategic IS are generally not suited to outsourcing as they require a high degree of specific business knowledge that a third party IT specialist cannot be expected to possess.

(b) Can the system be relatively isolated? Functions that have only **limited interfaces** are most easily outsourced, eg payroll.

(c) Do we know enough about the system to manage the outsourced service agreement? If an organisation knows very little about a technology it may be difficult to know what constitutes good service and value for money. It may be necessary to recruit additional **expertise** to manage the relationship with the other party.

(d) Are our requirements likely to **change**? Organisations should avoid tying themselves into a long-term outsourcing agreement if requirements are likely to change.

10.42 A key factor when **choosing and negotiating** with external vendors is the contract offered and subsequently negotiated with the supplier. The contract is sometimes referred to as the **Service Level Contract** (SLC) or **Service Level Agreement** (SLA).

10.43 The key elements of the contract are described below.

Contract element	Comment
Service level	The contract should clearly specify **minimum levels of service** to be provided. Penalties should be specified for failure to meet these standards. Relevant factors will vary depending on the nature of the services outsourced but could include: • Response time to requests for assistance/information • System 'uptime' percentage • Deadlines for performing relevant tasks
Exit route	Arrangements for an exit route, addressing how transfer to another supplier, or the move back in-house would be conducted.
Timescale	When does the contract expire? Is the timescale suitable for the organisation's needs or should it be renegotiated?
Software ownership	Relevant factors include: • Software licensing and security • If the arrangement includes the development of new software who owns the copyright?
Dependencies	If related services are outsourced, the level of service quality agreed should group these services together.
Employment issues	If the arrangement includes provision for the organisation's IT staff to move to the third party, employer responsibilities must be specified clearly.

10.44 After a supplier has been selected, and the contract negotiated and signed, the contract provides the framework for the **relationship** between the organisation and the service provider.

8: Selecting and managing information technology

10.45 The nature of the relationship between the organisation and the service provider will depend on the service that has been outsourced and the preferences and personalities of the people involved.

10.46 If full facilities management is involved, and almost all management responsibility for IT/IS lies with the entity providing the service, then a close relationship between the parties is necessary (a '**partnership**'). Factors such as organisation culture need to be considered when entering into such a close and critical relationship.

10.47 On the other hand, if a relatively simple function such as payroll were outsourced, such a close relationship with the supplier would not be necessary. A 'typical' supplier - customer relationship is all that is required. (Although issues such as confidentiality need to be considered with payroll data.)

10.48 Regardless of the type of relationship, a legally binding contract is the key element in establishing the obligations and responsibilities of all parties.

Question 4

Do any organisations with which you are familiar use outsourcing? What is the view of outsourcing in the organisation?

Answer

One view is given below.

The PA Consulting Group's annual survey of outsourcing found that 'on average the top five strategic outsourcers out-performed the FTSE by more than 100 per cent over three years; the bottom five under-performed by more than 66%'.

However the survey revealed that of those organisations who have opted to outsource IT functions, only five per cent are truly happy with the results. A spokesman for the consultants said that this is because most people fail to adopt a proper strategic approach, taking a view that is neither long-term nor broad enough, and taking outsourcing decisions that are piecemeal and unsatisfactory.

This lack of prescience is compounded by a failure to take a sufficiently rigorous approach to selection, specification, contract drafting and contract management.

The survey found that a constant complaint among many of those interviewed is the lack of ability of outsourcing organisations to work together.

Twenty-five per cent of those asked would bring the functions they had outsourced back in-house if it were possible.

Source: Business and Technology magazine

Advantages of outsourcing arrangements

10.49 The **advantages** of outsourcing are as follows.

(a) Outsourcing can remove uncertainty about **cost**, as there is often a long-term contract where services are specified in advance for a **fixed price**. If computing services are inefficient, the costs will be borne by the FM company. This is also an incentive to the third party to provide a high quality service.

(b) Long-term contracts (maybe up to ten years) encourage **planning** for the future.

(c) Outsourcing can bring the benefits of **economies of scale**. For example, a FM company may conduct research into new technologies that benefits a number of their clients.

(d) A specialist organisation is able to retain **skills and knowledge**. Many organisations would not have a sufficiently well-developed IT department to offer IT staff opportunities for career development. Talented staff would leave to pursue their careers elsewhere.

(e) New skills and knowledge become available. A specialist company can **share** staff with **specific expertise** (such as programming in HTML to produce Web pages) between several clients. This allows the outsourcing company to take advantage of new developments without the need to recruit new people or re-train existing staff, and without the cost.

(f) **Flexibility** (contract permitting). Resources may be able to be scaled up or down depending upon demand. For instance, during a major changeover from one system to another the number of IT staff needed may be twice as large as it will be once the new system is working satisfactorily.

An outsourcing organisation is more able to arrange its work on a **project** basis, whereby some staff will expect to be moved periodically from one project to the next.

Disadvantages of outsourcing arrangements

10.50 Some possible **drawbacks** are outlined below.

(a) It is arguable that information and its provision is **an inherent part of the business and of management**. Unlike office cleaning, or catering, an organisation's IS services may be too important to be contracted out. Information is at the heart of management.

(b) A company may have highly **confidential information** and to let outsiders handle it could be seen as **risky** in commercial and/or legal terms.

(c) Information strategy can be used to gain **competitive advantage**. Opportunities may be missed if a third party is handling IS services, because there is no onus upon internal management to keep up with new developments and have new ideas. Any new technology or application devised by the third party is likely to be available to competitors.

(d) An organisation may find itself **locked in** to an unsatisfactory contract. The decision may be very difficult to reverse. If the FM company supplies unsatisfactory levels of service, the effort and expense the organisation would incur to rebuild its own computing function or to move to another provider could be substantial.

(e) The use of FM does not encourage awareness of the potential costs and benefits of IS/IT within the organisation. If managers cannot manage in-house IS/IT resources effectively, then it could be argued that they will not be able to manage an arrangement to outsource effectively either.

Insourcing

10.51 Outsourcing involves purchasing information technology services or expertise from outside the organisation. Several factors have led some to believe this is not the best solution in today's environment.

(a) Many organisations have found there is a shortage of qualified **candidates** with the skills they require.

(b) The **cost** of acquiring people with high-tech expertise and business skills, whether employing or outsourcing, fluctuates due to factors affecting supply and demand.

8: Selecting and managing information technology

(c) Third, there is increasing recognition that to do a good job, IT professionals must understand the **business principles** behind the systems that they develop and manage.

10.52 Insourcing involves recruiting IS/IT staff internally, from other areas of the business, and teaching these business-savvy employees about technology. The logic behind the idea is that it is easier (and cheaper) to **teach technical skills to business people** than to teach business skills to technical people.

10.53 Supporters of insourcing believe it has the potential to:

(a) Create a better quality workforce that combines both technical and business skills.
(b) Reduce costs.
(c) Improve relationships and communication between IT staff and other departments.
(d) Increase staff retention.

10.54 Possible disadvantages include:

(a) The risk that non-technical employees will not pick up the IS/IT skills required.
(b) Finding staff willing to make the change.
(c) Replacing staff who do make the switch.

11 THE INTERNET

> **KEY TERM**
>
> The **Internet** is a global network connecting millions of computers.

11.1 The Internet is the name given to the technology that allows any computer with a telecommunications link to **send and receive information** from any other suitably equipped computer.

11.2 The **World Wide Web** is the multimedia element which provides facilities such as full-colour, graphics, sound and video. Websites are points within the network created by those who wish to provide an information point for searchers to visit and benefit by the provision of information and/or by entering into a transaction.

11.3 Most companies now have a **website** on the Internet. A site is a collection of screens providing **information in text and graphic form**, any of which can be viewed simply by clicking the appropriate button, word or image on the screen.

Current uses of the Internet

11.4 The scope and potential of the Internet are still developing. Its uses already embrace the following:

(a) **Dissemination** of information.
(b) **Product/service development** - through almost instantaneous test marketing.
(c) **Transaction processing** (electronic commerce or e-commerce) - both business-to-business (B2B) and business-to-consumer (B2C).
(d) **Relationship enhancement** - between various groups of stakeholders.
(e) **Recruitment** and job search - involving organisations worldwide.

(f) **Entertainment** - including music, humour, art, games and some less wholesome pursuits!

11.5 It is estimated that over 40% of households in the UK will have Internet access by the end of 2002.

11.6 The Internet provides opportunities to organise for and to automate tasks which would previously have required more costly interaction with the organisation. These have often been called low-touch or zero-touch approaches.

11.7 Tasks which a **website may automate** include:

(a) **Frequently-Asked Questions (FAQs)**: carefully-structured sets of answers can deal with many customer interactions.

(b) **Status checking**: major service enquiries (Where is my order? When will the engineer arrive? What is my bank balance?) can also be automated, replacing high-cost human service processes, and also providing the opportunity to proactively offer better service and new services.

(c) **Keyword search**: the ability to search provides web users with opportunities to find information in large and complex websites.

(d) **Wizards (interview style interface)**: these can help ensure people are directed to the information most relevant to them.

(e) **E-mail and systems to route and track inbound e-mail**: the ability to route and/or to provide automatic responses will enable organisations to deal with high volumes of e-mail from actual and potential customers.

(f) **Bulletin boards**: these enable customers to interact with each other, thus facilitating self-activated customer service and also the opportunity for product/service referral. Cisco in particular has created communities of Cisco users who help each other - thus reducing the service costs for Cisco itself.

(g) **Call-back buttons**: these enable customers to speak to someone in order to deal with and resolve a problem; the more sophisticated systems allow the call-centre operator to know which web pages the users were consulting at the time.

(h) **Transaction processing**: usually referred to as e-commerce.

Problems with the Internet

11.8 To a large extent the Internet has grown organically **without any formal organisation**. There are specific communication standards, but it is not **owned** by any one body and there are no clear guidelines on how it should develop.

11.9 The **quality** of much of the information on the Internet leaves much to be desired.

11.10 Speed is a major issue. Data only downloads onto the user's PC at the speed of the slowest telecommunications link - downloading data can be a painfully **slow** procedure.

11.11 So much information and entertainment is available that employers worry that their **staff will spend too much time** browsing through non-work-related sites.

11.12 Connecting an information system to the Internet exposes the system to numerous **security issues**.

Chapter roundup

- **Computers** can be classified as supercomputers, mainframes, minicomputers and PCs. The amount of **RAM** and the **processor speed** are key determinants of computer performance. Hard drive size is another important factor.

- The **operating system** provides the interface between hardware, software and user.

- There are a range of **input** and **output** devices available. The most efficient method will depend on the circumstances of each situation.

- Hard disks are used for internal **storage** - external storage may be on floppy disk, zip drive, CD-ROM or DVD.

- The term **system architecture** refers to the way in which the various components of an information system are linked together, and the way they relate to each other. A **centralised** architecture involves all computer processing being carried out on a single central processor. **Distributed** architectures spread the processing power throughout the organisation at several different locations.

- **Off-the-shelf software** is produced to meet requirements that are common to many organisations. The software is likely to be available **immediately** and **cost significantly less** than bespoke solutions. However, as it has not been written specifically for the organisation, it may not meet all of their requirements.

- **Bespoke software** should be written so as to **match** the organisation's requirements exactly. However, the software is likely to be considerably **more expensive** than an off-the-shelf package.

- An organisation that requires bespoke software to be written may issue an **Invitation to Tender (ITT)** to a range of potential suppliers.

- Some organisations **outsource** their IT function to external organisations. Outsourcing has advantages (eg access to specialised expertise) and disadvantages (eg lack of control over a key resource).

- Many organisations are now utilising **the Internet** as a means of gathering and disseminating information, and conducting transactions.

Quick quiz

1 List four reasons why manual office systems may be less beneficial than computerised systems.

   1 ....
   2 ....
   3 ....
   4 ....

2 What is RAM?

3 List five ways an organisation could input or capture data.

   1 ....
   2 ....
   3 ....
   4 ....
   5 ....

4 Distinguish between batch and real-time processing.

5 Why would an organisation issue an Invitation To Tender (ITT)?

6 What is a benchmark test?

7 What would you say is the main advantage of bespoke software?

Part B: Information technology and systems

8 What is the main disadvantage of bespoke software?

9 How could a weighted ranking system help choose between different software proposals?

10 Identify four broad classifications of outsourcing.

11 Do you agree with the statement 'information derived from the Internet is unreliable'? Justify your answer.

Answers to quick quiz

1 Manual systems may be slower, more prone to error, require more labour and may be unable to handle large volumes of data. (This assumes the computerised system is operating correctly, is reliable and that staff know how to utilise it fully.)

2 RAM stands for Random Access Memory. It holds the data and programs in current use. RAM and processor speed are important indicators of processing power.

3 [Five of]

Keyboard.	Mouse
Scanner and OCR.	Bar codes and scanner.
MICR.	OMR.
EPOS.	EFTPOS.
Touch sensitive screen.	Voice recognition software and a microphone.

4 Batch processing is the processing as a group of a number of transactions of a similar kind. Real-time processing is the continual receiving and processing of data. Real-time processing uses an 'on-line' computer system to interrogate or update files as requested, rather than batching for subsequent processing.

5 To invite tenders (offers to supply) for the system specified in the ITT.

6 A test of how long a machine and a program takes to run through a routine. Benchmark scores enable comparisons between systems.

7 As it is written for a specific purpose it should match user requirements very closely.

8 It's expensive when compared to off-the-shelf software.

9 A weighted ranking system involves establishing a number of factors important to a system, giving each factor a numerical weighting to reflect its importance, and using these weightings to calculate a score for each supplier (or software, or system).

10 Ad-hoc - a short-term requirement for increased IS/IT skills. Project management - eg an IS/IT project is outsourced. Partial -some IT/IS services are outsourced. Total - an external supplier provides the vast majority of an organisation's IT/IS services.

11 The Internet provides a means of accessing information from a wide range of organisations. Some of these organisations will provide good quality information (eg CIMA, BBC, etc), others may provide information that proves to be unreliable. Who is behind the information is a more significant indicator of reliability than the fact that the information was transmitted over the Internet.

The material covered in this Chapter is tested in Questions 11(b), 12, 15 and 20 in the Question Bank.

Chapter 9

EFFECTIVE COMMUNICATION

Topic list	Syllabus reference	Ability required
1 Co-ordination and communication	(ii)	Evaluation
2 The main communication tools	(ii)	Evaluation

Introduction

We have included communication within the information technology and systems part of this text to remain **consistent with the syllabus** structure.

Communication as a topic is applicable to many areas of business. This chapter starts with a brief outline of communication **theory**, then looks at communication in a **practical** business setting.

Learning outcomes covered in this chapter

- **Explain** the importance of effective communication and the consequences of failure in the communication process
- **Analyse** communication problems in a range of organisational situations
- **Recommend** changes or actions to avoid or correct communication problems

Syllabus content covered in this chapter

- The purpose and process of communication
- Communication problems and solutions
- The main communication tools, their features and limitations

1 CO-ORDINATION AND COMMUNICATION

Co-ordination

1.1 Central to the concept of organisation is the notion that the activities of the different people in the organisation need to be **co-ordinated**. So, the basic principle on which any idea of organisation is based is that of co-ordination.

1.2 *Mintzberg* lists the following ways in which work can be co-ordinated.

(a) **Mutual adjustment** co-ordinates work by informal communication. This is used for the most simple work, and the most complicated: simple, because it is an obvious mechanism for small groups; complex, as in some tasks it is impossible to plan very far ahead.

(b) **Direct supervision** achieves co-ordination by having one person responsible for the work of others. This person issues instructions and monitors performance. The division of labour is sharp.

(c) **Standardisation of work processes** occurs if tasks are performed according to strict rules and procedures, as in the operation of aircraft and railways.

(d) **Standardisation of outputs**. A standard output such as a component, a record or a service can be an input into a subsequent process with a minimum of co-ordination.

(e) **Standardisation by skills and knowledge** co-ordinates work by specifying the kind of training to perform the work. An example is a hospital. Doctors are trained in the necessary skills before being let loose on the patients. All teachers are trained, but they have considerable leeway in how they apply their knowledge.

1.3 The relative **complexity of the work affects the chosen method of co-ordination**. *Mintzberg* believes that the following relationships exist.

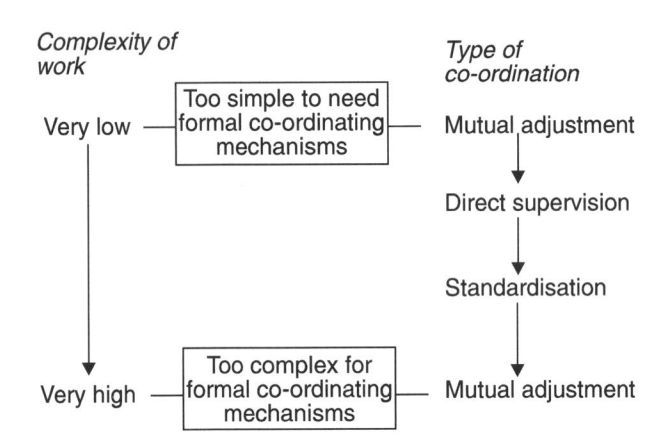

```
Complexity of                              Type of
work                                       co-ordination

Very low  ── Too simple to need       ── Mutual adjustment
             formal co-ordinating
             mechanisms
                                            ↓
                                         Direct supervision
                                            ↓
                                         Standardisation
                                            ↓
Very high ── Too complex for          ── Mutual adjustment
             formal co-ordinating
             mechanisms
```

1.4 The **organisation structure** and co-ordinating methods are responsible for the success with which a strategy is implemented, given that implementing strategy largely deals with the co-ordination and direction of individual work tasks.

1.5 As organisations grow in size, we have seen that some have a tendency to become complex. Co-ordinating the activities of people implies that the organisation **includes appropriate systems of communication**.

Communication 5/02

> **KEY TERM**
>
> **Communication** describes the process by which information is made available to others.

1.6 In any organisation, the communication of information is necessary to achieve co-ordination, whichever type of co-ordination is used.

(a) **Management**. Management need communication to make the necessary decisions for planning, co-ordination and control; managers should be aware of what their departments are achieving, what they are not achieving and what they should be achieving.

9: Effective communication

(b) **Departments**. All the interdependent systems for purchasing, production, marketing and administration can be synchronised to perform the right actions at the right times to co-operate in accomplishing the organisation's aims.

(c) **Individuals**. Employees should know what is expected from them. Effective communication gives an employee's job meaning, makes personal development possible, and acts as a motivator, as well as oiling the wheels of labour relations.

(d) **Organisational learning**. The communication system is necessary to enable the organisation to develop and disseminate new ideas. This links with the concept of **knowledge management** - that is ensuring the knowledge held by an organisation's staff is available to all.

Direction of communication

1.7 Communication is perhaps most routine between people at the same or similar level in the organisation (horizontal communication). It is necessary for two reasons.

(e) **Formal** to co-ordinate the work of several people, and perhaps departments, who have to co-operate to carry out a certain operation.

(f) **Informal** to furnish emotional and social support to an individual.

1.8 Communication within the formal organisation structure may be of the following types.

(a) **Vertical** ie up and down the scalar chain.

(b) **Horizontal or lateral**: between people of the same level or status – either in the same section or department, or in different sections or departments.

Horizontal communication is usually easier and more direct than vertical communication, being less inhibited by considerations of the organisation hierarchy.

(c) **Diagonal**. This is **interdepartmental** communication by people of different ranks. Departments in the technostructure which serve the organisation in general, such as Personnel or Information Systems, have no clear line of authority linking them to managers in other departments who need their involvement.

The communication process

1.9 The diagram below demonstrates in outline the process of communication.

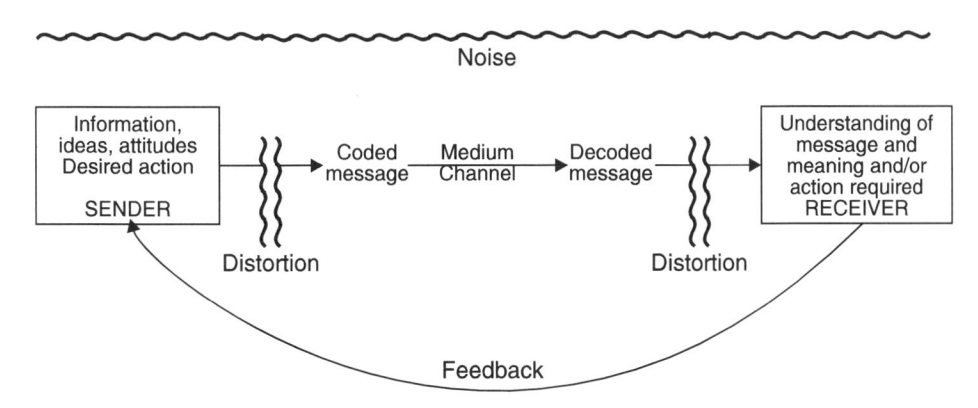

```
                              Noise
┌───────────────┐                                    ┌───────────────┐
│ Information,  │                                    │ Understanding │
│ ideas, attitudes│  Coded   Medium    Decoded       │ of message and│
│ Desired action│→ message  Channel →  message    →  │ meaning and/or│
│               │                                    │ action required│
│    SENDER     │                                    │   RECEIVER    │
└───────────────┘                                    └───────────────┘
              Distortion              Distortion
                         Feedback
```

A number of points can be noted.

(a) **Coding of a message**: the code or 'language' of a message may be verbal (spoken or written) or it may be non-verbal, in pictures, diagrams, numbers or body language.

(b) **Medium for the message**: there are a number of channels for communication, such as a conversation, a letter, a notice board or via computer. The choice of medium used in communication depends on a number of factors such as urgency, permanency, complexity, sensitivity and cost.

(c) **Feedback**: it is of vital importance that the sender of a message gets feedback on the receiver's reaction. This is partly to test the receiver's understanding of it and partly to gauge the receiver's reaction.

(d) **Distortion** refers to the way in which the meaning of a message is lost in 'handling', that is at the coding and decoding stages. In multinational, or global corporations, it might be caused by differences in culture.

(e) **Noise** refers to distractions and interference in the environment in which communication is taking place. It may be physical noise (passing traffic), technical noise (a bad telephone line), social noise (differences in the personalities of the parties) or psychological noise (anger, frustration, tiredness).

Barriers to communication

1.10 Good communication is essential to getting any job done: co-operation is impossible without it. Difficulties occur because of general **faults in the communication process**.

   (a) **Distortion** or **omission** of information by the sender.

   (b) **Misunderstanding** due to lack of clarity or technical jargon.

   (c) **Non-verbal signs** (gesture, posture, facial expression) contradicting the verbal message, so that its meaning is in doubt.

   (d) **Information overload** - a person being given too much information to digest in the time available.

   (e) Differences in social, racial or educational background, compounded by age and personality differences, creating **barriers to understanding** and co-operation.

   (f) People hearing only **what they want to hear** in a message.

1.11 There may also be **particular difficulties** in a work situation.

   (a) A general tendency to **distrust** a message in its re-telling from one person to another.

   (b) People looking for 'hidden meanings' in a message.

   (c) The relative **status in the hierarchy** of the sender and receiver of information. A senior manager's words are listened to more closely and a colleague's perhaps discounted.

   (d) People from different job or specialist **backgrounds** (eg accountants, personnel managers, IT experts) having difficulty in talking on a non-specialist's wavelength.

   (e) People **discounting information** from those not recognised as having expertise.

   (f) People or departments having **different priorities** or perspectives so that one person places more or less emphasis on a situation than another.

   (g) The supplying of **incorrect** or **incomplete** information (eg to protect a colleague).

   (h) Reluctance to give information which **conflicts** with the manager's assumptions or **expectations.**

   (i) Managers who are prepared to make decisions on a 'hunch' without proper regard to the information they may or may not have received.

   (j) Information which has no immediate use tending to be forgotten.

(k) Lack of opportunity, formal or informal, for a subordinate to say what he or she thinks or feels.

(l) Where there is conflict between individuals or departments, communications will be withdrawn and information withheld.

(m) The barriers to good communication arising from differences in social, racial or educational backgrounds, compounded by age differences and personality differences, can be particularly severe.

(n) The culture of the organisation. Some organisations prefer secrecy, especially bureaucracies.

    (i) Information might be given on a need-to-know basis, rather than be considered as a potential resource for everyone to use.

    (ii) The culture of some organisations may prevent the communication of certain messages. Organisations with a 'can-do' philosophy may not want to hear that certain tasks are impossible.

    (iii) Participative management styles inevitably encourage communication between members.

Overcoming the barriers

1.12 Many of the barriers outlined in the previous paragraphs occur as a result of general faults in the communication process.

(a) **Distortion** or **omission** of information by the sender.
(b) **Misunderstanding** due to **lack of clarity** in the information request.
(c) **Misunderstanding** due to **lack of clarity** in the information provided.

1.13 General **communication skills** can increase the chance of effective communication.

(a) **Skills in the selected medium of communication.**

Skills in **spoken** communication	Skills in **written** communication *(paper-based or digital)*	Skills in **visual** communication
Clear pronunciation	Correct spelling	Understanding of, and control over body language and facial expressions
Suitable vocabulary for the situation	Suitable vocabulary	Dress style, personal grooming and presentation
Correct grammar/ syntax	Correct grammar/ syntax	Drawing or computer graphics ability
Fluency	Clear writing or typing (layout, style, font etc)	Use of 'multimedia' applications (sound, video)
Expressive delivery	Suitable style eg formal or informal	Clarity of visual message (layout, colour)
Tone of voice	Suitable channel eg letter, fax or e-mail	

(b) **General skills in sending messages**

    (i) **Selecting and organising your material**, 'marshalling' your thoughts and 'constructing' your sentences, arguments and so on.

    (ii) **Judging the effect of your message** on the particular recipient in the particular situation. Cultural differences may need to be considered.

Part B: Information technology and systems

(iii) **Choosing language and media** accordingly.

(iv) **Seeking and interpreting feedback.**

(c) **Skills in receiving messages**

(i) **Reading** attentively and intelligently, making sure you understand the content, seeking clarification if necessary.

(ii) **Extracting relevant information** from the message, and 'filtering out' inessentials.

(iii) **Listening:** concentrating on the message - not on what you are going to say next, or other matters.

(iv) **Interpreting the message's underlying meanings**, if any, and evaluating your own reactions: are you reading in the message more or less than what is really there?

(v) Giving useful **feedback**.

> **Exam focus point**
> Communication is a topic that can cover many different areas of the syllabus, for example information systems (an important medium for communication within the organisation) and project management (eg keeping team members informed about what is expected from them).

2 THE MAIN COMMUNICATON TOOLS 5/01

2.1 The 'best' way to communicate a message depends on the nature of the message, the composition of the audience and the preferences of the sender. For example, if you wish to inform people that the organisation is to close and all will be made redundant, an informal conversation would not have the required level of formality or procedure.

Choice of communication medium

2.2 The choice of medium will depend upon numerous factors, including the following.

(a) **Time**

How long will be needed to prepare the message, and how long will it take to transmit it in the chosen form? This must be weighed against the **urgency** with which the message must be sent.

(b) **Complexity**

What medium will enable the message to be most readily understood? If detailed or highly technical information is to be exchanged or where a message has many interdependent parts, oral communication alone is not appropriate.

(c) **Distance**

How far is the message required to travel? Must it be transmitted to an office on a different floor of the building, or across town, or to the other end of the country?

(d) **Written record**

A written record may be needed as proof, confirming a transaction, or for legal purposes, or as an aid to memory. It can be duplicated and sent to many recipients. It can be stored and later retrieved for reference and analysis as required.

9: Effective communication

(e) **Interaction**

Sometimes instant feedback is needed for effective communication, for example when you are questioning a customer to find out their precise requirements ('small, medium or large?', 'green, red or blue?').

(f) **Degree of confidentiality**

Telephone calls may be overheard; faxed messages can be read by whoever is standing by the fax machine; internal memos may be read by colleagues or by internal mail staff; highly personal letters may be read by the recipient's secretary.

On the other hand a message may need to be spread widely and quickly to all staff: the notice-board, or a public announcement or the company newsletter may be more appropriate.

(g) The **recipient**

It may be necessary to be reserved and tactful, warm and friendly, or impersonal, depending upon the desired effect on the recipient. If you are trying to impress him, a high quality document may be needed.

(h) **Cost**

Cost must be considered in relation to all of the above factors. The aim is to achieve the best possible result at the least possible expense.

2.3 The syllabus identifies ten communication tools. We will look at the features and limitations of each.

Tool	Features / Advantages	Limitations
Conversation	Usually unstructured so can discuss a wide range of topics Requires little or no planning Gives a real impression of feelings	Temptation to lose focus May be easily forgotten
Meeting	Allows multiple opinions to be expressed Can discuss and resolve a wide range of issues Also see Chapter 3	Can highlight differences and conflict if not managed efficiently – have been known to turn into time-wasting confrontations 'Louder' personalities may dominate proceedings Costly in terms of personnel time A focused agenda and an effective Chair should prevent these limitations hindering the meeting - see Chapter 3
Presentation	Complex ideas can be communicated Visual aids such as slides can help the communication process The best presentations will leave a lasting impression Also see Chapter 3	Requires planning and skill Poorly researched or presented material can lead to audience resentment Also see Chapter 3

Part B: Information technology and systems

Tool	Features / Advantages	Limitations
Memorandum	Provides a permanent record of an internal message Adds formality to internal communications	If used too often or the message is too general people may ignore it Can come across as impersonal
Letter	Provides a permanent record of an external message Adds formality to external communications Use a clear, simple structure, for example • Letterhead • Reference or heading • Date • Recipient name and address • Greeting/salutation • Subject • Substance • Close • Signature • Author name and position • Enclosure/copy reference	If inaccurate or poorly presented provides a permanent record of incompetence May be slow to arrive depending on distance and the postal service
Report	Provides a permanent, often comprehensive written record Use a clear, simple structure. There is no one correct format. An example that could be adapted to suit the report requirements is… • Meaningful Title • Author name and position • Purpose/Terms of Reference • Procedure followed • Findings • Conclusion / Recommendations Where necessary use a hierarchy of headings to aid clarity. For example… • 1 Section heading • (a) sub heading • (i) sub point	Complex messages may be misunderstood in the absence of immediate feedback Reports that reach (necessarily) negative conclusions can lead to negative impressions of the author

Tool	Features / Advantages	Limitations
Telephone	Good for communications that do not require (or you would prefer not to have) a permanent written record	Receiver may not be available; 'phone-tag' is a frustrating pass-time! (Voice-mail may help)
	Can provide some of the 'personal touch' to people in geographically remote locations	Can be disruptive to receiver if in the middle of another task
	Conference calls allow multiple participants	No written record gives greater opportunity for misunderstandings
Facsimile	Enables reports and messages to reach remote locations quickly	Easily seen by others
		Fax machine may not be checked for messages
		Complex images do not transmit well
Electronic mail	Provides a written record	Requires some computer literacy to use effectively
	Attachments (eg Reports or other documents) can be included	People may not check their e-mail regularly
	Quick – regardless of location	Lack of privacy – can be forwarded on without your knowledge
	Automated 'Read receipts' or a simple request to acknowledge receipt by return message mean you know if the message has been received	Long messages (more than one 'screen') may best be dealt with via other means, or as attached documents
	Can be sent to multiple recipients easily, can be forwarded on to others	
Video-conference	This is in effect a meeting conducted using a computer and video system	The hardware is expensive compared to telephone
	Provides more of a personal touch than the telephone, but less than a 'physical' meeting	May be dominated by the most confident participant(s)
	Some non-verbal messages (eg gestures) will be received	Cross-border cultural differences may be unintentionally ignored as participants feel 'at home'
		Image quality is often poor – resulting in not much more than an expensive telephone conference call!

Part B: Information technology and systems

Chapter roundup

- Communication is vital in any organisation to achieve **co-ordination.**
- The relative complexity of the work affects the chosen method of co-ordination.. Co-ordinating the activities of people within an organisation requires appropriate **systems of communication**.
- Communication involves **transmitting information to others**.
- Communication may be **formal** or **informal**, **vertical** or **horizontal**.
- Effective communication involves ensuring **barriers to communication** do not prevent correct interpretation of the message.
- The **channel of communication** will impact on the effectiveness of the communication process. The characteristics of the message will determine what communication tool is best for a given situation.
- This is the final chapter in Part B of this Study Text. The **Mind-Map following the Quick quiz** brings together some of the main issues from Parts A and B of Text.

Quick quiz

1. What is 'noise' in communication theory?
2. List five factors that will influence the choice of communication medium.

    1 ……………………………………………………
    2 ……………………………………………………
    3 ……………………………………………………
    4 ……………………………………………………
    5 ……………………………………………………

3. Why should clear headings be used in a report?
4. Give an advantage and a limitation of a conversation.
5. Meetings have a significant hidden cost. What is it?

Answers to quick quiz

1. Distractions and interference in the environment in which communication is taking place.

2. [Five of]
   Time – the urgency of the message.
   Message complexity.
   Distance - how far the message is required to travel.
   Whether a written record is required.
   How quickly feedback may be required.
   Degree of confidentiality.
   Desired impression on the recipient.
   Cost.

3. A hierarchy of headings provides a structure which should aid clarity and understanding.

4. *Advantages*
   Unstructured so can discuss a wide range of topics.
   Gives an impression of feelings behind the message.
   Limitations
   Temptation to lose focus.
   No written record so may be forgotten.

5. The time of the attendees.

The material covered in this Chapter is tested by the *format and style* of answers required to Questions 5, 7, 8, 9, 10, 12, 13, 14, 15, 16 and 18 in the Question Bank.

Part B: Information technology and systems

INFORMATION SYSTEMS: POSSIBLE PROBLEM AREAS

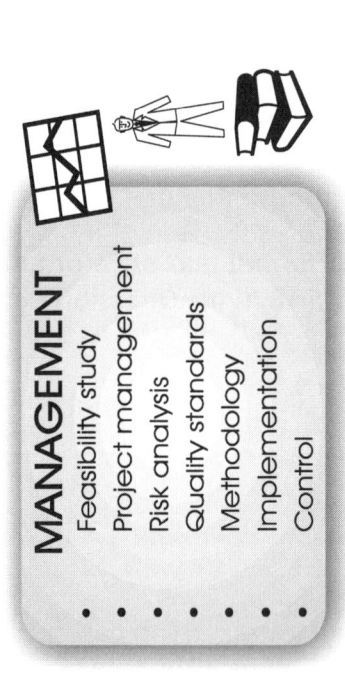

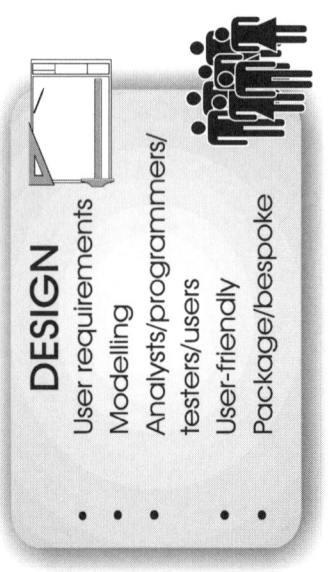

USER ACCEPTANCE
- User involvement
- Communication
- Realistic testing
- Training
- User-friendly

MANAGEMENT
- Feasibility study
- Project management
- Risk analysis
- Quality standards
- Methodology
- Implementation
- Control

INFORMATION SYSTEM
- ON-TIME
- TO SPECIFICATION
- WITHIN BUDGET

COST
- Cost/benefit
- Budget
- Monitoring
- Realistic
- Linked to quality

DESIGN
- User requirements
- Modelling
- Analysts/programmers/testers/users
- User-friendly
- Package/bespoke

258

Part C
Control

Chapter 10

CONTROL OF ACTIVITIES AND RESOURCES

Topic list	Syllabus reference	Ability required
1 Management writers and theories	(iii)	Evaluation
2 Control systems	(iii)	Evaluation
3 Control over employees	(iii)	Evaluation
4 Budgetary control	(iii)	Evaluation
5 Building controls into an information system	(iii)	Evaluation
6 The 'new' organisation and control	(iii)	Evaluation

Introduction

This chapter looks at the theory and practice of control. We start with the views of classical and contemporary management writers, then link control theory to systems theory before looking at some practical control mechanisms, including the controls that can be built into an information system. Finally, we look at control in a modern, flexible organisation.

Learning outcomes covered in this chapter

- **Evaluate** and recommend appropriate control systems
- **Evaluate** the control of activities and resources within the organisation (*Also see Chapter 11*)
- **Recommend** ways in which the problems with control systems could be avoided or solved
- **Evaluate** and **recommend** improvements to the control of Information Systems including those using information technology

Syllabus content covered in this chapter

- The way in which systems are used to achieve control within the framework of the organisation
- The views of classical and contemporary management writers relating to control
- The application of control systems and related theory to the design of management accounting systems and information systems in general
- The controls which can be designed into an information system, particularly one using information technology

1 MANAGEMENT WRITERS AND THEORIES

1.1 For as long as organisations have existed so have theories on how best to control them. We start this chapter with a summary of the views of **classical** (Fayol, Weber and Taylor) and contemporary management writers relating to control. Some **basic definitions** may help you to keep the theory that follows in perspective.

> **KEY TERMS**
>
> **Control** entails 'ensuring that what was intended to be actually comes to be'. (Roslender, *Sociological Perspectives on Modern Accountancy*, 1992)
>
> **Control** is 'the whole process by which management attempts to direct the efforts of the organisation towards the achievement of common goals'. (Coates, Rickwood and Stacey, *Control and Audit in Management Accountancy*, 1993)
>
> The aim of a **control system** is to make sure that the right things get done.

Classical school

Fayol

1.2 *Fayol* (1841-1925) was a French industrialist, who exemplifies the **classical school** of management thought. This popularised the concept of the **universality of management principles**: in other words, the same principles of organisation and management apply everywhere.

1.3 Fayol listed the following principles of organisation.

(a) **Division of work** ie specialisation.

(b) **Authority and responsibility**. The holder of an office should have enough authority to carry out all the responsibilities assigned to him.

(c) **Discipline**. A fair disciplinary system, with penalties fairly applied.

(d) **Unity of command**. A subordinate should receive orders from one boss only.

(e) **Unity of direction**. There should be one head and one plan for each activity.

(f) **Subordination of individual interests**. The interest of one employee or group of employees should not prevail over that of the general interest of the organisation.

(g) **Remuneration**. This should be 'fair', satisfying both employer and employee alike.

(h) **Scalar chain.** The scalar chain is the term used to describe the chain of command. Formal communication is up and down the lines of authority.

(i) **Stability of tenure of personnel.** A mediocre manager who stays is preferable to outstanding managers who come and go.

(j) **Team spirit.** Personnel should not be isolated, cohesion should be encouraged.

(k) **Initiative**. Must be encouraged.

1.4 Control should therefore be exercised following strict **policies, procedures and hierarchies.** Employees should be treated fairly, and should be encouraged to put forward their ideas, to 'superiors' who were better equipped to evaluate their merit.

Weber

1.5 The sociologist, *Max Weber* (1864-1920), developed the notion of bureaucratic administration. **Bureaucracy** was defined by Weber as a continuous organisation of official functions bound by rules.

1.6 Weber regarded an organisation as an **authority** structure. He was interested in **why** individuals obeyed commands. He identified three grounds on which **legitimate authority could exist**.

   (a) **Charismatic leadership**. A leader has some special power or attribute; decision-making is centralised in him or her, and delegation is strictly limited.

   (b) **Traditional, or patriarchal leadership.** In such organisations, authority is bestowed by virtue of hereditary entitlement, as in the family firm. Tradition is glorified.

   (c) **Bureaucracy.** Authority is bestowed by dividing an organisation into jurisdictional areas (production, marketing, sales and so on) each with specified duties. Authority to carry them out is given to the **officials in charge**, and **rules and regulations** are established in order to ensure their achievement.

1.7 Weber specified several general characteristics of bureaucracy.

   (a) **Hierarchy**: each lower office is under the control and supervision of a higher one.

   (b) **Specialisation and training**: there is a high degree of specialisation of labour. Employment is based on ability, not personal loyalty.

   (c) **Impersonal nature**: employees work full time within the impersonal rules and regulations and act according to formal and impersonal procedures.

   (d) **Professional nature of employment**: an organisation exists before it is filled with people. Officials are full-time employees, promotion is according to seniority and achievement; pay scales are prescribed according to the position or office held in the organisation structure.

   (e) **Rationality**: the 'jurisdictional areas' of the organisation are determined rationally. The hierarchy of authority and office structure is clearly defined. Duties are established and measures of performance set.

   (f) **Uniformity** in the performance of tasks is expected, regardless of whoever is engaged in carrying them out.

   (g) **Technical competence** in officials, which is rarely questioned within the area of their expertise.

   (h) **Stability**.

1.8 Weber regarded the role of **technical knowledge** in bureaucratic administration as the primary source of the superiority of bureaucracy as an organisation.

   (a) He acknowledged the deadening effect of bureaucracy and deplored an organisation of 'little cogs, little men, clinging to little jobs and striving towards bigger ones.'

   (b) He was less prepared to acknowledge the fact that bureaucracies do not always cope well with change.

Part C: Control

Taylor

1.9 *Frederick W Taylor* (1856 - 1915) pioneered the **scientific management** movement in the USA. **Scientific management** has some similarities with the ideas of bureaucracy, in that it supports the idea that there should be rational procedures governing each job.

1.10 Taylor argued that management should be based on 'well-recognised, clearly-defined and fixed principles.' Taylor's four principles of scientific management are given below.

(a) **The development of a true science of work.** All knowledge which had hitherto been kept in the heads of workmen should be gathered and recorded by management. 'Every single subject, large and small, becomes the question for scientific investigation, for reduction to law.'

(b) **The scientific selection and progressive development of workmen.** Workmen should be carefully trained and given jobs to which they are best suited. Although 'training' is an important element in his principles of management, 'nurturing' might be a more apt description of his ideas of worker development.

(c) **The bringing together of science and scientifically selected and trained men.** The application of techniques to decide what should be done and how, using workmen who are both properly trained and willing to maximise output, should result in maximum productivity.

(d) **The constant and intimate co-operation between management and workers.** 'The relations between employers and men form without question the most important part of this art.'

1.11 The practical application of the approach was the use of **work study techniques** to break each job down into its **smallest and simplest component parts**: these single elements became the newly-designed job. Workers were selected and trained to perform their single task in the most efficient way possible, as determined by techniques such as **time and motion study**. Workers were **paid incentives** on the basis of acceptance of the new methods and output norms.

1.12 Both workers and owners should **gain financially** from the increased productivity. At the Bethlehem Steel Works, Taylor said, the costs of implementing this method were more than repaid by the benefits. The labour force required fell from 400 - 600 men to 140 men for the same work. This effect on employment accounts for some of the hostility that scientific management encountered.

1.13 *Peter Drucker* made some useful comments about scientific management.

(a) Scientific management has contributed a philosophy of worker and work: 'human work can be studied systematically, can be analysed, can be improved by work on its elementary parts'.

(b) It depended on **financial motivation**: but people are motivated by many things, not just money.

(c) **Job design**. The idea that each separate 'motion' within a job should be done by a separate worker is dissatisfying to workers. Operations should be **analysed** in this way, but then **reintegrated** into a whole job.

(d) It divorces **planning** work from **doing** the work.

   (i) This has some advantages if the work is simple and the workforce unskilled. (At the time Taylor was introducing these ideas the US labour force included large numbers of first-generation immigrants; many had a poor command of English or were illiterate.)

   (ii) Where work is complex, it implies that managers know everything relevant there is to know, which is not necessarily true.

Human relations

1.14 In the 1930s *Mayo* (1880-1949) pioneered a new approach which emphasised the **importance of human attitudes**, values and relationships.

1.15 This was called the **human relations** approach. It was based on research into human behaviour, with the intention of describing and thereafter predicting behaviour in organisations.

1.16 This emphasis resulted from a famous set of experiments (the *Hawthorne Studies*) carried out by Mayo for the Western Electric Company in the USA. The company was testing the effect of lighting on productivity. They found that productivity shot up **whatever** they did with the lighting. The conclusion was that **the sense of being a group singled out for attention raised worker morale and productivity**.

1.17 The next stage involved interviews, and revealed that work relationships were considered very important. Work satisfied **social needs**.

1.18 Mayo's ideas were followed up by other psychologists - eg *Maslow, Herzberg, Likert* and *McGregor*. In a nutshell, they found that people are still the crucial factor in determining organisational effectiveness, but have more than merely physical and social needs. Attention shifted towards people's **higher psychological needs** for growth, challenge, responsibility and self-fulfilment.

Contingency theory

1.19 Contingency theory uses a scientific approach as a starting point to control systems theory, but focuses on factors that account for the **differences** between organisations and systems.

1.20 Contingency theory has been the basis of the majority of research carried out into management accounting control systems since the 1960s. Writers in this field include *Burns and Stalker* (1961), *Woodward* (1965) and *Pugh* (1976).

1.21 A scientific approach was emphasised in an attempt to find differences in control systems (eg management structure) between different organisations. The major factors identified by contingency theorists as affecting control systems are as follows.

- **The environment**
    - Its degree of predictability
    - The degree of competition faced
    - The number of different product markets faced
    - The degree of hostility exhibited by competing organisations

Part C: Control

- **Organisational structure**
    - Size
    - Interdependence of parts
    - Degree of decentralisation
    - Availability of resources
- **Technology**
    - The nature of the production process
    - The simplicity/complexity of the production process
    - How well the relationship between ends and means is understood
    - The amount of variety in each task that has to be performed

1.22 Not all organisations in the same environment will develop identical control systems, as different people will make different decisions.

Other theories of control

1.23 Four other perspectives of control are briefly explained in the following table.

Theory	Example theorist	Key points
Radical structuralist, also referred to as **Labour process theory**	*Braverman (1974)*	Is an interpretation of **economic history** from medieval times. Analyses the transfer of the control of work from the worker (medieval) to the capitalist (post-industrial revolution) to 'the management class'. Emphasises de-skilling, specialisation and the narrow skill-base of both workers and managers.
Structural functionalist, also referred to as **Conventional ideas**	*Woodward (1965)*	Societies/systems are complex and best understood by isolating them from other influences eg the people involved. System problem solving should focus on one area only, ignoring wider issues. Adopts a **scientific** approach.
Interactionism, also referred to as **Interpretivist**	*Giddens (1989)*	Attempts to understand systems and control by studying the interactions of **people** ('actors') in the system. *Giddens* emphases **structuration** as a way to deal with the issues of power and morality. Structuration distinguishes between social groupings, social conventions and norms - and individuals. Individual actions are viewed as reflex actions designed to conform with the group. Managers have power but not detailed technical knowledge. Subordinates have this knowledge but cannot be autonomous, as they do not allocate resources.

Theory	Example theorist	Key points
Foucault (there is no widely-used name for Foucault's views)	*Foucault* (1977)	Focuses on the relationship between knowledge and power.
		Emphasises the move towards a more complex, **knowledge-based** society.
		Discipline has played a large part in the development of organisations, professions and of society. For example:
		Space – enclosure, offices, partitions
		Time – timetables, schedules
		Methods – operations manuals
		Minds – examinations, professions, hierarchies

2 CONTROL SYSTEMS

Why bother with control

2.1 A system such as a business organisation must be controlled to **keep it steady** or **enable it to change safely**.

2.2 Control is required because **unpredictable disturbances** arise and enter the system, so that **actual results** (outputs of the system) **deviate from the expected results** or goals. Examples of disturbances in a business system would be the entry of a powerful new competitor into the market, an unexpected rise in costs, the failure of a supplier to deliver materials, or industrial action by employees.

2.3 To have a control system, there has to be a plan, standard, budget, rule book or any other sort of **target** or guideline towards which the system as a whole should be aiming.

2.4 **Control is dependent on the receipt and processing of information**, both to plan in the first place and to compare actual results against the plan, so as to judge what control measures are needed.

2.5 Within organisations, information may be received from a variety of sources.

(a) Formal sources, designed by managers of the organisation.
(b) Informally from sources within the organisation.
(c) Formal sources outside the organisation, ie from the environment.
(d) Informally from environmental sources.

2.6 Control is dependent on the receipt and processing of **information**. Organisations obtain information from a variety of sources.

Part C: Control

		Information type	
		Formal source	*Informal source*
Information source	*Within the organisation*	Budgetary reports, variance analysis, staff appraisals	The 'informal organisation' The 'grapevine'
	Outside the organisation	Market research, custom feedback, public databases	Surfing the Internet; informal conversations with customers or suppliers

Components of a control system

2.7 There are five main components of a control system.

Component	Description	Example
Standard	The targets at which the organisation is aiming	Budgeted material costs
Sensor	Device or person by which information or data is collected and measured	Sales force
Feedback	Covered later in this section	Covered later in this section
Comparator	Means by which the actual results of the system are measured against the predetermined plans or system objectives	Managers expected to make a judgement based on reported variances
Effector or activator	The device or means by which control action is initiated	A manager's instruction and a subordinate's action

The control loop

2.8 Control is exercised through a **control system**. All control systems can be analysed in the same way. The first distinction is between open- and closed loop systems.

(a) **Open loop system.** If control is exercised, it operates independently - it is not provided for within the system. Since information from **within** the system is **not** used for control purposes, control must be exercised by external intervention.

(b) **Closed loop system.** Part of the output is fed back, so that the output can initiate control action to change either the activities of the system or the system's input. A **feedback loop** carries output back to be compared with the input.

> **KEY TERMS**
>
> A **closed loop system** is 'A control system which includes a provision for corrective action, taken on either a feedforward or a feedback basis'.
>
> An **open loop system** is 'A control system which includes no provision for corrective action to be applied to the sequence of activities.' (CIMA *Official Terminology*)

10: Control of activities and resources

The diagram below illustrates such a system.

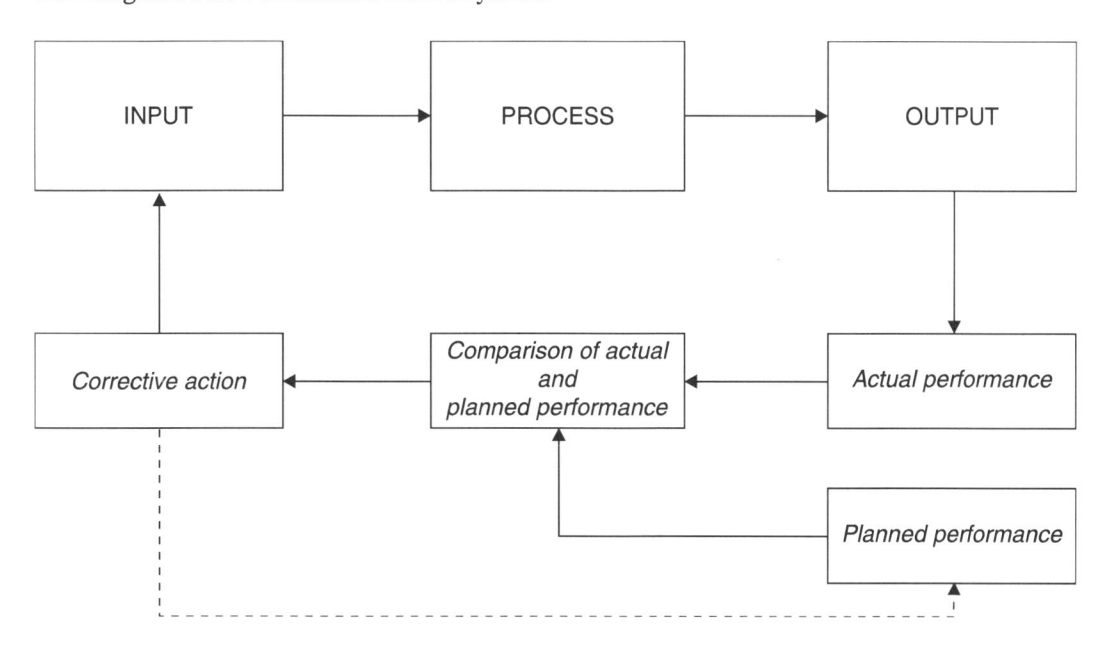

```
INPUT  →  PROCESS  →  OUTPUT
  ↑                      ↓
Corrective   Comparison of actual   Actual performance
action   ←   and planned         ←
             performance
                  ↑
             Planned performance
```

2.9 A business organisation uses feedback for control, and therefore has a closed loop control system. However, external and environmental influences should not be ignored. (See double loop feedback later in this section.)

2.10 The essence of control is the measurement of results and comparing them with the original plan. Any deviation from plan indicates that **control action** is required to make the results conform more closely with the plan.

Feedback control

> **KEY TERM**
>
> **Feedback control** is 'The measurement of differences between planned outputs and outputs achieved, and the modification of subsequent action and/or plans to achieve future required results.' (CIMA *Official Terminology*)

2.11 In a business organisation, feedback is information about actual results produced from within the organisation (such as management control reports) for the purpose of helping management with control decisions.

Negative feedback

2.12 **Negative feedback** indicates that results or activities must be brought back on course, as they are deviating from the plan.

> **KEY TERM**
>
> **Negative feedback** indicates that the system is deviating from its planned or prescribed course. This feedback is called 'negative' because control action would seek to reverse the direction of movement **back towards the planned course**.

2.13 For example, if budgeted sales for a department for June and July were £100,000 per month, and the final June sales report showed a total of £90,000. The report is negative feedback indicating that control action is required. Sales in July need to reach £110,000 to get back on to the planned course. Negative feedback in this case would necessitate July sales exceeding the budget by £10,000 because June sales fell short of budget.

Positive feedback

> **KEY TERM**
>
> **Positive feedback** results in control action which causes actual results to maintain (or increase) their path of deviation **away from planned results**.

2.14 For example, a company budgets to produce and sell 100 units of product each month.

  (a) Suppose feedback in the first month shows sales are 110 units, after only two weeks.

  (b) Action may be taken to increase sales further, encouraging further deviation of actual results from the plan.

Feedforward control

2.15 Feedforward control

> **KEY TERM**
>
> **Feedforward control** is 'The forecasting of differences between actual and planned outcomes, and the implementation of action, before the event, to avoid such differences'.
>
> (CIMA *Official Terminology*)

  (a) **Control delay.** A timelag may exist between the actual results and the corrective action. However these results might have been anticipated.

  (b) **Feedforward control** uses **anticipated** or forecast results, and compares them with the plan. **Corrective action** is thus taken **in advance**, before it is too late to do anything effective. Control is exercised before the results, rather than after the event.

Single loop feedback (primary feedback)

> **KEY TERM**
>
> Feedback which is based on past performance of a process and which is gathered to govern future performance is **single loop feedback** (or **primary feedback**).

2.16 Single loop feedback is concerned with 'task control' (the control loop). It has a narrow focus.

10: Control of activities and resources

Double loop feedback (secondary feedback)

> **KEY TERM**
>
> **Double loop feedback** (or **secondary feedback**) is control information which indicates both discrepancies between observed and expected results, **and** the need for **adjustments to the plan**.

2.17 **Double loop feedback (or secondary feedback)** is control information transmitted to a higher level in the system. It consists of information gathered from not only measuring outputs of the system itself, but also **environmental information**.

2.18 The term 'double loop' feedback indicates that the information is reported to indicate both discrepancies between the observed and expected results where control action might be required, and also **the need for adjustments to the plan itself**.

2.19 If a system is to react to a changing environment, which it must do to survive, then double loop feedback is essential.

A practical example of a control system

2.20 It may be helpful at this stage to relate the control system to a practical example, such as monthly sales.

(a) **Standard**. A sales budget or plan is prepared for the year.

(b) **Sensor**. The costing system records actual costs.

(c) **Feedback**. At the end of each month, actual results (sales units, revenue and so on) are reported back to management.

(d) **Comparator**. Managers compare actual results against the plan.

(e) **Effector**. Where necessary, managers take corrective action to adjust the workings of the system, probably by amending the inputs to the system. For example, salesmen might be asked to work longer hours or some new price discounts might be decided. Where appropriate the sales plan may be revised, up or down.

2.21 There are several other factors we should consider.

(a) The **influence of the environment** - such as government legislation or industrial action in a supplier industry.

(b) **Whether control action is possible**. For example, a sales manager cannot increase sales if the production department can't produce the desired output fast enough. Not all inputs to the system are controllable; a change in weather conditions which affects sales (such as ice creams or soft drinks) is outside the scope of management control.

(c) **How much information should be measured and fed back for comparison purposes**. Not all output is measured, either because it would not have any useful value as information, or because the system does not provide for its measurement.

(d) The **plan might need to be changed**. Environmental influences (such as an increase in income tax rates reducing the spending power of customers) could be responsible for the need to change the sales plan.

2.22 In the **design of a control system**, the following **factors** should be **considered**.

Part C: Control

(a) How much output should be measured, and in what ways should it be reported?

(b) What is the importance of environmental factors?

(c) What inputs should be regarded as controllable, and which of these would be worth attempting to control?

The practical application of control theory

2.23 Control theory may sound all well and good in theory, but there are a number of serious **problems to overcome** in applying theory to practice.

(a) **Preparing a standard or plan in the first place,** which is reliable and acceptable to the managers who will be responsible for the achievement of the standard or plan.

(b) **Measuring actual results with sufficient accuracy.**

(c) **Measuring actual results with suitable feedback periods.** The reporting cycle time must be kept sufficiently short to give managers a chance to take prompt control action when serious deviations from plan occur.

(d) **Providing non-accounting as well as accounting information** to help with the assessment of plans and results.

(e) **Identifying the causes of variations** between actual results and the standard or plan, and **distinguishing controllable from uncontrollable causes.**

(f) **Drawing the attention of managers** to a deviation between actual results and plan, and persuading them to do something about it.

(g) **Coordinating** the plans and activities of different departments in the organisation.

(h) **Informing everybody** who needs to be informed about how results are going.

Features of an effective control system

2.24 An effective control system should be:

(a) **Acceptable** to the organisation's members. The purpose of a control system is to stimulate control action, and it must therefore be tailored to the 'culture' of the organisation or the department within the organisation.

(b) **Appropriate.** Controls should be tailored to the capabilities and personalities of individual managers.

(c) **Accessible.** Controls should not be too sophisticated, using techniques of measurement and analysis which only a statistical or accounting 'expert' might understand.

(d) **Action oriented.** A control system will serve no useful function at all unless it leads management into taking corrective action.

(e) **Adaptable.** Controls should continue to be workable even when events show that original plans are unachievable (and should therefore be changed) perhaps due to unforeseen circumstances which arise. In other words, controls must be flexible and adaptable to new circumstances.

(f) **Affordable.** Controls should be economical and worth their cost in terms of the benefits obtained. Control will probably be economical if it is tailored to:

(i) The critical control points of the organisation's work.
(ii) The size of the organisation.
(iii) Areas where performance has a significant impact.

2.25 EXAMPLE

We now relate the control system to a practical example, such as **monthly budgetary control variance reports.**

(a) Standard costs and a master budget are prepared for the year. Management organises the resources of the business (inputs) so as to achieve the budget targets.

(b) At the end of each month, actual results (output, sales, costs, revenues etc) are reported back to management. The reports are the measured output of the control system, and the process of sending them to the managers responsible provides the feedback loop.

(c) Managers compare actual results against the plan and where necessary, take corrective action to adjust the workings of the system, probably by amending the inputs to the system.

2.26 Both negative and positive feedback information may result from two factors.

(a) **Controllable factors**, such as high labour turnover resulting from bad management.

(b) **Uncontrollable factors**, such as changes in the weather affecting production (eg of agricultural crops), a sudden rise in raw material prices.

2.27 It may be the case, especially with uncontrollable factors, that tinkering with inputs and processes may not be enough. **The plan itself may have to change** and so a comparison of actual results against the existing plan might be invalid.

2.28 EXAMPLE

A **budgetary control system** may need to change because of double loop feedback.

(a) **Unmeasured output** might include the morale and motivation of staff, the number of labour hours wasted as idle time or the volume of complaints received about a particular product or service.

(b) The **master budget** might have to be changed if it is realised that actual sales volumes will be radically different from those budgeted (eg as a result of a new competitor).

(c) There will be **environmental influences** (eg government legislation about safety standards) affecting both inputs to the system and also how the budget is established or amended.

(d) Some inputs to the system are uncontrollable or only partly controllable, as we have seen.

3 CONTROL OVER EMPLOYEES

3.1 Control is also exercised over individual employees.

3.2 There are two types of control strategies related to supervision.

(a) **Behaviour control** deals with the behaviour of individual employees. In other words, control is exercised over the procedures. Examples include standard policies and methodologies.

(b) **Output control** is where management attention is focused on results, more than the way these were achieved. Inspection of output is the most obvious example of output control.

Part C: Control

> **Case example**
>
> An example of behaviour control is that exercised by audit managers over their juniors. Audit procedures have to be followed for the information to be valid. Control must be exercised over how the work is done. The 'output' of the audit (whether or not to qualify the accounts) is completely dependant on the procedures used in the process.

3.3 Handy writes of a **trust-control dilemma** in a superior-subordinate relationship, in which the sum of trust + control is a constant amount:

$$T + C = Y$$

where T = the trust the superior has in the subordinate, and the trust which the subordinate feels the superior has in him or her;

C = the degree of control exercised by the superior over the subordinate;

Y = a constant, unchanging value.

Any increase in C leads to an equal decrease in T; that is, if the superior retains more 'control' or authority, the subordinate will immediately recognise that he or she is being trusted less. If the superior wishes to show more trust in the subordinate, this can only be done by reducing C, that is by delegating more authority.

Span of control

3.4 Span of control or 'span of management', refers to the number of subordinates responsible to a superior. If a manager has five subordinates, the span of control is five.

3.5 Classical theorists suggest:

(a) There are physical and mental limitations to a manager's ability to control people, relationships and activities.

(b) There should be tight managerial control from the top of an organisation downward. The span of control should be restricted to allow maximum control.

3.6 It is now accepted that there is no universally 'correct' size for the span of control. The appropriate span of control will depend on:

(a) **Ability of the manager**. A good organiser and communicator will be able to control a larger number. The manager's work-load is also relevant.

(b) **Ability of the subordinates**. The more experienced, able, trustworthy and well-trained subordinates are, the easier it is to control larger numbers.

(c) **Nature of the task**. It is easier for a supervisor to control a large number of people if they are all doing routine, repetitive or similar tasks.

(d) The **geographical dispersal** of the subordinates, and the **communication system** of the organisation.

Tall and flat organisations

3.7 The span of control has implications for the 'shape' of the organisation. An organisation with a narrow span of control will have more levels in its management hierarchy – the organisation will be narrow and **tall**. A tall organisation reflects tighter supervision and control, and lengthy chains of command and communication.

10: Control of activities and resources

3.8 An organisation of the same size with a wide span of control will be wide and **flat**. The flat organisation reflects a greater degree of delegation - the more a manager delegates, the wider the span of control can be.

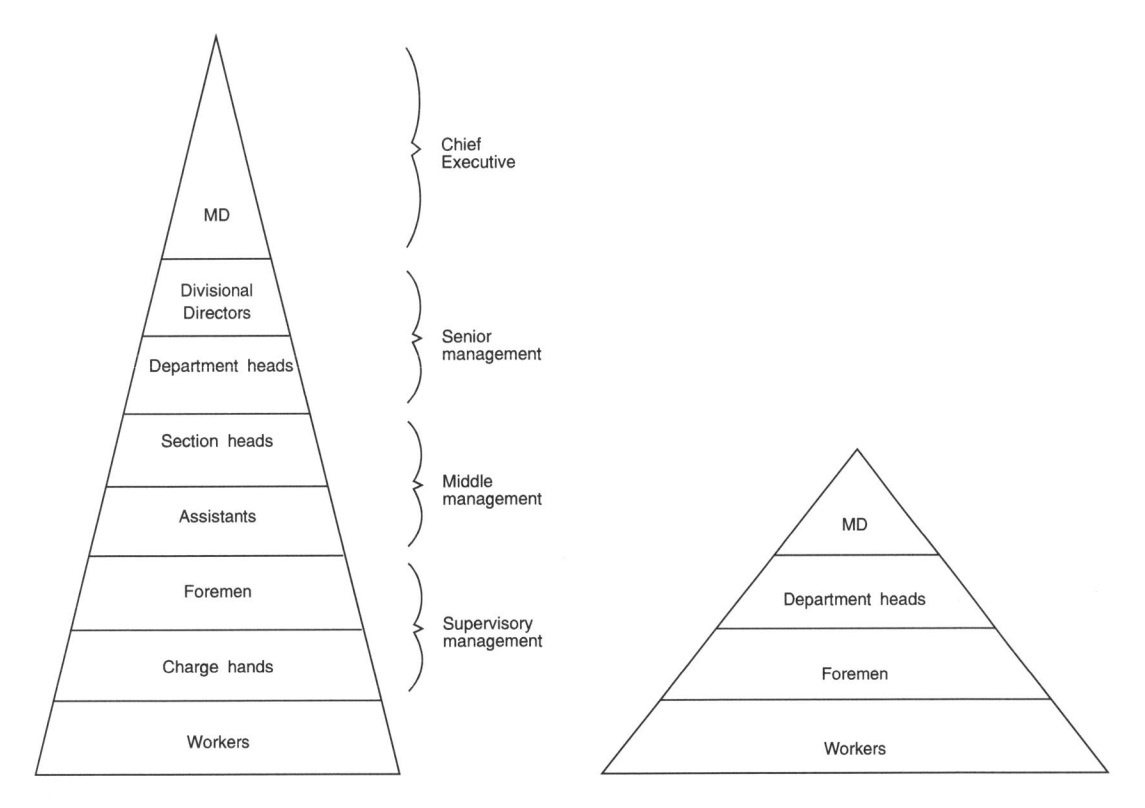

3.9 An organisation may be both **tall and flat**: the police force in the UK is a flat organisation up to inspector level (80% of all policemen are constables) but tall thereafter.

3.10 Classical theorists argued that a tall organisation structure is inefficient, because:

(a) It increases overhead costs.

(b) It creates a longer chain of communication. Management is more remote from work done at the bottom end of the organisation - information tends to get distorted or blocked on its way through the hierarchy.

(c) Management responsibilities overlap and become confused as the size of the management structure gets larger.

(d) The same work passes through too many hands.

(e) Planning is more difficult because it must be organised at more levels in the organisation.

3.11 Behavioural theorists add that tall structures impose rigid supervision and control and therefore block initiative and damage the motivation of subordinates. There may be more 'rungs' available in the promotional ladder, but there are unlikely to be real increases in responsibility between one and another.

Delayering and empowerment

3.12 Many large organisations in the 1980s and 1990s looked to cut costs through reducing the layers of middle management. This led to the process of **delayering** - removing whole layers of middle management - and **empowerment** of workers lower down. (The process has slowed in the new millennium – but there are now very few large organisations with tall structures.)

Part C: Control

3.13 The justification is that by empowering workers (or removing levels in hierarchies that restrict freedom), not only will the job be done more effectively but the people who do the job will get more out of it.

3.14 This thinking is in line with that of human relations theorists such as *Maslow* and *Herzberg* who believed that organisational effectiveness is determined by the extent to which people's 'higher' psychological needs for growth, challenge, responsibility and self-fulfilment are met by the work that they do.

Empowerment and control

3.15 *Ted Johns* has commented that 'Increasing needs for self-actualisation and autonomy among employees, coupled with fashionable notions of empowerment and delayering, have created organisations which are in danger of falling apart as the 'glue' of centralised control is weakened.'

3.16 Others believe that management control and workforce is commitment are **both** essential, and that the ideal type of organisation combines high levels of **commitment** of the **people** and control of the **processes**.

From compliance to commitment

3.17 The traditional system used by management to control the workforce based on **compliance**. This emphasised standard performance rather than continuous improvement or maximum performance.

3.18 The system relies on mechanisms such as policies, procedures and job specifications - which emphasise rigidity and inflexibility. The system is based on low levels of trust, tight supervision and careful inspection of work. The traditional assembly line is a typical example.

3.19 Such systems are suitable in a stable market environment. Nowadays, however, organisations must be **flexible** to be able to respond quickly to specific and varied customer demands. The workforce must therefore be more than merely compliant, it must be committed.

3.20 The following steps may help increase commitment.

   (a) Develop **identification** with the organisation and its values by means of:
   - Communications
   - Participation
   - Employees' ideas
   - Training
   - Profit sharing

   (b) Ensure that people **know what they have to achieve** and are aware of how their performance will be measured against agreed targets and standards.

   (c) Introduce a **reward system** which relates at least partly to individual performance.

   (d) Treat employees **as human beings**, not machines.

Employee appraisal

3.21 Employee appraisal can be viewed as a control tool as it aims to influence employee behaviour, and maximise the utilisation of the organisation's human resource.

3.22 The process of appraisal is designed to review performance over the past period, with a view to identifying any deficiencies, and improving it in the future.

> **KEY TERM**
>
> **Appraisal**: the systematic review and assessment of an employee's performance, potential and training needs.

3.23 The general purpose of any appraisal system is to improve efficiency. Personnel appraisal aims to ensure individuals are performing to the best of their ability, are developing their potential and that the organisation is best utilising their abilities. It may include:

(a) **Reward review**. Measuring the extent to which an employee is deserving of a bonus or pay increase as compared with his or her peers.

(b) **Performance review**, for planning and following-up training and development programmes, ie identifying training needs, validating training methods and so on.

(c) **Potential review**, as an aid to planning career development and succession, by attempting to predict the level and type of work the individual will be capable of in the future.

3.24 **Objectives of appraisals**

(a) Establishing the **key deliverables** an individual has to produce to enable the organisation to achieve its objectives.

(b) Comparing the individual's **level of performance against a standard**, as a means of quality control.

(c) Identifying the individual's **training and development needs** in the light of actual performance.

(d) Identifying areas that **require improvement.**

(e) Monitoring the organisation's **initial selection procedures** against subsequent performance.

(f) **Improving communication** between different levels in the hierarchy.

3.25 **A typical appraisal system**

Step 1. **Identification of criteria for assessment,** perhaps based on job analysis, performance standards, person specifications and so on.

Step 2. The **preparation by the subordinate's manager of an appraisal report**. In some systems both the appraisee and appraiser prepare a report. These reports are then compared.

Step 3. An **appraisal interview,** for an exchange of views about the appraisal report, targets for improvement, solutions to problems and so on.

Step 4. **Review of the assessment by the assessor's own superior,** so that the appraisee does not feel subject to one person's prejudices. Formal appeals may be allowed, if necessary to establish the fairness of the procedure.

Step 5. The **preparation and implementation of action plans** to achieve improvements and changes agreed.

Step 6. **Follow-up** monitoring the progress of the action plan.

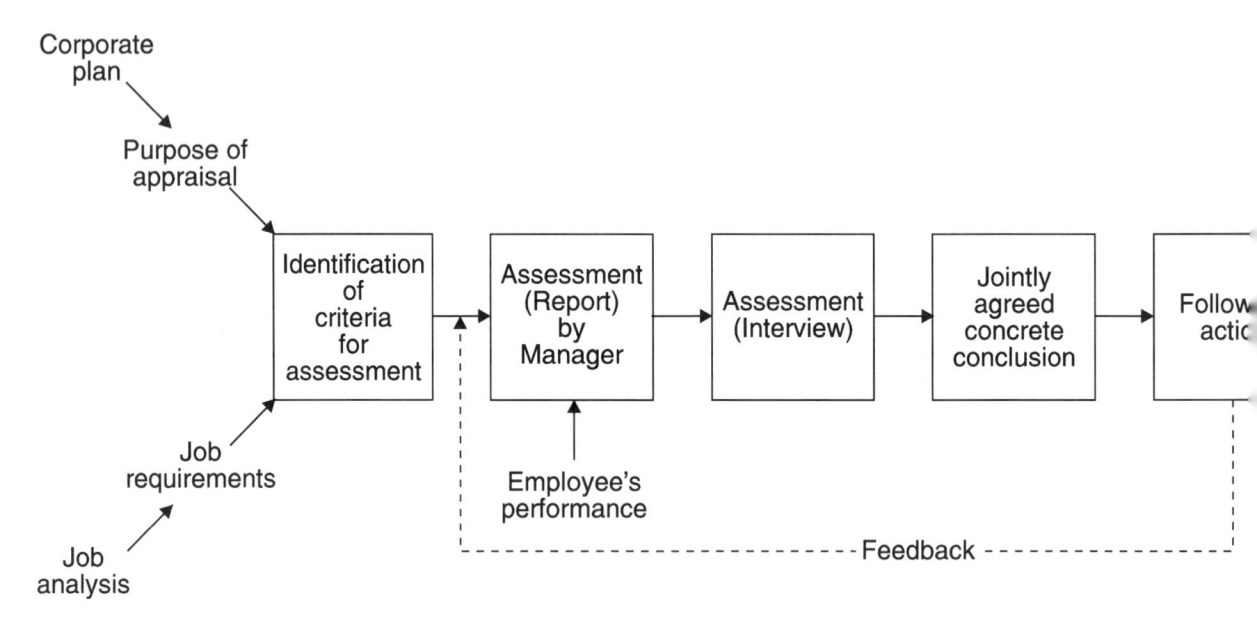

```
Corporate
  plan
     ↓
  Purpose of
   appraisal
        ↘
         Identification      Assessment                            Jointly
            of              (Report)       Assessment              agreed         Follow
          criteria     →       by       →  (Interview)  →         concrete    →   actio
            for              Manager                              conclusion
         assessment
        ↗                        ↑
    Job                      Employee's
 requirements                performance
    ↗
  Job                    ┆----------------------- Feedback ----------------┆
 analysis
```

3.26 Most systems provide for appraisals to be recorded, and report forms of various lengths and complexity may be designed.

3.27 *L Lockett* (in *Effective Performance Management*) suggests that **appraisal barriers** can be identified as follows.

Appraisal barriers	Comment
Appraisal as confrontation	Many people dread appraisals, or use them 'as a sort of show down, a good sorting out or a clearing of the air.'
	(a) There is a lack of agreement on performance levels.
	(b) The feedback is subjective - in other words the manager is biased, allows personality differences to get in the way of actual performance etc.
	(c) The feedback is badly delivered.
	(d) Appraisals are 'based on yesterday's performance not on the whole year'.
	(e) Disagreement on long-term prospects.
Appraisal as judgement	The appraisal 'is seen as a one-sided process in which the manager acts as judge, jury and counsel for the prosecution'. However, the process of performance management 'needs to be jointly operated in order to retain the commitment and develop the self-awareness of the individual.'

Appraisal barriers	Comment
Appraisal as chat	The other extreme is that the appraisal is a friendly chat 'without ... purpose or outcome ... Many managers, embarrassed by the need to give feedback and set stretching targets, reduce the appraisal to a few mumbled "well dones!" and leave the interview with a briefcase of unresolved issues.'
Appraisal as bureaucracy	Appraisal is a form-filling exercise, to satisfy the personnel department. Its underlying purpose, improving individual and organisational performance, is forgotten.
Appraisal as unfinished business	Appraisal should be part of a continuing process of performance management.
Appraisal as annual event	Many targets set at annual appraisal meetings become irrelevant or out-of-date.

Self-appraisal

3.28 Self-appraisal occurs when individuals carry out their own self-evaluation as a major input into the appraisal process.

(a) **Advantages of self appraisal.**

  (i) It **saves the manager time**.

  (ii) It offers **increased responsibility** to the employee being appraised - which may improve motivation.

(b) **Disadvantages**.

  (i) People are often not the best judges of their own performance – the supervisor may have a very different opinion.

  (ii) By the nature of the process, the **control aspect of appraisal is likely to be less** than 'downward appraisal'.

3.29 Many schemes combine the two - manager and subordinate fill out a report and compare notes.

Appraisal and reward

3.30 Another issue is the extent to which the appraisal system is related to the salary and reward system. There are drawbacks to linking salary or bonuses to appraisal.

(a) The **funds available** rarely depend on an individual's performance.
(b) **Continuous improvement** should perhaps be expected, not rewarded as extra.
(c) **Comparisons between individuals** are hard to make.

Improving the appraisal system

3.31 The appraisal scheme should itself be assessed (and regularly re-assessed) according to the following general criteria for evaluating appraisal schemes.

Criteria	Comment
Relevance	• Does the system have a useful purpose, relevant to the needs of the organisation and the individual? • Is the purpose clearly expressed and widely understood by all concerned, both appraisers and appraisees? • Are the appraisal criteria relevant to the purposes of the system?
Fairness	• Is there reasonable standardisation of criteria and objectivity throughout the organisation? • Is it reasonably objective?
Serious intent	• Are the managers concerned committed to the system - or is it just something the personnel department thrusts upon them? • Who does the interviewing, and are they properly trained in interviewing and assessment techniques? • Is reasonable time and attention given to the interviews - or is it a question of 'getting them over with'? • Is there a genuine demonstrable link between performance and reward or opportunity for development?
Co-operation	• Is the appraisal a participative, problem-solving activity - or a tool of management control? • Is the appraisee given time and encouragement to prepare for the appraisal, so that he or she can make a constructive contribution? • Does a jointly-agreed, concrete conclusion emerge from the process? • Are appraisals held regularly?
Efficiency	• Does the system seem overly time-consuming compared to the value of its outcome? • Is it difficult and costly to administer?

Upward appraisal

3.32 A trend adopted by companies such as BP and British Airways (and others) is **upward appraisal.** Subordinates appraise their 'superiors'.

3.33 **Advantages of upward appraisal**

(a) Subordinates tend to know their superior well, they have first hand experience.

(b) The chance of bias is reduced - the ratings of all the employees that report to a manager can be converted into a representative view.

3.34 **Problems with the method** include fear of reprisals, possible employee point-scoring or 'revenge' and a lack of authority - bosses may just ignore it.

Contracts of employment

3.35 Employment contracts are another tool used to achieve control within an organisation. An actual **written contract stating clearly what is expected** of employer and employee (including a job description) provides a visible control tool. (No written contract need exist for a contractual relationship to be established - a court would look at the reality of the situation, rather than the form of the arrangement.)

3.36 Considering how widespread and how important employment contracts are, the legal requirements as to form are remarkably fluid. This is because it is difficult to incorporate every situation which may arise during the course of work.

3.37 A contract of employment may be **written, oral or a mixture** of the two. At the one extreme, it may be a document drawn up by solicitors and signed by both parties; at the other extreme it may consist of a handshake and a 'See you on Monday'.

3.38 Each of these situations, subject to the requirements outlined below as to written particulars, will form a valid contract of employment, as long as there is agreement on essential terms such as hours and wages.

Written particulars of employment

3.39 In general a contract of employment need not be made in writing. However, under UK legislation an employer must give to an employee a written **statement of prescribed particulars** of his employment. (This information is provided as an example of the **type of information in many employment contracts**. Knowledge of the contents of legislation within a specific country is not required.)

3.40 The statement should identify the following.

(a) The names of **employer** and **employee**.

(b) The **date** on which employment began.

(c) Whether any service with a previous employer forms part of the employee's **continuous period** of employment.

(d) **Pay** - scale or rate and intervals at which paid.

(e) **Hours** of work (including any specified 'normal working hours')

(f) Any **holiday** and **holiday pay** entitlement.

(g) **Sick leave** and **sick pay** entitlement.

(h) **Pensions** and pension **schemes**.

(i) Length of **notice** of termination to be given on either side.

(j) The **title** of the job which the employee is employed to do.

3.41 If the employee has a **written contract of employment** covering these points and has been given a copy it is not necessary to provide separate written particulars.

3.42 Employees must also be informed of disciplinary and grievance procedures. These procedures may be designed to provide certain controls on employee behaviour.

3.43 As we are concerned with the use of employment contracts as a control tool, we will focus on the obligations the contract places on the employee.

Employee's duties

3.44 The employee has a **fundamental duty of faithful service** to the employer. All other duties are features of this general duty.

3.45 The **implied** duties of the employee include the following.

(a) **Reasonable competence** to do the job.

(b) **Obedience** to the employer's instructions unless they require him or her to do an unlawful act or to expose themself to personal danger (not inherent in the work).

(c) **Duty to account for all money and property** received during the course of his employment.

(d) **Reasonable care and skill** in the performance of work. What is reasonable depends on the degree of skill and experience which the employee professes to have.

(e) **Personal service** - the contract of employment is a personal one and so the employee may not delegate their duties without the employer's express or implied consent.

(f) The same duty of **fidelity** to an employer to whom he or she is seconded as to a **contractual employer**.

Effectiveness of the employment contract as a control tool

3.46 **Advantages** of employment contracts as a control tool:

- A well-written contract should spell out clearly what is expected of an employee
- It is a good starting point in the employer/employee relationship
- The boundaries of acceptable behaviour are spelt out
- Can bring other documentation into the employment relationship eg '.. will follow all procedures described in the Procedures Manual'

3.47 **Disadvantages** of employment contracts as a control tool:

- If not written well it can appear to be dictating to employees
- Tends to emphasise negative consequences
- If recourse to the contract is needed, it is likely the relationship has already broken down

4 BUDGETARY CONTROL

4.1 An organisation's control systems will incorporate an accounting element, such as a budget. However, as *Otley* says (*Accounting Control and Organisational Behaviour*) budgets 'do not and cannot provide a sufficient basis for the overall control of the enterprise, which must rest on broader foundations'.

4.2 All businesses need to record income and expenditure and keep financial records. Budgets have a number of control functions.

- To **authorise** expenditure
- To help **plan** expenditure
- To **communicate** and **co-ordinate** activities through the allocation of resources
- To **motivate**
- To **evaluate** performance

4.3 The purpose of any control system is to ensure that the organisation achieves its objectives. In theory a budgetary control system assists in this in several ways

- Breaking down plans into budgets for sections
- Collecting feedback information
- Motivating managers

4.4 If budgets are to be used to motivate performance, the following guidelines are useful.

10: Control of activities and resources

(a) Targets should be challenging but realistic, tailored to the circumstances and the personality of the manager.

(b) Participation can be useful provided that managers do not use participation to manipulate the process by one of the methods given below.

   (i) Building in budgetary slack.
   (ii) Setting conveniently low targets.
   (iii) Imposing difficult targets on other departments which they have not agreed to.

(c) Goals should be clear and simple.

(d) Feedback is necessary.

(e) Managers should be encouraged to experiment.

4.5 **Accounting information can be used** - and abused - in **appraising performance.** The performance appraisal system should consider the following matters.

(a) Trade-offs between measures (eg profit versus market share).

(b) Participation in budget setting.

(c) Qualitative indicators: 'what gets measured gets managed' even though factors which are hard to measure can be important.

(d) Other benchmarks and trends.

(e) Environmental factors: keeping inevitable losses to a minimum may be evidence of competence.

5 BUILDING CONTROLS INTO AN INFORMATION SYSTEM 5/01, 5/02

5.1 It is possible to **build controls** into computerised processing. A balance must be struck between the degree of control and the requirement for a user-friendly system.

5.2 Controls can be classified into:
- Security controls
- Integrity controls
- Contingency controls

Security controls

> **KEY TERM**
>
> **Security** can be defined as 'The protection of data from accidental or deliberate threats which might cause unauthorised modification, disclosure or destruction of data, and the protection of the information system from the degradation or non-availability of services'. (Lane: *Security of computer based information systems*)

5.3 The **risks** to data are:

- Human error
  - Entering incorrect transactions
  - Failing to correct errors
  - Processing the wrong files

- Technical error such as malfunctioning hardware or software
- Natural disasters such as fire, flooding, explosion, impact, lightning
- Deliberate actions such as fraud
- Commercial espionage
- Malicious damage
- Industrial action

5.4 Security can be subdivided into a number of aspects.

(a) **Prevention**. It is in practice impossible to prevent all threats cost-effectively.

(b) **Detection**. Detection techniques are often combined with prevention techniques: a log can be maintained of unauthorised attempts to gain access to a computer system.

(c) **Deterrence**. As an example, computer misuse by personnel can be made grounds for dismissal.

(d) **Recovery procedures**. If the threat occurs, its consequences can be contained (for example checkpoint programs).

(e) **Correction procedures**. These ensure the vulnerability is dealt with (for example, by instituting stricter controls).

(f) **Threat avoidance**. This might mean changing the design of the system.

Physical security

5.5 A system needs to be protected against **natural and man-made disasters**. Protective measures include the following.

- Site preparation, eg fireproof materials
- Detection equipment, eg smoke detectors
- Extinguishing equipment, eg sprinklers
- Use of uninterruptable power supplies (UPS)

5.6 Physical access controls are designed to prevent intruders getting near to computer equipment and/or storage media.

(a) Personnel, including receptionists and, outside working hours, security guards, can help control human access.

(b) Door locks can be used where frequency of use is low.

(c) This is not practicable if the door is in frequent use.

(d) Locks can be combined with:

(i) A keypad system, requiring a code to be entered.
(ii) A card entry system, requiring a card to be 'swiped'.

(e) Intruder alarms are vital.

5.7 Much computer equipment is easily portable and therefore susceptible to theft. Laptops and small printers are designed for portability; even desktops and laser printers can be easily carried by one person. Several protective measures can be taken.

- An equipment log, including booking out procedures
- Postcoding of equipment
- Bolts and/or locks to secure equipment to desks
- Secure storage of disks and CDs

Integrity controls

> **KEY TERMS**
>
> **Data integrity** in the context of security is preserved when data is the same as in source documents and has not been accidentally or intentionally altered, destroyed or disclosed.
>
> **Systems integrity** refers to system operation conforming to the design specification despite attempts (deliberate or accidental) to make it behave incorrectly.

5.8 Data will maintain its **integrity** if it is **complete** and **not corrupted**. This means that:

(a) The original **input** of the data must be controlled in such a way as to ensure that the results are complete and correct.

(b) Any **processing and storage** of data must maintain the completeness and correctness of the data captured.

(c) Reports or other **output** should be set up so that they, too, are complete and correct.

5.9 **Input controls** should ensure the **accuracy, completeness and validity** of input.

(a) **Data verification** involves ensuring data entered matches source documents.

(b) **Data validation** involves ensuring that data entered is not incomplete or unreasonable. Various checks can be used, depending on the data type.

   (i) **Check digits**. A digit calculated by the program and added to the code being checked to validate it eg modulus 11 method.

   (ii) **Control totals**. For example, a batch total totalling the entries in the batch.

   (iii) **Hash totals**. A system generated total used to check the reasonableness of numeric codes entered.

   (iv) **Range checks**. Used to check the value entered against a sensible range, eg balance sheet account number must be between 5,000 and 9,999.

   (v) **Limit checks**. Similar to a range check, but usually based on a upper limit eg must be less than 999,999.99.

5.10 It is possible for data to be mis-keyed, but still be accepted by the system as **valid** (because it is in the correct format).

5.11 **Processing controls** should ensure the **accuracy and completeness of processing**. Programs should be subject to development controls and to rigorous testing. Periodic running of test data is also recommended.

5.12 **Output controls** should ensure the accuracy, completeness and security of output. The following measures are possible.

- Investigation and follow-up of error reports and exception reports
- Batch controls to ensure all items are processed
- Controls over distribution/copying of output
- Labelling of disks/tapes

5.13 **Back-up controls** aim to maintain system and data integrity. We have classified back-up controls as an integrity control rather than a contingency control (see later in this section) because back-ups are part of the day-to-day procedures of all computerised systems.

> **KEY TERM**
>
> **Back-up** means to make a copy in anticipation of future failure or corruption. A back-up copy of a file is a duplicate copy kept separately from the main system and only used if the original fails.

5.14 The **purpose of backing up data** is to ensure that the most recent usable copy of the data can be recovered and restored in the event of loss or corruption on the primary storage media.

5.15 A related concept is that of **archiving.** Archiving data is the process of moving (by copying) data from primary storage, such as a hard disk, to tape or other portable media for long-term storage.

5.16 Archiving provides a legally acceptable **business history**, while freeing up **hard disk space**. If archived data is needed, it can be restored from the archived tape to a hard disk. Archived data can be used to recover from site-wide disasters, such as fires or floods, where data on primary storage devices is destroyed.

5.17 How long data should be retained will be influenced by:

- Legal obligations
- Other business needs

5.18 Data stored for a long time should be tested periodically to ensure it is **still restorable** – it may be subject to **damage** from environmental conditions or mishandling.

5.19 In a well-planned data back-up scheme, a copy of backed up data is delivered (preferably daily) to a secure **off-site** storage facility.

5.20 A tape **rotation scheme** can provide a restorable history from one day to several years, depending on the needs of the business.

5.21 A well-planned **back-up and archive strategy** should include:

   (a) A plan and schedule for the **regular back-up of critical data**.
   (b) **Archive plans**.
   (c) A **disaster recovery plan** that includes off-site storage.

5.22 As with archiving, regular tests should be undertaken to **verify that data backed up can be successfully restored**.

5.23 The **intervals** at which back-ups are performed must be decided. Most organisations back up their data daily, but back-ups may need to be performed more frequently, depending on the nature of the data and of the organisation.

5.24 Even with a well planned back-up strategy some re-inputting may be required. For example, if after three hours work on a Wednesday a file becomes corrupt, the Tuesday version can be restored – but Wednesday's work will need to be re-input.

10: Control of activities and resources

Passwords and logical access systems

> **KEY TERM**
>
> **Passwords** are a set of characters which may be allocated to a person, a terminal or a facility which are required to be keyed into the system before further access is permitted.

5.25 Unauthorised persons may circumvent physical access controls. A **logical access system** can prevent access to data and program files, by measures such as the following.

- Identification of the user
- Authentication of user identity
- Checks on user authority

5.26 Virtually all computer installations use passwords. Failed access attempts may be logged. Passwords are not foolproof.

- Standard system passwords must be changed
- Passwords must never be divulged to others
- Passwords must never be written down
- Passwords must be changed regularly, and changed immediately if there is any suspicion that a password is known
- Obvious passwords must not be used

Administrative controls

5.27 **Personnel selection** is important. Some employees are always in a position of trust.

- Computer security officer
- Senior systems analyst
- Database administrator

5.28 Measures to control personnel include the following.

- Careful recruitment
- Job rotation and enforced vacations
- Systems logs
- Review and supervision

5.29 For other staff, **segregation of duties** remains a core security requirement. This involves division of responsibilities into separate roles.

- Data capture and data entry
- Computer operations
- Systems analysis and programming

Systems integrity in a small company

5.30 By 'small' we envisage a company with, say, three **stand-alone PCs**. Possible controls are as follows.

(a) Installation of a **password** routine which is activated whenever the computer is booted up, and activated after periods of inactivity.

Part C: Control

(b) The use of additional passwords on 'sensitive' files eg employee salaries spreadsheet.

(c) Any data stored on floppy disk, Zip-disk or CD-R should be locked away.

(d) **Physical access controls,** for example door locks activated by swipe cards or PIN numbers, to prevent access into the room(s) where the computers are kept. This is probably not feasible in an open plan office.

Systems integrity with a LAN

5.31 The main additional risk on a system of this type is the risk of a fault or breakdown in one area **spreading across the system**. This is particularly true of **viruses**. A virus introduced onto one machine could replicate itself throughout the network. All software and disks coming in to the organisation should be scanned using proprietary **anti-virus software**, and all machines should have anti-virus software running constantly, especially if connected to a network.

5.32 A further risk, depending on the type of network configuration, is that an extra PC could be 'plugged in' to the network to gain access to it. The **network management software** should detect and prevent breaches of this type.

Systems integrity with a WAN

5.33 Additional issues, over and above those already described are related to the extensive communications links utilised by Wide Area Networks. Dedicated land lines for data transfer and encryption software may be required.

5.34 If **commercially-sensitive data** is being transferred it would be necessary to specify high quality communications equipment and to use sophisticated network software to prevent and detect any security breaches.

Contingency controls

> **KEY TERM**
>
> A **contingency** is an unscheduled interruption of computing services that requires measures outside the day-to-day routine operating procedures.

5.35 The preparation of a contingency plan is one of the stages in the development of an organisation-wide security policy. A contingency plan is necessary in case of some terrible **disaster** occurring to the system, or if some of the **security measures** discussed elsewhere **fail**.

5.36 A **disaster** occurs where the system for some reason breaks down, leading to potential **losses** of equipment, data or funds. The victim, however, cannot simply wait before continuing operations. The system **must recover as soon as possible** so that further losses are not incurred, and current losses can be rectified.

Question 1

What actions or events might lead to a systems breakdown?

10: Control of activities and resources

Answer

System breakdowns can occur in a variety of circumstances, for example:

(a) Fire destroying data files and equipment.
(b) Flooding.
(c) A computer virus completely destroying a data or program file or damaging hardware.
(d) A technical fault in the equipment.
(e) Accidental destruction of telecommunications links (eg builders severing a cable).
(f) Terrorist attack.
(g) System failure caused by software bugs which were not discovered at the design stage.
(h) Internal sabotage (eg logic bombs built into the software).

5.37 Any contingency plan must therefore provide for:

(a) **Standby procedures** so that some operations can be performed while normal services are disrupted.

(b) **Recovery procedures** once the cause of the breakdown has been discovered or corrected.

(c) **Personnel management** policies to ensure that (a) and (b) above are implemented properly.

Contents of a contingency plan

5.38 The contents of a contingency plan will include the following.

Section	Comment
Definition of responsibilities	It is important that somebody (a manager or co-ordinator) is designated to take control in a crisis. This individual can then delegate specific tasks or responsibilities to other designated personnel.
Priorities	Limited resources may be available for processing. Some tasks are more important than others. These must be established in advance. Similarly, the recovery program may indicate that certain areas must be tackled first.
Backup and standby arrangements	These may be with other installations, with a company that provides such services (eg maybe the hardware vendor); or reverting to manual procedures.
Communication with staff	The problems of a disaster can be compounded by poor communication between members of staff.
Public relations	If the disaster has a public impact, the recovery team may come under pressure from the public or from the media.
Risk assessment	Some way must be found of assessing the requirements of the problem, if it is contained, with the continued operation of the organisation as a whole.

5.39 The contingency plan is dependent on effective **back-up procedures** for data and software, and arrangements for replacement – and even alternative premises.

5.40 The plan must cover all activities from the initial response to a 'disaster', through to damage limitation and full recovery. Responsibilities must be clearly spelt out for all tasks.

Part C: Control

6 THE 'NEW' ORGANISATION AND CONTROL

6.1 In the past, the adoption of 'classical' management principles (exemplified by writers like *Fayol* and *Weber*) has meant that organisations developed the following characteristics.

(a) Belief in **universal laws** like the span of control principle (which states that no one brain can effectively control more than five or six other brains).

(b) Very **tall structures** (ie lots of different management levels) with **close supervision** at every level.

(c) **Hierarchical control** through adherence to a rigid chain of command.

(d) **Problem-solving** of a fragmented, directive, mechanistic kind, solely devoted to putting things right once they had gone wrong (instead of making sure they did not go wrong in the first place).

(e) **Single-function specialisms** like production and sales, with departmental barriers and careers concentrated in one activity.

(f) **Individualism** reflected in incentive systems and the encouragement of competitive behaviour.

(g) **Focus on tasks and responsibilities** in job descriptions rather than the concept of adding value and using initiative.

(h) **Systems which were reactive and procedure-bound** being seen as a very positive employee asset.

6.2 In an environment where there was little competition, business organisations and certainly public sector organisations could laze along, carrying superfluous employees, many of them under-utilised, under-developed and psychologically amputated.

6.3 The gradual but perceptible shift away from the traditional organisation has come about for the reasons below.

(a) **Everything global**: we now live in what has been described as a 'global village', with a global economy, a global marketplace, battered by global forces (political, economic, social, technological and religious).

(b) **Everything new**: organisations have come to appreciate that they are unlikely to survive unless they are responsive to the expectations of their customers; for some, there is a very new perspective if they previously operated in a monopolistic (or quasi-monopolistic) environment and did not regard their clients as customers at all (BT, for instance, used to call us 'subscribers').

(c) **Everything faster**: with techniques of **mass customisation**, it is now possible to order a tailor-made Toyota from a Tokyo car showroom and have the car delivered 24 hours later.

(d) **Everything different**: it is no longer sufficient to keep doing the same things but progressively to do them better. The world of work has entered a major paradigm shift towards entirely different expectations about performance, challenging the conventional assumptions of old.

(e) **Everything turbulent**: there is no going back to the peace and quiet of organisational stability in a world of slow social and technological change - instead, organisations nowadays must continue to cope with messy, paradoxical, ambiguous scenarios.

Re-engineering the organisation

6.4 The essential features for the new world of work are discussed by *Michael Hammer* and *James Champy* in *Re-Engineering the Corporation: A Manifesto for Business Revolution* (1993). *Hammer* and *Champy* envisage the following trends.

(a) **Work units**: from functional departments to process teams.

(b) **Jobs**: from simple tasks to multi-dimensional work. The old model (represented by 'Taylorism') offered simple tasks for simple people, whereas the new approach reflects complex jobs for smart people.

(c) **Roles: from 'controlled' to 'empowered'**. In a process team environment, people have the chance to learn more about the work process as a complete entity; performing the role becomes more satisfying, with a greater sense of completion, closure and accomplishment, and more learning and growth built in. The corollary is that jobs are more challenging and difficult as the older-style routine work is eliminated or automated.

(d) **Values**: from protective to productive. People in organisations have to believe that they work for their customers, not for their bosses.

(e) **Managers**: from supervisors to coaches.

(f) **Executives**: from scorekeepers to leaders.

(g) **Structures**: from hierarchical to flat.

6.5 The difficulty for most organisations is the need to manage the tension between two opposing sets of forces.

(a) The **centralising** impact of professional management, designed to produce a cohesive corporate strategy and the rational, efficient allocation of resources which will support this strategy.

(b) The **centrifugal** effect of the forces important for fostering entrepreneurship, empowerment, risk-taking and innovation.

Case example

Catalyst Technology Solutions

CTS provide disaster-recovery services for businesses. If a client is hit by fire or flood, or a computer malfunction, they can reload their companies' data onto the Catalyst system and continue to operate as if the crisis had never happened.

The Woking office stands empty, so if a client's premises have been destroyed, they can move in their whole operation. Catalyst's hi-tech house-bound employees do not have much in common with the traditional image of homeworkers - its networked workforce is only possible because of new technology. 'I know no other business that looks like this,' Mr Hixon says. 'Our competitors find it impossible to copy us because they are stuck in a culture which involves people sitting in offices with a manager in a glass-fronted office watching them and shouting when he wants attention.'

The modern equivalent of electrically-driven steam machinery is the outdated hierarchical structures most companies still rely on. Most have a command and control culture designed for a pre-IT age where information and instructions are handed from top layer of management down through the hierarchy. At Catalyst, information is disseminated throughout the company so everybody has access to all the documents relevant to the projects they are working on. Employees working without a manager peering over their shoulder involves a high degree of trust.

Businesses such as Catalyst could be ushering in the productivity revolution in the UK as companies start to base their structure around the potential of information technology.

Part C: Control

Mr Hixon has further plans for revolutionising Catalyst. A new telephone system will soon automatically route calls to workers' home numbers or another location, and divert them to a secretary if the call is unanswered.

Chapter roundup

- In this chapter, we have examined various **aspects of control.**
- Management writers have offered various **theories of control** - ranging from those who believe employees operate best under strict, autocratic leadership (eg **Taylor**), to those who emphasise the importance of human relationships (eg **Mayo**).
- A **control system** is necessary to ensure that the organisation's actual results, or the results of the subsystems which make it up, are in accordance with the plan.
- **Feedback** measures difference between planned and actual results.
- There is a **trust-control dilemma** in the employer-employee relationship.
- Employee **appraisal** and employment **contracts** can be used as control tools.
- **Budgets** are an example of an organisational control mechanism.
- **Information systems** that utilise information technology have some controls '**built-in**'.

Quick quiz

1. Max Weber pioneered the scientific management movement.

    True ☐
    False ☐

2. List the five components of a control system.

    1 ....
    2 ....
    3 ....
    4 ....
    5 ....

3. What is negative feedback?

4. What is positive feedback?

5. Explain two types of control strategies related to employee supervision.

6. Define 'span of control'?

7. List three advantages and three disadvantages of using employment contracts as a means of employee control.

    1 ....
    2 ....
    3 ....
    1 ....
    2 ....
    3 ....

10: Control of activities and resources

8   List four control functions of budgets.

         1   ....

         2   ....

         3   ....

         4   ....

9   What is the purpose of input controls in a computerised information system?

Answers to quick quiz

1   FALSE. Frederick W Taylor pioneered the scientific management movement. Weber developed the notion of bureaucratic administration.

2   Standard.
        Sensor.
        Feedback.
        Comparator.
        Effector or activator.

3   Negative feedback indicates that the system is deviating from its planned or prescribed course. This feedback is called 'negative' because control action would seek to reverse the direction of movement back towards the planned course.

4   Positive feedback results in control action which causes actual results to maintain (or increase) their path of deviation away from planned results.

5   Behaviour control deals with the behaviour of individual employees - control is exercised over procedures. Examples include standard policies and methodologies. Output control is where management attention is focused on results or output, rather than the process.

6   Span of control refers to the number of subordinates responsible to a manager or supervisor.

7   *Three advantages*
        A well-written contract should spell out clearly what is expected of an employee.
        It is a good starting point in the employer/employee relationship.
        The boundaries of acceptable behaviour are spelt out.

        Three disadvantages
        They can appear to be dictating to employees.
        Contracts tend to emphasise negative consequences.
        Recourse to the contract is often viewed as a last resort – after the employment relationship has already broken down.

8   [Four of]
        To authorise expenditure.
        To help plan expenditure.
        To communicate and co-ordinate activities through the allocation of resources.
        To motivate.
        To evaluate performance.

9   To ensure the accuracy, completeness and validity of input.

The material covered in this Chapter is tested in Questions 14(b) and 18(b) in the Question Bank.

Part D
Audit of activities and systems

Chapter 11

INTERNAL AUDIT

Topic list	Syllabus reference	Ability required
1 The process of internal audit	(iv)	Comprehension
2 Types of internal audit and risk	(iv)	Evaluation
3 Internal control systems	(iv)	Evaluation
4 The planning, controlling and recording of audit work	(iv)	Evaluation
5 The detection and prevention of fraud	(iv)	Evaluation

Introduction

The role of **internal audit** has undergone significant change in recent years. In this Chapter we explore the issues surrounding the internal audit function in the modern business environment.

The content reflects the 'new' focus of internal audit towards **risk management** and **process improvement**, as well as covering the traditional areas of accounting and financial **controls**.

Learning outcomes covered in this chapter

- **Explain** the process of internal audit
- **Produce** a plan for the audit of various organisational activities including management, accounting and information systems
- **Analyse** problems associated with the audit of activities and systems, **and recommend** action to avoid or solve these problems
- **Recommend** action to improve the efficiency, effectiveness and control of activities

Syllabus content covered in this chapter

- The process of review and audit of internal controls
- The role of the internal auditor and the relationship between the internal auditor and external audit
- The operation of internal audit, the assessment of audit risk and the process of analytical review
- The analysis of business risks and approaches to risk management
- Value for money audit and management audit
- The identification and prevention of fraud *(Also see Chapter 12)*
- The major tools available to assist with a review of internal controls *(Also see Chapter 12)*
- The different types of benchmarking, their use and limitations *(Also see Chapter 13)*

Part D: Audit of activities and systems

1 THE PROCESS OF INTERNAL AUDIT 5/01

1.1 Auditing is the most conspicuous form of internal control used in an organisation. Audit can be split into two categories:

- External audit
- Internal audit

External audit

1.2 It is a requirement of the Companies Act that all companies must appoint **external auditors** who will report to the members of the company on whether in their opinion, the annual statutory accounts give a true and fair view. The duties of the external auditor are imposed by statute and cannot be limited, either by the directors or by the members of the company. External auditors are not employees of the company.

Internal audit

1.3 **Internal auditors** are usually employees of the company whose duties are fixed by management, and who report ultimately to management. Many large companies have internal audit departments. However, internal audit services may be provided by an external accountancy firm. The external auditors may alter their audit approach to take account of the work done by the internal auditors.

1.4 There are several 'official' definitions of an internal audit.

> **KEY TERM**
>
> **Internal audit** is an independent appraisal function established within an organisation to examine and evaluate its activities as a service to the organisation. The objective of internal auditing is to assist members of the organisation in the effective discharge of their responsibilities.

1.5 The definition suggests that internal audit has a wider scope than external audit. External auditors consider whether a company's accounts give a true and fair view of its financial position. They need not comment on ways in which the company's results, systems or controls could be improved.

1.6 Internal audit usually operates in one or more of the following areas.

(a) **Review of the accounting and internal control systems.** The establishment of adequate accounting and internal control systems is a responsibility of the directors and/or senior management. Often, internal audit is assigned responsibility for reviewing the design of systems and processes (both manual and automated), monitoring their operation and recommending improvements.

(b) **Examination of financial and operating information.** This may include a review of the means used to identify, measure, classify and report information, and specific enquiry into individual items including detailed testing of transactions, balances and procedures.

(c) **Review of the economy, efficiency and effectiveness** of operations including non-financial controls of an organisation.

11: Internal audit

(d) **Review of compliance** with laws, regulations and other external requirements and with internal policies and directives and other requirements including appropriate authorisation of transactions.

(e) **Special investigations** into particular areas, for example suspected fraud.

1.7 There are **two main features of internal audit**.

(a) **Independence**. Although an internal audit department is part of an organisation, it should be independent of the line management whose sphere of authority it may audit. The department should report to the board or to a special internal audit committee (covered later in this section) and not to the finance director, as the finance director lacks the independence required. It is also important that internal auditors should have the authority required to carry out their responsibilities, and unrestricted access to records, assets and personnel.

(b) **Appraisal**. Internal audit is concerned with the appraisal of the work done and systems used in the organisation. Internal auditors should not themselves carry out any of the work that is being audited. The appraisal of operations provides a service to management, providing information on strengths and weaknesses throughout the organisation. Such information is invaluable to management when it comes to taking action to improve performance, or planning future activities of the company.

1.8 There are three main differences between internal and external audit.

(a) **Appointment.** External auditors are appointed by the shareholders (although they are usually only ratifying the directors' choice) and must be independent of the company, whereas **internal auditors are employees** of the organisation.

(b) **Responsibility**. External auditors are responsible to the owners (shareholders, the public or Parliament), whereas **internal auditors are responsible to senior management**.

(c) **Objectives**. The objectives for external auditors are defined by statute, whereas those for **internal auditors are set by management**. In other words, management - perhaps the internal auditors themselves - decide what parts of the organisation or what systems they are going to look at, and what type of audit should be carried out, for example a systems audit or a value for money audit.

Considerations relevant to the internal audit function

1.9 Consideration should be given to:

(a) **Staffing and training**

(i) The internal audit department should possess or have access to all the necessary skills for performing its function. It must be adequately staffed, and staff are likely to be drawn from a variety of disciplines.

(ii) Internal audit staff should be given the training to carry out their work competently.

(b) **Relationships**

Without surrendering their objectivity, internal auditors should try to establish good working relationships and mutual understanding with:

- Management
- External auditors
- The organisation's audit committee

Part D: Audit of activities and systems

Internal audit plans should be discussed with senior management. Individual audits should be arranged in consultation with the managers concerned, and audit reports discussed with management when they are being prepared.

Internal auditors should have regular meetings with the external auditors (who may be able to place reliance on some of the work done by the internal auditors). They should discuss their audit plans, so as to avoid unnecessary duplication in their work.

(c) **Due care**

The internal auditors should exercise due care in fulfilling their responsibilities. The chief internal auditor should ensure that his staff maintain standards of integrity and of adequate quality in their work.

(d) **Planning, controlling and recording**

The internal auditors should plan, control and record their work. These tasks are described in more detail later in this chapter.

(e) **Evidence**

The internal auditors should obtain sufficient, relevant and reliable evidence on which to base reasonable conclusions and recommendations.

Deciding just what evidence will be needed for any particular audit work calls for judgement by the auditors, with their judgement having regard to:

(i) The scope of the audit assignment.
(ii) The significance of the matters under review.
(iii) Just what evidence is available and obtainable.
(iv) What it would cost and how long it would take to obtain.

(f) **Reporting**

The internal auditors should report their findings, conclusions and recommendations promptly to management. The chief internal auditor should ensure that reports are sent to managers who have a direct responsibility for the unit or function being audited and who have the authority to take corrective action.

If the internal auditors find evidence of a serious weakness or malpractice, this should be reported immediately, orally or in writing, as soon as it is discovered, in an 'interim report'.

The internal auditors, having made recommendations in their report, should subsequently follow up their work by checking to see whether their recommendations have been implemented by management.

External/internal auditor relationship   Pilot paper, 5/01

1.10 There are a number of ways that the internal audit department can **assist the external auditors**. Examples of these are as follows.

(a) At an early stage in the financial period discussions can be held between the two parties to decide upon a **joint approach** which will enable both to restrict their tests to a minimum comparable with their individual responsibilities and to ensure that all important audit areas are covered.

(b) **Co-operation and sharing**, particularly in time-consuming tasks eg verifying stock counts.

(c) Work performed and information produced by the internal auditors can be used by the external auditors and will **prevent duplication** of effort, for example the debtors circularisation.

(d) The internal auditors' **detailed knowledge** of the company may be of assistance to the external auditors and the latter may be able to rely to a large extent on the internal auditors to monitor the continuous operation of the system of internal control.

1.11 To be able to **use work undertaken by internal audit,** external audit must be satisfied as to the standard and reliability of the information. Issues considered will include:

(a) **Organisational status**. Both the size of the organisation and the status allocated to the internal audit function should be considered.

(b) **The scope of the internal audit function**. Does the internal audit function have the authority to be pro-active in suggesting changes to policies and procedures, or is it concerned with review only?

(c) **Staff competence and qualifications**. Whether internal audit work is performed by persons having adequate technical training and proficiency as internal auditors (eg are they qualified accountants?).

(d) **Policies and procedures**. Is internal audit work properly planned, supervised, reviewed and documented?

Independence and audit committees

> **KEY TERM**
>
> An **audit committee** is established to assist the board to fulfil its responsibilities regarding internal control and the financial information provided to shareholders. The majority of members should be independent of the organisation. Consideration should be given as to the competency of those chosen to make up the committee.

1.12 Many large companies have an **audit committee**. An audit committee should provide an independent liaison between the board and the auditors (both internal and external). **Advantages** of having an audit committee include:

(a) Increased confidence in the credibility and objectivity of financial reports.

(b) By specialising in the problems of financial reporting it allows the executive directors to devote their attention to management.

(c) In cases where the interests of the company, the executive directors and the employees conflict, the audit committee might provide an impartial body for the auditors to consult.

1.13 In the UK, there have been major developments in the past decade identifying best practice in corporate governance. The initial work of the Cadbury Committee and Greenbury Report raised awareness and formulated a framework for addressing the major concerns of shareholders and companies. The Committee on Corporate Governance under the Chairmanship of Sir R Hampel has reviewed the work of Cadbury and Greenbury, and produced a report which the Stock Exchange incorporated into the Stock Exchange Listing Rules in 1998 as a new Combined Code of best practice. This recommended that audit

Part D: Audit of activities and systems

committees should consist entirely of non-executive directors, the majority of whom are independent of the company.

1.14 The committee must have the authority, resources and means of access to investigate anything within its terms of reference. The **duties of the audit committee** could include:

(a) Recommending to the board on the appointment of the external auditors, their resignation or dismissal and the audit fee.

(b) Review the half-yearly and annual statements before they are submitted to the board.

(c) Liase with external auditors.

(d) Review the internal audit programme and any significant findings.

(e) Review the external auditors' management letter and the company's statement on the internal control system.

1.15 The essential elements of the internal audit function are as follows.

(a) An appropriate reporting relationship should be established so as to achieve **independence**.

(b) Clear and comprehensive **terms of reference** and **objectives** should be established from the outset and regularly reviewed.

(c) Adequate **staff** of the appropriate levels of skills and experience should be provided. In most companies, it would be advantageous to include non-finance staff (such as computer specialists) in the internal audit team.

(d) An **audit programme** should be drawn up which identifies the organisational units to be audited and the topics to be covered.

(e) A set of operational auditing standards should be drawn up covering methodology, filing and recording, the procedures for preparing and clearing reports and methods of follow-up. This may take the form of an **audit manual**.

1.16 The **role of internal audit** comprises the following.

(a) Ensuring the adequacy of the system of **internal control** (accounting, financial and operating controls).

(b) Ensuring the reliability and integrity of **financial and operating information**.

(c) Ensuring the achievement of business objectives and goals.

(d) Ensuring efficient use of the organisation's resources.

(e) Preventing and detecting fraud.

(f) Co-ordinating with the external auditors.

Question 1

Outline the role of an internal audit department in a large organisation.

Answer

In the past an internal audit department devoted most of its time to accounting and financial matters but today there may be a considerable amount of time devoted to other areas, for example operational auditing. The job of the internal audit department is defined by the organisation of which it is a part. The internal audit department's work can embrace the following:

(a) Review of accounting systems and related internal controls.

(b) Examination of financial and operating information for management, including detailed testing of transactions and balances.

(c) Review of the economy, efficiency and effectiveness of operations and of the functioning of non-financial controls.

(d) Review of the implementation of corporate policies, plans and procedures.

(e) Special investigations.

2 TYPES OF INTERNAL AUDIT AND RISK

2.1 Internal audit can now be much broader in scope than investigation of financial systems and records, and so there are several different types of internal audit. As noted above, an internal audit department may be asked by management to look into any aspect of the organisation.

2.2 Which of the activities noted in Section 1 that an internal audit department carries out - and to what degree - depends on the type of audit being carried out. There are various different types of audit, but those of most concern to the internal auditor are likely to be:

(a) Systems audit (or more frequently now, risk-based audits).
(b) Value for money or VFM.
(c) Management audit.

We will now consider these in more detail.

Systems audit

2.3 This is the type of audit most commonly associated with the job of auditing. As its name implies, it is the audit of systems, although the term is commonly associated with the audit of accounting systems, such as cash and cheques, sales and debtors, fixed asset records and so on.

2.4 A systems audit tests and evaluates the internal controls within the system, to determine the following.

(a) How good the **internal controls** are.

(b) What **weaknesses** there might be in the system of internal controls.

(c) What **reliance** management can place on the internal controls that:

(i) The resources of the organisation are being managed effectively, and
(ii) The information being provided by the system is accurate.

2.5 The auditors must therefore investigate the nature of the control procedures within a system, and how well these procedures operate in practice. The main objectives of the internal control system are to:

(a) Ensure **adherence** to management policies and directives in order to achieve the organisation's objectives.

(b) **Safeguard** assets.

(c) **Secure** the relevance, reliability and **integrity** of **information**, so ensuring as far as possible the completeness and accuracy of records.

(d) Ensure **compliance** with statutory requirements.

Part D: Audit of activities and systems

Types of audit tests

2.6 There are two types of test that are used in systems audits.

(a) **Tests of controls**. These are tests that seek evidence that the internal controls are being applied as prescribed, and are functioning properly.

(b) **Substantive procedures**. After completion of the tests of controls, further detailed tests are carried out to verify:

   (i) The transactions and account balances.

   (ii) The existence of assets and liabilities, and their valuation (for example debtors, stocks, fixed assets).

These tests substantiate the figures in the accounts, and hence are called 'substantive' procedures.

2.7 The nature of **tests of controls** depends on the type of control being tested. Ideally the auditors will be looking for tangible evidence that the control has operated, for example completion of an invoice grid stamp on a purchase invoice. This is an instance of obtaining evidence by inspection.

2.8 Where a control does not leave permanent evidence of its performance it may be possible to test it by **observation** - or by testing it. Controls over the opening of post could be observed on a surprise basis; password controls on a computer terminal could be tested by attempting to defeat this control (by trying to gain access to a computer program or data file), as well as examining the record of passwords issued and password changes.

2.9 In any systems audit, the proportion of the work that is testing of controls and the proportion that is substantive procedures will depend on the **results** of the tests of controls.

(a) If tests of control find the internal controls are operating effectively, there will be no need for a great many substantive procedures (although some substantive procedures should be carried out). The figures in the accounts can be relied on as being accurate (or accurate enough).

(b) If tests of controls reveal faults or weaknesses in the operation of internal controls, then far more substantive procedures should be carried out.

2.10 However much testing of controls is carried out, it will always be necessary to perform some substantive work. Substantive procedures can be defined as those tests which seek **direct evidence** as to the completeness, ownership, valuation, existence or disclosure of particular account items. They comprise tests to discover material **errors** and **irregularities**, and tests to discover material omissions.

2.11 Tests which start with the accounting records in which the transactions are recorded and check from the accounting entries to supporting documents or other evidence serve to discover errors. Such tests should detect any **overstatement** and also **understatement** through causes other than omission.

2.12 Understatement through omission will not be revealed by starting with the record itself as clearly the items selected will not be ones which have been omitted from the record. Tests designed to detect omission start from outside the accounting records (the 'reciprocal population'), and the supporting evidence is checked to the entries in the accounting records.

11: Internal audit

2.13 In flowchart form, a systems audit can be summarised as follows.

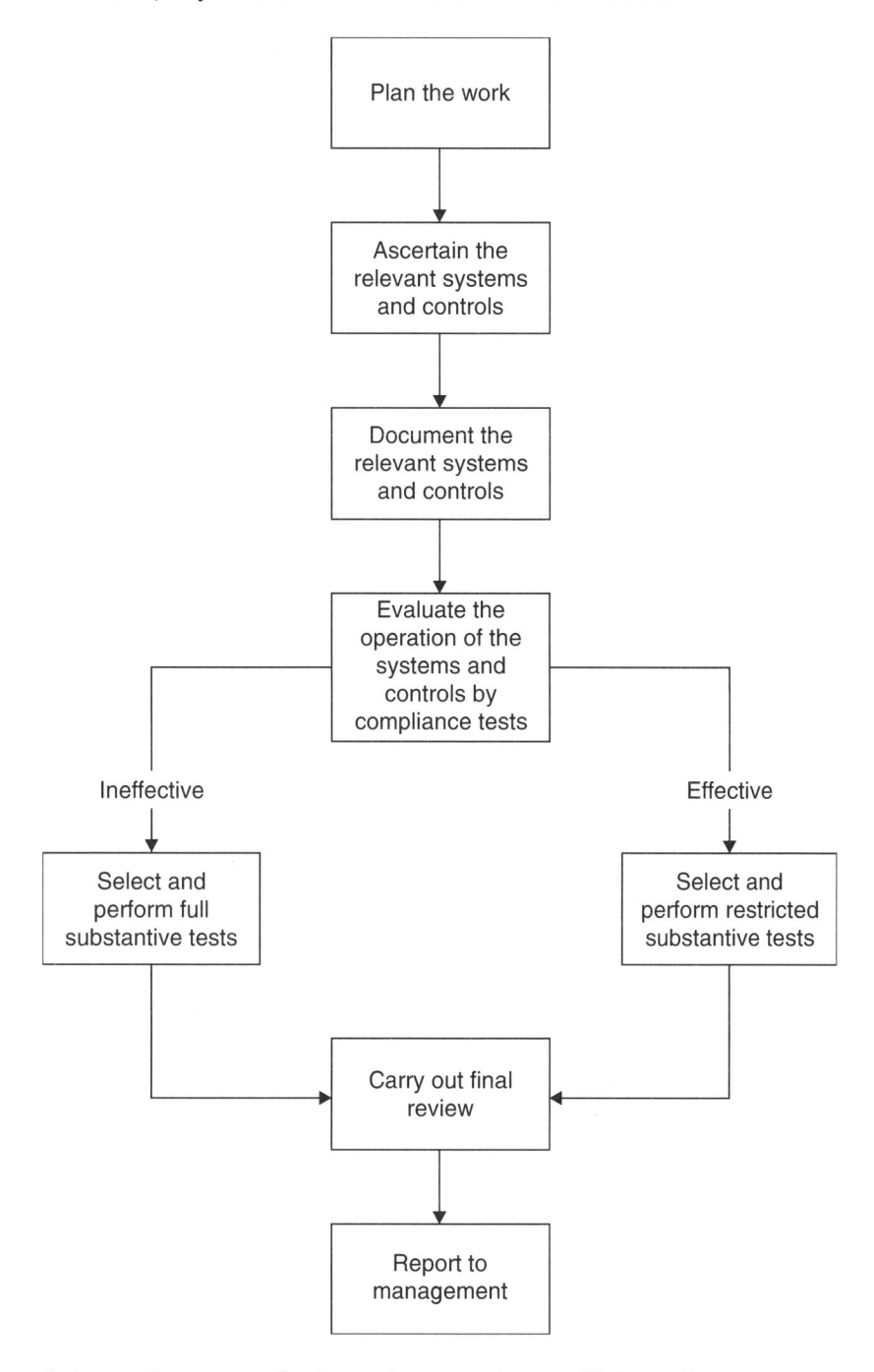

```
                    ┌─────────────────┐
                    │  Plan the work  │
                    └────────┬────────┘
                             ↓
                    ┌─────────────────┐
                    │  Ascertain the  │
                    │ relevant systems│
                    │   and controls  │
                    └────────┬────────┘
                             ↓
                    ┌─────────────────┐
                    │  Document the   │
                    │ relevant systems│
                    │   and controls  │
                    └────────┬────────┘
                             ↓
                    ┌─────────────────┐
                    │  Evaluate the   │
                    │ operation of the│
                    │   systems and   │
                    │   controls by   │
                    │ compliance tests│
                    └───┬─────────┬───┘
              Ineffective         Effective
                  ↓                   ↓
         ┌──────────────┐    ┌──────────────────┐
         │  Select and  │    │    Select and    │
         │ perform full │    │ perform restricted│
         │substantive tests│ │ substantive tests│
         └──────┬───────┘    └────────┬─────────┘
                └──────┐      ┌───────┘
                       ↓      ↓
                  ┌─────────────────┐
                  │ Carry out final │
                  │     review      │
                  └────────┬────────┘
                           ↓
                  ┌─────────────────┐
                  │    Report to    │
                  │   management    │
                  └─────────────────┘
```

As stated above, the extent of substantive procedures will depend on:

(a) How much reliance the auditors can place on the internal controls that exist, even if they work properly.

(b) The frequency with which internal controls appear to have malfunctioned.

(c) Whether other internal controls exist that act as a 'double check' to prevent errors in the financial records so that even if one control has malfunctioned, there should be no adverse consequences.

Audit risk

> **KEY TERM**
>
> **Audit risk,** in the context of internal audit, is the risk that the auditor(s) will issue an inaccurate statement on a matter in their area of responsibility.

2.14 Audit risk can never be completely eliminated. The preferred method of minimising audit risk has been to systemise the audit approach, so that all aspects have been standardised. This standardised solution grew out of a combination of external auditing standards and external audit firms' own manuals, but has 'crossed-over' into internal audit.

Risk-based audits

2.15 In recent years there has been a shift away from the systems-based auditing towards **risk-based auditing**.

> **KEY TERM**
>
> **Risk-based auditing** refers to the development of auditing techniques which are responsive to risk factors in an audit. In internal audit the auditor(s) apply judgement to determine the areas that place the organisation at greatest risk, and concentrate their resources on those areas.

2.16 This approach should ensure that the greatest audit effort is directed at the riskiest areas, so that the risks are minimised and greatest benefit is obtained from the internal audit resource.

2.17 The increased use of risk-based auditing reflects the growing complexity of the business environment. This has increased the danger of fraud, or more commonly, of simple mismanagement; factors such as the developing use of computerised systems and the growing internationalisation of business are relevant here.

A risk-based audit will follow the stages of systems-based audit shown in the diagram in paragraph 2.13. Risk-based refers to **what** is audited rather than how.

2.18 A **risk-centred methodology** is now 'the norm'.

Assessing audit risk and its components

2.19 **Audit risk** (AR) is made up of three parts:

- **Inherent** risk (IR)
- **Control** risk (CR)
- **Detection** risk (DR)

The relationship between the types of risk is: $\mathbf{AR = IR \times CR \times DR}$.

Inherent risk

2.20 **Inherent risk** arises from factors which may cause errors or irregularities to be present. The level of inherent risk will depend on various conditions existing **within the enterprise** as well as on conditions **outside the enterprise**. Examples of conditions existing outside the enterprise include:

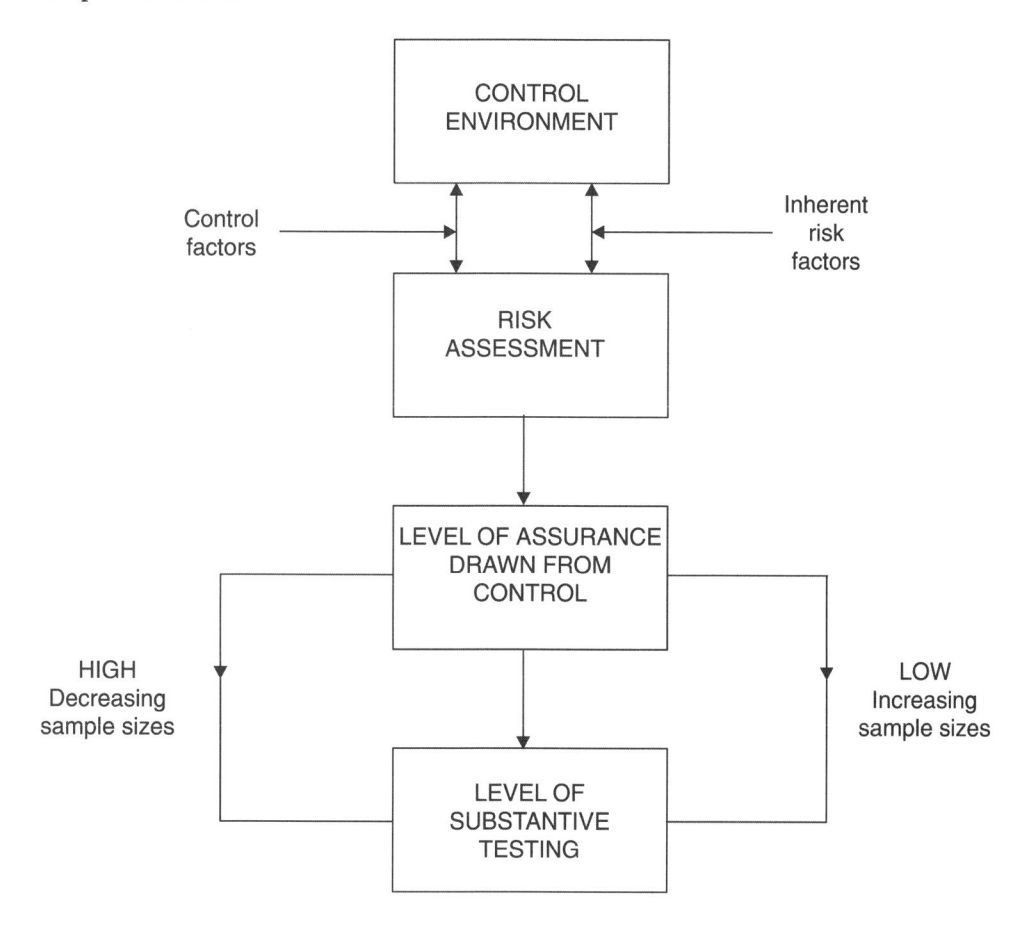

```
                    ┌──────────────┐
                    │   CONTROL    │
                    │ ENVIRONMENT  │
                    └──────┬───────┘
                           ↕
  Control   ──────→  ┌──────────────┐  ←──────  Inherent
  factors            │     RISK     │           risk
                    │  ASSESSMENT  │           factors
                    └──────┬───────┘
                           ↓
                    ┌──────────────┐
                    │LEVEL OF ASSURANCE│
             ┌──────│ DRAWN FROM   │──────┐
             │      │   CONTROL    │      │
             │      └──────┬───────┘      │
   HIGH      │             │              │    LOW
Decreasing   │             ↓              │  Increasing
sample sizes │      ┌──────────────┐      │ sample sizes
             │      │   LEVEL OF   │      │
             └─────→│ SUBSTANTIVE  │←─────┘
                    │   TESTING    │
                    └──────────────┘
```

(a) **Macroeconomic factors** such as general recession (this might, for example, threaten the collectability of debtors), or impending government legislation.

(b) Factors from **within the industry**, such as consumer demand conditions which might jeopardise future viability of the enterprise, or technological changes rendering stocks obsolete.

2.21 Examples of **inherent risk conditions** within the enterprise which could affect the auditors' assessment of audit risk include:

(a) **Poor management**, which could be affecting the business overall.

(b) Key personnel with a motive to **distort financial results**. For example, managers on a performance-related bonus scheme, or subsidiary company managers being pressurised by group management.

(c) The susceptibility of account balances to be misstated as the result of **fraud**.

(d) The risk that a very large **customer may not pay**. The bad debt (not previously provided for) would undermine previously stated results.

Control risk

2.22 The **control risk** is the risk that material errors will not be prevented or detected by internal controls. Even in the best system, some control risk will remain, for example because it will always be possible for management to override controls, or for fraudulent collusion between two or more employees to occur.

Part D: Audit of activities and systems

2.23 The assessment of the risk of material misstatements (inherent risk coupled with control risk) may be expressed as 'normal' or 'high' depending on the risk factors identified. It may be that an internal control is itself designed to minimise an inherent risk of the enterprise.

Detection risk

2.24 **Detection risk** refers to the risk of something adverse or irregular not being noticed. In internal audit this could relate to an inefficient and risky procedure not being challenged.

Business risk

2.25 Internal audit is increasingly being asked to take responsibility for all business risk. Business risk covers any risk that has the **potential to impact on a business**. The approaches to **risk management** covered in Chapter 2 in the context of a project, can also be applied to inherent risk, and to **business risk** in general.

> **KEY TERMS**
>
> **Risk** describes the consequences of situations or events which **may or may not occur**. A statistical estimation of the likelihood of the event **can** be made.
>
> **Uncertain events** are those whose outcome **cannot** be predicted with statistical confidence.

Risk preference

2.26 How an organisation deals with risk will depend on the attitude of the manager involved, and of the organisation on the whole.

> **KEY TERMS**
>
> A **risk seeker** is a decision maker who is interested in the best outcomes no matter how small the chance that they may occur.
>
> A decision maker is **risk neutral** if he or she is concerned with what will be the most likely outcome.
>
> A **risk averse** decision maker acts on the assumption that the worst outcome might occur.

2.27 The internal audit function should ideally **quantify the risks identified,** allowing informed decisions to be made as to whether the risk should be planned for, avoided (by adapting behaviour) or transferred (eg insurance).

Case example

What is an acceptable amount of risk will of course vary from organisation to organisation. For large public companies it is largely a question of what is acceptable to the shareholders. A 'safe' investment will attract investors who are to some extent risk averse, and the company will thus be obliged to follow relatively 'safe' policies. A company that is recognised as being an innovator or a 'growth' stock in a relatively new market, like Netscape or Yahoo!, will attract investors who are looking for high performance and are prepared to accept some risk in return. Such companies will be expected to make 'bolder' (more risky) decisions.

Allowing for uncertainty

2.28 **Conservatism** involves estimating outcomes in **a conservative manner** in order to provide a built-in safety factor. However, the method **fails to consider a range** of outcomes and, by concentrating only on conservative figures, may also fail to consider **the expected or most likely outcomes**.

2.29 Conservatism is **associated with risk aversion** and prudence. In spite of its shortcomings it is probably the most widely-used method in practice.

2.30 A more scientific version of conservatism is to measure the **most likely outcome** (or profit) from a decision, **the worst possible outcome, and the best that can happen**. This will show the **full range of possible outcomes** from a decision, and might help managers to reject certain alternatives because the worst possible outcome might involve an unacceptable loss.

2.31 EXAMPLE: WORST/BEST POSSIBLE OUTCOMES

Omelette Ltd is trying to set the sales price for one of its products. Three prices are under consideration, and expected sales volumes and costs are as follows.

Price per unit	£4.00	£4.30	£4.40
Expected sales volume (units)			
Best possible	16,000	14,000	12,500
Most likely	14,000	12,500	12,000
Worst possible	10,000	8,000	6,000

Fixed costs are £20,000 and variable costs of sales are £2 per unit.

Required

Determine which price should be chosen.

2.32 SOLUTION

Price per unit	£4	£4.30	£4.40
Contribution per unit	£2	£2.30	£2.40
Total contribution:	£	£	£
Best possible	32,000	32,200	30,000
Most likely	28,000	28,750	28,800
Worst possible	20,000	18,400	14,400

The **highest contribution**, based on **most likely sales volume**, would be at a price of **£4.40** but arguably a price of **£4.30 would be much better** than £4.40, since the most likely profit is almost as good, the worst possible profit is not as bad, and the best possible profit is better.

However, **only a price of £4** guarantees that the company would **not make a loss**, even if the worst possible outcome occurs. (Fixed costs of £20,000 would just be covered.) A **risk averse management** might therefore prefer a price of £4 to either of the other two prices.

Part D: Audit of activities and systems

Value for money audit

> **KEY TERM**
>
> A **value for money audit** is an investigation into whether proper arrangements have been made for securing economy, efficiency and effectiveness in the use of resources.
>
> *CIMA Official Terminology*

2.33 Value for money audits are often associated with one type of internal audit in the public sector (for example the work of local authorities, and central government departments). However, VFM audits are also used by companies, and are sometimes called 'operational audits' or 'efficiency audits'.

2.34 Although most internal audit work is probably still made up of systems audits, VFM audits have become more common and 'fashionable' in recent years. The purpose of a VFM audit is as follows.

   (a) To investigate a system or activity in the organisation.

   (b) To judge whether the objectives of the system are being achieved, and if not, why not. In other words, is the system operating **effectively**?

   (c) To judge whether the resources of the organisation are being used **efficiently** in achieving those objectives. Or is the system using too much manpower, is it too slow, does it use the most appropriate equipment, is there over-capacity in equipment or machinery?

   (d) To judge whether the system is being operated **economically**, or whether there is unnecessary overspending, for example is there excessive stockholding, are overtime costs excessive, are prices paid to suppliers too high, etc?

VFM audits look at **e**ffectiveness, **e**fficiency and **e**conomy in a system. These are referred to collectively as the '3 Es'.

2.35 A VFM audit will investigate the following.

   (a) Whether the management of an organisation has established proper arrangement for achieving value for money.

   (b) Whether those arrangements are applied in practice and whether they work successfully.

Management audit

> **KEY TERM**
>
> A **management audit** is an objective and independent appraisal of the effectiveness of managers and the corporate structure in the achievement of entity policies and procedures.
>
> *CIMA Official Terminology*

2.36 Many of the principles of VFM audits can be apply to management audits. The difference is that a management audit focuses primarily on the effectiveness of management in the organisation.

11: Internal audit

2.37 The aim of a management audit is to identify existing and potential management weaknesses and to recommend ways to eliminate them. A management audit will involve:

(a) An investigation into the effectiveness of managers and the corporate structure.

(b) A judgement as to whether management objectives are being achieved, and if not, why not. Are managers **effective**?

(c) To judge whether the organisation's management structure is **efficient?** Does the structure facilitate effective management activity?

(d) To judge whether the organisation is being managed **economically**, or whether there is unnecessary overspending, for example is there excessive middle management?

Benchmarking

> **KEY TERM**
>
> **Benchmarking** is described in the *Official Terminology* as 'The establishment, through data gathering, of targets and comparators, through whose use relative levels of performance (and particularly areas of under-performance) can be identified. By the adoption of identified best practices it is hoped that performance will improve.'

2.38 Benchmarking is sometimes utilised as part of the internal audit process - particularly in relation to value for money audits and management audits. In the context of internal audit, benchmarking against similar organisations is most likely to be used, with the aim of identifying areas of inefficiency.

2.39 Selecting a realistic organisation or set of organisations to benchmark against is vital. Unless the organisations are similar, or the measures used are adjusted to allow for differences in circumstances, the comparisons will be invalid. The process of benchmarking process, the different types of benchmarks and the advantages and disadvantages of benchmarking are explained in Chapter 13.

3 INTERNAL CONTROL SYSTEMS   Pilot paper

3.1 One of the main tasks of the internal auditors is to check the operational 'systems' within their organisation, to find out whether the system's internal controls are sufficient and are working properly. If they are not, it is the auditors' task to recommend improvements.

3.2 Internal audit thus acts as an internal control over other internal controls in the systems that are audited.

So what are the other 'internal controls' in a system that the internal auditors may wish to investigate?

3.3 An **internal control system** is defined by the Auditing Practices Board as follows.

> **KEY TERM**
>
> An **internal control system** comprises the control environment and control procedures. It includes all the policies and procedures (**internal controls**) that aim to ensure the orderly and efficient conduct of an organisation's business.

Part D: Audit of activities and systems

3.4 This definition includes adherence to internal policies, the safeguarding of assets, the prevention and detection of fraud and error, the accuracy and completeness of the accounting records, and the timely preparation of reliable financial information. The **internal control system extends beyond those matters which relate directly to the accounting system.**

3.5 Eight types of control which may exist in an organisation are listed below. One way of remembering them is to use the mnemonic SPAM SOAP).

S egregation of duties
P hysical
A uthorisation and approval
M anagement
S upervision
O rganisation
A ccounting
P ersonnel

Segregation of duties

3.6 This is one of the prime means of control; it is the separation of those responsibilities or duties which would, if combined, enable one individual to record and process a complete transaction. Segregation of duties reduces the risk of intentional manipulation or error and increases the element of checking. Functions which should be separated are:

C ustody
A uthorisation
R ecording
E xecution

3.7 A classic example of segregation of duties concerns the receipt, recording and banking of funds received. It is not good practise for the person who opens the post (and 'receives' cheques) to be the person responsible for recording the receipt of the funds and/or doing the banking. Dividing the duties so that no one person carries all these responsibilities is a form of internal control, in this case helping to safeguard cash receipts.

Physical

3.8 Physical controls include:

(a) Physical protection for assets, particularly those which are portable and valuable.
(b) Indirect protection for assets via documentation.
(c) Confidentiality of information.

Duties that aim to safeguard assets should be segregated from related responsibilities.

Authorisation and approval

3.9 All transactions should require **authorisation** or **approval** by an appropriate responsible person. The limits for these authorisations should be specified; limits will be delegated through budgets within departments. The important point is that **all** transactions should be authorised.

3.10 For example, a company might set the rule that the head of a particular department may authorise revenue expenditure up to £500, but that for anything more expensive they must

11: Internal audit

seek the approval of a director. Such authorisation limits will vary from company to company: £500 could be quite a large amount for a small company, but seem insignificant to a big one.

Management

3.11 These are the controls exercised by management outside the day-to-day routine of the system. They include:

(a) Overall **supervisory** controls.
(b) Review of **management accounts** and comparison with budgets.
(c) The **internal audit** function.
(d) Other special **review procedures**.

Supervision

3.12 Supervision control is important in order to:

(a) Compensate for the absence of other controls.
(b) Discourage **fraud** while improving **productivity** and accuracy.
(c) Sort problems out, thus allowing lower skilled workers to perform harder tasks.

Organisation

3.13 Enterprises should have a plan of their organisation, defining and allocating **responsibilities** and identifying **lines of reporting** for all aspects of the enterprise's operations, including the controls. The delegation of **authority** and **responsibility** should be clearly specified. This will help to prevent friction so staff work together well. It also means that no duties go unperformed or unchecked.

3.14 For example, it could happen that an employee in a company finds himself working for two masters, say a product manager (who is responsible for the production, marketing and profitability of one particular product) and a sales manager (who supervises the company sales policy for all products). A company which is organised in this overlapping fashion is said to have a **matrix** organisation. The point here is that the employee might be confused. He might not know who he is supposed to be working for at any one time; he might not know his priorities; he might work harder for one manager at the expense of the other. Such a state of affairs would be detrimental to the company, so it is sensible to set clear lines of authority and responsibility - in short, the company should utilise organisational controls.

Accounting

3.15 **All** transactions should be recorded **correctly**: ie completeness and accuracy are very important. Control totals can be used here, as well as reconciliations, trial balances etc.

Personnel

3.16 A system will not operate properly without appropriate personnel, ensured through:

(a) Recruitment of staff with appropriate **qualifications** and **qualities**.
(b) Internal **training** and **monitoring** for staff improvements.
(c) Proper **processes** for promotion and assessment.

Part D: Audit of activities and systems

3.17 As an example, a company accountant should be suitably qualified. Note that 'qualified' often means possession of a professional qualification, but it can mean qualified though work experience.

3.18 Other distinctions between types of financial control which you may come across are:

(a) **Administrative controls** (achieving objectives and implementing policies) and **accounting controls** (to provide accurate records and achieve accountability).

(b) **Detect controls** (to detect errors once they have occurred) and **prevent controls** (to stop errors occurring).

Internal control system

3.19 A company's operational systems (eg purchasing stock control, sales, capital expenditure planning, computerised management information systems and so on) will incorporate some internal controls from the SPAM SOAP list above. The controls that there are will depend on the particular circumstances of the company, but the range of internal controls it ends up with is called the company's or the system's internal control system.

3.20 An operational system need not possess all of the SPAM SOAP internal controls - or indeed the organisation may not be able to implement all of them, perhaps because they would be too expensive and so not worth having. For example, a very small organisation may have insufficient staff to be able to organise a desirable level of segregation of duties. In such cases some controls (eg supervision) might take the place of others.

3.21 Management has the responsibility for deciding what internal controls there should be. The internal auditors contribute to internal controls by measuring and evaluating the other internal controls installed by management and reporting to management on their effectiveness.

Inherent limitations of internal controls

3.22 Remember that no internal control system is foolproof. This is because internal controls have **inherent limitations**, as follows.

(a) The usual requirement that the **cost** of an internal control is not disproportionate to the potential loss which may result from its absence.

(b) Most systematic internal controls tend to be directed at **routine transactions** rather than non-routine transactions.

(c) The potential for **human error** due to carelessness, distraction, mistakes in judgement and the misunderstanding of instructions.

(d) The possibility of **circumvention of internal controls** through collusion with parties outside or inside the entity.

(e) The possibility that a person responsible for exercising an internal control could **abuse that responsibility** by overriding an internal control.

(f) The possibility that **procedures may become inadequate** due to **changes** in conditions or that compliance with procedures may deteriorate over time.

These factors show why auditors cannot obtain all their evidence from tests of the system of internal control.

11: Internal audit

Question 2

The internal auditors, in their report to the directors of A Ltd, commented adversely on the administrative control of fixed assets.

As the financial controller of A Ltd you are required to prepare a report in response to the auditors' comments, detailing those factors which require consideration in the administrative control of fixed assets other than those concerned with the control of operating efficiency and utilisation.

Answer

To: *The board of directors*
From: *Financial controller* Date: *16 October 20XX*
Subject: *A report on the administrative control of fixed assets*
General background

The administrative control of fixed assets should cover all movements of fixed assets including their acquisition, transfer, sale and scrapping. All decisions in relation to any of the above should be made by responsible officials of the company with an appropriate level of authority. No decisions should be taken without a proper appraisal of the situation. Full records of fixed assets must be maintained:

(a) To comply with statutory regulations.

(b) To ensure that management are able to take full advantage of any tax benefits and/or government grants available.

(c) To ensure that management are able to discharge properly their responsibilities to safeguard the company's assets.

Specific controls required

These should include the following.

(a) It should be established who may make proposals for the various types of fixed asset movement and who may authorise such movements.

(b) Standard requisition forms should be used for any proposed movement of fixed assets: these must be designed so as to ensure that all the necessary information for a proper appraisal of the request is available to the authorising official(s).

(c) A record of all approved proposals should be kept to ensure that these are properly dealt with.

(d) All further documentation relating to fixed asset movements (for example purchase orders, GRNs, etc) should be cross referenced using the proposal number allocated in the central record referred to in (c) above.

(e) Regular reports should be made to management of proposals approved, proposals completed, authorised expenditure contracted for and authorised expenditure contracted for but not yet paid.

(f) A detailed fixed assets register should be maintained showing the following for each asset.

   (i) Full description of the asset, including any identification numbers or marks, and details of its present location.

   (ii) Date of acquisition.

   (iii) Supplier.

   (iv) Original (historical) cost.

   (v) Current valuation of the asset (if appropriate).

   (vi) Expected date of disposal or scrapping.

   (vii) Depreciation or amortisation provided for the purpose of the accounts.

(g) The totals of the assets register should regularly be reconciled with the accounts in the nominal ledger.

(h) Periodically a physical verification of the assets should be carried out and agreed to the details in the assets register.

Part D: Audit of activities and systems

Evaluation of internal controls

3.23 The evaluation of internal controls within a system comes from the following sources.

(a) **System documentation:** deciding how the system works, and describing this 'on paper'.

(b) **Identification of potential errors:** recognising what can go wrong in this system. Potential errors can arise whenever there is a chance that one of the following objectives might not be achieved or satisfied.

   (i) Existence or occurrence - proof that something exists or has happened.
   (ii) Completeness - that an account balance contains every item that it should.
   (iii) Valuation or measurement - that a proper system of valuation has been used.
   (iv) Ownership - proof of ownership of assets.
   (v) Disclosure - that items are disclosed whenever disclosure is appropriate.

(c) **Identification of controls:** recognising the controls within the system that are designed to detect or prevent errors in the system.

3.24 Having identified potential errors and the controls to detect or prevent them, the auditor can assess whether the controls appear to be good enough to do their job sufficiently well.

3.25 When a control is evaluated, the auditors must assess the level of 'risk' that the control is inadequate or might not be properly applied. Factors to consider include the following.

(a) The nature of the control itself.

(b) The timing and frequency of the control check.

(c) Who performs the control, taking into consideration the competence, experience and integrity of staff, and the degree of supervision.

(d) What errors the control has succeeded in identifying and eliminating in the past.

(e) Whether there have been changes in the system or in staff, bearing in mind that control procedures might weaken and become slack in the early period of a new system or just after a change of staff.

3.26 When evaluating internal controls auditors may use **internal control questionnaires (ICQs)**. ICQs are detailed checklists of types of internal controls that are generally recognised as being required, in some form, in all systems. ICQs usually require a Yes/No answer, for example an ICQ could contain the question, 'back-ups completed daily?'.

3.27 A similar tool is an **internal control evaluation questionnaire (ICEQ)**. ICEQs may be used to develop an appropriate ICQ. ICEQs ask more general questions, such as 'is the contingency/disaster recovery plan adequate?'.

Question 3

You are the recently appointed internal auditor of Z Ltd and one of your first tasks is to investigate the procedure with regard to the receipt of customers' orders and the despatch of goods to them.

Your investigation reveals the following procedures, which are the only ones concerning the receipt and despatch of customers' orders. The orders arrive daily by post, either directly from the customer, or via the company's representatives. These go to the sales office where a pre-printed two-part un-numbered sales order set is made out for each incoming order. The sales office staff attach the second copy of the set to the original order and file this in alphabetical sequence.

11: Internal audit

The top copy is sent initially to the credit controller for approval. He checks it against a computer print-out of the current balances on the debtors' ledger and/or credit 'black list' reports. If credit is approved, the top copy is then sent to the finished goods warehouse where the items on the order are checked for availability.

If they are available the warehouse foreman then raises an un-numbered four-part pre-printed invoice/despatch note set. The individual copies of this set are distributed as follows. The top copy, valued by the warehouse, is sent to the customer as an invoice. The second copy goes to the accounts department to update the debtors' ledger. The third copy, unvalued, is used as a despatch advice note and included with the goods. The despatch clerk checks that no goods leave the company without this third copy. Finally, the fourth copy is retained on the warehouse file attached to the sales order copy.

Required

(a) Identify the internal control weaknesses of this system.
(b) Suggest improvements to overcome them.

Answer

(a) The internal control weaknesses of the current system are as follows.

  (i) There appears to be no formal system for dealing with orders received by telephone.

  (ii) There is no record logging receipt of an order.

  (iii) The sales order sets are un-numbered - it would therefore be possible to lose an order without its loss being obvious.

  (iv) The sales order sets are filed alphabetically - if pre-numbered they could alternatively be filed sequentially.

  (v) The credit controller is assessing each order before it has been valued by the warehouse – without knowing how much credit is being requested.

  (vi) There appears to be no system for dealing with part-satisfied orders, where only some of the goods requested are available.

  (vii) We are not told the system for what happens if the goods requested are not available in the warehouse.

  (viii) The invoice/despatch note set is un-numbered - it too could be lost without its loss being obvious.

  (ix) Since despatch notes are not numbered, it would be possible for the despatch clerk to be deceived by goods leaving the company with a despatch note which did not relate to an order.

  (x) The warehouse appear to value goods as a function on their own - this gives the warehouse foreman a large degree of personal responsibility that he may not deserve.

(b) Improvements could be made to overcome the weaknesses of the current system as follows.

  (i) Develop a pro-forma to be filled out in the case of orders received by telephone. These could trigger the order system along with the orders arriving by post.

  (ii) The sales order sets should be pre-numbered, with each set being entered by number in a sales order register. This would improve the physical control possible over orders and order sets.

  (iii) The second copies of the order sets should be filed sequentially if no register is to be kept. If a register is maintained, then they can remain being filed alphabetically.

  (iv) The credit controller must liaise closely with the warehouse department when making judgements concerning the granting of credit. The controller should ensure that the computer print-out of current debtors' balances gives an aged analysis of the debtors, as this will be of more use than just knowing the balances on each debtor's account.

  (v) A system for part-satisfied orders must be developed. Perhaps the warehouse foreman could raise his four-part set purely on the basis of goods available, and then return the sales order to the sales office making his comments on whether the balance of the order can be satisfied.

  (vi) The invoice/despatch note sets should be pre-numbered.

Part D: Audit of activities and systems

(vii) The warehouse foreman should value the invoices on the basis only of price lists approved by the accounts department. Otherwise there is no certainty that costs are being covered and a reasonable return being made on each order. Similarly discounts should only be possible after they have been approved by the head of the accounts department.

4 THE PLANNING, CONTROLLING AND RECORDING OF AUDIT WORK

Planning internal audits

4.1 As with any other activity or enterprise, an internal audit department must plan its work carefully if it is to achieve the audit objectives efficiently and effectively. The aim of audit planning is to:

(a) Decide priorities for audit work.
(b) Establish objectives (and apply control measures to ensure that objectives are achieved).
(c) Ensure that audit resources are used efficiently, effectively and cost-effectively.

4.2 Generally speaking, planning can be divided into three parts:

- Strategic
- Tactical
- Operational

Strategic planning of internal audits

4.3 The strategic plan sets out audit objectives in broad terms, including:

- Areas to be covered
- Frequency of coverage
- Rough estimate of resource requirements

4.4 Usually, the strategic plan covers a period of two to five years. It must be regularly reviewed and adjusted in the light of any changes in audit requirements or any information arising out of audit work. It is not the sort of plan which is worked through to the end and replaced by another: it is constantly amended to take account of changing circumstances.

4.5 The starting point for any strategic audit plan is a general awareness of the environment in which the internal audit department - and indeed the organisation as a whole - operates. The internal auditors need to be familiar with the following.

(a) The historical background of the company, and the characteristics of the company business, so that the present activities and performance of the company can be put into context.

(b) The structure of the company, including:

(i) The organisation chart of the company, showing the names, responsibilities and authority limits of the officials.

(ii) The location of the main operating and accounting centres, and any other centres where the company assets are held.

(c) How the company operates, including the:

(i) Flow of documentation including budgets and reports.
(ii) Books of account and ancillary records.

4.6 One of the problems with setting a strategic audit plan - or almost any plan, for that matter - is that it is often difficult to know just what areas are important enough to merit investigation or routine checking, and which are not. In practice, much of the long-term planning of internal audit is based on looking at what work has been done in the past and using common sense as to what needs to be done in the future, and having regard to the requirements of management. In order to prevent reliance on subjective judgement to such an extent, various risk analysis techniques have been developed.

Tactical audit planning

4.7 Once the internal auditors have set out their strategic plan, and agreed it with management, it is necessary to prepare a **tactical plan**. In many ways a tactical audit plan is the easiest type of audit plan to draw up. Basically, it takes the areas of work laid down in the strategic plan and matches them to audit resources and timetables. It covers a period of about six months to a year, and will include a:

(a) Programme of internal audits to be carried out.
(b) Detailed definition of the objectives of each audit.
(c) Detailed allocation of audit resources.

Operational audit planning

4.8 An operational internal audit plan will be drawn up for each individual audit. It is based on the objectives as broadly indicated in the strategic plan, on resource and timetabling considerations within the tactical plan, on results of previous audits, and any other relevant data. When completed, it should show the following.

(a) Detailed audit objectives.

(b) The extent of coverage and areas to be given emphasis (because, for example, of known weaknesses in internal control). This part of the plan will also consider the materiality of items examined in the course of audit and any special sampling methods required.

(c) Target dates for individual stages of the audit.

(d) Names of auditors responsible for or involved in the completion of the audit.

4.9 Nowadays, almost all operational audit plans include reference to an **audit programme**, or perhaps several audit programmes. An audit programme will comprise the following.

(a) Detailed audit instructions, including the amount of testing to be carried out.

(b) The actual amount of testing which was carried out, initialled and dated by the auditor.

(c) Cross-references to audit plans, internal control questionnaires and other working papers (so that a reviewer can follow the documentation of the audit easily, and so can anyone referring back to the audit in later years).

Although there are many advantages to the use of audit programmes (completeness, evidence etc) they should be used with caution; the auditors should not think that the audit consists only of completing all the tests in the programme, or that the same programme can be set each year.

Analytical review

> **KEY TERM**
>
> **Analytical review** is a substantive technique that can be used at the initial planning stage of the audit, during the course of the audit and at or near the completion of the audit when reviewing the financial statements. Analytical review procedures in respect of the financial statements will serve as an overall test of the reasonableness of the figures and are intended to corroborate conclusions formed during the previous stages of the audit.

4.10 They may highlight areas requiring further investigation where unusual matters or inconsistencies with earlier audit evidence are disclosed. Analytical review is a fundamental process in determining the important areas of the audit when planning a risk-based audit.

The techniques

4.11 It is meaningless to attempt a standardised approach to analytical review. Every industry is different and each company within that industry differs in certain respects. What can be stated for all audits is that the reviewer must have an in depth knowledge of the company, its history and the industry within which it operates.

4.12 To assist in analysing trends it is useful to make use of ratio analysis. The choice of accounting ratios is a matter of judgement, based on knowledge of the client, the industry, and the general state of the economy. In any event, ratios mean very little when used in isolation. Ratios should be calculated for previous periods and for comparable companies. This may involve a certain amount of initial research, but subsequently it is just a matter of adding new statistics to the existing information each year. The permanent file should contain a section with summarised accounts and the chosen ratios for prior years.

4.13 Important accounting ratios that could be examined include:

   (a) Gross profit margins, in total and by product.
   (b) Return on capital employed.
   (c) Gearing ratio (debt capital to equity capital).
   (d) Debtors ratio (average collection period).
   (e) Stock turnover ratio (stock divided into cost of sales).
   (f) Current ratio (current assets to current liabilities).
   (g) Quick or acid test ratio (liquid assets to current liabilities).

4.14 In addition to looking at the more usual ratios the auditors should consider examining other ratios that may be relevant to the particular business under examination, such as revenue per passenger mile for an airline operator client, or fees per partner for a professional office.

4.15 The further important technique is to examine important related accounts in conjunction with each other. It is often the case that revenue and expense accounts are related to balance sheet accounts and comparisons should be made to ensure that the relationships are reasonable. Examples of such related accounts are:

   (a) Creditors and purchases.
   (b) Stocks and cost of sales.
   (c) Fixed assets and depreciation, repairs and maintenance expense.

(d) Intangible assets and amortisation.
(e) Loans and interest expense.
(f) Investments and investment income.
(g) Debtors and bad debt expense.
(h) Debtors and sales.

4.16 Other areas that might be investigated in the analytical review include the following.

(a) In terms of sales, examine changes in products, customers and levels of returns, looking for any noticeable trends.

(b) Assess the effect of price changes on the cost of sales.

(c) Consider the effect of inflation, industrial disputes, changes in production methods etc, on the charge for wages.

(d) Where appropriate obtain explanations for all major variances analysed using a standard costing system. Particular attention should be paid to those relating to the over or under absorption of overheads since these may affect stock valuations.

(e) Compare trends in production and sales and assess the effect on any provisions for obsolete stocks.

(f) Ensure that changes in the percentage of labour or overhead content of production costs are also reflected in the stock valuation.

(g) Other profit and loss expenditure comparing:

   (i) Rent with annual rent per rental agreement.

   (ii) Rates with previous year and known rates increases.

   (iii) Interest payable on loans with outstanding balance and interest rate per loan agreement.

   (iv) Hire or leasing charges with annual rate per agreements.

   (v) Other items related to activity level with general price increase and change in relevant level of activity (for example telephone expenditure will increase disproportionately if export or import business increases).

   (vi) Other items not related to activity level with general price increases (or specific increases if known).

(h) Review profit and loss account for items which may have been omitted (eg scrap sales, training levy, special contributions to pension fund, provisions for dilapidations etc).

(i) Generally ensure expected variations arising from the following have occurred:

   (i) Review of minutes.

   (ii) Discussions with client officials.

   (iii) Industry or local trends.

   (iv) Known disturbances of the trading pattern (for example strikes, depot closures, failure of suppliers).

Control of internal audits

4.17 Control of the internal audit department and its work is necessary to ensure that audit objectives are achieved and that work is performed efficiently. The main features of control will be the management and supervision of the internal audit staff and the review of their work.

Part D: Audit of activities and systems

4.18 The chief internal auditor should undertake the following.

(a) Ensure that audit assignments are given to staff who have the necessary experience/training/competence to carry out the work.

(b) Ensure that the auditors for each assignment know what the audit objective is and what their responsibilities are.

(c) Agree a programme of work with each internal auditor.

(d) Provide supervision, review and guidance during each audit, and make a documentary record of this.

(e) Ensure that adequate working papers are prepared for each audit (see below).

(f) Ensure that internal audit results are in accordance with plans or that any variations between actual and planned results are explained.

(g) Evaluate the operations of the internal audit unit as a whole.

Recording internal audits

4.19 Internal audit work should be **recorded**.

(a) Working papers for each audit allow the chief internal auditor to check and confirm that the audit work has been properly performed.

(b) Working papers provide evidence for reference of the:

(i) Work done.
(ii) Problems encountered.
(iii) Conclusions that have been drawn.

(c) Preparing working papers encourages the auditors to adopt a methodical approach to their work.

(d) Working papers should contain sufficient detail to allow one internal auditor, if required, to step in and take over an audit from another auditor.

Quality control and internal auditing

4.20 Quality control should be of paramount importance in the internal audit department. It is difficult to criticise other departments for poor quality if the internal audit department is just as bad!

(a) The internal audit department should establish procedures for its audit work, and communicate them to all relevant staff. Audit manuals should be issued (and kept up-to-date) and standardised procedures applied.

(b) The department should remain satisfied that it has sufficient independence to perform its function properly.

(c) Procedures should be established to ensure that internal auditors adhere to ethical standards of independence, objectivity, integrity and confidentiality.

(d) Internal audit staff should have the skills and competence necessary to do their work. They should be given suitable training, and all staff must be kept up-to-date with changes (for example technical updating should be provided through courses, internal circulars etc).

(e) There should be procedures for consultation between audit staff, including a structured approach to the review of audit files and working papers.

(f) The effectiveness and application of quality control measures should be monitored. If any weaknesses are discovered, improvements should be made. Quality control is an on-going matter.

5 THE DETECTION AND PREVENTION OF FRAUD

5.1 While the vast majority of employees are honest, some employees may decide to act dishonestly. The incidence of financial fraud, particularly in a computer environment, is increasing. This presents a challenge to management and to internal (and external) auditors.

5.2 The mere presence of internal auditors will, to some extent, discourage fraudsters for fear of being discovered. The widely-held general perception that auditors should be expected to uncover all fraud is unrealistic, as it is not feasible to check every transaction and entry.

5.3 However, it is not unreasonable to expect fraud involving amounts that are **material** to be detected.

5.4 Everyone has their own idea of where an acceptable bending of the rules ends and fraud begins, so it is appropriate to start with a definition of fraud.

> **KEY TERM**
>
> **Fraud** means the intentional distortion of financial statements and/or other records carried out to conceal the misappropriation of assets, or any other type of gain.

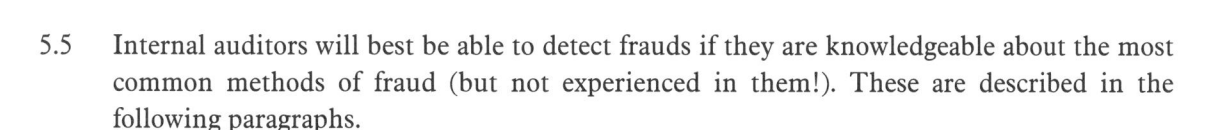

5.5 Internal auditors will best be able to detect frauds if they are knowledgeable about the most common methods of fraud (but not experienced in them!). These are described in the following paragraphs.

Ghost employees

5.6 These are imaginary employees whose 'wages' are paid and distributed amongst the fraudsters. This type of fraud is easier to perform if there is extensive reliance on casual workers, and minimal record keeping for such workers.

5.7 A detection tool that may indicate this type of fraud is a review of the numbers of employees required to achieve a standard amount of work. If at some times of the year a larger number appear to be required, there may be something amiss.

5.8 Scrutiny of signatures given as proof of receipt of wages should be made, together with an examination of bank direct credit schedules.

Miscasting of the payroll

5.9 This fraud involves 'skimming' a very small amount off each genuine wage or salary payment. For example, an employee who has earned £210.95 would receive only £210.90 in their bank account – the other £0.05 being skimmed off into the fraudster's account! The fraud relies on employees either not noticing or not complaining about the very small discrepancy. Over a large number of employees this can lead to substantial payments.

Part D: Audit of activities and systems

Stealing unclaimed wages

5.10 This is effectively confined to wages paid in cash and can occur when an employee leaves without notice or is away sick.

Collusion with external parties

5.11 This could involve suppliers, customers or their staff. Possible frauds are overcharging on purchase invoices, undercharging on sales invoices or the sale of confidential information (eg customer lists, expansion plans) to a competitor. Management should watch out for unusual discounts or commissions being given or taken, or for an excessive zeal on the part of an employee to handle all business with a particular company.

Teeming and lading

5.12 This is a 'rolling' fraud. It occurs when a clerk has the chance to misappropriate receipts from debtors or payments to creditors.

5.13 For example, when one employee has control of the sales ledger and recording debtors' cheques, they may, either by forged endorsement or by opening an account in a name similar to the employer's, pay cheques into a different bank account.

5.14 When the cashier knows that a reconciliation is to be performed, or that an audit visit is planned, the money is temporarily paid back. After the audit, the teeming and lading starts again.

5.15 Segregation of duties, surprise visits by auditors and independent checking of cash balances should discourage this fraud. This fraud can also be detected by independent verification of debtors, balances (eg by circulation). Sending out itemised monthly statements to debtors should act as a deterrent, although a really determined fraudster is likely to be able to avoid detection through statements alone.

Altering cheques and inflating expense claims

5.16 These are self-explanatory.

Stealing assets

5.17 Using the **company's assets for personal gain** and **stealing fully-depreciated assets** are both encountered in practice. Whether or not the private use of company telephones and photocopiers is a serious matter is up to the company to judge, but it may still be fraudulent.

Issuing false credit notes

5.18 Another way of avoiding detection when cash and cheques received from debtors have been misappropriated is to **issue a credit note which is not sent to the customer** (who has paid his account) but is recorded in the books. The issue of itemised statements monthly may show this up, as the customer should query the credit note. A similar tactic is to write a debt off as bad to cover up the disappearance of the payment.

Failing to record all sales

5.19 This fraud may be perpetrated in a business with extremely poor controls over sales recording and minimal segregation of duties. In such circumstances, a dishonest bookkeeper may invoice customers but fail to record the invoices so that the customer's payments never have to be recorded.

5.20 This type of fraud can occur where a customer is receiving large numbers of invoices from the business every month and so the bookkeeper's failure to record one or two invoices (if detected by auditors or his superiors) is simply put down to incompetence rather than fraud. A warning sign here is the perception by customers that 'your accounts department is a mess ... always getting things wrong ... we've given up trying to get our account right '.

The role of the internal auditors

5.21 The internal auditors should start their work by identifying the areas of the business most susceptible to fraud. These will include areas where cash is involved, and the other areas where the auditors' judgement is that the internal controls are insufficient to safeguard the assets. The existence of a properly functioning system of internal controls will diminish the incidence of frauds, so the auditors' opinion on the internal control system is of fundamental importance.

Whenever a fraud is discovered, the auditors should judge whether a weakness in internal controls has been highlighted, and if so what changes are needed.

Prevention of fraud

5.22 Fraud will only be prevented successfully if potential fraudsters perceive the risk of detection as being high, and if personnel are adequately screened before employment and given no incentive to turn against the company once employed. The following safeguards should therefore be implemented:

- A good internal control system
- Continuous supervision of all employees
- Surprise audit visits
- Thorough personnel procedures

5.23 The work of employees must be monitored as this will increase the perceived risk of being discovered. Actual results must regularly be compared against budgeted results, and employees should be asked to explain significant variances.

5.24 Surprise audit visits are a valuable contribution to preventing fraud. A cashier carrying out a teeming and lading fraud would be able to square up the books before a planned audit visit. But if the threat of a surprise visit is present, the risk of being discovered is usually sufficient to prevent the fraud.

5.25 Finally, personnel procedures must be adequate to prevent the occurrence of frauds.

(a) Whenever a fraud is discovered, the fraudster should be dismissed and the police should be informed. Too often an employee is 'asked to resign' and then moves on to a similar job where the fraud is repeated, often because management fear loss of face or investor confidence. This is a self-defeating policy.

(b) All new employees should be required to produce adequate references from their previous employers.

(c) If an employee's lifestyle changes dramatically, explanations should be sought.

(d) Every employee must be made to take his annual holiday entitlement. Often in practice the employee who is 'so dedicated that he never takes a holiday' is in fact not taking his leave for fear of his fraud being discovered by his replacement worker while he is away.

(e) Pay levels should be adequate and working conditions of a reasonable standard. If employees feel that they are being paid an unfairly low amount or 'exploited', they may look for ways to supplement their pay dishonestly.

Management fraud

5.26 So far, this chapter has concentrated on employee fraud. However, arguably more serious (and more difficult to prevent and detect) is the growing problem of **management fraud**. While employee fraud is usually undertaken purely for the employee's financial gain, management fraud is often undertaken to improve the company's apparent performance, to reduce tax liabilities or to improve manager's promotion prospects. Managers are often in a position to override internal controls and to intimidate their subordinates into collusion or turning a blind eye. This makes it difficult to detect such frauds. In addition, where the company is benefiting financially rather than the manager, it can be difficult to persuade staff that any dishonesty is involved.

5.27 This clash of interest between loyalty to an employer and professional integrity can be difficult to resolve and can compromise an internal auditor's independence. Management fraud often comes to light after a takeover or on a change of audit staff or practices. Its consequences can be far-reaching for the employing company in damaging its reputation or because it results in legal action. Because management usually have access to much larger sums of money than more lowly employees, the financial loss to the company can be immense.

Chapter roundup

- **External** auditors report to the members of the company on whether, in their opinion, the annual statutory accounts give a true and fair view.
- **Internal** auditors are usually employees of the company whose duties are fixed by management, and who report ultimately to management.
- There are various different types of audit, the main ones being systems or **risk-based** audits, **VFM** audits and **management** audits.
- The concept of **audit risk** (and its components) is very important.
- SPAMSOAP is a useful memory jogger when asked to consider **internal controls**.
- It is essential to **plan** and **control** audit work.
- **Detection of fraud** is an objective of auditing, (but by no means the only objective). Auditors should be aware of the common **types** of fraud, **signs** that may indicate fraud and **controls** that limit the opportunity to carry out fraud.

11: Internal audit

Quick quiz

1 What are the two main features of internal audit?

2 'A systems audit never uses substantive procedures'.

　　True　☐
　　False　☐

3 What is a risk-based audit?

4 The definitions in the table below are **NOT** alongside the corresponding risk. Match the four terms to the correct definition.

	Risk		Definition
(i)	Control risk	A	The risk that the auditors will issue an inaccurate statement.
(ii)	Audit risk	B	The risk of something adverse or irregular not being noticed.
(iii)	Inherent risk	C	The risk that material errors will not be prevented or detected by internal controls.
(iv)	Detection risk	D	Arises from factors which may cause errors or irregularities to be present. The level will depend on various conditions existing within the enterprise.

5 What is the purpose of a VFM audit?

6 What does SPAMSOAP stand for?

7 List five inherent limitations of internal controls?

　　1　…………………………………………
　　2　…………………………………………
　　3　…………………………………………
　　4　…………………………………………
　　5　…………………………………………

8 List four areas covered by the operational audit plan.

　　1　…………………………………………
　　2　…………………………………………
　　3　…………………………………………
　　4　…………………………………………

9 Define 'fraud'.

Part D: Audit of activities and systems

Answers to quick quiz

1. Independence and appraisal.
2. False.
3. An audit that concentrates on the areas that are deemed to pose the greatest risk.
4. (i) C.
   (ii) A.
   (iii) D.
   (iv) B.
5. A Value For Money (VFM) audit aims to establish that policies and procedures are in place to ensure resources are used efficiency and effectively.
6. Segregation of duties.
   Physical.
   Authorisation and approval.
   Management.
   Supervision.
   Organisation.
   Accounting.
   Personnel.
7. Possible limitations include: cost; directing controls at routine transactions; human error; collusion with external parties; abuse of responsibility; changes in conditions and a reduction in compliance with procedures over time.
8. Detailed audit objectives.
   Extent and depth of coverage.
   Schedule/timetable.
   Names and responsibilities.
9. Fraud means the intentional distortion of financial statements and/or other records carried out to conceal the misappropriation of assets, or any other type of gain.

The material covered in this Chapter, together with the material in Chapter 12, is tested in Questions 6 and 17 in the Question Bank. Study Chapter 12 before attempting these Questions.

Chapter 12

INFORMATION TECHNOLOGY AND THE AUDIT PROCESS

Topic List	Syllabus reference	Ability required
1 Information technology and internal audit	(iv)	Evaluation
2 Audit evidence and audit testing	(iv)	Evaluation
3 Computer assisted auditing techniques (CAAT)	(iv)	Evaluation
4 Computers and fraud	(iv)	Evaluation
5 The internal audit implications of other developments	(iv)	Evaluation

Introduction

The days of auditors studying piles of handwritten ledgers are long gone. Today, the vast majority of organisations utilise a **computer system** to perform a range of accounting and operational tasks.

This chapter examines the process of **auditing systems that utilise Information Technology**. Specific **problems** associated with the audit of systems which use Information Technology are evaluated, as well as how IT can be **used to assist** the audit process.

Learning outcomes covered in this chapter

- **Evaluate** specific problems associated with the audit of systems which use information technology

Syllabus content covered in this chapter

- The major tools available to assist with a review of internal controls (*Also see Chapter 11*)
- The identification and prevention of fraud (*Also see Chapter 11*)
- The techniques available to assist audit in a computerised environment
- The use of Information Technology to assist the audit process

1 INFORMATION TECHNOLOGY AND INTERNAL AUDIT

1.1 The vast majority of organisations now use computerised systems to organise their business activities. This has a number of implications for internal audit.

(a) Computers themselves (hardware and software) are **assets**, and so is the information held on them. Assets must be **protected**.

(b) In a **well-controlled** environment computers may make the job of internal audit easier because they are more **efficient** than humans at certain tasks.

(i) When designed and controlled correctly they improve the **accuracy** of records.
(ii) They are able to process data more quickly.

Part D: Audit of activities and systems

(c) In a **poorly-controlled** environment they may make the internal auditor's job more difficult.

 (i) Computers cannot make judgements regarding **honesty.** They will do whatever they are instructed to do by an employee.

 (ii) Computers **store data electronically (ie digitally)** in the form of binary 1s and 0s. Stored data is **not comprehensible** to the auditor (or anyone else) in its raw form.

 (iii) To be sure that data is processed in the way that was **intended** the auditor needs a logical mind and some **understanding** of **computer programs** and communications links.

Methodologies and audit

1.2 Systems developers often use a 'methodology' such as Structured System Analysis and Design (SSADM) to guide their work. Provided the methodology chosen is appropriate in the circumstances and it is properly applied this can have significant advantages.

(a) The **documentation** requirements are rigorous. SSADM and other methodologies use a variety of techniques such as entity modelling, data flow diagrams (DFDs) and entity life histories, which are designed to make a system understandable even to those with little technical knowledge.

(b) **Computer aided software engineering** *(CASE)* tools are available to check the logic and consistency of the system as it develops and ensure that the documentation is up-to-date.

(c) **Structured walkthroughs** mean that at each stage of development the designer 'presents' the system to those who are buying it, those who will use it, and those (such as Internal Audit) who will monitor its operation. Properly conducted, structured walkthroughs should ensure that responsibilities are clear, that users get the system they need, and that the project as a whole is properly authorised.

Modifications to existing systems

1.3 The same standards that apply to new systems should be applied to subsequent changes of the system. Internal audit needs to be alert to problems such as:

(a) **Lack of documentation** for modifications.

(b) **Inadequate documentation**, that does not clearly show how modifications fit into existing systems or how successive modifications fit in with each other.

(c) **Failure to train staff** in implications of modifications.

(d) **Inadequate arrangements** for introducing **modifications** and failure to consider what will happen when modifications are implemented.

User development and management decision making

1.4 A feature of modern computing is that users have significant power on their desks and users are becoming increasingly computer literate. Although this has brought increased efficiency to operations it has also brought dangers.

1.5 Entire applications (buttons, menus and all) can now be developed within office packages such as Microsoft Excel or Access. However:

12: Information technology and the audit process

(a) Different users may be using **different spreadsheet models** to help them with the same sorts of decisions, and perhaps coming to inconsistent decisions as a result.

(b) Users may **waste time** solving problems that other users have already solved but not shared.

(c) Models may be used by people who do not understand how they work, who may **overwrite** formulae, **corrupt variables**, and so on.

(d) User-developed applications are **rarely fully documented**.

1.6 The responsibility for ensuring that things like this do not happen may rest with IT managers or departmental managers. Individuals' use of their desktop PCs is certainly worth the attention of the internal auditor, who may wish to investigate matters such as training given, documentation kept, practice regarding back-ups and so on.

Around the computer?

1.7 Traditionally it was widely considered that auditors could fulfil their function without having any detailed knowledge of what was going on inside the computer.

1.8 The auditors would commonly audit '**round the computer**', ignoring the procedures which take place within the computer programs and concentrating solely on the **input** and corresponding **output**. Audit procedures would include checking authorisation, coding and control totals of input and checking the output with source documents and clerical control totals.

1.9 However, besides consuming vast amounts of paper and computer and printer time, the traditional approach does not reflect the modern reality of computerised accounting, where computers are used to manipulate and interpret data to assist in the management of the business. As the complexity of computer systems has increased there has been a corresponding *loss* of audit trail.

Through the computer

1.10 The 'round the computer approach' is now frowned upon. Typical audit problems include:

(a) Testing computer generated totals when no detailed analysis is available.
(b) Testing the completeness of output in the absence of control totals.

1.11 It is now accepted best practice for auditors to audit **through the computer**. This involves an examination of the **detailed processing routines** of the computer to determine whether the controls in the system are adequate to ensure complete and correct processing of all data. In these situations it will often be necessary to employ computer assisted audit techniques. (Covered later in this Chapter.)

Controls in computerised systems

1.12 When a business computerises its operations, the implications for the internal auditors are great. The nature of the audit will change and the auditors must obtain the requisite knowledge to audit the system.

1.13 The internal auditors may also be involved in the process of installing a computer system by giving advice and help. As with any system the organisation relies on, the internal auditor will also have an interest in its use and maintenance.

Part D: Audit of activities and systems

1.14 The procedure for implementing a new system is shown in the network diagram below.

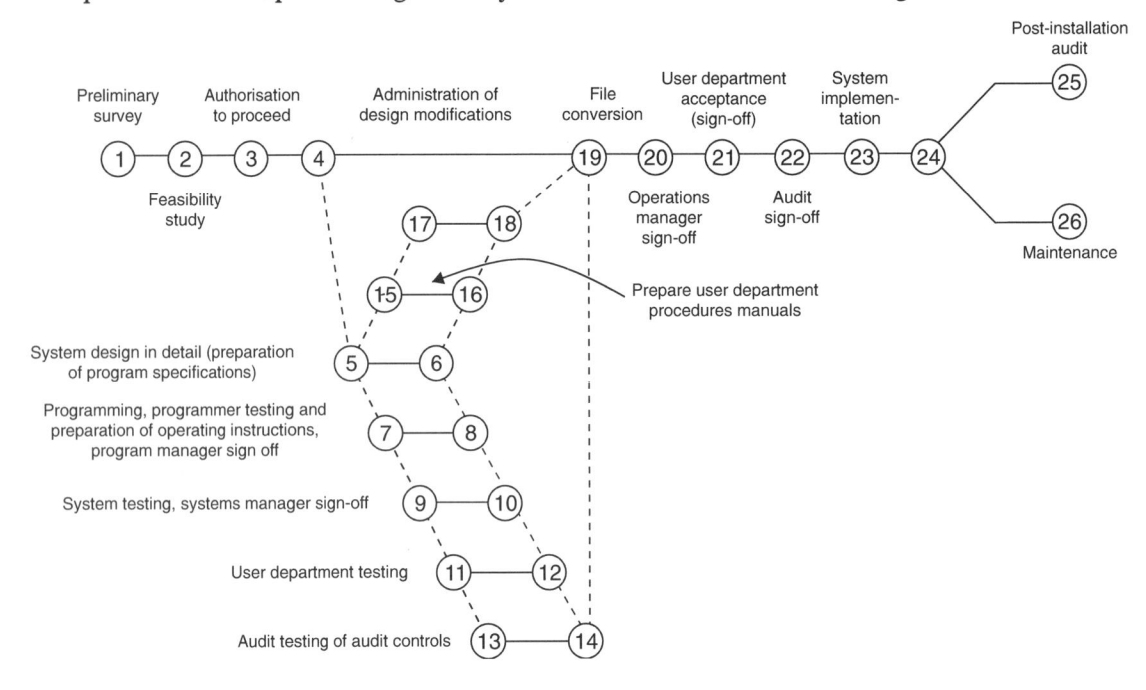

```
                Preliminary    Authorisation    Administration of    File        User department    System
                survey         to proceed       design modifications conversion  acceptance         implemen-    Post-installation
                                                                                 (sign-off)         tation       audit
                 (1)──(2)──(3)──(4)──────────────────────(19)─(20)─(21)─(22)─(23)─(24)─(25)
                      Feasibility                         
                      study           (17)─(18)           Operations    Audit              (26)
                                                          manager       sign-off           Maintenance
                                      (15)─(16)           sign-off
                                                          Prepare user department
                                                          procedures manuals
  System design in detail (preparation
  of program specifications)          (5)─(6)
  Programming, programmer testing and
  preparation of operating instructions,
  program manager sign off            (7)─(8)
  System testing, systems manager sign-off  (9)─(10)
  User department testing                   (11)─(12)
  Audit testing of audit controls           (13)─(14)
```

1.15 The auditors reviewing the development process will want to satisfy themselves that each of these stages is being completed in a controlled manner. They should also ensure procedures are in place that facilitate strong **user involvement** and influence during the development process.

1.16 The company should have a set procedure for the development of new systems. The **feasibility study** would usually be conducted by a **systems analyst** and the authorisation to proceed should be based on that study. The auditor should ensure that the matters which ought to be covered in the feasibility report are in fact included. The auditor should review the report for reasonableness.

1.17 The auditors will be involved at the systems design stage to check that various rules are clearly established, for example specific rules relating to access to different types of data.

1.18 The auditors should review the **program specifications** and ensure that they are formally accepted by the programmer. The auditors should also review the issuing of amendments to program specifications. If there are a large number of amendments, this may be an indication that something fundamental is wrong. The auditors will depend at this stage on the program specifications to indicate whether adequate controls are being built into the system to ensure the completeness, accuracy and security of data.

1.19 The auditors will review the programming work to satisfy themselves that standards laid down have been complied with. It is unlikely that they will review the program code itself, but they will confirm that all programming work has been test-checked by other programmers.

1.20 The programmer will **test the program** against test data. The auditors will review the **program file** which contains information on how each program works. The system should be tested in detail using the test data, not only by the programmer, but also by the user.

1.21 Audit can be invaluable in ensuring that no system goes live with inadequately **trained staff** or without a **full procedures manual**. Training can only be completed with hands-on experience once the system is up and running.

1.22 Good **file conversion procedures** are crucial and the auditors must ensure that the size and nature of the task has been allowed for. The auditors should enquire about the file conversion procedures very early in the system development.

1.23 Where they are required to **formally sign-off** the system, the internal auditors would only do so if they were satisfied that:

   (a) The system meets **user requirements**; programs **function satisfactorily**, have been **tested** thoroughly, have been developed **with adequate controls incorporated** and are **auditable**.

   (b) The **master files** are complete and accurate.

   (c) A satisfactory **implementation program** has been devised.

1.24 **Implementation** is often done in **phases**. Initially a pilot implementation may be followed section by section until implementation is complete. Parallel running of the old and new systems may be necessary, at least for the first sections to be implemented until confidence is built up. Parallel running doubles the task of the user department at a time when they are ill-placed to cope and may have lost staff due to a premature run-down in anticipation of staff savings through computerisation. The auditors should be vigilant for impending problems in the staffing of the user department.

1.25 After implementation, a **post-installation audit** should take place. This will usually be part of the **post-implementation review** (covered in Chapter 7 section 9). It is not the responsibility of the internal auditors to conduct this audit but they should conduct a review to ensure that it is done. The user department should be involved in this and approve the findings. The objective of this audit is to check that design objectives have been met.

1.26 The ongoing **maintenance** of the system must also be controlled. Good documentation, proper authorisation of all program modifications and the continued analysis of performance data of the system are the hallmarks of sound maintenance which the auditor will look for. In some cases the auditors may be part of the program change process.

1.27 A **summary** of the main control procedures over the in-house development of a system is as follows.

   (a) Adopt a recognised and documented system analysis and design method.
   (b) Full ongoing documentation must be completed throughout the development stage.
   (c) Review and approval should be carried out throughout the development stages.
   (d) Test data must be designed to impact on all system areas with pre-determined results.
   (e) Full testing should be carried out prior to implementation.
   (f) Approval of system documentation with external auditors.
   (g) Full training schemes should be set up.
   (h) User documentation should be reviewed prior to implementation.
   (i) Controlled file conversion from old to new system.
   (j) Review of ability of development staff.

1.28 A related control is the **segregation of duties**. The same person should not be responsible for receiving data, processing it and checking the resulting information.

2 AUDIT EVIDENCE AND AUDIT TESTING

Audit evidence

2.1 Internal auditors should **obtain sufficient appropriate audit evidence** to be able to draw reasonable conclusions on which to base the **audit opinion**.

2.2 Audit evidence can be obtained in many ways, often with a mix of tests of controls and substantive procedures, although sometimes only substantive procedures will be used; along with enquiries as to the adequacy of the accounting system as a basis for the preparation of the financial statements.

Sufficient appropriate audit evidence

2.3 'Sufficiency' and 'appropriateness' are interrelated and apply both to tests of controls and substantive procedures.

   (a) **Sufficiency** is the measure of the **quantity** of audit evidence.
   (b) **Appropriateness** is the measure of the **quality** or **reliability** of the audit evidence.

2.4 Audit evidence is usually **persuasive** rather than conclusive, so different sources are examined by the auditors.

2.5 The auditors' judgement as to what is sufficient appropriate audit evidence is influenced by factors such as the following.

   (a) The assessment of the nature and degree of risk of misstatement at both the financial statement level and the account balance or class of transactions level.
   (b) The nature of the accounting and internal control systems, including the control environment.
   (c) The materiality of the item being examined.
   (d) The experience gained during previous audits and the auditors' knowledge of the business and industry.
   (e) The findings from audit procedures, and from any audit work carried out in the course of preparing the financial statements, including indications of fraud or error.
   (f) The source and reliability of information available.

Tests of control

2.6 In seeking to obtain audit evidence from **tests of control**, auditors should consider the sufficiency and appropriateness of the audit evidence to support the assessed level of control risk. This is a very important point for internal auditors.

2.7 There are two aspects of the relevant parts of the accounting and internal control systems about which auditors should seek to obtain audit evidence.

   (a) **Design:** the accounting and internal control systems are capable of preventing or detecting material misstatements.
   (b) **Operation:** the systems exist and have operated effectively throughout the relevant period.

Substantive procedures

2.8 The terms 'substantive procedures' and 'substantive tests' are used to describe activities designed to substantiate (ie confirm) an accounting figure. Where tests of control provide satisfactory evidence as to the effectiveness of accounting and internal control systems, the extent of relevant substantive procedures may be reduced, but not entirely eliminated.

2.9 When seeking audit evidence from **substantive procedures**, auditors should consider the extent to which that evidence, together with any evidence from tests of controls, supports the financial statements.

2.10 The reliability of audit evidence is influenced by its source (internal or external) and by its nature (visual, documentary or oral). While the reliability of audit evidence is dependent on individual circumstances, the following generalisations may help in assessing that reliability.

(a) Audit evidence from external sources (eg confirmation received from a third party) is more reliable than that obtained from the entity's records.

(b) Audit evidence obtained from the entity's records is more reliable when the related accounting and internal control system operates effectively.

(c) Evidence obtained directly by auditors is more reliable than that obtained by or from the entity.

(d) Evidence in the form of documents and written representations is more reliable than oral representations.

(e) Original documents are more reliable than photocopies, telexes or facsimiles.

2.11 Consistency of audit evidence from different sources will have a corroborating effect, making the evidence more persuasive. Where such evidence is **inconsistent**, the internal auditors must determine what additional procedures are necessary to resolve the inconsistency.

2.12 The internal auditors must consider the cost-benefit relationship of obtaining evidence **but** any difficulty or expense is not in itself a valid basis for omitting a necessary procedure.

Procedures for obtaining audit evidence

2.13 Auditors obtain evidence by one or more of the following procedures.

- Inspection
- Observation
- Enquiry and confirmation
- Computation
- Analytical procedures

2.14 The reliability of audit evidence obtained by **inspection** of records and documents varies according to the nature/source and effectiveness of internal controls over their processing. Three major categories of documentary evidence exist, given here in **descending** degrees of reliability as audit evidence.

- Created and provided to auditors by third parties
- Created by third parties and held by the entity
- Created and held by the entity

Part D: Audit of activities and systems

2.15 **Inspection** of tangible assets provides reliable audit evidence about their **existence** but not necessarily as to their ownership or value.

2.16 The standard examples of **observation** are attendance at the stocktake, or at procedures which leave no audit trail.

2.17 **Enquiries** may range from formal written ones to third parties, to oral ones to persons inside the entity. Responses may provide auditors with:

- Information not previously possessed
- Corroborative audit evidence

2.18 Examples of **confirmations** include direct confirmation of debts by debtors of the entity or bank balances by the entity's bank.

2.19 **Analytical procedures** include ratio analysis and the examination of other relationships over time or between enterprises. For example, the gross profit percentage over a period of time may be analysed, or the level of bad debts, or stock levels etc for different accounting periods. Large unexplained differences may indicate the existence of error or fraud and are then followed up by substantive testing.

Sampling techniques

2.20 It is **impractical to examine every transaction** during the period under review. It follows that the auditors will wish to use some form of sampling. They must, however, take care to ensure that the uncertainties inherent in sampling are minimised. There are two types of uncertainty that can arise.

(a) The first is that auditors **may fail to recognise errors in the items they have examined**.

(b) The second is that errors will not be detected because **the items to which they relate have not been examined** – they are outside the sample.

2.21 A sample should be **representative of the whole population**. For example, a block sample of one week's purchase invoices may not be representative of the population for the whole year. Another point that must be considered is whether there is any built-in bias in the population. For example, when verifying debtors' balances, auditors should not just focus on high value accounts. They should select all accounts over a certain figure and a sample of the rest. This provides a representative sample but still allows a fairly high proportion of the population in money terms to be examined.

2.22 There are **two main methods of sampling** in common use:

- Judgement sampling
- Statistical sampling

2.23 The use of **judgement sampling** means that an **auditor's personal bias** may affect the choice of items (eg by selecting the purchase invoices that are easy to find). This means that the auditors will not know how representative the test has been and, consequently, it will be difficult to draw any useful conclusions relating to the population as a whole. Judgement sampling is, however, easy to understand and simple to use. It is also more appropriate to small audits as the use of statistical techniques is rather restricted when the population size is small.

2.24 Several statistical plans have been used in auditing. They are all based on the principle that useful quantitative conclusions for the whole population can only be drawn from sample results if **every item in the population has an equal chance of being selected** and the sample is free of personal bias. In other words random sampling (or an acceptable approximation to it) has been used. The main **advantages of using statistical sampling** can be summarised as follows.

(a) It provides an **estimate of the degree of probability that the sample is representative** of the whole population. This cannot be provided by means of judgement sampling.

(b) The **size of the sample required can be estimated** accurately on a scientific basis which enables the auditor to justify the number of items selected.

(c) The **samples may be smaller** than one selected by traditional means.

(d) The use of statistical methods of sampling enables the auditors to **predict the total number of errors** in a population from errors found in a sample, and also to estimate the maximum possible error rate.

2.25 The first steps to be taken by the auditors after examination of the population being tested for any built-in bias, is to decide on the **confidence level** they wish to employ. The confidence level is the degree of probability that the sample taken will represent the true condition of the whole population under examination. In sampling, 100% assurance is not possible and the auditors will usually decide on a confidence level of between 90 and 99 per cent.

2.26 At the same time the **degree of precision required** from the sample should be decided. This is a range (ordinarily expressed as plus or minus a given number of percentage points) within which the true answer concerning the population characteristics under study should fall, at a determined confidence level. For example, if auditors decided to use a 95% confidence level with a precision of 2%, and the sample showed an error rate of 4%, then the auditors can be 95% certain that the population error rate falls between 2% and 6%. As they are likely to be particularly concerned with maximum error rates this conclusion can be restated as follows.

The most likely error rate in the population is	4%
With 97.5% confidence, the maximum error rate is (4% + 2%)	6%

The confidence level has been increased to 97.5% as there is a 2.5% chance of the population error rate being greater than 6% and a 2.5% chance of it being below 2%.

2.27 For a given sample size the precision will vary with confidence level selected. So in the last example, it might be found that the maximum possible error rate was 6.4% with 99% confidence.

Question 1

Answer the following questions in relation to internal control.

Explain what you understand by the terms:

(a) Substantive procedures.
(b) Analytical procedures.
(c) Tests of control.

Answer

(a) **Substantive procedures** refers to those tests including tests of transactions and balances which seek to provide evidence about the completeness, accuracy and validity of the information contained in the financial statements or the accounting records.

Part D: Audit of activities and systems

(b) **Analytical procedures** involves the review of accounting data by ratio analysis, for instance by comparing average wages, age of debtors, gross profit percentage etc for different accounting periods. Large unexplained differences may indicate the existence of error or fraud and are then followed up by substantive testing.

(c) **Tests of control** are used when the auditors wish to examine a particular aspect of internal control, for instance that purchase invoices are signed to indicate management approval before they are paid. The auditors will select a sample of invoices and ensure that each has been duly signed. If the results are unsatisfactory, a more extensive test of controls may be required, or the auditors may carry out substantive procedures to ensure that purchases are *bona fide*.

The loss of the paper audit trail

> **KEY TERM**
>
> An **audit trail** has been defined as:
>
> 'a record of the file updating which takes place during a specific transaction. It enables a trace to be kept of all operations on files.'
>
> *(Glossary of Computing Terms of the British Computer Society)*

2.28 An **audit trail** should ideally be provided so that every transaction on a file contains a **unique reference** back to the original source of the input (for example a sales system transaction record should hold a reference to the customer order, delivery note and invoice). Where master file records are updated several times, or from several sources, the provision of a satisfactory audit trail is more difficult, but some attempt should nevertheless be made to provide one.

2.29 With an audit trail, the auditors can **trace a transaction** from beginning to end, to verify that it has been processed completely and correctly. In a manual system, an audit trail is created by hard copy evidence of transactions, with the hard copy of various documents being preserved and stored, for future checking or reference if required.

2.30 The CIPFA *Computer Audit Guidelines* includes the following comments.

> 'In a computer system the audit trail will not always be apparent as it would be in a manual system, as the data is often retained only on magnetic media and in a form that is intelligible only to the computer programs designed to access it.
>
> There may be occasions when the audit trail is not readily visible.
>
> (i) Output may be limited to a summary of items processed, thus making it impossible to trace an individual transaction right through the system from input to final resting place.
>
> (ii) Magnetic storage devices may be updated by over-writing the equivalent record with the result brought about by the newly input data, thus making visible reconciliation of start, change and finish position impossible.
>
> (iii) Reports may be on an exception basis only.
>
> Though such occasions may arise it should be remembered that though individual transactions are not visibly traceable through the system, the existence of adequate processing controls will ensure that at least an overall reconciliation of records/transactions input and processed can be made....
>
> The auditor may therefore have to be satisfied with a trail which, while not visible in detail, is nevertheless reconcilable throughout the system.'

12: Information technology and the audit process

2.31 An audit trail can be provided by a computer system in one of two ways.

(a) The system can be **designed to produce hard-copy output** of transactions at various stages in processing, including evidence of how each transaction adds to aggregate totals. However, such an audit trail would be administratively inconvenient and costly to produce and maintain.

(b) An audit trail could be preserved instead **on computer file**, with historical data 'dumped' on to back-up storage to provide audit evidence.

2.32 Even so, in a computer system, an audit trail might be 'lost' for a number of different reasons.

(a) Hardcopy evidence of transactions **might not be produced** by the computer system. Without hardcopy output at various stages in processing, the task of tracking transactions through the system becomes more difficult, especially in large volume systems. The sheer volume of processing in computer systems can make the tracking of individual transactions more difficult than in manual systems.

(b) Historical data might **not be retained** even on disk, because of the administrative difficulties of retaining many 'generations' of data on file.

(c) Data on disk or tape might become **corrupted**.

(d) With direct processing systems, transactions data will often be used to update a master file by writing over the data currently on file, without the use of a transaction file.

(e) With on-line input by keyboard, there might be **no hard-copy evidence** of an originating transaction.

(f) If several computer users share a common database, and each user can amend or update database records, it might be difficult to trace where an amendment originated.

Alternatives to reliance on an audit trail

2.33 A number of audit techniques can be used as an alternative to reliance on an audit trail.

(a) A 'round the computer' approach, although this is not best practice.

(b) CAATs (test data or audit software).

(c) Systems auditors can **check the programs** themselves to verify that they have been properly written to carry out their intended tasks.

(d) **Tests of controls** should be carried out to check that the internal controls over data input procedures are satisfactory, with further tests to confirm that the controls are properly operated in practice.

3 COMPUTER ASSISTED AUDITING TECHNIQUES (CAAT)   Pilot paper

> **KEY TERM**
>
> **Computer assisted audit techniques (CAAT)** are methods of using a computer to assist the auditor in the performance of a computer audit. The major categories are **audit software** and **test data**.

Part D: Audit of activities and systems

3.1 There is no mystique about using a computer to help with auditing. You probably use common computer assisted audit techniques all the time in your daily work without realising it.

(a) Most modern accounting systems allow data to be manipulated in various ways and extracted into an **ad hoc report**. The popular Sage Line 50 package allows its database to be quizzed in quite sophisticated ways, as illustrated below.

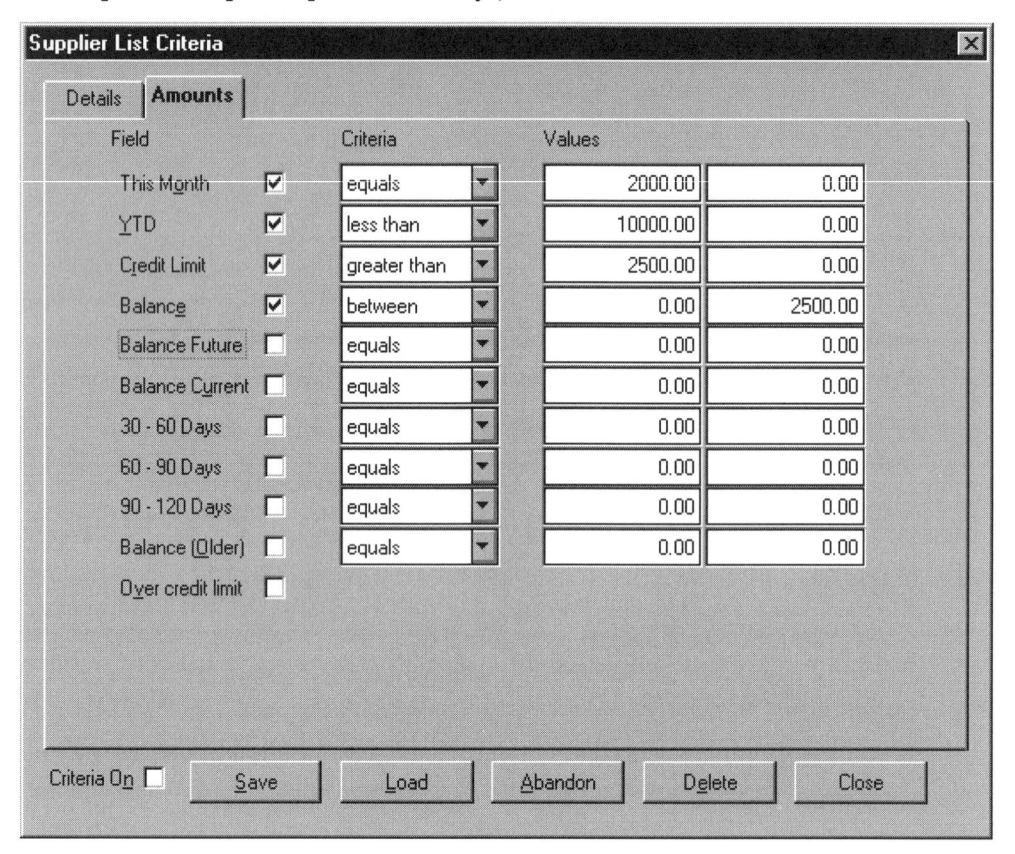

Field	Criteria	Values	
This Month ✓	equals	2000.00	0.00
YTD ✓	less than	10000.00	0.00
Credit Limit ✓	greater than	2500.00	0.00
Balance ✓	between	0.00	2500.00
Balance Future ☐	equals	0.00	0.00
Balance Current ☐	equals	0.00	0.00
30 - 60 Days ☐	equals	0.00	0.00
60 - 90 Days ☐	equals	0.00	0.00
90 - 120 Days ☐	equals	0.00	0.00
Balance (Older) ☐	equals	0.00	0.00
Over credit limit ☐			

Supplier List Criteria — Details / Amounts tab. Buttons: Criteria On, Save, Load, Abandon, Delete, Close.

(b) Even if reporting capabilities are limited, the data can often be exported directly into a **spreadsheet** package and then analysed. (For example by sorting in order of highest balances, or recalculating totals using the SUM function.)

(c) Most systems have **searching facilities** that are much quicker to use than searching through print-outs by hand.

3.2 There are a variety of packages specially designed either to ease the auditing task itself (for example selecting records to investigate, based on various statistical **sampling** techniques or calculating audit risk), or to carry out audit **interrogations** of computerised data automatically. There are also a variety of ways of testing the processing that is carried out.

3.3 Much of this work can now be done using PCs that are independent of the organisation's systems.

Using the right files

3.4 Before any audit software is run, the auditors should check the identity and version of the data files and programs used.

12: Information technology and the audit process

Audit interrogation software

3.5 Interrogation software performs the sort of checks on data that auditors might otherwise have to perform by hand. Programs may have to be written specially, in which case the internal auditor must take care not to rely to too great an extent on the IT staff whose systems and processing are being examined. However packages are available commercially from a variety of software suppliers and also from firms of external auditors.

3.6 The case example below will give you a clear idea of what interrogation software can achieve.

Case example: ACL for Windows

One of the leading CAAT products is ACL. ACL allows users to independently and interactively read, analyse, interrogate and report on data from virtually any mainframe, mini or microcomputer. Features:

Ease of use: An intuitive interface with pull down menus and point and click features

Built-in audit and data analysis functionality: Commands are specifically designed for audit and data analysis, requiring no additional programming or technical expertise

Interactive interrogation capability: Interrogate your data interactively, following your train of thought and investigating exceptions as they arise

Unlimited file size capability: Analyse 100% of your data file with complete confidence in your results

High quality reporting features: Once you've completed your analysis, create high quality, multi-line reports to support your findings

A few of the uses of ACL.

- Identify trends, pinpoint exceptions and potential areas of concern
- Locate errors and potential fraud by comparing and analysing files according to end user criteria
- Recalculate and verify balances
- Identify control issues and ensure compliance with standards
- Age and analyse accounts receivable, payables or any other time-sensitive transactions
- Recover expenses or lost revenues by testing for duplicate payments, gaps in invoice numbers or unbilled services
- Test for unauthorised employee/supplier relationships
- Automate repetitive tasks by creating custom ACL applications or batches

---

3.7 By using audit software, the auditors may scrutinise large volumes of data and concentrate skilled manual resources on the investigation of results, rather than on the extraction of information.

3.8 The level of expertise necessary for the use of audit interrogation software and its related techniques varies considerably.

(a) As a minimum auditors will require a **basic understanding** of data processing and the enterprise's computer application, together with a detailed knowledge of the audit software and the computer files to be used.

(b) Depending on the complexity of the application, the auditors may need to have a sound appreciation of **systems analysis,** operating systems and, where program code is used, experience of the programming language to be utilised.

Test data

3.9 An obvious way of seeing whether a system is **processing data** in the way that it should be is to input some test data and see what happens. The expected results can be calculated in advance and then compared with the results that actually arise. Alternatively auditors can attempt to input **invalid data** which the system should reject.

3.10 The problem with test data is that any resulting corruption of the data files has to be corrected. This is difficult with modern real-time systems, which often have built in (and highly desirable) controls to ensure that data entered **cannot** easily be removed without leaving a mark. Consequently test data is used less and less as a CAAT.

Embedded audit facilities

3.11 The results of using test data would, in any case, be completely distorted if the programs used to process it were not the ones **normally** used for processing. For example a fraudulent member of the IT department might substitute a version of the program that gave the correct results, purely for the duration of the test, and then replace it with a version that syphoned off the company's funds into his own bank account.

3.12 To allow a **continuous review** of the data recorded and the manner in which it is treated by the system, it may be possible to use CAATs referred to as 'embedded audit facilities'.

3.13 An embedded facility consists of audit modules that are incorporated into the computer element of the enterprise's accounting system. Two frequently encountered examples are Integrated Test Facility (ITF) and Systems Control and Review File (SCARF).

Integrated test facility

3.14 **Integrated Test Facility** involves the creation of a **fictitious entity** (for example a department or a customer) within the framework of the regular application. Transactions are then posted to the fictitious entity along with the regular transactions. The results produced by the normal processing cycle are compared with what should have been produced, which is predetermined by other means.

3.15 **Fictitious entities** must not become part of the financial reporting of the organisation and several methods can be adopted to prevent this. The simplest and most secure method is to make reversing journal entries at appropriate cut-off dates. ITF enables management and auditors to keep a constant check on the internal processing functions applied to all types of valid and invalid transactions.

SCARF

3.16 **SCARF** is a relatively simple technique to build into an application. It is best described by illustrating an example, in this case, a general (nominal) ledger application.

3.17 Each general ledger account would have two 'auditors' fields: a Yes/No field indicating whether or not SCARF applies to this account; and a monetary value which is a threshold amount set by the auditors. The system would be set up so that only the auditors could specify whether an account was a SCARF account or not and what the monetary value would be.

3.18 Subsequently all transactions posted to a SCARF account which had a value in excess of the threshold amount would also be written to a separate SCARF file. This technique thus

12: Information technology and the audit process

enables the auditors to monitor material transactions or sensitive accounts with ease and provides an assurance that all such transactions are under scrutiny.

Simulation

3.19 Simulation (or parallel simulation) entails the preparation of a separate program that simulates the processing of the organisation's real system. Real data can then be passed not only through the system proper but also through the simulated program. For example the simulation program may be used to re-perform controls such as those used to identify any missing items from a sequence.

Program logic and coding

3.20 Two further types of CAATs worth mentioning are:

(a) **Logical path analysis,** which will draw flowcharts of the program logic.

(b) **Code comparison programs,** which compare the original specified program to the current program to detect unauthorised amendments.

Knowledge-based systems

3.21 Decision support systems and expert systems can be used to assist with the auditors' own judgement and decisions. This is likely to save time and money as such methods increase the efficiency of the audit procedures used, and the maintenance of audit records. Other cost savings include the reduction in the number of staff required, and the fact that routine tasks can be assigned to technicians, who are helped by the expert system.

Question 2

Consider the following statements.

(i) Computer systems give rise to such possibilities as a lack of visible evidence and systematic errors.

(ii) The nature of computer-based accounting systems is such that the auditors are afforded opportunities to use the enterprise's computer to assist them in the performance of their audit work.

(iii) In choosing the appropriate combination of computer assisted audit techniques and manual procedures the auditors will need to take a number of factors into account.

(iv) In performing tests of control on application or general controls, the auditors should obtain evidence which is relevant to the control being tested.

Required

(a) Explain each of the phrases 'lack of visible evidence' and 'systematic errors' referred to in (i) above and state in respect of each three ways in which the auditors might attempt to overcome the problems arising from these two possibilities. You should illustrate your answer by reference to a stock control system.

(b) State briefly *two* computer assisted audit techniques (CAATs) which the auditors can use in the enterprise's audit. (Refer to (ii) above.)

(c) State and explain *five* factors which the auditors will need to take into account in choosing the appropriate combination of computer assisted audit techniques and manual procedures. (Refer to (iii) above.)

(d) Explain the words 'tests of control', 'application control', and 'general control' in the computer audit context. Illustrate your answer by outlining one relevant test of controls on:

Part D: Audit of activities and systems

(i) An application control.
(ii) A general control.

(Refer to (iv) above.)

Answer

(a) *Lack of visible evidence*

Some computerised accounting systems do not provide detailed audit trails. Many of the controls in the system are 'invisible' meaning users are unable to establish whether processing is conducted as intended.

In relation to a stock control system an example of the problem of lack of visible evidence might be the lack of hard-copy records relating to the processing of transactions, thus making it difficult for the auditors to carry out some of their normal tests of controls relating to cut-off procedures at the year end.

Three ways in which the auditors might attempt to overcome the problem of lack of visible evidence might be:

(i) The incorporation within the enterprise's software of a facility for special print-outs on behalf of the auditors in order to, on a test basis, 'plug some of the gaps' in the audit trail.

(ii) Testing the reliability of the computer-generated results by clerically recreating a sample of them, although this might prove to be both time-consuming and expensive.

(iii) Obtaining reliable audit evidence by other means, for example attendance at the company's physical stocktaking.

Systematic errors

Systematic errors in a computer system may result from errors in the software and/or standing data contained on master and reference files. Either type of error will be systematically repeated each time processing occurs until such time as the fault is identified and corrected:

In relation to a stock control system an example of the problem of systematic errors might be where a program fault resulted in the incorrect calculation of trade discounts for all customers instead of merely trade customers.

Three ways in which the auditors might seek to gain some assurance that such errors were not occurring would be:

(i) By examination and testing of the enterprise's program development and testing procedures to ensure that they were adequate.

(ii) By test checking the retained printouts of the enterprise's files from the time of their initial creation to ensure that the standing and reference data they contained was correct.

(iii) By test checking of the procedures for both program amendment and file maintenance.

(b) Two computer assisted audit techniques (CAATs) which the auditors could use in the enterprise's audit would be:

(i) The use of *computer audit software* to examine the contents of the enterprise's computer files.

(ii) The use of *test data* to test the operation of the enterprise's computer programs.

(c) Five factors which the auditors will need to take into account in choosing the appropriate combination of CAATs and manual procedures would be as follows.

(i) Computer programs often perform functions of which no visible evidence is available. In these circumstances it will frequently not be practicable for the auditors to perform tests manually.

(ii) In some cases, the auditors will need to report within a comparatively short time-scale. In such cases it may be more efficient to use CAATs because they are quicker to apply, even though manual methods are practicable and may cost less.

(iii) In many audit situations the auditors will have the choice of performing a test either manually or with the assistance of a CAAT. In making the choice, they will be influenced by the respective efficiency of the alternatives, taking into account:

12: Information technology and the audit process

  (1) The extent of tests of controls or substantive procedures achieved by both alternatives.
  (2) The pattern of cost associated with the CAAT.
  (3) The ability to incorporate within the use of the CAAT a number of different audit tests.

 (iv) There is a need before using a CAAT to ensure that the required computer facilities, computer files and programs are available. Furthermore, given that enterprises do not retain copies of computer files and programs for an indefinite period, the auditors should plan the use of any CAAT in good time so that these copies are retained for their use.

 (v) The operation of some CAATs requires frequent attendance or access by the auditors and this may not be possible.

(d) The terms given in the question can be defined as follows.

 (i) *Tests of controls*

  Tests to obtain audit evidence about the effective operation of the accounting and internal control systems, that is, that properly designed controls identified in the preliminary assessment of control risk exist in fact and have operated effectively throughout the relevant period.

 (ii) *Application control*

  Application controls relate to the transactions and standing data appertaining to each computer-based accounting system and are therefore specific to each such application. The objectives of application controls, which may be manual or programmed, are to ensure the completeness and accuracy of the accounting records and the validity of the entries made therein resulting from both manual and programmed processing.

 (iii) *General control*

  General controls are controls other than application controls which relate to the environment within which computer based accounting systems are developed, maintained and operated, and which are therefore applicable to all the applications. The objectives of general controls are to ensure the proper development and implementation of applications and the integrity of program and data files and of computer operations. Like application controls, general controls may be either manual or programmed.

  One relevant test of controls on each of the two types of control identified above might be as follows.

  (1) *Test on application controls.* Use of test data to test the effective working of a particular computer program.

  (2) *Test on general controls.* A review of computer logs to ensure that there is no evidence of breach of the security of the enterprise's system.

4 COMPUTERS AND FRAUD

Major categories of computer fraud

4.1 Computer fraud usually involves the theft of funds by dishonest use of a computer system. The type of computer fraud depends on the point in the system at which the fraud is perpetrated.

 (a) **Input fraud.** Data input is falsified; good examples are putting a non-existent employee on the salary file or a non-existent supplier to the purchases file.

 (b) **Processing fraud.** A programmer or someone who has broken into this part of the system may alter a program. For example, in a large organisation, a 'patch' might be used to change a program so that 10 pence was deduced from every employee's pay cheque and sent to a fictitious account to which the perpetrator had access. A 'patch' is a change to a program which is characterised by its speed and ease of implementation.

Part D: Audit of activities and systems

(c) **Output fraud**. Output documents may be stolen or tampered with and control totals may be altered. Cheques are the most likely document to be stolen, but other documents may be stolen to hide a fraud.

(d) **Fraudulent use of the computer system**. Employees may feel that they can use the computer system for their own purposes and this may take up valuable processing time. This is probably quite rare, but there was a case of a newspaper publisher's computer system being used by an employee to produce another publication!

Recent developments increasing the risk of fraud

4.2 Over the last few years there have been rapid developments in all aspects of computer technology and these have increased the opportunities that are available to commit a fraud. The most important of the recent developments are as follows.

(a) **Computer literacy**. The proportion of the population which is computer literate is growing all the time. Once people know how to use a computer, the dishonest ones among them may attempt computer fraud. It is much easier to 'hide' an electronic transaction: it is not 'visible', or not in the same sense as a paper-based one, in any case.

(b) **Communications**. The use of telephone links and other public communication systems has increased the ability of people outside the company breaking into the computer system. These 'hackers' could not have operated when access was only possible on site.

(c) **Reduction in internal checks**. The more computers are used, the fewer the tasks left to personnel to carry out. A consequence of this is often a reduction in the number of internal checks carried out for any transaction.

(d) Improvements in the **quality of software** and the increase in **implementation of good software** has not kept pace with the improvements in hardware. Distributed systems and networked PCs have become very common but this has caused the control over central databases and programs to be relaxed.

> **Exam focus point**
> A question in the May 2001 exam referred to problems auditing real-time systems and integrated systems. Remember that these systems require the same type of controls and audit as any other system – so 'general' controls are relevant. Additional problems could relate to gaining access to audit the system and isolating the cause/effect of any potential discrepancies.

Planned approach to counteract computer fraud

4.3 The management of every company must be conscious of the possibility and costs of computer fraud and everything must be done to avoid it. The company should attempt to prevent dishonesty by a comprehensive approach.

(a) All **staff** should be **properly trained** and should fully appreciate their role in the computer function. They should also be aware of the consequences of any fraud they might perpetrate.

(b) **Management policy on fraud** should be **clear and firm**. Management should have a positive approach to both the possibility and prevention of computer fraud.

(c) A **study** should be carried out to examine where the company is **exposed to possible fraud**. In the computer area itself, controls in the system and training will both be important. Other areas should also be examined, such as recruitment and personnel policies.

(d) As a result of the study undertaken, the company should map out an approach or **plan** in each area of the business **to tackle and prevent fraud**.

(e) The **plan** produced must be **implemented properly** across the company. Regular reports of progress should be made to the board. Particular attention should be paid to changes in programs and the purchase and implementation of new software and hardware.

Measures to prevent computer fraud

4.4 Here are some suggestions that should help prevent/detect fraud.

(a) **Physical** security of hardware.
(b) **Access** to the system should be **logged** and monitored eg through passwords.
(c) Input and output **controls** on processing.
(d) **Error logs** and reports should be monitored.
(e) Maintain control over **output documents** such as cheques.
(f) The use of **CAAT**s.
(g) **Staff recruitment** should include careful vetting, including taking up all references.
(h) Careful **supervision** of staff.
(i) **Separation** of duties.
(j) **Moral** leadership by management.
(k) Reduce the motive for fraud through good **employment conditions**.

5 THE INTERNAL AUDIT IMPLICATIONS OF OTHER DEVELOPMENTS

5.1 In this section we discuss developments in technology and working practices that have internal audit implications.

E-mail

5.2 E-mail may have numerous advantages in reducing office paperwork and speeding up communication, but it also has dangers from an audit point of view. For example, an employee may find it quite easy to send an e-mail from his or her boss's computer authorising a bonus or pay-rise.

Question 3

What controls could be put in place to prevent this (see 5.2) from happening?

Answer

(a) Requiring all computers to be 'logged on' using a unique user-name and password.
(b) The installation of 'screensavers' that automatically activate after a period of computer inactivity, and require the correct user password to deactivate,.
(c) Better staff recruitment procedures.

Part D: Audit of activities and systems

Networks and the Internet

5.3 Control of network systems is of the utmost importance. The auditors must be able to analyse the risks of unauthorised access such as line tapping or interception and to evaluate preventative measures.

5.4 **Authentication** programmes and **encryption** are used for security. The auditor must understand such matters and should be able to make recommendations on implementation. Password security is also extremely important, and the auditors may be called upon to recommend complex password procedures for sophisticated systems.

Electronic data interchange (EDI)

5.5 Electronic data interchange is now used very widely because it cuts out the task of re-inputting data that has already been input into a system in electronic form, saving time and improving accuracy.

5.6 However this raises a number of audit issues. How can the receiving organisation be sure that **data** transmitted by EDI is **authentic**? What **authorisation measures** are in place to ensure that transactions above a certain value are properly authorised before being transmitted or accepted? What is the **legal position** of the two parties if a transaction is disputed? Can an organisation rely on its EDI partner to operate adequate controls?

5.7 Again encryption and authentication offer some help, as do transaction logs that identify the originator of any transactions generated and transmitted.

Outsourcing

5.8 As we saw in Chapter 8, many organisations outsource part of their IT function to third parties such as Facilities Management companies. Internal audit should monitor outsourced activities, particularly (in relation to IT) in the areas of:

(a) **Security of data** (sensitive information such as names of customers and employees may have to be coded if necessary), and

(b) **Adequate facilities** for reconstruction.

5.9 Assuming a reputable facilities management company is used, it may be possible to use evidence collected by that company's own internal and external auditors for assurances about controls and procedures.

Chapter roundup

- The vast majority of organisations now use computerised systems. This has impacted greatly on the role of internal audit.

- Traditionally auditors audited '**around the computer**'. It is now recognised that to audit a computer based system it is necessary to understand the basic principles of how it operates. Therefore, audits are now conducted '**through the computer**'.

- The internal audit function should also ensure any new system has appropriate **controls built in**, and that it is implemented in a controlled manner.

- Auditors can obtain audit **evidence** through inspection, observation, enquiries, computation and analytical procedures.

- Auditors may use a number of **computer assisted audit techniques (CAAT)** including:
    - Audit interrogation software
    - Test data
    - Embedded audit facilities
    - Simulation
    - Logical path analysis
    - Code comparison programs

- **Computer fraud** includes:
    - Input fraud
    - Processing fraud
    - Output fraud
    - Fraudulent use of the computer system

- **Fraud prevention policies** should be **clear**, and involve training and recruitment controls, limitations on access and monitoring of errors and unusual transactions.

- **Modern developments** that improve access to data for end-users may undermine traditional controls. Developments in telecommunications require tight control.

Quick quiz

1. Why does an internal auditor need some understanding of computer programs and communications links?

2. What does auditing 'through the computer' involve?

3. Explain 'sufficiency' and 'appropriateness' in the context of audit evidence.

4. List five procedures which may be used to obtain audit evidence.

    1 ....
    2 ....
    3 ....
    4 ....
    5 ....

5. Name the two main methods of sampling.

    1 ....
    2 ....

6. What does CAAT stand for?

7. Name the two major categories of CAAT.

    1 ....
    2 ....

Part D: Audit of activities and systems

8   What does a code comparison program do?

9   List five controls that could be used to prevent computer based fraud.

   1   ....

   2   ....

   3   ....

   4   ....

   5   ....

10   'If computer facilities are outsourced, the internal audit function need not monitor activities'.

   True   ☐
   False ☐

Answers to quick quiz

1   So the auditor is able to establish that data has been processed in the way that was intended.

2   An examination of the detailed processing routines of the computer to determine whether the controls in the system are adequate to ensure complete and correct processing of all data.

3   Sufficiency is the measure of the quantity of audit evidence. Appropriateness is the measure of the quality or reliability of the audit evidence.

4   Inspection.

    Observation.

    Enquiry and confirmation.

    Computation.

    Analytical procedures.

5   Judgement sampling and Statistical sampling.

6   Computer Assisted Auditing Technique.

7   Audit interrogation software.
    Test data.

8   It compares the original specified program to the current program to detect unauthorised amendments.

9   Some possibilities are: physical security of hardware, controlled and logged access to systems, input and output controls, monitored error logs and reports, tight control over sensitive output, effective use of CAATs, thorough staff recruitment and vetting procedures, appropriate supervision of staff, separation of duties, moral leadership by management and good employee/employer relations.

10   False, although it may be possible to use evidence supplied from the third party company's own internal and external auditors.

The material covered in this Chapter is tested in Questions 6 and 17 in the Question Bank.

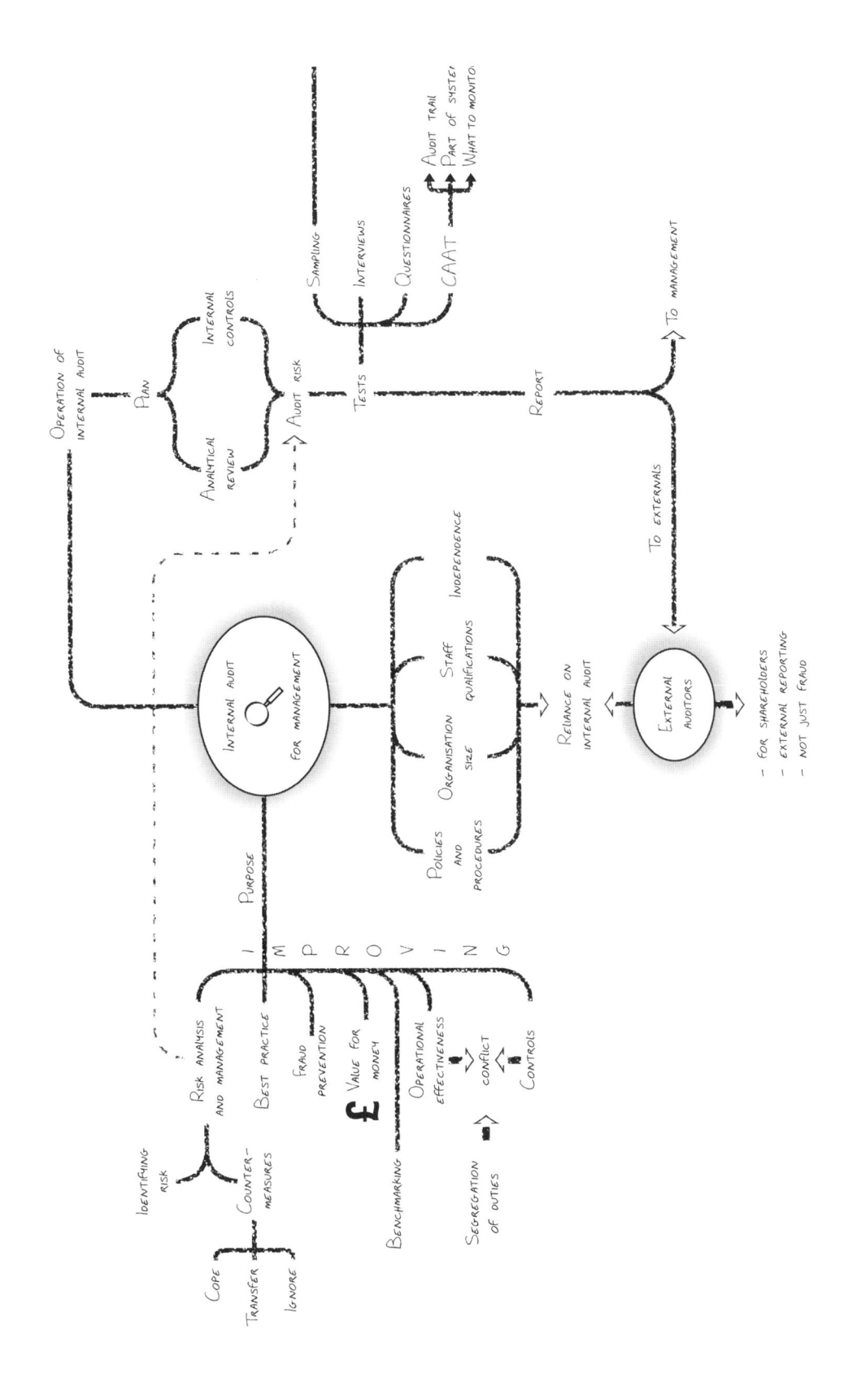

INTERNAL AUDIT

Internal audit (for management)

Purpose — IMPROVING
- **I** — Identifying risk → Risk analysis and management
  - Cope
  - Transfer
  - Ignore
  - Counter-measures
- **M** — Best practice
- **P** — Fraud prevention
- **R** — £ Value for money
- **O** — Operational effectiveness
  - Benchmarking
  - Segregation of duties ↔ conflict
- **V**
- **I**
- **N**
- **G** — Controls

Staff
- Policies and procedures
- Organisation size
- Staff qualifications
- Independence

→ Reliance on internal audit ↔ **External auditors**
- To externals
- For shareholders
- External reporting
- Not just fraud

Operation of internal audit
- Plan
  - Internal controls
  - Analytical review
- Audit risk
- Tests
  - Sampling
  - Interviews
  - Questionnaires
  - CAAT
    - Audit trail
    - Part of system
    - What to monitor
- Report → To management

Part E
Quality

Chapter 13

THE MANAGEMENT OF QUALITY

Topic list	Syllabus reference	Ability required
1 Control over quality	(v)	Evaluation
2 Traditional approaches to quality	(v)	Evaluation
3 Contemporary approaches to quality	(v)	Evaluation
4 Quality circles	(v)	Evaluation
5 Benchmarking	(v)	Evaluation
6 Other contemporary approaches	(v)	Evaluation

Introduction

A significant trend in all business sectors over recent years has been an increased **emphasis on quality**. In an increasingly **competitive** environment, quality is seen as vital to success. In this chapter we look at the **concept** of quality, before moving on to the various **approaches** used to ensure quality in both the product or service produced, and the systems used by the organisation.

Learning outcomes covered in this chapter

- **Analyse** problems with the management of quality in an organisation
- **Evaluate** the features, benefits and drawbacks of contemporary approaches to the management of quality
- **Produce** and communicate a plan for the implementation of a quality improvement programme

Syllabus content covered in this chapter

- The concept of quality and how the quality of products, services and activities can be assessed measured and improved
- Quality circles
- The use of benchmarking in quality measurement and improvement
- The various approaches to the management of quality
- External quality standards
- Contemporary developments in the management of quality
- The different types of benchmarking, their use and limitations.

Part E: Quality

1 CONTROL OVER QUALITY   Pilot paper, 5/01, 11/01

1.1 In an organisational context, quality is concerned with 'fitness for purpose', and **quality management** (or control) is about ensuring that products or services meet their planned level of quality, and conform to specifications.

> **KEY TERMS**
>
> **Quality**: 'the totality of features and characteristics of a product or service which bears on its ability to meet stated or implied needs'. *(Ken Holmes)*
>
> **Quality management** is concerned with controlling activities with the aim of ensuring that products or services are fit for their purpose, and meet specifications. Quality management encompasses quality assurance and quality control.
>
> **Quality assurance** focuses on the way a product or service is produced. Procedures and standards are devised with the aim of ensuring defects are eliminated (or at least minimised) during the development/production process.
>
> **Quality control** is concerned with checking and reviewing work that has been done. Quality control therefore has a narrower focus than quality assurance.

1.2 **Quality management** is a type of control system involving the activities outlined below.

   Step 1. **Plan**. Establish:

   (i) **Standards** of quality for a product (eg a software package) or service (eg performance and volume requirements).

   (ii) **Procedures** or production methods that ought to ensure that these required standards of quality are met (eg a systems development methodology).

   Step 2. Devise suitable instruments and techniques to **monitor** actual quality.

   Step 3. **Compare** actual quality with planned quality using **feedback**.

   Step 4. Take control action when actual quality falls below standard. **Quality auditing** involves a systematic inspection to establish whether quality objectives are being met. A quality audit could be carried out:

   (i) Internally, for example by staff from internal audit or a specific quality department.

   (ii) Externally, for example by a certified agency such as an ISO review (covered later in this chapter).

   (ii) On a supplier, or on the organisation itself by a supplier – to ensure compliance with the company's quality standards.

   Step 5. Review the plan and standards to ensure **continuous improvement**.

1.3 A goal for quality management in systems development should be the **prevention** of system defects. Examples of defects include 'bugs' that prevent the system operating correctly or a badly designed system that does not meet user needs.

2 TRADITIONAL APPROACHES TO QUALITY

2.1 In the past, 'quality' usually meant quality control – which meant inspection. Inspection was usually carried out at three main points.

- Receiving inspection
- Floor or process inspection
- Final inspection or testing

2.2 The problem with this 'inspection' approach is that it allows for built-in waste.

(a) The inspection process itself does not add value: if it could be guaranteed that no defective items were produced, there would be no need for a separate inspection function.

(b) The production of substandard products is a waste of raw materials, machine time, human efforts, and overheads (as the substandard production has to be administered).

(c) The inspection department takes up possibly expensive land and warehousing space.

(d) The production of defects is not compatible with newer production techniques such as just-in-time: there is no time for inspection.

(e) Working capital is tied up in stocks which cannot be sold.

2.3 Quality has increased in importance in recent years.

(a) **Growing affluence** in industrial societies has enabled customers to be more choosy. The growth of **consumerism** in affluent societies perhaps has encouraged greater attention to quality.

(b) Quality gave Japanese companies a **competitive advantage**, but these techniques have been **successfully imitated**. Coupled with freer trade, and increased competition from overseas, this has meant that quality is seen as necessary in **retaining market share**.

(c) Attention to quality can **save costs** and **enhance productivity**.

2.4 This demand for better quality has led to the acceptance of the view that quality management should aim to **prevent** defective production rather than simply detect it.

3 CONTEMPORARY APPROACHES TO QUALITY   5/01, 11/01

3.1 Most modern approaches to quality aim to assure quality in the production process, (quality assurance) rather than inspecting goods or services after they have been produced.

Total quality management (TQM)   11/01

3.2 Faulty output is costly - as it wastes resources and damages relationships. The essence of TQM is that quality should be 'built-in' to all processes and materials used within an organisation, with the ultimate aim of no sub-standard output.

3.3 **Total quality management** is a management technique which focuses on the belief that 'total quality is essential to survival in a global market'. Although referring to quality, it has been adopted as a business philosophy - one of the values that might be noted in a mission statement.

Part E: Quality

> **KEY TERM**
>
> **Total quality management** (TQM) is the continuous improvement in quality, productivity and effectiveness obtained by establishing management responsibility for processes as well as output.

3.4 **Principles of TQM**

Principle	Comment
Prevention	It costs less, in the long run, to prevent defective production than to employ teams of inspectors, to scrap materials or to rework shoddy output.

Principle	Comment
Right first time	Defective production is worse than no production.
Zero defects	The aim should be **no** defects. In products with **many** components, the defect rates in components should be extremely small.
Eliminate waste	This includes time, materials and money spent on dealing with customer complaints.
Everybody's concern	Quality is not just the concern of the production department, but is a culture for the whole business.
Internal customers	Each part of an organisation acquires services from other parts of the organisation. User departments are thus internal customers.
Quality chains	Internal customers are linked in quality chains – they are dependent on the product/service they receive from, and pass on to, each other.
Continuous improvement	TQM is not a goal that is achieved, but a way of managing. Firms should continually seek ways to improve their performance.
Employee participation	As so much attention is paid to the production process itself, the production workforce has a vital role to play in managing and improving quality.
Teamwork	'Managing quality involves systems and techniques, and requires the identification of individuals with company success through teamwork' (*Holmes*).

(Mnemonic, using first words in bold above: Prevention Rightly Zaps and Eliminates Everybody's Ineffective Quality, and Continuously Encourages Teamwork.)

Continuous improvement

3.5 Quality management is not a one-off process, but is the **continual examination** and improvement of existing processes.

(a) A philosophy of continuous improvement ensures that management **are not complacent**.

(b) **Customer needs change**; a philosophy of continuous improvement enables these changes to be taken into account in the normal course of events.

(c) **New technologies** or materials might be developed, enabling cost savings or design improvements.

(d) Continuous improvement **encourages experimentation**.

(e) Improvement on a continual, step-by-step basis is more prudent in some cases than changing things all at once.

3.6 *Holmes* proposes an eight-stage model for **improving quality**.

Step 1. **Find out the problems** (eg from customers and employees).

Step 2. **Select action targets** from the number of improvement projects identified in *Step 1*, on the basis of cost, safety, importance, and feasibility (with current resources).

Step 3. **Collect data** about the problem.

Step 4. **Analyse data** by a variety of techniques to assess common factors behind the data, to tease out any hidden messages the data might contain.

Step 5. **Identify possible causes** (eg using brainstorming sessions). No ideas are ruled out of order.

Step 6. **Plan improvement action**. Significant help might be required.

Step 7. **Monitor the effects of the improvement.**

Step 8. **Communicate the result.**

Question 1

You have just overheard the following conversation. The Board of a company are in a meeting and they are having a 'full and frank exchange of views'.

Marketing director: Customers are *our* department, and all this TQM nonsense is just another example of those jargon-spouting airheads in production affecting my ability to do my job!

Production director: Marketing people couldn't give a damn about quality, and we all know it's quality that sells the goods. Do you know the level of defects has been reduced from 10% to 4% in the last 12 months. Now that is quality!

Finance director: If all we get out of TQM is pointless rows like this, I might as well go back and do some real work!

What insights do each of the above characters have into TQM?

Answer

All of them miss the point as to the nature of TQM. The marketing director has a point in that TQM *does* imply a blurring of functional boundaries, but the marketing director *ought* to be pleased that, if TQM is implemented, the marketing concept will be brought into product design. The production director still has not grasped the concept. His idea of quality is 'technical excellence', not fitness for use. The finance director ought to care, as TQM has meaningful cost implications.

Organisational implications

3.7 Introducing TQM has **implications for the whole organisation**.

(a) TQM involves **giving employees a say** in the processes they are involved in, and in getting them to suggest improvements.

(b) TQM implies a **greater discipline to the process of production** and the establishment of better linkages between the business functions.

(c) TQM involves **new relationships with suppliers**, which requires them to improve their output quality so that less effort is spent rectifying poor input. Long-term relationships with a small number of suppliers might be preferable to choosing material and sub-components on price.

(d) It requires both **work standardisation** and employee **commitment**.

3.8 **Participation** is important in TQM, especially in the process of continuous improvement, where workforce views are valued. The management task is to encourage everybody to contribute. **Barriers to participation** include:

(a) An autocratic chief executive, who believes he or she is the sole key to the process.

(b) Individualism, in which people 'possess' ideas in order to take credit for them rather than share them for mutual benefit.

(c) Ideas of managers as leaders and directors rather than facilitators and supporters.

(d) Middle managers who feel their authority is threatened.

3.9 Managers find some aspects particularly hard to accept.

(a) Social and status barriers are removed with the removal of office partitions.

(b) Administrative functions must now be seen as **supporting the shop floor**.

(c) The **shop floor** is the most important area.

(d) Managers are judged by their contribution to team spirit, not 'the virility of their decisions'.

(e) Personal skills are needed (eg the ability to listen and communicate).

(f) A manager's role is in supporting and training, not disciplining and restricting.

3.10 As well as physical products, quality also applies to **service businesses** such as banks, restaurants or software developers. Quality issues arise in a number of areas.

- Customer expectations
- The process by which the service is delivered
- The attitudes and demeanour of the people giving the service
- The environment of the service encounter

Quality assurance schemes   11/01

3.11 The term 'quality assurance' is used where a supplier guarantees the quality of goods or services they supply. Quality assurance programs usually involve a close relationship between supplier and customer, which may extend to allowing customer representatives to view and/or monitor production procedures.

3.12 Quality assurance emphasises the processes and procedures used to produce a product or service – the logic being that if these are tightly controlled and monitored the resulting product and service will be high quality. As quality has been 'built-in', the routine inspection of goods **after** production should not be required.

13: The management of quality

Quality control

3.13 Quality control procedures focus on the product or service produced, rather than the production procedures.

3.14 Quality control involves establishing standards of quality for a product or service, implementing procedures that are expected to produce products of the required standard in most cases and monitoring output to ensure sub-standard output is rejected or corrected.

The cost of quality

3.15 Quality involves four types of cost. These are explained below, with examples referring to the development of an information system.

   (a) **Prevention costs** are costs incurred to ensure the work is done correctly – for example ensuring the system design is correct before beginning production. Prevention costs are the cost of avoiding poor quality.

   (b) **Appraisal costs** are the costs of inspection and testing – for example design reviews, structured walkthroughs and program testing.

   (c) **Internal failure costs** are the costs of correcting defects discovered before the system is delivered.

   (d) **External failure costs**. These are costs arising to fix defects discovered after the system has been delivered.

3.16 However, operating to high quality standards and procedures should also produce **savings**. Expenditure on failure prevention can reduce the cost of failure. Another saving is the reduction in quality inspection costs.

External quality standards   11/01

3.17 A number of organisations produce quality standards that can be applied to variety of organisations. The most widely used are those published by the International Organisation for Standardisation (ISO). (You would reasonably assume that it ought to be IOS, but it isn't. Apparently, the term ISO was chosen (instead of IOS), because 'iso' in Greek means equal, and ISO wanted to convey the idea of organisations using equivalent standards.)

3.18 ISO standards can be applied to many types of organisations - including those involved in producing software. The standards are updated periodically - the current standards are the ISO 9000 2000 series. The ISO 9000 2000 series of standards consists of four primary standards: ISO 9000, ISO 9001, ISO 9004, and ISO 19011.

3.19 ISO standards apply to many types of organisations - not just those involved in producing software. The standards are updated periodically - the current standards are the ISO 9000 2000 series. The ISO 9000 2000 series of standards consists of four primary standards: ISO 9000, ISO 9001, ISO 9004, and (the still to be finalised) ISO 19011.

   (a) ISO 9001:2000 contains ISO's new quality management system requirements. This is the standard you need to use if you wish to become certified (registered).

   (b) ISO 9000:2000 and ISO 9004:2000 contain ISO's new quality management system guidelines. These standards explain ISO's approach to quality management - ISO 9000:2000 presents definitions and discusses terminology, while ISO 9004:2000 is a set of guidelines for improving performance. These two guideline standards help

Part E: Quality

organisations implement quality management, but they are not intended to be used for certification purposes.

(c) ISO is working on a fourth new standard: ISO 19011. ISO 19011 will replace the old ISO 10011 quality auditing standards. The final version of this new standard is expected in the year 2002 or 2003.

What's the difference between being ISO certified/registered and being ISO compliant?

3.20 When a company claims that they are ISO 9000 certified or registered, they mean that an independent registrar has audited their quality system and certified that it meets the ISO 9001:2000 requirements (or the old ISO 9001:1994, 9002:1994, or 9003:1994 requirements). It means that a registrar has given a written assurance that ISO's quality management system standard has been met.

3.21 When an organisation says that they are ISO 9000 compliant, they mean that they have met ISO's quality system requirements, but have not been formally certified by an independent registrar. In effect, they are self-certified. Of course, an official Certificate does tend to carry more weight in the market place.

3.22 If an organisation that is certified or compliant, this does not indicate that their products and services meet ISO 9000 requirements. The ISO 9000 standards are process standards, not product standards. It is the processes that are use to produce that products or services that have been certified.

4 QUALITY CIRCLES

> **KEY TERMS**
>
> A **quality circle** is a team of workers from within the organisation which meets at intervals to discuss issues relating to the quality of the product or service produced.

4.1 Over the last two decades the demand for quality has permeated almost every area of business.

4.2 This has led to the design of systems through which quality can be effectively controlled using **internal resources**. In this context, Americans came up with the concept of **quality circles.**

4.3 A typical quality circle comprises employees from many levels of the organisation who meet regularly. The frequency of meetings varies across organisations – every three months would normally be sufficient.

4.4 Suggestions are encouraged regarding how the product or service produced could be improved, and how processes and working practices could be improved. Members are encouraged to analyse issues in a logical way.

4.5 Wider issues may also be discussed, as it is recognised that the complete working environment will affect quality levels. In some organisations this has led to quality circles having input on issues such as health and safety, employee benefits and bonuses and training and education programmes

4.6 The **benefits of quality circles** include:

13: The management of quality

(a) Employee involvement improves morale.
(b) Practical improvements/solutions are likely as workers know the processes involved.
(c) Organisation unity is fostered as the circle includes all levels.
(d) Suggestions can result in valuable savings.
(e) A 'culture' of quality is fostered.

4.7 Possible **drawbacks of quality circles** include:

(a) Employee 'power' is hard to control.
(b) The scope of influence can become very wide.
(c) Rejected suggestions may cause resentment.
(d) Business practicalities (eg cost) may not be fully understood.

4.8 The concept of quality circles has expanded to now include groups drawn from **separate organisations** but with a common interest. The example below describes one such group.

Case example

A new quality circle of European lawyers, (euroITcounsel) was launched this month in Milan. Members of the quality circle are drawn from major European commercial centres and leading IT law firm Tarlo Lyons is the co-ordinating member and UK representative. Its aim is to consider and advise upon legal issues affecting IT and telecomms clients in Europe.

euroITcounsel's first initiative focuses on the need for businesses to react to change in European law affecting inventions in software. US companies are adept at and willing to take advantage of this change because of their existing experience in patent protection for software which has been given by the US Patent Office for many years. European businesses ignore this at their peril.

euroITcounsel is a unique collection of lawyers with in-depth experience of advising clients in the Internet, computers and telecommunications (ICT) sectors, the members of which agree to maintain certain common standards of service for clients. These standards include response times, single point of contact and billing, Europe-wide coverage and advice from lawyers experienced in the IT sector and qualified in each state.

Clients of members of euroITcounsel have already benefited from the quality circle's work. euroITcounsel is promoting itself with a campaign based on communiqués which focus on strategic issues specific to the European IT and telecomms sectors developed at quarterly meetings of the quality circle.

Source: M2 Presswire 05-Aug-1999

5 BENCHMARKING 5/02

KEY TERMS

Benchmarking is 'The establishment through data gathering, of targets and comparators, through whose use relative levels of performance (and particularly areas of underperformance) can be identified. By the adoption of identified best practices it is hoped that performance will improve. Types of benchmarking include:

Internal benchmarking, a method of comparing one operating unit or function with another within the same industry.

Functional benchmarking, in which internal functions are compared with those of the best external practitioners of those functions, regardless of the industry they are in (also known as **operational benchmarking** or **generic benchmarking**).

Part E: Quality

> **Competitive benchmarking**, in which information is gathered about direct competitors, through techniques such as reverse engineering.
>
> **Strategic benchmarking**, a type of competitive benchmarking aimed at strategic action and organisational change.'
>
> (CIMA *Official Terminology*)

5.1 Benchmarking is basically an analysis of one's own performance compared with that of another organisation. Ideally the other organisation is one that is acknowledged to be the 'best in class' at the activity in question, and ideally the information is openly shared with the other organisation for the purpose of the benchmarking exercise. The **benchmarking process** is summarised in the following diagram.

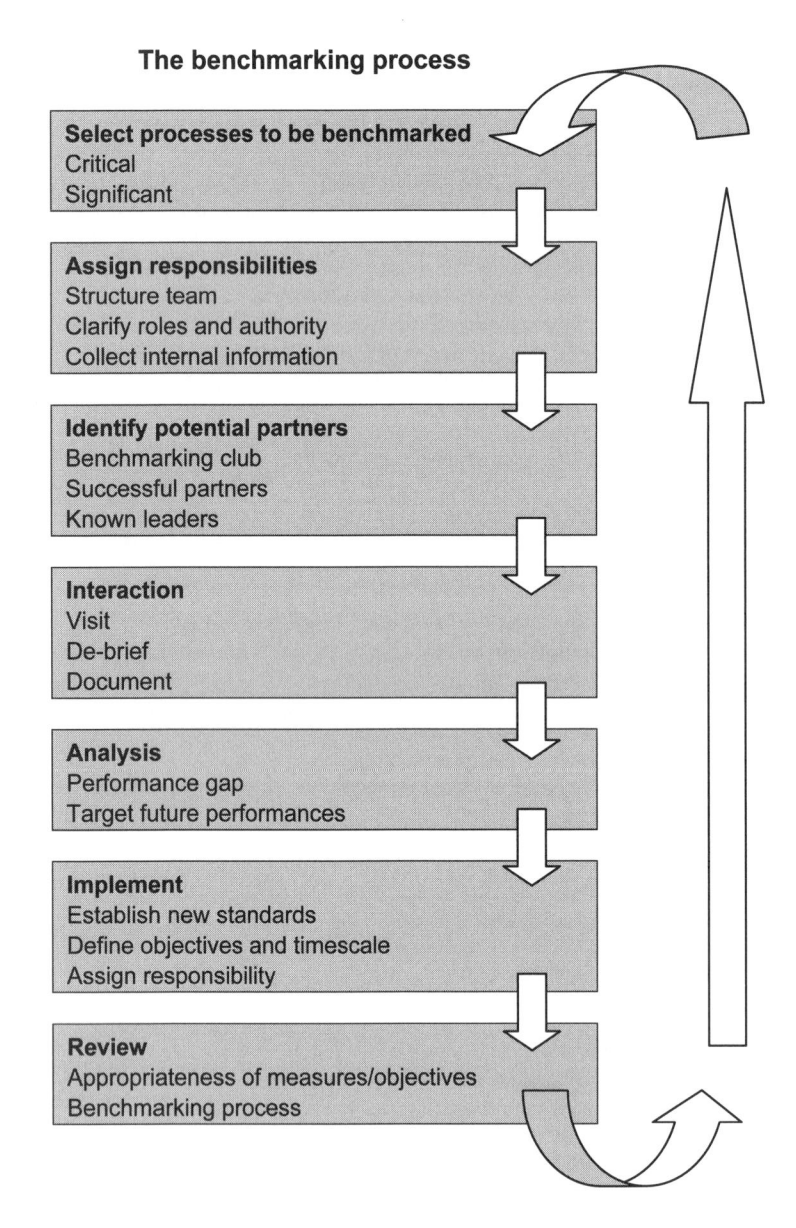

The benchmarking process

Select processes to be benchmarked
Critical
Significant

↓

Assign responsibilities
Structure team
Clarify roles and authority
Collect internal information

↓

Identify potential partners
Benchmarking club
Successful partners
Known leaders

↓

Interaction
Visit
De-brief
Document

↓

Analysis
Performance gap
Target future performances

↓

Implement
Establish new standards
Define objectives and timescale
Assign responsibility

↓

Review
Appropriateness of measures/objectives
Benchmarking process

(loop back to start)

5.2 A similar **approach to benchmarking** was described by *Richard Smith* in the February 1996 edition of *CIMA Student*.

Step 1. Consider whether the **benefits** to be gained from a benchmarking exercise **justify the time, money and effort involved**.

13: The management of quality

Step 2. Make sure that **those who actually carry out the activity to be benchmarked** form part of the **benchmarking team**.

Step 3. **Break down the chosen activity** into specific processes or outputs that are capable of measurement. At an early stage consider how any new information collected will need to be analysed.

Step 4. Carry out **internal measurement**.

Step 5. Gather **information**, perhaps by means of a pilot survey initially.

Step 6. Implement **changes** that are suggested by the exercise and monitor their success.

Step 7. **Repeat** the exercise periodically.

5.3 **Advantages** of benchmarking are as follows.

(a) It discourages **complacency.**

(b) It can **provide early warning** of future problems.

(c) It may **generate new ideas** from which all participants benefit.

(d) The comparisons are carried out by the people who have to live with any **changes** implemented as a result of the exercise.

(e) Improvement is seen to be **achievable:** managers can accept that they are not being asked to perform miracles if they have actually seen new methods working in another organisation.

5.4 However, benchmarking has a number of **problems**.

(a) Deciding **which activities** to benchmark. This could be a chicken and egg problem, since the organisation may not realise that there are better ways of doing things until it has seen what others do.

(b) Identifying **which organisation** is the 'best in class'.

(c) Persuading organisation to share information.

 (i) If it is a direct competitor, there is little incentive for it to give away its secrets or reveal its weaknesses. Worse, it may provide information that is not authentic.

 (ii) Even if it is not a direct competitor a rapport needs to be built up between the organisations and this will take time.

(d) Practices that get good results in one organisation **may not transfer successfully** to another organisation: they may depend on the talents or knowledge of particular individuals or on a particular culture.

Case example

This is a summary of the results of a 12 month research project to establish the potential for **benchmarking the finance function** in small and medium-sized enterprises (SMEs). The study measured the performance of over 600 firms across nine 'generic' finance function activities.

The key findings were:

Finance professionals viewed benchmarking as the preserve of large organisations, and for SME's, issues such as confidentiality and creating comparisons on a like-for-like basis cause major problems. Taking these reservations into account, the research has developed a methodology that can provide detailed performance analysis across the range of accounting activities.

The results compared the relative efficiencies of companies for each activity, with the most efficient defining the outer limits of performance at 100%. The average performance across all companies shows for example, that there is scope for a 42% saving in the use of staff resources in Management Accounting for the average firm.

Performance differences could also be identified between professional (qualified) and non-professional staff. On this basis, the study showed potential efficiency gains overall, of 37% for professional staff and 27% for non-professionals.

Less than 20% of companies reported using benchmarking to track the performance of their finance function. But those that do were more likely to be close to best practice than the others. Some activities were significantly more benchmarked than others; Purchase and Sales Ledger performance was twice as likely to be benchmarked as IT Management or Personnel support.

Many of the companies reporting performance measurements in finance activities were concerned with internal monitoring and not external benchmarking. Some 67% of best practice companies explicitly measure finance department performance using a number of informal metrics such as the number of errors reported, while only 30% of the less efficient businesses had comparable measures.

In summary therefore, the study clearly showed that significant potential exists for many companies to improve the productivity of their finance functions. Also, that the most productive firms are more likely than the less productive to use benchmarking to gain performance improvements.

Source: ICAEW Board for Chartered Accountants in Business - report commissioned from Manchester Business School

5.5 The concepts explained in this Chapter can be **applied to information systems**. For example, refer to 'benchmark tests' in Chapter 8, paragraphs 9.14 – 9.17.

6 OTHER CONTEMPORARY APPROACHES

6.1 We now take a brief look at two further approaches to quality.

5-S practice

6.2 This approach is based on five words – all starting with 'S'. The five words represent an approach intended to result in an organised approach to operations and management. 5-S practice is adapted from a similar approach devised in Japan.

S-word	Comment
Structurise	Introduce order where possible.
Systemise	Approach tasks systematically.
Sanitise	Be tidy, avoid clutter.
Standardise	Be consistent in your approach.
Self-discipline	Work hard when it is required. Do the above daily.

Total productive maintenance (TPM)

6.3 TPM aims to reduce equipment failure within an organisation. TPM involves:

- Equipment maintenance planning
- Equipment replacement plans
- Production planning
- Safety and environment planning

13: The management of quality

Chapter roundup

- **Quality management** is concerned with ensuring that products or services are fit for their purpose, and meet specifications.
- **Traditional approaches** to quality-focussed on **inspection**.
- **Modern approaches** to quality focus on the **prevention of defects** through quality standards and processes.
- Although quality may appear costly, a quality focussed organisation will **benefit** from improved customer retention, and savings associated with fewer rejected items.
- Modern approaches to quality utilise various tools including:
  - TQM
  - External quality standards
  - Continuous improvement
  - Quality circles
  - Benchmarking
  - 5-S practice
  - TPM

Quick quiz

1 Define 'quality'.

2 Does 'building quality in' cost money?

3 List five principles of TQM.

    1 ....
    2 ....
    3 ....
    4 ....
    5 ....

4 List four implications of TQM that could impact across the whole organisation.

    1 ....
    2 ....
    3 ....
    4 ....

5 What is a 'quality circle'?

6 List four possible benefits of quality circles.

    1 ....
    2 ....
    3 ....
    4 ....

7 List five advantages of benchmarking?

    1 ....
    2 ....
    3 ....
    4 ....
    5 ....

Part E: Quality

8   List four possible problems associated with benchmarking.

    1   ....

    2   ....

    3   ....

    4   ....

9   The comments in the table below are **NOT** alongside the corresponding 'S word'. Match the comments to the correct word.

5-S practice			Comment
(i)	Systemise	A	Introduce order where possible.
(ii)	Structurise	B	Work hard when it is required. Follow 5-S practice daily.
(iii)	Self-discipline	C	Be tidy, avoid clutter.
(iv)	Sanitise	D	Be consistent in your approach.
(v)	Standardise	E	Approach tasks systematically.

Answers to quick quiz

1   Quality may be defined as the totality of features and characteristics of a product or service which bears on its ability to meet stated or implied needs.

2   Building quality in (quality assurance) may involve producing a higher specification product or service, which is likely to cost more than producing to lower level specifications. However, high quality operating performance (ie conformance quality) should produce savings such as a reduction in inspection costs and in time spent on customer queries/complaints.

3   Any five from the following; prevention, principle, right first time, zero defects, eliminate waste, everybody's concern, internal customers, quality chains, continuous improvement, employee participation and teamwork. Re-read paragraph 3.7 for further details.

4   Four possible implications are: *TQM* involves giving employees a say in the processes they are involved in, and in getting them to suggest improvements. *TQM* implies a greater discipline to the process of production and the establishment of better linkages between the business functions. *TQM* involves new relationships with suppliers, which requires them to improve their output quality so that less effort is spent rectifying poor input. *TQM* requires work standardisation and employee commitment.

5   A quality circle is a team of workers from within the organisation which meets at intervals to discuss issues relating to the quality of the product or service produced.

6   Possibilities include; improved employee morale, practical improvements, organisation unity is fostered, suggestions can result in valuable savings and a 'culture' of quality is fostered.

7   Advantages include; discourages complacency, may provide early warning of problems, may generate new ideas from which all participants benefit, those involved are those who would be affected, encourages the attitude that improvement is achievable.

8   Possible problems; deciding which activities to benchmark, identifying which organisation is the 'best in class', persuading an organisation to share information, practices may not transfer successfully to another organisation.

9   (i)   E.
     (ii)   A.
     (iii) B.
     (iv)   C.
     (v)   D.

The material covered in this Chapter is tested in Questions 13(b) and 16(c) in the Question Bank.

Question bank questions

Questions 1-4 are **short** questions, intended to be used for revision purposes.

Questions 5-21 are based on **case study** scenarios. Ensure you have read the **'Tackling Scenario Questions'** section included in the front pages of this book before attempting these questions.

Case 1 (Q5-Q7) is approximately **half the size** of an examination standard case study, and includes 50 marks worth of questions.

Case 2 (Q8-10) includes 80 marks worth of questions.

Case 3 (Q11-14) is a **full-length** case study, with 100 marks worth of questions.

Case 4 (Q15-18) is the old style **Pilot Paper**, with questions totalling 100 marks.

Case 5 (Q19-21) is a shorter case study with 60 marks worth of questions. **Question 21** includes **detailed help** with the question and answer.

Question bank questions

1 NEW INFORMATION SYSTEM AND DECISION MAKING *24 mins*

'A new information system always aids decision making'.

Required

Discuss the validity of the above statement. (15 marks)

2 CRITICAL PATH ANALYSIS *22 mins*

You are the project manager responsible for a proposed new computer-based application for a medium sized retail chain.

You have drawn up an outline timetable for the introduction of the new system. The first draft of this is shown below.

Task	Description	Planned duration (weeks)	Preceding activities
A	Communication – inform staff at each shop of the proposal and indicate how it will affect them	1	–
B	Carry out systems audit at each shop	2	A
C	Agree detailed implementation plan with board of directors	1	B
D	Order and receive hardware requirements	4	C
E	Install hardware at all shops	4	D
F	Install software at all shops	2	D
G	Arrange training	3	D
H	Test systems at all shops	4	E and F
I	Implement changeover at all shops	10	G and H

Required

Produce a critical path analysis of the draft implementation plan. (This should identify the critical path and the total elapsed time.) (12 marks)

3 NEW SYSTEM IMPLEMENTATION *36 mins*

A new company is to be formed by the merger of two existing organisations to set up a national chain of cash and carry retail shops for cut-price furniture and kitchen units. A characteristic of the company policy is to be centralised stock control, with small local stocks and twice-weekly deliveries to each store. As management accountant you have been nominated as a member of a feasibility study team being formed to evaluate the proposals from different manufacturers for the supply of computer hardware and software to implement the required information system.

Required

(a) State who you would expect to see as the other members of a feasibility study team of five. (2 marks)

(b) Identify the major information requirements of the system. (4 marks)

(c) Describe the principal stages involved in the implementation of the proposed system in the 100 shops already open for business which, at present, use different systems. (10 marks)

(d) Explain the criteria used to evaluate the choice of system. (4 marks)

4 POST-IMPLEMENTATION AND CHANGE ISSUES *36 mins*

Required

(a) Describe the meaning and purpose of a post-implementation review. (5 marks)

The Human Resources Directors of a large company wants to measure the success of the application software he has commissioned and implemented for a personnel system.

Question bank questions

(b) Briefly describe three measures he could use to quantify the success of the application software and state what each of these three measures is attempting to assess. (8 marks)

It is expected that the user will define new requirements (and change old ones) throughout the life of the system.

(c) List the components of a procedure for recording, prioritising and implementing these changes.

(7 marks)

QUESTIONS 5 - 7 ARE BASED ON THE FOLLOWING SCENARIO   90 mins

SWM Ltd is a manufacturing company with three divisions, all of which operate from the same site. The company's main finished goods warehouse is located about one mile away. The main manufacturing site is the location for all other functions, including the IT department.

The company runs a corporate database on a mainframe computer with networked terminals. The terminals do not at present have any independent processing capacity. Departmental managers have become concerned at the speed of processing when several applications or users require computer time at the same time. The chief executive has also expressed concern about the high cost of software maintenance.

The warehouse stock records are maintained on a minicomputer in the warehouse. Each morning, details of the previous day's sales orders taken are sent by courier to the warehouse. The data, which is stored on a floppy disk, is downloaded to the warehouse system, which generates despatch documentation, including invoices, and picking lists. The warehouse's 'free' and 'allocated' stock records are updated.

At the end of each day, details of stock movements are sent to the main site and the mainframe's stock records are updated. These are referred to by sales order processing staff to ensure goods are in stock when booking orders. Copy invoices are also sent to the accounts department for posting to customer ledgers.

A recent review of software maintenance costs by the chief accountant has revealed the following.

(a) The mainframe has limited reporting capabilities. Recent requests for the provision of reports of sales by region and by product group have resulted in substantial reprogramming effort in order to add the required fields and routines.

(b) It is not possible to produce reports containing summary level information at the same time as routine reports are generated. This has meant that senior managers either content themselves with working with the long transactions listings used by operational staff in the relevant department or ask subordinates to prepare summaries 'manually', which the latter usually do with spreadsheet packages.

Required

5   SWM LTD: SYSTEM DEFICIENCIES   *36 mins*

Write a report to Departmental Managers identifying any information deficiencies in the current system and recommending ways in which the processing of data could be speeded up. (20 marks)

6   SWM LTD: SECURITY AND ITEGRITY CONTROLS   *27 mins*

Explain the controls that should be adopted to retain the integrity and the security of the data in the system? (15 marks)

7   SWM LTD: SOFTWARE MAINTENANCE   *27 mins*

Draft a report to the chief executive describing the types of software maintenance encountered in computer systems. (15 marks)

Total marks SWM Ltd scenario = 50

QUESTIONS 8 - 10 ARE BASED ON THE FOLLOWING SCENARIO

144 mins

You are employed by Metropolitan Financial Services (MFS), a company employing 1,200 staff based in your own country. As a Systems Accountant, one of your responsibilities is to improve the systems development process. In particular, the Managing Director has expressed concern at the length of time that systems development takes. The MD recently stated 'we have highly trained staff with excellent technical skills but we still seem to fall behind schedule on all of our systems development projects'.

Current systems development

Most concern at the moment relates to a project agreed upon nine months ago. The project goal is to centralise the management information systems for the three operational units by the installation of a new centralised server, and the consolidation of each unit's IT staff into a new IT team based at head office. It was planned that the transition would be completed within eighteen months. Interim plans were made to facilitate the change, for example one unit would deal with all payroll processing, one with all customer ledger activities and so on, using existing systems.

Problems encountered

At the end of nine months it has become apparent that the eighteen-month timeframe was over-optimistic.

The installation work on the new server at head office has progressed steadily, but the writing of the new software required for the centralised system is yet to start. As a result, a decision has been taken to defer the 'go live' date for the new system by six months, extending the transitional period to two years.

The redistribution of much of the back office and administrative work between units has proved difficult. The resulting operational problems have led to publication of regulatory body information being delayed. There is real concern that breaches of regulatory rules may occur.

Staff concerns

Senior management has been aware of the generally slow progress, and is now also becoming aware of the problems arising from the transitional arrangements.

In addition, users are concerned that they have had very little input to date on the development of new systems they will be dependant on. The disruption caused by the transitional arrangements has made users, jobs more difficult, for example staff often have to switch terminals depending on what type of information they need to access.

The three main areas affected by the changeover are:

(a) The MIS developed in-house. This includes 'front-office' functions such as dealing/trading, and 'back-office' functions such as settlement and reporting.

(b) 'Office' type software including spreadsheet, word-processing, e-mail and database.

(c) Access to a third party on-line information service.

The existing MIS has attracted user criticism. In particular, staff involved in dealing activities are unhappy with the way they have to navigate between screens when working in a high-pressure and fast-moving environment.

Users are satisfied with the office type software (running under Windows 98) and the access to, and information provided by, the third-party system.

Discussions with senior IT staff have revealed that the company uses a traditional systems development cycle and that requires minimal user involvement until the implementation stage.

Required

8 MFS: METHODOLOGIES AND PROJECT MANAGEMENT *72 mins*

Write a report to the managing director explaining:

(a) The features of a structured methodology and how MFS Ltd could benefit from the use of such a methodology. **(20 marks)**

(b) Possible reasons why systems development projects at MFS are not completed within schedule, and how this could be improved. **(20 marks)**

Question bank questions

9   MFS: CASE TOOLS AND PROTOTYPING   *27 mins*

The managing director has seen a technical article on CASE tools and Prototyping. He has requested you to write a memorandum containing a non-technical summary of the product features, and your opinion as to their suitability for use at MFS Ltd.   (15 marks)

10   MFS: SYSTEMS DEVELOPMENT AND PROJECT MANAGEMENT   *45 mins*

The managing director has also requested a report explaining the principles of project management and how these could be applied to systems development projects at MFS Ltd.   (25 marks)

Total marks MFS scenario = 80

QUESTIONS 11 - 14 ARE BASED ON THE FOLLOWING SCENARIO   *180 mins*

ABC Ltd supplies small tools, fixings such as nails and screws, paint and similar DIY materials to individual customers and small home improvement and decorating businesses. Sales are made from a central warehouse in a large city. Most sales to private customers are on a cash basis, although sales to small companies are on credit, with up to 30 days payment terms being offered. Most invoices are for a relatively low value, with £42 being the average invoice amount.

The company has been relatively successful, and has made a small profit in each of the last five years of trading. However, there has been a lack of investment in IT systems in particular in recent years, leaving ABC vulnerable to competition from the Internet.

Many of the employees at ABC (there are 24 full-time staff) have a long service history, and the directors tend to run the company on the basis of trust, rather than 'waste time', as they put it, introducing complicated and detailed control systems which, in their opinion, are not required. Similarly, staff tend to learn about customer service 'on the job', there have been no training courses for staff for the last seven years. Repeat business for ABC is generated because the staff have good working relationships with the customers and take time to understand their requirements.

Customers in return appreciate the personal service and are prepared to wait for the relatively slow service to obtain the correct goods required. ABC also carries an extensive product range and is willing to order any item not in stock, no matter how small in value. Some items appear to be sold at a minimal profit, but the directors accept that this does continue to provide good customer service and so accept the low margin.

Current systems and problems with them

ABC operates various computer systems; they are old, but generally reliable. The directors had no specific plans for upgrading the systems until a series of incidents which took place in the last few weeks:

1   Significant delays were noted and errors found in the credit sales system. These are explained in more detail in the section on existing sales system below.

2   Competitors have started offering on-line real-time stock availability and purchase to customers via the Internet. This has severely decreased ABC's sales in the last week.

3   A review of the stock system found that cost price of stock purchased for resale was based on the historical prices of five years ago, rather than the current price. As ABC sells many goods on a standard mark-up from cost price, this was in effect under-pricing goods being sold. In a few cases, goods were actually being sold at below the current purchase cost to ABC.

4   There are no up-to-date management accounts and a Management Information System proposed two years ago was not implemented due to lack of time on the part of the Chairman (who was also the nominal IT Director because no other Director wanted the job). This weakness became critical at a recent Board meeting when directors were unable to determine an effective strategy against Internet competition.

These issues are discussed in more detail below.

A report from the auditors recommended introducing an integrated accounts package to overcome some of these problems. The directors have asked the auditors for more information on the packages available and how these would overcome the errors identified by the auditors.

Part of the initial review of the systems by the auditors to produce a full report and plan the implementation of the new system was to record in some detail the existing credit sales system. Notes from the audit junior on this system are given below:

Existing Sales System – Credit sales

The system is partly manual and partly computerised, having been written in-house about 10 years ago by the Chairman's son as a software project at university. It is basically a recording system only, it lacks the detailed system level controls found as standard in most modern computerised accounting system packages. The main steps in the system are:

Step 1   Goods are despatched to customers using one despatch note per delivery. Despatches are made either by the customer collecting the goods from the company directly, or via a courier service.

Step 2   Despatch note information is transferred daily onto a Sales Invoice proforma maintained on a Word Processor. More than one Despatch Note can appear on one sales invoice where a customer places more than one order during a day. For example, Despatch Note numbers 10109 and 11092 for customer Jones both appear on invoice 66203. Transposition errors occur frequently when the Despatch Note numbers are entered onto the Sales Invoice.

Step 3   Despatch notes are filed in date order with no check to ensure the numeric sequence is complete.

Step 4   After printing out, Sales Invoices are re-input individually into the Sales Day Book and Sales Ledger. These computer systems are maintained in another department.

Step 5   Copy Sales Invoice are sent to each customer at the end of each week. More than one Sales Invoice may be sent to one customer if the customer has made purchases on more than one day during that week. For example, Sales Invoice 66203 for sales made on Tuesday will be sent to the customer with invoice 67321 for sales made on Friday.

Step 6   Customers pay invoices by cheque. Payments normally relate to more than one sales invoice. For example, cheque number 100976 from customer Jones may pay Sales Invoices 66203, 67321 and 68903.

Step 7   Cheque are recorded individually in the Cash Book.

Step 8   Cheques are also recorded in the Sales Ledger from CB information. However, some invoices are only partly paid where queries about individual despatches have not been cleared. For example, cheque 100976 paid invoices 66203 and 67321 in full, but only partly paid invoice 68903. The remaining amount on invoice 68903 will be paid on cheque 101076 in the following week.

Step 9   All cheques are grouped together and banked on a daily basis.

Step 10 A report of all overdue debts is produced on a weekly basis from the Sales Ledger. The part payment of invoices causes difficulties for debt collection, because the computer system flags a part payment as fully paying the invoice and moves the remaining balance into a global 'part-paid invoices' section of the ledger. This account was used because it was thought that part-payments would be relatively rare; however, about one in a hundred payments fall into this category making the system very difficult to maintain.

Internet purchasing

A major competitor has just opened an Internet site where customers can view stock availability and prices on-line, order those items and have them delivered to their home or work location on a next day delivery. Although the product range is not as comprehensive as ABC's, the pricing of goods is similar and delivery is free for orders over £30. This is providing a very attractive purchasing alternative, with some older established customers already suggesting to ABC that if a similar service is not provided then they will transfer their accounts. The major weakness with Internet trading is that competitors insist that payment is made via credit card over the Internet, and this appears to be limiting sales growth.

The directors have really no idea about the Internet and have employed a project manager to prepare various reports to help them understand this issue.

Lack of management information

The lack of management information has concerned the Board, although to date, provision of this information has not been a major objective. A project manager has been appointed to review the existing systems and implement at least a basic Management Information System for use by the Directors and other strategic managers. The main issues that the project manager will need to consider include:

- Linking the MIS with the new Integrated Accounts System
- The lack of effective computerised systems in other areas of the company such as stock control
- A lack of knowledge at Board level regarding what information a MIS can provide

Question bank questions

Required

11 ABC LTD: ERM, OFF-THE-SHELF SOFTWARE, INTEGRATED ACCOUNTS PACKAGE   *45 mins*

As part of the initial work of the Project Manager for ABC:

(a) Prepare an Entity Relationship Model for the Sales and cheque receipts system. (10 marks)

(b) Prepare extracts from a letter to the Board which:

    (i) Explains the benefits of purchasing an off-the-shelf accounting package. (5 marks)

    (ii) Explains how a computerised integrated accounts package can help to overcome the weaknesses in the sales and cheque receipts system. (10 marks)

12 ABC LTD: THE INTERNET   *45 mins*

Prepare slides and supporting notes for a presentation to the directors explaining:

(a) The Internet, and how the Internet can be used for Business to Consumer and Business to Business trading. (17 marks)

(b) The hardware that ABC would have to install to use the Internet for trading, assuming that the company hosts its own web-site. (8 marks)

13 ABC LTD: SWOT ANALYSIS, SERVICE QUALITY   *45 mins*

Prepare a report for the Board of ABC from the Project Manager of ABC Ltd, which:

(a) Presents a SWOT analysis for ABC. (15 marks)

(b) Provides recommendations on how the quality of service provided by ABC can be improved. (10 marks)

14 ABC LTD: IMPLEMENTATION STAGES, INFORMATION QUALITY AND CONTROL   *45 mins*

As the newly appointed Project Manager, prepare a memorandum for the Chairman which:

(a) Explains the stages for the implementation of a new MIS. (15 marks)

(b) Advises how the control of the business will be improved by the provision of higher quality information. (10 marks)

Total marks ABC scenario = 100

QUESTIONS 15 - 18 ARE BASED ON THE FOLLOWING SCENARIO *(From the Pilot paper)*   *180 mins*

You work for a firm of management accountants that specialises in implementing information systems. The latest assignment is to implement new systems at a small chain of ten shops managed by FRS Ltd and to integrate these into the systems of a multinational retail organisation (MRO Inc) that has recently acquired them. FRS Ltd sells a range of wines, spirits and groceries.

The chief executive of FRS Ltd is not particularly happy about the fact that, as part of the acquisition, FRS Ltd will be required to introduce new technology and be linked to the systems of MRO Inc. One of his favourite comments is to tap his head and say, 'That's the best computer, you don't need all this new technology.'

Your manager has asked you to prepare several documents in relation to this project. To assist you with this task you have been provided with the following information.

Extracts from notes of a meeting with the chief executive of FRS Ltd

Based upon previous experience the chief executive stated his fears about information systems (IS) projects. He gave the following as specific examples:

- Information systems staff do not talk to users
- Systems are always late, cost more than the original estimates and usually fall a long way short of user expectations
- Programs invariably contain errors

- Programmers do not always think about the practicality of their programs. One system he had experienced in the past utilised function key F3 to produce a look-up table in the sales-ledger program, but on the purchase-ledger program the F3 key was used to quit (exit) the program. The IS department refused to change it, saying that it was too late and too expensive to do
- Reporting facilities are often not flexible enough. At FRS Ltd they use a spreadsheet for management reporting

The organisation and information systems at MRO Inc

The chart below represents the department structure for each shop.

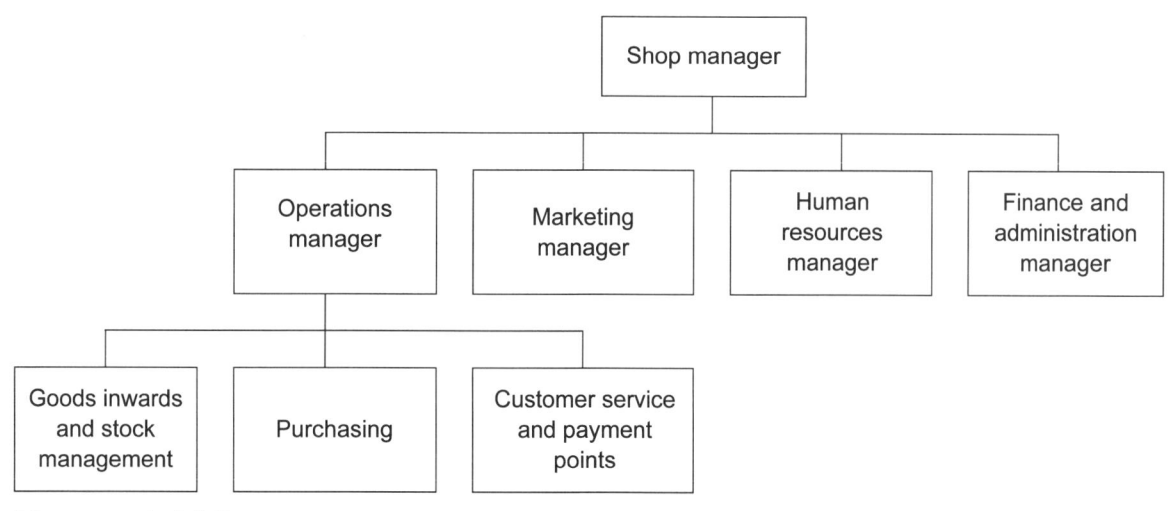

```
                          Shop manager
         ┌────────────────┬──────────────┬────────────────┐
    Operations        Marketing        Human          Finance and
     manager           manager       resources       administration
                                      manager           manager
    ┌────┼────────────┐
Goods inwards  Purchasing  Customer service
and stock                  and payment
management                 points
```

Management of staff

Each department has its own manager with a structure of support staff below, comprising supervisors and clerks. The operations department is split into three distinct areas of operation as indicated by the chart, each with its own supervisor and staff who work exclusively within that section.

Information systems

Each shop has a local area network (LAN), which uses a minicomputer as the central point.

The customer service/payment points operate electronic point of sale (EPOS) and electronic funds transfer at point of sale (EFTPOS) systems. These are connected to the minicomputer and update a database which holds stock and sales details.

The members of staff in each department utilise personal computers (PCs) with access to office software such as spreadsheets and word processing. They can also access the minicomputer, via the LAN, to gain information from the database required for their function. For example, the finance function is able to analyse the daily sales and information, the purchasing function has access to sales information by product line, and the marketing function is able to analyse sales trends and the effect of promotions on different product lines.

The stock and sales data are updated in real time.

All shops are connected to the head office computer network; they send a copy of the daily transactions to head office at close of business each day. This provides them with an additional copy for security purposes and enables members of the senior management team, who have access to an executive information system (EIS), to monitor the performance of the group as a whole and to investigate performance of individual shops if they wish.

There is an information systems department at head office, which provides support services to the shops and manages the wide area network (WAN). Email facilities are also provided between members of the group over the WAN.

Question bank questions

The organisation and information systems at FRS Ltd

The chart below represents the shop structure.

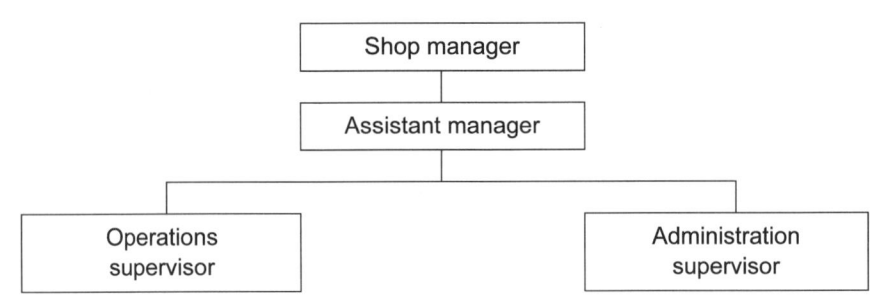

```
                    ┌─────────────────┐
                    │  Shop manager   │
                    └────────┬────────┘
                             │
                    ┌────────┴────────┐
                    │ Assistant manager│
                    └────────┬────────┘
                             │
                ┌────────────┴────────────┐
        ┌───────┴───────┐         ┌───────┴────────┐
        │  Operations   │         │ Administration │
        │  supervisor   │         │  supervisor    │
        └───────────────┘         └────────────────┘
```

Note. The operations supervisor is in charge of goods inwards, shelf stock and payment points. The administration supervisor is in charge of accounts and purchasing.

Management of staff

A manager and an assistant manage each shop with support from an operations supervisor and an administration supervisor. The operations supervisor controls the pool of staff that perform all the operations within the shop's retail activity. In some instances this means that the same members of staff could be involved in receiving goods into the stockholding area, replenishing stock on the shelves in the shop or manning a payment point.

Information systems

Head office has a computer system that is used for accounting transactions, and a PC that is used by the accountant to analyse the sales figures and to consolidate the data from each shop.

Information from the other shops in the group arrives in a variety of formats. Some shops use floppy disks, others send a hard copy from which the accountant enters the data manually to the PC. However, one shop sends the data via a dial-up link, which the manager had established from within his own budget.

Two shops do not use a computer at all. At the end of each month, they send to head office a copy of the cashbook, from which the data is extracted and entered into the PC.

The accountant at FRS Ltd, Mr Black, provides a summary of the profit and loss account for all shops at the end of each month. This is usually produced by about the twenty-first day of the following month, as he has to wait until all shops have sent the information.

Mr Black has been suggesting for some time that FRS Ltd should install computer terminals at each shop and connect them to a centralised mainframe computer at the head office. His argument is that all the information would be in the same format and it would make controlling it very simple. The chief executive is now keen to accept this idea to enable him to retain control over the individual shops.

Problems at FRS Ltd

A recent audit report from the auditors of FRS Ltd indicated problems in several key areas of the business.

Stock control was reported as being weak, with several instances being given as a particular cause for concern. These included:

- Stock discrepancies of high value items such as wines and spirits had been found on previous occasions, which resulted in stock losses being recorded in the accounts

- The stock management of perishable items, such as fresh vegetables and milk resulted in stock being written off on a number of occasions

- The local government health department had warned one shop that goods were still on the shelf after the 'sell by' date (the recommended date by which goods should be sold). This had only been by one day, but it had resulted in a strong warning being issued, and a reminder that legal action could result if additional infringements are discovered

Draft implementation plans

The information systems department of MRO Inc had drawn up an outline timetable for the introduction of the new system to FRS Ltd.

The first draft of this timetable follows.

Question bank questions

Task	Description	Planned duration (weeks)	Preceding activities
A	Communication – inform staff at each FRS shop and indicate how it will affect them	1	-
B	Carry out systems audit at each FRS shop	2	A
C	Agree detailed implementation plan with board of directors	1	B
D	Order and receive hardware requirements	4	C
E	Install hardware at all FRS shops	4	D
F	Install software at all FRS shops	2	D
G	Arrange training at premises of MRO Inc	3	D
H	Test systems at all FRS shops	4	E and F
I	Implement changeover at all shops	10	G and H

Required

15 FRS LTD: DISTRIBUTED AND CENTRALISED PROCESSING, INFORMATION FOR DECISION MAKING *45 mins*

Prepare a brief report for the chief executive of FRS Ltd that:

(a) Explains the difference between distributed processing and centralised, multi-user processing.

(6 marks)

(b) Explains the relative merits of adopting the information systems utilised by MRO Inc. (7 marks)

(c) Illustrates how information could be utilised for decision-making at the various levels of an organisation such as MRO Inc and the types of information system which support those decisions. (12 marks)

16 FRS LTD: STRUCTURED METHODOLOGY, INFORMATION SYSTEMS AND QUALITY *36 mins*

Prepare a memorandum to the chief executive of FRS Ltd that explains the following:

(a) The benefits of using a structured methodology to develop and implement new systems, indicating how this methodology will overcome the types of problems he has experienced in the past. (10 marks)

(b) How the concept of quality can be applied to information systems and how quality can be assessed and measured. (10 marks)

17 FRS LTD: SYSTEM DEVELOPMENT, PROJECT MANAGEMENT, CPA *54 mins*

Prepare a briefing paper for the management team of FRS Ltd that:

(a) Describes the major issues to be considered in managing the project to implement the new system at FRS Ltd. (10 marks)

(b) Evaluates the range of project management tools and techniques that can be used to justify and control the implementation of the information systems used by MRO Inc at FRS Ltd. (10 marks)

(c) Produces a critical path analysis of the draft implementation plan suggested by the IS department manager. (This should identify the critical path and the total elapsed time.) (10 marks)

18 FRS LTD: INTERNAL V EXTERNAL AUDIT, CONTROLS, IT AND AUDIT *45 mins*

Prepare outline slides and supporting notes for a presentation to be given to the shop managers of FRS Ltd explaining:

(a) The role of the internal auditor and the relationship between the internal auditor and external audit. (10 marks)

(b) The internal controls you would like to see implemented in the new system at FRS Ltd in relation to stock control. (10 marks)

(c) How information technology could be used to assist the audit process. (5 marks)

Total marks FRS scenario = 100

Question bank questions

QUESTIONS 19 - 21 ARE BASED ON THE FOLLOWING SCENARIO   *108 mins*

CAET Insurance offers motor, home, property and personal insurance. It has recently developed a holiday insurance product that it provides to the public. A potential customer is able to telephone a specially trained adviser who asks a number of pertinent questions. The answers to these questions are entered directly into a computer system that calculates and displays the premium. The adviser communicates the premium to the potential customer who may either accept or reject it. Accepted quotations are paid for by credit card and printed off and sent to the customer, along with the payment details.

The software to support the on-line holiday insurance quotation was developed in-house by the Information Systems (IS) department. It was developed in a GUI-based programming language and was the first system to be produced by the Information Systems department using this language. The project was delivered late and it exceeded its budget. The software has suffered many problems since it was installed. Some of these have been solved. However, there are still significant problems in the actual function that the advisers use to record the details of potential customers and produce the quotation.

In a recent meeting with the IS department, the advisers identified four main problems.

Illogical data entry

The advisers claim that the sequence is illogical. The questions jump from personal details, to holiday location, to travel details, back to personal details, to holiday location etc. There seems to have been little thought about logically grouping the questions and as a result potential customers become 'confused'.

Unclear field entry

Some of the information we ask for is mandatory and some is optional. Furthermore, the relevance of some questions depends on the answer to a previous question. For example, travel method is only relevant if the potential customer is travelling abroad. Unfortunately, the system does not show if a field is mandatory or optional and it shows all fields, whether they are relevant or not to a particular quotation.

Inconsistent cursor control

The information has to be entered very quickly. Many fields are filled completely during data entry. On some screens, the cursor jumps to the next field immediately after filing the previous field. In other screens, the cursor only moves after pressing the TAB key even when the field is filled. This inconsistency is very irritating, we often find ourselves over-typing completed fields and it is particular confusing for new advisers who are not used to the software.

Performance problems

One of the primary requirements of the system was the ability to process enquiries on-line and to produce instant quotations. However, at peak times the system is too slow to produce the quotation. Consequently, we have to promise to telephone the potential customer back and this destroys the immediate impact of the system. Hence the system is not fulfilling one of its primary requirements.

CAET Insurance has brought in a consultant to review the on-line holiday insurance system. The consultant has made a number of observations regarding the project and the developed software. Two summary paragraphs are repeated below.

Extract from the management summary

Project

The IS department failed to recognise that this was a very risky project. Three issues made it particularly risky.

- The users of the system had no experience in the holiday insurance industry hence they found it difficult to specify their requirements in advance.
- The decision to use a programming language that the department had not used before.
- The system had exacting performance requirements.

All projects at CAET Insurance are supposed to undergo a risk assessment as part of producing the Project Quality Plan (PQP). This risk assessment was omitted from this project for reasons that are still unclear. This was a serious omission.

The software

There is considerable evidence that the product is unstable and suffers from significant performance problems. My recommendation is that the bespoke system is abandoned and a suitable application software package is selected and installed. My research suggests that there are a number of possible solutions in the marketplace and these packages offer 'tried, tested, and error-free solutions'. It will be more cost-effective, in the long run, to adopt one of these packages rather than maintain the bespoke in-house software.

---

19 CAET INSURANCE: PROJECT MANAGEMENT *36 mins*

The consultant has pointed out that the project did not undergo the required risk assessment. This risk assessment would have required the project team to identify ways to avoid or reduce the chance of each risk occurring.

Required

(a) In retrospect what could have been suggested at the start of the project to avoid or reduce each of the following three risks identified in the consultant's report?

    (i)   The users of the system had no experience in the holiday insurance industry hence they found it difficult to specify their requirements in advance.

    (ii)   The decision to use a programming language that the department had not used before.

    (iii)   The system had exacting performance requirements.   (12 marks)

(b) The risk assessment is an important part of the Project Quality Plan (PQP). Two other terms used in the CAET Insurance PQP are:

    (i)   Project Sponsor.
    (ii)   Project Plan.

Explain the meaning and significance of each of these items.   (8 marks)

---

20 CAET INSURANCE: SOFTWARE DESIGN *36 mins*

One of the key requirements of the holiday insurance system was the need to speedily process requests for an insurance quotation over the telephone. The users have identified four specific problems with the on-line insurance quotation function.

(i) Illogical data entry.
(ii) Unclear field entry.
(iii) Inconsistent cursor control.
(iv) Performance problems.

The IS department still believes that these four problems can be solved and that there is no need to abandon the development of the bespoke system and use an application package solution.

Required

(a) Suggest how each of the following four problems could be solved, now that the system is live, and comment on the difficulty of implementing your solutions.

    (i)   Illogical data entry.   (2 marks)
    (ii)   Unclear field entry.   (2 marks)
    (iii)   Inconsistent cursor control.   (3 marks)
    (iv)   Performance problems.   (4 marks)

(b) Suggest how each of the following four problems could have been prevented or detected before the system went live.

    (i)   Illogical data entry.   (2 marks)
    (ii)   Unclear field entry.   (2 marks)
    (iii)   Inconsistent cursor control.   (2 marks)
    (iv)   Performance problems.   (3 marks)

---

21 QUESTION 21 ALSO REFERS TO CAET INSURANCE, AND INCLUDES DETAILED GUIDANCE - SEE THE FOLLOWING PAGE.

Question bank questions

21 CAET INSURANCE: QUALITY ASSURANCE AND TESTING *36 mins*

The consultant has suggested that one of the main advantages of the application software package approach is that the software is tried and tested.

Required

(a) Bespoke application systems developed in the IS department has to pass through the following three stages

   (i)   Requirements analysis.
   (ii) Systems design.
   (iii) Programming.

   Describe the quality assurance and testing associated with each of these three stages of the IS development process. (12 marks)

(b) Explain where quality assurance and testing should still be applied by the IS department when using an application software package approach and hence comment on the consultant's assertion that the software is 'tried, tested and error-free'. (8 marks)

Total marks CAET Insurance scenario = 60

Approaching the answer

You should read through the requirement, and then re-read and annotate relevant material from the scenario, highlighting points to include in your answer. An example is shown below.

CAET Insurance offers motor, home, property and personal insurance. It has recently developed a holiday insurance product that it provides to the public. A potential customer is able to **telephone** a specially trained adviser who asks a number of pertinent questions. The answers to these questions are entered directly into a **computer system** that calculates and displays the premium. The adviser communicates the premium to the potential customer who may either accept or reject it. Accepted quotations are paid for by credit card and printed off and sent to the customer, along with the payment details.

Annotations:
- Could customers enquire/purchase via a website?
- Could customers enter details direct via a website?
- Could existing insurance quotation software have been purchased and adapted?
- Did staff possess the required development expertise?

The software to support the on-line holiday insurance quotation was **developed in-house** by the Information Systems (IS) department. It was developed in a **GUI-based programming language** and was the **first** system to be produced by the Information Systems department using this language. The project was delivered **late** and it exceeded its **budget**. The software has suffered **many problems** since it was installed. Some of these have been solved. However, there are still significant problems in the actual function that the advisers use to **record the details of potential customers** and produce the quotation.

Annotations:
- Probably a 4GL
- Was this wise? Training provided to developers?
- Poor project management and system development procedures?
- Problems with an essential feature.

In a recent meeting with the IS department, the advisers identified four main problems.

Question bank questions

Illogical data entry.

The advisers claim that the sequence is illogical. The questions jump from personal details, to holiday location, to travel details, back to personal details, to holiday location etc. There seems to have been little thought about logically grouping the questions and as a result potential customers become 'confused'.

[Margin note: Were the advisors consulted during development?]

Unclear field entry

Some of the information we ask for is mandatory and some is optional. Furthermore, the relevance of some questions depends on the answer to a previous question. For example, travel method is only relevant if the potential customer is travelling abroad. Unfortunately, the system does not show if a field is mandatory or optional and it shows all fields, whether they are relevant or not to a particular quotation.

[Margin note: This is a basic requirement, shows a lack of user consultation in development process]

Inconsistent cursor control

The information has to be entered very quickly. Many fields are filled completely during data entry. On some screens, the cursor jumps to the next field immediately after filing the previous field. In other screens, the cursor only moves after pressing the TAB key even when the field is filled. This inconsistency is very irritating, we often find ourselves over-typing completed fields and it is particular confusing for new advisers who are not used to the software.

[Margin note: Was user-acceptance testing carried out?]

Performance problems

One of the primary requirements of the system was the ability to process enquiries on-line and to produce instant quotations. However, at peak times the system is too slow to produce the quotation. Consequently, we have to promise to telephone the potential customer back and this destroys the immediate impact of the system. Hence the system is not fulfilling one of its primary requirements.

[Margin note: This will cause potential customers to go elsewhere]

[Margin note: How was system developed and released with such a major flaw?]

CAET Insurance has brought in a consultant to review the on-line holiday insurance system. The consultant has made a number of observations regarding the project and the developed software. Two summary paragraphs are repeated below.

[Margin note: Understanding of business and system?]

Extract from the management summary

Project

The IS department failed to recognise that this was a very risky project. Three issues made it particularly risky.

[Margin note: Risk management]

Question bank questions

- The users of the system had no experience in the holiday insurance industry hence they found it difficult to specify their requirements in advance.

[Margin note: Research similar systems? Allow flexibility in the development process]

- The decision to use a programming language that the department had not used before.

[Margin note: If this language was most suitable, the project could have been outsourced]

- The system had exacting performance requirements.

[Callout: Essential these were met – they haven't been eg system response time]

All projects at CAET Insurance are supposed to undergo a risk assessment as part of producing the Project Quality Plan (PQP). This risk assessment was omitted from this project for reasons that are still unclear. This was a serious omission.

[Margin note: Indeed! Poor project management]

The software

[Callout: Post-project review?]

There is considerable evidence that the product is unstable and suffers from significant performance problems. My recommendation is that the bespoke system is abandoned and a suitable application software package is selected and installed. My research suggests that there are a number of possible solutions in the marketplace and these packages offer 'tried, tested, and error-free solutions'. It will be more cost-effective, in the long run, to adopt one of these packages rather than maintain the bespoke in-house software.

[Margin note: Availability? Modifications required?]

[Margin note: Very unlikely]

[Margin note: What about software quality?]

Required

(a) Bespoke application systems developed in the IS department has to pass through the following three stages

  (i)   Requirements analysis.
  (ii) Systems design.
  (iii) Programming.

Describe the quality assurance and testing associated with each of these three stages of the IS development process. (12 marks)

[Margin note: Six elements to include – QA and testing for each of the three stages.

'V' model links QA and testing]

(b) Explain where quality assurance and testing should still be applied by the IS department when using an application software package approach and hence comment on the consultant's assertion that the software is 'tried, tested and error-free'. (8 marks)

[Margin note: QA and testing still vital even when purchasing a package rather than developing in-house]

[Callout: In what environment? Different situation and users.

Very unlikely that software will be completely error-free.]

Answer plan

Organise the relevant points you have noted into a coherent answer plan. Not all the points you have noticed will have to go into your answer – you should spend a few minutes thinking them through and prioritising them.

(a) **Quality assurance and testing at three stages of systems development**

Intro
- Briefly link 'V' model to scenario

Requirements analysis
- Input, processing and output documentation
- Check against system

Systems design
- Based on business requirements
- Formal walkthroughs
- Testing – system, user acceptance

Programming
- Individual modules
- Unit test

(b) **Quality assurance and testing related to application package**

Intro
- Program design not required

Quality assurance
- Requirements specification still required

Testing
- User acceptance

Other points
- Software yet to be tested in this organisation
- Unlikely to be error free

You should flesh out the points contained in your plan and link them to form a coherent answer. Structured answers, with short paragraphs, should help ensure your answer remains focussed.

Question bank suggested solutions

Question bank suggested solutions

1 NEW INFORMATION SYSTEM AND DECISION MAKING

> **Tutorial note.** You should be wary of any statement that includes the word 'always'! It should be clear to you, after studying for this paper, that a poor quality information system is unlikely to lead to better decision making.
>
> A wide variety of points could have been made to answer this question – the solution that follows is only one possible answer.

Introduction

The statement 'a new information system always aids decision-making' is incorrect. A new information system that is poorly planned, designed and/or implemented is likely to be worse than the 'old system', and therefore result in poorer decision-making.

Possible problems with new information systems

Accuracy of systems specification

To provide accurate information to the users, any new system will need to be based on an accurate systems specification. This means that user requirements will be collected during the planning phase of the systems change, and these requirements incorporated into the systems specification and final systems design. If user requirements are omitted from the specification, or the final design is not based on the specification, then user requirements will not be met.

Type of system used

The type of system that is being used will limit provision of information by computer systems. Many systems, which are written to provide current or historical information, are unlikely to be able to give indications concerning future trends or events. Care is therefore required in implementing a system that is appropriate for the tasks being undertaken.

Provision of information

Information provided by the system may not aid decision making because it does not comply with the characteristics of good information.

Timeliness of information

The timing of provision of information from a system will have a major effect on its usefulness. Information that is provided late may not be particularly useful. For example, systems that are updated daily, rather than in real-time, may hold data that has become incorrect, possibly resulting in poor decisions.

Accessibility to information system

To aid decision making, information held on an information system must be accessible. There is little point in information being available if it cannot be used.

Accuracy of information

If information is not accurate, then incorrect decisions may be taken. Checks should be built into a computerised information system to minimise the chance of inaccurate data being input. Other, 'valid' data, may become inaccurate after it has been input - due to changing circumstances.

Other possible factors preventing information systems from aiding decision-making

Lack of training

To utilise a system, and the information held on a system, requires competent staff. Many new information systems are implemented without sufficient time being made available for staff training and familiarisation. Although the system may hold the information needed for decision making, users may be unable to access and use that information.

Conclusion

In conclusion, the statement should read 'a properly planned and implemented information system will always be able to aid decision-making'. As explained above, problems with the development process

Question bank suggested solutions

or other factors outside the control of the system mean there are limits to the effectiveness of information systems.

2 CRITICAL PATH ANALYSIS

> **Tutorial note.** This question tests your ability to produce a critical path analysis. This is a key technique - ensure you are able to apply it. Use the presentation style that you are most comfortable with – our answer shows both Activity on Node and Activity on Line presentations.

Critical path analysis [One of the following]

Activity on line presentation

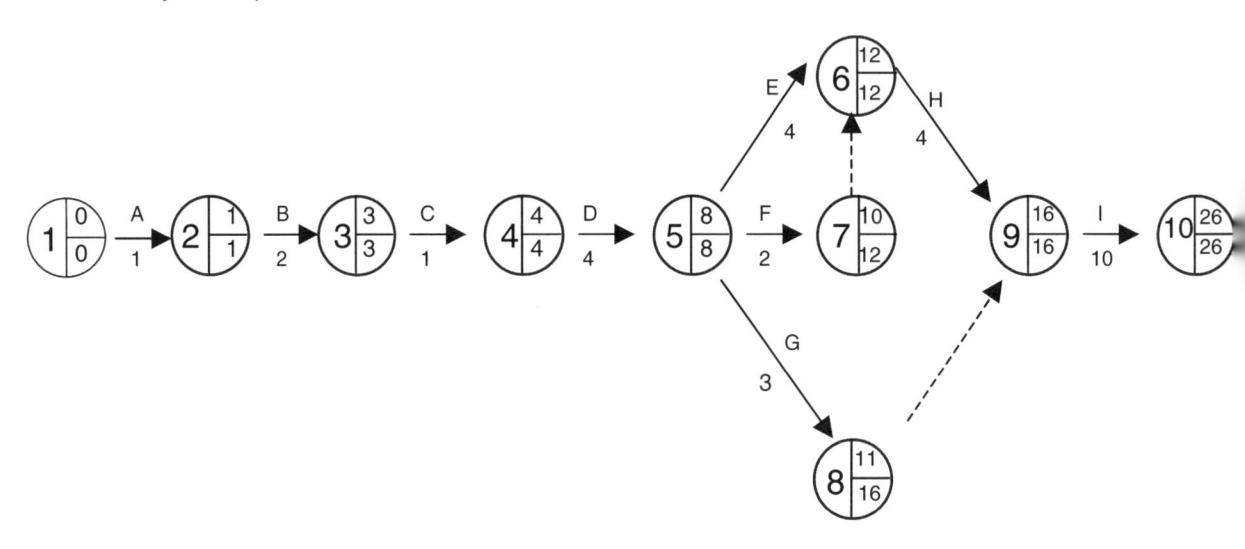

The critical path is A, B, C, D, E, H, I. The total elapsed time is 26 weeks.

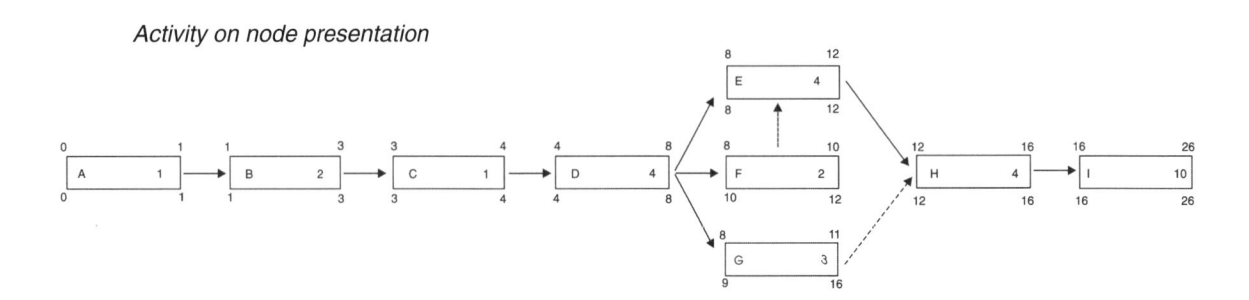

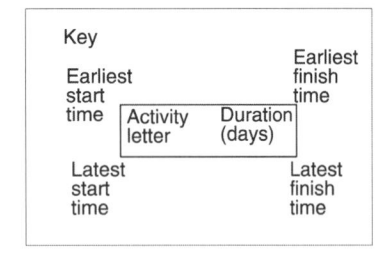

Activity on node presentation

Key

Earliest start time | Activity letter | Duration (days) | Earliest finish time
Latest start time | | | Latest finish time

3 NEW SYSTEM IMPLEMENTATION

> **Tutorial note.** When faced with a question that has a number of small parts, use the individual mark allocations as a guide to how much detail is required in your answer. In this question, your answer to part (c) should have taken half the time you spent on the whole question.

(a) The other members of the feasibility study team must bring their own particular knowledge and expertise to the study. There must be **operational expertise**, and this might be provided by three managers:

   (i) The central stores manager.
   (ii) The distribution manager.
   (iii) The manager of a store or group of stores in the chain.

The management accountant should have an understanding of the costs and financial aspects, and some IS knowledge too, but it would also be sensible to include the IS manager in the team (assuming of course that the organisation has an IS manager).

(b) Major **information requirements** of the system are as follows.

   (i) Current amounts of stock held centrally and locally, for each item, in physical quantities and value.
   (ii) Stock-outs in the central stores, and locally, and their duration.
   (iii) Periodic sales for each item, analysed by store and in total.
   (iv) Stock delivery requirements (each half-week) for each store - ie stock orders for each store and in total.
   (v) Delivery loads and schedules for each vehicle - ie delivery schedules.

(c) The **principal stages in the implementation of the proposed** system are as follows.

   (i) **Select the hardware and software** required, as a result of the feasibility study. Order the hardware and software, with agreed delivery dates. Arrangements for back-up and maintenance should be made.

   (ii) **Install the equipment** centrally and in the shops. If there is to be a staged implementation of the new system, equipment might only be installed in a few selected shops at first.

   (iii) There must be **staff training**, ideally provided by the supplier or dealer. If training is made to coincide with the delivery of the hardware and software, the staff can carry on training by practising on the company's own equipment after the training course has ended.

   One or two 'experts' in the system should be appointed. These would deal with queries from other operators of the system, and act as the link with the supplier's back up and maintenance service.

   (iv) **Testing**. Ideally, the new system should first of all be tested on 'dummy' data. The testing process could be used both to iron out operational snags with the new system and to continue the process of staff training.

   (v) **File creation**. Files for the new system must be created before the system can be operational. This can be a long and tedious process.

   (vi) **Changeover to the new system**. The changeover to the new system should be planned carefully. To start with, a few stores and head office could begin to operate the new system in a pilot run. Lessons could be learned from the pilot run and applied to the subsequent introduction of all the other stores to the system. (The option of parallel running would probably not be practicable for retailing operations, where stores staff would only have time to record sales once, using whatever point-of-sale hardware is introduced for the new system.)

   (vii) **Review and evaluation**. The new system should be reviewed and evaluated, once it has settled down, to determine whether or not it is achieving its intended objectives. Some amendments may be necessary, if so, the implementation of these changes should be carefully controlled.

Question bank suggested solutions

(d) **Criteria to evaluate the choice of system**

(i) **Reliability**. The reliability of the software and hardware should be checked, eg by following up references from other users of similar systems.

(ii) **Costs and benefits**. The benefits of the system should outweigh the costs. The costs would include software and hardware purchase costs and running costs such as maintenance and the rental of any data communication links that might be used etc.

The benefits might be difficult to evaluate but include:

(1) Lower stockholding costs
(2) Fewer stockouts and so more sales and profits
(3) Possibly, fewer staff costs

The **expected operational life** of the system would also be relevant to the comparison of costs and benefits.

(iii) **Better management information**. The quality of the management information will be a factor in the choice of system, although the benefits of a better MIS (apart from those listed above) would be virtually impossible to evaluate in financial terms.

(iv) The **flexibility of the system**. Will it allow the user to expand and modify the use of the system as operational requirements change over time?

4 POST-IMPLEMENTATION AND CHANGE ISSUES

> **Tutorial note**. Part (a) provides an opportunity to pick up easy marks for simply reproducing 'book knowledge'. If questions of this type appear in the exam, ensure you explain yourself sufficiently to pick up all the of the marks on offer. A wide range of measures could have been used in part (b). We provide four measures for study purposes – your answer should only include three. Part (c) is unusual in that it requires you to produce a list – always produce what is asked for.

(a) A post-implementation review takes place a few months after system implementation is complete. The review is to receive feedback from users on how well the system is working and to check that the objectives of the project have been met. The review normally takes the form of a meeting between the project sponsor, systems analyst, developers and users.

The review will investigate both the procedures used throughout the project and the systems that have been produced. The purpose of doing this is to identify what features of the project went well, and what went wrong or badly, so that future projects will avoid these problems.

In reviewing the objectives of the project, the review will also check whether or not the business benefits expected from the project have been achieved. Where benefits have not been achieved, or other objectives of the project have not been met, the review may also recommend remedial action to ensure that the required benefits are obtained.

(b) **Measures of success for application software**

(i) Number of calls to the help desk

Ascertaining the number of help desk calls per 100 employees (or some other useful number) will help to determine how useable and user-friendly the system is. The number of calls may also give an indication of the effectiveness of the training provided.

(ii) Number of errors reported

A log can be maintained, either by individual users or the help desk, of the number and type of errors found in the system. The actual error rate provides an indication of the quality of programming and the effectiveness of the different stages of testing (user acceptance, system and module).

(iii) Number of transactions processed

The original software specification will indicate how many transactions should be processed. Comparing the specification with the actual number processed will provide information on the usefulness of the system (if the system is not useful then presumably it will be used less than expected). A small number of transactions being processed could

Question bank suggested solutions

also be indicative of poor programming or inadequate hardware specifications, so further analysis may be needed to determine which of these is relevant.

(iv) Number of change requests

Users may request changes to the system, either where that system did not meet their original requirements, or where the system as implemented does not meet their expectations in some way. Changes requested due to initial specifications not being met provides some measure on the quality of the design and testing processes. Changes requested because the software is not meeting expectations may indicate weaknesses in this method of obtaining data for the initial specification.

(c) A procedure for recording, prioritising and implementing change requested for a live system are outlined below.

- A means for the user to record and request a change to the system
- A method of collating these change requests
- A means of providing an impact analysis and business case for each change
- A process for reviewing each request with agreed criteria for accepting or rejecting a request
- A method of prioritising requests that have been accepted
- Provision of appropriate documentation to record each change request with analysis and design implications for the existing system
- A method of allocating amendments to programmers
- A process for reviewing the work of programmers and ensuring that the change meets the initial specification
- A process for testing the change within the whole program suite
- Procedures for informing users date and nature of the change
- Procedures for updating system and user documentation prior to the release of the change
- A process for releasing that change into the live software

5 SWM LTD: SYSTEM DEFICIENCIES

> **Tutorial note.** You could have used the mnemonic 'ACCURATE' as a tool to kick-start your thinking relating to information deficiencies. The second part of this question demonstrates the need for an awareness of technical issues – although detailed technical knowledge is not required.

REPORT

To: Departmental Managers
From: Systems Accountant
Date: 4 May 200X
Subject: Recommendations for speeding up data processing

In response to the chief executive's memo of 21 April 200X, I have pleasure in enclosing a report on SWM's information system. The report focuses on current information deficiencies and how data processing could be speeded up.

Information deficiencies

The following information deficiencies are apparent in the system.

(i) The stock records held on the mainframe and used by the sales order team will inevitably show different positions from the warehouse's own stock control system on the warehouse minicomputer. Duplication of stock records in this way should be eliminated if possible.

(ii) The listings sent to the warehouse must sometimes include orders for out-of-stock items, as the records used for sales order booking are a day out of date at all times. Customers might be unhappy not to be notified that there is a problem when ordering.

(iii) It is not clear whether there is a procedure for same day despatch of urgent orders.

Question bank suggested solutions

(iv) Keying in of customer invoices in the accounts department is inefficient and provides a likely source of errors during input. Such re-keying of data should be eliminated.

(v) Provision of management information is, as noted in the company's own review, poor.

The first major issue is therefore for the company to ensure that the new database should hold a single set of stock records, available to all departments on both sites. Telecommunications links will eliminate the physical risks inherent in the use of couriers and will also allow all records to be updated at the same time. Similarly, billing details should be posted to ledgers without re-keying.

The second issue concerns management information. A system with a much more flexible reporting framework is required. A good database should allow this.

Speeding up processing

The comments above will enable all departments to have access to up-to-date data. Other suggestions for speeding up processing are as follows.

(i) An upgrade to the existing processor may be necessary. If the number of users or volume of transactions processed is higher than was ever envisaged when the existing system was purchased, it may be necessary to install a more powerful, and faster, processor.

(ii) An increase in available RAM (random access memory) would allow more relevant program files and data files to be stored in RAM. This would speed up processing.

(iii) The system could be redesigned so that more local processing is performed using PCs and perhaps minicomputers at local sites. The mainframe could then be used for the stock database and for bulk storage and printing applications. Local terminals could be replaced by processors and used for small/medium-sized local requirements.

(iv) An analysis could be performed of how time-critical various processing operations are. Batch processing of non-critical operations could be scheduled for overnight/weekend running: this might improve processing speeds for higher priority operations done during working hours.

(v) A new operating system (perhaps an open system) might be appropriate. This would be likely to provide improvements in processing speed. Of course, this might require the mainframe to be replaced too.

(vi) A separate processor designed specifically to deal with communications and related issues could be installed 'between' the mainframe and the terminals. This 'front-end processor' would deal with protocols, sending and receiving messages, terminal allocation, security and related technical matters, leaving the mainframe free to continue with processing.

Please contact me if you require further information.

6 SWM LTD: SECURITY AND ITEGRITY CONTROLS

> **Tutorial note.** If you have studied Section 5 of Chapter 10 you should have found this question straightforward. Remember to apply the theory to the situation at SWM Ltd.

Controls

Information is a vital resource of any organisation, and steps have to be taken to ensure its security and integrity as if it were any other valuable asset. Just as there are systems to ensure against theft or destruction of tangible assets, so too are measures taken to protect data and information.

Physical access

There are many possible threats to the integrity and privacy of data held in any system. There are basic physical dangers such as fire, which need guarding against. Controls to minimise risk include fireproof cabinets where important files are kept. Also, there are basic measures relating to physical access by unauthorised people to an organisation's premises. These physical controls relate both to the equipment and the storage media. Backup copies of data and programs, must be available in case of disasters.

Particular risks at SWM Ltd relate to the use of couriers and floppy disks to transfer data between sites. Even assuming back-ups are available, it is still possible that loss or corruption of disks could delay processing by 24 hours.

Question bank suggested solutions

In a new multi-user database system, the database will be held centrally, so the problem of physical access to the medium on which the data is stored will not be multiplied over several sites. Also, it will be easier to keep backup copies of one set of files than of several.

Logical access

The database contains data relating to a number of different applications, some of which might be for restricted viewing only. Access to the entire database should also be restricted. The type of control that will serve both functions is a password system, in which each user is given a unique code. The password can determine entry to the database, and also restrict users to specific views of it.

A further measure would be to restrict an individual user to one terminal, so that the password keyed in from that terminal could be checked to see that it corresponds in some way to the terminal itself.

For this system to work, passwords must be kept strictly confidential between users, and also as far as outsiders are concerned. Passwords should be changed regularly.

Communications

If data is transferred over a telecommunications link controls should aim to minimise the risks of hacking. Data sent over the link can be subjected to encryption and authentication procedures. Dial-back procedures can be used: they request callers to hang up and they then telephone the caller ensuring that the number is taken from a pre-set database.

Errors

The integrity of data can also be threatened by error. Human error can occur both in systems design and programming. Controls in the design stage, to avoid bugs, include adherence to programming standards, testing and so forth, before the database system is implemented. The same can be said for controls over system maintenance and updating. Proper documentation, testing and authorisation should minimise the risk of further design error.

Other forms of error can occur when the system is in use. To guard against this, there should be programmed controls over data input. These include check digits, range checks, format checks and so forth. The user interface can be so designed to make input of data strictly guided.

Personnel

Controls over personnel relate to a separation of functions as far as possible between programming staff and operational staff, so that operational staff do not have the opportunity to amend programs fraudulently, and so that programming staff do not get the opportunity to interfere with live data for fraudulent ends. For sensitive positions strict recruitment procedures should be followed.

With distributed systems, some of these controls are hard to maintain. In the situation outlined in this case, however, control over the database is maintained centrally so this is not so much of a problem.

7 SWM LTD: SOFTWARE MAINTENANCE

> **Tutorial note.** You should have found this question straightforward if you have studied Chapter 7 of this text. The answer below would have accumulated marks as follows:
>
> | | |
> |---|---|
> | Report format and clear layout | 2 |
> | Maintenance explanation | 2 |
> | Corrective maintenance | 6 |
> | Adaptive maintenance | 6 |
> | Perfective maintenance | 4 |
> | | 20 |

REPORT

To: Chief Executive
From: Management Accountant
Date: 10 May 200X
Subject: **Report on software maintenance**

Introduction

This report will explain the types of software maintenance necessary to ensure software remains efficient.

Question bank suggested solutions

Software maintenance is carried out for three possible reasons.

- To correct errors or 'bugs' (Corrective maintenance)
- To meet changes in internal operating procedures or external regulations (Adaptive maintenance)
- To keep up with new technical developments (Perfective maintenance)

We will look at each type of maintenance in turn.

Corrective maintenance

Testing procedures should identify most potential faults prior to installation. However, faults may not become apparent until certain combinations of conditions occur. Correction of these more obscure faults may be time-consuming and expensive.

Faults may also become apparent when consistently higher than expected volumes of data are processed. Volume limits are a key part of any transaction processing software and it is important that these are reviewed regularly to maintain efficiency. Increases in volume may require software and hardware upgrades (such as additional RAM).

Hardware failures can require changes to the operating system software. Additional warnings or error messages may be introduced. Procedures to back up files automatically when a system fails may be written into the software.

Some 'bugs' may only become apparent under certain hardware environments.

Adaptive maintenance

Software houses may regularly upgrade standard applications or general-purpose packages to provide additional features or make them user-friendlier. Customers need to decide whether to accept the upgrade, which is rarely supplied free of charge and will involve staff commitment to the new software. Non-acceptance of upgrades may lead to less effective support from the software supplier whose expertise is focused on the latest version of the package.

The operating procedures and needs of the user may change. This is very common with outputs such as reports and screen layouts, which are often changed to suit user requirements. Data processing operations are less often changed because they are more likely to reflect standard procedures whereas computer outputs evolve to meet the needs of the business. Many applications packages now allow users to customise the software (to a certain extent) themselves. For example, one person's 'standard' Excel spreadsheet screen may look different to another's - toolbars, the number of sheets, gridlines, the formula bar are all subject to user settings. Customised user generated reports are a common feature of accounting packages.

Hardware upgrades are common in larger systems and this often results in operating software being changed or entirely rewritten. Hardware changes range from a simple memory upgrade to changing from multi-user to networked systems.

External regulation often leads to mandatory changes in software, which can be quite extensive. A typical example is the change to various tax rates after the annual budget statement in the UK. These are normally straightforward and are often planned for in financial applications packages. However, the consequences of, for example, introducing multiple VAT rates would generally be complex and expensive for most businesses.

Perfective maintenance

Users may request enhancements to software which is not producing errors, but which could be made more user-friendly or improved in some other way. This may involve, for example, redesigning menu screens or switching to graphical user interfaces.

It may be possible to rewrite sections of programs to improve efficiency and response times. As noted above, output may be redesigned to provide better quality information. Off-the-shelf software products may undertake perfective maintenance in response to advances made in a competitor's product.

Conclusion

This report has explained the main types of software maintenance in general terms. Should you require more specific information, please ask.

Question bank suggested solutions

8 MFS: METHODOLOGIES AND PROJECT MANAGEMENT

> **Tutorial note.** Note how our answer is structured – a series of headings that match the question requirement, each followed by a short paragraph explaining the point being made.

REPORT

To: Managing Director MFS Ltd
From: Systems Accountant
Date: May 2000
Subject: Systems Development Projects

(a) The key features and benefits of a typical structured systems methodology are set out below.

Feature 1: Techniques

There is an emphasis on techniques. As an example, three techniques are used in SSADM: dataflow diagrams, logical data structures and entity life histories. For example, an event in an entity life history will match data flows which trigger processes on a dataflow diagram.

Benefits at MFS

These allow information to be cross-checked, and a 'picture' of the proposed system to be developed.

The emphasis on diagramming makes the system easier to understand for relevant parties, including users.

These techniques should ensure the system meets user data and information requirements. In other words, that the necessity for later enhancements is minimised.

Feature 2: Logical design

A logical design is produced that is independent of hardware and software.

Benefits at MFS

This logical design can be used as a basis for establishing what hardware and software is required.

It is unclear what information was used on which to base the purchase of the new server at MFS. This should be investigated, as should the actual suitability of the machine chosen.

Feature 3: User involvement

User involvement is a critical factor in the success of any development.

Benefits at MFS

A methodology provides a framework for communication between users and developers.

Feature 4: Documentation and development standards

Methodologies require documentation to be produced throughout the project, and provide a set of development standards that all parties must adhere to.

Benefits at MFS

This gives a comprehensive and detailed picture of the system and helps understanding of the system. The consequences of proposed changes can be seen clearly.

Feature 5: Methodology and control

The structured framework of a methodology helps with planning. It defines the tasks to be performed and sets out when they should be done.

Benefits at MFS

This allows control by reference to actual achievements rather than to estimates. Users are able to see progress clearly.

Where does this leave the current 'Centralisation Project'?

We need to let users know that the project will be proceeding, and emphasise the benefits it will bring. However, we should acknowledge that mistakes have been made in the implementation, and advise that the project is to be re-planned with significant user input.

Question bank suggested solutions

A more efficient way of working during the transitional phase has to be found. Regulatory reporting must take priority, something the amended project plan must allow for.

(b) Possible reasons why systems development projects at MFS are rarely completed within schedule are outlined below.

Drawback 1. SDLC approach is geared towards transaction processing

Currently at MFS, an early form of the Systems Development Lifecycle (SDLC) approach to systems development is used. The SDLC is efficient at automating operational areas within easily defined processing requirements, such as payroll, where the aim is to speed up high-volume transaction processing.

Such an approach is not entirely appropriate at MFS, where a management information system is the main new feature.

How could this be improved?

A methodology (as described in part (a)) is more suited to dealing with the more complex issues surrounding a MIS.

Drawback 2. User requirements poorly defined

User requirements ultimately determine the structure of the system. The initial system design aims to facilitate the production of output that the user has specified to be required.

If output requirements are altered during systems development, this can result in substantial design modifications. A simple change in user requirements costs over 10 times as much to rectify after acceptance testing than after the design phase This is likely to be a problem at MFS, given the lack of user involvement.

How could this be improved?

If a methodology were to be used, the user would be involved throughout the process, reducing the risk of differences between requirements and actual development.

A methodology that encourages user involvement and invites management at all levels to specify their requirements should be adopted. This may lead to a potentially beneficial rethink of the way the organisation carries out its activities.

Inadequate systems development documentation

Although no details of documentation standards are provided in the scenario, the lateness of many systems could be due to inadequately documented modifications causing confusion and 'bugs' elsewhere in the system.

How could this be improved?

A methodology should be adopted that includes clear documentation standards.

Applications backlog

Time overruns on old projects reduce the time key personnel can spend on new projects. At the same time, 'mission critical' old systems must be maintained so essential operations can continue (eg regulatory reporting).

How could this be improved?

A methodology would ensure that development is done in the same way each time and thus provides a realistic basis for estimation. More realistic schedules should reduce time overruns and provide a basis for management control.

Conclusion

The factors outlined above show that the current traditional systems development approach used at MFS is not producing the results required. Therefore, I recommend that we switch entirely to a structured methodology.

Recognised project-planning techniques such as work-breakdown structure and Gantt Charts should be used to enable a more realistic schedule to be established. The schedules for systems implementations in the past have been based on guess-work, resulting in unrealistic deadlines.

Question bank suggested solutions

9 MFS: CASE TOOLS AND PROTOTYPING

> **Tutorial note**. A straightforward question that is able to be answered using information from Chapter 5 of this book.

MEMORANDUM

To: Managing Director MFS Ltd
From: Systems Accountant
Date: May 200X
Subject: Prototyping and CASE TOOLS

Prototyping

Systems prototyping encourages the user to participate actively in the systems design and development process. Rather than producing a detailed specification the prototyping approach aims at producing a simplified version of the system, a prototype, which the user may then try out. Typically, the user might be able to try out data input screens or perform file enquiries.

The advantage of this approach is that the user actually sees a system in operation and can judge its usefulness and operation. This is extremely useful for users who are unfamiliar with information systems since they often revise their specifications as they become more familiar with the system's workings.

This approach greatly reduces last-minute system modifications or enhancements - users can notice deficiencies before systems are delivered so that specifications may more fully address user needs.

CASE tools

Structured methods are reasonably widely used in a number of organisations. They are mandatory in many government IT functions. Their use, although standardising many results, does impose quite an overhead in terms of increased demands for correct form filling at stages of the software production process, as well as a requirement for larger amounts of other paperwork particularly in relation to updates and standards.

CASE tools can reduce the effort required to perform some of the stages of the structured methodology by automatically producing the required stages. Many CASE tools go some way towards producing working programs.

The CASE tool should provide the following facilities.

(i) Support for the methodology used by the IT function.

(ii) Ability to interface directly to the central data dictionary.

(iii) Access and version control, to prevent unauthorised use and to ensure the right 'master' is being worked on.

(iv) Graphical prototyping facilities to assist in the production of reports, screens etc.

(v) Ability to assess the impact of changes and also to validate design work.

(vi) Facilities called code-generators to produce program output in a variety of programming languages.

(vii) Ability to function on a reasonable-specification PC while maintaining control for a multi-member team.

Conclusion

We should give serious consideration to the use of prototyping and CASE tools to speed up our systems development. Prototyping in particular will increase user participation, as will greater emphasis on a structured method. These measures should contribute significantly to the development of quality systems.

Question bank suggested solutions

10 MFS: SYSTEMS DEVELOPMENT AND PROJECT MANAGEMENT

> **Tutorial note.** As with many questions, there are a wide range of possible answers that could have scored well. The suggested approach to project management in the answer below shows how theories may be adapted to suit the circumstances described in the question.

REPORT

To: Managing Director MFS Ltd
From: Systems Accountant
Date: May 200X
Subject: Project management at MFS

The introduction of a new computer system has the potential to cause considerable disruption to an organisation.

Some problems are presently being experienced at MFS, particularly in connection with the transitional arrangements during the development of the new system. For example the 'going live' extension from 18 months to 2 years suggests that personnel costs will be at least one third over budget.

Project management techniques can help monitor and control projects. The principles are outlined below.

A **project** involves the management of a number of **disparate, yet interdependent tasks**, within a **timetable** and a **budget** set in advance. A particular project is unique, in that by its nature once done it is never repeated.

Efficient management of the resources and process of the project is vital if the project is to be completed successfully – that is on time, within budget and to the required quality.

The consistent lateness of IT related projects at MFS Ltd imply the organisation would benefit from the application of appropriate project management techniques. Workable policies need to be developed as soon as possible to prevent further damage being done to the company, for example through regulatory breaches and a further reduction in employee morale.

A suggested approach to project management

Step 1

> **Form the Project Board or steering committee.** A steering committee comprising senior user department personnel, a member of the finance department and various systems professionals should be appointed to oversee the project.

Step 2

> **Appoint a project manager.** This person will manage and oversee the execution of the project, and is responsible for its successful completion. The project manager presents the timetable and budget to the steering committee for their approval and authorisation.

Step 3

> **Plan the project.** The **goals** of the project are identified, and the **tasks needed to achieve them** are outlined. These are then matched to the manpower resources available, so that a **Project Plan** can be outlined and agreed. Tools such as work-breakdown structure, Critical Path Analysis and Gantt charts are useful aids. The schedule will indicate **when** each task has to be completed, and in **which order**. **Each stage** of the project is then planned in its own right. The stages of the project may be determined by the systems development methodology adopted.

Step 4

> **Control the project.** Actual outcomes are compared to the plan, and any discrepancies investigated and addressed as soon as they become apparent.
>
> The monitoring process should take into account four criteria.
>
> - **Time**, by reference to critical path analysis or Gantt charts.
> - **Resources**, by measuring available resources and percentage utilisation.
> - **Costs**, by reference to the MIS and budgets.

Question bank suggested solutions

- **Quality**, as appropriate.

Regular progress meetings should be held by the project manager with members of the project team to monitor performance.

Specified **documentation** is produced at the end of each stage for review and approval, in accordance with quality control criteria established.

At the end of each stage, progress will be reported to the steering committee. **Users** should be consulted, as their approval is necessary to demonstrate that the project is meeting its objectives.

Step 5

Complete the project. The resulting system must meet the technical criteria (Quality) specified (eg response times). All relevant documentation must be completed to an adequate standard, project files must be complete and there should be a clear relationship evidenced between the work done in the various successive stages of the project.

Step 6

Post-implementation audit. The project should be reviewed in terms of both the **technical quality** of the output, and the **efficiency** with which project tasks and management were carried out.

Stakeholders' feedback should be gained to ensure all viewpoints are covered.

Lessons that can be learned from the project should be documented to prevent the same mistakes being made on similar projects in the future.

11 ABC LTD: ERM, OFF-THE-SHELF SOFTWARE, INTEGRATED ACCOUNTS PACKAGE

> **Tutorial note**. Ensure you are able to apply diagramming techniques such as ERM, DFD and ELH – they crop up regularly in examination questions.

(a) See the ERM on the following page.

Question bank suggested solutions

(a) (i)

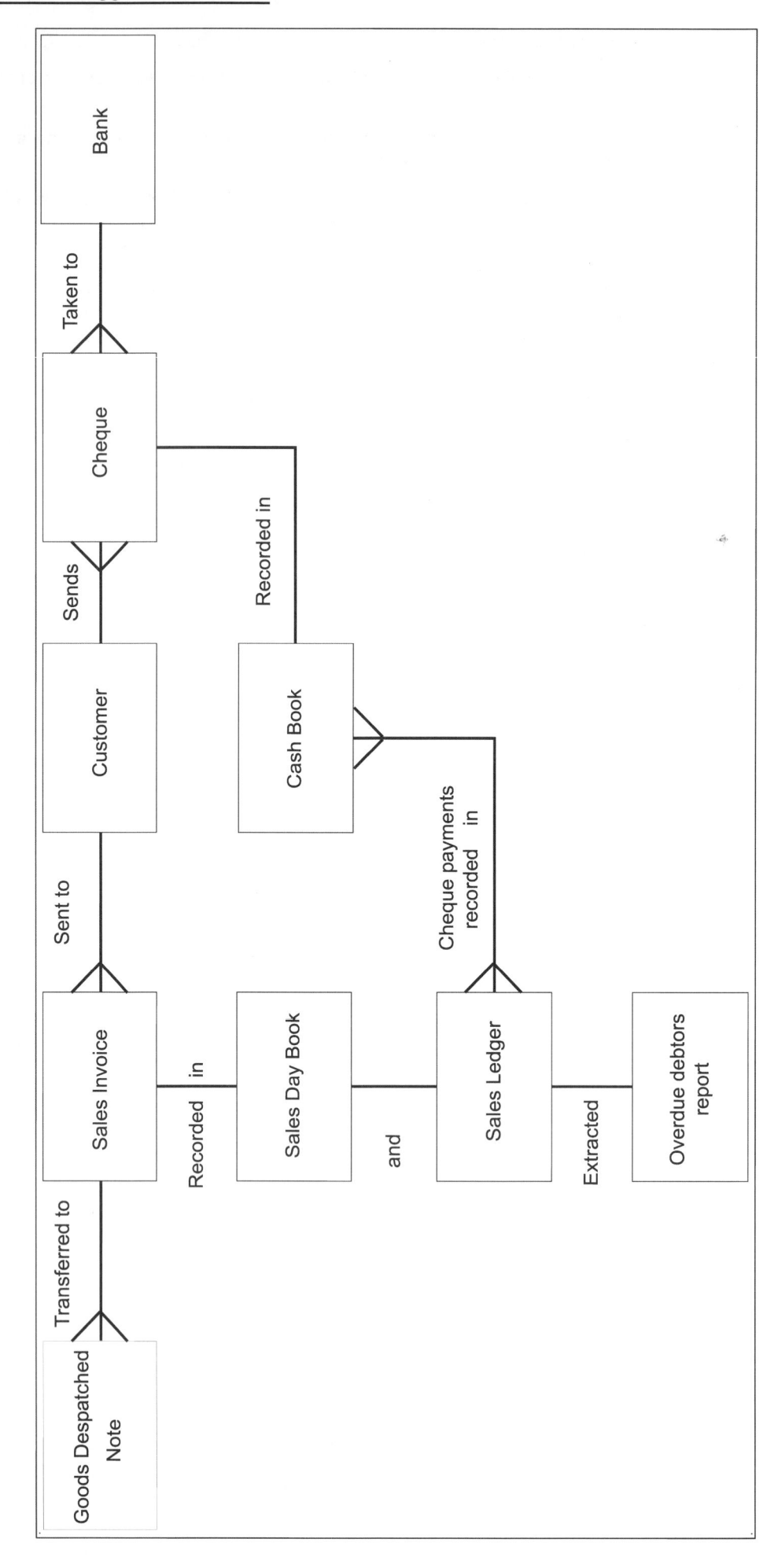

Entity Relationship Model - ABC Ltd Sales and cheque receipts

Goods Despatched Note —Transferred to→ Sales Invoice —Recorded in→ Sales Day Book —and→ Sales Ledger —Extracted→ Overdue debtors report

Sales Invoice —Sent to→ Customer —Sends→ Cheque —Taken to→ Bank

Cheque —Recorded in→ Cash Book —Cheque payments recorded in→ Sales Ledger

402

Question bank suggested solutions

(b) (i) The benefits of purchasing an off-the-shelf accounting package will include:

- **Fewer errors**

The current software package has at least one major programming error in it, namely the lack of appropriate updating of the cost price of stock items. Off-the-shelf packages will be extensively tested before being released, which will help to ensure that these types of errors are eliminated. Releasing a package with errors would very quickly undermine the integrity of the package, with sales falling and the company writing the software potentially not being able to continue in business.

- **Automatic updates**

The software in ABC has remained unchanged since it was written. During this time, there could have been amendments to accounting policies, presentation of information etc. which would not have been reflected in the software. A third party package would be automatically updated for these changes with updates to the software being distributed as and when required. The software will be technically up-to-date.

- **Telephone support when necessary**

It appears that staff in ABC were unaware of the errors in the software, and even if the errors were discovered would be unsure about the appropriate course of action. A third party vendor will normally provide telephone support so queries about the software can be quickly and easily resolved.

- **Documentation and Training**

There is no reference to the provision of appropriate documentation on the software (either technical or training material). Again, a third party would be able to provide appropriate documentation to support the use of the software, and may even provide training courses in the use of that software for staff. This will help implementation and decrease the learning curve and errors made in using the software.

(ii)

Weaknesses in the sales and cheque receipts system, and how a computerised integrated accounts package could help to overcome them:

- **Numeric Sequence of Despatch Notes**

The Despatch Notes are currently filed in date order, with no check on the numeric sequence. It is possible that goods have been despatched, but the Despatch Note lost; in this case a sales invoice will not be raised. This error will not be identified due to the lack of numeric sequence check on Despatch Notes.

A computer system will be able to track the actual numbers of Despatch Notes entered into the system and provide an exception report on any missing numbers. The report can be produced whether or not the Despatch Notes are entered in sequence or not. Missing Despatch Notes will be identified and input to avoid loss of sales revenue.

- **Transposition Errors on Sales Invoices**

When Despatch Note information is entered onto the sales invoices, transposition errors can occur. If the Despatch Note number is not recorded correctly, then it will not be possible to check back from the sales invoice to the Despatch Note in case of queries with the invoice.

Entering Despatch Note information onto an invoice pro-forma will allow the computer to check that number for accuracy. Including a check digit within the number (so that any keying errors result in the check digit calculation being incorrect) is a standard way of providing this check. Any Despatch Note numbers highlighted as being incorrect can be re-input using hopefully the correct number.

- **Re-inputting of sales invoice information**

Sales invoices are recorded and printed out from a Word Processor, before being re-input into the main Sales Day Book and Sales Ledger systems. This wastes time of the staff in ABC as well as increasing the possibility of input errors taking place.

Using an integrated system will mean that after the sales invoice has been completed, it will be stored within the system and the SDB and S/L will be updated automatically; there will be no need for re-input of information. This will provide significant decreases in time taken to input sales details and decrease error rates.

Question bank suggested solutions

- **Access to stock ledgers**

When sales invoices are produced, all the Despatch Note information including stock details and quantities sold are entered by hand. This may take a significant amount of time, because many items such as stock codes and descriptions will have to be entered onto each invoice.

Linking the invoicing system with the stock system will eliminate this work; entering a stock code will allow the appropriate sections of the sales invoice to be completed by transferring relevant details such as description and price charged from the stock system. If necessary, the stock quantities could also be updated with the items sold.

- **Incorrect information**

There does not appear to be an adequate facility to allow for the part-payment of invoices on the current computer system. If a part payment is recognised as a full payment, then income may be lost because the debt cannot be located easily in the 'part payments' section of the debtors report.

A modern computerised system will allow part payments, and show part paid invoices against the main debtor name. This will help maintain a better control over debtors in ABC because all amounts outstanding will be allocated to specific debtors.

12 ABC LTD: THE INTERNET

> **Tutorial note.** Note the simple slide design in the answer that follows – you are not expected to produce elaborate slides under examination conditions. Often, a series of heading is all that is required.

(a)

```
Internet basics
Technology
www
Web browsers
Websites
Internet Service Providers
```

Technology. The Internet is the name given to the technology that allows any computer with a telecommunications link to exchange information with any other suitably equipped computer.

The Internet is also called the World Wide Web (**www**), information superhighway or cyberspace, although technically it is the 'Web' that makes the Internet easy to use

Web browsers are the software loaded on Internet enabled computers to allow them to view information from the Internet.

Internet information is contained on **Websites**, which range from a few pages about one individual to large sites offering a range of services, such as Amazon.co.uk and Lastminute.com.

Access to the Internet is provided by Internet Service Providers (unless the organisation is large enough to run its own web connection). For a small fee, an Internet connection is made via the telephone line to the ISP and then onto the www itself.

Question bank suggested solutions

Obtaining information

Web browsers

Search Engines

Advertising

Page design

Cookies

As noted above **Web browsers** allow www pages to be displayed on the users' computer. The most common browsers are Internet Explorer and Netscape Navigator.

Because the Internet contains millions of pages of information, **Search Engines** can be used to locate the information you need. Popular search engines include Yahoo! and AskJeeves. Search engines obtain their income by selling advertising space and 'links' to other web pages on their information pages.

An attractive **page design** is needed to attract people to a site, while the information must be provided quickly and accurately to maintain interest and ensure that the site is visited again.

Many Internet sites store **cookies**, or small files of information, on the users' computer. The cookies act as a signal to the web site that the user has been to the site before, so the content of the site can be tailored to that users' preferences.

Other Internet information

Security

Viruses

Anti-virus programs

e-mail

Security on the Internet can be poor because most Internet communications can be copied without the user knowing this has happened. Additional security is needed if the Internet is to be used for trading, rather than just viewing information.

Because the Internet has no official regulation system, some potentially dangerous programmes called computer viruses can be found on it. A virus is a computer program which is designed to damage the software or hardware of the computer receiving the virus.

To guard against viruses damaging software or hardware, you need to have an **anti-virus program** running when the Internet is accessed. This program detects and warns the user about virus programs before they can do any damage.

The Internet also allows communication via **e-mail** between individuals. E-mail is not secure (because the Internet is not secure, as noted above) so any communication must be treated like a post-card, that is it can be read by anyone intercepting the e-mail.

Using the Internet for Business to Consumer trading

What does this mean?

Benefits to customers

Benefits to the organisation

Hardware requirements

Software requirements

Allow payments over Internet?

Question bank suggested solutions

What does this mean? Trading on the Internet from Business to Consumer means providing goods or services for sale via an Internet site.

Customers access the organisation's web page, select the goods or services required and then order (and sometimes pay for) these items on the Internet, without reference to any other individual.

The **benefits to customers** are normally the ability to check stock levels quickly, obtain competitive quotes for goods and then order those items direct from their computer without having to go to a shop.

The **benefits to the organisation** are normally increased sales with fewer overheads (less sales staff needed). However, there are other factors to take into consideration such maintaining the web site, comparing competitors' prices and ensuring goods are delivered on time.

There are also significant **hardware requirements** which are explained in part (ii).

Software requirements can also be extensive. Software needed will include firewall (to stop unauthorised access and prevent computer viruses entering the company's computer systems), on-line stock system and Internet software to provide this link between the stock system and customers.

If **payments over the Internet** are allowed, then additional software and security systems for taking credit card information and encrypting this for transfer over the Internet, will also be required.

Using the Internet for Business to Business trading

What does this mean?

Benefits to purchasers

Benefits to sellers

Hardware requirements

Software requirements

What does this mean? Selling Business-to-Business is similar to selling Business-to-Consumer, although now the trading is carried out between different organisations. The trading normally means exchanging electronic information such as sales and purchase orders and invoices, with goods being transferred in the normal way. In most situations, information is exchanged via secure links to a central trading site where orders are placed and bids are received from suppliers.

The main **benefit to purchasers** is that they can obtain competitive quotes quickly from a number of suppliers, and then place orders quickly and efficiently, rather than relying on the post (with delays in waiting for letters to be received) or telephone where order information may be transferred incorrectly).

The main **benefit to sellers** is that they can access a worldwide market, rather than a local or national market. Sellers may also be at a disadvantage because price competition will become more acute, while not having an Internet site may limit sales if customers expect to trade in this way.

Hardware requirements are similar to business-to-consumer trading, explained in part (iii).

Software requirements are likely to be more onerous than business to consumer trading because there may be specialist software trading programs already in use by organisations, and the protocols in these programs will have to be matched to enable ABC or any other company to start trading here.

Conclusions

Internet

Business to Consumer

Business to Business

On-line payments

The **Internet** provides a new trading medium.

Business-to-Consumer trading should be considered by ABC Ltd because competitors are already using this medium and ABC may lose significant amounts of sales if it not adopted.

Question bank suggested solutions

Business-to-Business trading in terms of exchanging order information is less important for ABC because Business-to-Consumer trading can be used for these activities.

Providing **on-line payment** systems will be more complicated than just order information; allowing payment by invoice will allow some competitive advantage over competitors.

(b)

The hardware that ABC will require for Internet trading will include:

- A server with sufficient capacity to maintain the Internet software, including firewall, stock database and links to the other hardware.

- On-line terminals to be used by staff in ABC to update the stock database with new stock lines and deliveries of existing lines so that the database shows correct balances of stock available.

- A connection to the Internet, probably using a telephone connection with a modem or equivalent device, although hopefully with digital rather than analogue transmission. Digital transmissions are quicker than analogue.

- A printer to produce hard copies of customer orders to act as a picking list in the stock room and possibly an input document to the sales system. It is possible that the Internet server will be kept completely separate from ABC's other computer system to provide additional security against viruses etc. If this is the case then some method will be required to transfer sales information from the stock server to the sales system. The hard copy picking list is one method of doing this.

- Appropriate cabling to join all the other items of hardware together.

13 ABC LTD: SWOT ANALYSIS, SERVICE QUALITY

> **Tutorial note.** SWOT analysis is a key technique – ensure you are able to apply this framework to a wide range of situations.

REPORT

To: Board of ABC Ltd
From: Project Manager
Subject: SWOT analysis and quality control
Date: May 200X

(a) **SWOT analysis**

As requested in your Board meeting of April 1st 200X, I present a SWOT analysis for ABC Ltd.

A SWOT analysis involves looking at the Strengths, Weaknesses, Opportunities and Threats facing an organisation. While this analysis may not be complete, it does provide appropriate guidance on these areas and therefore indicates courses of action that the Board should consider taking to build on the strengths and opportunities and guard against the weaknesses and threats.

- **Strengths**

    Customer relations

    ABC has excellent relations between its staff and customers, because staff are willing to take the time to find out exactly what customers want. However, service can be slow and the Internet may provide a threat in this area.

    Workforce

    The workforce are on the whole loyal to ABC, with the high retention rate pointing to good staff management policies.

Question bank suggested solutions

Product range

The product range is extensive, with more lines available than competitors, apparently including those with Internet sites.

- **Weaknesses**

   'Old' feel to company – personal service

   The provision of relatively slow personal service may be seen as a weakness in some situations. Most businesses today try and combine service with speed of delivery, hence the use of Internet sites. ABC needs to provide some formal staff training to start to introduce these concepts of service while investigating Internet selling as a method of keeping up with competition and possibly providing some advantage.

   No recent investment in technology

   There has been very little investment in computers for the last few years. While the systems may appear adequate to support the current business, they are inadequate to support new areas such as Internet selling and the MIS / integrated accounts package that are needed to run the company efficiently. There will be limits to how far personal service can be relied upon to overcome these weaknesses.

   Internal pricing issues

   The problem noted with stock pricing is worrying, especially as this means that prices may have to be increased. Whether price increases will adversely affect trade remains to be seen. However, there is also the issue to address that there may be other errors in the company's systems that have not yet come to light. Some additional expenditure may be needed to check the integrity of all systems currently being used.

- **Opportunities**

   Use Internet for better service product range.

   While the use of the Internet provides a threat, it also provides an opportunity. ABC should be able to set up a trading site on the Internet comparatively quickly. Providing the option for customers to pay by cheque, rather than by credit card over the Internet will decrease the time needed to build the website as security protocols will be less complicated. Allowing this option will also provide some competitive advantage for ABC (as long as competitors don't follow suit).

   Similarly, ABC's extensive product range may be another source of competitive advantage. If other companies cannot match the range, then hopefully customers will be more attracted to ABC's site.

- **Threats**

   Internet service of competitors

   The provision of Internet service by competitors is a threat to ABC because at the moment, the company cannot match this service. If Internet trading becomes more of a standard, then sales in ABC will almost certainly decline. The directors have made an appropriate move by employing a consultant to investigate this area. The provision of a timely report should be recommended.

   ABC's customers

   ABC has a loyal customer base; however other trading options like the Internet or more attractive prices may start to erode this loyalty. The challenge is knowing how to maintain customer loyalty, while trying to implement systems which appear to duplicate competitors and may therefore decrease that loyalty.

   Culture at ABC

   The main threat to ABC is the continuation of business. With influences like different selling media becoming more important, ABC may need to update its culture to be technologically up-to-date and provide a much faster service if it wants to survive.

(b)

Quality of service

The quality of service currently being provided by ABC is good. In fact some customer loyalty has been built up around good quality service. However, just because quality is good now, does not mean that actions cannot be taken to enhance that quality in the future. In particular, the Board need to take account of trends in service, such as speed of delivery, that will impact severely on the quality provided by ABC in the next few years.

Specific actions that the Board can consider now include:

- **Starting a Total Quality Management system**

    The idea of Total Quality Management (TQM) is to implement a system of continuous improvement which focuses on the need to meet customer expectations. One of the basic principles of TQM is that the cost of preventing mistakes is less than the cost of correcting them. If customers are going to be attracted by other forms of selling, or require more efficient service, then the 'mistake' for ABC will be not to start to put systems into place now that will meet those expectations.

    The Board of ABC Ltd can start preparing staff now by:

    ○ Establishing quality circles or other similar discussion groups to discuss the quality of customer service and implement methods of improving this

    ○ Providing appropriate training in current best practice in customer service

    ○ Asking customers to record instances of good service

    ○ Providing positive feedback to staff on the success of any initiative, such as increases in sales or increases in customer satisfaction ratings.

    ○ Implementing these actions now rather than later will help staff prepare for any necessary change in the method of service.

- **Training in how to use new technology**

    Other initiatives within ABC will involve the use of up-to-date computer technology. As it is likely that staff in ABC are relatively senior (low staff turnover implies an ageing workforce), then there may be some fear of both the introduction of this technology from the point-of-view of job losses or actually using the technology. The Board need to provide re-assurance that job losses will not take place, and also provide appropriate training in the use of the new systems. This will help to alleviate any concerns from staff, while helping them enhance their skills.

- **Investors in People**

    With an increase in investment in staff training and development, ABC could apply for recognition of this with schemes such as Investors in People (or an appropriate local or country based scheme). Obtaining the award would be recognition for ABC of its care for the workforce and provide an incentive to employees to continue to enhance their skills as ABC Ltd would presumably assist them.

- **ISO 9001**

    There are also various International Standards Organisation (ISO) schemes that ABC Ltd can apply for. ISO 9001 is the standard for quality management systems. Applying for and obtaining this award will reassure all that deal with ABC that they are dealing with a reputable, well-run organisation.

Question bank suggested solutions

14 ABC LTD: IMPLEMENTATION STAGES, INFORMATION QUALITY AND CONTROL

> **Tutorial note.** Both parts of this question are 'typical' in that they require you to explain a theory or concept and **apply** it to a given situation.

MEMORANDUM

To: Chairman of ABC Ltd
From: Project Manager
Subject: MIS and quality of information
Date: May 200X

This memorandum aims to provide an overview on how any new MIS would be implemented into ABC Ltd and also provides a summary of the benefits that can be expected from the provision of higher quality information from the MIS.

(a) *Stages for the implementation of a new MIS*

The implementation of any new system tends to follow a set procedure. I will outline the stages of the Systems Development Life Cycle in this memo, although other techniques are just as valid. After providing a brief explanation of each stage, I will show how that stage is relevant to ABC Ltd.

- Identification of a problem

This stage involves an analysis of an organisation's information requirements. The analysis is carried out in conjunction with the users of the system so that the actual requirements, rather than likely requirements, can be determined.

Within ABC Ltd you have already recognised the need for a MIS, although time has precluded any effective system from being implemented. Recent errors within the stock system also highlight the need for additional management control. Having accepted that additional management information is necessary, I will need to have discussions with the various managers / Board members to identify exactly what information they require. These discussions will normally take place after I have reviewed the objectives and systems within ABC so I am aware of what your company does, and the different sources of information available to any new MIS. It is possible that I may be able to suggest additional information that will be useful, but managers have not considered simply due to lack of knowledge of what is available from a MIS.

- Feasibility study

This stage normally involves a review of the existing system and the generation of a range of possible solutions for the new MIS. One system will be selected based on the costs and benefits of the available systems.

As there is no existing system, this will make the feasibility stage easier. Taking the requirements from the *problem identification* stage I will review what MIS's are available and provide a summary of the costs and benefits of each system. The Board will need to make a decision at the end of this stage on which system to implement, although you will have cost information to assist you. Given that there is no existing system, and very few information systems to provide data for the MIS, any solution is likely to be relatively expensive compared to a situation where a MIS is being replaced.

- Systems investigation

This is a detailed investigation into the existing system to obtain information on response times, data volumes and other key indicators.

Given that there is no existing MIS, this stage will actually focus on checking what information is already produced by the current systems in ABC, and then determining how this can be incorporated into the new MIS. It is likely that the MIS will have to generate a lot of the required information. However, as other computerised systems are improved, then these can be designed to feed additional information into the MIS so enhancing the value of information obtained from it.

However, it will be important now to set standards for information to be produced by the MIS and further discussions with the Board and managers will be required to ensure that the detailed information provision will be appropriate.

- Systems analysis

Systems analysis involves a detailed analysis of existing systems to determine why methods are being used, what the alternative methods are and what the performance criteria for the systems should be.

Again, due to the lack of up-to-date systems within ABC, in this stage I will actually be checking documentation like the Entity Relationship Model (from question 1) to check how systems in ABC actually work. In particular, I will be reviewing the specification of the integrated accounts package that will be purchased to ensure it fits the current working methods and also provides appropriate outputs that the MIS can use. In other areas like stock control and sales, I will check that the output from these systems are appropriate, and possibly recommend enhancements to other areas of ABC to provide better or more up-to-date management information.

- Systems design

Having obtained all the information about the existing systems, the proposed accounts package and the possible MIS's, this stage involves producing a detailed systems design for the new MIS.

Here, I will concentrate on showing precisely what outputs will be produced, how those outputs will be produced by the MIS, and what inputs will be expected to provide the outputs. Where possible, electronic links to the accounts package will be provided, with manual links to other less computerised systems for now. Again, as other systems are upgraded, more direct links into the MIS can be made.

- Systems implementation

As the name suggests, in this stage the MIS will be implemented into ABC Ltd.

The main issues with implementation are likely to be the linking to other accounts packages, and ensuring that staff are aware of the inputs that will be required to ensure that the MIS functions effectively. As the MIS is not replacing any existing system, it can be tested during implementation without affecting existing processing, although some overtime may be needed to trial the input of data and understanding and checking of the accuracy of management information output. When both the users and myself are happy with the quality of information being produced, it can formally 'go live' to start to provide the information you require.

- Review and maintenance

This is an ongoing process which checks that the objectives set at the beginning of the feasibility study have been met, and that the performance of the system is satisfactory.

At this stage, I will need to check again with managers / Board members that they are receiving the information they expect. I will also need to review other areas of ABC to start feasibility studies to upgrade the information systems there.

(b) *How the control of the business will be improved by the provision of higher quality information.*

Providing information via the MIS will enhance your control of ABC in various ways.

In general terms, the overall focus of your management style will become more 'hands on' or proactive. The situation to date appears to have been to let the company 'run itself', whether this has occurred by accident or design. In the future, you will have more information and can therefore be more pro-active in your approach to business management. This change may need discussing with your fellow directors and staff first so that the change in management style can be seen as a positive attitude rather than have the appearance of not trusting staff.

Having up-do-date information will mean that business decisions can be made more quickly. This will be particularly important if the Board decides to start trading on the Internet. This medium tends to be very price sensitive, so more frequent revisions to prices in response to competitors' actions may be necessary.

The MIS can be programmed to generate exception reports to highlight unusual or large items. For example, when access to the stock files is obtained, the problem of selling goods below cost price can be identified as being 'unusual'. Similarly, warnings can be generated on items with very low stock levels, or items with high stock levels that are no longer selling particularly well. Appropriate action can be taken to amend the selling price or quantities ordered for those items. In other words, management can focus on the important aspects of the business rather than wasting time reviewing detailed reports to find these exceptional items for themselves.

Over time, historical information about the performance of ABC will be accumulated. This will assist the Directors in production of business plans as trends in profits, sales etc. will become apparent.

Question bank suggested solutions

Planning will also be assisted now as a model of the business can be built within the MIS. The effect of changing key variables such as standard mark-up on items sold can be determined. The effects of amending strategy, for example to move into new product areas or different methods of selling (such as the Internet) can also be modelled with estimates of profits at different levels of sales being generated.

The Integrated accounts package should provide information on aged debtors. However, this information can also be used by the MIS to track debtors ageing over time to try and match this to changes in credit terms offered, pricing or even methods of selling. An analysis of this information will enable the board to make more effective decisions to limit the amount of debtors in the future.

15 FRS LTD: DISTRIBUTED AND CENTRALISED PROCESSING, INFORMATION FOR DECISION MAKING

> **Tutorial note.** This is an excellent question requiring the application of book knowledge to the question described at FRS Ltd. The answer provided is also of a very high quality – both in structure and content.

REPORT

To: Chief Executive FRS Ltd
From: Management Consultant
Date: 29 April 200X
Subject: Introduction of IT systems

(a) The new Information system at FRS could be set up to process data using either distributed or centralised multi-user processing. An outline of the differences between the two follows.

Distributed processing utilises multiple processing units distributed around the system. The processors are linked (preferably via dedicated ISDN lines), enabling the transfer and utilisation of data held at different locations. Distributed processing is characterised by:

- Computers spread over a wide geographical area
- Shared data files
- The processing of data at more than one location

MRO Inc operates a form of distributed processing. Each local shop has its own processing capability (usually a PC). These processors are linked together with neighbouring outlets forming a Local Area Network (LAN). Each LAN is linked to MRO head office, forming a Wide Area Network (WAN). This network provides a means of communication between all shops and each other, as well as with head office.

Centralised multi-user processing describes the situation where all data is processed in a central location, such as head office. At the head office there will be a reasonably powerful computer (probably a mainframe) holding all the program and data files utilised by the system.

The hardware at individual shops would therefore not require processing or data storage capability. This would enable the installation of 'dumb terminals' – essentially a keyboard and screen linked to the central computer.

Many users are able to access the central processing unit at the same time, and process data simultaneously. If FRS Ltd adopted a multi-user system the terminals would be located in individual shops, and connected by an external data link.

(b) The **relative merits** of implementing the type of information system used by MRO Inc include:

Sharing of information

The MRO network solution would enable the sharing of information through the use of e-mail, bulletin boards and if justified the setting up of a group intranet. The IT infrastructure could be used as a tool to provide cohesion to the group, and encourage communication between individual shops.

Enhanced management information

Head office will be able to view summary level information using the Executive Information System (EIS). If further detail is required, management would be able to 'drill down' to view underlying data, such as the performance of individual shops.

More relevant information

Under the MRO system, each shop would have access to its own data and information, allowing more informed decisions to be made. The EPOS and EFTPOS systems would allow each shop to capture sales and customer data, which could be used in stock management and marketing promotions.

Less risk of complete system failure

Each shop has its own processing capability, so a problem in a single location will not prevent operations continuing as normal elsewhere. If centralised processing as suggested by Mr. Black was adopted, a problem with the central computer would affect all shops.

Greater flexibility

Distributed processing allows for greater flexibility in systems design. If an individual shop has a specific requirement this can be built into the system. For example, an individual shop manager may have the ability and inclination to use spreadsheet software as a management tool. Office software could be purchased and offered to be installed on the shop PC. Greater flexibility is also provided regarding possible future changes to the system.

(c) **Information for decision making**

There are three levels of information within an organisation: strategic, tactical and operational.

Strategic information is 'high level' information relating to the organisation as a whole. It is used to plan the medium- to long-term objectives of the organisation to monitor and control progress towards those objectives. Strategic information should include external as well as internal data, as the external environment is a major influence on organisation performance. Some strategic reports should be produced on a regular basis, eg a monthly summary of group performance.

Strategic decisions have to take into account a wide range of variables. A system that gathers and analyses information relating to those variables is required to support strategic decision making. An **Executive Information System (EIS)** is used for this task. The EIS is in effect a corporate model, which enables key information to be analysed.

At the other end of the information spectrum is **operational information**. Operational information is:

- Related to day-to-day operations (transaction-based)
- Derived from internal sources
- Detailed
- Prepared regularly, preferably in a standard format
- Transaction-based

For FRS Ltd this would include the daily recording of (for each shop):

- Employee hours
- Stock levels
- Daily sales
- Banking and cash 'float' details

The majority of operational information would be recorded on transaction-based systems. In FRS Ltd sales transactions would be captured electronically at the point of sale, while other data such as employee hours would require manual input. The data would feed into the relevant modules of an **integrated accounting system** (eg sales ledger, purchase ledger, cashbook and payroll).

A real-time integrated accounting system such as that used by MRO provides the advantages of easy posting and reconciliation between modules and constantly up-to-date information on which to base decisions eg stock items that require re-ordering, quick or slow moving product lines.

Between strategic and operational information is **tactical information**. Tactical information is:

- Wider in scope than operational data - but still mainly internal
- Short- to medium-term based
- Usually summarised (eg monthly sales of a singe shop, delicatessen profitability over a range of shops)
- Often presented in the form of a comparison (eg actual against plan)

Question bank suggested solutions

Tactical decisions are often based on data that is summarised and processed in such a way that will aid decision making eg a **spreadsheet** model utilising 'what if' functionality could quickly calculate profitability based on various sales mixes. A package such as Microsoft Office provides spreadsheet (Excel), database, and word-processing facilities, and a user-friendly e-mail interface (Outlook).

16 FRS LTD: STRUCTURED METHODOLOGY, INORMATION SYSTEMS AND QUALITY

> **Tutorial note.** Part (a) of this answer provides an excellent summation of how structured methodologies may be used in the systems development process. Note also how the answer is structured in such a way that enables the marker to easily identify the point being made.

MEMORANDUM

To: Chief Executive FRS Ltd
From: Management Consultant
Date: 29 April 200X

(a) There are a wide range of structured methodologies that can be applied to systems development and implementation. Each methodology recommends a logical step-by-step approach. Structured Systems Analysis and Design Methodology (SSADM) is a methodology that distinguishes between logical and physical design.

- Logical design refers to how the system is designed to meet user needs, eg screen layout, menu structure

- Technical design refers to the 'hidden' aspects of the system that enable the logical design to operate, eg file structures

The type of problems experienced in the past should either be avoided or their impact minimised through the use of a structured methodology.

Problem: Information staff do not talk to users

Solution: A structured methodology involves users at all stages of design and implementation. Users are the 'customer' the methodology aims to satisfy. ('Users' means just that - the people who use the system hands-on. It is not good enough to include only the managers of users). User sign-off is required at key stages of development, before further work commences. Communication between developers and users is key, and encourages the development of good working relationships. The relationship should be formalised through user-representation on the project implementation team.

Problem: Systems are late, over budget and under-perform

Solution: A structured methodology acts as a form of project control. Key milestones in development are highlighted and scheduled with the participation and agreement of all involved. Unrealistic timetables should not be accepted.

A major reason systems are often delivered over-budget is that they are late (ie more staff time is required than budgeted for). A realistic timetable that is agreed to by all should prevent this. User involvement at all stages should prevent costly reworking being required as a result of something being overlooked.

Systems often give the perception of under-performing due to unrealistic expectations. These expectations may be built up by systems personnel making unrealistic promises, or may be due to a lack of user knowledge regarding what computer systems are capable of. User involvement in the process at every stage should ensure expectations are realistic, and discourage unrealistic statements being made.

Problem: Programs contain errors

Solution: Structured methodologies include comprehensive testing procedures in conditions designed to replicate the actual operating environment. Users are heavily involved in testing, and user authorisation is required before implementation. Even with this emphasis on testing, some errors may only be discovered after the system 'goes live' - when a unique set of circumstances occurs. Post-implementation testing should locate these errors enabling them to be corrected with minimum disruption.

Problem: Inconsistency

Solution: The inconsistent application of function keys is a basic error. The standardisation of function keys across modules is accepted practice in accounting packages, and would be developed in consultation with users if a structured methodology were used.

Problem: Inflexibility in reporting

Solution: A combination of user involvement and a flexible report writer should ensure the information required can be obtained from the system direct – without the need for further manipulation in a spreadsheet.

(b) Quality and Information Systems

Quality can be defined as 'fitness for purpose'. The purpose of an information system should be defined by developers and users before development work begins. Quality can then be measured against this agreed purpose.

Quality can be split into two components: design quality and conformance quality.

- In relation to an information system, design quality relates to the user-friendliness of the system. Not only should the system be capable of doing what is required, operation of the system should be logical, consistent and easy to learn.

- Conformance quality means the ability of the system to do what is required of it, for example the absence of any major bugs.

The concept of quality can be applied to information systems in three steps.

Step 1 - set measurable objectives

Realistic objectives must be set that are measurable in terms of time, cost and performance. Objectives for system reliability and speed can be developed fairly easily. Qualitative factors such as user-friendliness and customer satisfaction also require objectives to be set.

Step 2 - monitor progress

Hardware quality can be assessed by monitoring response times, number of system crashes, downtime and network traffic.

Programming quality can be measured via monitoring error reports during testing and the faults reported by users.

The use of the features within the package can be monitored to establish how often users utilise them. For example, if the main customer enquiry screen is rarely accessed it is likely that either users don't know how to use it or are unaware of it, and require further training, or that it is faulty. Both illustrate a reduction in quality of the system and should be rectified.

Software user-friendliness can be monitored through contact with users, and the tracking of customer support calls to helpdesks.

Overall customer satisfaction could be monitored using a user-satisfaction scale.

Step 3 - monitor the overall effect of the system

Systems are not produced for their own ends. In the case of FRS the overall aim of the new information system is to improve shop productivity, through the provision of more accurate and timely information. For example, if a reduction in inventory holding costs is noted, this could be a result of more accurate and timely stock information. Although the establishment of a direct relationship between a new system and improved business performance can be difficult to establish, an educated attempt should be made as that is the true indicator of system quality.

Question bank suggested solutions

17 FRS LTD: SYSTEM DEVELOPMENT, PROJECT MANAGEMENT, CPA

> **Tutorial note.** A wide range of answers could have scored well in parts (a) and (b). The answer provided here is only one possible approach. Ensure you understand the logic behind the CPA diagram in part (c) – use the notation that you are most comfortable with.

BRIEFING PAPER

To: Management team of FRS Ltd
From: Management Consultant
Date: 29 April 200X

(a) The major issues to be considered in managing the project to implement the MRO Inc system at FRS Ltd are outlined below.

The project manager and the project team

It is important to establish who has overall responsibility for a successful implementation. The scope of the project needs to be established, and then a person with the required motivation and skills appointed as project manager. The composition of the project team is vital – particularly ensuring sufficient user representation. (Including actual 'hands-on' users, ie not only management.)

What the implementation hopes to achieve

The project team requires a focus. What the implementation is supposed to achieve should be spelt out clearly. The statement may seem like stating the obvious, but it provides a reference point which all issues that arise should take into account.

How successful completion will be achieved

The project must be properly planned and controlled if it is to achieve completion on time, within budget and to required performance specifications. The availability of required resources must be established. Tasks need to be scheduled and allocated providing a framework for monitoring progress and exercising control.

Communication

Communication between developers and users is essential. The project team must establish lines of communication between team members (eg meeting, e-mail links) and between the team and all personnel affected. What the implementation hopes to achieve, from both a users, and an organisation-wide perspective, should be communicated to the personnel of FRS Ltd.

User training

The survival and prosperity of FRS Ltd is dependant on shop transactions. It is therefore essential staff are able to use the system before it 'goes live'. Training requirements should be planned as part of the overall implementation plan. 'Hands-on' sessions using the new system in a test environment are vital.

Method of implementation

How will the new system be implemented? Will a phased implementation be followed or is it practical to have a straight cut-off of the existing system. Will all shops change over at the same time?

Contingency plan

A contingency plan must be drawn up that enables business to continue in the event of system failure. This may involve utilising the old system or reverting to manual procedures.

(b) There are a range of project management tools and techniques available to manage the implementation project. The major tools that would be applicable are outlined below.

A **Strengths, Weaknesses, Opportunities and Threats** analysis could be undertaken to assess whether the implementation fits with FRS Ltd's overall business objectives. A cost-benefit analysis could be included in this process to establish the economic feasibility of the project. The technical aspects of the project should also be evaluated as to its practicality and suitability to the businesses, operations. A **contingency plan** should exist containing strategies for those risks identified as posing a material threat to the project. It may be necessary to transfer some risk via insurance.

Question bank suggested solutions

The process of project selection and the measuring of the financial performance of a project can be achieved through **investment appraisal** techniques. Techniques such as Net Present Value, Internal Rate of Return, Accounting Rate of Return and PayBack can be used to evaluate whether the project should be undertaken. Expected costs and returns should be able to be estimated reasonably accurately based on the experience of MRO Inc.

Control over the implementation can be helped through the use of a **structured methodology** and a close relationship with users. An **external quality management system**, such as ISO 9001 can help maintain control and quality.

The project planning can be carried out with the aid of **project management software** such as Microsoft Project. The project should be broken down into individual tasks using **Work Breakdown Structure**. These tasks and projected completion dates together with available resources form the major input into the software package. The package is then able to produce a **Critical Path Analysis** detailing the sequence and inter-relationship of tasks and **Gantt Charts** highlighting the resources required and the activities for which team members are involved in. Actual progress can then be reported against the plan as a means of control.

The tasks identified during Work Breakdown Structure also form the building blocks for the construction of the **project budget**. Financial control should be exercised through the budget using variance analysis and exception reporting.

(c) Critical path analysis *[One of the following diagrams]*

The critical path is A, B, C, D, E, H, I. The total elapsed time is 26 weeks.

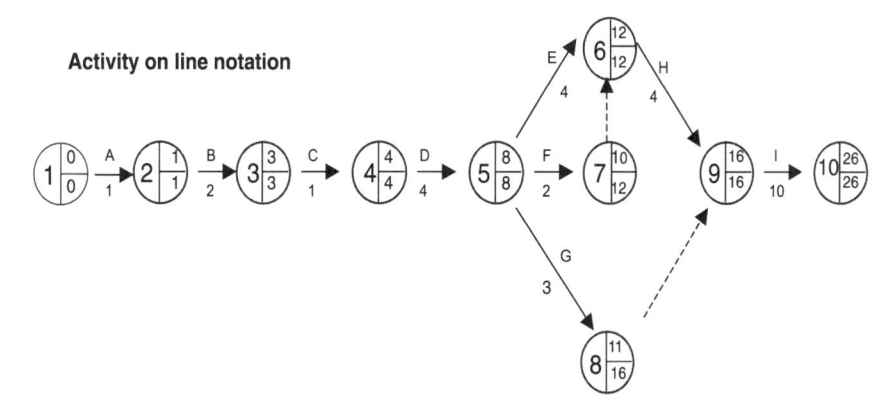

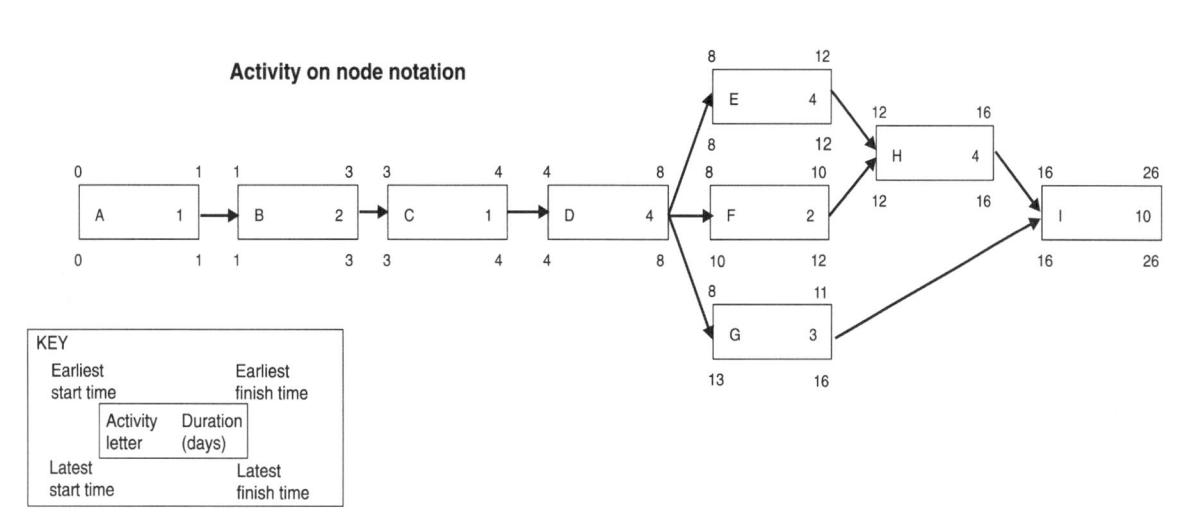

Activity on line notation

Activity on node notation

KEY

Earliest start time		Earliest finish time
	Activity letter	Duration (days)
Latest start time		Latest finish time

Question bank suggested solutions

18   FRS LTD: INTERNAL V EXTERNAL AUDIT, CONTROLS, IT AND AUDIT

> **Tutorial note.** The relationship between internal audit and external audit is highly examinable, particularly as there have recently been a number of high-profile auditing cases in the news (Enron, Worldcom).
>
> Ensure each heading you provide on your slides is sufficiently explained in the corresponding note.

(a)   The role of the internal auditor and the relationship between the internal auditor and external audit.

Slide 1

Internal audit

- Independence
- Internal
- Evaluates the adequacy and effectiveness of controls
- Responsible to management

The primary function of internal audit is to examine and evaluate the adequacy and effectiveness of **controls**.

Internal audit is established **within** an organisation, and is ultimately responsible to management and directors.

The wider role of internal audit encompasses ensuring **best business practice** is followed in the operation of the business.

Slide 2

The internal auditor

- Review accounting and internal control systems
- Examine financial and operating information
- Review economy, efficiency and effectiveness of operations
- Identification of risks
- Investigations as required

A primary concern of an internal audit is to review the **accounting and control** systems.

Includes the design and operation of **financial and non-financial controls**. For example the computerised stock updating routine and physical stock controls could be evaluated and the cash receipt and banking procedures checked.

Examination of the **financial and operating information** would ensure that information was correctly reported to the appropriate level within the organisation. The systems that financial information is based on should be reviewed for accuracy and efficiency.

A review of the **economy, efficiency and effectiveness** of operations would enable the internal auditors to recommend appropriate improvements. This may include areas such as job descriptions and the segregation of duties to strengthen control. For example, the same person should not be responsible for receiving payments, processing them and banking them.

Applying the same principle to a higher level, the auditor would check that systems are designed to promote the achievement of **overall organisation objectives**. For example, ensuring that the methodology and procedures followed to facilitate the implementation of a new information system meet the requirements of users and of the overall organisation.

Risk management is an important element of internal audit. Risk is a wide-ranging concept. For example, there is risk in not providing employees with a workplace that complies with Health and Safety legislation as this could lead to costly financial penalties (as well as employee injury). Where risk exists, adequate controls must be put in place to reduce risk to acceptable levels.

The internal auditor is in an excellent position to develop a meaningful overview of the company and its operations. It is likely that some area of operation will appear to be either inefficient or exposed to risk. The auditor should use initiative and decide whether an **investigation** into this area is warranted. Management may also request a review of an area or process they suspect could be improved in terms of efficiency or control.

Slide 3

External audit

- Independent third party – protect shareholders
- Focus on the accounts and records of an organisation
- Compliance with accounting standards and legal requirements
- Overriding concept is a true and fair view
- Overlap with internal audit

External audit is carried out by an **independent** third party and is accountable to the **shareholders** of the organisation. It's focussed towards establishing an opinion regarding the compliance of the external accounts with accepted accounting practice.

To establish their opinion it is necessary for external auditors to review the **systems and procedures** used to produce the accounts. This means there will be some **overlap** with the work of internal audit, and that external auditors may be in a position to recommend improvements to operations and controls. Co-operation between internal and external audit should keep the duplication of work to a minimum and ensure the best use of resources.

To be able to use work undertaken by internal audit, external audit must be satisfied as to the standard and **reliability** of the information. Issues considered will be:

Slide 4

External audit utilising internal audit work

- Organisation status
- Scope of internal function
- Competence of staff
- Policies and procedures followed

Organisational status. Both the **size** of the organisation and the **status** allocated to the internal audit function should be considered.

Scope of function. Does the internal audit function have the authority to be pro-active in suggesting changes to policies and procedures, or is it concerned with review only?

Staff **competence**. Whether internal audit work is performed by persons having adequate technical training and proficiency as internal auditors (eg are they qualified accountants?).

Policies and procedures. Is internal audit work properly planned, supervised, reviewed and documented?

(b) Internal controls

Slide 5

Internal controls and stock control

- Segregation of duties
- Physical security
- Authorisation
- Management and supervision
- Accounting
- Staff

Question bank suggested solutions

Segregation of duties

The present system at FRS Ltd allows one person to be involved in handling of goods inwards, the placement of stock on shelves and cash handling for goods sold. These duties should be **segregated** to reduce risk of fraud. If in very small outlets the size of the labour force means this is not possible, close supervision and strict reconciliation procedures should be implemented.

Physical security

Stock and cash are typical targets for **fraud**, so should be subject to tight controls. A daily cash reconciliation should be carried out, and stocktakes completed at least monthly. In outlets experiencing significant stock discrepancies weekly stocktakes may be required. Tight control and detailed documentation is required for the transfer of stock between outlets. Access to stores should be controlled to reduce the risk of pilferage.

Authorisation

Authorisation levels need to be established and all transactions subject to the **required level of authorisation**. For example, all goods purchased require a correctly completed and authorised purchase order.

Management and supervision

Some degree of control can be exercised through a review of FRS Ltd's **management accounts**. eg variance analysis, stock levels and turnover. Management should ensure procedures are in place to effectively manage **perishable stock** items as stock held past its sell-by date could cause substantial losses. Each days transactions should be subjected to a **supervisor review**, reducing the risk of falsification or errors.

Accounting

Stock levels are recorded on the accounting system. **Accurate recording and processing** of transactions is vital if control over stock is to be maintained. The system should provide an **audit trail** showing who is responsible for each transaction. Some transactions should require **authorisation** by a separate person of the required level of authority, eg stock adjustments.

Personnel

All personnel should be **reference checked** before being employed. **Staffing levels** need to be adequate to enable correct procedure to be followed, and training needs must be addressed.

(c) Information technology and the audit process

Slide 6

Information technology and the audit process

- Computer Aided Auditing Techniques
- Audit interrogation software
- Test data
- Embedded audit facilities - Integrated test facilities – SCARF
- Simulation
- Knowledge based systems

Computer Aided Auditing Techniques is a catch-all phrase that describes automated auditing techniques such as:

Audit interrogation software

Interrogation software performs checks on data looking for transactions outside of normal limits or procedures. This enables large volumes of data to be examined, although this is on a fairly superficial level. FRS Ltd would find this particularly helpful for its transactions-based system.

Test data

Test data is used to establish if the system is processing data in the way that it should. A separate test ledger should be set up to facilitate this testing.

Embedded audit facilities

An embedded audit facility consists of audit software incorporated into the accounting system. This allows a continuous review of data entered into the system, and the manner in which it is treated by the system Two examples are Integrated Test Facility (ITF) and Systems Control and Review File (SCARF).

(1) Integrated test facility

Integrated Test Facility involves the creation of a fictitious entity (for example a supplier) within the framework of the regular application. Transactions are then posted to the fictitious entity and results analysed for 'correctness'.

(2) SCARF

SCARF involves auditors choosing accounts to be monitored in detail.

Simulation

Simulation involves using a separate program that simulates the processing of the actual system.

Knowledge based systems

Knowledge based systems are more complex and are used to estimate the effect of a change in the operation of the business. For example, the expected effect of a general increase in the cost price of stock items on the performance of FRS Ltd could be estimated. Simulation systems are useful in highlighting potential areas for investigation.

Question bank suggested solutions

19 CAET INSURANCE: PROJECT MANAGEMENT

> **Tutorial note**. For part (a) your answer should use the elements described in (i), (ii) and (iii) as headings. Our answer includes sub-headings within each of these, relating to avoiding risk and reducing risk. This is not necessary, but does help ensure a wide range of points are included.
>
> If you have studied Chapters 1 and 2 of this text you should have found part (b) straightforward.

(a) (i) **Risk: Lack of user experience in the holiday industry**

Avoiding risk

Experience in the holiday industry could be obtained by either recruiting new staff with the appropriate experience, or by helping existing staff obtain that experience, through their work and possibly by attendance on some appropriate training courses. However, using the latter option will almost certainly have delayed the systems project.

Reducing risk

Involving users throughout the design process could reduce the risk of implementing an incorrect or partly functional system. Specifically, system prototypes and pilot testing could be carried out to check the appropriateness of any system design.

Reviewing similar systems that may already be available on the market or at third parties may also reduce risk. The latter will be difficult to achieve where third parties do not want to share their knowledge although a review of propriety software will at least indicate the functionality that can be included in any new system.

(ii) **Decision to use a programming language with no experience of that language in-house**

Avoiding risk

This risk can be avoided, either gaining the appropriate experience in-house, or by using a different programming language that in-house already have experience in. The choice will depend on how important it is to use the functionality in the chosen language.

Reducing risk

If the unfamiliar language has to be used, then risk of failure can be reduced firstly, by allowing more time in the project plan for training or hiring of staff. Another alternative is to put back the project delivery time to recognise that problems may occur in writing and testing the software. These alternatives may be more appropriate than implementing software that fails or causes errors shortly after implementation.

(iii) **Exacting performance problems**

Avoiding risk

Performance problems can be avoided by decreasing the use of the computer system at busy times. This may mean storing customer telephone calls in a queue and only taking the number of calls that the system will process or promising to call customers back at a less busy time. As a last resort, CAET could stop giving quotes on-line, although this may not be an acceptable option, given CAET's commitment to using the system.

Reducing risk

Checking that high specification hardware is installed to provide adequate processing power can reduce the risk of poor performance. Faster hardware will decrease the waiting time for response from the system.

Alternatively, prototypes can be produced during the design and build phase to test the system response times. If performance cannot be improved, then at least expectations of users and customers regarding performance can be managed.

(b) (i) **Project sponsor**

The project sponsor is the customer for the system. This person is not necessarily the finance director, but the manager of the business unit or department where the new system will be implemented. The sponsor will have made the business case for any new or revised system, and will seek to ensure that those benefits are delivered in the final system.

As the project sponsor is responsible for delivering the benefits of the project, that person will also be promoting the project prior to implementation. Promotion in this case will mean ensuring that appropriate resources are allocated to the project as well as ensuring potential users are aware of the project and are briefed on the benefits of that project. Lack of a project sponsor will increase the risk of project failure, due to lack of co-ordination of the activities of the project and possible lack of priority for the project within the organisation.

(ii) **Project plan**

The project plan provides an overall picture of the project showing the activities to be carried out, the time of those activities and how the different activities are related to each other. Most project plans are presented as some form of chart (eg GANTT chart) or network so that interconnections between the activities can be seen clearly.

The project plan is used to estimate the total time to complete the project and identify those activities, which must be completed on time to avoid the whole project being finished late. The effect on total project duration from changes in activities can also be estimated by entering revised times for activities into the plan. If no plan is produced, then the overall project time and critical activities will be difficult to predict. There will also be an increased risk of late completion due to overall lack of control.

20 CAET INSURANCE: SOFTWARE DESIGN

> **Tutorial note.** Look at our answer below – note how the lengths of different parts of the answer differ. For example, Part (a) (iv) includes the most material. This is because this part of the question is worth 4 marks, while many of the other parts are worth 2 marks. Of course, to earn marks what you write must be relevant to the question asked – but with short questions often the key is not to write too much, and to gauge the length of your answer by the marks on offer.

(a) (i) **Illogical data entry**

The logical order to input data into the system needs to be ascertained from the users of the system. This error could have been identified in a prototype and the screen design amended at this time. However, given that the correct fields appear to be available, rather than some fields actually missing, the screen should be fairly easy to amend. Within the GUI interface, each field will have its own placeholder (similar to those in Microsoft Access), so these can be dragged to a new location and the order of using the fields amended to reflect the user requirement.

(ii) **Unclear field entry**

Mandatory fields should be easy to identify, possibly by using a different colour to shade the field or providing a darker boarder around the input box. Similarly, displaying some fields should be made dependent on entries actually made in previous fields. Again, using the GUI interface tools, amendments to field properties should be fairly easy to accomplish.

(iii) **Inconsistent cursor control**

Inconsistent cursor control is difficult for the user as the action of the cursor is difficult to predict, as the case study shows. A survey of users will help to identify which action on the completion of each field is actually appropriate. Pressing the tab key may be the easiest option because the software may not always identify when a field is complete (eg when does an address end?). However, as long as the action is consistent and logical, then the actual alternative chosen is irrelevant.

The change should again be easy to implement by ensuring that the properties for completion of input in each field are the same.

Question bank suggested solutions

(iv) **Performance problems**

Performance problems are more difficult to remedy as they may require amendments to hardware or software, which are simply not possible post-implementation. However, it may be possible to:

Add additional disk space, RAM memory or upgrade network cards to a higher specification or install a more recent processor to try and improve overall system performance. All of these alternatives should help to reduce the response time.

Alternatively, the actual use of system resources in terms of which programs are being run at specific times can also be reviewed. If resource-intensive programs, such as file re-organisation, are being run during the day, then these can be deferred to a less busy time. This will free up system resources for more important programs such as the on-line insurance system.

(b) (i) **Illogical data entry**

Ensuring that the screen correctly reflects the method of work would normally be checked during the design stage of a system, specifically by using a prototype of the screen layout. At this time, amendments to the screen design could be made prior to the final system being built, avoiding these errors at the user acceptance test. However, given that this is a new system, even a prototype may have been of limited use because users could still have been uncertain about how they wanted to input data.

(ii) **Unclear field entry**

The issue of some fields being optional could again have been detected at the build stage using a prototype to check which fields actually needed to be completed for each data record. Alternatively, data collection during the building of a logical model during system design may also have detected that some fields were optional.

However, in the current situation, some design standard is required to distinguish optional from mandatory fields. This will ensure that optional fields will only be shown when they are required.

(iii) **Inconsistent cursor control**

The lack of consist use of the cursor again implies a lack of standards during the design phase of the software. Stating the action to take on completion of a field in a style manual would help to ensure this error did not occur, or if it did, the manual would show which style should be applied.

Design errors would be detected during systems testing, as this is now a systems standard.

(iv) **Performance problems**

The performance of the system should be checked during system testing; specifically checking system response time when processing increasingly large amounts of data. It is possible that this load testing was not carried out, or that the system was inadequately tested at this time, with only a small number of transactions being processed. If the problem had been detected during testing, then the software could have been amended to try and enhance performance prior to going live.

It is also possible that performance problems were not detected before the system went live because system testing was carried-out in an environment that did not match the live environment. For example, testing may have been performed on hardware with different specifications.

21 CAET INSURANCE: QUALITY ASSURANCE AND TESTING

> **Tutorial note.** Compare this answer to the marked-up question and the Answer plan we provided in the question bank – this should show the thinking process used to produce this answer.
>
> You could have drawn a simple 'V' model to explain your answer to parts (i) – (iii). If you did, you should still break the explanation part of your answer up into the separate parts of the question.
>
> Structuring your answer exactly as the question was structured means it is less likely you will omit to answer all areas of the question – and makes it easier to mark (and therefore easier fro the marker to give you marks).
>
> In part (b), ensure your answer covers all areas. The requirement may be broken down into three areas; software packages and testing, software packages and quality assurance; and the consultant's statement.

(a) The three areas of application development mentioned in the question relate to the three stages of testing outlined in the 'V' model of system development. In this model, analysis and testing are linked at three specific points: *[Brief introduction including mention of the 'V' model]*

1. Requirements analysis and user acceptance testing
2. Systems design and systems testing
3. Program design and unit or module testing.

(i) **Requirements analysis** *[Structure your answer around the question requirements]*

In the requirements analysis stage, documentation is produced to show what the system is required to do in terms of input, output and processing. The documentation will be produced in text or graphical form, and then checked to ensure that it is complete and adheres to appropriate design standards.

In user acceptance testing, the requirements analysis is re-visited and checked against the new system. The new system should fulfil the requirements previously defined in the requirements analysis; if it does not, then further amendments may be required before the users sign-off the system.

(ii) **Systems design**

During system design, the architectural software design is produced from the business requirements and technical specification for the software. Documentation is produced to specific design standards so it can be checked using formal walkthroughs. *[For each of the three stages, include points relating to quality assurance and testing]*

In systems testing, all of the individual programs are tested together as one integrated suite of software. The integrated software is compared back to the original design specification to check that the programs work as outlined in this design. If the design is not met then the systems testing fails and amendments to the overall design of the software may still be required. When the systems testing is complete, the integrated software is forwarded for user acceptance testing.

(iii) **Programming**

At this stage, the individual programs or modules of the software are designed. The actual designs will again be produced in accordance with specific design standards and tested prior to the program itself being written.

After the program is written, it is checked back to the program specification to ensure that this has been met. This testing is normally called unit testing. Any errors in the program modules are corrected or debugged before the individual programs are sent for systems testing.

Question bank suggested solutions

> Start with a brief explanation of the application software package approach

> Emphasise the fact that steps must be taken to ensure the packaged software is suitable, and must be tested

> It is unlikely that any large software package is completely error-free, it is important that there are no major errors

(b) Using an application software package approach means that software is purchased from a third party supplier ready for use within the organisation. This means that systems design and program design and their associated testing phases are not required because the software house will have already performed this testing.

However, a specification of requirements will still be required, and therefore user acceptance testing will also be required. The specification of requirements is necessary because the software must still meet the business needs of the organisation. The requirements must therefore be listed and compared to the specification for the program. It will be very difficult to amend the application software after it has been implemented, so checking requirements is essential.

User acceptance testing is also necessary to ensure that the requirement specification is met, and that the software adequately supports the business needs of the users as well as the volume of transactions.

The comment concerning 'tried, tested and error free' may be incorrect.

Firstly, the software has not been tested in the organisation, so it may not meet the specific requirements of users. The testing to date has been against the requirements of designers in the software house, not the organisation where the software is being implemented.

Secondly, the software is unlikely to be 100% error free. The software house may not have been able to test all combinations of the different software modules or with the specific transactions that will be used in the organisation in a live situation. Errors may still occur.

Index

Note: **Key Terms** and their references are given in **bold**.

5-S practice, 366

Absorption, 55
Access, 135
Accessibility, 74, 203
Accounting, 313
Accounting controls, 314
Accounting information, 283
Accounting records, 98
ACL for Windows, 341
Activator, 268
Activity, 24
Activity-on-node diagrams, 34
Actual Cost of Work Performed (ACWP), 30
Adaptive maintenance, 189
Addendum, 66
Adjournment, 66
Administrative controls, 314
Agenda, 65, 69
Amendment, 66
Analogy, 77
Analysis, 13
Analysis and design, 140
Analysis tools, 124
Analysts' workbenches, 124
Analytical procedures, 335
Analytical review, 320
Anecdote, 77
Application Service Providers (ASP), 239
Applications backlog, 121
Appraisal, 277, 299
Appraisal and pay, 279
Appraisal as annual event, 279
Appraisal as bureaucracy, 279
Appraisal as chat, 279
Appraisal as confrontation, 278
Appraisal as judgement, 278
Appraisal as unfinished business, 279
Appraisal barriers, 278
Appraisal costs, 358, 362
Appraisal procedures, 277
Archiving, 286
Around the computer, 331
ASCII, 206
Ashby, 104
Audience, 73
Audit committee, 301
Audit evidence, 334
Audit interrogation software, 341
Audit risk, 303, **306**, 341
Audit trail, 338
Authorisation and approval, 312
Authority and responsibility, 262
Avoidance, 55

Back-up, 286
Barriers to communication, 250
Batch processing, 213
Behaviour controls, 273
Benchmark tests, 227
Benchmarking, 311, 363
Bespoke applications, 212, 223
Bespoke development risks, 228
Bespoke software, 221, 223, 228
Beta version, 180
BIOS, 206
Bit, 206
Bottom-up budgeting, 29
Brainstorm, 74
Braverman, 266
Budget, 5
Budget Report, 31
Budgetary control, 282
Budgeted Cost of Work Performed (BCWP), 31
Budgeted Cost of Work Scheduled (BCWS), 30
Budgeting Worksheet, 30
Bugs, 189
Bulletin boards, 244
Bureaucracy, 263
Business risk, 308
Business system, 90, 168
Byte, 206

C++, 126
Cache, 206
Cadbury Committee, 301
Call-back buttons, 244
CASE repository, 124
CASE tool, 124, 150
CAST, 180
CD-R, 211
CD-ROM, 211
CD-RW, 211
Central processing unit (CPU), 205
Central server, 218
Centralisation, 236
Centralised, 236
Centralised architecture, 215
Chairperson, 64, 67
Champy, James, 291
Change control, 58
Character, 206
Charismatic leadership, 263
Check digits, 285
Chip, 205
Choice of medium, 252

Index

Classical management principles, 290
Classical theorists, 274
Client, 218
Client applications, 219
Client workstation, 218
Client/server, 204
Client-server architecture, 218
Closed loop system, 268
Closed system, 101
Coates, Rickwood and Stacey, 262
Code comparison programs, 343
Code generators, 125
Coding of a message, 249
Collusion with external parties, 324
Common methods of fraud, 323
Communication, 6, 248, 249
Companies Act, 298
Comparator, 268
Competitive benchmarking, 363
Completing Phase, 29
Completion, 29
Completion Report, 53
Completion stage, 29
Compliance tests, 304
Computation, 335
Computer aided software engineering (CASE) tools, 330
Computer Aided Software Engineering (CASE), 124
Computer Aided Software Testing, 180
Computer assisted audit techniques (CAAT), 340
Computer fraud, 346
Computer manufacturers, 239
Computer Output on Microfilm (COM), 209
Computer-based monitoring, 195
Computerised systems, 203
Conduct of meetings, 64
Confidence level, 337
Confidentiality, 253
Connections, 90
Conservatism, 309
Constituting a meeting, 66
Consultancies, 99
Consultancy firms, 238
Consulting activity, 238
Context diagram, 153
Contingency plan, 55
Contingency theory, 265
Contingency, 55, 288
Continuous improvement, 279, 358
Control, 262
Control of internal audits, 321
Control procedures, 333
Control risk, 307
Control system, 262, 267
Control theory current thinking, 266

Control totals, 285
Controlling, 93
Controlling phase, 28
Controls in computerised systems, 331
Convening a meeting, 65
Conventional ideas, 266
Co-ordination, 247
Copyright, 231
Copyright, Designs and Patents Act 1998, 231
Corporate applications, 219
Corporate appraisal, 25
Corporate Over-Use, 231
Corporate server, 218
Corporate systems, 100
Corrective maintenance, 189
Cost control, 56
Cost variance, 31
Cost, 253
Cost-benefit analysis, 144
Coupling, 103
Credibility, 74
Criteria for evaluating appraisal schemes, 279
Critical activities, 32, 40
Critical path analysis, 28, 33

Data dictionary, 124, **133**, 233
Data flow, 152
Data flow diagram, 152
Data independence, 131
Data integrity, 285
Data process, 152
Data processes, 152
Data processing, 212, 234
Data redundancy, 131
Data store, 152
Data structure, 157
Database, 131
Database administrator (DBA), 132, 233
Database management system (DBMS), 131
Database systems, 131
Databases, 167
Decentralised, 217, 236
Decentralised architecture, 217
Decision making, 94
Decision Support System (DSS), 110, 343
Decision tables, 160, 178
Decoupling, 103
Defining phase, 22
Definition, 76
Degree of precision, 337
Delayering, 275
Deliverable, 24
Departmental level systems, 101
Departmental server, 218
Description, 76

Index

Design and development stage, 28
Detect controls, 314
Detection risk, 308
Deterministic systems, 102
Development costs, 145
Diagnostic software, 235
Diagramming tools, 124
Digital Versatile Disk (DVD), 211
Direct changeover, 187
Direct supervision, 248
Discipline, 262
Dispute resolution, 16
Disputes Review Board, 16
Distance, 252
Distortion, 250
Distributed architecture, 217
Division of work, 262
Divisional level systems, 100
Document generators, 125
Document review, 151
Documentation, 184, 190
Double loop feedback, 271
Downsizing, 204
Drucker, 264
Dual command, 262
Due care, 297
DVD, 211
Dynamic testing, 177

Ecological feasibility, 144
E-commerce, 243
Effectiveness, 193, 194
Effector, 268
Efficiency, 193, 194
EFTPOS, 208
EIS, 109
Electronic commerce, 243
Electronic data interchange (EDI), 99, 345
Electronic Point of Sale (EPOS), 208
E-mail, 344
Embedded audit facilities, 342
Employee's duties, 281
Employment contracts, 281
Empowered, 291
Empowerment, 275
Empowerment and control, 276
Enquiry and confirmation, 332
Enterprise servers, 204
Entity, 157, 159
Entity life history (ELH), 159
Entity modelling, 157
Entity relationship model (ERM), 157, 158
Entropy, 105
Environment, 92, 100
Environmental scanning, 99
EPOS, 208
Equipment cost, 145

Errors, 189, 203
ESS, 109
Estimates, 30
Evaluation
Exaggeration, 77
Executive Information System (EIS), 109
Executive Support System (ESS), 109
Expert systems, 112
External audits, 298
External data sources, 99
External entity, 152
External failure costs, 358, 362
External information, 98
External/internal auditor relationship, 297
Extranet, 114

Facilitator, 150
Facilities Management (FM), 237
Facilities, 65
Fact finding, 147
Failing to record all sales, 324
Fayol, 262, 290
Feasibility and fact finding stage, 24
Feasibility study, 25, 119, 141, 332
Feasibility study report, 146
Feedback, 250, 252, 268, 269
Feedback basis, 268
Feedforward control, 268, 270
File conversion, 185, 333
File creation, 185
File, 212
Filtering, 103
Financial feasibility, 144
Flat organisations, 274
Flat structure
Flipcharts, 80
Float time, 42
Floppy disks, 210
Formation stage, 23
Foucault, 267
Fourth generation language (4GL), 127
Fraud, 322, 323, 324, 325, 346
Free float, 42
Frequently-Asked Questions (FAQs), 244
Full procedures manual, 332
Functional benchmarking, 363

Gantt chart, 28, 31, 39, 43
Ghost employees, 323
Giddens, 266
Gigabytes, 206
GigaHertz, 205
Global forces, 290
Goal, 23
Greenbury Report, 301

431

Index

Handheld, 204
Handouts, 81
Handy, 274
Hard disks, 210
Hardware, 232
Hash totals, 285
Hawthorne Studies, 265
Help desk, 235
Herzberg, 265
Hierarchy of systems, 100
Hierarchy, 263
Higher level feedback, 271
Human relations, 265
Humour, 77

Impact analysis, 133
Implementation stage, 28
Implementation, 333
Implementing phase, 28
Incremental approach, 239
Independence, 299
Independent float, 42
Individualism, 290
Inflating expense claims, 324
Information bureaux, 99
Information centre (IC), 137, 234
Information overload, 250
Information services, 99
Information superhighway, 243
Information System controls, 283
Information theory, 93
Informix-4GL, 129
Inherent risk, 306
Initiation stage, 22
Initiative:, 262
Inkjet printers, 210
Input devices, 206
Inputs, 91, 198
Insourcing, 242
Inspection, 335
Installation costs, 145
Installation of a mainframe, 174
Intangible, 146
Integrated circuit, 205
Integrated Test Facility (ITF), 342
Intel, 205
Interaction, 253
Interactionism, 266
Interest, 77
Internal auditing, 298
Internal benchmarking, 363
Internal control system, 311, 314
Internal control questionnaire, 316
Internal control evaluation questionnaire, 316
Internal data sources, 98

Internal failure costs, 358, 362
Internal information, 97
International Organisation for Standardisation, 361
Internet, 100, 137, 243
Interpretevist, 266
Interpreting, 252
Interviews, 148
Intranet, 114
Invitation to tender (ITT), 224
ISO, 361
Issuing false credit notes, 324
Iteration, 160
ITT, 224

Java, 126
Joint Applications Development (JAD), 137
Joint venture sourcing, 239
Judgement sampling, 336
Justification, 143

Key field, 212
Keyword search, 244
Kilobytes, 206
Knowledge management, 249
Knowledge Work Systems (KWS), 111
Knowledge Workers, 111
Knowledge-based systems, 343
KWS, 111

Labour process theory, 266
Laptop, 204
Laser printers, 210
Law of requisite variety, 104
Leadership styles, 8
Levelled DFDs, 153, 154
Libraries, 99
Licences, 230
Life histories, 159
Likert, 265
Limit checks, 285
Limited entry, 162
Local applications, 219
Local area network (LAN), 216
Local server, 218
Lockett, 278
Logical cues, 75
Logical data structure, 157
Logical design, 122, 168
Logical path analysis, 340
Logical structure, 167
Logs, 195
Lower CASE tools, 125

Magnetic Ink Character Recognition (MICR), 208

Index

Magnetic stripe cards, 208
Maintenance, 13, 192, 333
Management audit, 310
Management by exception, 9, 55
Management fraud, 326
Management Information Systems (MIS), 110
Management Information Systems, 110
Management theories, 261
Management, 313
Managing conflict, 11
Managing meetings, 69
Manual systems, 203
Many-to-many relationship, 158
Many-to-one relationship, 157
Maslow, 265
Master file, 213
Mayo, 265
McGregor, 265
Mediation, 16
Meeting, 63
Megabytes, 206
Megahertz (MHz), 205
Memory, 205, 206
Message, 75
Methodology, 121, 330
Metrics, 194
Michael Hammer, 291
Microfilm, 209
Milestone, 50
Minutes, 68
Miscasting, 320
Monitoring
Monitors, 195
Motherboard, 205
Motion, 66
Mouse, 207
Multiple sourcing, 239
Mutual adjustment, 247

Negative entropy, 105
Negative feedback, 269
Negotiation techniques, 12, 16
Nerves, 82
Network analysis, 32
Network diagram, 24, 32, 43
Networks, 348
Noise, 250
Non-programmable decision, 106
Normalisation, 166, 167, 168

OAS, 111
Objective setting stage, 23
Objective, 23
Object-oriented Programming, 127
Observation, 150, 335

OCR, 208
Office Automation System (OAS), 111
Off-line testing, 177
Off-the shelf package, 221, 229
Off-the-shelf applications, 212
One-to-many relationship, 157
One-to-one relationship, 157
On-line processing, 214
On-line testing, 177
Open loop system, 268
Open system, 101
Operating costs, 145
Operating systems, 212
Operational audit planning, 319
Operational decisions, 107
Operational feasibility, 144
Operational information, 107
Operational level systems, 101
Operations control, 234
Optical character recognition, 208
Optical mark reading (OMR), 208
Optical mouse, 207
Option evaluation, 143
Organisation, 313
Otley, 282
Output control, 273
Output devices, 209
Outputs, 91, 197
Outsourcing, 237, 348

Parallel running, 187
Parallel simulation, 343
Participants for a meeting, 64
Partnering, 16
Passwords, 287
Peer-to-peer architecture, 220
Perfective maintenance, 189
Performance measurement, 93
Performance review, 196
Performance testing, 179
Performance, 196
Personnel, 310
Personnel costs, 145
Phased changeover, 188
Physical design, 122, 169
Physical security, 284
Pilot operation, 188
Planning internal audits, 315
Planning phase, 24
Planning, 93, 265
Point of order, 67
Portables, 204
Positive, 270
Positive feedback, 270
Post-completion audit, 53, 54
Post-implementation review, 198
Post-implementation review report, 199

Index

Post-installation audit, 333
Post-installation review, 333
PowerPoint, 79
Preparation, 174
Presentation, 72
Prevention controls, 311
Prevention costs, 357, 362
Prevention of fraud, 322
Primary cache, 206
Printers, 210
Prioritise, 74
Probabilistic systems, 102
Problem definition, 142
Problems/requirements list, 142, 167
Processes, 91
Processor, 205
Productivity, 203
Program file, 332
Program specifications, 332
Program testing, 176
Programmable decision, 106
Programmers' workbenches, 125
Programmers, 13
Programming tools, 212, 230
Progress report, 50
Project, 4
Project Board, 23
Project Brief, 45
Project Budget, 29
Project change procedure, 57
Project Charter, 45
Project documentation, 45
Project Evaluation and Review Technique (PERT), 40
Project evaluation and review technique, 28, 40
Project evaluation meeting, 72
Project Initiation Document (PID), 22
Project Initiation, 22, 45
Project Initiation Meeting, 45
Project Life Cycle, 20
Project management plan, 45, **46**
Project management process, 6
Project management software, 37, 42
Project management tools, 5
Project management, 4, 17, 140
Project manager responsibilities, 7
Project manager, 5, 6, 7, 55
Project meetings, 71
Project objectives, 23
Project owner, 15
Project phases, 21
Project plan, 45
Project planning, 6
Project problem solving meetings, 72
Project quality plan, 49
Project scope, 23

Project sponsor, 15
Project stages, 21
Project stakeholders, 14, 17
Project status meetings, 71
Project supplier, 15
Project support team, 15
Project team, 9
Proposal, 66
Props and demonstrations, 81
Prototype, 129, 150
Purpose of meetings, 63

Quality, 5, **356,** 359
Quality and costs, 361
Quality assurance, 356
Quality auditing, 356
Quality circle, 362
Quality control, 6, 322, **356,** 361
Quality management, 356
Quality standards, 361
Quality of output, 203
Query languages, 135
Questionnaires, 149
Questions, 76, 83
Quorum, 66
Quotation, 77
QWERTY, 207

Radical structuralist, 266
RAM, 206
Random Access Memory (RAM), 206
Range checks, 285
Rapid applications development (RAD), 137
Ratio analysis, 320
Read-Only Memory, 206
Receiving, 252
Recipient of a communication, 253
Record, 212
Recording internal audits, 322
Reduction, 55
Re-engineering the Corporation
Regression testing, 191
Relational data analysis, 168
Relationship models
Relationships, 157
Relevance, 74
Remote diagnostic software, 235
Remuneration, 262
Repetition, 77
Report generator, 125
Report production, 135
Requirements specification, 168
Requisite variety, 104
Resolution techniques, 12
Resolution, 16, 66
Resource histogram, 28, 41

Resources, 4
Review and maintenance, 119
Review stage, 29
Review, 13
Reward system, 279
Rhetorical questions, 77
Risk, 20, 308
Risk management, 54
Risk neutral, 308
Risk seeker, 308
Risk-based auditing, 306
ROM, 206
Roslender, 262
Round the computer, 331, 339

Sample size, 337
Sampling techniques, 336, 341
Savings, 146
Scalar chain, 262
Scanners, 208
Scenario building, 26
Schedule variance, 31
Scientific management, 264
Screen layout generator, 125
Scribe, 150
Secondary feedback, 271
Secondary, 271
Secretary of the meeting, 68
Security, 283
Segregation of duties, 312, 333
Selection, 160, 174
Self-appraisals, 279
Self-organising systems, 103
Semi-structured decision, 106
Sensor, 268
Server types, 218
Server, 218
Service bureaux, 237
Service Level Agreement (SLA), 240
Service Level Contract (SLC), 240
Settlement, 16
Sign-off, 31
Simulation, 343
Slides, 78, 79
Smart cards, 209
Social feasibility, 144
Socio-technical systems, 101
Software choice, 222
Software contracts, 230
Software houses, 238
Software licences, 230
Software supplier proposals, 225
SPAM SOAP, 312
Span of control, 274
Specialisation, 263
Specification, 13
Speed of processing, 203

SSADM, 122
Staff appraisal system, 277
Stage-fright, 82
Stakeholder matrix, 15
Stakeholders, 14, 15
Standard, 268
Standardisation by skills and knowledge, 248
Standardisation of outputs, 248
Standardisation of work processes, 248
Standby equipment, 175
Static analysis, 178
Static testing, 177
Statistical sampling, 336
Statistics, 77
Status checking, 244
Stealing, 323, 324
Steering committee, 233
Strategic benchmarking, 363
Strategic decisions, 106
Strategic information, 108
Strategic planning, 318
Strengths and weaknesses analysis, 26
Stress testing, 179
Structural functionalist, 266
Structuration, 266
Structure, 248
Structured and unstructured problems, 106
Structured data, 131
Structured decision, 106
Structured English, 167
Structured problem, 106
Structured Systems Analysis and Design Method (SSADM), 122, 330
Structured walkthroughs, 136, 330
Study team, 141
Subordination of individual, 262
Substantive procedures, 335
Substantive tests, 304
Subsystems, 92, 100
Supervision, 313
Support centre, 234
SWOT analysis, 25, 27, 146
System, 90
System analysis, 119
System boundary, 91
System design, 119
System investigation, 119
System testing, 175, 177, 181
Systems analysis, 152
Systems analyst, 13, 332
Systems audit, 303
Systems concepts, 103
Systems Control and Review File (SCARF), 342
Systems development life-cycle, 119
Systems development staff, 234
Systems evaluation, 193

Index

Systems implementation, 119
Systems integration, 237, 240
Systems integrity, 285
Systems investigation, 147
Systems maintenance lifecycle, 190
Systems theory, 90
Systems view, 100

Tactical audit planning, 319
Tactical control, 106
Tactical decisions, 107
Tactical information, 107
Tall organisation, 274
Tall structures, 290
Tape storage, 211
Tape streamers, 211
Task, 24
Task planning stage, 24
Taylor, 264
Team spirit, 262
Teambuilding, 5, 6
Technical feasibility, 143
Technical manual, 184
Technical system options, 168
Teeming and lading, 324
Terms of reference, 22, 142
Test data, 342
Test script, 178
Testing methods, 177
Testing plan, 181
Testing strategy, 181
Testing, 13, 175, 177, 181, 332
Tests of control, 334
Through the computer, 331
Time share, 237
Time/Cost/Quality Triangle, 57
Title, 81
Top-down budgeting, 29
Total float, 42
Total productive maintenance (TPM), 370
Total quality management (TQM), 357, 360
Touch screens, 209
Touch sensitive pads, 207
Trackball, 207
Traditional leadership, 263
Training, 182, 263
Training plan, 182
Transaction file, 213
Transaction Processing System (TPS), **111**
Transactions, 93
Transference, 55
Trust-control dilemma, 274

Uncertain, 311
Uncertainty, 20, 311
Unit testing, 176
Unit integration testing, 176
Unity of command, 262
Unity of direction, 262
Unstructured decision, 106
Unstructured problem, 106
Upper CASE tools, 124
Upward appraisal, 280
Usability testing, 179
User acceptance testing, 177
User groups, 137
User involvement, 135
User manual, 184
User requirements, 121
User validation, 136
Users, 15, 121
Utilities, 212

V model, 175
Value for money audit, 310
VDU, 207, 210
Visual aids, 75, 78
Visual Display Unit (VDU), 207
Voice recognition, 209
Voting, 67

Weber, 263, 290
Website, 243
Weighted ranking, 227
Woodward, 266
Work breakdown structure, 28
Working papers, 321
World Wide Web (www), 243

Zip disk, 210

CIMA – Intermediate Paper 10: Systems and Project Management (7/02)

REVIEW FORM & FREE PRIZE DRAW

All original review forms from the entire BPP range, completed with genuine comments, will be entered into one of two draws on 31 January 2003 and 31 July 2003. The names on the first four forms picked out on each occasion will be sent a cheque for £50.

Name: _____ Address: _____

How have you used this Text?
(Tick one box only)
☐ Self study (book only)
☐ On a course: college (please state)_____
☐ With 'correspondence' package
☐ Other _____

Why did you decide to purchase this Text?
(Tick one box only)
☐ Have used BPP Texts in the past
☐ Recommendation by friend/colleague
☐ Recommendation by a lecturer at college
☐ Saw advertising
☐ Other _____

During the past six months do you recall seeing/receiving any of the following?
(Tick as many boxes as are relevant)
☐ Our advertisement in CIMA *Insider*
☐ Our advertisement in *Financial Management*
☐ Our advertisement in *Pass*
☐ Our brochure with a letter through the post
☐ Our website www.bpp.com

Which (if any) aspects of our advertising do you find useful?
(Tick as many boxes as are relevant)
☐ Prices and publication dates of new editions
☐ Information on product content
☐ Facility to order books off-the-page
☐ None of the above

Which BPP products have you used?

Text	☐	MCQ cards	☐	i-Learn	☐
Kit	☐	Tape	☐	i-Pass	☐
Passcard	☐	Video	☐	Virtual Campus	☐

Your ratings, comments and suggestions would be appreciated on the following areas.

	Very useful	Useful	Not useful
Introductory section (Key study steps, personal study)	☐	☐	☐
Chapter introductions	☐	☐	☐
Key terms	☐	☐	☐
Quality of explanations	☐	☐	☐
Case examples and other examples	☐	☐	☐
Questions and answers in each chapter	☐	☐	☐
Chapter roundups	☐	☐	☐
Quick quizzes	☐	☐	☐
Exam focus points	☐	☐	☐
Question bank	☐	☐	☐
MCQ bank	☐	☐	☐
Answer bank	☐	☐	☐
Index	☐	☐	☐
Icons	☐	☐	☐
Mind maps	☐	☐	☐

	Excellent	Good	Adequate	Poor
Overall opinion of this Study Text	☐	☐	☐	☐

Do you intend to continue using BPP products? Yes ☐   No ☐

On the reverse of this page are noted particular areas of the text about which we would welcome your feedback.

Please note any further comments and suggestions/errors on the reverse of this page. The BPP author of this edition can be e-mailed at: barrywalsh@bpp.com

Please return this form to: Nick Weller, CIMA Range Manager, BPP Publishing Ltd, FREEPOST, London, W12 8BR

CIMA – Intermediate Paper 10: Systems and Project Management (7/02)

Please note any further comments and suggestions/errors below.

FREE PRIZE DRAW RULES

1 Closing date for 31 January 2003 draw is 31 December 2002. Closing date for 31 July 2003 draw is 30 June 2003.

2 Restricted to entries with UK and Eire addresses only. BPP employees, their families and business associates are excluded.

3 No purchase necessary. Entry forms are available upon request from BPP Publishing. No more than one entry per title, per person. Draw restricted to persons aged 16 and over.

4 Winners will be notified by post and receive their cheques not later than 6 weeks after the relevant draw date.

5 The decision of the promoter in all matters is final and binding. No correspondence will be entered into.

See overleaf for information on other
BPP products and how to order

CIMA Order

To BPP Publishing Ltd, Aldine Place, London W12 8AW
Tel: 020 8740 2211. Fax: 020 8740 1184
www.bpp.com Email: publishing@bpp.com
Order online www.bpp.com

Mr/Mrs/Ms (Full name)

Daytime delivery address

Postcode

Daytime Tel

Email

Date of exam (month/year)

POSTAGE & PACKING

Study Texts
	First	Each extra
UK	£3.00	£2.00
Europe***	£5.00	£4.00
Rest of world	£20.00	£10.00

Kits/Passcards/Success Tapes
	First	Each extra
UK	£2.00	£1.00
Europe***	£2.50	£1.00
Rest of world	£15.00	£8.00

Breakthrough Videos
	First	Each extra
UK	£2.00	£2.00
Europe***	£2.00	£2.00
Rest of world	£20.00	£10.00
MCQ cards	£1.00	£1.00

Grand Total (Cheques to *BPP Publishing*) I enclose a cheque for (incl. Postage) £ _____

Or charge to Access/Visa/Switch

Card Number _____

Expiry date _____ Start Date _____

Issue Number (Switch Only) _____

Signature _____

Order Items

		7/01 Texts	1/01 Kits	1/01 Passcards	9/00 Tapes	7/00 Videos	8/01 i-Pass	7/01 i-Learn	MCQ cards
FOUNDATION									
1	Financial Accounting Fundamentals	£20.95	£10.95	£5.95	£12.95	£25.95	£24.95		£5.95
2	Management Accounting Fundamentals	£20.95	£10.95	£5.95	£12.95	£25.95	£24.95		£5.95
3A	Economics for Business	£20.95	£10.95	£5.95	£12.95	£25.95	£24.95		£5.95
3B	Business Law	£20.95	£10.95	£5.95	£12.95	£25.95	£24.95		£5.95
3C	Business Mathematics	£20.95	£10.95	£5.95	£12.95	£25.95	£24.95 1/02 i-Pass	£19.95 1/02 i-Learn	£5.95
INTERMEDIATE									
4	Finance	£20.95	£10.95	£5.95	£12.95	£25.95	£29.95	£19.95	£5.95
5	Business Tax (FA 2001)	£20.95 (9/01)	£10.95	£5.95	£12.95	£25.95	£29.95	£19.95	
6	Financial Accounting	£20.95	£10.95	£5.95	£12.95	£25.95	£29.95		
6I	Financial Accounting International	£20.95	£10.95	£5.95	£12.95	£25.95	£29.95	£19.95	
7	Financial Reporting	£20.95	£10.95	£5.95	£12.95	£25.95	£29.95		£5.95
7I	Financial Reporting International	£20.95	£10.95	£5.95	£12.95	£25.95	£29.95		
8	Management Accounting - Performance Management	£20.95	£10.95	£5.95	£12.95	£25.95	£29.95	£19.95	£5.95
9	Management Accounting - Decision Making	£20.95	£10.95	£5.95	£12.95	£25.95	£29.95	£19.95	
10	Systems and Project Management	£20.95	£10.95	£5.95	£12.95	£25.95	£29.95	£19.95	
11	Organisational Management	£20.95	£10.95	£5.95	£12.95	£25.95	£29.95	£19.95	
FINAL									
12	Management Accounting - Business Strategy	£20.95	£10.95	£5.95	£12.95	£25.95			
13	Management Accounting - Financial Strategy	£20.95	£10.95	£5.95	£12.95	£25.95			
14	Management Accounting - Information Strategy	£20.95	£10.95	£5.95	£12.95	£25.95			
15	Case Study								
	(1) Workbook	£20.95			£12.95	£25.95			
	(2) Toolkit for 11/01 exam: available 9/01		£19.95						
	(3) Toolkit for 5/02 exam: available 3/02		£19.95						

Total _____